Allan Mills

Winnipeg

1979.

THE SICKLE SIDE OF THE MOON
The Letters of Virginia Woolf
VOLUME V: 1932—1935

THE LETTERS OF VIRGINIA WOOLF

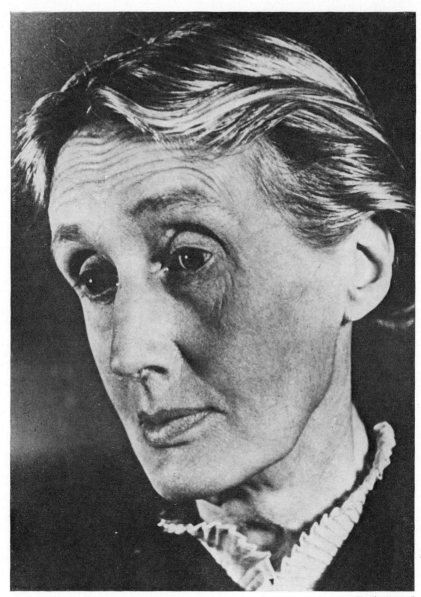

Virginia Woolf in her 50s

THE SICKLE SIDE OF THE MOON

The Letters of
VIRGINIA WOOLF

Volume V: 1932-1935

Editor: Nigel Nicolson
Assistant Editor: Joanne Trautmann

1979
THE HOGARTH PRESS
LONDON

Published by
The Hogarth Press Ltd
42 William IV Street
London WC2N 4DF

*

Clarke, Irwin & Co. Ltd
Toronto

British Library Cataloguing
in Publication Data

Woolf, Virginia
The letters of Virginia Woolf.
Vol. 5: 1932-1935. The sickle side of the moon.
1. Woolf, Virginia—Correspondence
2. Novelists, English—20th century—Correspondence
I. Nicolson, Nigel II. Trautmann, Joanne
III. Sickle side of the moon
823'.9'12   PR6045.072
ISBN 0-7012-0469-9

Printed in Great Britain by
T & A Constable Ltd
Hopetoun Street, Edinburgh

"When a person's thick to the lips in finishing a book . . . its no use pretending that they have bodies and souls so far as the rest of the world is concerned. They turn the sickle side of the moon to [the] world: the globe to the other."

Virginia Woolf to Ethel Smyth

9 *February* 1935

Contents

Frontispiece

Editorial Note

ANY edition of letters must be selective because many are inevitably lost, and the chance of survival does not seem to us an imperative reason for printing all we have found. Nearly fifty of Virginia Woolf's letters and postcards have been omitted from this volume because they concern social arrangements or small business affairs which are often mentioned again in another context, and throw no new light on her character or life. A postcard which reads *in toto*, "Would you like me to come to tea tomorrow? Or not?", cannot be worth publication, particularly when her diary confirms that the tea-party never took place.

The number of such omissions in this volume is slightly larger than previously, but it does not represent a change in editorial policy. It means only that more letters of that type survive because as Virginia Woolf's fame mounted, more people kept them.

This volume is unillustrated except by a frontispiece, because as people grow older they tend to photograph and be photographed less. The few pictures which exist of the Woolfs in their later married life are often of poor quality or have already been published elsewhere.

The copyright in the letters belongs to Quentin Bell and his sister Angelica Garnett, and we are increasingly grateful for the help which they and Mrs Bell have given us. Olivier Bell is simultaneously editing the volumes of Virginia Woolf's diary, and it is to her that we have addressed the majority of our questions. The letters can be regarded as skirmishers ahead of the more compact body of the diary, and the editors of both sets of documents have had the benefit of the others' work. Not only are there many clues in the published diary and its annotations which throw light on Virginia Woolf's later life, but Mrs Bell has never been daunted by our enquiries about a period often ten years ahead of the one on which she is currently working, and she has allowed us to read typescripts of the full diary ahead of publication. For this facility we are also indebted to Dr Lola L. Szladits, Curator of the Berg Collection, New York Public Library, which owns the originals. But we have quoted almost nothing from the diary that has not already been published.

Our research-worker for this volume has been Lorraine Helms, and we acknowledge with thanks her industry in discovering the sources of many obscure allusions and publications mentioned in the letters.

Three books in particular have been of great help to us. *A Bibliography of Virginia Woolf*, 1967, by B. J. Kirkpatrick; *A Checklist of the Hogarth*

Press, 1976, by J. Howard Woolmer; and *The Pargiters*, 1978, edited by Mitchell A. Leaska.

For allowing Professor Joanne Trautmann to spend part of her academic year working on this volume we are grateful to the Department of Humanities, The Pennsylvania State University College of Medicine, Hershey, Pennsylvania, and for the continuing support of its Chairman, E. A. Vastyan.

Mrs Norah Smallwood of the Hogarth Press has again been the most understanding of publishers, and T. & A. Constable of Edinburgh the most painstaking of printers.

The following have willingly responded to our requests for help or information: Barbara Bagenal; Dr Wendy Baron; Mrs Mary Bennett; Professor Richard Braithwaite; John Burt (Sussex University Library); Lady Darwin; Gloria Glicken Fromm; P. N. Furbank; David Garnett; Victoria Glendinning; Harmon H. Goldstone; Jeremy Hutchinson; Virginia Isham; Milo Keynes; Catherine Lacey (Tate Gallery); Sir Henry Lintott; the staff of the London Library; Jean O. Love; Jane Marcus; Kathleen Miller (Harvard University Archives); Isolda Moon; Dr Madeline Moore; John U. Nef; Adam Nicolson; Robert T. Oliver; Dr David Parker (Dickens House Museum); Mrs Ian Parsons; Frances Partridge; Dr Kathleen Raine; Professor David Rodes; Kenneth Rose; Professor S. P. Rosenbaum; George Rylands; Daphne Sanger; Elaine Sharland; Richard Shone; George A. Spater; Stephen Spender; Thomas F. Staley; Angelica Thevos (George T. Harrell Library, Hershey Medical Center).

The typing of the letters has been shared between Valerie Henderson (assisted by Ann Erikson), Gretchen Hess Gage and Joan Bernardo in the United States; and Pamela Kilbane and Jane Carr in England. In preparing the book for press we have owed much to the secretarial help of Jane Carr.

NIGEL NICOLSON
JOANNE TRAUTMANN

Erratum: Letter 2971 (to Elizabeth Bowen) is misplaced. The correct date is 6th January 1934.

Introduction

THE fifth and penultimate volume of Virginia Woolf's letters covers four years, 1932 to 1935, when she was between the ages of 50 and 53. She published no major book, but wrote and nearly finished *The Years*, and meanwhile sustained her reputation and income with *The Common Reader* (Second Series), *A Letter to a Young Poet, Flush,* her essay on Walter Sickert and a small amount of journalism. She also revised her play *Freshwater*, which was performed at a Bloomsbury party in 1935. These were the years scarred by the deaths of Lytton Strachey and Roger Fry, and of less intimate friends like Carrington, Goldsworthy Lowes Dickinson and Francis Birrell. Virginia's health remained, on the whole, good, her creative and social life undiminished. She made new friends like Elizabeth Bowen and Victoria O'Campo, and an old friendship like Lady Cecil's could be blown to life by a chance letter to which she would immediately respond. In the four successive summers she and Leonard went on holiday abroad, to Greece, France, Italy, Ireland, Holland and Germany.

They were not, however, such happy years for Virginia as those which immediately preceded. The writing of *The Years* became a torment. The Hogarth Press imposed a strain that was at times intolerable. She minded the death of Lytton Strachey terribly, and the suicide of Carrington, whom she had seen only the day before, made his loss seem even more dreadfully complete. "As long as you are there", she had written to her (No. 2542), "something of the best part of his life still goes on." So much had been said between Virginia and Lytton, and only when he was dead did she realise how much there was left to say. Years afterwards she was still thinking as she wrote, "Oh but he won't read this!", and what made it harder to bear was the thought that so few other people seemed to care. Critics began to savage his character and reputation. In one of her angriest letters (to Francis Birrell, who was himself dying) she wrote:

> "How my gorge rises at the new generation of virtuous young men . . . who have learnt all their tricks from Lytton, and then accuse him of not loving mankind! Lytton had more love in his little finger than that castrated cat in the whole of his mangy stringy partless gutless tailless body." (2787)

Then Roger Fry died, which affected her scarcely less. There was a double pain there, for herself and for Vanessa. "He was the most intelligent of my friends, profusely, ridiculously, perpetually creative: couldnt see 2 matches without making them into a boat" (2978), as she had found when they went to Greece together two years before.

As her friends died, she felt that her own life was beginning to fray. In the concluding section of *The Years*, when the Pargiter family was crumbling apart, leaving sentences bitten-off and affections unspoken, there is some hint of her own melancholy. All those letters written, all that talk, all those arrangements fixed—for what? To be laughed at, sneered at, as Chelsea laughed and sneered at Bloomsbury. But unlike the Pargiters, she drew tighter her own family affections: with Vanessa, unshakeably loyal though only intermittently communicative; with Leonard, zealous, stubborn, just, truthful, rocklike in her life; with her nephews, Julian and Quentin, whose expanding lives she rejoiced to share, teasing them into confidences; with Angelica Bell, alternately a sprite and an angel, whose holidays she alchemised, as she did with all children, into necklaces of delight.

Then there were her own annual holidays with Leonard. Seldom did she return from one of them without pronouncing it the happiest of her life, without saying that she wanted to live in the country she had just visited. She never fell ill when abroad, but she was not a very adventurous traveller. Apart from two short visits to Turkey before her marriage, she never strayed outside western and southern Europe. More than once she was tempted by invitations to visit the United States, but they came to nothing, unfortunately, because her preconceived notions of America (see, for example, Letter 2694 to Vita, who was on an American lecture tour), and her unconcealed prejudices about the character of its people, might have been changed by first-hand knowledge of its loveliest districts and its most intelligent men and women. Although she read foreign literatures and made several valiant attempts to speak French and Italian, she was temperamentally an insular person as far as personal relations went. Her only close foreign friend was Jacques Raverat, who was semi-anglicised by education and marriage to an Englishwoman. While travelling in Europe, she would exchange a few halting words with hotel-servants and peasants, but barely concerned herself with a country's history, art or people. She was not a Baedeker traveller. In later life she seems seldom to have visited a château, a church, a picture-gallery or an historical site, unless it was one associated with a great writer like Montaigne, or unless she was dragged there by a more energetic fellow-traveller like Roger Fry. What she enjoyed most was the countryside and the life of small towns, the smell of aromatic plants on low hills "where no one has ever been before" (2735), picnicking under cypresses and olives, and always the delicious release from London, the exhilaration of being unavailable. Few people have benefited more from holidays than Virginia, and few letters from abroad have conveyed such intense pleasure more economically than hers.

During these years her most intimate friends remained Vita Sackville-West and Ethel Smyth. Although she was probably fonder of Vita than of

Ethel, it was Ethel whom she saw more frequently and with whom she most regularly corresponded. Ethel maintained a pressure on her which Virginia found difficult to resist, while Vita, due to her involvement with other women, her growing love of solitude and her reluctance to intrude on other people's, drew gradually more distant, and Virginia felt a reciprocal hesitation to disturb her. Her infrequent visits to Sissinghurst were now made with Leonard, and were daytime visits only, as generally were Vita's visits to Rodmell, also accompanied. After one such visit, Virginia summarised for Ottoline Morrell her current opinion of Vita, not unkindly but with explicit reservations that leave little doubt that their love-affair had burnt itself to cinders:

> "Vita came with her sons, one Eton, one Oxford, which explains why she has to spin those sleepwalking servant girl novels. I told her you would like to see her. I remain always very fond of her—this I say because, on the surface, she's rather red and black and gaudy, I know: and very slow; and very, compared to us, primitive; but she is incapable of insincerity or pose, and digs and digs, and waters, and walks her dogs, and reads her poets, and falls in love with every pretty woman, just like a man, and is to my mind genuinely aristocratic; but I cant swear that she wont bore you" (2841),

which meant that Virginia herself was rather bored by Vita. She now felt about her what she might have felt in the first place had there been no physical attraction. In her eyes Vita had lost "the beaming beauty I first loved her for" (3084), and her modesty and gentleness, combined with a slightly lurid private life, were qualities that no longer aroused in Virginia much enthusiasm. She did not understand that Vita was now alarmed by her, having lost her love, and did herself less than justice when they met, and that far from becoming a more superficial person, a mere scribbler and gardener, as Virginia believed, she was moving into a new phase of her mental life, reflecting deeply on the meaning of religion, as her poems *Solitude* and *The Garden*, and her biographies of Joan of Arc and the Saints Theresa, reveal. This was territory into which Virginia could not follow her, and indeed she was ignorant of it, for Vita made no attempt to entice her there.

With Ethel Smyth it was quite different. She revolved round Virginia like a moth round a lamp, loving her and being unfrightened by her, and was capable of rallying from a snub in a way that Vita never could. In her mid-70s, in spite of increasing deafness, she was approaching the climax of her career as a composer. Her pertinacity, which people had once thought a nuisance and unwarrantably vain, now paid off. In January 1934 she was awarded a Smyth festival of her music and banquets in her honour, which Virginia, half-admiring, half-contemptuous (because they involved Royalty and self-advertisement), attended out of friendship. To Ethel's slight consternation this belated recognition of her talents robbed her of a life-long complaint that she was unrecognised, but in a new wave of autobiographical books she still maintained it. Again and again Virginia begged her to moderate her grievances, correcting her manuscripts (while admitting their "swing and ease") to exclude the note of petulance. Ethel rarely consented. Nor did she for one moment consider that she might be trespassing too far on another artist's time. If she wrote a book, Virginia must correct it. If she composed a ballet, Vanessa must design the scenery. Life was a perpetual conflict, with allies and enemies. Virginia was recruited as the main ally, and the main enemy were men. At one moment Virginia could write to her, "I find your atmosphere full of ozone; a necessary element" (2502), but at another she could accuse Ethel of "beating up quarrels for the sake of dramatising herself" (2859). Rows between them became half, but only half, a joke. Although Virginia often claimed that their natures were incompatible, "incorrigibly different", reconciliation was worth the certainty of fresh trouble. Virginia found it difficult to repulse adoration, unlike Vanessa, who on the telephone could pretend to be her own maid, without even disguising her voice, telling the unwelcome caller that Mrs Bell was abroad. If Virginia was loved, she would respond with a sort of love, "a limpet childish attachment" (2543). She always sought to calm Ethel, fascinated by her ambition but at the same time horrified by it. It was, in its selfish way, obscene.

While Ethel complained that she was ignored, Virginia complained that women were ignored. There was no point in personalising the issue. In *A Room of One's Own* she forced herself "to keep my own figure fictitious; legendary. If I had said, Look here am I uneducated, because my brothers used all the family funds which is the fact—Well theyd have said: she has an axe to grind; and no one would have taken me seriously" (2746). She wanted to be taken seriously. *A Room of One's Own* was light-hearted, based upon two lectures she gave to Cambridge undergraduates, but its wit and sarcasm were expressions of her deeply held belief that women had been placed at a humiliating disadvantage by men, and still were. She determined to expand her ideas in several different ways. Her first opportunity came in a speech on women's professions to the London-National Society for Women's Service in January 1931, when she shared the platform with Ethel, and eighteen months later she began *The Pargiters*, a "novel-essay" on feminism, combining fiction with argument in alternating sections. When she had written some 60,000 words, she dropped the essays, thinking the two art-forms incompatible, and developed the fictional passages into *The Years*, published in 1937. She re-worked and greatly expanded the didactic essays into *Three Guineas*, which appeared the following year.

Thus during a large part of the 1930s Virginia Woolf was preoccupied with the position of women in a man's world, but in her published writing only, for it was a rare theme in her letters, diary or conversation. She regarded *The Years* and *Three Guineas* "as one book" (AWD. p. 295). *The Years* dealt with the harmful effects of a Victorian upbringing on both men and women. *Three Guineas* was an attack on contemporary militarism, which she attributed in large part to the historical role of men and their denial of a proper education to women. The two subjects, however, did not merge easily. The Victorian patriarch and the 20th-century fascist were men of different worlds, and Virginia's attempt to link them did not carry conviction. Maynard Keynes thought *Three Guineas* "a silly argument and not very well written" (Quentin Bell, II, p. 205).

It is worth investigating why Virginia took up the cause of women so heatedly. There is no doubting her strength of feeling, but nothing in her own life, nor in the lives of her close friends, quite explains it, which makes her protest unselfish and therefore all the more impressive. It is true that she and Vanessa had not been sent to Universities, as both her brothers were, but Vanessa went to art-school and Virginia was taught Greek and Latin professionally, and both had the run of their father's library, with his strong encouragement. Later she sometimes admitted that she was glad not to have had a University education. Her intellectual development would have been limited by it. Whenever she visited Oxford or Cambridge she returned disgusted by the narrow-mindedness of academics, by the supine dullness (or what was worse, the self-assertiveness) of undergraduates, and in the Oxford chapter of *The Years* she lampooned both brilliantly. She was entirely justified in stressing the importance of education for women, and a modest room and income of their own, but she had not herself been seriously deprived of them. In the 1930s, when her anger boiled over, she was in every sense one of the most liberated women in England, and had been so for twenty years. Among her friends, only Ethel Smyth considered that her career had been thwarted by male dominance, and Virginia thought her wailing embarrassingly strident. Virginia liked men, and since her childhood had had no upsetting relationship with any of them. Her husband had every male quality that she most admired in them. Nor was she concerned in these three books with the position of women less fortunate than herself. She confined her argument to the daughters of educated men, who came from comfortable homes, and she thought the working class pitiable but uninteresting.

She stated women's grievances with such power that readers overlooked the fact that her argument was to a large extent anachronistic. The professions *were* opening to women: to give but one example of the trend, both Virginia's doctors in middle and later life were women. The Universities *were* open to them. In 1927 there were 8,000 women students in higher education, equal in status to the men at all Universities except Cambridge. School-education for girls had been compulsory since 1870. Most women had had the vote since 1918, and all by 1928. Today the newspapers print every week the obituaries of women who began distinguished careers at the very time when

Virginia was protesting that few opportunities existed for them. She drew most of her examples from the past, but presented them in such a way as to suggest that they were still equally relevant.

She found in men qualities which she deplored—aggressiveness, arrogance, self-satisfaction. The corresponding defects in women she scarcely mentioned. Men shoot beasts and birds, but women wear their fur and plumage. Victorian matriarchs could be as ruthless to their children as the patriarchs, and very few of them made use (as Virginia did) of the opportunities for self-education which leisure and financial security afforded them. They were lazy and self-indulgent, and most of them actually welcomed their dependence upon men. It saved them from responsibility.

Virginia not only overstated the case, but muddled it. She often appeared to despise the very professions she wished women to enter. If many men had the qualities she ridiculed, they were not the most estimable men. If they wore robes, wigs and uniforms of different rank (a frequent object for her scorn) it was for historical reasons, to which women were by no means indifferent when they qualified to wear them too. She seems to have found little merit in ambition, and to sneer at the skill and effort required to win acceptance for causes in which people of both sexes deeply believe. Her anger was focused not on men of mean attainments, but on the successful. Not on the intrusive bureaucrat, the bullying sergeant or the hack scholar, but on the statesman, the General, the Professor and the Judge. Their eminence was itself suspect to her. The Chairman was morally a feebler creature than the idlest and most taciturn member of his committee. What, one would like to ask her, was the man or woman of legitimate ambition to do? Refuse all honours, responsibility or advancement? Virginia's own actions were not always consistent with her doctrine. She refused the offer of Companion of Honour, a degree at Manchester University and the Clark lectureship at Cambridge. Her refusal of the titular honours one can understand; but proudly to turn down the Clark lectures, when she was the first woman to be invited to give them, only weakened the cause of women in general, and contrasts with her natural eagerness to win literary recognition, to accept, for example, the award of the Femina prize for *To The Lighthouse*. Applause for a serious lecture delivered in a college hall is not different in kind from applause for a book in the *Times Literary Supplement*, but she persuaded herself that it was, perhaps rationalising her dislike of lecturing, or because it would have been inappropriate for the audience to boo.

The central subject of *Three Guineas* was war. Ever since Homeric times there has been a sexual element in war, encouraged by women, to whom a warrior (even a pay-clerk in a remote headquarters) appears a more virile figure than the same man at home. It was women who distributed the white feather. Virginia conceded that they were much to blame, and asked how both sexes could be cured of their militant patriotism. First, she answers, by education, negatively. The "arts of dominating other people" should not be taught in the ideal University (p. 62)[1]; there should be no examinations or degrees, which simply stimulate a nasty form of pride. Nor should the students study any of the arts or sciences which encourage war (p. 67), which would presumably include the study of the military aspects of history and the physical sciences. Secondly, women must adopt "an attitude of complete indifference" to the militant posturing of men. But not always. They must be active pacifists as well. When they see £30 million spent annually by their Government on weapons of war which all sane people would refuse to use, they must protest at the criminality of it. But what would have happened, in the context of the 1930s, if the money had not been spent, the arms not used? In reply Virginia took refuge in nonsense, in saying that no appeal can be made to women to contribute to their country's defence, as their country had done nothing for them in return. "If you insist upon fighting to protect me, or 'our' country, let it be understood soberly and rationally between us that you are fighting to gratify a sex instinct which I cannot share; to procure benefits which I have not shared and probably will not share" (p. 197). All women, in fact, should regard themselves as stateless until men cease to make war, for whatever reason.

It was at this point that she lost her audience. Her argument was neither sober nor rational. It was not even qualified by satire, like the *Lysistrata*. Leonard (whose silence on all this in his autobiography may be indicative of what he thought at the time) gradually eased her out of her untenable position. When war came, she still maintained that 'they' made wars. 'We' as usual remained outside and had no voice in our fate. "Better win the war than lose it", Leonard grimly replied, and Virginia more than half agreed (Quentin Bell, II, p. 211). By October 1939 she had brought herself to the point of writing to Edward Sackville-West, "With a solid block of unbaked barbarians in Germany, whats the use of our being comparatively civilized?" That was the question she never asked herself when *Three Guineas* was in its crucible.

I have carried this discussion beyond the time-limit of this volume because in 1932-35 all her ideas on these two subjects germinated, and while she gave expression to many of them in *A Room of One's Own* and *The Years*, she was banking her fires for the even angrier book she was contemplating, *Three Guineas*. She wrote it with passionate conviction, not just to annoy, but to challenge. She threw a stone through the window, which is often a valuable thing to do. The three books have been widely re-read. In many passages they express with great eloquence the legitimate aspirations of women, which in many respects are still not satisfied. She was an imaginative, emotional writer, and in *Three Guineas* attempted to use for the first time the apparatus of logic, scholarship and politics, and the scope and shape

1. The quotations from *Three Guineas* are taken from the Hogarth Press edition, 1977.

of it were not suited to her particular cast of mind. "She was the least political animal that has lived since Aristotle invented the definition", wrote Leonard in *Downhill all the Way*. She lacked and even despised the means that would have helped her to convince the neutral reader, the technique of irrefutability, the ability to make him react constantly, "That is true". Her argument was weakened by inconsistency, incoherence, selective quotation and abandoned trails.

When Q. D. Leavis wrote of *Three Guineas* as devastating a review[1] as Virginia received for any of her books, she commented, "I read enough to see that it was all personal—about Queenie's own grievances and retorts to my snubs" (AWD. p. 301). Why did she not mind more that her argument was pulled to pieces? Because she *knew* that what she had written was true. It had all welled up from her childhood—the horrid masculinity of Leslie, George and Gerald which had humiliated her and weakened her sexual nature (a recurrent theme in *The Pargiters*), the pathetic image of her mother's last years, of Vanessa forced to do the household accounts, and herself to hand round buns at tea-parties. She was describing a world which had evaporated, but which to her was still real. She who had won free of it so young, so defiantly, so successfully, was almost alone in imagining that nothing had basically changed.

NIGEL NICOLSON
Sissinghurst Castle, Kent

1. Reprinted in *Virginia Woolf: The Critical Heritage* (ed. Robin Majumdar and Allen McLaurin), 1975, pp. 409-19.

Abbreviations at foot of letters

Berg: The Henry W. and Albert A. Berg Collection of English and American Literature in the New York Public Library (Astor, Lenox and Tilden Foundations).

Sussex: University of Sussex Library, Brighton.

Texas: The Humanities Research Center, The University of Texas, at Austin, Texas.

King's: King's College Library, Cambridge.

Letters 2501-2572 (January–April 1932)

On 25 January Virginia Woolf reached the age of 50, but her birthday passed almost unnoticed, because four days earlier Lytton Strachey had died of cancer. She missed him dreadfully, and found consolation only in talking and writing about him to his brothers and sisters, and to some of his more intimate friends like Ottoline Morrell, Ralph Partridge and, above all, Ralph's wife Dora Carrington, whom she tried to sustain against suicide, but in vain. Carrington killed herself on 11 March, the morning after Virginia and Leonard had visited her at Ham Spray. In spite of these two successive blows, Virginia maintained an active social life in London, and visited Ethel Smyth at Woking, Vita Sackville-West at Sissinghurst, George Rylands at Cambridge, Maurice Baring at Rottingdean and Roger Fry in Suffolk. She had not yet embarked on the novel which was fermenting in her mind (The Pargiters, which later became The Years), and laid aside Flush, which she had begun the previous August. In early February she finished A Letter to a Young Poet, addressed to John Lehmann, who was still working in the Hogarth Press, and revised old articles and wrote some new ones for the second volume of The Common Reader, but refused the flattering invitation to give the Clark Lectures at Cambridge.

2501: To Ethel Smyth   [*Monk's House, Rodmell, Sussex*]

Postcard
[1 January 1932]

Lytton still better   Hope to write tomorrow or possibly ring up about 1 from London

V.W.

Berg

2502: To Ethel Smyth   *Monks House,* [*Rodmell, Sussex*]

Monday [4 January 1932]

No time to write, owing to the exigencies of the post and the need of catching this moment of sun. But very glad of your letters; and will return

I

Elth[1] and send the number of the invaluable flask. It strikes me—did you pluck the leather from your own heart—was it *your* bottle? And did you catch cold for want of it? Never was there such a pelican. Eh on Dickens exactly hits my view: but I'll enlarge later—the maid wading through the long grass is a masterpiece that has always stuck in my mind.[2] And I want to develop the theory that I am really like Dickens myself, had it not been for the nerve in my spine—I mean endlessly prolific—I have now 5 books in my mind and given another set of nerves cd. write day in day out! London was rather a scrimmage: but I'm better I'm sure; and can write lines in my head. And dont please die, lying down like an Indian, and saying 'death'; for really I find your atmosphere full of ozone; a necessary element; since in my set they never praise me and never love me, openly; and I admit there are times when silence chills and the other thing fires. So dont die I repeat, in a hurry as I say. Lytton rather better. I saw Oliver, the brother, in London, who was majestic with the 18th century good sense and intelligible integrity of all the Stracheys; with passionate family love well battened down. Like the Balfours. Its going to be a long fight for Lytton. He remains reasonable, calm, will even argue about truth and beauty and thus vindicates the race of scholars

Goodbye
V.

Berg

2503: To V. Sackville-West   *Monks House, [Rodmell, Sussex]*

6th Jan. [1932]

Yes dearest Creature I cant deny that I have a sort of dying ember in my heart for you—what they call affection, and if it dies it will be because you suffocate it with the no doubt satisfactory but to me rather too substanial [*sic*] figure of Jones[3]—of whom I'm rather jealous, and so call her Jones all short.

Here was I at Rodmell and you with her—but I cant really think Enid with all her seductions can be as nice, or as interesting, or as much of a lark as—someone I could touch with a stick at this moment. So this is to ask

1. Probably letters written to Ethel Smyth by her great-niece Elizabeth Williamson (grand-daughter of her sister, Mary Hunter), who was then aged 29 and taught astronomy at University College, London.
2. The scene occurs in Chapter 18 of *Bleak House*.
3. Enid Bagnold, the novelist and playwright, who married Sir Roderick Jones, Chairman of Reuters, in 1920. They lived at Rottingdean, a few miles from Rodmell, where Vita was visiting them.

if you'll come and see me on Monday next—(because you said [you] wanted
to see me and it was only modesty if you didn't ask, so in future I shall ask
you, without thinking you'd rather be with Jones)—and if so what time?
I expect I'm alone for lunch, and in for tea and dinner—since we only go
back on Sunday and the worlds slow toil, or whatever the phrase is,—
torture toil and treason—will not have corrupted me by then. Yes, I am
very very fond of you, and whats more I was very much touched, almost
to the point of tears by Harold's farewell in Action.[1]—So honest, so straight-
forward, and like a small boy taking a caning. I hope he didn't really mind,
but I expect he did, more than he lets on. On the other hand I thought
Mosley's farewell oily, bragging, crafty, pompous, insincere and flamboyant.

I wish you and Harold could live on sober literature—poems and
biographies—and let him become, incidentally, minister for foreign affairs,
as he would. Really I believe, if you would curb your ancestral sumptuosity
which I love—George [butler] and Champagne, bath salts and kidneys for
supper with mushrooms at midnight and the walls of Long Barn[2] reeling
and the voice of twenty budgerigars peeling (didnt I always say I was a
poet?—thats a rhyme) I say, if you'd draw in your ancestral horns I believe
you need neither of you lap out of Beaverbrooks dish and send your sons
to Eton all the same. Anyhow I'm glad you showed Rothermere the door.[3]
But since you've married an explosive, heaven knows where he wont effulge
in crimson and gold next. I was sent a notice of 5 Gordon Square to look
at—is it a nice house? Rather noisy I suppose.

Yes, I knew you'd feel unhappy as I did about Lytton. I should mind
it to the end of my days if he died but they think he may get through now
—Like all Stracheys he has a fund of Anglo Indian tenacity, besides which
he remains perfectly calm, collected and cheerful and likes to argue about
truth and beauty—you must admit that this is admirable—while about 20
Stracheys are collected in The Inn [at Hungerford], with varieties of mistresses, who all quarrel, as you may suppose. No, I wish one's friends were
immortal—I'm greatly at their mercy—and then you go flaunting off with
the widow Jones—I always endow dull stodgy commonplace women with
widowhoods. I'm sending this—which is not what you may call an interesting, rather an affectionate letter, to Long Barn, somehow wishing to

1. *Action*, the weekly newspaper of Sir Oswald Mosley's New Party, had been
   edited by Harold Nicolson since October 1931. For financial reasons it ceased
   publication at the end of December after only thirteen issues. In his valedictory
   article Nicolson wrote: "We recognise with cold calm that our failure is for the
   moment complete."
2. Although the Nicolsons bought Sissinghurst Castle in April 1930, they still
   lived until 1933 for much of the time at Long Barn, their house near Sevenoaks.
3. Harold Nicolson had rejected Lord Rothermere's invitation to edit the gossip
   column in the *Sunday Dispatch*, and Lord Beaverbrook's to write the weekly
   book-review for the *Sunday Express*.

evade Penns. What on earth is wrong with Dotty?[1] She now refuses to answer L's [Leonard's] letters, couched though they are in the most conciliatory terms.

Its a torrent and a gale, and I'm sitting over the fire reading Lady Curzon[2] with enthusiasm—empty headed as I suppose she is: but what an adorable aristocrat. I like Aunts to collect foxes teeth for necklaces.

So let me know, honey, about Monday.

V.

We've just been put on the telephone—385 Lewes—but this is dead secret. I wish you'd ring me up for fun.

Berg

2504: TO ETHEL SMYTH   [*Monk's House, Rodmell,*
                                         Sussex]

Wednesday [6 January 1932]

Here are E's letters.[3] My word are you travelling today? But this kind of remark is no pleasure in a letter, and I've written so many as its useless walking, that I cant go on even to you. I'm better though—oh yes: I wrote this morning: a vast plate of saddle of mutton did the trick: I'll tell you the story some time. Is it any good for your pain—plain roast meat in masses?

Well Lytton is improving, and we go back [to London] on Sunday I think and I hope this blasted season of misery is more or less over.

V.

Berg

1. Dorothy Wellesley, later Duchess of Wellington, edited for the Hogarth Press the *Hogarth Living Poets* series and was herself a poet. She lived at Penns-in-the-Rocks, near Withyham, Sussex.
2. Lady Cynthia Curzon was the daughter of the Marquess Curzon of Kedleston, and married Sir Oswald Mosley in 1920. Virginia had read her article published in the last number of *Action*. She died in 1933, aged 34.
3. Elizabeth Williamson. See p. 2, note 1.

Wednesday [13 January 1932]

The news is very bad about Lytton tonight, though not quite hopeless. We're going to Hungerford early tomorrow, as they think it may be some help—I shall come back on Friday—perhaps late tomorrow.

I'm much better so there's not the least risk for me.

Take care of yourself

V.

Berg

2506: To Vanessa Bell   52 *Tavistock Square, W.C.1.*

Thursday [14 January 1932]

We're just back from Hamspray, so I thought you might like to hear. Lytton is better again, though they thought he was dying on Sunday. In fact the Dr. said it was hopeless, but he suddenly got better—like last time [December, 1931]. He's now fearfully weak, but not actually losing strength. They've got a new specialist [Sir Arthur Hurst] who thinks the disease is running its course, but cant say how long it will be. Nobody has ever seen a case like it and nothing goes as they expect. We took Pippa out and had tea with Carrington Ralph and Frances at Hamspray.[1] They all seem worn down, but inclined to be hopeful again. Except for the general feeling that nobody knows what may happen. Lytton is conscious and determined to do all he can, and they said he liked our coming. His temp. went down to 99 this afternoon.

Perhaps you've heard from James [Strachey].

We shall be here this week end

B.[2]

Berg

1. Lytton Strachey was dying of cancer at Ham Spray, his house near Hungerford, in Wiltshire. He was too ill to see Virginia and Leonard, but was told that they had come. Among those who gathered round his death-bed were his sister Philippa ('Pippa'), Dora Carrington and her husband Ralph Partridge, and Frances Marshall, who married Partridge after Carrington's suicide in March 1932.
2. 'Billy', derived from 'Goat', the name by which Virginia was known to her sister and brothers in childhood.

2507: To Lady Ottoline Morrell

[52 *Tavistock Square, W.C.*1]

Friday [15 January 1932]

Dearest Ottoline,

Yes, I feel hopeless about ever seeing you—partly I've been away and retired from life into obscurity—then Lytton's illness. We were at Hungerford yesterday, and saw them all. He is desperately ill, but they think there is some hope—he recovered again, when they thought him dying on Sunday. Pippa [Strachey] is with him all the time, and says he is wonderfully composed and does all he can to help. But what an awful time they're having—and nobody seems to know how long the illness lasts, and what course it takes.

I wish I could come next Friday, but I think we go to Rodmell, and perhaps to Hungerford again.

Might I come one day the week after? I should so much like to. London is a handfull—here I'm interrupted and made to write nonsense by William Plomer.[1]

Love Virginia

Texas

2508: To Lady Ottoline Morrell

52 *Tavistock Sqre,* [*W.C.*1]

[mid-January 1932]

Dearest Ottoline,

I would love to come in one day next week, perhaps Thursday or Friday, at my usual time, between the lights, if it suited you. But I cant be quite sure of days at the moment, because if the Stracheys should want us to go down again we would of course. One feels numbed and desperate —yet perhaps theres still hope. The doctors say everything is sound in Lytton—if only the illness would slacken.

Yes, I was very glad you liked the Waves. I'm very proud if you do like what I write—It was much beyond me, and I failed of course. I didn't mean real people, only ghosts—but perhaps real people have ghosts. I wanted too to say how sorry I was about your brother.[2] But, as usual, I was afraid of hurting you if I wrote: O dear what a fool one is!

yr V

Texas

1. The novelist, poet and auto-biographer (1903-73), many of whose books the Hogarth Press had published, including *Turbott Wolfe* 1926 and *Sado* 1931.
2. Lord Henry Cavendish Bentinck, who died in October 1931. He was a soldier and Member of Parliament, and the half-brother of the Duke of Portland.

Monday, 18th Jan. [1932]

Dearest Carrington,

Please, please dont bother to write if we send Lytton a few flowers—
its such a pleasure to the old Wolves, but not if it adds to your burdens.
Not but what I love getting a letter from you, if only for the sake of the
hand [writing]—my ideal in the way of hands.

I wrote to Julia[1] immediately asking her to come, but have had no
answer. Perhaps she's away, or perhaps, being a Strachey, and as astute as
an eel, she's got wind of my intentions and wont come near me. I shall try
again in a day or two. I wish I could understand the psychology of Julia.
Think of writing a whole book and then swallowing it back into the womb!
—what a disgusting metaphor—the result of 3 hours talk with Ethel Smyth.
Now its a queer thing, but all old women of high distinction and advanced
views seldom talk of anything but the period and the W.C. How do you
account for it? I rather think its the final effort at complete emancipation—
like a chicken getting rid of egg shell.

We had two South Africans to dinner last night—one William Plomer,
the other Alice Ritchie,[2] both novelists, and they discussed Mrs Kapp; who
is Yvonne Cloud, and lives, with Benita Yaeger under Morgan's [Forster]
bath, which leaks, as you might expect—hence a vast novel by Cloud, all
about sapphism, so dull, so improper,[3]—do you meet with those figures—
Benita and Kapp?—I expect so: and now William Plomer is living in sin,
as I suppose with Tony Butts[4] and they're giving a party to which Miss
Susan Glaspell[5] is going and Walter Sickert. But I'm too old for parties.
Once they were so exciting my head reeled. Now—though you wouldn't
think it—I can only see through everybody to the truth. Raymonds Letter
—which the Bagmen [book-travellers] call Mortimers French Letter[6]—

1. Julia Strachey, Lytton's niece, had married Stephen Tomlin, the sculptor, in
   1927. She was one of Carrington's most constant friends.
2. Whose books, *The Peacemakers* (1928) and *Occupied Territory* (1930) had been
   published by the Hogarth Press, for whom she had also acted as a traveller.
3. Yvonne Cloud's Sapphic novel was *Nobody Asked You* (Willy-Nilly Press,
   1932). With Benita Jaeger (Clive Bell's constant companion in the 1930s), she
   rented the ground floor and basement of 26 Brunswick Square, where Forster
   occupied the first floor. His scalding bath water overflowed into her yard, and
   she protested, with the result that they became friends.
4. Anthony Butts, the painter, had travelled with Plomer throughout Europe, and
   they then shared a house in Canning Place. For a time Butts was a pupil of
   Sickert.
5. The American short-story writer and playwright, 1882-1948.
6. *The French Pictures. A Letter to Harriet*, by Raymond Mortimer, published by
   the Hogarth Press in January 1932 as No. 4 in *The Hogarth Letters* series.

booms and booms. Nessa and Duncan are enraged at the mere mention. Lord I'm glad I'm not a painter—their taste is so pure; theres no getting round them.

Oh how I envy you Ham Spray! Really it is the loveliest place in England. I can hardly bear to think of my poor spotted downs after yours. The trees—the downs—yours I mean. I want very much to come again. Forgive this prattle, dearest Carrington.

V

Robert H. Taylor

2510: To Dora Carrington   [52 *Tavistock Square, W.C.*1]

Thursday [21 January 1932]

Darling Carrington,

We are all thanking you for what you gave Lytton.[1] Please Carrington, think of this, and let us bless you for it.

This is our great comfort now—the happiness you gave him—and he told me so.

Virginia

[*in Leonard's handwriting:*]
I think you know that I feel the same.

Leonard

Robert H. Taylor

2511: To Philippa Strachey   [52 *Tavistock Square, W.C.*1]

Postcard
Thursday night [21 January 1932]

Darling Pippa,

I sit thinking of Lytton and Thoby and how Lytton came to me when Thoby died[2] and I feel more than ever your sister now, darling Pippa, if you will let me. You know how we loved him.

Virginia

Strachey Trust

1. Lytton Strachey died in his sleep at 2.30 p.m. on 21 January.
2. Virginia's brother, Thoby Stephen, died of typhoid in 1906, aged 26.

2512: To Pernel Strachey   52 *Tavistock Square, W.C.*1

Friday [22 January 1932]

Dearest Pernel,[1]

Here are a few flowers for you and Pippa with our love.

We are going to Rodmell this afternoon, but shall be back on Sunday at tea time: I shall ring up to hear how Pippa is.

                                                    Yr Virginia

If theres any chance you would like to see me, leave a message—I would come any time.

Strachey Trust

2513: To Ethel Smyth   52 *T.[avistock] S.[quare, W.C.*1]

[26 January 1932]

Well, I didn't write, but was grateful for your note and rest secure on your understanding my silence and all the rest. As you may suppose, I've been rather involved in the usual miseries of this sort of occasion—Lord, how people suffer, and how human beings torture each other unnecessarily —But I cant go into this now: and its all over,—not the tortures, no, but after this week, I suppose we shall be again as usual. I've had to see a good many people, one way and another.

How are you? Well, dont bother to write if you're as I'm so often, in the dumps: but I should like to hear that you're not stiffening or sickening or anything horrid

                                                    V.

Berg

2514: To Donald Brace   52 *Tavistock Square, W.C.*1

Typewritten
27th Jan 1932

Dear Mr Brace,

I am afraid that there is no chance that I can let you have the second volume of the Common Reader to bring out this spring. I have now gone through the material, and I find that there is more work to do upon it than

1. Pernel Strachey (1876-1951), the fourth of Lytton's five sisters, was Principal of Newnham College, Cambridge, 1923-41.

I expected. I think I could make a more complete book of it also by adding one or two fresh articles, and as these would not have beeen printed before they might be an added attraction. But this will take time; and I see that I must postpone until the autumn. I am very sorry if this should make any difficulty for you; but I hope I prepared you for it in my last letter. I will of course let you know directly I can be certain of dates. I thought my sister's jacket very attractive.[1]

I believe I never told you how much I liked your edition of the Waves. It has done much better than I expected, and I hope it still sells a little.

With kind regards,
yours sincerely,
Virginia Woolf

Harcourt Brace Jovanovich

2515: TO ETHEL SMYTH   52 *Tavistock Sqre.* [*W.C.*1]

Jan. 29th 1932

No, we're not at Rodmell, and I cant say I ever wish to go there again. Factories are rising on the river bank [at Ashham]—cement works— huge, vast, about as big as the Albert Hall. And the woman next door keeps spaniels that bark all the morning. I'd much rather stay here, or in White-chapel, or in any suburban slum where theres no down and marsh to be murdered inch by inch by these damnable buggers. Only I generally like buggers; I cant think of a word to fit them—thats all. My walks ruined for ever.

Otherwise I have little or nothing to say. The poor dear Stracheys are so miserable and so reasonable—we have them to dinner, and I try to crack jokes; and then nothing happens, and I feel age and gloom and sterility and resentment settling over them, for Lytton was their pride and their joy; and they're all aging and most of them growing poorer, and then violence and jealousy sprang up, even before Lytton died, so that there were scenes upon scenes; and the Stracheys fled, leaving the house to these unhappy mistresses, and desolated wives to quarrel in.[2] But I cant explain: anyhow its been a tragic and sordid week, and here's Oliver [Strachey], the brother you met, coming in a minute to dine—What am I to joke about tonight? I've been walking across Hyde Park in the dusk; a desert of wide eternity it looked to be sure, with all the trees dark as cinders, a negro sitting on a

1. Both the English and American editions of *The Common Reader: Second Series* were published in October 1932, and both had jackets designed by Vanessa Bell.
2. Dora Carrington and Frances Marshall remained at Ham Spray after Lytton's death, with Ralph Partridge, Stephen Tomlin and (temporarily) Gerald Brenan.

seat alone, and a woman opening a packet of sanitary towels, on an arm chair by Park Lane, and avenues stretching on and on, till I thought I should walk for ever and never reach humanity again But I did—Marble Arch that is to say—I daresay I get an infinity of pleasure from the intensity of my own emotions. But I cant write without thinking of Lytton— never mind: I won't go into that. I liked hearing you shout—I mean your letter. I'm glad that you're buffeting about as usual.

Lord! I must go and wash.

V.

Berg

2516: To Gwen Raverat   52 *Tavistock Square, W.C.*1

Sunday [31 January 1932]

Dear Gwen,[1]

I ought to have written before, but I've been in a rush. Yes do come— not this week; but what about next—Tuesday or Wednesday, 4.30—(I think they're the 9th and 10th) Let me know if one of those would do; and come here if you will.

Your Virginia

I'm sure you understand what Lytton's death means to us.

Sussex

2517: To Dora Carrington   52 *Tavistock Sqre.,* [*W.C.*1]

Sunday [31 January 1932]

Carrington dearest, I hope you dont mind my writing to you sometimes— it is such a comfort because there is nobody to talk to about Lytton who knew him as you did—and of course dont answer. One hates so the feeling that things begin again here in London without him. I find I cant write without suddenly thinking Oh but Lytton wont read this, and it takes all the point out of it. I always put away things in my mind to say to Lytton. And what it must be for you—I wish some time I could see you and tell you about the time, after Thoby's [Stephen] death, before you knew him, when I used to see him. But I could never give him what you did. I used to laugh at him for having grown so mellow and good tempered (you know

1. Gwen (*née* Darwin) was the wife of the French painter, Jacques Raverat, who died in France in 1925. Virginia had been very fond of him, and continued to befriend Gwen in her lonely widowhood. She had first known her when both were young women.

11

how I loved laughing at him) and he said, "Oh but you know, it is rather wonderful—Ham Spray and all that—and its all Carrington's doing." This is no help to you now, but it is for us. Before he knew you, he was so depressed and restless—and all that changed when you had Tidmarsh.[1]

Tell Julia that she's still got to come and see us, and bring her book.[2] Please do the pictures for it. I know Lytton would have liked that.

Yes of course I'll write about him some day, but it must be for you, only.

And some time I want to come to Ham Spray again (if this is not being like [Sibyl] Colefax). How lovely it was that night—I shall never forget it. Pippa dined here the other night—she seemed well; but very broken, I thought.

Well, Carrington, I must stop and please forgive me for droning on— but you are the person who understands best about Lytton.

Virginia

Leonard sends his love.[3]

Robert H. Taylor

2518: TO RALPH PARTRIDGE   52 *Tavistock Square,* [*W.C.*1]

Sunday [31 January 1932]

Dearest Ralph,

I hope you wont mind my writing—I didn't like to write before. But as time goes on the loss of Lytton seems to get harder and harder to bear, and if this is so for me, what must it be for you? My only comfort is to think that you and Carrington gave him all those last years—I am sure of greater happiness than he had ever known. I shall always bless you for this and love you for what you were to him.

I dont know if you're in London, and would ever come and see us. Perhaps you and Frances [Marshall] would dine one night?

But dont bother to answer—this is only to send you our love.

Your affate
Virginia

Robert H. Taylor

1. In 1917 Lytton and Carrington had leased the Mill House at Tidmarsh on the River Pang, Berkshire.
2. In September 1932 the Hogarth Press published *Cheerful Weather for the Wedding* by Julia Strachey (Tomlin).
3. Carrington replied (4 February, *Sussex*): "There are only a few letters that have been any use. Yours most of all, because you understand."

Tuesday [2 February 1932]

No, as I expected, I cant come tonight.[1] There's a farewell dinner to Clive [Bell], who's returning to Rome tomorrow to prosecute an affair with a rich American—rather halfheartedly I think, but what would you? —Turned 50 as he is. So I've given your ticket to a musical clerk in the office, which I grudge her, as I should like to hear you, with your gift for solidifying the connection between you and the audience—May I read it? In return I'll copy out an old memoir that tumbled out of a box when I was looking for something else that I wrote ten years ago about our doings with George Duckworth when we were so to speak virgins.[2] It might amuse you: but it needs copying—such a mess its in.

Yes, I liked seeing you—you didn't ask me—but I tell you on the chance you have my passion for being assured of small facts like this. I daresay I'm even vainer than you are—

V.

Berg

2520: To Julian Bell   [52 *Tavistock Square, W.C.1*]

Typewritten
3 Feb [1932]

My dear Julian,

I have made enquiries about the Nonesuch Dryden, but they are not such as encourage me—the answers I mean—to buy it. Clive says Summers is an obscene knave;[3] even old Desmond [MacCarthy] has nosed out some misprints, which considering the state of Desmond's brain, shows that the text must be a pullulating mass of maggots. So I have bought you some books instead—God knows if you want them; but here they are (or the post will bring them). First Drydens Miscellany[4] which I am told is interesting as a light on his taste; then the other mans miscellany—whose name

1. To a lecture which Ethel was giving on musical criticism at King's College, London.
2. 22 *Hyde Park Gate*, written for the Memoir Club in 1920 or 1921, and published in *Moments of Being* (ed. Jeanne Schulkind, 1976). George Duckworth was Virginia's half-brother.
3. *The Dramatic Works* of John Dryden, edited by Montague Summers in six volumes. Nonesuch Press, 1931-32.
4. Dryden's *Critical and Miscellaneous Prose Works*, edited by Edmund Malone, 1800.

escapes me is it Dodsley[1]—the famous one, in which I think the Elegy was first collected; and it is a great test of taste to see if you can spot which poem is by whom. Then a small shabby [George] Crabbe—but it has a charm for me who worship him, as you know, illegitimately but with passion. You share my taste that way I think and with more reason, since you tell the truth and I never could. Then theres a little book of the kind of mild rustic melody I also like—Then some modern French but I'm in a tearing hurry—John[2] rampant—must go to tea with Ottoline—so only add that Birrell and Garnett will change any book for any other if you have it already.[3]

Many happy returns of the day—and to think it was tomorrow 24 years I saw you first in your native vice, and took the measure of your skull! Shall we see you soon?

Virginia

[*handwritten*]

John seems to think you have Crabbe—if so, let me have him, as I want one.

Quentin Bell

2521: To Lady Ottoline Morrell

52 *Tavistock Square, W.C.*1

Thursday [4 February 1932]

Dearest Ottoline,
    Many thanks for Mrs Cameron's address.[4] I would like to see her again some time and will write. You bamboozled me into dreadful boasting I'm afraid—I never meant that my own writing is aristocratic, only my attitude to writing in general—but I daresay thats boasting too: I mean I dont

1. Robert Dodsley (1703-64), who first published *Gray's Elegy written in a Country Churchyard* in his *A Collection of Poems by Several Hands*, 1750.
2. In January 1931 John Lehmann had joined the Hogarth Press as assistant to Leonard, with a view to becoming a partner later. He had been a friend of Julian Bell at Cambridge, where Julian was now writing a dissertation on Pope, hoping to win by it a Fellowship at King's.
3. The bookshop, patronised by most of Bloomsbury, which David Garnett and Francis Birrell had founded in the early 1920s. In 1927 it had been bought by Graham Pollard, the bibliographer.
4. Elizabeth Bowen, the novelist (1899-1973), who had married Alan Cameron in 1923. Virginia had first met her at tea with Ottoline.

think I could go about scribbling in papers: thats all it amounts to: or admire the [J. C.] Squires and the [J. B.] Priestleys. I put my boasting down to the fumes of your aristocracy, overpowering me yesterday.

I liked talking about Lytton to you—so many things come to my mind I want to say to him. Carrington has written again—She says Lytton left a diary of a tour he took in France last summer, and it is a very happy one; and that is some comfort to her—poor Carrington.

Leonard is out, and I dont know whether he could come on the 19th— I know he would like to. May we, as they say, leave it open?

I'll send the Waves; and dont buy [Samuel Johnson's] the Lives of the Poets until I've seen if I can find you a copy.

And do—as I meant to insist—finish your Memoirs, and confound your enemies and let me read it.[1]

V.

Texas

2522: To Ethel Smyth   [52 *Tavistock Square, W.C.*1]

Typewritten

Friday [5 February 1932]

I think I dislike them both equally—so clumsy—Where musical criticism sideslips—where musical criticism derails—I think it a mistake to be colloquial, vernacular, unless you hit it off exactly. Why not, simply and dully, Some fallacies of m. c. 'Failings and fallacies of the Musical Critic.' 'Where Musical Criticism is at fault—' no I certainly dont like where musical criticism derails. I leave it at that. Skids is better.[2] But I think to drop smartness best of all. About next week —I'm rushed by person after person (and then you call me a hermit!) Every day Im out or have someone here. Wednesday would be best; if you came latish—say 5.45 or 6. Gwen Raverat has asked out of the blue to come that day, after a years absence. She comes to see me alone, I expect, to talk of her difficulties, I suspect; but that should be over by 5.45, and it would be a first rate tonic for her poor woman to meet you; so I wish youd come and talk to her. Really, there is a sympathy between you, I believe—shes everything thats brave and angular and honest and downright—a far better character than mine. But not so appealing to the lower senses, perhaps.

1. In the early 1930s Ottoline began to write her Memoirs based on her diaries, but they were not published until after her death, when they were edited in two volumes by Robert Gathorne-Hardy (1963 and 1974).
2. Ethel was sending Virginia, one by one, articles which she had previously published and was now rewriting for her collected essays *Female Pipings in Eden*. This article was eventually called *Where Musical Criticism Goes Astray*.

We are off to Rodmell this afternoon not that I see much point in it.
I shall walk out and find another acre of my view spoilt for ever. And the
dogs bark, and then I cant work, and I've masses upon masses of work to
do, after my six weeks holiday. I admit I think it a very good thing, this
working. Ive been toiling over Donnes poetry all the morning[1]—with
antlike assiduity; for the Common Reader. Are you working? I hope so.
Sing me the Jacobite song one of these days.

V.

Berg

2523: To Lady Ottoline Morrell
52 Tavistock Square, W.C.1

Feb 8th [1932]

Dearest Ottoline,

I am very glad to have the photograph of Lytton—how exactly it brings
him back! I wonder if you can get other copies. Pippa was asking for
photographs the other day. (But she's gone abroad now).

Alas—Friday the 19th is the day we go to Rodmell; otherwise Leonard
would have liked very much to meet the bull dog man[2]—perhaps he'll come
again: and you'll ask Leonard.

Yes, that was what I was thinking too the other day—I mean that now
Lytton is dead how comforting it is to be with you who loved him. We
must always hoard the memory of him up together—that will be something
real—otherwise, running about London and finding everything going on,
I am aghast at the futility of life—Lytton gone, and nobody minding. But
with you, who loved him, some reality comes back. So you must let me come
sometimes. How can *you* complain of your own failure? I've been writing
about Donne all the morning and wondering what use it is. And then people
who read and exist beautifully and generously like you, seem to me so
enviable: and then you complain—and I throw up my hands in amazement.
So little do we understand each other!

yr V

Texas

1. *Donne After Three Centuries*, the second article in *The Common Reader: Second
Series*.
2. A man named Hodgson, who bred bull-dogs.

52 *Tavistock Square, W.C.*1

11th Feb. [1932]

Dearest Ethel,

Of course I would make an exception for Nan and Ethel,[1] if only they wouldn't ask me for Friday 26th! Thats the day we go to Rodmell in the afternoon, and that particular day we have to start early and go by Tunbridge Wells to travel our books—so I don't see how I can. But I would have liked to meet Nan, Hugh [Walpole] and David [Cecil]: and many thanks for asking me.

Anyhow you'll come this next Thursday.

Yours aff
V.W.

Wendy Baron

52 *Tavistock Sqre,* [*W.C.*1]

Feb 11th [1932]

My dear Hugh,

Yes I'm quite recovered again and immersed in the usual business—manuscripts—and Mr Simpson[2] who sits near me sighing O Providence, like a gnome: Miss Belcher[3] has been telling me about the horrors of life in Hilldrop Crescent. John Lehmann—how exciting it would be to be 23 [24] and in love! But I cant go into all that.

I'm delighted by your account of Prince George[4] among the books—He seems to me to keep up the George 3rd tradition and I love him for it. Really it would be awful, catastrophic, if the royal family took to art. However, as you say these matters must be gone into over a pot of honey. If I'm meeting you at Ethel's we can settle dates. And please remind me to ask you to give me fully and confidentially the true story of Mr Thring and

---

1. Nan Hudson and Ethel Sands were both Americans and both painters. They divided their time between Auppegard, their house in Normandy, where Virginia had visited them, and 15 The Vale, Chelsea, where they entertained lavishly.
2. John Hampson Simpson's new novel *O Providence* was published by the Hogarth Press in February 1932.
3. She had been an assistant in the Hogarth Press since March 1928.
4. Prince George (1902-42), fourth son of King George V and Queen Mary, was created Duke of Kent in 1934. He had been opening a book-exhibition under Hugh Walpole's chairmanship.

the society of authors,[1] for reasons I can't give now, being tipsy with having just bought a divine screen by Duncan Grant.

So hoping to meet

Yr V.W.

Texas

2526: TO LADY OTTOLINE MORRELL

52 *Tavistock Square,* [*W.C.*1]

Sunday [14 February 1932]

Dearest Ottoline,

It is more than good of you to send me the photographs. I suppose the one with Yeats was taken last summer. How tremendously vivid Lytton becomes in them—one can hear him speak. I'm sure Pippa [Strachey] would like them. We've been looking through his old letters, but cant find the ones we want, of course, What wouldnt one give for another hour—so much was not said. But I know that's foolish.

But you need never doubt his affection for you. Apart from the whole atmosphere, which was the right setting for some of his emotions—Garsington I mean, and Bedford Sqre[2]—I know he had a peculiar feeling for you yourself. But you know this too. I saw Mary—she's terribly bereft, I think: after the break with Clive she depended most on Lytton.[3]

I've got Richard Braithwaite (Cambridge)[4] and Lord David,[5] I think, on Wednesday—if you would come in any time about 5 it would be very nice—but I dont suppose you can. But try.

Forgive this scrawl—foolish but affectionate.

yr Virginia

Texas

1. Herbert Thring, Secretary of the Authors Society.
2. Garsington Manor near Oxford, and 44 Bedford Square, London, Ottoline's pre-war houses. She now had no country house, and lived at 10 Gower Street in Bloomsbury, where Virginia had met Yeats in November 1930.
3. Mary Hutchinson, wife of the barrister St John Hutchinson. Her long affair with Clive Bell came to a painful close in 1927-28. She was related to Lytton Strachey through her grandfather.
4. He was a Fellow of King's, and University Lecturer in Moral Science, 1928-34. In 1953 he became Professor of Moral Philosophy at Cambridge.
5. Lord David Cecil, the biographer and literary critic, aged 29. Later this year he married Rachel, daughter of Desmond and Molly MacCarthy.

2527: To Jonathan Cape   *The Hogarth Press,*
                                          52 Tavistock Square, W.C.1
Typewritten
14th Feb 1932

Dear Mr Cape,
    Many thanks for your letter and the suggestion that I should write an introduction to one of Jane Austen's books. I am sorry to refuse again, but the truth is I do not care about writing introductions—to me a very difficult proceeding—and in this case I have already said all that I am able to say. But please accept my sincere thanks for the suggestion.

                                          Yours sincerely
                                          Virginia Woolf

Jonathan Cape Ltd

2528: To William Plomer   *52 Tavistock Square, W.C.1*
Wednesday [17 February 1932]

Dear William,
    Could you come in tomorrow, Thursday, night, anytime after 9? We've got Derric Leon[1] coming, the novelist who's written a novel in about 10 vols: which I find fascinating. Here's a scrap of his hand, for you to diagnose —I'm so half-conscious I can't write. Remind me to give you a card from a Japanese.[2]

                                               yr
                                               V.W.
Texas

2529: To Helen McAfee   *52 Tavistock Square, W.C.1*
Typewritten
Feb. 19th 1932

Dear Miss McAfee,
    Many thanks for your letters and for returning the article.[3] I am afraid that I cannot make any suggestions for articles at the moment, as I am

1. Derrick Leon (d. 1944), author of *Livingstones: A Novel of Contemporary Life,* which the Hogarth Press published in February 1933. It was in one volume, but 653 pages long.
2. Plomer had spent nearly three years in Japan, 1926-29.
3. Miss McAfee, managing-editor of the *Yale Review,* had rejected Virginia's article on the Rev. John Skinner (1772-1839), the Rector of Camerton, Somerset, and author of voluminous diaries. But Virginia published the article in *The Common Reader: Second Series.*

already committed to other work which will keep me busy for some time to come. The suggestion you make about an article upon Queen Elizabeth is of course attractive; but I fear that I could not undertake it. My knowledge of English history is rudimentary in the extreme, and to write anything of interest about Elizabeth one would have to make a far more serious study of the time than I have leisure for.

It was very good of you to pass on my request for a copy of one of the Yale Shakespeares—I have been sent a delightful volume, and have sent on the information to the friend—a Fellow of Kings [George Rylands]—who first spoke to me about it. But they have not told me what I owe. I hope they will remedy this omission—or I should not have asked for the volume.

Believe me, yours sincerely
Virginia Woolf

Yale University

2530: To Margaret Llewelyn Davies

52 Tavistock Square, [W.C.1]

Typewritten
19th Feb [1932]

Dearest Margaret,

I have been in an awful rush or I would have answered your letter before. The book [*unidentified*] sounds most interesting—the sort of thing I like best. The difficulty at the moment is that I dont think I could manage to come up and see her in the morning; I am as usual very much behind hand with some essays I am doing, and have to give up the mornings to work. Would it be possible for your friend to send her MS. to me here, and I would read it as soon as I can? That would save time, and I suppose she is anxious to get it published as soon as possible. As you know, there are often unfortunately obstacles which make it impossible to publish books that one likes—but from your account this one certainly sounds promising. So please let me see it. I am so glad she liked our little book.[1]

We have been living in rather a whirl—an idiotic Polish Count[2] has

1. *Life As We Have Known It* (1931), a volume of working women's reminiscences, with an Introduction by Virginia, and edited by Margaret Llewellyn Davies, who had been Secretary of the Women's Cooperative Guild.
2. Count Geoffrey Wladislaw Vaile Potocki de Montalk, who was descended from a Polish aristocratic family but claimed to have been born in New Zealand, was charged on 8 February with publishing a group of obscene poems, one of which was dedicated 'to John Penis in the Mount of Venus'. His defence was that it was 'a literary experiment', intended for private circulation. He was found guilty and sentenced to six months' imprisonment. He appealed, and Leonard offered to contribute £20 towards his bail.

got himself into prison for writing silly indecent poems and Leonard is getting him out, which takes incessant interviews, calls from other poets in sandals and plush trousers—how can the young be so silly and egotistical. Shelley is at the bottom of it—but they write in the style of Mrs Hemans[1] save for indecency. Then we have been rather involved with the poor Stracheys—as you can imagine there is a mass of things to be read and talked over. But someday we must meet—I shall hope to visit the Russian—if an afternoon is ever possible. Love to Lilian[2]—I do hope her eyes are better.

Yrs Virginia

Sussex

2531: To William Plomer   52 *Tavistock Square, W.C.*1

Typewritten
Friday [19 February 1932]

Dear William,

Here is the post card—will you let me have it back with your instructions as to what I'm to say—if anything.

I am still shivering with alternate emotions of anger, laughter, and utter boredom from the Count [Potocki] last night. What an incredible combination—the count and Mr [Derrick] Leon!

Please be a man of kindness and send me your graphological diagnosis—I think it must be called that—of Leons hand writing, with any comments upon the Count that occur to you.

We must have another party without the Count—one evening will last me a lifetime with the count.

Yours ever—but always now on the type writer I'm so afraid of your discoveries—

Virginia Woolf

Texas

2532: To William Plomer   52 *Tavistock Sqre,* [*W.C.*1]

Monday [22 February 1932]

Dear William,

I'm so sorry, but we're already dining out on the 1st and 3rd March—this is bad luck, and I hope you will ask us another night later, as we should so much like to come.

---

1. Felicia Dorothea Hemans (1793-1835), whose sentimental poems were immensely popular in her day.
2. Lilian Harris had been Margaret's Assistant Secretary in the Women's Co-operative Guild.

There's not much to await in my letter to a young poet.[1] I find one can hardly broach the subject in 4,000 words; and then some space has to go in the amenities of letter writing. But who is your man?—a don called something like Leaven[2]? I've not read him, but have submitted to cross examination from, perhaps, his wife. The truth about the modern poets seems to me to be that they have all the virtues, and none of the gifts—but then I'm hopelessly wrong about poetry, like most prose writers.

Yours
V.W.

Texas

2533: To Ethel Smyth   52 *T*.[*avistock S*.[*quare, W.C*.1]

Tuesday [23 February 1932]

Lord Ethel, what a silent grub I've been—but I cant describe the rush last week, and the complications. Did I tell you about the Polish Count, and his invocation to the male organ—for which he's in prison and L. is trying to get him out, for which reason I've not had time to buy suspenders: my stockings sag down; nor nibs: I've none left to write with—nor boots— oh nothing. and all because of the Polish Counts male organ sticking in the Mount of Venus.

What can I suggest at the moment? Wait a day and I'll see. Thursday is my last sitting,[3] praise God: Friday we have [Sibyl] Colefax and [Hugh] Walpole. Saturday—thats the only chance: but thats threatened at the moment. But as I say, wait a day and let me collect my wits. Also I may have to rush down to Ham Spray (the Stracheys). Where there is every sort of misery at the moment, that I cant go into. I repeat, wait till tomorrow: I can always telephone. And I'm moody and broody, but my star is inclined to you; Its not *that* mood thats wrong. Yes I liked Maurice B.[4]

V.

Berg

1. *A Letter to a Young Poet* was suggested to Virginia by John Lehmann, and addressed to him. It was first published in the *Yale Review* in June 1932, and by the Hogarth Press in July.
2. F. R. Leavis (1895-1978). He was Editor of *Scrutiny*, a quarterly, and later a Fellow of Downing College, Cambridge. He and his wife, Q. D. Leavis, a teacher of literature, were occasional critics of Bloomsbury in the 1930s. In the first issue of *Scrutiny* (1932) Virginia was censured for "some cerebral etiolation" in her novels.
3. For a portrait by Vanessa.
4. Maurice Baring (1874-1945), the poet and novelist. He was an intimate friend of Ethel Smyth, who wrote his biography (1938) during his lifetime.

Friday [26 February 1932]

I've only got 3 minutes—Colefax and Hugh have just gone: I've swallowed dinner: I've got to dress and go to L.'s mother's party—good God![1] My mind is dizzy with talk. I cant settle any plans at the moment. This is only, though you wouldn't think it, the voice of affection. I will write or ring up tomorrow. Apologies for this incoherence. And yesterday was awful: I ended the evening in black despair—

V.

Berg

Sunday [28 February 1932]

No dearest Ethel, you cant feel more of a wretch than I do. Perhaps you never said you felt a wretch—I impute my own miseries to you. Lord, lord, what time wasted in talk last week—talk, talk, talk, and all save perhaps 2 hours and 10 minutes utter waste. When the 10 Jews sat round me silently at my mother in laws, tears gathered behind my eyes, at the futility of life: imagine eating birthday cake with silent Jews at 11. pm:

But this is to say what if I came to you[2] for the night on Thursday next —that is the 3rd? Can you have me? I think I can manage it. But every day till Thursday is useless—I mean if you want an hour alone. theres always somebody coming, except I hope to God on Tuesday when I must sit down to the pile of MSS. which has heaped itself up. If I cant read between 5 and 7 thats what happens—a pile.

Consider Thursday next. and let me know. I could catch a train about 5.30 or 6, and be down for dinner and come up next morning in time to go to Rodmell. So then we could stretch our legs out and talk alone, uninterrupted from about 7. pm to about 4. am. But now you'll be engaged.

Yr
V.

Berg

1. Marie Woolf, the mother of ten children, was 82.
2. At Coign, Woking, Ethel's house. It was Virginia's first overnight visit there.

Sunday [28 February 1932]

Dearest Dadie,

Of course we're coming to Hamlet [at Cambridge]. Could you get us tickets for the Saturday night performance—March 12th that is; and I command you to send me the bill. I'm longing, without exaggeration, to see it.

I've been sent a volume of the Yale Shakespeare you told me of—I wish the type wasn't American, that's all. They have also sent this prospectus—you see they have an interleaved edition too.

Yes, I want to see you too. Life seems awfully empty without Lytton.

Your
Virginia

George Rylands

Sunday 28th Feb [1932]

Dear Hugh,

Yes of course I should think it a great honour if you dedicated your Scott book to me.[1] Indeed I woke at 3 this morning and said what was the nice thing that happened last night?—and remembered your letter—Here is Mr Edwin Muir[2] accusing me of a perverted passion for Scott—well, I admit it: and I want very much to see what you say about this infirmity of ours—when will it be out? What are you saying—lots of things I hope. And do you really want another copy of the Waves? If so, you've only got to hold up the little finger of your left hand and I will send one. (I have a sensibility about sending people my books: they'll have to say they like them: so I dont, unless asked)

I was rather cross at Sibyl's [Colefax] coming. She seemed to create an atmosphere of amiable insincerity instantly—not but what I like her. Its only—what? I wonder if you felt what we felt. And I wanted to explain my violence about Morgan.[3] I'm sure I'm wrong, at least I think it highly likely. I suspected him of wrapping up tame little reputable platitudes in

1. Walpole wrote a 15,000-word Introduction to his anthology of Walter Scott's novels, *The Waverley Pageant*, which was published in 1932 in connection with Scott's centenary. Its dedication read, "For Virginia Woolf who does not scorn Sir Walter".
2. The novelist, poet and critic, 1887-1959. His article was in the *New Statesman*.
3. Charles Morgan (1894-1958). He had just published his most famous novel, *The Fountain*, which won the Hawthornden Prize.

words of twenty five syllables, and thus posing, and thus undermining the health of English letters, as Mrs Ward[1] did and others: with their damnable pretence of fine writing: and so threw the book out of the window half read. But I explode so easily against fiction that I have hardly any trust in my own vehemence. Anyhow, dont dismiss me as an etiolated, decadent, enervated, emasculated, priggish blood-waterish 'ighbrow: as Arnold Bennett used to say. Yes: I think a letter to Trollope would be first chop.[2] (I'm now trying to acquire a red-blood style) I think the Small House at Allington perhaps the most perfect of English novels along with Jane Austen—I cant explain now why.

Also, what I couldn't say before Sibyl—and how does she insist upon being spelt?—I am much concerned about your health. May I visit you in the Nursing Home:[3] or will you be able to come and take a cup of tea only before you go? Let me know if there's an afternoon free.

And I'm fearfully pleased to think of Virginia Woolf upon your dedication page.

Yrs affate
Virginia

Leonard wants me to say that he thinks he may hit on a better idea for a letter than A. T. [Anthony Trollope]. He will write himself.

Texas

2538: To Dora Carrington   52 *Tavistock Sqre.*, [*W.C.*1]
[28? February 1932]

Carrington dearest—that is very good of you, to send me the photograph. I have only some small ones Ottoline gave me. This is extraordinarily good I think. I didnt mean that I doubted that Lytton knew we cared—because I always felt that however seldom we met, our feeling was so deep it couldn't change: no—I only feel now desperate sometimes that one let time slip and didn't see him. For instance last winter—But I was ill all November. And I used to think he was so happy with other people, and so—but you know all this: one always feels it: and I had come to think that we had so many years together still, and we should see more and more of each other. I'm wondering if one day I may see some of his letters. I begin to think I would write something perhaps of my feeling about him for you—how we used to talk when we were young.

1. Mrs Humphry Ward (1851-1920), the popular novelist and philanthropist.
2. Walpole did not pursue this idea, but in July the Hogarth Press published his *A Letter to a Modern Novelist*.
3. He was about to undergo a thorough medical examination for diabetes.

This is only to thank you: Ralph was very good and kind and tender the other day.

Yr loving Virginia

Julia [Strachey] has just sent her story.

Robert H. Taylor

2539: To Ethel Smyth   [52 *Tavistock Square, W.C.*1]

Postcard
[29 February 1932]

The wireless people are:—

E. M. G. Gramophone.
11 Grape Street
Shaftesbury Avenue

I think Eddy[1] has one of their gramophones, which are far the best; and now we have added the wireless, also the best. Mention Mr Woolf if you like.

V.W.

Berg

2540: To Clive Bell   52 *Tavistock Square,* [*W.C.*1]

29th Feb. 32

Well, dearest Clive, this is very generous of me, because I dont much think I shall get an answer. But look at the date—leap years day—certain rights are mine. Also I'm encouraged by the fact that since our generation's letters cant be published, this can be a wild scribble between the lights. (Its cold, cold, damnably cold in London): and thats a great relief to me, because we're all so famous now. You would think that this was leading to a boast, wouldn't you? And so it is. Didnt I get a letter this morning from the Master of Trinity in person asking me to be Clark Lecturer next year[2]—

1. Edward Sackville-West, Vita's first cousin, was already, at the age of 30, becoming well known for his novels and music-criticism. E.M.G. gramophones had enormous horns made of papier-maché. Roger Fry and Vanessa each had one too.
2. The Master of Trinity was Prof. Sir Joseph Thomson. The Clark Lectures on English Literature were founded in 1883 (when Leslie Stephen gave the first course of lectures) in honour of William George Clark, the Shakespearean scholar and Vice-Master of Trinity. Desmond MacCarthy had lectured on Byron in 1929, and Virginia was the first woman to be honoured by an invitation to give the lectures. For a fuller explanation why she considered that writers should refuse to lecture, see her *Three Guineas* (1938), Part One, note 30.

Yes I did: but I shant do it—think of writing six lectures, and standing on a platform at my time of life. I shall only tell as many people as I can in a casual sort of way, and pass on to something else. Indeed, as Desmond was once a Clark lecturer, the honour is not overwhelming, even to a vain woman like myself—Lord!—what stuff he does write—now about Lytton —like an old spaniel dribbling down its chops.[1] He made no use of your article, which I copied, and sent him and thought very well of.

I could tell you a mint of literary gossip—if it weren't so repulsive— having just seen Hugh: chiefly about the Book Society and how but this is a profound secret,[2]—Hugh has: ahem. Well then the indecent novel by Mrs Gerald Brenan[3] has come our way, and from half a sniff I dont see much to it—trembling like an aspen, she says that men co-co-copulate with women. Thats a fact. Did you know it? On the other hand Julia Tomlin [Strachey] has delivered a very cute, clever, indeed rather remarkable acidulated story, which we shall publish.[4] In the social line, Harold and Vita are going to America, lecturing [in early 1933]; I met Anrep[5] last night at the Camargo [ballet] and was introduced to his daughter and mistress— which reminds me that Roger is said to be making heavy weather with his cargo of Russians, and Nessa predicts what we all secretly desire. The old chief [Maynard Keynes] and Lydia dined here, and the talk was all very amiable, and about the past, and how he met Barbara Hiles[6] and did more than meet her 50 years ago. They're doing Hamlet at Cambridge and we are going up to haunt that windy tomb—how I shall shiver and shake, and avoid talking to Peter who's novel lies by me, but I cant abear Peter's novels.[7] Why cant he be coupled with Webster, or Jonson or some other text that wants correcting, for ever and ever, in sickness or in health amen? And on Monday we attend the law courts. Did you ever hear of a Count Potocki[8]? Well he went and wrote a poem about Penis in the mount of Venus; and O what luck to sit and fuck: and Come and Hunt in Pegg's Cunt: for which

1. Desmond MacCarthy's article on Lytton Strachey was published in the March issue of *Life and Letters*.
2. J. B. Priestley had resigned from the Selection Committee of the Book Society (of which Walpole was Chairman), and was replaced by Edmund Blunden.
3. Mrs Brenan was Gamel Woolsey, the American poet, whom he married in 1931. Her novel was *One Way of Love*, which was accepted by Gollancz, who then took fright over *The Well of Loneliness* case, and it was never published. (See *Personal Record* by Gerald Brenan, 1974, p. 223).
4. *Cheerful Weather for the Wedding*, 1932.
5. Boris Anrep, the Russian mosaicist. He was estranged from his wife Helen, who was living with Roger Fry.
6. Barbara Bagenal (*née* Hiles) had been the Hogarth Press's first assistant in 1917-18, and married Nicholas Bagenal in 1918.
7. F. L. ('Peter') Lucas, (1894-1967), the poet, novelist and scholar, and Fellow of King's College, Cambridge.
8. See p. 20, note 2.

he was given 6 months imprisonment, and we've had to employ Jack Hutchinson to get him out. Such is English life at the moment. Write, please, and tell me about Rome. Write fully and give my love wherever its desired.

Virginia

Quentin Bell

2541: To Ethel Smyth   52 *T.[avistock S.[quare. W.C.*1]

Wednesday [2 March 1932]

I hope to catch the 5.38 tomorrow [to Woking], and will come up by the 6.15 bus: arriving as far as I can see at 6.30. I shall bring no clothes, and a hot water bottle.

So no more till then. Remember, I never drink wine at home; and am more than glad to get up for breakfast.

Berg

2542: To Dora Carrington   52 *T.[avistock] S.[quare, W.C.*1]

2nd March [1932]

I loved those little pictures, darling Carrington. How it seizes upon one, the longing for Lytton, when one sees them. But then how happy he looks —that is one comfort—and then again I thank you. We would always have come to Ham Spray: it was only the feeling we had that that belonged to another side of Lytton's life: I dont mean that you didn't want us, but that it was simpler for him to come here. But heavens—how I wish we had brushed aside all that, and come and stayed: or made him come here oftener. Of course one gets involved in things, and there is always the press, and Leonards different things—how worthless it seems now compared with one hour of being with Lytton. Yes, I think it does get harder—I cant describe to you the sense I have of wanting to tell Lytton something. I never read a book even with the same pleasure now. He was part of all I did—I have dream after dream about him and the oddest sense of seeing him coming in the street.

Oh but Carrington we have to live and be ourselves—and I feel it is more for you to live than for any one; because he loved you so, and loved your oddities and the way you have of being yourself. I cant explain it; but it seems to me that as long as you are there, something we loved in Lytton, something of the best part of his life still goes on. But goodness knows, blind as I am, I know all day long, whatever I'm doing, what you're suffering. And no one can help you.

I've read Julia's story. I think it astonishingly good. We shall publish it I hope: but will you try to keep her at it—and will you do pictures? I'm sure thats what would make it a success—Couldn't there be woodcuts in the text? It seems to me full of scenes that want illustrations. Its extraordinarily complete and sharp and individual—I had no notion it would be so good. But I feel she may tear it up at any moment—She's so queer: so secret, and suppressed.

Goodbye, darling Carrington

your old attached friend
Virginia

Robert H. Taylor

2543: To Ethel Smyth   [52 *Tavistock Square, W.C.*1]

Friday afternoon. 2.10 p.m. [4 March 1932]

Look dearest Ethel, I am sitting down at once to express my sense of gratitude—never have I enjoyed a chaste night more [at Woking]. Please live 50 years at least; for now I've formed this limpet childish attachment it cant but be a part of my simple anatomy for ever—wanting Ethel—I say, live, live, and let me fasten myself upon you, and fill my veins with charity and champagne. Of course you'll go and spoil all my plots about Trinity—talking over the fire to Lady B.[1] I shall meet ghosts of your irreticence in the courts of Cambridge—never mind I forgive you the sin before you've committed it; and you cant say I didn't warn you, can you? all Woking in the 3rd class carriage is witness to that. Did you see the woman's face when you vociferated about sitting in the lavatory?

Well—here's an interruption: I'm only scribbling, without I fear that exemplary economy of adjectives that you so rightly admire, before I once more draw the strip [*sic*] of my case and plunge off with L. to the wilds.

But these are the moments which one should give thanks for—when one feels cheered and warmed, and thinks that it was Ethel who created that happiness; so live another 50 years; and dont please be put off by terrible irregularities—my spasms of one emotion after another—those spikes I drive into my fingers. Heavens how I admired your practical sense: typical of so much: the taxi; the dr: the pincers: the splinter out: mushrooms and champagne.

V.

And let me know the cost of the taxi.

Berg

1. Lady (Elizabeth) Balfour, Ethel's friend and neighbour, a daughter of the Earl of Lytton, who married the 2nd Earl of Balfour in 1887.

2544: TO ETHEL SMYTH   [*52 Tavistock Square, W.C.1*]

Typewritten
Sunday [6 March 1932]

1 . . . L. says just what I said about Peter Davies—hes a very good,
exclusive publisher, who would give great attention to a book like yours,[1]
which is out of the common run. Therefore he advises you strongly to go
to him. He gets up his books extremely well into the bargain.

2 . . . The Counts trial. Weve no news of this; nor do we know who is
trying it. But the thing to do would be to look in the law list in the paper
tomorrow. It is an appeal case, and the defendant is Count Potocki de
Montalk.[2]

Just back from Rodmell.   V.

Oh the chocolate came and is absolutely delicious. What a good thing I
made that joke!

Berg

2545: TO DORA CARRINGTON   *52 Tavistock Sqre.*, [*W.C.1*]

Tuesday [8 March 1932]

Carrington dearest—We have a day off on Thursday—day after tomorrow.
We want to come down and discuss Julia's book and see you. Might we?
Would you give us lunch?—then we'd come back in time for dinner, like
last time. This would be a great treat for us—perhaps I might wander up
the down, and look at some of Lyttons books. Anyhow, if we may, we will
come about lunch time. With our love

                                                      yr Virginia

Robert H. Taylor

2546: TO ETHEL SMYTH   [*52 Tavistock Square, W.C.1*]

Typewritten
[8 March 1932]

No dearest Ethel I dont think Friday can be managed, since L. is out;
and I have to sit [to Vanessa]. But the EMG would let you hear a later
model than ours: [*handwritten*] and L. says a much better one.[3]

1. *Female Pipings in Eden*, Ethel's latest volume of autobiographical essays,
   published by Peter Davies, 1933.
2. The Count lost his appeal.
3. See Letter No. 2539.

We go down to Hamspray on Thursday and may I suppose stay the night; but hope to be back late. No; its not the [Master's] Lodge I'm staying at—its only with the Fellow of Kings [George Rylands], or rather at an Inn. And then we shall travel our books on the east coast for a day or two—back Tuesday or Wednesday—oh lor, how Id like to stay here and write—too many people, too many people. Mrs Keppel[1] tomorrow. Eddie [Sackville West] just gone—enthusiastic and affectionate about you; in which I joined. about Coign too and the comfort of staying there

V.

[*handwritten*]
and he abused The Waves, and I abused Simpson[2]

P.T.O.

L. says he *could* be in by 6.30 on Friday and would be pleased to play you Beethoven Opus. 31 No 3 if you could come *punctual*.

Berg

2547: To Elizabeth Bowen   52 *Tavistock Sqre.*, *W.C.*1

8th March [1932]

Dear Mrs Cameron,
    Yes of course I was hoping I might see you again. This Thursday unfortunately I have to go away; but would Wednesday or Friday next week suit you at 4.30? (I think they're the 16th and 18th). If you could send me a card I should be grateful.

Yours sincerely
Virginia Woolf

Texas

2548: To Dora Carrington   52 *Tavistock Square*, *W.C.*1

Thursday night [10 March 1932]

Carrington dearest, we are just back [from Ham Spray] and had our dinner, and I cant help scribbling one line to thank you—oh just for being yourself. You cant think how close Lytton comes when you're there: you keep him for me more than anyone. So go on, dearest, devilish though it is for you;

1. Mrs George (Alice) Keppel, the beautiful and discreet mistress of Edward VII. In 1932 she was aged 63, and died in 1947, two months before her husband. Virginia met her lunching with Raymond Mortimer.
2. Edward Sackville-West's novel about a children's Nanny, 1931.

because you do what no one else can do. I'm so lonely sometimes without him, so old and futile and merely dried up, and then with you I feel come over me—its so odd—what I was when Lytton was there.

And then its so lovely—the rooms, the carpets, the trees outside, every little object. How do you do it? I felt consoled walking under the trees.

And look what ugly paper this is! When am I going to have the drawings[1] and the book plate?

D'you know there was a coin, silver, Italian or French, in the little box?[2] I must send it back. So good night dearest Carrington, from your attached old friend who would do anything if she could.

Robert H. Taylor

2549: TO LADY OTTOLINE MORRELL

[52 *Tavistock Square, W.C.*1]

Friday [11 March 1932]

Dearest Ottoline,

This is just to tell you that Carrington died this morning. We were there yesterday and talked and she seemed quiet and very gentle. That is all I know now, but I wanted you to know.

My love
Virginia

Texas

2550: TO RALPH PARTRIDGE [52 *Tavistock Square, W.C.*1]

Saturday [12 March 1932]

Dearest Ralph,

This is just to give you our addresses: tonight (Saturday) the Bull, Cambridge. On Sunday after lunch we go to Norwich, and spend the night. Address. Post Restante. Monday night, at Rogers. Rodwell.[3] Tuesday 52 Tavistock Square.

Let us know if we can help in any way, and all our love.

Virginia
Robert H. Taylor

1. For Julia Strachey's story, which was published unillustrated. Carrington shot herself next morning, and died in great pain six hours later. She read Virginia's letter just before her suicide.
2. Which Carrington gave to Virginia. Carrington had herself given it to Lytton.
3. Virginia and Leonard spent the night of 14 March at Roger Fry's house, Rodwell House, Baylham, near Ipswich.

52 *Tavistock Square, W.C.*1

Typewritten
12th March 1932

Dear Miss McAfee,

You were so kind as to ask me to send you an article for your June number. I have just heard from Harcourt Brace that they are not publishing the enclosed essay for some months. We shall publish it over here in early June. But if it suited you, perhaps you would like it for the June number.[1] Harcourt Brace are bringing it out as a booklet later.

Would you be so very kind as to cable your decision, as I have not much time in which to arrange for American publication?

Believe me,
yours sincerely
[no signature]

Yale University

52 *Tavistock Square, W.C.*1

[14? March 1932]

My dear Julian,

I hope you are all right again. We missed you greatly, Norman Angell[2] was rather fun.

I saw Dadie [Rylands] yesterday and he praised your Pope[3] highly. He seemed to think it full of ideas and orginality and wanted you to go on with it. I hope you'll let me see it.

I dont think it much matters not getting the fellowship—I expect I am foolish—but still I dont like Fellows, as fellows. Much better write on your own.

Anyhow come and see us soon

Virginia

Friday

I have just got this back from Cambridge—address not known—God knows why—so am sending it via Nessa

Quentin Bell

1. *A Letter to a Young Poet*, published in the June issue of the *Yale Review*.
2. Author of *The Great Illusion* (1910) and many other books on politics and economics.
3. Julian's dissertation on Pope. It failed to obtain for him a Fellowship at King's, and when it was offered to the Hogarth Press for publication, Leonard turned it down. (See *Journey to the Frontier*, by Peter Stansky and William Abrahams, 1966, pp. 89-92.)

[52 *Tavistock Square, W.C.1*]

Tuesday [15 March 1932]

Dearest Ottoline,

I've been away till this evening or I would have written. Yes, of course it was suicide, but at first I didn't like to say so, as they were anxious to get the verdict that it was an accident. She had borrowed a gun from Brian Guinness,[1] and shot herself early on Friday morning. She died in 3 or 4 hours. Ralph arrived while she was still conscious. She told him it was an accident—that she had been shooting at a rabbit and had slipped. But she had already tried once before when Lytton was dying. That was why we went down—the only chance seemed to be to give her some interruption. But I felt, as we sat talking about Lytton in Lytton's room that afternoon, that she could not go on much longer. She said she had failed with everything except with Lytton—she was very gentle and affectionate. I could only tell her how much we all needed her—indeed, she kept so much of Lytton that her death makes his loss more complete. But she had suffered so terribly and could not believe that there was anything to come in life. I feel that he would have hated it—Pippa came back last night on hearing of it. Carrington made every preparation and rang up Ralph after we had gone to say that she felt more cheerful. But it was terrible leaving her alone that night, without anybody in the house.

yrs
Virginia

Texas

52 *Tavistock Square, W.C.1*

15th March [1932]

Dearest Dadie,

We decided to go to Kings Lynn, so had to start early, so missed seeing you,—alas. But perhaps you'll be round here next week and will let us know. It was a charming dinner—how fascinating it is to meet complete strangers—and I'm dumbfoundered [*sic*] at your brilliance as a producer [of *Hamlet*]. Talking of brilliance—d'you know Trinity has asked me to be Clark lecturer! Isn't that a compliment for an illitertrate (who cant spell)

1. Bryan Guinness, (later 2nd Lord Moyne), the poet and novelist. He lived at Biddesden House, Andover, where Carrington, with Ralph Partridge, Frances Marshall and David Garnett visited him on 29 February, and she borrowed his gun 'to shoot rabbits' at Ham Spray.

of my sex? But no—I leave all that to you. And that reminds me—what about your dialogues[1]—and shall we have the honour of printing them?

Yr Virginia

George Rylands

2555: To Ethel Smyth [52 *Tavistock Square, W.C.1*]

[17 March 1932]

No I think its really a pity for you to come tomorrow unless you're absolutely on the doorstep, because its so tantalising that running in and out, and feeling one cant start anything, and Miss [Elizabeth] Bowen stammers and blushes.

But do as you like—only there's also your cold, and you'll get late and so on and so on: and die on my hands. O what a rush—dining out

V.

Berg

2556: To V. Sackville-West [52 *Tavistock Square, W.C.1*]

Thursday [17 March 1932]

Dearest Creature,

I dont think I ever thanked you for the dogs[2]—may I keep it and perhaps use it in my story?

I've been rather submerged in tragedy—Carrington killed herself the day after we were there. I dont think anything could have stopped it—still.—

But what I say now is, I'm going to the Old Vic on Monday night to see Duncan's ballet.[3] Will you come! I believe its ravishing.

Let me know. We are here this week end: Oh and I've been seeing such divine country, untouched, unspoilt, unknown—where I mean to retire, on the wolds, by the sea, with great clumps of cypresses planted by Coke of Norfolk.[4] But enough. Will you come too?

Y
V.

Berg

1. Rylands had begun to compose a dialogue on Poetic Style, following his *Words and Poetry* (Hogarth Press, 1928), but he later abandoned it.
2. Possibly a photograph of Vita's spaniels, which Virginia proposed to use in *Flush*.
3. Duncan Grant had designed the scenery and costumes for *The Enchanted Grove*, with music by Ravel and Debussy, presented by the Vic-Wells Ballet.
4. Thomas William Coke, Earl of Leicester (1754-1842), the great agriculturist who lived at Holkham Hall, near Cromer, Norfolk.

2557: To V. Sackville-West   52 [*Tavistock Square, W.C.1*]

[19? March 1932]

Come on as early as you can on Monday: The Old Vic is in the Waterloo Road, Donkey, and not Hammersmith; and there won't be a dress in the house. I dont know what time it begins.

V.

O and dont let Ethel know we're going, or she'll come too.

Berg

2558: To Harmon H. Goldstone

52 *Tavistock Square, W.C.1*

Typewritten
19th March 1932

Dear Mr Goldstone,[1]

I have only just received your letter; and I am afraid therefore, as you say that your essay has to be finished by the 1st of April that I am too late to be of any help to you. But I will answer your questions as far as I can— I do not think however, as you can guess, that a writer is able to say much about his life or work.

I have not studied Dr Freud or any psychoanalyst—indeed I think I have never read any of their books; my knowledge is merely from superficial talk. Therefore any use of their methods must be instinctive. As far as I remember, the character of Septimus in Mrs Dalloway was invented to complete the character of Mrs Dalloway; I could not otherwise convey my whole meaning about her. I have never written a line of verse. But the decision to write prose and not verse was made without any deliberation. So far as I know, my methods are my own; and not consciously at any rate derived from any other writer. No 'life' of me has been written; the only facts are to be found in the books of reference that you name. The name "Bloomsbury Group" is merely a journalistic phrase which has no meaning that I am aware of. I may have printed a few newspaper reviews of novels in the Times literary supplement between 1905 and 1908 but nothing else.

---

1. Goldstone was at this date a senior student at Harvard, aged 21. He had written an essay on Virginia for a college competition (which he did not win), and considered developing it into a whole book, but abandoned the idea when he discovered that Winifred Holtby and Floris Delattre had already written books about her. He later became an architect in New York City and was Chairman of the New York Landmarks Preservation Commission 1965-73.

The titles of the two stories published by the Hogarth Press [in 1917] are The Two Jews, by my husband; and The Mark on the Wall by myself.

I am afraid that this is all the light I can throw on the questions you ask; and may I request that you will consider this letter as private? I should of course be much interested to read your essay; and with best wishes for your success.

Believe me,
yours sincerely
Virginia Woolf

Berg

2559: TO WILLIAM PLOMER   52 *Tavistock Sqre, W.C.*

Sunday [20 March 1932]

Dear William,

It is very good of your friend, (of course I remember him) to have verified M. Delattre for me. He sounds highly respectable. His book has now arrived.[1] I can't say I find it lively reading, but then its difficult to see one self as a mummy in a museum: even a highly respectable museum. Never mind: you'll join me soon.

I'm sorry M. Janin[2] is disappearing—the people one likes always do. And I wanted, among other things, to ask him about coffee, for which I have a passion. I must wait. Will you convey my thanks and regrets.

Please suggest a night at Monks House—Early September would be best.

Leonard says Cambodia[3] is doing well: I'm so glad; and rather suspect that your fortune is made. And how did you know Rosamund [Lehmann]? Where? why? This letter must stop.

V.W.

Texas

2560: TO ETHEL SMYTH   52 *T.[avistock] S.[quare, W.C.1]*

Monday [21 March 1932]

Dearest Ethel,

I was, and am, very sorry you couldnt, no wouldn't come today. But I expect you were right—Anyhow Leonard has a violent cold, and you'd

---

1. *Le Roman psychologique de Virginia Woolf*, by Floris Delattre. Paris, 1932.
2. René Janin, the son of a French general and a translator from German into French. Virginia had met him dining with Plomer on 17 March. He was also a friend of Stephen Spender.
3. Plomer's novel *Sado*, which the Hogarth Press had published in September 1931.

have caught it. Perhaps, for this reason, I shall put off the people—the Stracheys again—tomorrow; but I dont know.

Anyhow I've accepted M.B.'s [Maurice Baring] invitation to tea on Easter Monday [at Rottingdean], and shall see you then, which will be nice —oh yes, nicer than seeing you here, where I feel hemmed in and depressed and haunted by poor Carrington. That last visit and talking to her in Lyttons room and saying goodbye in the evening in the garden and thinking of her going back into the house alone: and then waking and fetching her letters and shooting herself—how they come back and back. Not that I could have done anything; but when we were talking, perhaps I could have said more in praise of life—I wonder. Only I couldn't lie to her—But I think I've told you all this. She held to it, even to her husband as she died that it was an accident—how strange the human mind is—considering she'd done it once already, or tried to. But she won her point—I mean, they [the Coroner] brought it in an accident, and its said all the servants and so on suspect nothing, which saves him, poor man some little added misery. But heaven knows now what he can do; or his unfortunate mistress—This is all very dismal, and if you came I should only infect you. I'm taking Vita to the Old Vic. Oh and we think of flying to Greece for a month; please please rake up all your advice, and memories. and let me have the benefit.[1]

I'm scribbling with Leonard sneezing, and the effect is of a hen pecking up here one grain, there another—MB has sent me his book,[2] and I've snatched up his praise of your singing, which is all to my mind I mean what I would say myself, on the strength of half one of Schuberts songs that morning. Arent you happy to have that gift as well as the others? I've now got a huge book on V.W.: [Delattre] but cant read it, because I hate my own face in the looking glass.

Well then write to Rodmell. and dont altogether forget—as she deserves—your Virginia—And I never told you all about Cromer on Sunday evening and the moors, and the sea, and heaps of lovely things I saw.

Berg

2561: To George Rylands   52 *Tavistock Sq,* [*W.C.*1]

Wednesday [23 March 1932]

No: Dearest Dadie, you mistook me, as I wrote carelessly. I refused the Clark lectureship—I was only boasting that they'd offered it me. How could I mug up 6 lectures when I know nothing of the subject? So I said to the

1. Ethel had published *A Three-legged Tour in Greece* in 1927.
2. *The Puppet Show of Memory*, Maurice Baring's autobiography (1922). He describes Ethel's singing on pp. 139-40.

Master that I was profoundly touched and gratified, which I am: but incapable: which I am.

Why this modesty about life? Arent you one of those enviable people who have it both ways? Books 6 months, life 6 months: so dont dally, but write the dialogues instantly.[1] We think of going to Greece in April. Any advice to offer? What's the best way of going? Expenses? Inns? above all, are there Bugs? There used to be, 25 years ago; but people say they no longer bite. Thats my chief recollection of Corinth[2]—bugs to right, bugs to left.

We are just off to Monks House. If you shd ever see any fellow of Trinity, please, emphasise my gratitude. It was extraordinarily nice and generous and open minded of them; and I wish I could have done it. And let us see you.

Yr Virginia

George Rylands

2562: To Ethel Smyth

Monks House, [Rodmell, Sussex]

April fools day [1932]

Well my dear Ethel. since you will only write me postcards about facts I suppose I must take my pen and stir your embers. Lord if you knew how difficult I find it to write! There's always someone here between tea and post—oh such heaps of people, yesterday the Keynes's, today my nephew and his lady, tomorrow Brighton and the labour party. So I forget what I was going to say. Something about Greece. By God, what a sport or trump or card you are—I'm trying to snatch the sort of slang your Captain Grant[3] would use at Newmarket—you know how I love that style—to care about your friends' journeys far more than they care! Its an amazing magnifying glass you carry under your hat. But I was saying we shall go to Greece via Venice; and fly back; and want to hire a car in Athens.

None of this is very real to me at the moment because I'm raked and rasped and altogether out of spirits—those buildings. My view is ruined for ever. They've now put up 3 iron sheds, literally the size of St Pauls and Westminster Abbey on the down which overlooks my marsh. Hence the entire flat is commanded by these glaring monstrosities and all my walks that side, not only the downs ruined: and the view from the terrace: the view I always swore was eternal and incorruptible. Its like losing £200 a year for life—worse. And wherever I walk this monstrous abortion intrudes

1. See p. 35, note 1.
2. Virginia's previous visit to Greece was in September 1906.
3. Alistair Edward Grant, a partner in Peter Davies, the publisher, whom Virginia had met when she visited Ethel and Maurice Baring at Rottingdean on 28 March.

itself. This is what they call civilisation—and its to produce cement, of which England has already more than she can use: so they'll smash, in a year or two, and there the horror will be for ever.[1] This has swept me on to a second page, which I cannot fill even at my pace which is 100 miles an hour, as the post is about to go and my nephew to come.

We go back on Sunday night, and perhaps somehow I shall get my week straight and somehow see you and somehow finish my articles which bore me to a kind of dancing agony at the futility of all criticism, and mine more than all—such childs play. Such caper cutting about folly they are. (The 2nd Common Reader this is) And then I must buy shoes and gloves and a jersey and some bug powder, and nightgowns and hats and—this is the prelude to all the joys of travel. Are you in fact going to Greece too? With whom? Why? Where?

I've invented the skeleton of another novel: but it must wait, buried, at least a year.[2]

This egotism must cease: but I hope its poked your ashes and caused a fan among them so that you'll seize your pen, and plunge it deep, and cross page after page at your nursery table—the one that comes in Imps. that masterpiece.[3] What a good book it is I will have a little marble square let in to your writing table to say so, in case you wrote it there. Where did you write it. And were you ever in love? and whats your notion of life?

V.

and why do you go to Torquay, and with whom; and who is the person you like best, and why, and what was the compliment to your beauty, and was Maurice ever in love with you and did you go to bed with more than one man?[4]

Berg

2563: To V. Sackville-West   Monks House, Rodmell,
                                                    [*Sussex*]

Friday 1st April [1932]
April fools day: and I was had completely by Leonard

Listen, long ears.

An American dealer has written to me to say that a Collector wants to buy the MS of Orlando. For my part I think it would be a very good thing

1. The sheds remained until 1978, when they were partly demolished after the cement-works ceased operation.
2. Probably *The Pargiters*, her novel-essay about feminism, which she later developed into *The Years*.
3. *Impressions that Remained*, Ethel's two-volume autobiography, 1919.
4. Virginia is referring to Henry Brewster, the Anglo-American poet and philosopher, with whom Ethel was intimate until his death in 1908.

if you sold it *now*—you might get a hundred or two; and it seems to me far better to sell now, when the dollar is worth whatever it is worth, than to keep it mouldering at Long Barn: and it will moulder still more at Sisst.[1] What I should like would be that you should start your library on the proceeds. So let me know. I will write another book and give you the MS. instead—about turning into a rusty, clotted, hairy faithful blue-eyed sheepdog.

Are you coming up on Monday, and if so are you coming my way? We return Sunday night—I was going to say damn: but my happiness here is almost entirely ruined. You can't think what horrors—vast galvanised iron sheds, 3 of them, about the size of the Albert Hall, aren't rising right in the middle of my marsh. The terrace is irretrievably ruined. What is the point of staying on here? I've been walking on the downs, but everywhere one comes on the horror, and it works a sore on one's mind. It makes me rage and wake in a hellish misery at dawn. I daresay this kind of outrage is among the real sorrows of life.

So I want comforting.

V.

We go to Greece on the 14th I think, flying one way. Its only £5 more than train, and 2 days quicker. I say—we hope you will dine too on Thursday next with Harold. Kingsley Martin[2] is coming. Apart from the pleasure of your society, I think the effect would be all to the good.

Berg

2564: To Ethel Smyth   [52 *Tavistock Square, W.C.*1

Monday [4 April 1932]

I doubt if I made my meaning clear on the telephone:

The dr. says that as last time I was done [inoculated] my temp. was 102 next day this may happen again and therfore advises no engagements. I think probably this was an accident and there'll be no after effects whatever. So choose: if Wednesday is much more convenient for you come then to

1. Virginia had given Vita the bound manuscript of *Orlando* soon after its publication in 1928. It remained in her writing-room, first at Long Barn and then at Sissinghurst, until her death in 1962, when it was given by her sons to the National Trust, to be kept in perpetuity at Knole. Virginia also bequeathed to Vita in her Will any other of her manuscripts she wanted, and she chose *Mrs Dalloway*, now in the British Library.
2. He had been appointed Editor of the *New Statesman* when it amalgamated with the *Nation* in February 1931, and remained Editor until 1960.

tea: and risk being put off. Or if its indifferent, come tomorrow (Tuesday) and be certain. Unless I hear, I shall expect you tomorrow (Tuesday) 4.30.

V.

Berg

2565: To Ethel Smyth [52 *Tavistock Square, W.C.*1]

Wednesday [6 April 1932]

Well it would have been no good your coming here tonight. Its not been nearly as bad as last time, but I'm as drowsy as a bear—even a little temp. completely dulls my mind. I'm now crawling off to bed, and shall wake tomorrow. And no dinner—only fish and toast, so I hope you've dined on quails and champagne

Will write later V.

Berg

2566: To S. S. Koteliansky [52 *Tavistock Sqre, W.C.*1]

9th April 1932

Dear Kot,[1]

It was very good of you to write, and I cant help answering though you tell me not to. Yes, what you say is true. Lytton's death is very hard to bear. But all the more one needs the friends that are left, and I am grateful to you for saying that you think of me with affection. Do you remember giving me a wooden box once when we came to see you? I have it now before me, and often think of you—We are now going abroad till May, but if you should ever care to come and see us please understand that it would be a pleasure to us both to see you again.

And again, thank you for your letter.

Your affate

British Library Virginia Woolf

2567: To V. Sackville-West 52 *T[avistock] S.[quare, W.C.*1]

Sunday Night [10 April 1932]

This was found under your chair tother night and is therefore supposed to be your's[2] Please, please write to me—if addressed here it will be for-

---

1. Samuel Koteliansky (1882-1955), was a Ukrainian émigré who had a few friends in Bloomsbury, and collaborated with Virginia on translations from the Russian in the early 1920s.
2. A book of stamps.

warded: I mean *they* will: I mean you must write every week, or whenever you think of me, or see the moon in a huddle, or hear a dog howling or tread on grass. I've refused the £5,000 for Orlando, on your behalf— What a donkey! This would have built you a library to last for ever. Yes I'm taking the 2 saddles for you and Ethel; one's a mans; for thats, as I understand, to be your relation.

Shall we ever meet again?

This time next week I shall be floating past the lights of Dalmatia— looking out of my porthole window I shall see—no, this is too cruel; since all you'll see is the BB.C: Siepman's[1] earnest and perspiring forehead, Langham Place, omnibusses and so on. But Lord! I've got to do a mint of things before I go: Sybil, Nan Hudson, and so on

So goodnight and Potto's love.

V.

Berg

2568: To Ethel Smyth   [52 *Tavistock Square, W.C.*1]

Typewritten
Sunday [10 April 1932]

I return Millgate [*unidentified*]
The name is:—
London and National Society for Women's Service.[2]
We shall certainly go to Giolmann[3] first thing. We are having our letters addressed to Poste Restante, Athens. If we change, we shall inform the Hogarth Press. So at any time they will give you our whereabouts. As I have another inoculation on Tuesday and have to go down to Rodmell for the day and buy every sort of minute object I write this now; but shall try to write before we start if only a line. And hope for letters.

V.

Berg

1. Charles Siepmann succeeded Hilda Matheson as Director of Talks, B.B.C., 1932-35.
2. The feminist society which Virginia and Ethel had addressed on 21 January 1931. Philippa Strachey was its Secretary from 1914 to 1951.
3. The tourist-agency in Athens.

Typewritten
April 10th 1932

Dear Miss McAfee,

Many thanks for your kind letter. I am so glad that you liked the article.[1] Since I sent it you we have decided to go to Greece for a months holiday and shall start on the 15th April. I expect to be back about May 15th; I am afraid from what you say therefore that I shall not be here when the proofs arrive. If you would send them to me addressed Poste Restante, Athens, I think I should probably get them safely. But of course there is always some risk of missing letters when one is travelling. If I do not let you have them back in time would you therefore be so very kind as to correct them for me? I have noted only one error so far of importance—Gera*l*d for Gera*r*d Hopkins, but I fear there may be others.

> With our kind regards
> yours very sincerely
> Virginia Woolf

Yale University

Monday, April 11th 1932

Dearest,

It was a great indeed divine pleasure hearing from you[2]—which I did this morning. Lord knows, though, if I can finish this—Nan Hudson has just gone—Sibyl Colefax is about to come. It is a windy rainy evening turned 6 o'clock. And tomorrow we start at dawn to deposit Pinka at Rodmell, and then I'm inocculated, and we leave for Greece on Friday. Not by air though. That turned out a fraud. They only fly one to Paris, and pick one up again at Brindisi; so we go to Venice, and sail down the Dalmatian coast, and so reach Athens about Tuesday. We start with Roger and Ha-[3] Helen [Anrep], whose ticket I offered to pay towards, has some mystic objection. I see its all likely to end in bugs, quarrels, playing chess, disputing about expeditions and so and on and so on—but I shall feel this all

1. *A Letter to a Young Poet.*
2. Vanessa was staying in her house at Cassis, in the south of France.
3. 'Ha' was Margery Fry (1874-1958), Roger Fry's youngest sister. She was Principal of Somerville College, Oxford, 1926-1931, and a lifelong worker for penal reform.

makes bones for your pot: that is still the cauldron in which my life is brewed

Barbara [Bagenal] takes the cake. Never never can there have been a woman so sealed from birth to all the subtleties sensibilities and harmonies of civilised life. To dump her mumpish brat [Judith] on you at the last moment seems the last straw. Couldnt this be tactfully conveyed her, by Duncan say, on a card? Of course its a form of morbid love for you—thus to inflict these scars. Any contact is some sort of ecstasy to her—But after this, dont despise me for Ethel Smyth and the rest. Nan [Hudson] has been humbly rhapsodising about your genius for art—a subject that leaves me cold. But she says you are one of the 3 people she loves. The third is a dog. Would you believe it, she has altered all her plans because her summer bull dog might have been left with an unsympathetic servant; was about to start for Cannes, and is going as it is to live at Dieppe alone with him for a fortnight. She told me a long story about a Swiss who copulates with cows. I take this to mean that she has relations with Peter [the bull-dog]. I dont blame her, save that he's old, blind and smells. Then she said people take her for a Sapphist. By dint of praising incontinence as an aid to landscape painting I almost brought her to admit that she has, once or twice, on a pale May night, embraced Ethel [Sands] in a coppice. But she flitted off to a party—I like her though, and feel that there is brick beneath the—is it called rubble?—which I doubt with Ethel.

I've been seeing the usual sort of people—that, is the Keynes' at Rodmell, and Ethel [Smyth] and Vita and Harold. We went over to Sissinghurst which is now a complete 15th Century Castle, with moat, drawbridge, seneschal, greyhound, ghost, bowling green and I daresay buried treasure. Its rather a lovely rose-red though. Then we had tea with Maurice Baring at Rottingdean—2 dirty footmen to hand anchovy sandwiches, which I loathe and so had to put in my bag. When asked for a match by Baring I handed him my sandwich. Ethel Smyth was there, straddled like a major in front of the fire. Then I saw James and Alix;[1] James rather dried up and stratified I thought: Alix flowing with a queer phosphorescent beauty. Old Mrs S. Florence has just proved in 10 vols. that colour is the same as sound: the question is who will publish it?[2] James is Lyttons executor, and has found masses of poems and plays, mostly unfinished, also box upon box of letters. We advised him to have the letters typed and circulated among us. He says Lytton said very unpleasant things about us all. But as we all do that, I dont see that it matters. Ott [Morrell] and Roger Senhouse neednt be included, if it hurts their feelings. Our letters aren't there—it was an

1. James Strachey (1887-1967) was Lytton's youngest brother, and is best remembered for his translation of Freud's *Complete Psychological Works*. His wife Alix (*née* Sargant-Florence) studied with him under Freud in the early 1920s.
2. In 1940 Mary Sargant-Florence published, in a single volume, *Colour Coordination*.

earlier series. James says that Lytton meant to write one more book on George Washington; and then retire, probably abroad, and write violently, proclaiming his sodomy, and cutting adrift from society. I must say I doubt it.

By the way, did Angelica get a pound from me?[1] I dont want thanks—only to know if it reached her. If not, I'll send another. I may have missed you at Fitzroy Street. Lottie [maid] has heard from Clive, and apparently starts cleaning on Friday. I'm in despair about Rodmell. Theyve now run up 3 incredibly vast galvanised sheds at the foot of Asheham, which completely ruins our view, and the rumour is that they are building 60 workmen's cottages. I suspect our part is doomed, and we had better go now—at least if we could sell the house. But perhaps we shall be more sure this summer: still its bound to be destroyed, though Maynard says the factory will go bankrupt. Thank God, theres Colefax ringing up for the 18th time to say she cant come. But the incoherence of this letter and the fact that the hand is less legible than print are due to the imminency that brooded over me. The weather is incredibly vile: rain, snow, hail, gales, fog all at once.

Now to business. We shall call at Poste Restante Athens for letters. I imagine Athens will be our headquarters. We shall be in Greece about a fortnight—from April 19th to May 14th: and stay perhaps in Italy on the way back and be home on 4th. So please *write write write*. If you write direct send to Poste Restante Athens: but the Press here will always forward. Nor need I remind you of the excitement of any letter in foreign parts. Please ask Duncan to write. As for that wretched false hearted Pixy [Angelica] I hardly expect a letter from her. No doubt Judith [Bagenal] is tenderer-hearted. I shall alter my will accordingly. No one has died. Florence Burke[2] has written. Her husband has broken his knee cap. [Walter] Sickerts show is said by Nan to be very bad. Lady Diana is appearing in The Miracle.[3] What is Julian doing about his fellowship? Write, write write, good Dolphin; and I will remember you to your blue brothers in the Aegean. Leonard sends love.

B.

Berg

---

1. Angelica Bell, Vanessa's daughter, was thirteen.
2. Florence Burke (*née* Bishop) was a friend of Leslie and Julia Stephen who married a naval doctor.
3. Lady Diana Cooper first appeared as the Madonna in Max Reinhardt's American production of *The Miracle* in 1923. In 1932 she revived the role at the Lyceum Theatre in London, and subsequently in many cities of Britain.

12th April [1932]

Dear William,

I like Miss Bowes Lyons' poems very much.[1] They're handmade not shop made—a great relief, I find, after the general run. I like the Hare especially—its so spare and angular and individual. No wonder she prefers doing this to writing novels. I hope she'll write some more and let us see them. Sometimes as you know we can print very small books ourselves. I'm sending them back tomorrow.

We are off to Greece on Friday as I think Leonard has told you. Many congratulations on the Book Society choice[2]—at last a good one. So we can forgive Hugh [Walpole] some of his other sins.

I suppose, by the way, I didn't leave a blue silk spectacle case at your house the night we dined there? I'm afraid not—but there's just a chance.

Yours
Virginia Woolf

Texas

2572: To Ethel Smyth   52 *T.[avistock] S.[quare, W.C.*1]

Typewritten
Thursday [14 April 1932]

Such an infernal rush. Still have to get a macintosh. Well, this is merely by way of goodbye. I'll speak to Giolmann in high terms of you. We'll try to do Meteora[3] if any hope exists. They say motoring is very difficult. We're taking—L. is going to study—your book. 3 legged tour. We shall float down the Adriatic and in that peace I hope to write to you perhaps— Last typhoid more unpleasant than first—the wrong way round. Here are some cuttings. Theres Virginia in the year 1911. I'm glad you beat Elgar.[4] No, I dont want to be in large letters anywhere. I think this is sincere. Mrs [Miss] Craig[5] gives me distinct pain. And what a donkey— think of taking my fun deadly serious. I can see your rooms. and envy you

1. Lilian Bowes-Lyon (1895-1949), a niece of the future Queen Elizabeth (wife of George VI) was the author of several volumes of poems and one novel, but she was never published by the Hogarth Press.
2. Of Plomer's novel *The Case is Altered*, published by the Hogarth Press in July 1932.
3. The group of medieval monasteries in Thessaly.
4. Presumably a joint billing of Ethel's music and Edward Elgar's, which she disliked.
5. Edith Craig, Ellen Terry's talented daughter and a theatrical producer, who greatly admired Ethel's music.

rather. Itll pour on the Parthenon and as you say what can I see in Greece—purblind worm that I am? The one serious delight is to be beyond the telephone—no need to 'see' anyone for four weeks. This is a cry—because every day in this rush someone has sat me down for two hours talk—no escaping ones kind, much though I love and respect them. Even now—someones waiting. So good bye not for so very long and I shall pounce on letters from Bath.

Virginia

Berg

Letters 2573-2585 (April–May 1932)

On 15 April Virginia and Leonard went on holiday to Greece with Roger Fry and his sister Margery. They were away until 12 May. Travelling by train through Paris, they embarked at Venice on a ship which took them down the Adriatic and round the southern coast of Greece to Athens, where they spent several days, visiting Daphne, Sunium, Aegina and Marathon. Then they drove to the Peloponnese—Corinth, Mycenae, Nauplia, Sparta (Mistra) and so back to Athens. Finally came an expedition to Delphi. They abandoned a plan to visit Thessaly or Crete, and returned by train from Athens through Belgrade to England, leaving the Frys in Greece. Their companionship had been an almost untarnished pleasure. The Frys were indefatigable, knowledgeable, loquacious. They explored, painted and botanised, while Virginia, though tired by long drives over atrocious roads and blistered by the sun, found it "by far the best holiday we've had for years".

2573: To Vanessa Bell

[*On board the Lloyd Triestino s.s. Tevere*]
19th April [19]32

Well here we are floating past the Greek islands. Not a ripple on the sea, so hot one can sit naked on deck—an occasional fowl settles on the masts—Roger comes running to say thats Corcyra [Corfu] which it isnt—a Greek gentleman corrects him—asked his name he says he is Christ son of Christ. There is also Mr Hutchinson,[1] the archaeologist, who plays chess. But we are in the first class, and all this seething life surrounds the Frys in the Second. I have withdrawn to our palatial writing room, where there are only bald headed merchants. The truth is it is impossible to do anything at sea. We were to reach Athens this evening, but rocks have fallen and blocked the Gulf of Corinth so we have to go round, and shant arrive till 6 tomorrow morning—rather a bore, as there is a limit to ones love of sea life. We have a cinema in the evening: tray upon tray of ham sandwiches; beef tea half hourly; and an occasional melancholy waltz. So far, the Frys and the Wolves have been as sweet as nuts and soft as silk, and I daresay we haven't stopped talking, completely, for half an hour. There was dinner in Paris, at a little place where Roger took his wife 36 years ago: and then a night and half day at Venice. Roger oozes knowledge, but kindly warmly like an aromatic—what? Shower bath, it'll have to be, as my wits are dazed.

1. Perhaps Richard Wyatt Hutchinson, best known for his excavations at Nineveh.

We only had time for 3 churches and part of the Academia—and Florias Ha—[Margery Fry]—(I've once called her so, by mistake) dressed like an elderly yak in a white pelt constrained by a girdle, is admirable in bearing the brunt of aesthetic criticism. I've heard her even contradict Roger about Bellini, and she always has a feeling about a sky or a pillar or the use of bald heads in design which turns the blade off the poor ignorant Wolves. I did however, attack Titian and Leonard says he made a point about a diagonal —anyhow, it doesnt matter, as Roger is urbanity itself, and realised from the first that one must let pass Venice and concentrate upon Greece.

We drove round Brindisi yesterday, in search of a dome that Roger had seen from the boat, but we only found the railway station and one locked church. This was a diversion however, as Leonard had beaten Roger twice at chess, and I gather there was some feeling,—what Roger does is to take his Queen back, and then says—which is exasperating,—he cant play well when Leonard is so slow. But this is the only rub. We talk, talk, talk. Sometimes Ha and I (but I must call her Margery) pace the deck discussing Herbert Fisher,[1] or Pamela,[2] I think she suspects me of being an intellectual and moral and social snob; so I do my best to climb off my perch and roll on the floor; and sometimes she likes me; and then she's fearfully humble. When I say "but Ha—I mean Margery—you know all about politics" she says "My dear Virginia, when will you get that silly illusion out of your head? I'm merely good at bluff. That's how I take people in."—I think she was probably a good deal chastened by Rogers infatuation with Blooms-bury, and suspects me of being in conspiracy against her, But Lord lord—I know nothing about anyone; and merely advance my antennae and generally get snubbed—yesterday I lost my spectacles, (but had packed them): this morning I came down to breakfast holding my sponge bag, and have once wandered, in my night gown, into the barbers shop. This is what comes of dreaming of Duncan all night. Why dream of Duncan? He never dreams of me, nor thinks of me either; nor writes to me into the bargain. Yet my lust for love remains undiminished by the Greek islands. We are just in time for Easter in Athens. Christ the son of Christ—how Roger picks up dusky jews at every turn, and Ha too. We shall have a following like a bitch on heat—says we must spend the 1st of May night in the churches and the streets: all lights but one go out. That is the Easter rite, and more beautiful he says than any other. Roger has a special box of canvases; Ha is also going to sketch. We think of going to Crete. Roger thinks of meeting Helen [Anrep] at Venice. What thoughts are in your head? Well this, though a terrible letter from a born writer—which you cant deny I am—not a good one but a born one—that's the sort of thing Roger and I argue about—

1. H. A. L. Fisher, the historian, formerly President of the Board of Education, and Warden of New College, Oxford, 1925-40. He was Virginia's first cousin.
2. Roger Fry's daughter, then aged 30, who married Micu Diamand.

is long, and adoring and full of the most tender if unexpressed—but aren't the tenderest feelings precisely those—emotions. This is whats called 'crossing' a letter. Please, please write, Poste Restante, Athens Greece.

I could have described the scenery but I know of old how you hate that.

B.

Leonard is still playing chess. No—here he is—has beaten Roger again. Lord!

Berg

2574: To Ethel Smyth   *Hotel Majestic, Athens*

April 20th Wednesday [1932]

Well, you'll have to put up with an illegible scrawl. We're just arrived; the gulf [Corinth canal] was blocked with rocks, and so we came round spending another night. So far all has been easy and warm and airy, and successful. One night at Venice then on down the Adriatic with Venizelos[1] on board, passing the islands all day yesterday, comfort, air, quiet, sitting on deck reading Wells, Shakespeare and a screaming gull called Middleton Murry.[2] Roger and his sister went 2nd; hes coagulated various greeks and Jews—its their way—Rogers and M's I mean; so have a thousand pieces of good advice. Its blazing white in Athens, with donkeys sagging on either side with black tulips and red anemones. We're now changing into thin clothes and going up to the Acropolis. Your letter arrived very welcome; and pleasant to think of Bath and Ethel at her window a Much Muckle.[3] We go to Giolmann [travel-agent], who met the boat, tomorrow. I will speak of you, or show your book—I doubt if we shall manage Meteora. The Frys incline to Crete, said to be the loveliest land in all Greece. First we must knock down Greek art—Roger thinks poorly of it. I still hold up the Temples; and shall argue tonight—never were such chatterers; oh and we learn Greek, and count out money, and Venice was divine, oaring about from church to church in the evening and the islands, elephant grey with rose red stains, and the ships passing at night, and a lighthouse suddenly

1. Eleutherios Venizelos (1864-1936), the Greek patriot and statesman. He was then, for the fourth time, Prime Minister of Greece.
2. The critic and editor, with whom Virginia had conducted a sort of running fight ever since his marriage to Katherine Mansfield in 1918.
3. Possibly a reference to the large-mouthed woman in Browning's poem *Muckle-mouth Meg*. Or from Scott's *Bride of Lammermoor*: "I think it might pass, if they winna bring it ower muckle in the light o' the window."

opening as we sat at a movie with Venizelos. There—thats all—L's going to the post—and this is only like a wag of Pan's[1] rudimentary tail. I think we shall stay here some days.

V.

Berg

2575: To V. Sackville-West   [*Hotel Majestic*] *Athens*

April 24th [1932]

Well, you haven't written to me, not one word, not one post card, so perhaps Sissigt. is blotted out—the Tower fell, crushing the daughter of the Sackvilles to pink pulp—a very fitting end for a woman who forgets old but humble, humble but old, friends. Its Sunday at Athens; we've been lunching, not too well, and looking for 2 hours at Byzantine relics—because its a sultry wet day; and now we're off to Hymettus, and yesterday we went on a ship to Aegina, and saw the loveliest temple, and an island all carved in terraces with olives and wild flowers, and the sea running into the bays (it was pouring wet, I must admit, and we were herded with 50 American archaeologists) Still it is a beautiful island, and I padded to the hill top, picking wild irises and unknown yellow stars, and little purple, violet, blue, white, pearl flowers, all about as big as the stone on your ring no bigger. And we went to Daphnis, and wandered in olive woods, and to Sunium, the Temple on a cliff, which cliff is soft with flowers, all again no bigger than pearls or topazes. Margery Fry is a maniacal botanist, and squats— she's the size of a Russian bear—on the rocks digging with a penknife. And we saw the Greek shepherds huts in a wood near Marathon, and a lovely dark olive, red lipped, pink shawled girl wandering and spinning thread from a lump of wool from her own flock of sheep. There! Thats to make you feel envious. (I see you've got foot and mouth disease in Kent.)

Our drawbacks—these you'll want to know—are bitter winds, stormy grey skies, and vast helpings of soft sweet pudding. Also Roger has the piles—cant walk, also Margery suffers, like all spinsters aged 63 [60] from unrequited loves 20 years ago for Englishmen who were killed in the war. But this means that she is full of the most obsolete and erudite information about archaeology; has everything an invalid can want in a huge wooden box, and makes arrowroot for those who like arrowroot the last thing at night. Tomorrow, if the rain stops, we're off for 3 nights in the Peloponese. (cant spell) and then back here, and then, I think to Crete, and then, I suppose home. But I dont want Tavistock Sqre at the moment: I like the life here—you should see the donkeys, with paniers full of anemones; and the Square, all ablaze with flowers, and the Acropolis. Have I described our

1. Ethel's sheep-dog.

afternoon on The Acropolis—when a storm rushed up from the Aegean, black as arrows, and the blue was as blue as hard china, and the storm and the blue fell upon each other and 10 million German tourists rushed across the temple precisely like suppliants in their grey and purple mackintoshes—no I haven't described the Acropolis—You may thank your stars I know my place as a prose writer and leave all that to someone who, about this time 4 years since, won from Jack Squire, a silver beaker to drink her pop from.[1] There! Thats my revenge for your not thinking of me. Ethel thinks of me. The first thing I got here from Giolmann the tourist agent was a sheet from Woking bidding him buy a man's saddle 2nd hand for her to ride on this autumn "as I'm growing stiff and rather past middle life now". I picture you and Ethel jogging up Hymettus together on a second hand man's saddle. By the way, who is a sandy middle aged red faced ex-diplomat, married to an Italian wife, who was minister in Norway[2] and talks at top of his voice about Austen, Bill Bentinck, Lascelles, Billy Tyrrell and so on?[3] He almost got to you, but caught me listening and drew his horns in. He was travelling on the boat from Venice. Lord, how wearisome diplomatic talk is—d'you know Bill Bentinck—etc etc—you are well out of it. But it is not well that you shd. forget me. Please write. Roger is angelic, and exudes knowledge of the most sympathetic kind.

L sends his love—but is catching a flea— V.

Berg

2576: To Ethel Smyth   *Nauplia, [Greece]*
Postcard
April 26th [1932]

Here we are safe, very cold, very hot, driving all day, seeing Corinth Mycenae, on to Epidauros now, breakfasting on a quay, red and blue boats mountains, sun, incredibly lovely; Giolmann [travel-agent] superb.

V.

Berg

1. J. C. Squire was founder-editor of the *London Mercury*. In 1927, as Chairman of the Hawthornden Prize Committee, he awarded the prize to Vita's poem *The Land*.
2. Virginia may have her facts wrong. None of the more recent British Ministers in Oslo married an Italian. She may have met Sir Archibald Clark Kerr (1882-1951), who was British Minister in Stockholm and a friend of all the other diplomats mentioned, including Harold Nicolson. His wife Maria was not Italian, but Chilean.
3. Austen Chamberlain, Foreign Secretary, 1924-29; William Cavendish Bentinck, H.M. Minister in Athens, 1932; Sir Alan Lascelles, Private Secretary to George V; Sir William Tyrrell, H.M. Ambassador in Paris, 1928-34.

May 1st 1932

Dearest Quentin,

It was a great joy to get your letter at Athens, and it served very well to cheer us all up that night. Not that we want cheering particularly—save that some part of Roger's inside is coming through, so that he cant sit or stand—but this makes little difference. Its merely a question of going behind a hedge now and then with a buttonhook. There is often not a soul in sight for 20 miles. The roads are incredible—mere tracks between pits. We motor from dawn to dusk. Now we are at Delphi, with a torrent rushing down the street, 6 vultures, or golden eagles soaring above us, and whole sheep roasting over woodfires on poles because it is for some reason Easter Sunday. All the Greeks are therefore singing wild incantations and marching about with candles and corpses on biers. We have put Greek art in its place—rather lower than it was: on the other hand, their architecture is better than it was reputed. But the Byzantines are the real swells. (This is a quotation from Roger). Roger is a fair shower bath of erudition—Not a flower escapes him. And if it did, Margery would catch it. Between them every bird beast and stone is accounted for. We talk almost incessantly, and yesterday had the great joy of smelling a dead horse in a field. No sooner smelt than 12—no—15 vultures descended from the azure and proceeded to pick it. They have long blue bald necks like snakes. Sometimes a tortoise crosses the road—sometimes a lizard.

But we travel from Athens to Corinth and so to Nauplia without any human intercourse. I will not describe the scenery, as I know you cannot read more than one word in ten of what I write, and that one is probably wrong. This is a pity as the scenery is marvellous, miraculous, stupendous —save for the olive groves however, it is not very plastic, and Rogers paintings suffer he says from this deficiency. But he never puts his nose out without hanging himself round with easels, canvases and paint boxes. Margery also paints. But even so, they talk. They never stop talking. They talk Greek, on a system, so that tonight we were almost landed with two black kids and a pail full of sour milk, owing to a misunderstanding between Margery and a shepherd. I can only write now because Leonard is playing Chess with Roger, and Roger has just had his Queen back.

Tomorrow we are motoring to a monastery [Hosios Loukas] along a road that is almost always impassable—one either falls off the ruts or into the pits—But R has persuaded the chauffer [*sic*] that it is perfectly easy. So pray for us, and at the same time forgive the dulness of this letter, and its illegibility. We shall be back in about a fortnight—shall hope to see you—if that is Mary Butts[1] hasn't butted you. I cant go into this as there's no room.

1. The novelist and short-story writer. She was the sister of Anthony Butts, William Plomer's friend, and married John Rodker, the poet and translator.

Roger is now hopelessly beaten. The Greeks are playing bagpipes and serenading the bleeding body of Christ in a very sensual minor key. So goodbye—

Virginia

Quentin Bell

2578: To Vanessa Bell   *Delphi, [Greece]*

Monday, May 2nd [1932]

Well its almost impossible to write because of the heat, and being half asleep after lunch but I must admit you deserve some thanks for writing such a masterpiece on the human species.[1] I read it (carefully selected extracts only) at lunch: and as the doleful tale of Stracheys Partridges Tommies [Stephen Tomlin] and Wogan[2] curled its length the house—we were lunching in Athens—rocked with laughter. Still it seems to me certain your final trial was not Ralph, but Mary (Hutchinson) She told me she meant to go to the Huxleys.[3] As you observe, since its France she'll be bound to come and see you—and Clive—and Duncan. And there'll be the devil to pay. Pray God you write and tell me about it.

Here we are in Delphi, all well except for Roger's inside falling out and my skin peeling in great sores. The wind and sun, the bitter cold and violent heat, the driving all day along rocky or pitted roads, make one feel like a parboiled cactus. All the same, it is so far a great success—I mean from our point of view. No quarrels, no accidents,—in fact, we live in considerable comfort, and have a car to drive in, instead of pottering about in trains and flies as we used.[4] The Inns are now clean as new pins—not a bug, or even a flea to be seen; no corpses on the wall, and the food about as good as English—too many olives and sardines for me; but Leonard and Roger love them and plunge into octopuses and lizards,—I mean they eat them, fried—oily lengths like old rubber tires cut into squares. There's not an

---

1. See Roger Fry's letter to Helen Anrep, 4 May 1932, from Athens (*Letters of Roger Fry*, ed. Denys Sutton, 1972): "Virginia in particular doesn't seem to want to talk. . . . I think she gets immense pleasure from just having experiences. Only when Vanessa's grand letter from Cassis came denouncing the human race ('mice are easier to get rid of') Virginia launched out about how she would write to Vanessa about the Frys." Vanessa's letter of 19 April survives (*Berg*), but in so mutilated a condition as to be almost illegible.
2. Wogan Philipps, the painter and farmer, who married Rosamond Lehmann in 1928. He succeeded his father as 2nd Lord Milford in 1962.
3. Aldous and Maria Huxley lived at Sanary in the south of France.
4. During Virginia's previous visit to Greece, with Vanessa, in 1906.

English man or woman to be seen; our only society is our own, and some peasants, but as Roger learnt Greek out of the wrong book, most of our talk gets wrong, and when I correct with pure Classical Greek—as my way is—the only result is that we are supposed to have bought 2 kids. No, I haven't probed Margery: old age brings its sad wisdoms—I see one cant eviscerate the elderly unless one wishes to have decomposing carcases hung round one's neck. There is the less need, however, as she has told us all about her emasculated life, with the old Frys—how her father dismissed her lover, and her mother never let her laugh at any story a man told lest it should be thought fast. The dulness of her youth and the 6 sisters was she says worse than a convent. At the age of 97 Lady Fry, having shut them all up in so many band boxes pouring out tea and watering flowers owned that her policy had been a mistake.[1] But it was then too late—Margery has missed having a child, and has to paint and botanise and watch birds and philanthropise for ever instead. I daresay it would be better if she married Roger as you suggest. They hum and buzz like two boiling pots. I've never heard people, after the age of 6, talk so incessantly. Whats more, there's not a word of it what you and I might call foolish: its all about facts, and information and at the most trying moments when Roger's inside is falling down, and Margery must make water instantly or perish, one has only to mention Themistocles and the battle of Platea for them both to become like youth at its spring. The amount they know about art, history, archaeology, biology, stones, sticks, birds, flowers is in fact a constant reproof to me. Margery caught me smiling the other day at my own thoughts and said no Fry had ever done that. "No" said Roger, "we have no power of dissociation." which is why of course they're such bad painters—they never simmer for a second. R. has done about 20 pictures under incredible difficulties, but for some reason oil paint wont dry here so they'll all be smudged. As for his amiability and indeed docility its astonishing as he cant walk and cant sit our doings have to be very mild—This is a great mercy—most of the day they paint and we sit about under the trees. I admit we've done most of the museums, but far from thoroughly. The great discovery is that the Greeks were far inferior to the Byzantines. So we search out obscure mosaics and mosques and neglect all we used to see with Violet Dickinson[2] Lord what ages ago that seems!

I spare you the truth—which is that Greece is far and away the loveliest country now left—quite unspoilt—in fact, uncivilised. I spare you all account of Delphi and Nauplia. The day before we came here they found the body of Cochrane, whats her name Ilberts son, on a tree in the cliff

1. Lady Fry died in 1930 at the age of 97. Her husband, Sir Edward Fry, a distinguished jurist, died in 1918, aged 91.
2. Violet Dickinson, Virginia's most intimate friend in her adolescence and early youth, had accompanied them to Greece in 1906.

opposite.[1] He fell over and broke his back, and—here I was called off, and now we are back (May 4th Wednesday) in Athens after driving 13 hours yesterday. He broke his back on a tree, and they found his skeleton with a watch between the ribs.

It is blazing hot and gets steadily hotter. I wear my thinnest dress and a vast shady hat, and still its too hot to sit in the sun. This letter is so dull and disjected that I think I ought to stop, and try to darn my stockings and mend my suspenders: still I cant resist a little dessiccated gossip, if you've not anyone on you at the moment, no Tommies or Ralphs. But I'm always in danger of running on about the beauty of Greece which is far better than I remembered—in fact, we can't have seen it at all. Nothing is spoilt—its as wild as a pole cat—every inch is a different flower—mostly minute and like sparks of emerald and so on: Margery grubs in the earth like a grizzly bear to get roots to send home to the stone deaf Agnes[2] whenever she's not fixing a hawk or vulture with her glance or arguing or doing any one of the things the Frys do. But she's as sweet as milk and pathetic—about her lost life, and no children but only endless university honours. But as I was saying its the beauty—if ever I had a turn towards Sapphism it would be revived by the carts of young peasant women in lemon red and blue handkerchiefs, and the donkeys and the kids and the general fecundity and bareness: and the sea; and the cypresses. (This sentence reads wrong: but I leave it to you to disentangle.) We've just been to the Post office and found no letter from you but one, of the most enchanting nature from Angelica [Bell], who seems to sum up all the gifts as well as graces. Are you rid of Judith [Bagenal] at last? Isnt she like a very round hard boiled egg?

Yesterday we had a fine sample of Fry tenacity—Roger had heard of a monastery [Hosios Loukas] with mosaics near Delphi—the driver pointed out that it would add 3 hours to our 10 hour journey, also climbing a mountain at midday on mules. Roger found a shorter way. But, the man said the road is impassable. Not a bit of it said Roger. So it was planned; and we got up at 5 ready to start. At the last moment news came that a car had rolled over the precipice owing to the bad road, and the driver absolutely refused to go. So we compromised and went the long way and rode up the hill in the heat of midday and the mosaics were very inferior and the Monks were very annoying, and we didn't get back to Athens till 8.30 at night, having broken a spring, punctured a tire, and run over a serpent. But we saw an eagle. And Roger said it was only by these experiments that one could get real insight into the people—However he's in the best of tempers:

1. He was David Cochrane, son of Margaret ('Mora') Ilbert and Sir Arthur Cochrane (Clarenceux King at Arms), and a nephew of Mrs H. A. L. Fisher. As an undergraduate in 1931 he went on a walking-tour in Greece, and fell down a cliff near Delphi. His body was found exactly a year later.
2. Agnes Fry (1868-1957), sister of Roger and Margery. She had been deaf since childhood.

and though we were almost speechless with dust we had a very good dinner and so to bed.

We start back on Monday I think, and shall be home it is thought on the 15th or 16. when the greatest indeed the only pleasure will be to see Dolphin [Vanessa]. I cant think why we dont live in Greece. Its very cheap. The exchange is now in our favour. There has been a financial crisis and we get I dont know how many shillings for our pound. The people are far the most sympathetic I've ever seen. Nobody jeers, or sneers. Everybody smiles. There are no beggars, practically. The peasants all come up across the fields and talk. We can't understand a word and the conflict between Roger's book and Leonards often makes it impossible for us to get a drop to drink, because they cant agree what is the word for wine.

But it is now nearly 12, and I must stop. The Frys suggest that we should make a final dash to Olympia, and if so we shall go on Friday for 2 nights. They stay on another week.

So farewell.

B.

Leonard sends love. The Frys are painting the Parthenon
Ethel Smyth writes that she has met a man who is an enthusiastic admirer of your painting. She says would you therefore decorate a ballet she is writing.[1] She doesnt think you'll answer her. But the truth is the Camargo wont accept her ballet. However now I've asked you. And the man's wife "raved about a portrait by Vanessa".
I didnt mean that I wanted *thanks* for the [Angelica's] pound: only I thought I'd lost it: however I'm very glad of A's letter. What a born writer!

Berg

2579: To Ethel Smyth   [*Hotel Majestic, Athens*]
Wednesday May 4th 1932 A.D.

There, whats wrong with that date? Whats Einstein got to do with it? For your further information I will add 11.35 on a blazing hot morning. I'm sitting on my bed with my ink pot on the po-cupboard, a large boil on my chin, result of wind and sun, a sore throat, result of cold and dust, but almost perfectly happy all the same. Why did you never tell me that Greece was beautiful? Why did you never mention the sea and the hills and the valleys and the flowers? Am I the only person who has eyes in my head? I solemnly inform you, Ethel, that Greece is the most beautiful country in the whole world; May is the most beautiful season in the whole

1. *Fête Galante*. Vanessa did the décor for it in 1934.

year; Greece and May together—! There were the nightingales for example singing in the cypresses where we sat beside the stream: and I filled my lap with scarlet anemones; Yes, but you want facts; Baedeker. Well then, we went from Athens to Corinth; town being rebuilt after earthquake; gulf [canal] stopped owing to heavy fall of rock; six donkeys engaged in carting fall away; will take 6 months or year: all traffic meanwhile held up: Delphi cut off; oranges unobtainable in hotel: from Corinth (all this in a great open car of Giolmann's perfectly driven over roads like coagulated craters by enchanting driver) to Mycenae: my word. magnificent. Bees booming in the Tomb of Agamemnon. (What is the line about "his helmet made a hive for bees")[1] tea at Belle Helene;[2] among the plains, with frogs barking: so to Nauplia in the evenings; oh and then next day up the most nerve racking pass, shooting like an arrow along a razor with caverns of rock in abysses a million feet deep under one's left eye, and donkeys emerging round the corners to Mitrovitza; so to Mistra; Byzantine church magnificent; peasants delightful; coffee in a peasants room; so to Athens again; all the time the heat increasing and the wind, and the flowering trees visibly opening and making tassels of violet and white and crimson (dont ask me to document these facts) against a sky of flawless blue. Then a day at Athens, which was good Friday according to their barbarian reckoning, but Lord, Ethel, how infinitely I prefer their barbarian reckonings to your protestant orthodoxy! At night, in the still heat, we stood on the balcony and saw the procession go by, singing in a minor key, some, to me, impressive and solemn dirge round a bier; and the clergy with beards and long hair and stiff catafalque like robes sang, and I can assure you all that is in me of stunted and deformed religion flowered under this hot sensuality, so thick, so yellow, so waxen; and I thought of the lights of the herring fleet at sea; everyone holding a yellow taper along the street and all the lights coming out in the windows. Why, we almost wept, we pagans.

So on to Delphi; another vast journey; and saw a stork lodged on the head of the stone lion which marks the battle is it of Cheronea, where the Greeks, as you know, were beaten for all time,[3] and Leonard read an account of it in the Greek, for my husband is a most cultivated man—so's Roger; and Roger, whom I meant you to rise at, with his rather cautious admiration of the Greek statues in the museums, is far and away the best admirer of life and art I've ever travelled with; so humane; so sympathetic, so indomitable: though, unfortunately, part of his inside is hanging down, and another part is screwed up, so that he cant ride or walk, and our adventures therefore have to be circumscribed: still as I was saying he never boggles at a terrific

1. "His helmet now shall make a hive for bees" (George Peele, 1558-97, *Polyhymnia*).
2. The inn at Mycenae: *Hôtel de la Belle-Hélène et du Roi Ménélas*. The names of the four travellers can still be seen written in the visitors' book.
3. By Philip of Macedon in 338 B.C.

expedition like ours yesterday and has nosed out all the Byzantine Churches and Greek Temples (which he thinks sublime: its only the museum statues of muscular boys and cowlike women that remind him of the Royal Academy) and can feel his way along a pillar or a carving or a mosaic with a sensibility and vigour that make one think of a prodigiously fertile spider, where we are ants, hard, shiny, devoid of all filament whatsoever. This faculty of his is a constant marvel to me, and I buttonhole him and say, as at Aegina, "Now Roger tell me why?" and then he quivers his eyes and says how the things a matter of inches—its life, its individuality: thus it differs from Sunium built 6 inches t'other way, as an Arab from a carthorse. Meanwhile Margery his sister has her glass on a bird. An Eagle! I cry. Nonsense. A vulture. She says, or it may be a bee eater. Then Roger shouts, Oh come and look at this! My word thats swell—very swell—and we all gaze up, (This scene takes place at Daphnis in the Byzantine Church) at some annunciation or Crucifixion: and I steal away to the marble door and see the olives and the pines baring their heads and letting the sun and shade darken and illumine them and think how theyre like waves on the grey hill side. But Baedeker. So we reached . . . [*last page missing*].

Berg

2580: To Julian Bell   *Athens*

Postcard
May 5th [1932]

We have seen vultures, buzzard, eagles, bee eaters, blue thrushes, temples, ruins, statues, Athens, Sparta, Corinth—and are just off to a monastery. So goodbye.

Virginia

Quentin Bell

2581: To Lady Ottoline Morrell   *Athens*

Postcard
May 7th [1932]

Love from Leonard and Virginia. This is where we are, not much like Gower Street. Roger raves about the Byzantines.

Virginia

Texas

May 8th [1932]

Well I have just got your letter, and it was very nice to get your letter though I cant help feeling, being as you know a very polyp for emotion, that you're somehow rather saddened worried, bothered—why? Why is life so complicated at the moment?[1] Money? Dotty [Dorothy Wellesley]? Writing? God knows. Its no use asking questions at this distance, nor indeed much use writing letters, since we start back tomorrow—

But I will just have my little fling, since your letter was such a nice one, like a beautiful Borzoi, Queen Alexandra's favourite dog, writing with an eagles quill. Did you ever see a Borzoi write a poem? A sextet? Well, if you haven't you've missed one of life's most seductive sights. At Sandringham I'm told they were at it all night long—But to return. I was going to tell you how we've been off in a car jolting and jumping to Nauplia, Mycenae, Corinth, Mistra, Delphi and so on. And there were bees in Agamemnon's tomb, and I thought of you—such a booming they made in a stone hollow like a vast beehive. Sea was round us at Nauplia—the waves lapped my balcony and I looked down into the hearts of fish. And then we crossed an appalling pass, winding round and round, every sweep higher, and one wheel or the other perpetually balancing over a precipice 3,000 feet of sheer rock beneath. How I trembled! Then suddenly swooping round a corner to come upon a flock of goats or another car, and to have to back, with the hind wheels brushing the tops of pine trees. But we got through safely and so to Delphi, where an Englishmans skeleton, the son of my oldest friend [Margaret Ilbert], had been found, dangling from a tree in a gorge, with a gold watch between the ribs. There I bathed my feet in the Castalian spring [Delphi]; and all the rocks were covered with pale purple campanula —but whats the use of talking of flowers to an Englishwoman? You buy them in bunches: here they toss them at our heads. I've never seen so many —at Aegina yesterday the whole hill was red with rock roses, and yellow sea poppies, one of which I picked for you—here are its decaying petals. The sea gets in everywhere—you come to the top of a hill and there's the sea beneath. And snow mountains beyond, and bays as they were when Eve—no it should be Persephone—bathed there. Not a bungalow, not a kennel, not a tea shop. Pure sea water on pure sand is almost the loveliest thing in the world—you know how many times I've said so, and brought in old women with baskets. So yesterday we plunged into the sea and swam about in the Aegean, with sea urchins and anemones, all transmuted, waving red and yellow beneath our feet. Then the hills—they aren't green, but

1. "Life is too complicated—I sometimes feel that I can't manage it at all" (Vita to Virginia, 25 April, *Berg*). Her depression was due to cumulative causes— the failure of *Action*, money-worries, Lady Sackville's bullying, and lumbago.

marble, always with flying veils of purple and blue. But I wont run up a bill for words (I'm writing in a rush, about to go out for the last time in Athens) We must at all costs come here next year. Do you mean you would have come this? I never thought it possible, what with Eton[1] and so on. But next year is already marked for Crete—damn America[2]. Seriously, its a folly to waste one's prime acquiring gold when there's this perfectly wild and yet very civilised and entirely beautiful place without an Englishman or woman in it to be lived in. And when shall I see you? Before I see Ethel? Please say yes. We stay a day or two at Rodmell.

Yes it was so strange coming back here again I hardly knew where I was; or when it was. There was my own ghost coming down from the Acropolis, aged 23: and how I pitied her! Well: let me know if you're up and forgive scrawling scribbles

V.

Berg

2583: To John Lehmann   [*Hotel Majestic*] Athens

May 8th [1932]

My dear John,

I have written to you several times (in imagination) a full account of our travels with a masterly description of Byzantine and Greek art (Roger is all for Byzantine) but I'm afraid you never got it. The truth is its almost impossible to put pen to paper. Here am I balanced on the edge of a hotel bed with Marjorie and Roger popping in and out to suggest excursions, and Leonard ranging the sponge bags with a view to packing.

I'm afraid you've had the devil of a time with Belsher[3] away, and the door standing open to bores of every feather. I've often thought of you with sympathy when one wheel of the car has been trembling over a precipice 2,000 feet deep, and vultures wheeling round our heads as if settling which to begin on. This refers to the road into the Peloponnesus.

Then we went to Delphi, to Nauplia, to Mycenae—its all in the letter I never wrote. I can assure you Greece is more beautiful than 20 dozen Cambridges all in May week. It blazes with heat too, and there are no bugs, no inconveniences—the peasants are far nicer than the company we keep in London—its true we can't understand a word they say. In short I'm setting on foot a plan to remove the Hogarth Press to Crete.

1. Vita had two sons at Eton College.
2. Vita and Harold were committed to a lecture-tour of the United States in early 1933.
3. Miss Belsher had been an assistant at the Hogarth Press since 1928.

Roger is the greatest fun—as mild as milk, and if you've ever seen milk that is also quicksilver you'll know what I mean. He disposes of whole museums with one brush of his tail. He plays chess when the dust is sweeping the pawns from the board. He writes articles with one hand, and carries on violent arguments with the other. It has been far the best holiday we've had for years, and I feel duly grateful to you, for sitting in your doghole so stalwartly meanwhile. Excuse scribble.

Love from us both.
Virginia

John Lehmann

2584: To Pamela Diamand   *Trieste, [Italy]*

Postcard
Wednesday [11 May 1932]

The Wolves have missed the Frys greatly.[1] Otherwise a comfortable dull journey: rain yesterday and cold. Threw most of our lunch to beggars in memory of you. V. is being taught chess. Love from both. O to stay in Venice!

Leonard and Virginia

Pamela Diamand

2585: To V. Sackville-West   *Monks House, [Rodmell, Sussex]*

Friday [13 May 1932]

Your letter just come. Yes we're back—came last night—safe and sound and in robust health save for a sore throat which is the result of dust, and heat. Think of that—dust and heat! What a dream it seems now! I assure you the beauty was unbelieveable.

Are you [broad] casting on Monday? Shall I see you? We go back on Sunday so as to grapple with I daresay 10 miles of MSS

Let me know—because there's one person in England I do rather want to see—at least Potto does—is it Ethel?

V.

I'm so sleepy after 3 days train I cant write.

Berg

1. Roger and Margery Fry remained in Greece while Virginia and Leonard returned to England by Orient Express. Pamela Diamand, Roger's daughter, was then staying in Venice, and the Woolfs had met her there on their way back.

Letters 2586-2615 (May–July 1932)

On her return from Greece, Virginia spent the spring and early summer months in London, and went for frequent weekend visits to Rodmell. She was feeling profoundly depressed, still shaken, one supposes, by the effort of writing The Waves and by the deaths of Lytton Strachey and Carrington. But there were more immediate causes. Leonard and John Lehmann were finding it increasingly difficult to work together in the Hogarth Press, and there was a constant barrage of visitors to Tavistock Square who had to be 'seen', interrupting Virginia's work and placing on her a strain which culminated in her fainting in a restaurant, and in two furious letters (12 and 14 July) to Ethel Smyth, herself a main culprit, which might have ended their friendship. Virginia's A Letter to a Young Poet was published on 7 July, and four days later she finished her second volume of The Common Reader. Apart from a little journalism she wrote nothing else during these months.

2586: To Ethel Smyth   52 T[avistock] S.[quare, W.C.1]

Thursday [19 May 1932]

1   Very well then, lets put it off till another time.
    Friday is all taken up with a dreary business talk so I shouldn't be in a good mood—Anyhow I'm in a vile one,—the transition from freedom and Greece to endless conversation in London makes me itch all over. I daresay I shall settle down to civilisation in the course of a week or two.
2   I dont know if to be glad or sorry about M. H. [Mary Hunter?]
3   And I cant go into our particular crises as they involve co-respondents, business, money. and so on.[1]
4   And now I've got to go up and wash and change and sit in my arm chair and talk, and dine out and talk and go to a party and talk. Yes, my voice is the voice of one in perfect health and bad temper. Boils gone—superficially that is—inwardly no.

Berg

1. John Lehmann was reconsidering the Woolfs' offer of a partnership in the Hogarth Press. He feared that he might not work happily with Leonard on terms of equality, and he needed a higher salary. (For his account of the difficulties, see his autobiography, The Whispering Gallery, p. 195, and Thrown to the Woolfs, 1978, pp. 32-4).

2587: To V. Sackville-West 52 T.[avistock] S.[quare, W.C.1]

Sunday [22 May 1932]

This is just to say Are you coming to the [Chelsea] flower show? We
are going on Tuesday afternoon; so do lunch with us and go with us and
dry your pen for the moment. As posts seem to be so much worse in Kent
than in Greece would you ring up.

Lunch 1.

V.

Berg

2588: To Mrs Franks 52 *Tavistock Square, W.C.1*

Typewritten
23rd May 1932

Dear Mrs Franks [*unidentified*],

I am needless to say greatly interested by your letter telling me that
you have a letter from my father which gives a description of my mother.
And what you say is quite true—I have read many accounts of my mother
—she died when I was 13—but what my father said about her would be
of peculiar interest to my sister and myself. Thus if you would be so very
kind as to let me have the letter I should be most grateful and would return
it to you safely. Although as I say I was only a child when she died, I have
a very vivid memory of her.

It is extremely kind of you to have thought of this. Please accept my
best thanks.

Yours sincerely
Virginia Woolf

Columbia University

2589: To Vanessa Bell 52 *Tavistock Square, W.C.1*

Tuesday [24 May 1932]

The Wolves are giving you a Frigidaire with their love for your birthday.[1] Would you ring up tomorrow morning and say when you can see
the man about installing it. It is already ordered so protest is useless.

Virginia
Leonard

Berg

1. Vanessa was 53 on 30 May.

2590: To V. Sackville-West   [52 *Tavistock Square, W.C.*1]

Wednesday [25 May 1932]

Dearest Creature,

Are you coming up on Monday? If so are you coming to see me—lunch, tea, dinner, what? The flower show was a mass of cold mud and blazing blossom and petrified faces. Oh the country gentlemen of England and their riddled, raddled, foxhunting wives! Theres only one person I want to see, and she has no burning wish for anything but a rose red tower and a view of hop gardens and oasts. Who can it be? Its said she has written a poem and has a mother, a cow, and a moat. I'm so illiterate—I've seen so many people—life offers so many problems and there's a hair in my pen.

So let me know about Monday.

V.

Would you like to give [the manuscript of] Orlando to the Bodleian? Aren't I vain?

Berg

2591: To Edward Sackville West

52 *T[avistock] S[quare, W.C.*1]

Wednesday [25 May 1932]

Dear Eddy,

Many thanks for your characteristic letter. I'm sorry you think I didn't "put it at all well" the other night—Still more sorry that I ever tried to 'put it' at all. (By the way, I did it entirely off my own bat—Duncan had nothing to do with it). As for what you call the "cheapness" of my remarks about "behaving like a gentleman" I never said anything of the kind. I urged you to behave like a British nobleman, an intentionally half-humorous remark and no doubt in your eyes a vulgar one. To urge either you or Duncan to behave like a gentleman is too silly even for me.

Anyhow I've had my lesson and wont interfere in your affairs again—that I promise you.

Yours

Berg   Virginia Woolf

2592: To Ethel Smyth   52 *T.[avistock] S.[quare, W.C.*1]

Thursday [26 May 1932]

Well Ethel dear this is very sad—that you're not with me at this moment but hitting some ball about on a cold grey lawn. Do you dress in white?—

Do you wear a little straw hat with a blue ribbon, and a blouse fastened by a dragon fly in turquoises? Those are my ancient views of lawn tennis seen over a paling in Cornwall 30 years ago. But enough of these recollections. Were you here, in the arm chair opposite, we wouldn't recollect: we would—how d'you call it?—present. So you were very wrong-headed not to come. Yet I dont blame you. I cant tell you how down in the mud and the brambles I've been—nearer one of those climaxes of despair that I used to have than any time these 6 years—Lord knows why. Oh how I suffer! and whats worse, for nothing, no reason thats respectable. Only coming back from Greece here to the incessant rubbing and rasping; and then one thing going bad on my hands after another—here's one friend in a divorce case, another fallen in love; and an odious quarrel fastened on me;[1] and the whole Press upset and in process of death or birth, heaven knows which— these I suppose were reasons why I answered you so grumpily: and was incapable of any vision of hope. This evening is the first evening, nearly, I've had to myself; and slowly I'm renewing my soul. I'm reading over the fire. Can it be possible I shall one day wish to write again—Can there be peace and hope on t'other side of this blazing cauldron? I repeat—how one suffers: and why? No doubt you have a reason when you suffer. I wouldn't live last week again for £33.10/- and 6d.

This is only by way of apology: I doubt that even you, who so well know even me, can understand why I'm such a damnable whirled dead leaf blown by in an invisible sandstorm. Let us hope for a day next week— God knows.

V.

Berg

2593: To Ethel Smyth   [52 *Tavistock Square, W.C.*1]

Typewritten
[29 May 1932]

What about dining with me on Thursday—next 2nd I shall be alone. But cant manage Tuesday afternoon. Dinner 7.30. Let me know; but dont bother, as I'll arrange another day if this is a difficult one.

V.

Oh thank you for your understanding letter—just back from Rodmell— its so spoilt, my marsh, I can hardly bear to walk there.

[*handwritten*] forgot to post this

Berg

1. With Edward Sackville West.

2594: To Mrs Franks   52 *Tavistock Square, W.C.*1

4th June 1932

Dear Mrs Franks [*unidentified*],

I return herewith my father's letter. I have read it, and my sister also has read it, with very great interest. Although as you say, it does not describe my mother directly, it gives a sense of their life at the time which is very vivid and brings him before us as only a letter can.

I must thank you again very sincerely for the kindness which led you to send it me.

It has struck me that as you are interested in Thackeray relics you might like this photograph of the drawing of him by Samuel Lawrence which was, I think, given by George Smith, the publisher, to Thackeray's daughters when he went to America.[1] The original drawing is in our possession. I am therefore sending you a copy.

> Believe me
> yours sincerely
> Virginia Woolf

Columbia University

2595: To Kingsley Martin   52 *Tavistock Square,*
                                                           *W.C.*1

Typewritten
5th June 1932

Dear Mr Kingsley Martin,

Leonard tells me that you asked him if I would consider writing the World of Books page in the New Statesman for a few weeks.

It is very good of you to suggest it, and I have been thinking it over. But I have come to the conclusion, not for the first time, that it would be a mistake for me to try. I used to write regularly for the Times Lit Sup; but I was very glad when I could give it up. For one thing I am not an expert journalist—that is, it takes me three or four mornings to write an article that most people do in one. Then books one wants to write about dont appear every week, so that one has to write about boring books out of ones line. And then I feel the worry of being up to time a great burden. So for these reasons I have decided not to bind myself to regular journalism again. But I am very grateful to you for having given me the chance.

> Yours sincerely
> Virginia Woolf

George Spater

1. The Samuel Laurence drawing was done in 1852. Thackeray's daughter Harriet was Leslie Stephens's first wife.

2596: To Ethel Smyth   [52 *Tavistock Square, W.C.*1]

[9 June 1932]

No, I dont see how I can manage Wednesday unless it suits you to come late—We've another Hogarth Press discussion—God damn it—that afternoon. And this afternoon 7 to tea—all at 6s and 7s too—and I'm too dazed to write.

Eli[th] last night very refreshing[1]

V.

Berg

2597: To J. D. Hayward   52 *Tavistock Square, W.C.*1
                    Copy of a Testimonial

Typewritten
June 9th 1932

I have known Mr Hayward's[2] work as an author and journalist for a considerable time. Ever since he used to write for The Nation when my husband was Editor.

I have always thought highly of it and followed it with interest.

Virginia Woolf

King's

2598: To Edward Sackville West
                    52 *Tavistock Square, W.C.*1.

14th June [1932]

My dear Eddy,

I was much touched to hear from Vita that you wanted to come and see me again. I was very sorry we quarrelled. My only wish was to make it up between you and Duncan, but no doubt I was clumsy in the way I did it. And certainly your letter broke off all relations quite emphatically—as I read it. But there is no need to go into this—quarrels are very foolish things.

At the moment it is rather difficult to suggest a meeting. I'm only allowed by the dr to do a little work on condition I see practically no one. Sometimes we're here—sometimes at Monks House. If you should be down there would you either write or ring up—Lewes 385—I dont want you to make a journey in vain, and I find it difficult at present to settle plans beforehand.

1. Elizabeth Williamson. See p. 2, note 1.
2. John Davy Hayward (1905-65), the bibliographer and anthologist.

But it will be a great pleasure to see you, whenever it is, and to begin again a friendship which I enjoyed greatly. May it never lapse again!

yr affate
V.W.

Berg

2599: To Ethel Smyth [*Monk's House, Rodmell, Sussex*]

Saturday, and Sunday [18 and 19 June 1932]

Yes Ethel, I was deeply touched by thinking of your picking pinks for me—I thought the time of pinks was over—emotionally, I mean; and I remembered the day you brought them in cardboard boxes, two years ago, and you said this marked the honeymoon and would soon be over. Isnt it odd what romance certain scenes hold for one—you this hot evening in your garden. picking pinks. Its the thought of the evening, and me coming in at the door, and shelling peas with you and the pinks smelling, and then a little dinner in the fading light Please if ever I come again, dont meet me —I meant to tell you this—but let me find you among your things—you cant think what a shock of emotion it gives me—seeing people among their things—I've lots such scenes in my head; the whole of life presented—the other persons life—for 10 seconds; and then it goes; and comes again; so next time dont meet me.

By the by, how amused, yet outraged I was crossing the road the other night, by your violent rejection of my arm. 'No succouring' What an old applewoman you are underneath—all Whitechapel is under your blue ascot frock—yes—is it the cursing gambling Indian sires;[1]—How did you brew this violence? In another moment you would have felled me to the ground with your fist. Weren't you like a woman sitting squat on a public house steps, with a little clay pipe and a basket of matches No thats not quite it and I'm writing in the devil of a hurry: must stop.

Monday

Your letter: Oh Tuesday and Wednesday is Ottoline and going out. I could be in late on Tuesday 6.30: but is that worth it? What about a real conversation on Wednesday week, wh. I promise to keep free if I possibly can?

Let me know

V.

Berg

1. Ethel's father, Major-General J. H. Smyth, had begun his career as an artillery officer in Bengal.

52 *T*[*avistock*] *S*[*quare, W.C.*1]

Wednesday evening [22 June 1932]

Oh dear, oh dear—no sooner had your letter come than the telephone rings—Tom [Eliot]. May he come and see us. 'Oh yes, do'. 'But Vivienne [his wife] wants me to say may she come too—to tea, to dinner, this week, next week?' Evidently she was at his elbow—So its hopeless. I cant face it. We put them off till the week after the week after next. The ether, the whistle, the dog—its too sinister and sordid and depressing. How did you live through it. One must simply let him drown, wrapped in swathes of dirty seaweed. If she weren't so malodorous and tousled it would be more tolerable—No, nothing could make me see them again together. This is only a cry from the heart in answer to yours.

Now I must change and go and dine with Margery Fry off cheese, at the other end of London, and tomorrow dine with Mary [Hutchinson] and go to the Zoo; and on Monday have Mirsky[1] and his prostitute, and on Tuesday dine with Americans,[2] and on Wednesday have old Ethel Smyth— thats what London is, a perpetual catcall and cry. But this didnt apply to our old crony tea, which was delicious and healing to my heart. Oh yes, you must sell all you possess, even the yellow pearls, and go to Greece. How you would love it—stretching in the sand among the asphodel. I believe we both had Greek grandmothers, and this cage in Bloomsbury with the poets and their prostitutes is only an interlude. But heavens, I must change.

I wasted an hour very happily this afternoon looking for a [Fanny] Burney for you in an old bookshop—I almost bought Shakespeare, Byron, and the works of [William] Hayley instead. But no doubt Burney will turn up in time. Dont get one just yet anyhow.

Love from us both   V.

Texas

1. Prince Dmitri Mirsky, the Russian literary historian, who left his native country after the Revolution and became Lecturer in Russian literature at King's College, University of London.
2. Richard Clarke Cabot (1868-1939), Professor of Clinical Medicine and Professor of Social Ethics at Harvard University. He was the author of standard medical textbooks and was writing *The Meaning of Right and Wrong*, 1933. His wife was Ella Lyman Cabot (d. 1934), a teacher of ethics and psychology in Boston private schools.

52 *Tavistock Square*, [*W.C.*1]

[end-June 1932]

My dear Rosamund,

It was melancholy indeed that you didn't come up the other day, but just as well, because I was stupid as an owl; but do come properly another time and let me know: is dinner any good? Are you always catching the last train? That is my impression of you, flying across London to the shades of Oxfordshire—oh how nice! Still, we've just been swimming Pinka in the Serpentine, and it was incredibly lovely—every housemaid a dab of pure colour. Why cant the summer last forever? and housemaids be for ever blue and yellow.

No: I was slightly shocked at my own verbosity the other night. Nessa and I get off upon our old days and chatter like magpies, elderly white magpies; when its you—the humming birds—is Miss Morris [*unidentified*] a humming bird?—who ought to be singing to us.

I hope and think things are settled with John to all our advantage.[1] We must meet, you and I, and have a talk soon.

Yr Virginia

Now I've forgotten how you spell Rosamond let alone Phillips.[2]

King's

2602: To Ethel Smyth
52 *Tavistock Square*, [*W.C.*1]

Tuesday [28 June 1932]

Look here, it is much too hot to think of making a special journey to London tomorrow. Put it off until there's a breeze. Its silly to come panting —exhausted here—we shall transact no business and I shall feel guilty. Choose another day and I'll keep it.

I had meant, if time had been willing which it wasnt (2 Russians, [Mirsky] Vita, and a stark honest sad Strachey woman [Alix] all on top of each other yesterday) to explain my idiotic or rather childish refrain "Do you like me better than—?"

This is not to be taken seriously. It is only a relic of childish days when I used to pull Nessa's amethyst beads. Say, please say you love me best: and then she'd shake her head; and then I'd go over her friends and relations, like beads; and so on. This habit comes over me still with you and Vita:

1. The Woolfs had agreed with John Lehmann (Rosamond's brother) that he would remain temporarily as an 'adviser' to the Hogarth Press.
2. Rosamond Lehmann had married Wogan Philipps in 1928.

and its not to be taken as a serious demand that you should soberly search your affections. Far from it.

Now I must wash and change and go and dine with Katherine Furse,[1] whom I've not seen since Charles died, or thereabouts—How I dread the moment when the door opens and I have to go in. I assure you I'm almost sick with fright at this moment—To you this would mean nothing—I mean you wouldn't feel afraid.

Berg   V.

2603: To V. Sackville-West   52 *Tavistock Square*, [*W.C.*1]
Friday [1 July 1932]

Your friend from America, or rather your friend Pearnie,[2] is coming to see me about The Pictorial World.[3] What I want to know is how much did you say they paid you: because, though naturally much inferior, I still think, being so much older and sadder, I ought to be paid the same—if that is, I'm paid anything: which I doubt.

What about The Miracle?[4] Thursday next week would suit me best—indeed, it seems, God help me, the only day. Let me know and dont entirely throw off one who loves you.

Did you go West as you said? To Cornwall? And buy another castle; or is it only Avebury Manor House [Wiltshire] this time?

Why must one see so many people? Today a child of 2, my Godchild, daughter of Rupert Brooke's old love;[5] and streams fell from her woollen drawers. So they did from mine once when I was bridesmaid, at her age. But I like that better than luscious and intense Russians—better than Colefax among her pots.[6]—though I respect her too. L. brought 3 chairs. Someone was highly praising a book called Noble Godavary.[7] I must read it.

Berg   V.

1. A daughter of John Addington Symonds and a friend of Virginia's youth. She had married Charles Furse, the painter, in 1900, and he died of tuberculosis in 1904, aged 36.
2. Nancy Pearn of Curtis, Brown Ltd., the literary agents.
3. Virginia's name for *Pictorial Review* (New York), to which Vita contributed several articles in 1932-33.
4. The Max Reinhardt production at the Lyceum Theatre, in which Diana Cooper appeared as the Madonna.
5. Virginia Richards, third child of Noel (*née* Olivier) and Arthur Richards, the doctor whom she married in 1921.
6. Lady Colefax had founded an interior-decoration business in which she was later joined by John Fowler.
7. *The Death of Noble Godavary*, Vita's long story, published by Ernest Benn in early June.

July 1st [1932]

All right, I will pick out the letters and you can fetch them any time on Sunday morning.[1] I let them go grudgingly, though I admit I have no cause on the face of it to be aggrieved. You've given me time and enough; and I've read enough to begin to get the feeling that I want to sink down alone, for a month, with the letters round me and absorb them and all their circumference. What I grudge is that a month is out of the question; and its out of the question largely owing to my own complete incapacity to rule my own time. Talk of dress, my dear Ethel—thats a mere flea bite: that I can settle and dismiss in a second: its the plague of people that really worries me: if you could lay that cloud of stinging gnats, or tell me how, I should be eternally grateful. Every day its the same—somebody insists upon being seen; has a claim; will be hurt if I dont. Three letters to this effect already last night and this morning. The days loom ahead of me. Each with its "seeing' its being at home and sitting here and talking, its arranging visits and dinners—and the end is I cant read what I want or write; and the people I do want to see—wonderful that the faculty should still exist—I see only in a crush: and some I never see at all. But still they go on: 4 to tea today: and its never over; each week, like a wheel, brings up a fresh crop. There! Thats my wail. How would you deal with a lady [Noel Richards] who's called her baby Virginia after me, and must bring it to tea; and then—no, I cant recount the lot. Think out a method, please. And forgive the usual exacerbated egotism.

V.

I couldn't resist peeping into the letters again: how fascinating: I feel the tug of innumerable psychological filaments, which I believe, obtuse as I am, I could unravel and knit up in a remarkable picture—but whats the use of dreaming? I've 20 MSS to read for violent blood thirsty authors.

Berg

Thursday [7 July 1932]

I find we've made such a mass of money this year—we've just done our half yearly accounts—that I'm sending you a very small crumb,[2] as I've

1. The letters of Henry Brewster, Ethel's lover (d. 1908), which she had lent to Virginia in November 1930.
2. A cheque for £100.

nothing whatever to buy with it. So this is nothing to do with Angelica; its Dolphin's solely. So be a good beast and say no more about it. Lord— what a party it was last night!

B.

Berg

2606: To V. Sackville-West   [52 *Tavistock Square, W.C.*1]
Thursday [7 July 1932]

I've just asked Stella Benson to dine,[1] so I wont come on Tuesday; but many thanks. And for the book [*Noble Godavary*] which I shall read: at the moment I'm in bed, having been faint (it was so d—d noisy and hot) at a party at the Ivy last night and convoyed home by Clive the oddest scene: but not a pleasant place to faint in. Oh if there were no more parties except with sheep dogs who just give paws. How I envy you the Lake [at Sissinghurst]: London is intolerable; but I hope we go to Rodmell for Sunday tomorrow where I shall sit in the garden. Oh dear yes—and theres heaps of things I want to talk to you about. Did you think there was any *sense* in my letter—anything true about poetry?[2] I shall be much interested to read Harold:[3] what about Hugh's letter?
But I'm half asleep.
Monday then, as early as you can.

V.

I never rejected Godavary? Ethel says its magnificent

Berg

2607: To Mrs Thomas Hardy   52 *Tavistock Square, W.C.*[1]
July 11th [1932]

Dear Mrs Hardy
I was very much disappointed not to come to your lunch the other day. I had been dining out the night before and fainted, owing to the heat, so

1. The novelist (*Tobit Transplanted*, 1931, etc). She had married J. C. Anderson of the Chinese Customs Service in 1921, and died in Tongking, Indo-China, in December 1933.
2. *A Letter to a Young Poet* was published on this day.
3. In the *New Statesman* of 9 July Harold Nicolson reviewed Virginia's *A Letter to a Young Poet* and Hugh Walpole's *A Letter to a Modern Novelist*. About Virginia's letter he wrote, "It will be read by posterity with curiosity and pleasure."

that it seemed unwise to go out again next day. Indeed I stayed in bed. But I am quite well again now, and hope very much I may see you later.

I have always wanted to tell you how greatly I enjoyed your life of Mr Hardy. It gave a wonderful picture of him. My husband and I have never forgotten the day we spent with you.[1]

With kind regards from us both

Yours sincerely
Virginia Woolf

Frederick B. Adams Jr.

2608: To Ethel Smyth   [*52 Tavistock Square, W.C.*1]

Typewritten
Tuesday [12 July 1932]

Oh my dear Ethel I'm not quite such a fool as you think me (this refers to your long kind entirely mistaken letter) That is if the problem were what you state—a question of "aspirants for interviews" then Ive solved it long ago. I never never see them.—or people who ask to come because they like my books, or schoolmasters, or bringers of Mss—or societies that want me to speak. I merely type in two minutes—Ive just done it three times—"Mrs Woolf is sorry, but her engagements" and Miss Belsher of the Hogarth Press signs it; and theres an end. Indeed if I saw people who want to consult me I should *deserve* your laughter and pity and contempt.

But its not *them*—what I find impossible to solve is the problem of personal friends, and the friends of personal friends. All these cases, for instance, are waiting solution at the moment; R;[2] a very old friend; ill; in a home; will I go and see him; Nellie Cecil;[3] stone deaf; will I come over to Gale and see her (She was divine to me twenty years ago;) my mother in law—at Worthing; when am I coming?: Mrs Hardy, widow of Thomas, will I lunch; her husband was an old friend of my fathers; Katharine Furse,[4] will I dine any time before August 1st; to meet her dear friend, Mary Follett;[5] Dorothy Bussy,[6] Lyttons sister; will I see her to discuss Lyttons letters— etc etc. All these people I like; some have been good to me years ago when

1. In July 1926. Thomas Hardy died in January 1928, and his second wife, Florence, published two memoirs of him, *The Early Life* (1928) and *The Later Years* (1930).
2. Roger Fry had had an operation.
3. Lady (Robert) Cecil, who lived at Gale, Chelwood Gate, Sussex.
4. See p. 73, note 1.
5. The American philosopher, author of *Creative Experience*, etc.
6. Dorothy Strachey (1866-1960) was Lytton's elder sister. She married the French painter, Simon Bussy, in 1903. She translated Gide, and published *Olivia* in 1949.

I was a gawky tongue tied impossible girl; how can I say to them "Owing to the ever increasing MSS a publisher has to read . . . I am forced to set apart definite afternoons . . . The next available day is . . ." It's impossible. And its not my vanity and weakness as you make out; its simply the way of human beings—look at yourself. There you are saying do come and meet Mrs Woodhouse;[1] do lunch with Mary Dodge;[2] do come over to Maurice [Baring] at Rottingdean; do arrange to see Ronald Storrs.[3] And why you think I'm foolish and ridiculous to dine at the Ivy on a hot night with people I've known twenty years, and not foolish, but wise and adorable to dine with you at Coign in order to meet Barings and Storrs whom Ive known ten minutes and dont care a straw for—I cant imagine. However I never expected sympathy for that unlucky faint; and shouldnt have told you myself. But as you see the problem isnt the problem you imagine.—thats all I want to make clear to you. Not to claim sympathy.

Many thanks all the same. I'll keep your form and use it on your friend Lady Oxford who's just rung up. But not on Nelly Cecil nor Stracheys nor my poor old 82 year old mother in law.

I say, what do you mean by calling the Benson Bronte[4] first rate; fifth I should say, if that. This reads hot. But then I am.

Virginia.

Berg

2609: To Ethel Smyth   [52 *Tavistock Square, W.C.*1]

Typewritten
Thursday [14 July 1932]

Well I'm sorry if you think I wrote with undue vehemence or unfairly. But I think I have reason to feel exacerbated—not only in my vanity—that you, who protest you like me, should still think, after two years, that I'm capable of wasting time and strength on 'admirers', on what you call 'aspirants for interviews' and then complain I dont get time for work—I do feel nettled—whether from vanity or not I dont know—to think of you and Miss Dodge sitting in judgment on me and writing to quote your own words "I do rather doubt whether you have the department of character which is necessary (to refuse aspirants to interviews.) And the reasons are

1. Violet Gordon-Woodhouse, the harpsichordist, with whom Ethel often stayed in her beautiful house, Nether Lyppiat, in Gloucestershire.
2. A wealthy American, who settled in England and greatly admired Ethel's music. Coign (Woking) was built on a plot of land given to her by Miss Dodge.
3. Sir Ronald Storrs (1881-1955), the orientalist and at this time Governor of Cyprus. Another admirer of Ethel's music.
4. *Charlotte Brontë*, by E. F. Benson, 1932.

(1) you are kind and want to gratify these people. (2) You are flattered at their wanting so desperately to consult you. (3) There is a magpie element in you."

All this time youve been thinking I'm that sort of person—thats how I spend my time, in a rose coloured tea gown, signing autographs. I'm so vain of having prestige, which, as you remark, any fraud or fifteenth rate person may have, that I cant resist gratifying it; and then complain and then faint; and then am surprised when the austere Ethel is 'coldly angry'. As for your discovery that I "like going out", whereas the unsociable Ethel [*handwritten*] the unsociable Ethel who sees more people, stays in more houses, and enjoys it more than anyone I know [*typewritten:*] prefers complete solitude, I think I had better follow your advice "Since thy servant may not speak and live, let it be left at that".

Let us agree that it was I who thrust myself upon the Barings and the Dodges in my insane and insatiable desire for flattery. Seriously, I dont blame you, or Katharine Furse or myself, for the amiable impulse which prompts one to say 'Oh do come and meet my friends—' I never meant to imply that I did. All I say is that these adorable impulses are the devil— because one cant deal with them coldly with printed forms—they rouse one's feelings: one sees that it is goodness and kindness that prompts it. [*handwritten*] I admit that I'm so made that I get one of the most intense pleasures in life from "seeing people"—Dodge and Barings that is, not Scarboroughs and Huges [?] [*typewritten:*] And hence my difficulty; hence my fainting.

But, to exonerate myself, here are two of the letters that I get most days —and heres the answer I invariably send. Now no more. The whole thing is insoluble. As you say.

V.

[*handwritten*]

By the way, it strikes me that the last "aspirant for an interview" to whom, unwisely as I come to think, an interview was granted was—who d'you suppose—Ethel Smyth! Do you know that lady? If so, tell her with my love, not only has she blasted my belief in the possibility of friendships but whats more next time she talks of loving me, knowing me, wishing to see me, I shall understand that she refers to a lady in a rose coloured tea gown, with a lap dog, a fountain pen, and a habit of writing her name with a flourish across what she calls photos of a celebrated authoress.

Berg

2610: To Harmon H. Goldstone

52 *Tavistock Square, W.C.*1

Typewritten
20th July 1932

Dear Mr Goldstone,

I am much interested to hear that you think of developing your essay into a book on my writings.[1] Of course I shall be delighted to give you any help that I can; though I may add that I have found that it is generally much better for the author who is being criticised to stand as far apart from the book as possible; and for the writer to judge as impersonally as possible. But if there are any questions of fact that I can settle, I will willingly do so.

Unfortunately, I shall not be in London at all before October. If, however, you liked to send me your outline to the above address it would be forwarded; and I would give you any help that I can. M. Delattre has just published a book upon me in French; I do not know if you would find this useful. The title is Le Roman Psychologique de V.W. Librairie J. Vrin.

Believe me, yours sincerely
Virginia Woolf

Berg

2611: To Elizabeth Bowen

52 *Tavistock Square, W.C.*1

July 22nd [1932]

Dear Mrs Cameron,

It is very good of you to send me your novel,[2] which I am keeping, as a treat, for next week, when I get into the country and forget for a time the masses of manuscript that I ought to be reading. What a relief it will be to find a real book after all this rubbish, and I hope you will carry out your idea of a diary of books, not events—I mean not tea parties but Milton and so on.

With thanks, yours sincerely
Virginia Woolf

Texas

2612: To Helen McAfee

52 *Tavistock Square, W.C.*1

Typewritten
July 25th 1932

Dear Miss McAfee,

I should have thanked you before for the cheque for my letter to a young poet.[3] Many thanks and also for the copies of the Yale Review. I

1. See Letter 2558.
2. *To the North* by Elizabeth Bowen, 1932.
3. Virginia's essay was published in the *Yale Review* in June.

79

was told the other day by a very critical Englishman that in his opinion the Yale Review is the best of all American magazines, Certainly this number seems to me—if I am not prejudiced in its favour—full of good things, and I hope it will continue to flourish in spite of the general depression. Our papers struggle along with difficulty.

We are just off to Sussex for two months but shall be up and down in order to see to the Hogarth Press.

With kind regards from us both
yours very sincerely
Virginia Woolf

Yale University

2613: TO LADY CECIL   52 *Tavistock Square*, [*W.C.*1]

Monday [25 July 1932]

Dear Nelly,

Well you may call me a liar, but you cant deny I have a lovely heart—to sit down when I should be packing and answer you, instantly.

I daresay E. F. Benson [*Charlotte Brontë*] was all right—its only I detest the collocation (is that the word?) of that tubby ruddy fleshy little Clubman with Charlotte. Its impure. Its like cats marrying dogs—against the right order of things. Let him stick to Dodo.[1] I cant follow the Bronte enthusiasts. A lunatic, living I think near Hatfield, has sent me a book proving that Branwell [Brontë] wrote Wuthering Heights[2]—the work (her work that is,) she says, of years. One of Benson's points was that Charlotte had *no* feeling of any kind for the other sex; but was entirely decimated (is that a word?) by passion for one of those obscure old frumps—Hussey, [Ellen] Nussey—what was her name? Yet I can remember, or think I can, old George Smith preening himself—hundreds of years ago—when my mother said—oh this is millions of years ago, I may well have invented it—"I am sure Charlotte was in love with *you* Mr Smith".[3]

You see, I'm becoming senile, and can only think of the drawing room at Hyde Park Gate when, as I say, I should be packing. By this you may know that we're off to Rodmell tomorrow. Its all very well to ask my sister

1. E. F. Benson's novel *Dodo*, which created a sensation when it was published in 1893. It was generally supposed to be based on the character of Margot Tennant (later Lady Oxford). He published *Dodo the Second* in 1914, and *Dodo Wonders* in 1921.
2. Alice Law, *Emily Jane Brontë, and the Authorship of 'Wuthering Heights'*, 1925.
3. George Smith (1824-1901), a partner in the firm of Smith & Elder, who published *Jane Eyre*, etc. In 1882 he founded the *Dictionary of National Biography*, which Leslie Stephen edited.

to bring me, to Gale, but how do I know that you wont be at Geneva?[1] You mostly are. Whenever I ring you up the Butler says her Ladyship has just started for Geneva. I'm afraid its no use writing this letter any longer: I must pack.

About the Bookseller—was his name Glaisher? Did he put his head in a gas oven? Thats the trade gossip. He died owing us £1.10.6 I think. To lay dust upon his ghost I'm sending you the Letter to a poet: poor Lady Cecil! Thats what comes of writing to authors and telling them they're hardhearted abandoned liars—coals of fire, by every post. But you needn't refer to it. If you should write a letter ignoring the coal of fire it would naturally be welcome.

V.W.

The Marquess of Salisbury (Cecil Papers)

2614: To Ethel Smyth   *Monk's House, Rodmell,*
                                          [Sussex]

[28 July 1932]

I'm sorry to have been so long in writing, but this is the very first evening I've had to myself since I saw you. But I've been thinking over what you say, and the whole position. And what I want to make clear at once is that I dont think that the actual cause of the quarrel is of any importance. I entirely accept your statement that you did not mean to hurt me by what you said—indeed I am sure nothing was further from your mind. But that doesn't do away with the fact which I admit seems to me much more serious—that these misunderstandings between us do happen—one last summer, one this. And as you say that you never quarrel with your friends, and as I certainly never quarrel with mine, the fact does seem to point to some incompatibility between us. But that again would not so much matter to me at least, though it is of course a very unfortunate fact. What I do find harassing and unnerving and odious to an extent that I dont think you realise is the resulting 'scene'. I think I told you last summer how I loathed it. Last week after our letters I was in dread that the same thing might happen again. I purposely told you that I could only see you for an hour and a half; and I did my best to avoid the subject. I think you will admit that it was entirely owing to you that it was discussed at all. And to me the memory of that discussion is one of such horror—it makes me feel so degraded—so humiliated—as I used to feel, after a scene with Nelly[2]—that—well, I dont see how I'm to see anyone easily, or write, or

1. Lord Cecil was chief British representative on the Disarmament Conference there.
2. Nelly Boxall, the Woolf's cook since 1916.

speak freely to anyone who may insist upon a scene like that again. At the same time I quite understand that you may be perfectly right to wish to clear things up in talk—that its not your fault if you are violent as you say you are—that I am, quite probably, unnecessarily disgusted and sickened (not only by you—by myself also) when such scenes take place. But, given our obvious tendency to misunderstand each other more than we misunderstand other people, and given the fact that such scenes are not particularly hateful to you, or that you feel them to be necessary, I admit that the future does seem to me full of difficulty.

But please dont think that in saying this I blame you. I dont. I have the highest admiration for you. besides affection. But it is useless to conceal what I know to be my own peculiarities: or the very great effect they have on me. Last night for instance I dreamt through the whole of that scene again and woke with a horror of you and a horror of myself. But I expect you will understand the position without further description—all I want to make clear is that the difficulty for me lies there, and not in the misunderstanding which I have no doubt was fantastic, as you say.[1]

V.

Berg

2615: To John Lehmann

Monks House, [Rodmell, Sussex]

July 31st [1932]

Dear John,

I am a wretch not to have answered your very interesting letter before.[2] But London was an unholy racket, what with Americans, manuscripts, the Common Reader—oh the dulness of that book—and so on. Now it is pouring, and the Vicars wife is dead, and I must see, in spite of the bells tolling and the trees dripping if I can defend myself (I'm rather annoyed by the way that we've succumbed to [*nine words omitted*] Quennel:[3] but Leonard thought we must have him if anyone: I'd much rather be answered and torn up and thrown in the waste paper basket by you or [Cecil] Day Lewis: but it cant be helped.)

Now for your points: of course dressing up may have some advantages; but not more than gin and bitter or evening dress or any other stimulant. Besides it becomes a habit, and freezes the elderly, like Wyndham Lewis,[4]

1. Ethel replied: "I've just got your wonderfully fair and temperate—and as I said—generous letter" (*Berg*).
2. About *A Letter to a Young Poet*.
3. Peter Quennell, the poet, critic and literary biographer. His *A Letter to Mrs Virginia Woolf* was published by the Hogarth Press in October 1932.
4. The author and painter, and a persistent critic of Bloomsbury.

into ridiculous posings and posturing. But its not a matter of great importance. I admit your next point—that is that my quotations aren't good
illustrations: but as usual, I couldn't find the ones I wanted when I was
writing; and was too lazy to look. Anyhow my impression is that I could
convince you by quotations: I do feel that the young poet is rather crudely
jerked between realism and beauty, to put it roughly. I think he is all to be
praised for attempting to swallow Mrs Gape;[1] but he ought to assimilate
her. What it seems to me is that he doesnt sufficiently believe in her: doesnt
dig himself in deep enough; wakes up in the middle; his imagination goes
off the boil; he doesnt reach the unconscious automated state—hence the
spasmodic, jerky, self conscious effect of his realistic language. But I may
be transferring to him some of the ill effects of my own struggles the other
way round—writes poetry in prose. Tom Eliot I think succeeds; but then
he is much more violent; and I think by being violent, limits himself so
that he only attacks a minute province of his imagination; whereas you
younger and happier spirits should, partly owing to him, have a greater
range and be able to devise a less steep precipitous technique. But this is
mere guesswork of course. As for publishing,[2] I dont see your point that
it is salutory because it wipes clean the slate: I think, on the contrary, it
engraves the slate, what with reviewers and publicity. And if, as is quite
likely, the best poems are written before 30, they wont spoil with keeping.

But the fact is I'm not at all satisfied with the Letter, and would like to
tear up, or entirely re-write. It is a bad form for criticism, because it seems
to invite archness and playfulness, and when one has done being playful
the times up and there's no room for more. However the B.B.C have caught
on to the idea and want to have a series of letters to unknown Listeners in
the autumn. I suggested Stephen Spender[3] to an Uncle about Everything.
But they're so inconceivably timid they wont ask any but old duffers—for
instance Maurice Baring on being late for dinner.

It is now Bank Holiday [1 August], and has stopped raining, and here
is your second letter. But I never meant you to *read* Orlando: only to sell
it. The green copy was worth £10 I think in America before the smash.[4]
Please sell it and buy—I dont know what. I nibble at Flush,[5] but must
correct my proofs [of *The Common Reader*]: anyhow, I feel the point is
rather gone, as I meant it for a joke with Lytton, and a skit on him. But
I'll see. I do hope you're better. Is it colitis? Thats what Dotty [Dorothy

1. A symbolic charwoman. See *A Letter to a Young Poet*, pp. 6 and 14.
2. "For heaven's sake, publish nothing before you are thirty." *A Letter* . . . .,
   p. 26.
3. Spender was then 23. Virginia had met him in 1931, but the Hogarth Press
   published none of his books.
4. The first, limited, edition of *Orlando*, published by Crosby Gaige, New York,
   in October 1928.
5. Which Virginia had started to write in the summer of 1931.

Wellesley] has: and I wouldnt like to share a disease with her. But please recover entirely—I know once having 40 million pneumonia bugs daily how they eat one's heart out.

Leonard wants me to thank you for your letter.

V.W.

You see, from enclosed, that you have a double at Eastbourne [*unidentified*] What am I to say?

Texas

Letters 2616-2639 (August-September 1932)

The Woolfs, as was their normal custom, went to Monk's House for August and September. It was a very hot summer, and Virginia fainted one evening in the garden, partly from heat-stroke, and partly from the recurrence of her heart-trouble. She recovered quite quickly, and was able to finish correcting the proofs of The Common Reader, Second Series, *and write the greater part of her short book* Flush, *about Mrs Browning's dog. There were frequent visitors to Rodmell, among them T. S. Eliot and his distracted and distracting wife. On the day of their visit (2 September) John Lehmann sent in his resignation from the Hogarth Press. Virginia lost another of her old friends, Goldsworthy Lowes Dickinson, who died on 3 August.*

2616: TO ETHEL SMYTH

Monks House, [Rodmell, Sussex]

Sunday 7th and Monday 8th August [1932]

I was just about to write to you when I heard of Goldie Dickinson's death.[1] I hadnt even heard he was ill. This has rather spun me round into another mood. I had known him off and on, for ever so many years; and become much more intimate lately—the same sort of intimacy I had with Lytton and some others; though of course not nearly so close as with Lytton. Still—he was the most charming of men—the most spiritual.— Isnt it odd how the curtain seems about to fall sometimes? What with Lyttons death, Carrington's death, now Goldie's death—all people who have gone in and out of my life these past twenty years.—But no more.

I only wanted to explain how I cant at the moment pick up what I was going to say—cant get back into the mood. The main thing was I think that though I quite accept what you say—that you can control yourself, that there'll be no more scenes—still I'm left doubting—isnt it rather a cribbed and confined sort of friendship when one has to be controlled and on one's best behaviour? Doesn't the need point, as I said, to some queer, no, not queer, natural,—incompatibility between us? I dont see that this is to be wondered at, after all. We are both extreme in character. And then we met late in life, and then, as you say, I dont know your friends nor you

---

1. Goldsworthy Lowes Dickinson (1862-1932), the historian and philosopher, and lecturer in Political Science at Cambridge. Virginia had recently been drawn closer to him by his perceptive appreciation of *The Waves* (Vol. IV, pp. 397-8). He died on 3 August in a London hospital, of a haemorrhage.

mine, so that the natural background is missing. But what is important is that I suspect that your violences are part of your virtues—and so are my exaggerations and obtusenesses part of mine. If we have to control ourselves and to control ourselves so much more than we need with other friends, aren't we diminishing our own peculiar light? You see, I dont understand the system on which your mind works, by nature. When you say for example that you're going to write something about me and publish parts of my letters—I am flabbergasted. I swear I couldn't do such a thing where you're concerned to save my life. Yet to you it seems natural—right—amusing— a joke? I dont know what. I mean, I dont blame: I don't praise: I simply dont understand. I give this as an instance as the sort of thing that happens between two people as different as we are; and how bewildering it is. I'm not attempting to sum up, nor coming to a conclusion. I make these rough notes for your information, and solely because I feel the value of the thing itself—our relationship.[1] Obtuse and variable as I am, I still think, seriously nothing more important than relationships—that they should be sound, free from hypocrisies, fluencies, palaver—

Well: as Mrs Pankhurst[2] used to say; so conveniently making an end of one topic and going on to another. Its very hot here: I am correcting proofs [of *The Common Reader*]: we have a good many visitors one way or another. Though none yet, praise be the Lord, sleeping in the house. Tomorrow is our London day. And then my mother in law comes over. And then and then—I've got a mass of things I want to write, but cant get down to them till I've done the sheer, unutterable drudgery of proof correcting—in this case more than ever dreary: for I quote Donne: and they misquote; and I have to look up Donne, and Sidney, and Spenser—oh how I hate facts: but still more, misquoting facts.

No: I thought Elizabeth [Williamson] looking particularly well; but then it was the evening and we were chattering. Anyhow, looks dont count much either way. My brother is yatching [*sic*]; and his lady wants to break with him;[3] and Nessa thinks she ought to tell him so. That is what is happening in Sussex at the moment. And the Labour party is meeting in the drawing room tonight, and I must politely greet the man who built the bungalow.[4] And now for more proofs. I ought to write this scrawl again; but leave it to you to decipher, not only the hand, but the meaning.   V.

Berg

1. Ethel had written to Virginia: "My relation to you is the most precious thing in my life" (30 July, *Berg*).
2. Mrs Emmeline Pankhurst, the suffragette leader, for whose cause Ethel had been to prison in 1912, in a cell next to Mrs Pankhurst's.
3. Adrian and Karin Stephen separated temporarily, but did not divorce.
4. F. Hancock, who stood as Labour candidate for Lewes in 1931 and 1935, and built a disfiguring bungalow on the top of the down above Rodmell. (See Vol. IV, p. 380.)

Monks House, Rodmell,
Lewes, Sussex

Sunday [7 August 1932]

My dear Roger,

We want just to send one line—there was nobody like Goldie and I know what his death must mean to you. How I hate my friends dying! Please live to be a thousand. You cant think what you mean to us all.

Love from us both
your
Virginia

Of course, no answer.

Sussex

Monks House, Rodmell,
Lewes, [Sussex]

Aug 8th [1932]

Dear Alice,[1]

I think you said that you might be willing to come down here for a night in August. Will you suggest one? We should very much like to see you, if you don't mind a very small bedroom. But my view is spoilt for ever—did I tell you? Vast iron sheds for cement, ruining the entire valley.

How is the novel? Are you in process of jumping from the window, as I advised?

Yours
Virginia Woolf

Mrs Ian Parsons

Monks House, [Rodmell,
Sussex]

Aug. 9th? [1932]

Well, dear Mrs Nicolson, when are you coming over—for I dont count meeting you in Lewes high Street buying wines.

Oh how hot it is! I've been mooning on the downs with Pinka—in

1. Alice Ritchie had already published two novels with the Hogarth Press, and had travelled books for them.

spite of houses, still its the loveliest country in the world, with the corn ripening, and yellow butterflies and—I forget how the sentence ends. I daresay you've got enough scenes stored in your great forehead to finish all my sentences. Yesterday we were in London—the devil; tomorrow my mother in law: Saturday poor distracted Siepmann.[1] By the way, how good your husband is in the N.S. I entirely agreed with his BBC. article [*unidentified*]: still more with his Yeats Brown, which fizzled up and made melted butter of all the other mild eulogists.[2] Max [Beerbohm] for example. The divine delight of a really good review is that one has read the book: now I needn't bother myself with Yeats Brown ever again. But while your husband slices the heads off the daisies I wish his wife (not to be too euphemistic, thats you) would write me, for me only, a long long, solid solid, tough, tight trenchant poem—say about a wagon; or a bull—the one who ranges your sheds for ever unsatisfied. Do please. I cant bear the patter of meritorious prose any more—so thin—such gruel and water. Its not a food for the mature—only for pink babies like dear old Hugh. That reminds me: I've not answered him, at Sark;[3] nor Ethel—Oh my God Ethel! I should think I had had 6 reams of notepaper crossed, underlined, red pencilled, starred, since you made your famous remark about my being faint. I'm getting at my wits end. Happily its very cheap, her notepaper, and I really believe she gets a kind of mild continuous orgasm from this flux. And that reminds me, who is Mrs Ralph Ivers, or Dorothy Easton,[4] of Sevenoaks— who has sent me a story, rather, indeed, very, good, to whom Sackville West has been "so kind"—who is she, and why does she write me a drivelling letter about her small boy and her motor car—and I think call me Virginia. The wonders of authors will never cease: I've had such a packet of letters lately, one from a Sodomite who has discovered his perversion all owing to that bad book The Waves and therefore says I must find him a job or he will cut his throat on my doorstep.

Well, I think, delightful as this letter is, I must go and put my pie in the oven; then we have ice cream to follow—you know we have a frigidaire —with fresh raspberries. Then we turn on the loud speaker—Bach tonight —then I watch my baby owls learning to fly on the Church tower—then I read Lord Kilbracken[5]—what a good book—then I think what about

1. See p. 43, note 1.
2. Harold had reviewed *Golden Horn* by Francis Yeats Brown in the *New Statesman* of 6 August. He wrote: "Clearly he is talented, honest and agreeable. He should do better."
3. Hugh Walpole was on holiday in Sark, one of the Channel Islands.
4. Mrs Ivers (Dorothy Easton) wrote novels, books on gardening, and an autobiography *You Asked Me Why*, 1936.
5. *Reminiscences of Lord Kilbracken*, 1931. As Arthur Godley, he was Gladstone's Private Secretary, and later Under Secretary of State for India. He had died in June 1932.

bed—on which note, as I chastely put it, I end. But when are you coming? Sibyls [Colefax] pending, so do be beforehand.

V.

Berg

2620: To Ethel Smyth

Monks House, [Rodmell, Sussex]

Sunday 14th August [1932]

Well Ethel dear be a kind Christian woman and write me a friendly letter and dont be a sleek tabby but my old uncastrated wild cat. Here am I in bed after falling in a faint among the roses on Thursday evening precisely as I fell 2 years ago [29 August 1930]. Really it wasn't my fault this time. We had L's mother and brother to lunch—it was that very hot day— we sat out in the garden: The old lady was ravishing—almost brought tears to my eyes—gave me an old pair of pearl ear rings of hers; and then, as I say, I dropped down: but it wasn't as bad as last time, except for being muddled in the head, I'm all right today and shall get up for luncheon. L. rang up our dr. in London who says its clearly nothing but the heat, and if I stay quiet for a day or two I shall be all right. So thats all the medical details.

I've been thinking meanwhile that I probably wrote with undue acerbity about your intended letter and article. I didn't catch your meaning—I thought it was to be about me, seriously: I mean one of your brilliant and searching streaks of memory: and, you being a born writer, I thought you'd put in a great deal more than I'd like people to see. I'm rather nervously pernickety about personalities, as I get so much heckled by journalists for Bloomsbury Highbrowism and so forth. But if its about Lady B. Maurice Baring. Eth, Pan[1] and so on, why not go ahead? and leave me out? I should enjoy *that*—them in and me out—quite immensely. You'd do it brilliantly and they wouldn't mind: its only one of my perversities—dislike of personal appearances: you will understand. If I didn't figure as a novelist I shouldn't mind.

Well—(how I bless [Emmeline] Pankhurst for that convenience of style) I am seriously contemplating getting up and finding stockings and dress cast to the winds on Thursday. It was so odd, lying in the grass, and seeing the flowers dance above my head. I'm reading masses of pigsticking books; and how Edgar Wallace dictated 70,000 words in a week end:[2] and

1. Lady (Elizabeth) Balfour, Maurice Baring, Elizabeth Williamson and Pan (Ethel's dog).
2. The novelist and playwright. He had died on 10 February, 1932. Many of his novels and his best play, *On the Spot* (1931), were dictated during single weekends.

I'd like to read one of Ethels most violent, disruptive, abruptive, fuliginious, catastrophic, panoramic, I cant think of any other adjectives—effusions. It is deliciously shady and cool. My room is nothing but door window and garden. Tomorrow I shall be up and correcting proofs.

V.

Monday
Forgot to post this. Up: recovered; correcting proofs.

Berg

2621: To Alice Ritchie   *Monks House, Rodmell,*
                                           Lewes, Sussex

14th August [1932]

Dear Alice,

I'm so sorry not to have answered: like many people I toppled over into a flower bed in a faint that hot day and have been in bed. Could you possibly come on Monday 22nd? The other days you give are difficult as Leonard has to go to London this week, and the next week, alas, we have to go to Essex. But if Monday doesn't do, make other suggestions: only not the 20th, not the 25th.

Bring the novel and finish it up here in my room.

Yours
Virginia Woolf

Mrs Ian Parsons

2622: To Harmon H. Goldstone   *Monk's House, Rodmell,*
                                            Lewes, Sussex

Typewritten
16th August 1932

Dear Mr Goldstone,

I must apologise for my delay. I left your address in London, and did not like to return your Outline[1] to the hotel address [in Paris]. Also I have been laid up, owing to the heat, and fear that my comments on your Outline will be of a very scrappy kind. But such as they are I will make them.

It is very difficult to give an impartial opinion of a book devoted to ones own work; but the Outline seems to me to suggest some very interesting questions; and I should certainly read it with great pleasure if it were about somebody else. I am a little doubtful as to your reference to "VW's own statement of the problem of aspect." I dont know exactly to what it refers;

1. Of his proposed book about Virginia. See Letter 2610.

but I should like to enter a caution against anything that I have said as a critic being taken as evidence of my own views, or of my aims. I am much of Hardys opinion that a novel is an impression not an argument. The book is written without a theory; later, a theory may be made, but I doubt if it has much bearing on the work.*

The Bloomsbury Period. I do not want to impose my own views, but I feel that Bloomsbury is a word that stands for very little. The Bloomsbury group is largely a creation of the journalists. To dwell upon Bloomsbury as an influence is liable to lead to judgments that, as far as I know have no basis in fact.

I may say that I have never read Bergson[1] and have only a very amateurish knowledge of Freud and the psychoanalysts; I have made no study of them.

Money and a Room of ones own. Some writers have taken my statements literally in a Room of Ones Own, and have inferred that I myself was left £500 by an aunt; and worked as a journalist etc. It is perhaps thus worth saying that this is purely fictitious.[2] I have had an independent income ever since I was of age; and have never had to write for money or to pursue any profession.

Education and early reading. Partly from reasons of health I was never at any school or college. My father allowed me to read any book in his library when I was a girl; and it was a large library.

With regard to the translations—I scarcely like to claim that I 'translated' the Russian books credited to me. I merely revised the English of a version made by S. Koteliansky.[3]

Since writing to you, I see that Miss Dorothy Richardson, the novelist, is engaged upon a study of my books, which should be interesting.[4]

I enclose the Outline, and must thank you for letting me see it. I am sorry not to be more helpful; but as I think I have already said, I am sure you will write better if you are fettered as little as possible by the views of the author.

Yours sincerely
Virginia Woolf

Berg

* Virginia wrote against this paragraph *Not for quotation.*

1. Henri Bergson (1859-1941), the French philosopher.
2. Not quite fictitious. Virginia's aunt, Caroline Emelia Stephen, left Virginia £2,500 (gross) when she died in 1909; and between 1916 and 1921 Virginia contributed almost weekly articles to the *Times Literary Supplement.*
3. Of Dostoevsky's *Stavrogin's Confession*, Tolstoy's *Love Letters*, and Goldenveizer's *Talks with Tolstoy*, all 1922-23.
4. There is no evidence that Dorothy Richardson even contemplated a study of Virginia's work, and certainly none was published. Later she was invited to review *The Years*, but declined because she did not like it.

2623: To Sir Henry Newbolt   *Monks House, Rodmell,*
                                            Lewes, Sussex

16th August 1932

Dear Sir Henry,

I have entirely forgotten writing to you!—but as you say that there is nothing discreditable in the letter I am delighted that you should print it, and am much flattered that you should have taken the trouble to keep it.[1]

I am delighted quite apart from that, to think that you have written your memoirs and much look forward to reading them.

Yours sincerely
Virginia Woolf

George Spater

2624: To Hugh Walpole   *Monks House, Rodmell,*
                                            [Sussex]

Aug 17th [1932]

My dear Hugh,

I am a wretch—I know it. But the more I love getting letters, the more I hate writing them. And I've had the excuse of being laid low with a heat stroke. Have you ever fallen down among your dahlias as if felled by the Lord Almighty? Its an odd experience—interesting, acute, unpleasant. I am all right again—only making this serve as an excuse. And you wont be in Sark any longer. Henry's love affair will be over, or, as they call it, consummated.[2] But where you may be now—whether in the Isle of Man, or Bucharest, or Timbuctoo or merely Piccadilly—heaven knows. How I envy you your mobility! I'm contemplating a voyage to Ireland—where I've never been—in September: but thats all; and no doubt that wont come off; the garden, the owls, Leonard's flowers, my room—out on the terrace, where there's nothing between me and Caburn—these are all too nice: but they cant mean anything to you: when I say 'terrace' and 'garden room' you see something—that I'm sure—but something plunged in the splendour of your own romance.

1. Henry John Newbolt (1862-1938), the poet, was best known for his *Drake's Drum*, which Leslie Stephen often declaimed to his daughters. Virginia's letter was written to him in about 1902 (Vol. I, letter 41), and was printed in his Memoirs, *My World as in my Time*, 1932.
2. Virginia may have written 'Henry' for 'Harold'—Harold Cheevers, Walpole's man-servant and companion since 1926, who accompanied him to Sark. Or possibly a reference to Henry James, on whom Walpole was writing an essay for his book *The Apple Trees*, 1932.

Vita and Harold were here on Sunday, very flourishing, with the boys [Ben and Nigel]: overflowing into every corner of life—Vita's book has been made into a play, at Croydon (Passion Spent I mean)[1]—forgive this telegraphic style—its not particularly modern—though Harold would say so—its only heat, laze—economy of effort. And Vita said Hugh's Scott is out with a dedication to you![2] Damn the man—why haven't I got it? I cried. Calm yourself, she replied: its only out to the Trade. What excites me even more is the rumour in some paper that you're publishing your Memoirs, If thats so, tell me the exact moment and I'll wire to Bumpus [bookseller]. Now if I were you, I would add that to my days work—autobiography for 30 minutes daily; please do write a colossal book—sweep every crumb in to it—the days work: and everybody, what you eat, read, think, love, hate, laugh at,—all: considering your mobility and your versatility, and how many loves and hates you have—what a book! what a book! I cry, green with envy. Please, by the way of instalment tell me the true story of James Agate.[3] When I read the Review I said, in my hardened way, now what infamy is at the back of that? Aren't these reptiles shortsighted? a child in arms could have seen that the whole thing was spawned by some livid and lurid serpent in the pit of his soul—not by any love, as he pretended, for the art of fiction—are we all incurably corrupt? with which I must end.

V.W.

Texas

2625: TO ETHEL SMYTH

Monks House, [Rodmell, Sussex]

Aug 18th [1932]

Yes it was very nice to get your letter Ethel, your uncastrated letter and I laughed heartlessly over the lunch party, and Lady Rayleighs heels in the air.[4] My Cambridge friends insist that Mr Sidgwick[5] is a miracle of intellect still—only inclined to be silent. But my brain is all dust and ashes

1. It was not Vita's *All Passion Spent* which was dramatised, but her novel *The Edwardians*, produced by the New Croydon Repertory Company on 17 September.
2. See p. 24, note 1.
3. James Agate, the dramatic and literary critic (1877-1947), had violently attacked Hugh Walpole in the *Daily Express* for his *A Letter to a Modern Novelist*, but not surprisingly, because the Letter contained a ferocious attack on Agate.
4. She was the second wife of the 4th Lord Rayleigh, the distinguished physicist.
5. Virginia must have been referring to the great Henry Sidgwick (1838-1900), the Professor of Moral Philosophy at Cambridge who had a strong intellectual influence on his generation. In the 1930s there was no living Sidgwick at Cambridge who could be described as 'a miracle of intellect'.

and I shant get a spark with a poker today. Lord how hot it is here—the downs fizzling across the marsh: the village sunk in portentous silence. I'm much better but dont do more than creep from my bedroom to my lodge, holding a parasol to placate L. who follows me like a dog—About the faint —I wish I could gratify your morbid curiosity, but one packs about 10 lives into these moments—I could write 3 volumes—how odd it is to break through the usual suddenly and so violently. It wasn't in the afternoon; but after dinner, sitting on the terrace, in the cool. I was looking at Caburn and thinking how the night of a hot day differs from cool nights—thinking about all that was cool and quiet—the white owl crossing the meadow when suddenly my heart leapt; stopped; ran away, like a four in hand. I cant stop it, I said. Lord, now its in my head. This pounding must must must break something. So I said "I'm going to faint" and slid down and lay flat on the grass at L's feet. He dashed into the house and came back with the ice tray of the frigidaire, which he put under my neck. And then I thought of everything under the sun: he says it lasted 30 minutes. Then the pounding lessened; and he helped me up; and I felt very faint—trees; flowers, stretching, fading: and I thought I could never get to the house—really that was painful, walking and fainting, but I did; and flopped on the bed; and said to L. with my usual sense, Would it be a good thing to use the Po? Certainly he said and I used it: and began shaking and he said can you take your temperature? But I couldnt hold the tube in my lips; however, I did later, and instead of being very high as the dr. expected, it was very low: and gradually I became sleepy and comfortable, only afraid to move, as if all my limbs were separate, and so fell asleep and woke, drowsy, sleepy, content—and thats all. L. rang up the dr. who is seeing a specialist who knows about heat fainting and will inform us. But there's no need. There is nothing whatever wrong with me. I've always had what they call an intermittent pulse, and this—so a heart dr told me—tires the heart and makes it sensitive to strain, but the heart is perfectly sound, strong, and loving as you know. And this pulse too is infinitely better now than it was 10 years ago. Are these facts enough?

I'm seeing Lydia and will ask her about the Ballet.[1] She is rather touchy now about her dancing and apt to say she must retire; but sometimes is overcome, like an old warhorse, by the sound of music and goes back. What Vanessa's up to, I dont know: but I'm sure she'll do the scenery if its decided on, since she likes that sort of job;[2] and I've just made myself a life member of Sadlers Wells; and everybody seems in favour of new ballets

1. Lydia Lopokova, the ballerina, who married Maynard Keynes in 1925. The ballet was Ethel's *Fête Galante*.
2. Vanessa did two ballet-designs in 1932: for *High Yellow* produced by the Camargo Ballet, and for the Sadlers Wells production of *Pomona* in January 1933. In the following year she did the décor for *Fête Galante*.

and modern decoration. I say, my father used to go to lectures by Professor Smyth[1] in order to see him burst into tears at the mention of Marie Antoinette.

V.

Berg

2626: TO LADY CECIL   *Monks House, Rodmell,*
                                       [Sussex]

Aug 18th 1932

My dear Nelly,

What a charming woman you are! (I forget what this refers to—it is merely a general observation that sprang to Nessa's and my lips when we were talking about you the other day) Yes of course we will come over or up, as you call it, but may we leave the day at the moment doubtful? I've been celebrating the heat by tumbling in a faint among Leonard's dahlias, and the doctor says I am to stay quiet in a shady room at present. As I dont want to fall down among your dahlias, may we leave it till the sun has gone back into the clouds?

I was greatly interested by the quotation you sent me from Hale Wright[2] about my mother. I never knew that he was a friend of my father's: why he gave her the photograph I cant imagine. But oddly enough I've been thinking about him lately. Among our authors is a girl of 17 who writes poetry. Her name is Easdale,[3] and she and her mother—who's name was Adeney—came over the other day; and the mother who's an incredible goose and chatterbox but simple-minded and rather touchingly idiotic, informed me, as we were wandering round the garden, that the reason why she had left her husband was that he was so jealous of her friendship with Mark Rutherford. "But of course he was *merely* a friend and guide to me" she said. "I have heaps of his letters in a box at home. And then he married a woman I detested [Dorothy Vernon]. Why are men so jealous, Mrs Woolf? It was the greatest thing in my life—my friendship with that good man. .Yet your father left me, Joan, because of it." "Yes it was dreadfully sad" said Joan—who has the face of a cherub on a chocolate box. "These sort of things dont happen nowadays" said Mrs Easdale—"not among you young people". And so they went on chattering. I rather think she's sending me his letters. Did you ever hear of her? She is now not notably attractive, either in body or mind, except that one loves complete geese, being so sensible oneself.

I liked the boy who thinks I know about school life.[4] I seem to be a

1. Ethel's great-uncle, William Smyth, Master of Peterhouse, Cambridge.
2. William Hale White (1831-1913), the novelist, philosophical writer, literary critic and civil servant, who wrote under the name 'Mark Rutherford'.
3. Joan Easdale, whose two books of poems the Press had published in 1931-32.
4. Which he had deduced from reading Virginia's *A Room of One's Own*.

95

well known authority upon Eton and Roedean. A cutting has just come which says that ignorant as Mrs W. is about everything else, she is an admitted expert on girls schools—nobody knows them so intimately. And I've only had the tip of my nose in one once, taking Nessa's child there. Aren't reviewers——well, well, its a hot day, and I'm to keep cool. So I won't launch out; and I remember too, how we used to review books together, 100 years ago, for that long faced old lantern jawed man, who kept Charlotte Brontes socks in a glass case in his drawing room.[1]

Now, Lady Cecil, (this is meant to mark a change of tone, from the gossiping to the hortatory) whatever you do, write your Memoirs, bringing in all that romantic past; please do: I loathe novels; nobody will write poetry: here am I told to keep quiet: write your memoirs and send them to me instantly.

                                                              Yr Virginia W.

Marquess of Salisbury (Cecil Papers)

2627: To Ethel Smyth   *Monks House, [Rodmell,*
                                                              Sussex]
Sunday 21st Aug. [1932]

Ah-hah-the heat wave has broken and we are all cool again. This happened quite suddenly here—a cold, sinister yellow wind rushed through the garden about 2: as if a lid had been opened and air escaped from a cauldron. Our thermometer fell I dont know how many degrees: then rose; then fell with a thud. So we went to Lewes after tea and bought our weekly groceries and after that walked on the down above Lewes, and everybody was walking out too, like prisoners escaped—dogs bounding, horses galloping, wind blowing—everything released—how queer it looked: and I saw one old vagabond sitting under a furse bush, making a cushion of flowers' heads, either by way of thanksgiving, or a wreath for his wife, as you like it. All the little red blue and purple down flowers were strewn round him. We had thunder at night of course, but not very tremendous, only enough to spoil the Promenade [Concert] to which we were listening. Odd—there was a crack of lightning over Caburn, and instantly Mozart went zigzag too. Modern life is a very complicated affair—why not some sudden revelation of the meaning of everything, one night?—I think it might happen.

Are you, in a more humble way, appearing at Queen's Hall?[2] I must

1. Reginald Smith (1857-1916), who married the daughter of George Smith, Charlotte Brontë's publisher. In 1898 he became editor of the *Cornhill Magazine*, and Virginia and Nelly Cecil had both contributed to its book reviews in 1908.
2. The overture to Ethel's opera *The Wreckers* was conducted by Sir Henry Wood at the Queen's Hall on 22 August.

make a note to listen—As you gather, I'm much the better for this relief, and cant pretend to any kind of illness now, though L. insists upon treating me like the Princess who feels a pea through 6 mattresses. I think these fainting fits are much more alarming to the onlookers than to oneself. He wanted, against my wish, to have our London dr, Elly Rendel,[1] Lyttons niece, down the other day: but she said that would be useless, and I refused to have the local man who tinkers one as a plumber would a very fine watch. The specialist is I think away. Anyhow its passed off now. And the only interesting symptom—my spine swollen and burning and tender at the 3rd knob from the top—no doctor can account for. Its nerve exhaustion they say; and dont know what it means. My tongue is so pure Leonard is green with envy: all my ills come from the lump of nerves in my spine, which are tied to my heart. But enough of health. I've done my proofs[2] in spite of the heat, and am lolling and languishing in a luxury of indolence.

The Keynes's came over; and she was most anxious that you should realise that she cant dance in your ballet [*Fête Galante*] simply because it stirs such wild jealousy in the hearts of other dancers if she does. She's in the awkward position of being the patroness, and has to take great care to share out the work equally, as they're all starving and she rich. They hadn't heard your music yet, but were highly appreciative of you, in your capacity of uncastrated cat. Maynard was much impressed; and thought your military descent must account for the dominating masterful energy with which you vanquished even those who agree with you. This is a great compliment from Maynard, who rules all Cambridge and has the whole of Kings in his pocket.[3] Was your father a good general by the way?— did he ever kill a man—the father of the uncastrated cat? Are you, as I hope, going on with your cesspool, Lady Balfour, M Baring, pot-pourri— if thats what they're called? [*Female Pipings in Eden*] Please do, just to show there's no ill feeling. With all of them in, I'm just as well left out. And my feeling against these personal appearances is really no fake; my publicity is already too much for me—not that I'm modest: not at all. But limelight is bad for me: the light in which I work best is twilight. And I'm threatened with 3 more books upon me: Holtby[4] has induced another publisher to print her follies: [Dorothy] Richardson is producing another; and a man from America [Harmon H. Goldstone] a third. All this means to me a kind of fuss and falsity and talking about my husband, mother, father, and dog which I loathe. But I should love to read you on other people.

1. Dr Elinor Rendel had been Virginia's doctor for many years. She was the daughter of Lytton Strachey's eldest sister, also named Elinor.
2. Of *The Common Reader: Second Series*.
3. Maynard Keynes had been Bursar of King's College since 1926, and spent most weekends there.
4. Winifred Holtby's *Virginia Woolf* was published this year by Wishart & Co. For Richardson see p. 91, note 4; for Goldstone, p. 36, note 1.

My brother is still enamoured and deluded and is getting up a weekly Club, for the purpose of meeting his very dull lady [Dora Chapman]. I am subscribing 2/6 for this reason. We have to go Essex next week to spend the night with him,[1] and I hope to go round by way of Canterbury, as a spree. But happily I'm not in Adrian's inner confidence, and so shall talk about boats and dogs and so on, not love and death.

What good letters you write—always: but specially to convalescents—I've written this one in 10 minutes: 3 days ago it would have taken 60. So I'm cured

V.

Berg

2628: TO LADY OTTOLINE MORRELL   *Monks House, [Rodmell, Sussex]*

6th Sept. [1932]

Dearest Ottoline,

I wish I could write you as nice a letter as you wrote me, but I have been out walking on the Downs, with a black spaniel who will chase sheep —hence my hand with which I tried to hold him in, shakes like an aspen. But you must try to decipher—only it wont be worth while.

Do you think people (I'm thinking of Lytton and [Hugh] Walpole) do write letters to be published? I'm as vain as a cockatoo myself; but I dont think I do that. Because when one is writing a letter, the whole point is to rush ahead; and anything may come out of the spout of the tea pot. Now, if I thought, Ottoline will put this letter in a box, I should at once apply the tip of my finger to the end of the spout. When one was very young perhaps one did: perhaps one believed in immortality. I think Lytton's letters were freer as he got older and rid of this illusion: hence they're not printable; but James is bringing out a little book of his essays this autumn.[2] Only scraps, but there's an essay on letter writing, which, considering he was about 22 seems to me amazing—not as thought but as cabinet making —putting little bits of wood side by side in their right places. That is why one gets so sick of essay writing. I feel sticky all over when I've done, measuring, fitting, and using glue. (The dog has not only made my hand shake; but upset all the letters in my head).

I cant say we have had a quiet summer, because Sussex is really only an extension of Oxford Street, and as we are on the way side, anybody drops

1. At Thorpe-le-Soken.
2. *Characters and Commentaries*, edited by James Strachey, 1933.

in. And I long for a house in a wood, approached by a two mile drive, with deep lakes at frequent intervals. People stay so long in the country. And I never have enough butter, or the milk has gone sour, or the cat has eaten the only fish. What you must have suffered at Garsington! I believe London on the whole is more retired. We went off about July 26th—did you come and knock after that? I wish I'd been there.

I had meant to discuss Tom and Vivienne Haigh Eliot with you; but its now an old subject and stale, and perhaps you have seen him or her: I hope the separation is complete and final, as it promised to be when I last had news. Poor V. was running amok all over London. Did she come to you? He is coming here one of these days—I mustn't say which, or where he is, for fear V. should put on her crazy old hat and follow after.[1]

Francis Birrell[2] has been very ill—a tumour on his brain—but mercifully the operation is over and said to be successful. Why is one so fond of one's friends? Partly egotism, I suppose. I felt that if Francis died I should be 50 years older. So please dont get ill, or let Philip [Morrell] get ill, not that I have the least affection for either of you—why should I?—haven't you always been very good to me?—(So I'm putting you in my next book) but dont get ill because I dont want to die myself; and thats what happens when other people die.

Yes, I wasted most of my youth on Greek plays. I used to be able to read Aeschylus in a kind of hop skip and jump way: and the other day I thought I'd try Sophocles again: but found all the words withdrawn like clouds into the sky. Still I always feel—but no, the dog has put it beyond my power to go on, and I have to wash, and write to Ethel Smith—she's back, fuming and foaming and furious from the Hebrides—and drive over to Charleston to dine with Nessa and Duncan. Its a lovely pale yellow, pale blue, red, purple evening, with all the corn in stacks, like cakes, and the swallows, and the apples,—apples hanging are the most beautiful of fruits; so forgive this scrawl, which is not to be put into a box, but burnt in the Dukes garden,[3] where I daresay you are sitting. How are the memoirs getting on?

V.

Texas

1. T. S. Eliot and his wife had called at Monk's House on 2 September.
2. He was the son of the author and Liberal statesman, Augustine Birrell. He died on 2 January 1935.
3. The Duke of Portland's house, Welbeck Abbey. He was Ottoline's half-brother.

Monks House, [Rodmell, Sussex]
7th Sept 1932

Yes I am a wretch never to write letters, but considered carefully, this is a compliment, because if I felt I had to write it would mean that you were one of those horrid old bores who expect answers (oh there's such a pile of them on my table.) Your adventures fill me with horror—of course everybody changes when they get to Brighton: even I know that, and do it by light of instinct. But then I should have cracked the guard over the head with [Ronald] Storr's thick umbrella—and so solved the question of leaving it in London: because I should have killed the guard and broken the umbrella. I like to think of myself doing these violent acts. While the mild and timid Ethel sips a cup of tea in a restaurant. You seem to be as busy as a girl in her first season—going about conducting. Does it mean—if so you wont admit it—that fame, no not fame—mere vulgar success, has at last crowned your bald head? (Metaphorically, you are bald; according to Ethel's version of Ethel, not a single laurel leaf has ever grown there; and like the Pelican she has plucked out all her feathers on her breast for champagne drinking chicken eating relations; so she is not only bald on the head, but bare on the breast—what a repulsive object, when one comes to think of it, So let us change the subject)

I've been asked to write in the Times about my father for his Centenary.[1] Shall I or shall I not? I cant resist trying because he was such a very remarkable figure: but you wont see it: indeed I cant make it visible, in only 1500 words, so I shall give up, I think; but at the moment my head is full of him. One thing you would have liked—his extreme sincerity; also unless I'm partial, he was beautiful in the distinguished way a race horse, even an ugly race horse, is beautiful—And he had such a fling with his hands and feet. Also he was a great climber. Also he was completely unworldly. Also he begot me: but then you prefer Vanessa.

I have been doing a lot of odds and ends—seeing anybody who chooses to knock at the window. The other day in walked the T. S. Eliots—he's the poet, and she, poor raddled distressing woman, takes drugs. On a wild wet day she dresses in white satin, and exudes ether from a dirty pocket handkerchief. Also she has whims and fancies all the time—some amorous, some pornographic. Meanwhile he sits there, as trim as a bank clerk, making exact, but rather laboured conversation—for instance about his motor car. But as you've never seen him or read him this means less than nothing to you. Isnt it odd that you read Maurice Baring and not Tom Eliot? Where's your rudimentary sense of English literature Ethel? I would give all MBs copious cool works for one of Toms least and most brittle phrases. So there.

1. Virginia's article about Leslie Stephen was published in *The Times* on 28 November, the centenary of his birth.

Never tell me we are twin souls, cast out of one mould, of identically the same plaster again.

Oh I'm so fascinated by the Empress and her mother.[1] Did the E. ever talk to you about Mérimée? about Stendhal? To think that she knew them both, and that you knew her! If you've one duty, this side of the grave, it is to go on memorialising—not me; but all these disappearing Kings and Queens. Then there have been any number of odd adventures at the Hogarth Press: unrepeatable now: then I've been racing [at Brighton] and lost 12/6: then I want to buy a house in Essex: then Colefax was coming and put me off, and now puts me on, and I wont be put on and off, all because of Prince Somebody, and so tell her on the telephone; then—but Lord its 7 and I've forgotten to put our pot in the oven. I must rush in. This is only a wild scribble of unmitigated affection.

V.

Berg

2630: To Lady Cecil   *Monks House, Rodmell,*
                                       Lewes, Sussex
8th Sept [1932]

My dear Nelly,

At last I have succeeded in cornering my sister—I met her in a wool shop today in Lewes—and arranged that if it suits you may we come over next Wednesday, which is I think 14th, to tea—that is about 4.30 if the cars dont break down—Leonard, Vanessa and I? But of course you will have gone to Geneva, or the Butler (I insist upon a butler) will say so. Couldn't you let Geneva rule itself for once in a way? or change your butler? It is a howling storm in this part of Sussex, and we had meant to spend tomorrow on a picnic at Canterbury.

Well, what do you think of your nephew marrying I was going to say my niece—but she isnt that—Rachel MacCarthy I mean.[2] Anyhow she's in the 7th Heaven, and it will be very good for David, whom I think a most charming young man, so kind to old women like me. I dined with him the other night and took all the asparagus by mistake. A less refined nature would have given him back a dozen sticks—I ate them all—Which reminds me—years ago you told me to read Stella Benson. And I loathed her—And you were quite right. She is a nice woman—bleached like a skull and long suffering with a husband in China, which he deserves, and long

1. The Empress Eugénie (1826-1920), widow of Napoleon III. On the collapse of his Empire, she lived first at Chislehurst and after her husband's death, at Farnborough, where Ethel met her in 1890 and became her constant companion.
2. David Cecil married Rachel MacCarthy, the only daughter of Desmond and Molly, on 13 October.

may he stay there. On the other hand I like her very much, and am going, after 20 years to begin to read the books you read. And do you know Cornelia Sorabji?[1] because I am to meet her. I have masses to say but no paper.

So goodbye V.

By the way, it is my father's Centenary in Novr. and the Times want me to write an article about him—but I dont think I can. Anyhow, do tell me what you thought of him. Was he very alarming? charming? eccentric? rude? or what?

Marquess of Salisbury (Cecil Papers)

2631: To V. Sackville-West   *Monks House, [Rodmell, Sussex]*

Friday [9 September 1932]

I meant to ask—and forgot—if you would lend me the [Lenare] phogh which I gave you (of myself) because that devil [Winifred] Holtby wants one for her book in a hurry, and this might do. They'd return it. Could you bring it—but doubtless now, with your other attachment, its down the coal hole. Oh alas.

    Never mind come on

Monday and
all
shall
be
forgot
and
forgave.

I dont suppose therell be time to look in

V.

Berg

2632: To Ethel Smyth   *[Monk's House, Rodmell, Sussex]*

Sunday [11 September 1932]

Yes I'm a mole—Look at my week—today Nessa and the children: tomorrow Vita comes and will stay over Tuesday afternoon: Wednesday

---

1. Cornelia Sorabji (1866-1954) was the daughter of an Indian teacher, and was educated at Somerville College, Oxford. She became a barrister in London, did much for women's causes in India, and was a prolific author and lecturer.

I've got to go over and see deaf Nelly Cecil—it might be London. I dont think, knowing my own moodiness, I can talk to you with happiness in the intervals of this hubbub.—no I dont think it would be worth your while. But later? in London? here? I'm racing to catch the post so leave this question standing. And I cant think of what's in my head: and the dog barks; and Pinka stole the ham: can one eat a ham licked by a dog? is it hydrophobic? You were right about Lehmann's mouth by the way—quite right.

And so farewell

V.

Berg

2633: TO WILLIAM PLOMER   *Monks House, Rodmell,*
                            [Sussex]

Sunday Sept 11th [1932]

Dear William,

We shall like it very much if you would come for the week end next Saturday—17th that is: I rather think Charles Siepman of the B.B.C is coming—d'you know him?

I'm quite recovered—fainting is such an odd experience its almost worth it. But all experiences will wait till you come: we've a lot we want to talk about.

They've built cement works and spoilt the view—damn them—There's a train that gets in about 4.30 I think. Let us know if you'll catch it or which.

V.W.

Texas

2634: TO HUGH WALPOLE   *Monks House, Rodmell,*
                            [Sussex]

Sept 12th [1932]

My dear Hugh,

I've been roaming about in various places, but passing through London last week I looked in at the Press, and there lying on the table was the Scott —my Scott—from you.[1] Really my dear Hugh you are much too generous —this is said soberly as a fact, but also with warmth. What have I done to deserve such goodness? I dont conceive (this refers not only to your Scott, but to ever so many other things—your letter the other day for instance) I carried off my Scott and have been browsing partly in him, partly in you. As you know the complete works of Sir Walter, in a fine large copy, in which my father used to read him to us, are lined up on my

1. Walpole's *The Waverley Pageant*, dedicated to Virginia.

103

shelves. I don't know him accurately and minutely as you do, but only in a warm, scattered, amourous way. Now you have put an edge on my love, and if it weren't that I must read MSS—how they flock!—I should plunge —you urge me almost beyond endurance to plunge once more—yes, I say to myself, I shall read the Monastery again and then I shall go back to [*The Heart of*] Midlothian. I cant read the Bride [*of Lammermoor*], because I know it almost by heart: also the Antiquary (I think those two, as a whole, are my favourites). Well—to inspire a harassed hack to this wish to kick up her heels—what greater proof could there be of your powers of persuasion and illumination? My only complaint is that you pay too much attention to the arid gulls who cant open their beaks wide enough to swallow Sir Walter. One of the things I want to write about one day is the Shakespearean talk in Scott: the dialogues: surely that is the last appearance in England of the blank verse of Falstaff and so on! We have lost the art of the poetic speech—

But I didn't mean to begin on this, only to thank you. I wish my ink would flush red to show my gratitude, instead of which it runs as black as Styx. And I hope, without wishing to be intrusive, that life has been treating you better, as you, of all people deserve—that things maynt turn out as bad as they seemed [his diabetes].

We go back in October—and that reminds me, a swarm of wild Italian bees, that sting everybody within a mile, have made 30 lbs of wild Italian honey—some of which will be on the tea table, so come soon and eat it.

Your affate
Virginia

Texas

2635: To Lady Cecil   52 *Tavistock Square, W.C.*1

Tuesday [13 September 1932]

Dear Nelly,

I am so sorry that you aren't well. Otherwise we might have been sitting over the fire at this moment, which I should have enjoyed. Please suggest another day, or let me come and see you.

It is extremely bleak and cold at this moment in London—if thats any consolation to you for being in bed. I hope you are writing your memoirs, and that you'll send them to me to read.

I saw David and Rachel the other day—they talked and talked—ever so happy, like two birds on a bough.

Yr aff
V.W.

The Marquess of Salisbury (Cecil Papers)

2636: To Ethel Smyth

Monks House, Rodmell,
[Sussex]

Thursday [15 September 1932]

I have the Hell of a weekend—two people staying here, one at his own invitation in order to disburden his soul—a shallow vessel, but full of storms, so he says.[1] Therefore, whats the good of your putting yourself on a train? God knows. We go up to London on Tuesday—after that?—but we shall be back for good on the 1st: however, as you know, I'm incapable of making a plan. The general's daughter must buckle to and do that, if its to be done.

Oh I'm so flea-bitten!—no, its harvesters, the result of the most divinely lovely walk through stubble this afternoon. I found the loneliest of valleys with silver sheep clustering on the sides, hares leaping from my foot, and, great horses slowly dragging wagons like shaggy sea monsters—but corn was dripping instead of sea weed—Oh how happy, content calm sunned amorous peaceful I was—in a biblical frame of mind. My word, when one shuts off the villas, this land is I think the fairest far in all Arabia. The Mérimée book is 2 quarto vols: Letters to Csse de Montijo:[2] I get it from the London Library: he is a smooth sharp clear minded man, with an edge to him; and I accumulate, reading largely, little hints about that life time which I let into my general view rather happily. And I like thus gradually —letters begin in 1846 or so—approaching your Empress [Eugénie]. She's still unmarried. What she she [*sic*] think of her mother?

Yr
V.

Berg

2637: To Frances Marshall

Monks House, Rodmell,
[Sussex]

Sept 15th [1932]

My dear Fanny,
I dont believe I have any right to this familiar speech, but I hope you dont mind—
Here is the second letter from your friend[3]—I thought you might like to see it as you so much enjoyed the other. I answered him at considerable

1. Charles Siepmann, Talks Director of the B.B.C. The other guest was William Plomer.
2. La Comtesse de Montijo (1794-1879) was the wife of a Spanish grandee, and mother of the Empress Eugénie. She was a friend of Prosper Mérimée, and their correspondence was published in two volumes in 1930.
3. Mrs Partridge has now (1979) no recollection of this man, nor of "the lady with swollen eyes" mentioned later in the paragraph.

length and gave him a great deal of good advice—among other things I told him that every second young man and woman in Newcastle-on-Tyne was either a bugger or a sapphist—you see with what result. Heaven help me I've not yet answered the lady with swollen eyes whose son wont have his house treated as an hotel—nor can I face it. Why dont you set up a bureau in Bloomsbury for the treatment of such cases? I assure you the Hogarth Press has a waiting list a yard long.

It is an incredibly lovely evening and I wish you and Ralph were here to beat us soundly at bowls. Instead we have just visited an old woman [Mrs Grey, Rodmell] who made me feel a hump on her back and said it was full of water. But we should very much like to come to Ham Spray sometime whether you beat us or not.

I cant help wondering whether possibly Ralph could not do something with Carrington's letters—I mean if they give a daily account of Lytton and Ham Spray it would be such a boon to us all.[1] And if I could help in any way you know how gladly I would. But perhaps its impossible. But dont you think something might be done? Anyhow beg him to finish the Greville.[2] And please come and see us when you're in London—we go back in October.

Love to Ralph from us both
Yr V.W.

Frances Partridge

2638: To Lady Ottoline Morrell   *Monks House, Rodmell,*
                                     [Sussex]

Sept 16th [1932]

Dearest Ottoline,

I hear that you wanted Riley's[3] address—I wish I knew it, but when I looked for him in July he was gone—And I owe him several shillings: and want more books bound.

But what I wanted to ask is Have you got Fanny Burney's diary? I find there are two editions—the old one [1842] and Austin Dobsons [1904],

---

1. Carrington's letters were not published until 1970, when they were edited by David Garnett.
2. In 1928 Lytton Strachey had begun to edit a full edition of Charles Greville's memoirs (1814-60), and he was much helped by Ralph Partridge and Frances Marshall, who transcribed it from the original in the British Museum. After Lytton's death, the work was continued by the Partridges, helped by Roger Fulford, and it was published in 1938.
3. Robert Edward Riley, the bookbinder of 19 Woburn Buildings, Tavistock Square.

much the fullest—but I expect though not so elegant to look at. I've found copies of both in the old shop here, and want to send you one (if you'd like it) but dont know which you'd prefer. Let me have a line to say.

So David [Cecil] is to marry Rachel [MacCarthy]—well, thats a blessing fallen out of the sky. I feel Desmond is now secure, with Salisburys behind him. And the other day we had a sudden apparition—Tom and Vivienne [Eliot]. She became increasingly distraught as the afternoon wore on, changing her mind every second, and flying from one extreme to the other. Poor Tom—anyhow he escapes tomorrow.

Its incredibly beautiful here at the moment, in spite of the devils who plant red boxes on the top of the downs. I sit down in a hollow and look and look—one becomes an opium eater in ones eye—merely sitting and looking at cornfields, blue wagons and sheep is enough. But I like human beings too—this is a compliment—though you wouldn't guess it—to you.

yr
V.W.

Texas

2639: To Ethel Smyth

[*Monk's House, Rodmell, Sussex*]

Wednesday [28 September 1932]

Here's the synopsis.[1] I see it should include everything in the whole world—how fascinating to have a little theme like that that includes the whole world. But I cant, at the moment, pretend to deal with it or you or Pan or anything, owing to the curse that is on me of packing, tearing up, finding lost MSS (a woman has sent me her whole life and I think I've lost it) and trying vainly to write the 30 letters I ought to have written in the past 10 days. So excuse—Yes I enjoyed the other day. Which day? Why? Ah I cant say.

V.

Berg

1. Of Ethel's ballet, *Fête Galante.*

Letters 2640-2687 (October–December 1932)

On leaving Rodmell at the end of the summer holiday, Virginia went to the Labour Party Conference in Leicester, an event in which she had no interest whatever, except to support Leonard, the delegate from Lewes. Almost as soon as they returned to London, Virginia had renewed heart trouble, and again a month later. But it was more because of, than in spite of, her illness that she was able to make such rapid progress with her new book The Pargiters. *She had an excuse to avoid unwanted visitors and parties, and in nine weeks wrote 60,000 words, an unprecedented rate for her, although, as it turned out, she published none of them. At Christmas in the country she took a break from the book, and resumed* Flush *as a relaxation. The second* Common Reader *was published on 13 October. Ottoline Morrell was again an occasional visitor to Tavistock Square during Virginia's enforced 'rest', and so was Logan Pearsall Smith, to whom she wrote some sharp letters which marked the virtual end of their friendship.*

2640: To Ethel Smyth   52 T[avistock] S.[quare], W.C.1]

Thursday [6 October 1932]

Well Ethel dear, I enjoyed your letter immensely—about Ly Betty [Balfour] and the hidden picture. Yes—thats your line—writing letters to amuse me. I'm sorry Nelly [Boxall] gave you an exaggerated report—I've been so worried by furious authoresses ringing up. I told her to pitch my illness rather high—But I'm better—only if I walk or get over hot or merry —now Holtby's book,[1] just glanced at made me roar with laughter—that set my pulse off—if I laugh too much I get whatever it is—deranged action —systolic something—its nothing serious at all. I lie down between tea and dinner, and take cabs; and thank the Lord, must avoid hot rooms and parties. But I write every morning, and I'm enjoying my writing [*Flush*], word by word, hugely. How you'll hate it!

The dr's coming to have a thorough tap, listen, look tomorrow afternoon. I dont know what time: and she'll find nothing wrong. So I cant be sure when I can see you: but L. says you're ringing up, or he is.

Heres the 7/-

Well, Ly B[alfour]. may be right about my cousin Herbert.[2] All I can

1. *Virginia Woolf* by Winifred Holtby.
2. H. A. L. Fisher. See p. 50, note 1.

say is that he denounced me, as a writer, at a lunch party: next said Nessa had put herself beyond the pale; wrote me an angry letter about the Dreadnought[1] "vulgar playing tricks on the King's ships—for God's sake keep your name out of it" damn my name—his name he meant—he was so proud of it—and I say V. Woolf is every bit as good: but I admit he adored his poor stuffed beast sisters[2]—they all do that—thats one of the things I most dislike in them: so I was tempted to bury him, but didnt.

Yr
V.

Berg

2641: TO ETHEL SANDS   52 *Tavistock Square, W.C.*1

Friday [7 October? 1932]

Dearest Ethel

Why am I a bad woman?—and if I am, why ask me to dinner? However, I will come with pleasure, good or bad, on the 12th. 8.30.

I didn't send you Cecil on disarmament, or Strong on Yeats[3] because (between ourselves) they seem to me d——d dull.

Yrs
Virginia

Wendy Baron

2642: TO STEPHEN SPENDER   52 *Tavistock Square, W.C.*1

9th Oct [1932]

Dear Mr Spender,

We are only just back as we went up to the Labour Conference at Leicester, but I hope you may be still in London.

Would you dine with us on Tuesday (11th) at 8? Dont change of course —I expect we shall be alone.

Yours sincerely
Virginia Woolf

Texas

1. The famous hoax, organised in February 1910 by Horace Cole. Virginia, Adrian and four friends visited H.M.S. *Dreadnought* at Weymouth in the disguise of the Emperor of Abyssinia and his suite. The ship's flag-commander was William Fisher, Herbert's brother and Virginia's first cousin.
2. The word 'sisters' is uncertain in the manuscript.
3. Viscount Cecil, *A Letter to an M.P. on Disarmament* (1931) and L. A. G. Strong, *A Letter to W. B. Yeats* (1932), both published by the Hogarth Press.

Monday [10 October 1932]

In the horrid rush this evening I forgot my only message—to say how immensely I enjoyed The Waterfall.[1] I thought it read even better (but this is usual) in print than typing; and how suavely and subtly and yet with what a leap and a dash you skirted the subject and slipped over—No, I cant, with my brownpaper mind, give the effect. I rather regret the Empress [Eugénie]—if she were to be 30,000 words equalling the Waterfall. What a loss. *Also* my bill for the books.

                                                                V.

Berg

2644: To V. Sackville-West   52 *T.[avistock] S.[quare, W.C.1]*

Wednesday [12 October 1932]

I've just bought the 6,000th copy of Family History—6000 sold before publication—my God![2] And my fingers are red and whealed with doing up parcels for 3 dys incessantly. Miss Belsher ill—orders pouring in—we all working till 7.30—thought we were just finished—then a last batch of orders discovered hidden in a drawer another hours work—clerks panting —telephones ringing carriers arriving—parcels just finished in time to catch the vans—Oh Lord what it is to publish a best seller—when shall I be able to hold a pen again? But its been great fun—and a very good excuse for not going to Arlington Street [Hugh Walpole?] today.

Yes, I'll come to Sissinghurst. But when will you come here—all covered with gold as you are? You must sign my 6 thousandth copy—so sleepy I cant write and a red forefinger, and a cut, too, from tearing open cardboard with a knife—so goodnight—I'll write later

                                                                V.

What fun it all is to be sure—selling 6,000.

Berg

1. A story which Ethel included in *Female Pipings in Eden* about an incident in her childhood when she wore boy's clothes.
2. Vita's new novel, published by the Hogarth Press on 13 October, the same day as *The Common Reader: Second Series*.

Tuesday 18th [October 1932]

Yes dearest Creature—that was very nice of you. Pinka and I sat erect, blushing, as our praises poured forth from the trumpet.[1] I think you gave me too much—I hope the three you suppressed weren't listening too. But anyhow, you soothed my vanity—there are people who say I'm vain—did you know it?—like cream poured onto the sore nose of a feverish—I shall say cat—having just had tea with two cats. (Nessa brought up the Charleston cat; as we drank tea it split into two—one of those miracles that do happen in peoples studios) Anyhow you said what I most wanted—not that I'm an enchanting gossip, but that my standard is high. I loathe being called enchanting. Did you see Priestly on Harold you and me?[2] I thought if I were a cat I should not split so much into two as into one glutinous stream of unadulterated disgust. You would have been still nicer if you had told me you were in London, and come here. I prefer you, bodily, to you vocally.

Oh I was in such a rage of jealousy the other night, thinking you had been in love with Hilda that summer you went to the Alps together![3] Because you said you werent. Now were you? Did you do the act under the Dolomites? Why I should mind this, when its all over—that tour—I dont know. But I do. D'yu remember coming to confession, or rather justification, in my lodge? And you weren't guilty then were you? You swore you werent. Anyhow my Elizabeth [Bowen] comes to see me, alone, tomorrow. I rather think, as I told you, that her emotions sway in a certain way. (thats an elegiac) I'm reading her novel to find out. Whats so interesting is when one uncovers an emotion that the person themselves, I should say herself, doesn't suspect. And its a sort of duty dont you think—revealing peoples true selves to themselves? I dont like these sleeping princesses. Talking of the upper classes, I went to the David–Rachel wedding. To see Lady Salisbury with Desmond was entirely worth 5/6 white gloves. And Molly with Ld. Salisbury:

So when are you coming to see me!

V.

Berg

---

1. On 17 October Vita reviewed *The Common Reader* in her radio-talk about new books, scrapping three other books in order to make room for a full treatment of Virginia's.
2. This article has not been traced.
3. In July 1929 Vita and Hilda Matheson (at that time Talks Director of the B.B.C.) had gone on a walking tour of the Val d'Isère.

Typewritten
Oct 18th 1932

Dear Mr Cape,

Many thanks for your letter suggesting that you should reprint my introduction to a volume of Gissings Selections for a fee of five guineas.[1]

I shall be very glad to give you permission; and I would suggest that you should print from the version just issued in the second series of my Common Reader. I have altered it to a certain extent. I do not think that I could alter it any further. I have not read By the Ionian Sea [1901]; but I imagine that the introduction is sufficiently general to serve as it stands.

Yours sincerely
V. Woolf
(Mrs Woolf)

Jonathan Cape Ltd

2647: To Ethel Smyth   [52 *Tavistock Square, W.C.*1]

Friday [21 October 1932]

I wish I were at the Opera with you—cant be helped. It was my fault for going to the motor show before a dinner party. I've been drowsy all day—have read perhaps 2 pages. No I dont think your Benson—as we are —is up to much.[2] Perhaps its my head. I want to hear about Camargo[3] I want—many things. I think I shall either stay quiet or go off for a country drive tomorrow. I want—oh yes—do *criticise* The C. R: that I should like. I've met about a dozen people who burst into praise of the Waterfall— clever young men, old women and so on.

Please please please write more—also write the Empress. I could write a book about your memoirs. Surely, if you sat over the fire o'nights, after music, you could drop out some more, like pearls—pearls that have got into one's underclothes. Oh I'm so sleepy. Thank you for coming.

V.

Berg

1. Virginia's Introduction to George Gissing's *Selections Autobiographical and Imaginative* (1929) was first published as a review in the *Nation & Athenaeum* in February 1927.
2. E. F. Benson wrote two volumes of reminiscences—*As We Were* (1930) and *As We Are* (1932).
3. The ballet Company named after the great 18th-century ballerina. Ethel hoped that they would perform *Fête Galante*.

10.20 [21 October 1932]

I've just had a most confused and agitated telephone from Nessa, who says that Maynard tonight tells her that the Ballet must be postponed. He has written to you, but she thinks you wont get it, owing to some mistake of his secretarys till tomorrow late—and therefore doesn't suppose you'll want to come up to Ly Dianas [Cooper] tomorrow; and *so wont expect you.* (She was dining out and rang me up, and asked me to tell you—which I do in some confusion, as people are dining here—and talking.) All I mean is, I suppose if you're *not* coming to Diana, you wont come to the Gilbert and Sullivan.[1]

Forgive this confused scrawl. I could come on Monday if that suits you better

V.

Berg

2649: To H. A. L. Fisher   52 *Tavistock Square, W.C.1*

23rd Oct. 32

My dear Herbert,

It is very nice of you to ask us. Weekends are rather difficult, but might I come for the night of Tuesday November 22nd?[2] I'm afraid Leonard wont be able to get away for the night, but if you dont mind having me alone, I should like it very much.

Your affate
Virginia Woolf

Bodleian Library, Oxford

2650: To Ethel Smyth   [52 *Tavistock Square, W.C.1*]

Wednesday [26 October 1932]

No, I dont think tomorrow is worthwhile. I've been summoned to attend Herbert Stephen's funeral—God knows why, but I suppose I must go, dried up old haddock, that he was.[3] Thats a.m: Then we dine out, 7.30:

1. *Iolanthe*, at the Savoy Theatre.
2. To stay with him at New College, Oxford.
3. Sir Herbert Stephen, 2nd Bt. (1857-1932), the son of Leslie Stephen's brother James Fitzjames Stephen, 1st Bt. He was a lawyer and author of two legal text books.

then go to Adrians halfcrown Club—damn it all. Without undue flattery, I'd rather talk to the uncastrated cat. But I should be dry as Herbert by tea time. But come *Thursday* next week—I'm longing to go to the Gilbert and Sullivan too. And theres my mother in laws annual birthday. But—remark how emphatically every sentence begins—I will write to you, and listen in to you God willing. I met Eth W^n [Williamson] last night—I thought her 'looking' extremely well—but it was so hot we were all lobster colour. Talking of which, the specialist after 3 months cogitation pronounces my faint due to 'heat exhaustion' and wants to see me at 71 Harley Street. Not if I know it

So goodnight
V.

Berg

2651: TO HUGH WALPOLE   52 *Tavistock Square, W.C.*1

Oct 26. 32

My dear Hugh,

I have signed the petition with pleasure,[1] leaving a discreet place for some body to sign in front of me. I've no alterations to suggest, and am giving it to Leonard, to get his signature, Of course there are any number of people who might be got to sign, but I suspect it is best to depend on a few. I hope the poor woman gets something out of it—I'm told amazing stories of the state A. B. left his various variety of dependents in. Poor man! and last time I met him, just before his death, he seemed the image of prosperity stability and longevity. I am longing to hear, naturally, about the vicar and the wife and the W.C. and trust you to come and tell me next time you're in London.

No, I've not read Miss Holtby: Prof Delattre (in French) almost did for me; I suppose Winifred has merely added another kind of tombstone. She is the daughter of a Yorkshire farmer and learnt to read, I'm told, while minding the pigs—hence her passion for me.[2] I'm so glad you are slashing

1. The petition was not published, but was probably an appeal to the Home Secretary on behalf of Arnold Bennett's wife Marguerite. Bennett left £36,000, of which most went to Marguerite, but she disputed the part of his Will which bequeathed his manuscripts to his mistress Dorothy Cheston.
2. Winifred Holtby (1898-1935), the novelist, was born in Yorkshire, and graduated from Somerville College, Oxford. She came to London in 1921 and lived with Vera Brittain. Her last novel *South Riding*, 1935, was generally regarded as her best. She met Virginia only once while she was writing her short book about her.

about at your book[1]—how I love tearing things up—it gives one such a sense of power. But, if I ever do read a novel again—d'you know I read 600 mss a year now—I shall read Herries.[2]

Yr aff V.W.

Texas

2652: To LOGAN PEARSALL SMITH

52 *Tavistock Square, W.C.*1

Oct. 31st [1932]

Dear Logan,[3]

I am sorry not to have written before, but I have been very busy—our clerks always fall ill at the critical moment—and indeed all I have to say is that for my part I was not conscious that we are 'enemies' as you suggest. My memory is probably as bad as yours, and I have no recollection of not answering your suggestion that you should come and see me. I am very sorry if I was so forgetful—it was not intentional. Nor do I remember giving you a 'frosty answer'—I mean a purposely frosty answer. I think it possible, though, as we live in a world of gossip, that some rumour had reached me that you were not favourably disposed to Bloomsbury—why should you be? —and I felt that there would be a certain discomfort in meeting, at least on my side. This is the only explanation that occurs to me of our not meeting oftener, and of course I regret it as much as you do.

Yours very sincerely
Virginia Woolf

Frederick B. Adams Jr.

2653: To ETHEL SMYTH

52 *T.[avistock S.[quare, W.C.*1]

Tuesday [1 November 1932]

But you told me you could *not* manage Thursday PM. and so I said I would go to a party [Mary Hutchinson's], 5, at Sadlers Wells to which I'm entreated to bring you. But the devil is that having had a long day

---

1. Hugh Walpole had just scrapped 50,000 words of his current novel *Vanessa*, but within ten days had rewritten them.
2. *Rogue Herries* (1930), Walpole's most ambitious novel.
3. Pearsall Smith, author of *Trivia*, etc., had known Virginia since 1910, but in 1925 they had a dispute about the morality of Bloomsbury writers contributing to glossy magazines like *Vogue*, and had seldom met since then. He had written to ask her whether the Hogarth Press intended to reprint his pamphlets *Stories from the Old Testament* (1920) and *The Prospects of Literature* (1927).

yesterday I got a mild faintishness last night—L. made me see the dr. today, who says its only that I've tired my heart—nothing wrong with it. This usual intermittent pulse in a different form—and recommends quiet. So I'm altogether vague about my doings on Thursday, tho' I'm practically all right today. Perhaps if you rang up Thursday? And wd you come to Sadlers Wells? I promised to bring you if I'm able.

V.

Berg

2654: To Ethel Smyth   [52 *Tavistock Square, W.C.1*]
Wednesday [2 November 1932]

I dont think there's much chance that I shall be able to go to Sadlers Wells tomorrow. I'm rather done up today. I think I shall stay absolutely quiet tomorrow—if possible I want to go to Schnabel;[1] but I dont expect I shall be able to see you, or anyone, if thats so, in the afternoon. This is only to save you bother, or the possible change of plan. There's nothing really the matter, only these attacks, even slight ones, leave one very drowsy and inert, by the fire. I am to drink digitalis—as I used to do years ago. Well I hope your concert is coming off well this afternoon.

V.

A scrawl to catch country post

Berg

2655: To William Rothenstein
                                        52 *Tavistock Square, W.C.1*
Nov 2nd 1932

Dear Sir William,[2]
    It is very good of you to write to me about my book [*Common Reader*]. I always feel apologetic about publishing my own criticism, because I dont know that there is much excuse for adding to books about other books, unless one has something like knowledge to impart. And that I haven't. But I do claim to be a lover of reading, and it is a great reward and encouragement to me if I can send a little shock across to you who care so much

1. Artur Schnabel (1882-1951), the Austrian pianist, was giving a series of Beethoven recitals at the Queen's Hall.
2. Rothenstein (1872-1945), the painter and principal of the Royal College of Art, had known Virginia's parents, and done drawings of each of them.

for the other art. Why there aren't more critics, or better, of painting, I cant make out. It must be easier, with a picture in front of you—but there too I am very ignorant.

Thank you so much for writing.

Yours sincerely
Virginia Woolf

Houghton Library, Harvard University

2656: To Lady Ottoline Morrell

*52 Tavistock Square, W.C.*1

Thursday [3 November 1932]

Dearest Ottoline,

I wonder if you could possibly come here tomorrow at 5.30 instead of my coming to you?

I've had rather a rush lately what with one thing and another, with the result that I have upset what is called the rhythm of my heart—a thing I've always had more or less, and of no importance; but it tends to make me get faint; and I dont want to get faint in your drawing room. I shall be all right in a week or two, if I'm quiet, the dr says, so if its the least bother to you to come here, let me know, and I'll come later. But it would be very nice to see you, and if you could bring me your D.H.L. memoir, that would interest me immensely. I've finished his letters:[1] no, I'm not enthusiastic: I dont think its the real thing, though of course he was so hounded by those brutes the army and public that one's entire sympathy is with him. But what a thin, exaggerated affair it is to be sure! and all on the same string.

V.W.

If I dont hear I shall expect you at 5.30.

Texas

2657: To Kingsley Martin

*52 Tavistock Square, W.C.*1

Typewritten
[4th November 1932]

Dear Mr Kingsley Martin,

I am so sorry to return this book again. I've no doubt it is charming, and it was very nice of you to think of sending it me. But I have developed such a repugnance to the thought of writing a review, that I dont think I

1. The *Letters of D. H. Lawrence*, edited with an Introduction by Aldous Huxley, 1932.

shall ever write one again. If I ever feel inclined, of course I will let you know, in case you have a book you would send me. But as things are, I feel it is wasting your time to let you send me books—kind though it is of you. Also of course the 1500 or 2,000 word limit, necessary as it is in the New Statesman, is a very great drawback—if one has anything to say about a book, one wants, I find, more like three or four thousand words to say it in.

I am sending back the book today therefore.

Yours sincerely
Virginia Woolf

George Spater

2658: TO LOGAN PEARSALL SMITH   52 *Tavistock Sq.* [*W.C.1*]

Typewritten
[6 November 1932]

Dear Logan,

Do not be alarmed, to quote your own words, by the thought that I am proferring an olive branch. And excuse the typewriter, but my hand is getting too illegible for prolonged use. Confined to my sofa at the moment —how apposite your reference to a heart specialist was!—I have been pondering your letter, certain aspects of which interested me greatly; so that I cant resist writing, though I fear longwindedly, but then I'm rather knocked up.

I agree with you that one can admire a set or group and at the same time indulge a malicious desire to laugh at it.[1] Am I not just as guilty as you are? Only of course I laugh at Chelsea whereas you laugh at Bloomsbury. And I feel great admiration and respect for Chelsea as you do for Bloomsbury—indeed I can't see any reason for you to prefer Bloomsbury, as you intimate that you do—but then, alas, so much of what you say is ironical. And I too have always thought and I have often said (to quote you again) to the great annoyance of people like Lady Desborough and Mrs [Alice] Keppell (you know what great ladies are) sometimes sneer at Chelsea—that in my opinion it is full of delightful people and brilliant gatherings. How could

1. Pearsall Smith had written to her on 2 November (*copy in the Library of Congress*): "I don't think I have ever been really hostile to Bloomsbury. I have always thought and sometimes said (to the intense annoyance of my hearers) that I regarded Bloomsbury as the only group of free spirits in the English-speaking race. I may have mocked at Bloomsbury, because mockery is my favourite pastime, and also perhaps . . . because I was not admitted to its conclaves. That I have told funny stories about it is possible, nor is it utterly unconceivable that I may have invented one or two."

it not be? I need only mention, besides yourself, Desmond, Maurice Baring, Ethel Sands, Bob and Hilda Trevelyan, Mr Connolly,[1] Mrs Hammersley,[2] and then theres Sibyl Colefax round the corner. How can you, even out of politeness, put us in Bloomsbury above you? I'm sure you dont. Its only your fun. But much though I admire Chelsea, I freely admit that I have mocked at you all because mockery is 'my favourite pastime,' just as it is yours. And I may have made up a story or two about you into the bargain.

Up to this point then there is not much difference between us. Now comes the interesting distinction. I have known Chelsea for many years. For many years they have asked me to tea and dinner and I have asked them to tea and dinner. And then I discovered that they were laughing at me and my friends behind my back; and they discovered that I was laughing at them and their friends behind their backs. So I gave up asking them; and I gave up accepting their invitations. This is not due to having a good heart—it is simply that such intercourse seemed to me dull, barren, fruitless, uninteresting.

Now what I find so interesting is that you, who are, as far as I can make out, in the same case as I am, will yet take the trouble to write to me and say "perhaps we are enemies? . . . I seem to recollect that I received but a frosty answer the last time I suggested coming to see you. Or was it perhaps no answer at all?"—you will write like this implying—but again, in dealing with so ironical a mind how careful one must be not to exaggerate—still such words do seem to me to imply that you would actually like to come and see me. Yes, I turn to your first letter, and there you say in so many words 'I often regret that I never see you'. Now is this true, or is it ironical? And how can you like seeing me, if you laugh at me and my friends behind my back?

Those are some of the questions that I ponder as I lie here. And, thus pondering, it seems to me possible that you are right—at least to this extent. That is, why should not Chelsea and Bloomsbury meet and laugh at each other to their faces and quite genuinely enjoy themselves? It seems to me worth trying. Then again, you say 'critics resent criticism, and mockers being mocked' But do they, if it's done face to face? Surely both sides might benefit greatly if it were done in that way.

I am ashamed to see that I have written all this without making, or quoting, a single aphorism. And how delightful your little galaxy of them from—is it Fulke Greville?—is at the end of your letter![3] I have racked my brains to think of one to end with; but am relieved to have it on your

1. Cyril Connolly, the author, critic, future Editor of *Horizon*, was then aged 29.
2. Violet Hammersley, the patron of Wilson Steer, the painter, and a friend of Duncan Grant.
3. One of them (supposed to have been written by Mrs Greville) was, "Those who listen to themselves, are not listened to by others".

authority that 'no woman (except George Eliot) was ever mistress of this delicate art'. So be it, I will leave aphorisms to your sex. With regard to the pin-prick—"with this little pin-prick to end my letter"—to quote you again—my trouble is that either through age or habit I have become almost impervious to pin-pricks. If you weren't (this is only going to be a very small sheet) you will have to prick a good deal harder. And I promise, if you will come and see me, that I'll rummage in my dressing table for a few pins of my own. I'm sure you dont intend to claim pin-pricking as an exclusively masculine art.

There, to quote you once more, we must leave it, Come and laugh at me and my work and my friends to my face, and I'll do the same by you. No doubt we shall both profit. I am not allowed at present to do much entertaining, but in two or three weeks I shall be delighted to see you on the terms stated, I fear rather diffusely, above.

Yours very sincerely
Virginia Woolf

[*handwritten*]

In reading this over, I see that the molehill has become a mountain—but then the molehill was raised by you.

Frederick B. Adams Jr.

2659: To H. A. L. Fisher   52 *Tavistock Square, W.C.*1

7th Nov. 32

My dear Herbert,

I am so sorry but I am afraid I must put off coming to you [at Oxford] on the 22nd. We've been having rather an exhausting autumn, with the result that I have somehow strained my heart. It is nothing of the least importance and will soon be cured with quiet, but the doctor refuses to let me do anything at all tiring during the next few weeks, and has knocked off all staying away. I had very much looked forward to seeing you again. I hope if you are in London, and not too busy, you will suggest a visit here. Please make my apologies to Lettice [his wife]. It was so nice of you both to ask me.

Your affate
Virginia Woolf

Bodleian Library, Oxford

[8? November 1932]

Well, my faithless sheep dog,—yes, you'll be turned into a very old collie if you dont look out, blind of one eye, and afflicted with mange on the rump—why dont you come and see me? Poor Virginia can't come to you. She—that is, I suppose, I—had another, very slight though, fainting; and Elly Rendel brought her misanthropic stethoscope, and says the systolic action of my heart—what used to be called my intermittent pulse—is too wild; and thats why I faint; and I must be quieter, and drink digitalis, and there's nothing whatever wrong with my heart! And I mustn't go into hot rooms, like Sibyls. So I doubt if I can come to Sst. [Sissinghurst] at the moment—not that its a very hot room—the bedroom might be though— For which reason I ask again (I'm in such a rush) when could you come and see me? I'm divinely happy, because I wrote all the morning—Oh how you'll hate my new novel, and how it amuses me!—and then I go for a walk, or drive, and then I come back to tea, carrying one muffin which I eat, with honey, and then I lie on the sofa, and—who d'you think came and talked to me t'other night? Three guesses. All wrong. It was Violet Trefusis—your Violet.[1] Lord what fun! I quite see now why you were so enamoured— then: she's a little too full, now, overblown rather; but what seduction! What a voice—lisping, faltering, what warmth, suppleness, and in her way —its not mine—I'm a good deal more refined—but thats not altogether an advantage—how lovely, like a squirrel among buck hares—a red squirrel among brown nuts. We glanced and winked through the leaves; and called each other punctiliously Mrs Trefusis and Mrs Woolf—and she asked me to give her the Common R. which I did, and said smiling, By the way, are you an Honourable, too?" No, no, she smiled, taking my point, you, to wit. And she's written to ask me to go and stay with her in France, and says how much she enjoyed meeting me: and Leonard: and we positively must come for a whole week soon. Also Mrs Keppel loves me, and is giving a dinner partly [sic] solely for me in January. How I enjoyed myself! To be loved by Mrs Keppel, who loved, it is said—quite a different pair of shoes [Edward VII].

Well, what I was going to say, but have no time, is that I dont altogether agree with you (on the wireless) about Lawrence. No, I think you exaggerate. Genius, I admit: but not first rate genius. No. And such a cad to Ottoline. My word, what a cheap little bounder he was, taking her money, books,

---

1. Vita and Violet Trefusis (daughter of George and Alice Keppel) had eloped to France together in 1920, to be pursued and reclaimed by their husbands. She was now aged 38, and was already a leading figure in Parisian and Florentine society. Her husband, Denys, had died in 1929.

food, lodging and then writing that book.[1] And the other night they broadcast a poem, writer unknown; and L and I listened in; and we said who's that? some modern, quite 2nd rate, but trying to be first rate—pretentious —not genuine. Behold, Lawrence again, so they say. I admit the genius, in Sons and Lovers: but thats the sum and pinnacle of it all (I've not read anymore) the rest is all a dilution, a flood, a mix up of inspiration, and prophecy—which I loathe—Oh yes, a genius, but not first rate. So there.

And come and see me

V.

Berg

2661: To Ethel Smyth   52 *Tavistock Sq.* [*W.C.1*] *Bulletin*

Tuesday [8 November 1932]

It was a bore the dr. coming this afternoon. L. didnt want me to see anyone, as we're trying to go to the first part at any rate of Schnabel tonight. I shall leave if its too hot. The dr. quite pleased—says my blood pressure is normal, better than last time; and tho' my pulse is still too fast—d'you like these details?—there's nothing wrong with the heart—only strain: and probably that is mere nerve exhaustion; and is instead of a headache. The present theory, so brilliant are drs, is that if I have my usual headache, thats nerve exhaustion; so my little temperature; so my racing pulse—all nerve exhaustion. And what is nerve exhaustion? I ask. Ah, that we cannot say.

Anyhow I needn't see a dr. for a fortnight; am to lie down; between tea and dinner, but can write as much as I like and read all day and talk a certain amount.

Heavens what an egotistic medical scrawl! Now I'm going to dine and drive to the Q. Hall.

Well then one day next week? between tea and dinner?

V.

I enjoyed Miss S's jokes immensely [*unexplained*]. L. threw away the last L. Mercury, before I'd read you.[2] Cd. you lend me a copy? Have you begun the Empress?[3]

Berg

1. *Women in Love*, 1921, in which he cruelly portrayed Ottoline in the character of Hermione Roddice.
2. Ethel's article in the *London Mercury* for November was entitled *Delirious Tempi in Music*, protesting that conductors played Gilbert and Sullivan music too fast.
3. Ethel's essay on the Empress Eugénie for *Female Pipings in Eden*.

9th Nov. [1932]

My dear Hugh,

Yes do come, *Tuesday* 4.30. That will be very nice—you wont mind if I lie on a sofa between tea and dinner? I've been fainting in hot rooms, and the dr. says I've been what they call—I cant remember—upsetting the systolic something? intermittent pulse?—something to do with the hearts action; but nothing serious, only requires rest.

What terrific people you and Vita are—bursting out on the stage! I think I could hardly face the excitement of seeing bodies to ones ideas— What is your play? One of your books or an original venture?[1] There again I long to become a playwright. But we will discuss this on Tuesday—also the clergyman's wifes W.C, also James Agate, also—we've got millions of things to discuss.

                                                                    V.W.

Texas

Thursday [10 November 1932]

Yes, my kind clever colly—come to lunch on Tuesday next *here* at 1. I'm told not to lunch or dine in hot restaurants—anyhow, here is much nicer, and you can stay on a bit later and talk. Then I'll tell you all about Violet [Trefusis]. It was her novel[2] that brought her—I think she's been rather silly about it—but we'll tell you, if you'll keep it secret.

Publishers mustn't gossip. Yes, I see now, in a flash, a chapter in your past I never saw. Frightfully queer. She wasn't what I expected—but no time to say more now.

I've seen Elly [Rendel] again and had all kinds of tappings and listenings, and she says there's nothing wrong with my heart, but this usual old inter-mittent pulse that I've had since I was a baby has gone a step too far— hence my faintings in the heat, at the Ivy etc: and that I must lie down and rest and not get excited and not walk too far and not talk too much and not go out to parties: but I can write all the morning; and talk all the evening; and read all night. So I'm very happy. And my draught of digitalis is rapidly slowing up my pulse;—its already better

---

1. Walpole's own dramatisation of his novel *The Cathedral*, which opened in the Embassy Theatre, Swiss Cottage, on 21 November.
2. *Tandem*, 1933. Violet had previously written two other novels in French.

So there—is that the kind of detail you like? Oh how nice to see you again! You're the only person I ever ask to come here—if person you can be called

V.

Berg

2664: To Margaret Llewelyn Davies
52 *Tavistock Square*, [*W.C.*1]

Typewritten
10th Nov. [1932]

Dearest Margaret,

Yes it was an age since we heard from you; and we missed every time we were in London together. Do let us meet when your back. You must ring and settle a good time. What a miserable thing about Lilians [Harris] eyes—I cant conceive any affliction I could less well endure; and sure she never says a word or does a thing but whats sensible, wise, discreet, virtuous, and everything it ought to be. But then I've long nourished a secret passion for Lilian, and tried, vainly, I admit, to imitate her qualities. Thats what comes of being Berties cousin—I suppose—a natural fund of unending goodness, which is not so much credit to her, because if ones Bertie's cousin it comes by nature. Such is my theory at least. You see, it leaves me free to be a monster because I'm not Berties cousin. (I rather think Lilian is not either—I mean the man who's connected with Mary, the man who lives at Las Palmas [*unidentified*].

We came back from the Labour Conference at Leicester—did we tell you we'd been there?—theres a lot to say about it—I sat in the gallery—Leonard down on the floor among the delegates—he was sent by Lewes—but this must keep.

Then of course our head clerk [Miss Belsher] fell ill on the day of publication; we all had to work like mad doing up 6000 copies of Vitas new book, Family History, to get them out in time; at the last moment Miss Cashin [clerk] casually opened a drawer, and found a whole bundle of orders that had been stuffed away and forgotten. So we had to set to again —with the last van waiting in the street. It rather reminded me of some of your scampers with politics—the things I never understood—deputations to the Prime Minister and so on.

After this I was rather done up—I had been rather faint in the heat wave, and the dr. tells me I have slightly upset my usual old heart. So that I must lie down, but only after tea. Its nothing to speak of. Janet Case[1] is

---

1. She taught Virginia Greek in her youth, and was now living in the New Forest, writing nature notes for the *Manchester Guardian*.

coming here today—indeed I must go and toast her muffin now. L. is in the Press or he would send all kinds of messages to you both. But let us know when youd like to see us. [Winifred] Holtby is a farmer's daughter and I'm told her book is bad—, vain though I am, I cannot read about myself, and my parents and my education—all lies too.

So goodbye. Love to Lilian.

V.

[*handwritten*]

I have, of course, forgotten the main thing I wanted to say. Do you remember showing me a letter from W. Bagehot to your aunt, about women being servants, or something like that?[1] I am re-writing a speech I made to some young professional women, and want to quote it. May I? Have you got it? I'll ask you when we meet.

Sussex

2665: To Ethel Smyth   52 *Tavistock Square, W.C.*1

[13 November 1932]

The Book [*The Common Reader*] should have been posted on Friday, or Saturday. I left it in the Press on Friday and told them to send it Oh Ethel! Ethel! Where is your taste, your judgment—I ask in all solemnity (I'm rocking with laughter)—"The Austens are of your very best"—do you really think so?[2] Well, the article may be a masterpiece—I thought it feeble in the extreme, and said to L. 'heres someone trying my tricks in the Times—" No, of course I didn't write it. Surely—"But the little things must hold out their little things to one another"—my dearest Ethel, do you really think I write like that? and is that what you think my 'very best" —'the frame provided by a great artist'—"but I could quote half the article" —I thought it the feeblest little poke that ever was. And its my best! I've just got the Austen letters—I was so much irritated by that article that I

1. For Walter Bagehot's letter to Emily Davies see *The Pargiters*, ed. Mitchell A. Leaska, 1978, p. 34 *n*. Virginia used this quotation in *Three Guineas*, chapter I, note 23. Emily Davies (1830-1921) founded Girton College, Cambridge, in 1873.
2. A review in the *Times Literary Supplement* on 10 November of *Jane Austen's Letters* (ed. R. W. Chapman). The author of the review was E. M. Forster (See Letter 2672).

thought I must see if there wasn't a good deal more in them than he or she made out.

My very best! ! ! ! ! ! ! !

Really—I quite understand—I should be just as much out about music. And I'm better and we're back, but I'm going to be very quiet

Berg

2666: TO CLIVE BELL   52 *Tavistock Square, W.C.*1

Tuesday [15 November 1932]

Dearest Clive,

I did meet Rebecca a year or two ago at Todds' board,[1] but I'd very much like to meet her again at yours. Only might it be tea, not lunch? I find lunch now impossibly comatose; whereas by tea time, I brisk up. Still this may be the very opposite case with you. So let me know if tea will suit or not. Lottie [Hope, maid] could, I suppose, say yes or no. 22nd Nov: Tuesday. 4.30. or 5.

By the way, Rebecca is said to be doing a cure abroad. But as she is making excuses for being 9 months and ten days late with a manuscript[2] this may well be what my old nurse called a tarradiddle. What d'you think that word comes from? And, by the way, Elly says if I get faint again I must give up all parties, even tea: but I dont for a moment think I shall get faint again.

                                                                          Yr Virginia

Quentin Bell

2667: TO ETHEL SMYTH   52 *T*[*avistock*] *S.*[*quare, W.C.*1]

Sunday 20th November [1932]

I know I have been a wretch, as usual, not to write before, if only to indulge you in your mad Jane Austen mood, which amuses me immensely. Why on earth should you mind coming a howler once in a way about that article? As I said, I should be far more howling if I wrote to you about your music. Its only your d——d rashness thats at fault—and as you know

1. In May 1928 Virginia met Rebecca West, the novelist and journalist, at a party given by Dorothy Todd, the former editor of *Vogue*. But it was not their first meeting.
2. Rebecca West, *A Letter to a Grandfather*, Hogarth Press, 1933.

I rather admire that quality in you—if you'd been a Professor's daughter, you would have said, casually, "By the way did you write an article in the TLS? I didn't think it one of your best, but . . ." and so have been safe either way. As you'r a general's daughter you jumped straight in; and really came an awful cropper; which I prefer; Because one knows where one is. As a matter of fact two people, Hugh Walpole and Vita, both said, off their own bats, "Did you read an article imitating you in the T.L.S?" And they both went on to say how for 3 lines they had thought it might be me, and then thought well, she must have been very ill to write like that, and then decided that I hadn't written it. But then they both spend such wits as they have in writing. What I thought about the article—and I read it again, after your letter—was that the man or woman was so much engaged in imitating, first me, then someone else—for it went on differently—that he or she had never got away from the looking glass at all, and therefore had quite forgotten to say anything about Jane Austen. This being so, I bought Jane Austen, and find as I suspected that the man or woman is entirely flatly and absolutely wrong, and that the Austen letters are so important and interesting that I fear I shall have to write about them one of these days myself. And, again Ethel dear, you're entirely wrong—whatever "Bloomsbury" may think of JA., she is not by any means one of my favourites. I'd give all she ever wrote for half what the Brontes wrote—if my reason did not compel me to see that she is a magnificent artist. What I shall proceed to find out, from her letters, when I've time, is why she failed to be much better than she was. Something to do with sex, I expect; the letters are full of hints already that she suppressed half of her in her novels—Now why? But I've only read 30 pages: I've no time—ever so many MSS to read.

I had to spend 2 days last week in bed with this jumping heart—not bad though: only the dr. happened to come, and said that if I didn't stay quiet I should have to stop my mornings work, which I really cannot endure: so I put off everything; didnt even go round to Nessa, and now am much better again and writing furiously. That is why I can't write letters. I've written nearly 2,000 words (oh how you'll hate them!—since the T.L.S. is my very best—ah hah—you shant hear the last of that!—how you'll hate them!) But the effect of writing 2,000 words is that my hand staggers like a drunk crow in the evening; and I still have 20 letters I ought to write —They shall go to the typewriter though—I've entirely lost count of your movements. I cant keep my own plans in my head, let alone other peoples —so I must send this—and the L. Mercury article—ah hah![1] I wont tell you what I thought of it—to Coign, in the pious hope that you may resurrect there one of these days. Or here. But God knows when. I am honestly and soberly trying to be as quiet and dull and recumbent as I can. The dr. says I ought to have been much worse than I was, the other day, seeing that

1. See p. 122, note 2.

I sat up till one thirty howling with laughter and rage at L's polish Count[1] —the man who wrote the water closet rhymes, and turns out to be an appalling bore, dressed in flowing purple, with hair down his shoulders, conviction that he is King of Poland; and the accent and manners of a Cockney stable boy.

V.

Berg

2668 To Dora Sanger   52 *Tavistock Square, W.C.*1

Typewritten
Nov. 20th [1932]

Dear Dora,[2]
(I must apologise for typing, but my hand is so illegible that I write out of kindness to you in type).

It was very nice to hear from you again. I wish we could have arranged a meeting. But at present I am doing my best to obey my doctor and see hardly anyone and only for a short time. So I hope you will suggest another visit later when I shall be all right and we need not hurry. As a matter of fact I am already much better—it is an old bother, that I have had before after influenza, and I am taking care more by way of precaution than anything—it can be such a bore, and means lying down for weeks. Many thanks for telling me about Mrs Gray. I think Goldie[3] told me about her last year— I will certainly remember and suggest it to my doctor if I dont get right as soon as I should. But I found last time it was only a question of rest—they say theres nothing wrong.

I hope this means that you are much better than you were. I suppose you arent much in London now; and I dont know what Daphne is doing. It seems an age since we saw either of you. Please give her my love, and Leonards—we often think of you. And it would be nice to see you in the flesh some day also.

Yours affectionate
Virginia Woolf

Daphne Sanger

1. Count Potocki de Montalk. See p. 20, note 2.
2. The widow of C. P. Sanger, the barrister and editor of the standard work on Wills. He had died in 1930. Daphne was their daughter.
3. Goldsworthy Lowes Dickinson, the historian and philosopher, who had died in August.

Thursday [24 November 1932]

Dearest Duncan,

I must seize my pen, though I am reeling with excitement, to tell you that we have just unrolled your carpet and it is perfectly magnificent. (I seldom underline a word, but on this occasion I must). It seems to me a triumphant and superb work of art, and produces in me the sensation of being a tropical fish afloat in warm waves over submerged forests of emerald and ruby. You may well ask what sort of forest that is—I reply it is the sort of fish I am. As you know, it is the dream of my life to be a tropical fish swimming in a submerged forest; and now this is permanently gratified —with what effects upon my morals, my art, my religion, my politics, my whole attitude to reality, God only knows. For the moment I feel kindly disposed even towards Eddy [Sackville West] himself (whose last letter is a masterpiece—I must show it you) and further, I feel perfectly sure that I am not paying you a penny or even a halfpenny for all this subdued yet gorgeous riot (the forest that is)—you have made me a tropical fish gratis and for nothing—so that no expression of mine can really convey adequately my gratitude, which must remain as a lump of entire emerald (I said it would get into my style—thank God, my article on Sir Leslie is finished) until death us parts. I've just had a paean of praise of the room from Ott: Everyone seemed enthusiastic. I hope some cash will result.

Now I am going to swim in my forest.

V.W.

Duncan Grant Estate

[25? November 1932]

Dearest Ottoline,

Its very good of you to send round another lot of Lytton's letters. I get a queer feeling I'm hearing him talk in the next room—the talk I always want to go on with. I wonder how many talks I've had with him—sometimes I think I never talked so much to anyone, except Leonard. I daresay that was why one saw less of him lately—we had said so much. And then, of course, life is so exacting—one cant fit it all in. The last time we were to go to Ham Spray I was tired and put it off. I expect this must happen, when one has known one's friends for 20 years; and it doesnt mean one drifts or parts; only that the main things have been said—And yet, now I have a million things to tell him, and never shall. I rather think your silence

was of this kind too; and then your link was so burning hot at one moment[1]
—mine never was so intricate and triangular—; and when Henry went fizz,[2]
Lytton must have been affected. And then Carrington—after Lytton died
James [Strachey] told me, what I guessed, that she had been jealous of
Lytton's old friends; and that was one of her sorrows, when he was dead,
that she had kept us from him. Indeed she said so to me herself: but as she
was so precarious herself in her hold on him, and depended so completely,
one cant blame her. And then there was Roger Senhouse,[3] who bored me
so much that I could never cultivate him, as Lytton wanted. All this was
much the same with you I expect: that is how one loses hold on people.
My only regret is that Lytton himself was beginning to feel again the young
men and Carrington were not after all his old friends; and so we were about
to meet again, much more often—and then he died.

No, I wasn't in the least tired by your visit—not at all: rather the other
way. My heart is a very good judge of character and I only faint when Polish
Counts [Potocki] with long hair come here. That reminds me—you must
come to a quite ghastly party that Nessa and I are giving on Wednesday.
Its a purely commercial (dont whisper it) affair, to induce the rich to buy
furniture, and so employ a swarm of poor scarecrows who are languishing
in Fitzroy Street.[4] You are NOT to buy, but you (and Philip [Morrell]) are
to come: and what you're to do is to sacrifice yourself once more to the
cause of these delightful people who always treat you so well and swim
through the rooms trailing glory in your wake and entertain Margot
[Asquith], Lord Sud[e]ley, Lord anybody—as you know how. I look
forward with horror and despair, but perhaps we may have a crack in a
corner. Anyhow come again here soon. The mercy of having my heart
wrong is that it entirely cures me of headache so thus I can write 3 hours
daily instead of 1½. Mrs Carswell wants me to puff the new edition of her
D.H.L.[5] Not if I know it!

yr VW

Texas

1. Lytton's friendship with Ottoline began before the First War. "Each seemed to
   fulfil a real need in the other; one hungering after secret confidences, the other
   so eager to impart them" (Holroyd, *Lytton Strachey*, II, p. 12). At one moment
   there were rumours that they were romantically attached.
2. Henry Lamb (1883-1960), the painter, with whom both Ottoline and Lytton
   had been in love.
3. Senhouse was the last of the young men whom Lytton loved. He was a co-
   founder of Secker & Warburg, the publishers, and the translator of Colette.
4. The party (on 30 November) was given by Virginia and Vanessa at the Lefevre
   Gallery to open a Music Room which Duncan and Vanessa had designed,
   down to the carpets, chairs and mirrors. The room, and the party, are described
   by Richard Shone, *Bloomsbury Portraits*, 1976, pp. 237-42.
5. *The Savage Pilgrimage: A Narrative of D. H. Lawrence* by Catherine Carswell,
   2nd edition, 1932.

Typewritten
27th Nov. 1932

Dear Logan,

I am a wretch not to have thanked you before for your letter and the tract.[1] I have read it with great amusement, and only wish it were longer. Leonard has now read it too—we have over 600 MSS to read yearly now, which accounts for our extreme slowness; and it strikes him that you perhaps might add an introduction? and let us print it. But no doubt you wont want to do this. But perhaps if you will come and see us one day—on the terms agreed on—we might discuss it. It is certainly edifying in the extreme; and the portrait is delightful.

Yes I agree about Chelsea. I dont like the mix up of letters and coronets. But I'm afraid there are a good many coronets in Bloomsbury now—the peerage seems to have taken us up—but as long as we dont become peers ourselves, I find the peerage intoxicatingly beautiful—the old English peerage I mean—not the rich peerage, nor—I was going to say the American peerage—would that have been a pin prick? or an aphorism?

Yours very sincerely
Virginia Woolf

Frederick B. Adams Jr.

2672: To Ethel Smyth   [52 *Tavistock Square, W.C.*1]

Tuesday [29 November 1932]

This is not a letter, so dont be alarmed; only to say I have a letter from the publisher of the Austen letters saying they had been told *I* wrote the T.L.S. article—hoped I hadn't—are much relieved to find the "culprit is E M. Forster".[2] Lord—I never guessed it could be him. Well, you were right in thinking it by a man who can write; though I dont think he did more than a few simple tricks this time. The letters are to me fascinating—for what they dont say largely. But *dont* say anything about EMF: he'd be hurt if he heard I'd been declaiming: its all Hugh Walpoles gossip I imagine: he disliked the article so much. Are you coming to Nessa's tea party show tomorrow? I'm going: I'm much better: havent been out for 14 nights but this tea party will be the dreariest thing conceivable—Margot [Oxford] etc: convened to buy; and they wont buy; and they'll drink, and no doubt steal. No more. I'm ever so much better

V.

Berg

1. *How Little Logan was Brought to Jesus*, which his father, a well-known evangelist, had published many years before. The Hogarth Press did not reprint it.
2. See Letter 2665.

2673: To H. A. L. Fisher   52 *Tavistock Square, W.C.*1

29th Nov. 1932

My dear Herbert,

I am greatly pleased that you liked my article,[1] and it was very good of you to say so. I was reluctant to write it, but Vanessa and Adrian wanted me to—and I did it in the fear that I should make a complete failure of it.

Yes, I too remember Hyde Park gate very well, and your coming— and mother saying you had won a fellowship and asking her what that was.

Yrs affate
Virginia Woolf

Bodleian Library, Oxford

2674: To Elizabeth Bowen   52 *Tavistock Sqre.*, [*W.C.*1]

Nov. 30th [1932]

Dear Miss Bowen,

I am very much better and think there is no doubt that I shall be quite well on Thursday if you would come then at 5. (and wouldn't mind perhaps finding me in a dressing gown.)

The bother is that these headaches sometimes come back suddenly and then I'm not able to talk. But if so, I would ring you up at the address you gave,—and I dont think its likely as I've lain here for 6 days in perfect obedience.

But please say if you'd rather wait till there's no chance of being put off —I expect you are very busy.

Yours sincerely
Virginia Woolf

If I dont hear I shall expect you.

Texas

2675: To Dorothy Bussy   52 *Tavistock Square, W.C.*1

[end-November 1932?]

My dear Dorothy,

This is my annual invitation to tea on the 15th June: and also to ask if you take in paying guests? A friend (male) [*unidentified*] of Francis Birrell's wants to convalesce near Mentone, where he is at the moment, and

1. On the centenary of Leslie Stephen's birth. *The Times*, 28 November.

suggested possibly you would take him, which was jumped at. I suppose he wants to come soon, and I dont think he needs any special care.

But if you would be so angelic as to inform me, or Francis Birrell, 70 Elm Park Road, S.W., whether there is any chance of this, all particulars would be sent you.

I got into the clutches of your niece Ellie [Rendel] earlier in the autumn, and have spent many weeks in bed, wishing you would walk in—No such luck! But remember June 15th.

Yours affate.
Virginia Woolf

Texas

2676: To Lady Ottoline Morrell

52 Tavistock Square, W.C.1

Friday [2 December 1932]

I'm involved, owing to that awful party with Mary [Hutchinson], with Morgan [Forster] (no, he wasn't the party) with Rebecca West and I don't think I can keep off Logan. You won't want to mix again with these nice but rather too numerous people—and then Lady Oxford,—says she must have a picture of me next Lord Rosebery in her book—So come if you will alone if you will, the next week. That's the worst of parties—people—but I'm much better in spite and thought your distinguished black, or was it purple? a merciful relief in that parrot house of screeching chocolate boxes— Why is the current fashion of bald heads and tight hips so depressing? I didn't like Mary's version of a lady jockey at all.

Nessa and I went to Brixton today to see our old family cook[1] and she said, sitting in her bedsitting room, This is better than any party—which indeed it was.

Texas

2677: To Logan Pearsall Smith

52 Tavistock Square, W.C.1

Typewritten
4th Dec. 1932

Dear Logan,

I am afraid that, as this week is very full, it will have to be the week after. Perhaps tea, 4.30, on Thursday 15th will suit you.

1. Sophie Farrell.

I am quite ready to 'love' as you suggest; the idea of fighting originated with you, I fancy. At least I seem to remember a remark of yours to the effect that we must have quarrelled because I had not asked you to tea. Let it be 'love' by all means.

And of course, though I am unable to invent aphorisms, I try to understand those of others, and I take the meaning of your latest and loveliest—"If you are losing your leisure, look out!—it may be you are losing your soul" to be that these letters waste a great deal of time; and that it is extremely good of you to lose still more leisure, and imperil your soul still further by coming all this way to tea. I do so profoundly agree.

Therefore do not trouble to answer. We shall look forward to seeing you on Thursday the 15th unless I hear to the contrary.[1]

Yours very sincerely
Virginia Woolf

Frederick B. Adams Jr.

2678: To Elizabeth Bowen   52 *Tavistock Square, W.C.1*

Wednesday [7 December 1932]

Dear Miss Bowen,
    I'm so sorry, I'm afraid I shant be able to see you tomorrow. I've got knocked up and am being made to stay in bed and see nobody. Is there any chance that you would come another day?—Early next week I am sure I shall be all right again. I am so disappointed, and I hope this wont upset your plans.

Yours sincerely
Virginia Woolf

Texas

2679: To Ethel Smyth   [52 *Tavistock Square, W.C.1*]

Sunday [11 December 1932]

    Here are the cuttings back—very impressive, and I hope operative.[2] I'll send the Book as soon as I can.[3] I laughed aloud over you: unalloyed:

1. Logan Pearsall Smith noted on this letter: "The visit was of course a failure. I never went again." And in a note attached to it (*Library of Congress*): "It was hardly worth while (as she herself had hinted) to make further attempts to cross the differences of age and tastes and friends that lay between us."
2. Ethel had sent Virginia a set of press-cuttings about her recent musical triumphs.
3. *Little Innocents*, 1932, a miscellany of childhood reminiscences by various authors, including Ethel, Vita, Harold Nicolson and Edward Sackville West. It was edited by Alan Pryce-Jones.

at the others I laughed, but with a private comment that the authors would not have enjoyed. Vita of course is always such gold, pure, to the heart, that I love her at her most innocent. And I've not read them all: but it seems to be a field for posturing—this of infantile anecdotage: very illuminating. Just back from Rodmell—why we went, God knows. It was merely exposing myself to a thousand steel knives, and such a roaring in the trees by night that I thought of God and Ethel.

Nessa says she is sending me a letter of yours, so thats all right—I went to Dido and Aeneas [Purcell] at the Wells and thought it absolutely and entirely satisfying: so come away before the English opera.[1] My taste is very limited. I cant judge music any more than someone else can judge articles in the T.L.S.[2]

Berg

2680: TO THEODORA BOSANQUET   52 *Tavistock Square, W.C.*1

Typewritten
11th Dec 1932

Dear Miss Bosanquet,[3]
    I should have thought that there could be no doubt that the National Portrait Gallery ought to have a picture of Katherine Mansfield. I have never seen the picture you mention (nor indeed any picture), but I should be ready to help to secure it if in the opinion of people who knew her it is a good likeness. Of course there is always something in a picture that a photograph cannot give.

    I see you say that there is to be a private view of the portrait some time in January and perhaps I shall be able to come and see it. At any rate I am certainly in favour of buying a picture of Katherine Mansfield for the National Portrait Gallery.[4]

Yours very sincerely
Virginia Woolf

Houghton Library, Harvard University

1. *The Devil Take Her* by Arthur Benjamin.
2. See Letters 2665 and 2672.
3. Theodora Bosanquet had been secretary to Henry James in his last years, and the Hogarth Press had published a memoir of him by her in 1924.
4. There is no portrait of Katherine Mansfield in the National Portrait Gallery.

[12 December? 1932]

Heres the cheque for 61.15.7. I think its ridiculously little—I think its absurd, for example, to charge only £5.5. for the desk—which means that you're charging nothing for painting or designing. However I send the cheque; and think we had better discuss the details. I suppose there's more furniture to come in. You've not used up to £100 anyhow.[1] I cant help thinking too that some of the things might sell. But we'd better discuss it by word of mouth. Does fender mean the fire stool? Lots of the things I want at Rodmell.

But we must meet

B.

Also I dont think you and D[uncan]. can have charged anything for your carpet designs. Why not?

Berg

Sunday [18 December 1932]

This is the usual scrawl, pending time to write at length (Thank God— off to Rodmell on Tuesday) And only to say, *dont* take any steps whatever, even imaginary, as yet about the MS of Room[2]—I'm dealing cautiously with it and want to consult Pippa Strachey privately first. By a miracle, I've found all the pages. Also, dont take my word about the Womens Service Society. I'm so inaccurate. They wrote to the Times though about a month ago; and if you want any information, the address is Miss P. Strachey Women's Service House 29 Marsham Street Westminster. They'd be enchanted naturally to hear from you: but all their plans are subtle, secret and full of diplomatic guile

We've been seeing a flamingo in Richmond Park—How much I prefer seeing flamingoes to seeing Mr. Pearsall Smith!

Your name is spelt with a y. So write to Monks House

V.

Berg

1. Virginia had guaranteed to spend £100 on buying furniture, etc., on sale at their party of 30 November.
2. Virginia's *A Room of One's Own*, 1929. She was considering the sale of the manuscript for the benefit of the London-National Society for Women's Service, of which Philippa Strachey was Secretary.

Monks House, [Rodmell, Sussex]

22nd Dec. 1932

(When it gets near the end of the year, I always remember, and write the date in full)

As I wrote 20, no more and no less, letters two days ago, you can't complain that I didn't write to you. My hand staggered like a tipsy crow. The waits have just done singing: L. has given them 2/6—but I cant say I caught the music of old England, though I listened—which reminds me, is Vernon Lee's book on music good?[1] Ought I to order it? I like her trailing clouds of sub fulgent ink—why cant she write tighter though?—thats what trips me up—like falling over one's train, coming upstairs, after dinner, No, I didn't read Eddy—Yes, I did read the article in TLS (not by me, for a wonder) on L.S. [Leslie Stephen] Quite good I thought, in its surface way: but then they'd no space. It is ironical that my father thought nothing of his criticism, and secretly believed himself a great philosopher. No one mentions the philosophy; all the criticism.

Have I answered all your questions? I'm reading Jane Austen [Letters] in this heavenly solitude over the log fire: and whether its my luxurious state, anyhow I find her steadily improve. I think her little fame at the end brisked her up—good Lord, she died at 42: the best to come. Have you read them? No. L. has turned on the wireless, and a gent. is talking about International measures.—curse him.

I am taking a few days holiday: I have cut off the book [*The Pargiters*] which you will unreservedly hate. And its very dull—taking a holiday. very pointless; I look at the cows and watch one lick its ear—a thing I've not done (watch a cow lick its ear) since I started the book you'll hate. But its a good thing to turn off the lights and look at the world now and then. How odd that the world goes on just the same whether I look at it or not! Do you find that when you're writing—the world goes out, except the precise part of it you want for your writing, which becomes indeed indecently clear. I'm reading 20 books at once—masses of books—and feel like a walrus taking to the sea—so vast, so calm, so indifferent, with the whole Atlantic to wallow in—but that's an illusion because the Keynes's will be over: then the Gages;[2] then the Bells: and the poor Walrus will climb on to its rock and bark—How is your cold? What are you working at? Oh do tell me all about your suffrage life one of these days.

V.

Berg

1. Vernon Lee (1856-1935), whose real name was Violet Paget, published *Music and its Lovers* in 1932. She was an intimate friend of Ethel.
2. 6th Viscount Gage, the owner of Firle Place and of Charleston, and his wife Imogen (*née* Grenfell).

Monks House, Rodmell,
[Sussex]

Dec 23rd [1932]

Dearest Dolphin

I cannot think of any news—my last contact with civilised life was with Barbara and Saxon and Judith.[1] Naturally the admirable Barbara made it an excuse to sit down with me for 1 hour and ½ before Saxon came—being as she said and I can believe, tired of trailing round shops. I bear her no ill will; though Angelica and I had a mint of things to say. Angelica is becoming a woman of great taste and discernment. We were just discussing Mrs Gaskell and Thackeray and I was finding her exactly of my way of thinking when, as I say, in pushed that lamentable troupe, and for the rest of the time we talked of canning fruit and bottling eggs and I generally got the impression of grime and grasp and drudge and extinction—not altogether alleviated by poor dear Saxon, who could not think where they were to dine. I said the Ivy. Finally they trapesed off to some dismal pot-house in Fitzroy Street. Barbara was sleeping with Mrs Sickert:[2] the bassoon is laid between them. But bassoons when touched by Barbara merely rattle like tin cans— I told her fruit always goes bad in tins: tins, she said, cost ½ each when bought by the dozen gross. Angelica disgraced herself—Lord, what a time is coming for us, now that the last of the Brats is of an age to whisper comments into ones ears!

All this is deadly dull. Were you very dull with Raymond [Mortimer] —a trashy, meretricious dulness; mine was dulness pure and simple. It is blazing hot here: the flowers are out; the bees threaten to swarm; L. and Percy[3] spend the day pruning. Mr Robinson[4] has bought the farm down, and is going to farm it, so I shall have no excuse to buy another house as I had intended. Asheham Cement is now all smoke by day and light by night and will soon go smash. The Wolves went to Brighton and bought you 4 red buttons—which anyhow dont take much room and may come in on some stitchery of yours. As my small and unregarded present I enclose this very dull cheque: I want to pay the cocktail bill entire: now, dont lash your tail: otherwise you should have had a gramophone or an evening dress: this is less and need not be mentioned. Send bill for upholstery. Needless to say, Duncans stuff is not to be had for a fortnight. The Turkey has come. I'm afraid poor old Ethel has met with a final reverse about her ballet—

B.

1. Barbara Bagenal and her daughter Judith; Saxon Sydney-Turner had loved Barbara in his youth, but remained a bachelor working in the Treasury.
2. Thérèse Lessore, the painter, the third wife of Walter Sickert.
3. Percy Bartholomew, Leonard's gardener.
4. J. C. Robinson, who lived at Oatlands, Iford, near Rodmell.

By the way, the screen would be magnificent here—I cant bear the old curtains much longer.

We sent Julian [Bell] 2 books—Tom, and Aldous:[1] let me know if they dont come. Our new Perkins [Hogarth Press clerk] always puts Essex instead of Sussex, so letters go wrong. But my God, how heavenly to see nobody! But the Keynes' will be on us. And when is your party? (that I should enjoy—but doubtless you cant ask me, quarrelsome as I am)

Berg

2685: To Lady Ottoline Morrell

Monks House, Rodmell,
[Sussex]

Boxing Day [1932]

Dearest Ottoline,

It was very good indeed of you to send me three such lovely scarves; but very rash. Three beautiful gifts—how many lashes wont they earn you? Lady Ottolilia Morrett—look out for that flamboyant female in my next book. At present, just to take you in, I'm very grateful. The Keynes's came over to lunch yesterday: I was at the lowest gasp even of my dishevellment, I rushed in, pinned a scarf to my neck—and lo and behold—a thrill ran through the company. They said they couldnt think where my beauty and the lovely scent came from. So a thousand (provisional) thanks.[2]

I'm reading the new edition of Carswells D.H.L. book: hence these reflections. It is a miserable scratchy edgy raw ill conditioned book: God knows why I ever told her it was interesting—save as an exhibition of what sour love and malice and ill breeding mixed can do. Why cant she speak out if she wants to? Thats what is so malodorous—her hints and nods and becks: and then the servile and supine adoration: as of a mangy—it must be—bitch. But I've read so many books since we came, this one is happily buried under.

It has been balm to the heart, escaping London, and the 25 people I saw the last week, till my brain was like a 20 times exposed film—Logan's horrid nose obliterating all. I dont like Logan: he's coarse and rank and would, if he were a fish, stink, to put it plainly. But dont tell Ethel, whom I'm afraid I may have offended about Logan already. Anyhow here there

1. T. S. Eliot's *Sweeney Agonistes* and Aldous Huxley's *Brave New World*, both 1932.
2. Ottoline replied (28 December) that they were not scarfs but handkerchieves. "The chiffons were for your Nose's use! To cut out Mary . . . but wherever you use them I shall be proud" (*Sussex*).

are barns and marshes. I startled a great swan sleeping on the river bank this afternoon—no doubt about it, nature is incredible—flocks of little birds, grey green downs—my little river silver—and the hay stacks like half eaten cakes. And now the firs and books. A thousand (provisional) thanks. Are you better?

V.W.

Texas

2686: To Ethel Smyth   *Monks House, [Rodmell, Sussex]*

Dec. 28th or thereabouts [1932]

All right Ethel Smyth; I'll answer your questions if you'll send me them and Eddy's story.[1] But first, answer me these: 1. Why are you so insistent about Eddy's story? Did he ask you to show it me? (2) If I tell you what I think of it, are you going to repeat my words to him? Now these are two questions that you must answer with that rough British honesty that befits a general's daughter.

I am actually writing the very day I get your letter—a proof of the divine peace of Monks House. Nobody but the postman can possibly interrupt me between today and tomorrow. Therefore I am sunk deep in books. Oh yes, I write in the morning—just a little joke [*Flush*] to boil my years pot: but from 4.30 to 11.30 I read, Ethel. Isn't that gorgeous? And not only those damned flimsy MSS: no: books: printed, solid, entire: D'you know I get such a passion for reading sometimes its like the other passion—writing—only the wrong side of the carpet. Heaven knows what either amounts to. My own brain is to me the most unaccountable of machinery—always buzzing, humming, soaring roaring diving, and then buried in mud. And why? Whats this passion for? You, who love questions, answer me that. No—nobody can. And then this passion, which has been so well advised, lands me tonight in a book like the reek of stale cabbage and cheap face powder—a book called The Story of San Michele by [Axel] Munthe [1929]. Now dont say its your favourite work. A book more porous with humbug, reeking more suddenly with insincerity, I've never read. I'm at page 50. I rather suspect you of knowing him. My mother in law loves him—his d——d sentimental book, she being the mother of 9 children, and used to darn their socks on waking in the time of her calamity. And I'm reading Stella Benson:[2] with pleasure, and—oh so many books—doesn't it break your heart almost to think of me, with this passion, always consumed with the desire to read, chopped, chafed, bugged, battered by the voices, the

1. In *Little Innocents*. Edward Sackville-West told the story of a car accident at Knole when he was a child.
2. *Christmas Formula*, 1932.

140

hands, the faces, the bodily presence of those who are pleased to call themselves my friends? Its like knocking a bluebottle off its lump of sugar perpetually. I am in an exaggerative mood. I should qualify all this with a thin red line signifying 'exaggeration'—but God knows if Ethel Smyth—I think of calling you so in future—cant read Virginia by this time, let her eyes fall into a well and there drown.

You sound a little raucous—your cold I suppose: and I hope its gone; and I hope you're writing music; and I hope you're thinking of me; and thinking how you will tell me all about Mrs Pankhurst and the suffrage. Why did you militate? I am turning over that other little book [*The Pargiters*] in my mind; and want to know a few facts.

And tomorrow my dear Vita sails, and I shant see her till April.[1]

Yes, that saddens me: it takes away a lamp and a glow, and a shady leaf and an illuminated hall from my existence.

But enough, as old Lady Ponsonby used to say when she threw the soup tureen at Queen Victoria. And do you remember Lady Radnor, a vast stout woman, who had you to lunch in Venice, so she says; and did she sing well; and what was the truth of her—her memoirs[2] are mostly lies, but only because a pen is to her what a tassel is to a blind Arabian mare on Tuesday morning in the desert. Guess what I mean—surely I must mean something?

Oh its so lovely on the downs now—a dewpond like a silver plate in the hollow; and all the hills, not distinct as in summer, but vast, smooth, shaven, serene; and I lie on the ground and look; and then the bells tinkle, and then the horses plough; and then, forgetting all the days to come and days past and this day and tomorrow,—well, you know the mood; only I incorporate better with earth than you do, because I'm—well I'm not nearly as fine a figure as you are. *You* resist: you rebut; you insist—I lie back on the wind and lend myself—I was going to say to the waves: but you never could abear that book. Do you say 'abear?' So goodnight

V.

Berg

2687: To Hugh Walpole   *Monks House, Rodmell,*
                                                    [Sussex]
28th Dec [1932]

My dear Hugh,
    I can assure you that I liked your present better than any—better than the peach fed Virginian ham even, for literature, if you wont think me too

1. On 30 December Vita and Harold embarked at Southampton on the German liner *Bremen* for their lecture-tour of the United States.
2. *From a Great-Grandmother's Armchair*, 1927.

high brow, is something—not I suppose if you are starving on a desert island—I was going to say that literature—but I become too self conscious to go on—is more than ham. Well, anyhow, this book of yours[1] is to me, anyhow, more than ham, first because I love finding myself quoted and called mysterious on the first page—considering I'm wallowing in ham and grilled turkey—and then because as you know, of all literature (yes, I think this is more or less true) I love autobiography most.

In fact I sometimes think only autobiography is literature—novels are what we peel off, and come at last to the core, which is only you or me. And I think this little book—why so small?—peels off all the things I dont like in fiction and leaves the thing I do like—you. Seriously, soberly (I'm staggering from a walk alone, starting a swan, a heron, fieldfare and so on) I do think this is a very charming and attractive book: I think Henry James is entirely delightful;—why dont you give us the whole of him and Mrs [Lucy] Clifford and all their fascinating shades:—and the hat delighted me, and Cumberland, and [Arnold] Bennett. Do go on. Do make a quatuorology of it. I think it your duty when Herries is finished to do Hugh. But anyhow this instalment is delightful—as a beginning. Only think what it might lead to—what a volume for me to read. Think of me, dying as you so kindly suggested of heart failure over a teapot and crying with my last breath, He never wrote his autobiography! Wouldn't that wring your heart? (curse this pen—its like an old spade held in the hand of a rheumatic sexton—I'm so cold).

One word more: what about Livingstone?[2] Derrick Leon's novel? did you read it? with what result? But you're off to the Indies: and about to write your autog. Thank God.

Love from us both V.

Texas

1. Hugh Walpole's *The Apple Trees*, a volume of reminiscences, which was published for Christmas 1932. The first words of the book are: "There is a fearful passage in Virginia Woolf's beautiful and mysterious book *The Waves*, which, when I read it, gave me an acute shock of unanticipated reminiscence." He then quotes a long passage from *The Waves* (pp. 19-20 in the Penguin paperback edition), which contains the sentence: "The apple-tree leaves became fixed in the sky; the moon glared".
2. *Livingstones: a novel of contemporary life* by Derrick Leon, 1933.

Letters 2688-2733 (January–April 1933)

Virginia finished the final typescript of Flush *in January, and returned to* The Pargiters *with "a flood of creativeness". By the beginning of May she had written 50,000 words. She was enjoying the experiment of mixing fact with fantasy, but it was the only one of her books which she totally transformed after making such good initial progress with it. Vita was lecturing in the United States until the very end of this period, and Virginia was finding Ethel Smyth an almost intolerable burden upon her time and patience. "It's like being a snail and having your brain cracked by a thrush", she wrote to Vanessa on 19 February. She refused the offer of an Honorary Degree at Manchester University, calling such academic honours 'Mumbo Jumbo'. From February onwards she conscientiously took lessons in Italian, and it was to Italy that she and Leonard drove in their new car at the beginning of May.*

2688: TO ETHEL SMYTH   *Monks House, [Rodmell, Sussex]*

1st Jan. 1933

Here is Vita's address—it will, she says, always find her.

> c/o W. COLSTON LEIGH.
> 521 Fifth Avenue New York[1]

Here, enclosed, is the paper of questions.[2] But the fact that I myself would not have said this or that, only means that whats right in one sentence is wrong in another. I dislike the expressions separately—in their context, bathed in Morgans very peculiar sensibility they may be all right—I'm not Morgan. Thats one of the puzzles of letters—how an atmosphere—person—taste—pose—can transform the good into the bad.

I have also read Eddy's story [in *Little Innocents*]. It seems to me competent and charming and effective and well told—its a good anecdote too—but I could not by any possibility bring myself to call it a 'little masterpiece'. The effect, on me, is far too slight and fugitive. I shall have forgotten it tomorrow. A masterpiece is I think something said once and for all, stated,

1. The lecture agency which arranged Harold's and Vita's American tour.
2. Ethel, stung by Virginia's ridicule that she should have mistaken a review of Jane Austen's Letters by E. M. (Morgan) Forster for one by herself (see p. 125), sent Virginia a list of stylistic comments on the review.

finished, so that its there complete in the mind, if only at the back. This remains, for me, on the surface.

But as you see, I emphasise the 'for me'. Its quite true, and I've said it before—I cannot feel any certainty in my own judgment of living writers. I'm too twisted and distorted by my own preoccupation. I mean I know this is, for me, good or bad: but of the dead I know (heaven forgive me!) This *is* good or bad: Probably you're much closer the mark than I am with living writers. I daresay both Eddy and Maurice [Baring] are far better than I think. Its M's superficiality that distresses me—compare him with Turgenev now thats a masterpiece maker, now and then, in M's own line too: but M. B seems to me to go out like candleshine before it. Never mind—I daresay you see more of the whole than I do. I rather jib at giving criticism of the living for this reason. And I'm now (I think this is true) almost indifferent to criticism of myself.—Since we're all living. I dont think you're either right or wrong about The Waves: no two people think alike about it. And, for anything I know, I may be better as a critic as you say than as a novelist. Its too late to change anyhow; and I follow my mood in that as in other things—which reminds me, I'm off to London to go to a 'party'! must see some people after 10 days solitude; then shall come back to books: then rush to society. Which is better? which do I need most? God knows, I cant say—a common predicament of mine all my life. But instead of developing this interesting theme, I must stop or the post will go and you want Vitas address—Yes, its odd how strongly I miss her—miss her presence in the green fields of Kent, even without seeing her there. I'm afraid she hated going when it came to it—said she loathed leaving Long Barn. Well good day—its New Years day too

V.

Berg

2689: To Elizabeth Bowen   52 *Tavistock Sqre.*
(*Monks House, Rodmell*)

3rd Jan 1933

Dear Elizabeth,

What a dangerous friend you are! One says casually I like shortbread—and behold shortbread arrives. Now had I said I like young elephants, would the same thing have happened? I suspect so. The only way to neutralise the poison is to cancel it with something you dont want, here's a book therefore. But be warned—I often make tea caddies in magenta plush—that will be your fate on the next occasion. I embroider them with forget-me-nots in gold.

As a matter of fact, nothing could have come in more handy. I rushed up here last night to go to a party and found the cupboard entirely bare.

There was a parcel. Opening it in a disillusioned way, expecting some MS of a novel, lo and behold, there was shortbread. So I fell on it and having the digestion of an ostrich made a splendid meal all solid—but Heavens what delicious rich ripe shortbread! Being ill should have been my fate—not at all—I dressed up as Queen Victoria on her wedding night and fell into the arms of the Prince Consort.[1] The effect upon the royal line has yet to be discovered. But it will be laid to your door.

Excuse this scrawl. We are just off again, and I am still spinning with last night's debauch. And this pen is in the last stage of disintegration. How did the tea party with Logan go off? Mine [on 15 December] was the dampest and dreariest of wet—no merely moist—fire works. Not being an Irish fox, you see, I can't get at the ripe grapes. I cannot re-write this letter, so the mixed metaphors must remain.

Texas   yr VW

2690: To Virginia Isham   *Monks House, Rodmell,*
                                         Lewes, Sussex
Typewritten
4th Jan 1933

Dear Virginia,

Your letter has been sent on here. I shant be back in London, I'm afraid, until the 15th. And then you will be gone. But if you were in London on the 17 which is Tuesday and could come in any time after nine thirty, we shall be at home (at 52 Tavistock Sq.) and it would be very nice to see you and discuss the Waves. Oddly enough I met somebody who wants to film it the other night.[2]

Would Giles[3] come in too? I dont know his address. And we shall be unchanged—I mean in clothes.

                                         Yours ever
                                         Virginia Woolf

[*handwritten*]

by this I mean that we dont dress.

Northamptonshire Record Office

1. It was a fancy-dress party for about 50 people given by Vanessa for Angelica's 14th birthday. Leonard went as the Prince Consort.
2. Virginia Isham, an actress who was distantly related to Virginia, hoped to broadcast part of *The Waves*. The 'somebody' who wished to film it was Wogan Philipps, Rosamond Lehmann's husband, whom Virginia had met at Vanessa's party.
3. Sir Gyles Isham Bt. (1903-76), her brother, who had played several Shakespearean roles at the Old Vic and Stratford-on-Avon.

[52 *Tavistock Square, W.C.*1]

[early January 1933]

Dearest Ottoline,

Oh dear, Tuesday and Thursday are my only free days, as we now go away on Friday, but what about Wednesday 11th?—that I will keep for ever, if I survive Ethel Smyth. Lord!—what a plague of locusts the woman is!—fine, vigorous insects, whom I respect and admire, but they leave me bent and broken. I look forward with hope to Wednesday 11th—in spite of her.

V.

Texas

2692: To Ethel Smyth   *Monks House, [Rodmell, Sussex]*

Friday Jan: 6th [1933]

No my dear Ethel, I shant be able to come up on the 9th or 10th,[1] because—I forget if I told you—we have bought a brand new and very expensive car [a Lanchester]. This has been promised us weekly since Dec 10th. As now arranged it will be delivered here on the 14th. We must have one spin. It is the apple of L's eye. It is on the fluid flywheel system. It will cruise—how I love technical words—at 50 miles an hour. Unless I can persuade him to dash me up to London for the night—but no: that one night of mine was the limit. He grudges every moment not spent here. The buds are opening. It is like May: the moon is like June, and the blackbirds tune—so I shant be there. But I shall listen in next time—dear me, its all very badly arranged. And I agree with you—the wireless is a humbug—a mere travesty and distortionment—I get more pain from it than pleasure. What with the Germans cutting in, and the voice of your friend God Almighty—growling and grumbling. That reminds me—why do you think Vernon Lees views on the war detestable?[2] What would you say to mine? And what are yours? So you'll have to write another letter, willy nilly. But I still wish I could see you conducting and hear the tunes you think I might like. I suspect that we shall be forced to come back on the 15th. Needless to say Miss Belsher has influenza; her fur coat has been stolen from the Press—in short we embroil ourselves again in the buzzing of gnats

1. Ethel was conducting the music of her ballet, *Fête Galante*, at the Queen's Hall on 10 January.
2. Vernon Lee (Violet Paget), an intimate friend of Ethel. On 12 January Ethel replied to Virginia: "I hate her utter lack of patriotism—either innate or acquired" (*Berg*).

instead of floating sublimely between Heaven and the hills—as at this present moment—Why, I can assure you, the loveliness of the sight makes even my tough heart tremble—the marshes, the clouds, the birds and June. But human life is also valuable. I met the mistress of a headmaster in Lewes high St—a hare faced pale eyed woman and felt my ardours revive

Your letter just come. Yes I'm much better and no more digitalis.

Berg

2693: To Vanessa Bell

[Monk's House, Rodmell, Sussex]

Postcard

Friday [6 January 1933]

We may inflict ourselves on you for tea tomorrow, which is, you wont know, Saturday. But its so freezing all our pipes are frozen here, and the LeFevre [Gallery] have sent me things that dont belong to me and not the things that do, But I will tell you all when we meet.

B.

The carpet [by Duncan Grant] has come }
The glass is up } both are beyond all dreams.

Berg

2694: To V. Sackville-West

Monks House, Rodmell, [Sussex]

7th Jan 1933

Well, dearest Creature, it is a lovely spring evening. The thrushes are singing—no, not singing but chattering in the tree—you know the squawk they make. Leonard is pruning the fig tree; it is just upon five o'clock and so soft and fine and pink that we can hardly settle in. Yet I swear this is only Jan: the 7th: and L. picked me a snowdrop this morning.

This prelude is intended to make you jealous, as you observe. For next to Ethel Smyth, you're jealous of the English fields, at this moment—so I diagnose your case. O Lord that I could see you, as you are—sitting on a tight plush seat in a car, I imagine, with views of the Middle West—an unattractive land, largely sprinkled with old tin kettles—racing across vast slabs of plate glass. For you are now travelling across America; the negroes are spitting in the carriage next door; and after 25 more hours, the train will

147

stop at a town like Peacehaven, only 75 times larger, called Balmoralville [*invented*], where you will get out, and after a brief snack off clams and iced pear drops with the Mayor, who is called, I should think Cyrus K. Hinks—but thats a detail I leave to you, you will go to a large baptist Hall, and deliver a lecture on Rimbaud. Oddly enough I'm doing the very same thing myself, only in another part of America—see enclosed [*missing*]—thats why I'm so startlingly accurate.

I was seized with gloom when you left—ask Ethel. Isn't it odd what tricks affection—to leave it at that—plays? I dont see you for six weeks sometimes; yet the moment I know you're not there to be seen, all the fish-mongers shops in the world go dark.[1] I always think of you as a pink shop with a porpoise in a tank. Now there are no porpoises. No, Sissinghurst is grey; Sevenoaks a drab coloured puce. Here I sit at Rodmell, with a whole patch of my internal globe extinct. Yes—thats a compliment for you.

I didn't expect to see you on Christmas day. We slumped through the mud with the Keynes's.

What other news is there? Heaven be praised, I have seen no one. I read; I walk; I put dinner in the oven; I sleep. And next week we go back—dear me—to London; where Miss Belsher has influenza and her fur coat, valued at £30—was stolen off the peg outside the W.C. door she says by an unemployed consumptive man a friend of Miss Scott Johnsons[2] As you will deduce, Miss Belsher and Miss S. J. are not on the best of terms. And Hugh Walpole is coming to dinner. And Violet Trefusis sent me a vast nodding bunch of lilac; to which I replied—as you would have me. No, I'm not spending the New Year between her and M- de Polignac.[3] I wave the banner of chastity and cry upward. Then theres Ethel (Sands) then there's Nan Hudson, then theres Raymond, then there's Rosamond Lehmann, Roger Fry and myself all sitting on the studio floor [Vanessa's] and eating ham and chicken. Ah, says Nan, this is the sort of life I really love. Then, my good woman, why dont you lead it? I say, being in a truculent mood just now, snipping the wigs off these elderly heads, as I daresay you've observed. This was at Angelica's party—this brilliant wit, these flashing epigrams. By the way, are you lecturing on me at Albertvilleapolis Pa [*invented*]? If so, do send me your notes. Please do. And let them say something of love, and Horne the butler [at Long Barn]. Let them slip in one word to say Vita loves Virginia better than the whole world wrapped in a

1. Virginia often returned to her memory of Vita imperiously ordering fish in a Sevenoaks shop in December 1925.
2. Who, after John Lehmann's departure, became Leonard's manager at the Hogarth Press, but stayed only a few months.
3. Winnaretta (Winnie) Singer, daughter of the American sewing-machine millionaire, married as her second husband Prince Edmond de Polignac in 1893. They were friends of Marcel Proust and leaders of Parisian intellectual society, particularly of musicians. He died in 1903.

nutshell. Better than all those ardent but anaemic herring grillers with whom—Lord love her soul!—she consorts. Because Virginia is so clever, so good; and Virginia—this is a fact, not merely an idle boast—Virginia has been asked to write for the London Mercury by Jack Squire. What he says is, Will I send him a story and he'll see if it'll do.[1] Oh my God—how I envy you, slipping off your skin and adventuring through fields where the flamingoes rise in flocks and the old black women stand at the doors, a baby at each breast! Thats what I adore and honour and cherish the Nicolsons for—sloughing their skins, every spring in a heap of drab scales and plunging naked into nothingness. Yes; you are a venturous woman, and make me envious. Please, for Gods sake, dont catch the flu, or the pneumonia—both I see rampant in New York. Dont do a thing that can diminish your splendour in my eyes, Come back soon, before I start, as I intend, for the East.

I'm told that Bunny Garnett's book on Pocahontas is very good.[2] Is it? Please tell me. I can read nothing but my own novel [*The Pargiters*], which is just as well, because nobody else will ever get through it.

Shall you now clear a space among the spittoons and write to me? Describe everything, down to the lace on womens nightgowns. Then add a terse but compendious statement why I love Virginia next best to my husband and sons.

And take great care of yourself.

V.

Berg

2695: To Virginia Isham   *Monks House, Rodmell,*
                                         Lewes, [Sussex]

Typewritten
8th Jan [1933]

Dear Virginia,

I am so sorry you cant come on Tuesday. Do let me know when you are in London again and suggest a visit. I think we shall be there till Easter. Of course I should be delighted if you could make anything of the Waves on the wireless. I'm afraid you will find it very difficult to get it taken, unless you know somebody there who would be interested. Let me know if I can do anything to help. Yes of course be Susan if you like her; and I should be delighted if Gyles [Isham] would be Bernard. We must meet and discuss it—I am rather in the dark as to what you think could be done. The only other suggestion was from a man called Wogan Phillips—the

1. She refused this request.
2. *Pocahontas, or The Nonpareil of Virginia*, by David Garnett, 1933, a biography of the American-Indian princess written in fictional form.

149

husband of Rosamond Lehmann, who wanted to make a film of it. But I dont think this will come to anything. Also, your idea is quite different, for I suppose a film would be all dumbshow. However please consider that you have my permission and blessing for whatever they are worth. It would interest me immensely to see what you could do with it.

I wonder what you're acting at Oxford? If I come there I shall drop in and see. The Fishers[1] did ask me to stay last term; I'm rather terrified of going. And I never thanked you for the tickets for Schnitzlers play.[2] We enjoyed it greatly—I dont think its a good play, but it was a very interesting experiment. I dont think you can do thinking as well as speaking on the stage—or not like that.

So let me know if theres a chance of meeting.

Yours ever
Virginia Woolf

Northamptonshire Record Office

2696: To T. S. Eliot

Monk's House, Rodmell,
Lewes, Sussex

Typewritten
15th Jan 1933

My dear Tom,

I am shocked to see that your letter is dated 20th Nov. 1932. Here it is 1933. And you are now on the Santa Fe Railway.[3] But why? Where are you off to? Anyhow in Feb. you are starting English 26, a course limited to 15 students. But why? I cant imagine any possible answer, so I must leave this among the unsolved riddles.

Here we are rather damp, and to speak plainly, Leonard has the itch. That is, we went to a fancy dress party at Vanessas; and he had the temerity to dress up as an English gentleman of the old school in hired clothes. I say it served him right; the itch was in the stock. Naturally, it would be. I should tell this story to your Americans. But thats the sad part of our story. The other and brighter side is that we have bought a new Lanchester—with a fluid fly wheel. It came after two months delay, last night. We drive up this afternoon. I wish we had the English professor with us.

Your letter told me all I can absorb of life at Harvard. The Cabots and

1. H. A. L. Fisher, the Warden of New College, Oxford.
2. *La Ronde* by Arthur Schnitzler, which was performed in French at the Arts Theatre.
3. Eliot was appointed the Charles Eliot Norton Professor of Poetry at Harvard University, 1932-33.

the Sedwicks and the Wolcotts[1] and the soap. And the sponge shaped like a brick. London is much as usual, or was when I left it on Dec. 20th. Ottoline was giving her parties; but I dont go because of Mr Stephens.[2] Ottoline alone is much better than Ottoline mixed. If you are going to talk about Bloomsbury—if they gave you the 250 dollars—I should say this. Woburn Square is falling down falling down. London University is rising. I saw Mary Hutch. Jack [Hutchinson] has been defending Compton Mackenzie.[3] Roger [Fry] is off to Tangier because a gentleman of Tangier wants to know whether his grandmother's ceiling is painted by Tiepolo or not—a fact which Roger alone can certify. And of course we go on reading MSS; and of course they are mostly about a man called Eliot; or in the manner of a man called Eliot—how I detest that man called Eliot! Eliot for breakfast Eliot for dinner—thank God Eliot is at Harvard. But why? Come back soon; and write again, to your old humble servant Virginia.

Ella Strong Denison Library, Scripps College, Claremont, California

2697: TO ETHEL SMYTH   [52 *Tavistock Square, W.C.1*]

Thursday [19 January 1933]

Well Ethel dear I'm awfully sorry, and yet rather glad too. I like people to die with dignity standing up, as Mary did.[4] And I'm not such a fool as to deny the strength of affections—the strongest perhaps the MOST secret—stealing out in dreams, or coming, like yours for her, when you say you dont feel it. But isn't it a mercy she is quit of dying standing after all these months? I had that impression of her very deeply—the last time I saw her was the day before her sale, when she was sitting at her table (about to be sold) and didn't know me, but received me, of course, like a Queen, and then suddenly smiled and said "Oh Mrs Woolf! Do sit down. Such a pleasure to see you."—Well, I call that, the day before one's sale a very fine attitude.

1. For the Cabots, see p. 71, note 2; Ellery Sedgwick (who married Mabel Cabot), 1872-1960, Editor of *The Atlantic Monthly*, 1908-38; and perhaps one of the four socially prominent sons of Roger Woolcott, formerly Governor of Massachusetts and benefactor of Harvard University.
2. James Stephens, the Irish poet, an incurable chatterbox.
3. Compton Mackenzie, the novelist, was charged at the Old Bailey on 12 January with an infringement of the Official Secrets Act in his war-time memoirs *Greek Memories*. He pleaded guilty, and was fined £100.
4. Ethel's sister, Mary Hunter, died in poverty, having lived very extravagantly and been declared bankrupt in May 1931, when Virginia attended the sale of her possessions.

She was as smart as could be—with a new hat, I should say, beautifully placed, costing at least £10.10. and the chairs and tables all ticketed round her. Oddly enough I passed her house today. But no more. and live to be 100 at least please

V.

Berg

2698: To V. Sackville-West   52 *Tavistock Square, [W.C.1]*

Jan 24th 1933

Yes, dearest Creature, I did write to you [letter 2694] but I called you Nicolson, and did not say forward; so you may not have got it. As it was the very most passionate letter I ever wrote, and the loveliest and wittiest what a pity. (This is trusting you never got it.)

You wrote to me from the high seas. How like you—to have waves 80 miles high, and to stand on the Bridge with the Captain [of the *Bremen*].

Now the point of you is that everything is like you—thats very profound. Here it is freezing, sneezing. You knew we had June last month—well, all the roses will be burnt by frost. Leonard is always talking about his buds. And the pipes are frozen here, and when I've had my bath Nelly [Boxall] and I have to bale it down the w.c. filling a pail with a tumbler. Heaven be praised, the w.c. is not yet frozen; but tomorrow the pipes will burst. I tell you all this to bring you in touch with England. I daresay you're eating clams on a skyscraper at this moment—5:30 on Tuesday evening, the time you should be with me. And we wasted our last evening. I raging against Eddy [Sackville West], you very honourably upholding him. Did you ever discuss it with him? I've not seen him since; nor ever shall, I daresay, for I cant maneuvre my friends tempers.

They're all dying, my friends—only Mrs Hunter, I mean, and George Moore and Alan Parsons[1]—none of them my friends, but the air is full of funerals, and old Ethel is in the highest glee.

She was here, pounding the arm of the chair the other night, and I said Wont you be late for Mrs Hunter? Dont care if I am said Ethel. At last I packed her off, and Mrs. Hunter died 10 minutes after she got there. I'm rather pleased; she was such a time dying, and yet, if one has to die—as they say—I like her drinking champagne on yellow satin as well as anyway.

1. George Moore, the novelist, died on 21 January; and Alan Parsons (1889-1933), formerly a civil servant, and later dramatic critic of the *Daily Mail*, died on 15 January.

I am writing all the morning: and I like writing; but you wont much care for it. Never mind. Oh and tonight theyre dancing Orlando on the ice,[1] and I shant be there. Its a remarkable fact—the whole British peerage says they descend from the Courtiers I invented, and still have the snow boots which they wore on the frost which I invented too. Its all true, every word of it.

They charge 30/- a ticket, and I would willingly have gone and hired skates if you'd have come. But now my porpoise no longer crowns the fishmongers shop—thats a quotation from the Scholar-Gypsey.[2]

Dotty (excuse this leaping and jumping—I have to dine out) has given up the Poets Series[3]—I'm afraid she's grumpy, but oh dear, I cant smooth out all her grumps and glooms. She should be mated with a stallion and pour her humours down that sink, And the Press badly wants a filip of some sort. Shall you have your new novel ready for October?—its about America;[4] and it has a storm at Sea. We've had an American—head of Macmillans—here today.[5] Thats my boast. Oh I must boast, for I cant bear to think of all you're doing and seeing, and I not there, and I not there! Please, please, write down every scrap for me; you know how not a tassel on a table or a stain on a mat comes amiss. And how I miss you! You wouldn't believe it. I want coloured windows, red towers, moats and swans, and one old Bull walking up and down an empty stable: you, in short. But you dont want me. You are enchanting, chiefly with the glamour of your title and the glow of your pearls, all the Coons in Canada. Tell me that too: about the white soft women and their blazing eyes. I wish I couldn't see them so clearly couched on glittering frosty grass with the daughter of The Sackvilles.

Now I must dress. We are dining in Addison Road with the Laskis. Who is Mrs Laski?[6] What shall I say to her? And the pipes are frozen.

1. "A Gawdy on the Frozen Thames" (but actually on the Grosvenor House ice-rink) was organised by Lord Riddell, Lady Newnes and Lady Burney in recollection of James I's ice-carnival in 1604, described in *Orlando*. Lady Newnes appeared in an ice-sleigh as Queen Anne of Denmark, and there were skating ballets performed by debutantes.
2. Matthew Arnold—but of course it was not a quotation.
3. The *Hogarth Living Poets* series which Dorothy Wellesley had edited and subsidised since 1928.
4. Vita's next novel was *The dark island*, 1934, which was not about America. But in 1942 she wrote *Grand Canyon*, which was.
5. The President of Macmillan's Publishing Company, New York, was then George Brett (1858-1936).
6. Harold Laski (1893-1950) was Professor of Political Science at the London School of Economics from 1926 until his death. In 1911 he had married Frida Kerry, the daughter of a Suffolk landowner, against the strong opposition of his parents to so early a marriage.

Hail and Farewell—that was the one book of G.M's[1] I admired wholly.
Write to me—write.

V.

Its today—and we dined with the Laskis and I didn't like her, or Mr Saxon
or Harper [*unidentified*], or the dinner or the drinks and I'm so cold, and
the pipes are still frozen.

Berg

2699: TO ETHEL SMYTH   52 T.[*avistock*] S.[*quare, W.C.*1]

Friday [27 January 1933]

Well, dame Ethel, I've only got 5 minutes before we start. Lord the
cold! But the new car is sealed like a Pulman—I feel ever so rich, conservative, patriotic, religious and humbuggish when I drive in it. and I enjoy
this new Virginia immensely. She's one of the nicest people I know, and
would love a party at Lady Roseberys above everything.

I thought your letter in the D.T. very good.[2] Did they cut it? Anyhow
it was given the front row of the stalls, as it deserved. When is the F.G.
[*Fete Galante*] to be given? Not till June?

As you were abusing old G M [George Moore] he died. I rather regret
him. I liked his incorruptible conscience in art, combined with the corruption
of all the rest. And—oh I'm so cold—but I shall bring back your warmer—
I cant remember to boil it—I've not the right temperament for your boiler
—and I went into a great shop and bought a coat and a leather jacket so
that I'm rigged up and look like Nansen discovering the Pole. Well, one
day you'll see me discovering Coign [Ethel's house at Woking].

Yr
V.

L's mother is still very ill, but at 83 she entirely refuses to die, and so they
say, will persist in living[3]

Berg

1. George Moore published his autobiography in three parts, *Ave* (1911), *Salve*
   (1912) and *Vale* (1914), which he called collectively *Hail and Farewell*.
2. Ethel's letter in the *Daily Telegraph* of this date complained that a performance
   of Gilbert and Sullivan's opera *The Mikado* had been played too fast.
3. Leonard's mother did not die until 1939.

Typewritten
27th Jan 1933

Dear Mr Brace,

It was very kind of you to tell me about the sales of the Common Reader with you. I think we have sold almost exactly the same number here. We feel quite satisfied, as the sale of that kind of book is very limited, and no books are doing well over here. I hope to send you a short and simple little book [*Flush*] soon—that is if my husband thinks it successful. It is by way of a joke. And then I want to get to work on a longer novel.

I hope things are doing well, or better, with you. The slump seems to be telling on our publishing more now than before.

With best wishes,
yours sincerely,
Virginia Woolf

Harcourt Brace Jovanovich

29th January 1933

Dearest Dadie,

It is angelic of you to ask us, but alas, we can't manage the 18th week-end, and days in the week are impossible for L. But we propose coming up [to Cambridge] book selling one day this term. May we let you know? But aren't you ever in London, also? Please, please, come and dine. There's a mass of things we want to talk about—to wit, your book, the dialogues I mean, and all sorts of other things. Don't tell me you're secretly married to the Head of Girton,[1] like the rest of your friends. L. says our books won't be ready in time to advertise in the programme.[2]

Love from your attached, if elderly, friends,   Virginia
                                                       and
                                                       Leonard

We have a new car, shaped like a fish, green on bottom, silver on top.

George Rylands

1. A characteristic joke. The Mistress of Girton College, Cambridge, 1931-42, was Helen Wodehouse, a highly respectable woman of 52 who published a number of books of sermons. But two Cambridge friends of Virginia and Rylands had recently married graduates of Girton, Richard Braithwaite and F. L. Lucas, both as second marriages.
2. Rylands was producing a series of plays for the Marlowe Dramatic Society.

[10 February 1933]

No I cant come today—we're going early, to travel books on the way [to Sussex].

Sorry I was so glum. Its nothing but the truth. I'm in a cursed mood and cant bear the human face—so put off coming here, I advise you, as long as possible. Perhaps by the end of the week I shall be thawed—God knows.

V.

I shall listen in.

Berg

Feb. 14th [1933]
(Valentines day but no valentine)

Yes—yes, it was very nice indeed to get your letter "I am just about to dine with the President"[1]—these were the last words of the last chapter. I see you've learnt how to end chapters—rather as if I wrote And now darling Vita, the Prince of Wales being outside in his new streamline car, I'm off to dine with King George—except that nobody, not even a blue snob like myself, could whip up much excitement over that—but do continue your story. What new dress? What did the President say?—and what did you drink?

Now two things have to be said at once before Ethel, who's been lunching at the German Embassy comes in—but I'm afraid I was so huffy on the telephone that she won't. First: I've given, in a generous moment, the MS of A Room of O. O. to the Women's service Club. They want me to sell it for them in America—its to stave off their bankruptcy.[2] If you do in truth speak well of Virginia in Pineappopolis [*invented*], do you think any of the collectors there would buy it? Or what collectors are there? This is a mere question—if it comes your way, ask: but dont conceivably bother.

I've gone and lost the name of the man who wanted to buy Orlando[3] But they say no one buys anything now in the USA.

1. On 27 January Vita and the British Ambassador's wife, Elizabeth Lindsay, dined at the White House with President Hoover, who was succeeded five weeks later by President Franklin D. Roosevelt.
2. Philippa Strachey was Secretary of the Society, which Virginia had addressed on 21 January 1931.
3. See p. 40.

2nd. We have our new car. Isn't it pathetic, the trust of human nature, to think that you'll be interested in that—with Niagara churning at your door and the wolves howling and the Indians chasing each other with tomahawks up and down snow mountains? Call on Brett[1] if you're in Mexico and give her a kiss from me. She's stone deaf, and carries a trumpet wreathed in ribbons but was kissable once on a time. Here the Lawrence lice still propagate. Murry on Carswell on Lawrence[2]—a disgusting pullulation—Finally, Frieda [Lawrence] is going to speak in public herself. No I dont think I can ever look at Lawrence again—they've cheapened him so. Think if I died, and left as my only friends, Logan and that little pimp [Cyril] Connolly: But you won't agree. And I am interrupted.

I was going to say our car has come—silver and green, fluid fly wheel, Tickford hood—Lanchester 18—well what more could you want? It glides with the smoothness of eel, with the speed of a swift, and the—isn't this a good blurb?—the power of a tigress when that tigress has just been reft of her young in and out up and down Piccadilly, Bond Street. The worst of it is we cant live up to it. I've had to buy a new coat. But whats the good? Theres my hat. Thats all wrong—thats a Singer[3] saloon hat.

Lord, I wish you'd come back. Tell me this is your last long voyage—you may take short ones with me when la mer est brusque[4]—which reminds me, I'm learning Italian.[5] Yes, as soon as I can stop writing to you—and I like dribbling on, for then I see a porpoise in a shop window at Christmas and pearls and a pink coat—a jersey was it? —anyhow you wore gaiters, and it was the sight of the gaiters—dont tell this to your audience—that inspired Orlando [on 18 December 1925]—the gaiters and what lies beyond —well: when I can stop I shall learn Andare to go. Its damned irregular. And my teacher is called Bianca, and she teaches me for love, and she's the mistress of Mr Stoop—did you know Big Bertha?[6] She went off in an apoplexy and now Bianca has inherited the pearls. And I dined with Mary [Hutchinson] and she told me all about Charlie James the man milliner who was dropped by Heaven into her hands just as she was sighing one day to Todd[7]—Oh what I want is a young man to devote his life to dressing me.

1. Dorothy Brett, the painter, a daughter of Lord Esher. She had been an intimate friend of Katherine Mansfield and D. H. Lawrence, and followed Lawrence to Taos, New Mexico, where she remained until her death in 1977, aged 93. Vita met her in March, "and gave her your love. She blushed all over. I met her in a crazy household, at a place called Carmel, [California]" (Vita to Virginia, 28 March 1933, *Berg*).
2. See p. 130, note 5.
3. Both their previous cars had been Singers.
4. See Vol. IV of this edition, p. 197, note 2.
5. Virginia was taking Italian lessons twice a week from Bianca Weiss.
6. Bertha and Frank Stoop, art collectors and patrons of music.
7. Dorothy Todd, the former Editor of *Vogue*.

This Charlie does in Ryder Street—Her new dress is like that cold dish at Fortnums all white with black dice, or like Christabel's[1] hall, or like anything that's symmetrical, diabolical and geometrically perfect. So geometrical is Charlie James that if a stitch is crooked, Vita, the whole dress is torn to shreds: which Mary bears without wincing though she has to dine with Diana [Cooper], which seeing Charlie comes to Albert Road with a white cat (in rubber) as a gift. This is my smartest piece of gossip. It wont interest you; but then I should get it all wrong if I told you about the primulas and the perifoneums, and how the peach has put out 3 inches of bud since we were last in Sussex—last week end that is. Its a very fine cold bright spring day here, and my being is troubled with all those vague desires which— oh I think—yes I know—yes it is—Ethel. Oh my God on the contrary it was Leonards new suit I think

So farewell.

No, there's no news. Have you seen Tom Eliot? Are you worn to a bone? How's Harold? Which of you is the favourite? Do send me some cuttings describing you. What sort of looking place is Virginia? And the Blacks? Lady Cunards house was burnt—by Nancy some say.[2] Raymond is much as usual. Clive has gone to Jamaica Dont ask if he's alone; or if not with whom. Roger's gone to Tangier; Vanessa to Charleston—London is so silent one sometimes hears a man blow his nose in Kensington High Street —which reminds me, this house may be pulled down next year; and we may flit this very March, to Gordon Square: so it may be you'll never see me again sitting surrounded by my pictures. I'll tell you. The D of Bedford has refused us once more; just as I had been with a measuring tape round 15 rooms, 3 wcs and 2 bathrooms[3]—God damn the dukes—David Cecil came here with Rachel—very happy, thats enough; how one thing leads to another.

So love and farewell.

V.

Vado, vai va andiamo, andate vanno. Is that right? Scott Johnson going [from the Hogarth Press]; poor depressed woman, not much as a manager though a heart of gold.

Love to Sibyl Colefax when you meet her at White House

Berg

1. Christabel McClaren, whose husband succeeded as the 2nd Lord Aberconway in 1934, She was a patron of the arts and had a salon in Mayfair.
2. Lady (Emerald) Cunard, the American hostess who was the intimate friend of George Moore. Nancy was her daughter, who ran the Hours Press in Paris.
3. Virginia had been viewing 35 Gordon Square, with the idea of leasing it from the Bedford Estate. But the Woolfs remained in 52 Tavistock Square until 1939.

Tuesday Feb 14th [1933]

Dearest Ottoline,

I'm so sorry to hear through that old wild cat Ethel Smyth, that you're ill again and going into a home. What a bad time of it you've had this winter! Will they cure you? I do hope so. I should have written but lapsed into complete lethargy and assumed that every one was in the same state—with the exception of Ethel Smyth of course, whose conduct is that of a very large moth in a room with a lamp. I write this expecting her any moment— She's been lunching with the German ambassador and had hoped to lunch with you. I tried to shunt her on to Molly [MacCarthy], and hope she didn't reach you in person.

Well this is only by way of meeting you in the street and waving and passing on. You mustn't bother to write. I wish I had anything amusing to send you. English literature, though I can read the least scrawl of any old char so long as its not fiction—which alas it generally is—seems at its worst and weakest at the moment. I wish I could read in the Times Lit Sup Lady Ottoline Morrell's memoirs in 5 vols will be out on Tuesday next. Then I should sit on a campstool with a thermos flask and a bag of oranges outside Bumpus [bookshop] all night. Have you done the Garsington Chapter? Murry's last spurt of oil and venom and other filth seemed to me his foulest.[1] What does Frieda say of it all? I heard you were in your red cloak divinely beautiful in the Courtyard of the Brit. Museum the other day with a short stout lady who turned out to be Frieda—I see Frieda finally is to lecture on Lawrence after which I think the government should declare partridge shooting ends. Does it?

I am trying to learn Italian, and trying to write, and trying to believe that (I cant think how this sentence was going to end)—here I was interrupted by a surveyor. In two weeks we shall know if they're going to pull this house down. I've been househunting too; but the Duke [of Bedford] always says at the last moment I wont have vans at the door, and off we go again.

                                                                                    VW

Texas

2705: To Vanessa Bell   52 *Tavistock Sqre, [W.C.1]*

Sunday [19 February 1933]

Well dearest Dolphin—not that you deserve to be called so, considering your hardness to a tender request of mine the other night. Still you dont

1. *Reminiscences of D. H. Lawrence* by John Middleton Murry, 1933.

mind me so much in writing as in fact. The truth is, I suspect, you dont read. What with one thing and another I daresay you haven't what you call opened a book this six weeks. But I'm so bored with Italian irregular verbs—and then I have such a passion for you—Yes, its rather a case of Ethel Smyth and me over again. Once more she's gone off in a dudgeon, because she says I'm so cold. But in fact I almost died last Friday. Its like being a snail and having your brain cracked by a thrush—hammer, hammer, hammer; and she pulls her chair up to an inch of my nose, and she's getting deaf as a post—and there I had to sit for 2 hours and more. I gather she's going to be diddled again by the Camargo [Ballet]; but I cant make head or tail of it.

We've seen a great many old friends for some reason—Desmond, Morgan [Forster] and so on. I call it the homing of the rooks: we're all settling on the trees. But the Rook Desmond was in great spirits, chiefly I think because he was about to prevent the Rachel David marriage—that is he thought it hopeless—and had arranged with Cynthia Asquith[1] to tell David to go—but at the last moment he was too lazy to settle the matter, and so didn't tell Cynthia; and so one night he came in late and there was David engaged to Rachel. But the wedding cost him over £250. Rachel had to go to the dentist; they all lost their heads and bought too many new clothes: then there was a lunch party with sandwiches on the sideboard and champagne: and so Desmond has never been quite so poor in his life as he is at the moment: Morgan also was in high feather, because he's never enjoyed anything so much as writing Goldie's life.[2] Therefore I propose to die next year, and you must oblige the year after. And we've been asked to a party at Lady Astor's to meet the Prince of Wales. I do hope they haven't asked all Bloomsbury, because then I cant mention it.

It is a wet winter day—no, its dry, but the snow is so thick on my skylight it might be rain. Oh dear when shall I see you? Never. Because I suppose we must go to Rodmell on Friday. I wanted to go to Angelica with you. Can it be arranged? I suppose not. Such is life. Then you'll retire for another fortnight, and so we go on. But you dont mind. I mean nothing to you, as Ethel says, Except what Pinka [dog] means. Poor old lady—she has the rheumatism at the base of the spine, and cant sit down, or stand up. and naturally therefore accuses me of being a fish, since I can swim. And on Tuesday we go to tea with Harry and Ba:[3] but I shant tell you about it unless you answer this. I'm dropped by the [Ethel] Sands'—but on the

1. Cynthia Asquith (1887-1960) was the daughter of the 11th Earl of Wemyss and March, and married Herbert Asquith, second son of the Prime Minister. She was a friend of D. H. Lawrence and Ottoline Morrell.
2. Forster's life of Goldsworthy Lowes Dickinson, the Cambridge humanist, was published in 1934.
3. Harry and Barbara Stephen (née Nightingale). He was Virginia's cousin, and had been a Judge in Calcutta until 1914.

whole, as it would mean buying part at least of a new dress, I bear up, and shall ask Nan [Hudson] to tea, and so plant a fiery feather in Ethel's flank. Nelly is in a huff with Leonard about getting breakfast punctual. Lottie[1] is installed of course; the Bedford Estate never cease surveying this house, but so far we haven't heard anything; and I cant think of much else to say, except that I'm passionately in love with a woman who treats me like an old glove in the gutter—oh and I've got to be photomatoned[2] tomorrow— and I washed my head, and my hair is in my eyes, and Nessa never writes to me, or thinks of me—Lord Lord, what a farce life is, a passing of phantoms, a crowing of cocks—we ought to be at Cambridge at this moment— so there are some mercies remaining

Please kiss Quentin, as you wont kiss me.

B.

Berg

2706: To Vanessa Bell   [52 *Tavistock Square, W.C.*1]

[23 February 1933]

Yes. delighted to dine with you (this is because you'll never come to us) on Friday wh. is tomorrow at 7.30 about. No I think I did very well out of the show,[3] and only wish I'd got my screen. Curse Duncan for letting it go.

Addio carissima sorella mia

Berg

2707: To Lady Ottoline Morrell
                                    52 *Tavistock Square, W.C.*1
Feb. 23rd [1933]

Dearest Ottoline,

Yes do say when you're back—Come round in the owling time or let me come. I recovered, down at Rodmell—the dr seems to think I needn't faint ever again, unless I'm rash. And I am writing, but a dull book this time, I think. Never mind—it keeps me bubbling like a very small but cheerful black kettle. Flush is only by way of a joke. I was so tired after the Waves, that I lay in the garden and read the Browning love letters, and

1. Lottie Hope had worked for the Woolfs as a parlourmaid between 1916 and 1924.
2. Photographed in a booth where the sitter takes her own photograph.
3. The party-exhibition which Virginia and Vanessa gave on 30 November 1932.

the figure of their dog made me laugh so I couldn't resist making him a Life. I wanted to play a joke on Lytton—it was to parody him. But then it grew too long, and I dont think its up to much now. But this is all very egotistical.

I was talking about you twice yesterday—once to Bianca Weiss who teaches me Italian—and says she taught you; Bianca she called herself, and was, and is, somehow attached to the Stoops: second, I talked to Duncan about you. And really I dont think you would have been ashamed. No I think you should have been behind the door. What we admired, we said, was your outrageous passion for—is it life? art? Anyhow we said that woman is a great liver:—and think how seldom talkers talk to one's advantage! No, I wouldn't like to overhear my friends on me. Please finish Garsington [her memoirs]; and let yourself flow, and dont tidy up stragglers. You cant think what a joy to me your unpruned dew wet moon lit phrases are—and then that fishing foxhunting Duke [of Portland] thinks he can take a carving knife and cut off the thorns!

yr VW

Texas

2708: To Mrs Norman Grosvenor

52 Tavistock Square, W.C.1

25th Feb 1933

Dear Mrs Grosvenor,[1]

It is delightful of you to write to me, and I'm so glad that you call me Virginia! I always remember my father taking me to dine with you. I think it was the first time I dined out in evening dress, and I was very shy. I could still tell you what we talked about. My father I think had a special affection for you, and I know it was a great pleasure to him to see you in those years when he was very lonely. I'm so glad you liked what I wrote about him in The Times [on 28 November 1932]. I found it very difficult to say anything and feared it was not much like him. And I am so glad too that you like my Common reader articles—it seems rather foolish to write articles about books sometimes—but at anyrate I shall remember that you like them.

Please give my love to Susie and thank you again for writing.

Your affate
Virginia Woolf

Lady Tweedsmuir

1. Caroline Grosvenor (*née* Stuart-Wortley) married the third son of Lord Ebury, and was active in women's causes until her death in 1940. She was also a novelist and painter in water-colours. Her daughter Susan (mentioned in the last line) married John Buchan, the novelist, who was created Lord Tweedsmuir in 1935.

52 *T[avistock] S[quare. W.C.*1]

Monday [27? February 1933]

Dearest Ottoline,

Wonderful woman—to have gone to Woolworth and retrieved these machines![1] A thousand thanks. I'm sitting as neat as a coot at this moment, Leonard having mastered the principle. No, no, I had no intention of letting any Italian curl or frizz me, only in the desert of Bianca (who's a good woman, but shouldn't stay so long or depart from Italian grammar,) I let my fancy play with hair. I never seriously dream of being tidy, and for Gods sake remain as you are, and let us hold hands, in unity, untidy. It was my fault, muddying the waters with Bianca, and I've no more intention of falling into the Brett[2] snare than of being curled by the Queen's hairdresser. As a matter of fact, Brett is the vaguest dream to me—I scarcely see her in colours at all; and she will fade completely—except that I like to think of your insect with the long nose.

Please come again soon and mount on your pinions.

I've been listening to Jelly[3] playing Bach in the [Westminster] Abbey; but the crowd was too great, and the violin took in gulps of air.

yrs V

Shall I send you ear-stoppers? I always use them.[4]

Texas

52 *Tavistock Square, W.C.*1.

28 Feb: [1933]

Enclosed cheque for Angelica.

Hope to see you some time, but you must let us know.

L. has a bad cold from the wetting in the snow. Tommie[5] came in last night, and I'm taking him to the Cranium[6]—if indeed we go—I rather dread so much inspissated male virtue—not altogether my line, Quentin must kiss me. I went to the Stoops[7] today—what a queer little Dutch weather clock couple they are—He showed me all the pictures from top to bottom

1. For waving or curling hair.
2. See p. 157, note 1.
3. Jelly d'Aranyi who, with her sister Adela (Fachiri), were the two most famous Hungarian violinists of their day.
4. As an aid to sleep.
5. Stephen Tomlin, the sculptor.
6. The convivial society founded by David Garnett in 1925.
7. See p. 157, note 6.

—Lord knows I can't say the right things. Bianca [Weiss] sways the footmen with complete composure. I rather like her—with her hat off, she's rather a figure. But its an endless circle of Chelsea magnates—she lunches out daily. Last night I saw Ethel [Sands] and Nan at a distance—at a distance Ethel was cordiality itself, but no invitations. I shant tell you any more news, or you wont come and see me

B.

Berg

2711: To Ethel Smyth   52 *T.*[*avistock*] *S.*[*quare, W.C.*1]

1st March [1933]

Yes, after you left the other night I was certain that you had decided never to see me again. Perhaps I'm right. After all, there are tides in the affairs of men—an ebb and a flow: why should not the tide of Ethel recede, there, from the hall, that night, in the gaslamps, with the taxis drifting by, and the ruby light from the restaurant cloaking it—our friendship—in flowing purple? Why do these moments, all draped and aparelled, overwhelm me so completely? and then recede? To witness tonight, when again perhaps I think Ethel was not so completely damned towards me—I mean the crack was not so complete—as I thought. And so, instead of dreaming in my chair I write almost as dreamily. Lord I've forgotten everything, everybody A chrysalis must feel as I do. You know how their tails twitch—well mine just does that tonight. It is the cold, the spring. Oh we were caught in a storm on Friday and came back to London, with our windows thick in ice and a car loomed up; we almost crashed—rather beautiful it was, crossing the river.

But this is all very remote. Do you die as I do and lie in the grave and then rise and see people like ghosts? And all my friends are dead—Gwendolen Cecil,[1] one of my first: and then I never went to lunch when she asked me. You know, life is too multitudinous: I feel I've been living ever since there was a crocodile in the Nile.

To come down to this very instant, what are you doing? Bath? And what about Mrs Jones and the letters.[2]

Oh but you're angry with me—won't write—I got the most startling conviction of that in the hall—

1. Lady Guendolen Cecil (*née* Godolphin), a daughter of the Duke of Leeds and niece of Nelly Cecil. In 1923 she married Algernon Cecil, the historian. She died on 25 February 1933.
2. Alice Jones (1878-1970), formerly Leonard's assistant on the *Nation*, and Philip Morrell's secretary during the First War, was typing Henry Brewster's letters for Ethel Smyth.

Well, well, anyhow I send you my blessing in whatever world you may be. I suppose a very vigorous world—unlike mine.

Dont write unless you want to.

V.

I'm making a shot at your address.

Berg

2712: To Jonathan Cape   52 *Tavistock Square, W.C.1*

Typewritten
3rd March 1933

Dear Mr Cape,

I am sorry to hear that Mr Gissing objects to my introduction.[1] I have a vague recollection that he wrote to me when the introduction first appeared[2] and said that I had exaggerated his father's lack of education—or something of the kind. But I did not gather that he objected to the article as a whole; and he certainly did not ask me to alter it or suppress it. Nor did he write to me when I reprinted it in the Common Reader a few months ago.

From what you say I gather that his objections must be much stronger than I realised. And until I see what they are I cant of course say whether I can answer them or not, Certainly I meant no disrespect to his father— and I dont think that any impartial person who read my article would think so. If he should write to the papers, I will see what steps I can take and let you know.

Yours sincerely
Virginia Woolf

Jonathan Cape Ltd.

2713: To Lady Cecil   52 *Tavistock Square*
[*Monk's House, Rodmell, Sussex*]

March 4th [1933]

My dear Nelly,

I have been thinking so much about you and Guendolen.[3] Do you remember asking me to meet her hundreds of years ago at Grove End Road?

1. A. C. Gissing took exception to Virginia's Introduction to *Ionian Sea*, by his father George Gissing (1857-1903), which Cape republished in 1933.
2. In the *Nation & Athenaeum*, 26 February 1927.
3. See p. 164, note 1.

We sat on the sofa in the window with the trees outside. What an exquisite and enchanting human being she was! And she was just as lovely, a few years ago when I met her somewhere. It was a peculiar charm, so gentle, and yet so acute. I wish I had seen more of her—one always wishes that.

But this is only a line to say how sorry I am. She always talked so much about you—years ago I mean when she was quite a girl—about staying with you; about your goodness to her.

Dont bother to write.

As a matter of fact, though I say Tavistock Square, we're at Monks House this weekend. And I say its the first spring evening—one can walk up and down the garden path after tea—thats my definition of spring.

Please let me come and see you some day.

yr aff

V.W.

Marquess of Salisbury (Cecil Papers)

2714: To Ethel Smyth   52 *T[avistock] S.[quare, W.C.1]*

March 12th [1933]

You are such a kind hearted woman that my little defalcations in not writing, dont matter Nor do I bear you a grudge for having left a stout umbrella here. Rose Macaulay[1] left gloves and a brooch. I am feeling content at the moment—At twelve today we started for Ivinghoe Beacon;[2] and I had an hours walk in some silent green beech woods; and a great fox got up; and there was not a sound in all the world. Its a lovely valley, open, very classical. The way the trees grow, in groups, makes me think of Virgil. And so home, with even the Bye Pass Road glorified in the spring, which is hot enough to have peeled the skin off my nose. Lord, how lovely England is! if one could take a carving knife and cut off the villas. I'm practising a surgical eye, which shaves landscapes till they are as they were in Chaucer's day. I allow only 300 year old houses, mules, and waggons. Its not so difficult, if you make a habit of it.

I am too sleepy and too contented to write a better letter. I cant tell you about my Princess even—a stolid idol looking woman—Patricia Ramsay[3]—who could only move this way and that: unjointed, like a vast doll. Poor woman! She let me tease her about being royal for an hour. "We

1. The novelist and essayist, 1881-1958.
2. In the Chiltern Hills, near Tring.
3. Lady Patricia Ramsay (b. 1886), a daughter of the Duke of Connaught, and grand-daughter of Queen Victoria. She renounced her title "Princess" on her marriage to Admiral Sir Alexander Ramsay in 1919.

are all very shy" she said; "but the others are small. I'm an elephant"—but she hadn't the protruding eyes, as I told her.

I am trying to write and trying to read and trying to keep a steady head among parties. Lady Rhondda[1] has cropped up again. I liked her book—an honest woman, I should say; but not subtle. Oh dear me, how can I write this letter? I'm burning all over—I'm sleepy: and yet, here I swear it shall go to the City on the 7 hills.[2] Tell me about Lawrence. I never meant to say a sweeping thing about him—indeed I'm sure of his 'genius'; what I distrust is the platform; I hate the "I'm right" pose in art. But Lord, I've read so little; and his fame is a muddy river, trampled by oxen and pigs. Ottoline ended, I think, by finding Mrs D.H.L. a lump—but then there's an old sore; as with most of O's friends. She writes me vast letters on violet scented paper, contorted, but to me pathetic, like the flight of owls on a hot day—so unsteady, topheavy, furtive, ill judging, but in their way beautifully balanced

Yes I will write again, more fully?

Yr V

Berg

2715: TO FREDERICK B. ADAMS

52 *Tavistock Square, W.C.*1

Typewritten
14th March 1933

My dear Mr Adams,

You have no reason at all to apologise for your charming letter which gave me great pleasure.

I am very glad to think that you share my sympathy for Flush. The idea came to me that he deserved a biography last summer when I was reading the Browning letters. But in fact very little is known about him, and I have had to invent a good deal. I hope however that I have thrown some light upon his character. —the more I know him, the more affection I feel for him. The dog who acted his part here was black—but there can be no doubt that Flush was red.

I do not know what to say about selling the MS. I had not thought of it—indeed I have never sold any of my MSS. I do not know what it is worth. Perhaps the best plan therefore would be if you would say what you would give—I dont know how else to settle it. I think the book is about 30,000 words in length. I write my books in paper covered volumes, and re-write

1. The Editor of *Time and Tide*, the journal which she founded in 1920. She had just published her autobiography, *This was my World*.
2. Bath, where Ethel was staying for five weeks.

them a good deal in typescript. But the manuscript is of course the foundation for the final version; and I have only one manuscript.[1] Harcourt Brace will publish the book, probably this summer.

I must also thank you for your appreciation of my other books—I am very glad that you like them.

I think my father, Leslie Stephen, must have known some of your family in America.

Believe me,
yours sincerely
Virginia Woolf

Frederick B. Adams Jr.

2716: To Ethel Smyth   [52 *Tavistock Square, W.C.1*]

Thursday [16 March 1933]

Yes a first rate article[2]—very supple—sonorous and shooting its shafts this side and that till the old brute is fairly lit up. Very good indeed I think. I envy you your use of the vernacular—so free—springy: and certain words—'wrath—' in that connection give me a little rasp of pleasure:[3] wrath is perfect; anger, wrong. And I kept saying what word'll she use there (I'm writing in a rush and cant remember how the sentence went) Oh yes very good indeed, the airiness and solidity mixed: I like corners to figures: your Brahms one might stub one's toe against.

I should leave out 'the heart' in the last sentence;[4] seems to me the rhythm is more direct, and strong—(as its a high note this is important) unencumbered.

So sorry I'm too sleepy to write, but I've had a long day

V.

Berg

1. Mr Adams (director of several American railroad corporations), 1878-1961, did not buy the manuscript of *Flush*, which is today in the Berg Collection, New York. Instead, he bought some corrected typescript pages of *Orlando*.
2. *Recollections of Brahms*, which Ethel first wrote for the *London Mercury* on the centenary of Brahms's birth, 7 May 1833, and later republished in *Female Pipings in Eden*. She had known him well in Leipzig in the 1880s.
3. "Frau Schumann failed to do him [Wagner] justice. But who cared? What mattered was the quality of the phrase forged in the molten lava of her wrath." (*Female Pipings*, p. 66).
4. "The heart" does not occur in the last sentence of the published article.

Monks House, [Rodmell, Sussex]

March 18th 1933

Well, do you remember me? I wrote you a very long and passionate letter the other day, but stuck it in my case, forgot it, left it, and found it so out of date—it was all about earthquakes and banks failing[1]—that I can't send it. How difficult it is to write, with all the spring birds singing and the garden full of blue and white crocuses—We've been walking on the downs at Falmer.[2] The woods there are like Greek horses manes—d'you know the look? brushed, red, brisk—oh so lovely at this moment. I only wish I were a poet, so that I could describe a team of brown horses ploughing red brown earth, and a grove of trees reflected in a great pond there is there under the church, with two swans swimming: you must write it for me.

To turn to Americans—your horror, the publisher, is coming alas. There's no sense in it, since I've no plans to share with Houghton Mifflin;[3] still if come he must, he must come. Anyhow I owe you that at least—I'll ask Sibyl [Colefax] to meet him—after your all too noble efforts about my MS.[4] I never meant you to trouble to write—only to suggest a name. Anyhow it is obviously hopeless at the moment. Oddly enough an American Adams wants to buy the MS. of Flush—that foolish witless joke with which I solaced myself when I was all a gasp having done The Waves. (You remember that very bad book?)

I saw Sibyl the other day; and she had seen Harold, and Harold had said you are a roaring raging success; which, I said, dont matter a straw with Vita. She'll shake her coat, and the grease and the oil will run down her. A great compliment to you. Shall you net anything after all—with the dollar collapsed?—There'll be the experience, as they call it—all those virgins you've ravished—teas you've eaten, shrines you've visited, fat old women you've intoxicated. I liked the maid's letter—but what a very cultured woman to have had darning one's stockings!

You know Sibyl is naturally, congenitally, an American. She can hardly tolerate the lowness of London houses, the age of the earth, any longer. But I doubt that worldliness pays—I never saw anyone so suspicious. I cut one of my silly jokes, and she takes umbrage, like a dog—I mean, you

1. Vita's lecture tour coincided with a grave economic crisis in America, and at one time there was talk of cancelling the tour itself. She and Harold were now in California.
2. Between Lewes and Brighton.
3. Harold Nicolson's American publisher. The managing director was Roger L. Scaife (1875-1951), who in 1934 became President of the Boston publishing house, Little, Brown. He was the author of several books including *What Daddies Do, Muvver and Me,* and *Cape Coddities.*
4. Of *A Room of One's Own.* See p. 156.

know how huffy dogs look if you laugh at them. So do women of the world. Oh but I'm going that way myself. Who is my latest friend? A Princess of the Blood royal—poor stuck Patricia [Ramsay], as large, impassive unjointed as a doll made all of china. D'you know I had to talk to her for an hour, and asked her all sorts of questions about being Royal and why she hadn't married the King of Spain. She balanced herself like a vast idol, slowly sweeping her eyes round the room—this was at a party given by the Queen's secretary in Duncans studio.[1] And I was asked to meet the Prince of W.— but I think, in my effort to keep up with your triumph, I told you that before. No, I said, I wont.

Please Vita darling come back soon. We shall be off in the car to Italy if you dont—we want to try the fluid fly wheel on the Alps. Please come snuffing up my stairs soon, just the same, in your red jersey. Please wear your pearls. Please bring Sarah [dog]. And then ask me to Sissingt. Lord, how you'll love your first night there and sun rise seen from the pink Tower! Write to me.

V.

I think Italian is frightfully difficult—to speak. Bianca is not your Bianca; but Weiss.

Berg

2718: To V. Sackville-West   52 *Tavistock Square, W.C.*1

March 21st [1933]

Oh dear I forgot to post this again—too many people—my dear Dadie [Rylands] for 2 hours made me all in a rush, you'll like to hear.

Your nice letter all about Burlington Barbie has just come. How we roared! And the psychologist on your passions—I could have told that without going into a trance in the W.C.[2]

But here is my business: about the MS [of *A Room . . .*]. I dont know what Pippa Strachey has done. I'll ask her and write and let you know. Sybil, in her great kindness, went to an expert, about the MS of Flush; and the expert says that that ms. is worth £1,000—I doubt it. But I'll write as soon as I hear.

Also: can you give us any private information about a woman called Ivy (I think) Davison?[3] She's said to be an old friend of yours, wants a job,

1. By a courtier-friend of Duncan Grant, Timothy Chichester.
2. Vita's letter to Virginia does not survive to explain these two allusions.
3. Editor of *The Geographical Magazine* in the 1940s.

and may be coming to see us about the Press. Please excuse all this bother. Your friend Scaife [of Houghton Mifflin], hell take him, is coming.

So farewell and write soon

V.

Berg

2719: To the Vice-Chancellor,
University of Manchester   52 *Tavistock Square, W.C.*1

Typewritten
26th March 1933

Dear Vice Chancellor,[1]

I need not say how deeply I am honoured by the proposal of the University of Manchester to confer upon me the degree of Doctor of Letters.

I very much regret that I feel myself unable to accept the proposed honour. But, as I have always been opposed to the acceptance of honours, whether civic or academic, by writers, I feel that I should be acting with great inconsistency if I accepted any such honour myself. I am sure that you will understand my point of view.

But I am of course deeply grateful to the Council and Senate for desiring to confer upon me a degree, and to yourself for the kindness with which you have written to me.

Believe me,
yours sincerely
Virginia Woolf
(Mrs Woolf)

University of Manchester

2720: To Shena, Lady Simon   52 *Tavistock Square, W.C.*1

26th March 1933

Dear Lady Simon,[2]

It is extremely kind of you to ask us to stay with you, and nothing would have given us greater pleasure. But, as I have just written to the Vice

1. Sir Walter Moberly.
2. Lady Simon was the daughter of John Potter, a ship-owner, and in 1912 married Ernest Simon, who was knighted in 1932 and in 1947 became the 1st Lord Simon of Wythenshawe (1879-1960). He was widely known as an expert on smoke-abatement, housing, local government and education, particularly in Manchester, where they lived. Lady Simon was his collaborator in all this work, and their partnership has been compared to that of the Webbs.

Chancellor [of Manchester University] I feel that I cannot accept the University's offer to give me a degree because I have always been opposed to honours of all kinds, for writers, and thus feel that I cannot consistently accept one for myself.

I am sure you will understand my point of view, and will believe that I am, all the same, extremely grateful to those who wished to honour me in this way.

One of my chief reasons for regret in refusing is that I shall lose the chance of making your acquaintance. But I hope that this need only be postponed. If you should at any time be in London it would give us great pleasure to see you here. Meanwhile, may I thank you very sincerely for your kindness and generosity?

Yours sincerely
Virginia Woolf

Sussex

2721: To Ethel Smyth   52 *T.*[*avistock*] *S.*[*quare, W.C.*1]

Sunday [26 March 1933]

Well my dear Ethel, this cant even be a spider crawl, because, oh I have written so many letters (one to refuse such an honour as you think one ought to accept[1]—but then you're a base honour corrupted woman—going up to 'honour' women, when the only honour is blue blank air, no more and no less—whats the point of this honour worship? Mumbo Jumbo!) Yes; I'm really only answering your competent fact demanding fingers— about Mrs Braithwaite.[2] Privately, confidentially, I thought it a flimsy flopsy ill written sprawly niggly piece of work—wanted to be shot through a rifle in one bullet—Anyhow, we have stopped that series, at the moment as I said; and the only suggestion that occurs to L. is that she should print it in Cambridge as a pamphlet. That is how it would reach the right quarter. If dissolved in the sea of London nobody would notice it. Moreover 9000 words is an impossible length for any magazine: Desmond MacCarthy would not look at it—he's the only one who prints at length [in *Life and Letters*]. A pamphlet is far more effective—but she ought to shorten, to tighten. And its so damned provincial in tone—another argument in favour of a small printer at Cambridge. But for Gods sake *dont hand on a word* of this: I wrote a polite version to her. She's married an old friend of mine.

1. See preceding letters.
2. Margaret Mary (*née* Masterman), wife of Virginia's old friend, Richard Braithwaite. He was Cambridge University Lecturer in Moral Science, 1928-34. Her pamphlet was never published.

I say what weather! And I'm in such a hurly burly—Lady Rhondda drags me to Hampstead tonight—then there's—oh well, there's the Prince and the Princess [Ramsay]—you shant boast of David [The Prince of Wales] without rousing my little frog chorus. but what a bore, after all, royalty turning Bohemian is—if it werent for the lark once in a way. If you will write, I'll try to.

V.

Berg

2722: To Ethel Smyth   52 *Tavistock Square*, [*W.C.*1]

Thursday 30th March 1933

But I cant possibly write a full account of my life—here I am just in from taking my mother in law round Richmond Park—She has shrunk to the size of a shrew mouse, after her illness, but is still indomitable, and was married 67 years ago tomorrow. After that, now in fact, I must wash, being inkstained mud stained, and dress, which means changing even stockings, and go off in a hansom cab or taxi this wild blowing night to Pall Mall to dine at a Club with an old friend [Saxon Sydney-Turner] who should know better than to ask Americans to meet me—And when asked to choose the dinner I was too shy to say only Pate de foie gras, champagne, mushrooms and chocolate ice, or welsh rarebit. So now about Monday or Tuesday. I've got to spend Tuesday at Bedford, book selling, so thats no good. On Monday I have an Italian lesson (at Hugo's)[1] till 5.30: but shall be back here by 6. Would you like to come say at 6.5? by which time I shall have taken my hat off and lit the fire? If so let me know and come.

Lord Lord, why cant I what is called seize life by the forelock and ride it like a race horse? Why must I eat through a vast incoherent dinner now this instant? Why is it cold, why am I fated to wear silk stockings for the American friends of a friend who is the dumbest man in the world? Why must Leonard put on a dinner jacket and a black tie? I liked old [Lady] Rhondda—but she must have had a fright as a child—nothing else explains her humming and hawing—her indecision, her incapacity; but a nice woman, all the same.

So goodbye

V.

Berg

1. Hugo's Language Institute in Oxford Street.

Monks House, [Rodmell, Sussex]

April 1st 1933 (fools day)

I had a very nice letter from you the other morning, written from top of a mountain, where all the streams run backwards.[1] I deserved it, because while you were seeing the streams, I was seeing Mr Scaife [of Houghton Mifflin]. No I dont think I altogether like Mr Scaife. He's a blotchy looking toad like man, who tells stories about his dog's tricks. However he seemed consumed with admiration for you and Harold, and didn't stay long. He seemed to have an idea that I should write a life of my father. Good God!

This is the month in which you'll come back. That will be very nice I admit. You'll find any number of flowers out—There were 7 days like June, and by looking steadily even in Tavistock Square, one could see little green frills coming out of black iron boughs. This is a fact. Now its blowing a white wind over the downs,—d'you remember how white the fields get about this time? We've been walking over the downs, and then we came in and turned on the loud speaker, heard Cambridge beat Oxford—the boat race. I lost 6d. to Leonard. And the night before we dined at a Club and met 2 diplomats, Called Atherton,[2] Americans, who said they more or less knew you. Lord! I'm glad Harold left the Embassy, or whatever you call it. Quite nice, both of them, but like tin, biscuit tin, empty, shiny. Yet no positive fault to be found. I mean they both seemed very nice people, only you gave a tap—that is I said something very intelligent, and the poor man, who was sleek as a trout, merely brushed his eyes over me, as if I, your most lovable Virginia and Potto, were pebbles at the bottom of a river. How I wish any illusion would abide! After meeting Princess Patricia [Ramsay], I cant any longer pretend, even at midnight when I dream of things I should like to do, that I wish to overhear the Royal family at dinner. Very little therefore remains.

I am going to be painted, stark naked, by a woman called Ethel Walker who says I am the image of Lilith.[3] She has a rough raddled charm, is something like Phil May[4] to look at, has 3 fox terriers, one blind of the right eye, and lives, eats, sleeps, drinks I should say in one room overlooking the river. Swans float practically in at the window. Vast lorries full of tin cans go by—

1. Vita had written to Virginia on 16 March in a train which was crossing the watershed of the Rocky Mountains. (*Berg.*)
2. Ray Atherton, Counsellor of the American Embassy in London, 1927-37.
3. Dame Ethel Walker (1861-1951), a member of the New English Art Club who was much influenced by the French Impressionists. She had a studio in Cheyne Walk, Chelsea. Lilith was an Assyrian-Jewish demon, a screech-owl, who appears in *Isaiah* xxxiv, 14. The portrait was never painted.
4. Phil May (1864-1904), the caricaturist, particularly of London costermonger life.

to Rat Island—d'you remember seeing the tins when we went to the docks [in March 1931]? She is 73—that is the only thing against her; and has lived a regular herring griller's life, which as you know, I love. And I have been to dine with Lady Rhondda, because I liked so much her story of how she swam under water when the Lusitania sank [in 1915]. Why do none of these adventures ever happen to me? But dont take the hint and let them happen to you. No please let this be your last adventure. You cant, as you say, go much further away. Keep a globe in your room at Sisst: and ink your tracks, and then when anyone says anything, you can say But theres nothing I haven't seen: which is true; and then settle on your estates, and preserve the woods, and ride a white horse, and breed dogs, and have me to stay, and write poetry.

We have just passed our publishing season, but nothing has sold violently well. Do you ever read a book on the train? If so, get Livingstons, our monster novel.[1]

Why do they say Italian's easy? Bianca [Weiss] tears her hair because I get my subjunctives wrong and then there are those damned possessive pronouns. Now I must put our dinner to cook; oh why dont you swoop down the road, and draw up at the gate, with a great washing basket full of figs, as you once did, when your mother loved me, and sent me a bottle of vermouth!

So goodbye—
V.

Do do please write us another book as soon as ever you can.

Berg

2724: To Ethel Smyth   52 T.[avistock] S.[quare, W.C.1]

5th April 1933

No time to write—no time. And no brain. I dont think Friday would be worth it—Ottoline is coming at 5.30. and as she's very deaf, poor woman, and I haven't seen her since before Christmas, I've said I will be alone. But we dont go to Rodmell till Thursday week. Why not perhaps one day next week? And we're only there a week; and shall come here between and only be 3 weeks in Italy.—So there are many chances of eliciting whatever it may be. What I call a winkle talk. Now d'you see why?

I've just bought a bath, and now Lord O: is coming, and I have a lesson. I leave Lord: O. to your imagination.[2]

1. *Livingstones: A Novel of Contemporary Life*, by Derrick Leon, published by the Hogarth Press in February. It was over 650 pages long.
2. Lord Olivier, the Fabian Socialist and former Governor of Jamaica, whose four daughters Margery, Brynhild, Daphne and Noel had been friends of Virginia.

I will try to write, but the Italian craze, and so on steal what remains of time—and yesterday we were at Bedford and St. Neots and I'm so sleepy today—so sleepy, so hot, so dreamy so full of emotion that I shall never never be able to express

V.

Typewritten

I will ask L. about the typing, but its really only a question of buying a new ribbon. Tell her; its a shame not; its a dodge they will try to be cheap; but its a damned shame.[1]

Berg

2725: To Ethel Smyth   [52 *Tavistock Square, W.C.*1]

Sunday [9 April 1933]

No Ethel dear, I'm afraid I must put you off till we come back. That is, I've been headachy and L. has now become so testy saying I shall spoil the time at Rodmell that I'm going to be quiet these next 3 days. I daresay he's right. Its been rather a rush—and whats the point of seeing you and not being able to respond? But we come back on 27th and shall have a fortnight before Italy: so come then, quietly and properly. I'll write again. I'm in fact and sincerely, in spite of irreligion sorry about your sister.[2] Lord what sorrows there are in the world
    Please live to 108

                                           Yr
                                             Virginia

Berg

2726: To Hugh Walpole   *Monks House*, [*Rodmell, Sussex*]

Saturday April 15th [1933]

My dear Hugh,
    It was a great pleasure to hear from you—I've heard of you, rather vaguely, from Clive Bell who followed your steps in Jamaica, was always hearing of you, and never seeing you. He says its the one place to live in—

1. Ethel had complained of typing done by Alice Jones: "too brown." She added "You always type when you are furious with me" (4 April 1933, *Berg*).
2. Alice Smyth, who married Harry, brother of the Archbishop of Canterbury, Randall Davidson. Alice died on 1 October 1933, at the age of 82.

but then he had I gather the young, of the other sex, naked, in the cabin—so he says: I begin to throw salt on all these elderly fakes.

Anyhow, I cant find much fault with England at the moment. Its hot, its blue, its green, the flowers are breaking through, about 3 inches a night, the fish are swimming and I have just had the strength of mind to refuse to dine with a rich banker in Lewes.[1] Thus it is inconsistent to say that we're off to Italy for 3 weeks; but then Leonard has bought a new car, with a fluid fly wheel, so we must run it over the Alps. But shant we meet some day soon? Are you rooting in Keswick? No, you must flower at tea in Tavistock Sqre. I've a new carpet to show you.

Oh yes, quote as much as you like of Orlando—I shall be proud. I'm going to read the last Herries,[2] whatever you may say to the contrary. I shall like our own times—its some deficiency of mine that I cant like fiction with a historical date to it. But what I really want is your autobiography, and that must be in 15 not 4 vols. Flush is only a joke—done by way of a lark when I had finished the Waves: but its too long—got out of hand—and not worth the trouble.

I entirely agree about Mr Roberts. But he's convinced himself that the laboured dull idiotic satire is a work of genius.[3] Livingstone's[4] sells more or less: the Press should have made it sell, they praised unanimously, and we still have hopes.

This is merely a croak, like the noise the rooks are making: now I must learn my Italian irregular verbs.

V.W.

Texas

2727: To V. Sackville-West   *Monks House, [Rodmell, Sussex]*

Wednesday [19 April 1933]

I say this is exciting!

You're back[5]—Thank the Lord my porpoise is in the fishmonger's again! But when shall I see her? We are here (Lewes 385) till Sunday after-

1. Sir Eric Hambro (1872-1947), formerly a partner in Hambro's Bank and a Conservative M.P.
2. *Vanessa*, (1933), the last of Walpole's four novels describing a family's history over a period of a century, of which the first volume, *Rogue Herries* (1930), was often regarded as his best book.
3. Michael Roberts, *Non-Stop Variety: The Intellectual Ferment of the Post-War Years*. Published in *New Country: Prose and Poetry by the Authors of New Signatures*. Hogarth Press, March 1933.
4. See p. 175, note 1.
5. Vita and Harold returned from America on 20 April.

noon. Then London for 10 days: then Italy. Could you ring up—dont tell me you've changed your voice too—and suggest any time, which I'll keep even if it means murder.

Ah but you've missed the spring of one thousand years, all gone now. But we sat and roasted—brown as berries—lovelier than any desert sewn with roses and Brett[1] into the bargain

Now you must attend to your world. Lord how I envy you the pink tower after all America

V.

Love and congratulations from us both to Harold.[2]

Berg

2728: TO ETHEL SMYTH

Monks House, [Rodmell, Sussex]

Wednesday 19th April 1933

This is not a letter, only a scrawl, we're off to Brighton about the car. I'm quite recovered; but I've been lying at the bottom of the pool till now; not speaking, reading or writing except when forced. Now its all gone (the headache) thank the Lord. London was the devil before Easter—always is like water rushing down a drain. We come back on Sunday. I dont mean to be swept off my feet again this six months:

What a spring! Yes—what a time, merely sitting in the garden and watching. I heard from Vita last night that she will be back on the 21st—oh but you dont mean to see her, as she'll remind you of the dead, the lost Virginia. I'm amused to be dead—one of those ghosts that people talk of respectfully: rather a dignified position: you can't speak ill of the dead. And the dead dont write letters, but they do read them, at least Ethel's. Yes, I intend to be a dead in future; the dead have so many rights; and what a joy you snubbed Delius,[3] and that the sister said the same here [*unexplained*]. Is it usual for village children to copulate in school? Do ask Ly Betty.[4] Thats what they do here; and the chief village gossip, a lady, sits at her cottage window and observes them through an opera glass. But no time for more

V

Berg

1. Dorothy Brett. See p. 157, note 1.
2. For finishing his book *Peacemaking*.
3. Frederick Delius, 1862-1934.
4. Lady Balfour. See p. 29, note 1.

2729: To Vanessa Bell   *[Monk's House, Rodmell, Sussex]*

[24 April 1933]

Just a line to say wont you seriously consider coming to Siena: starting May 5th back 26th: as my guest? (if you're not too d——d proud)

Please do

B

Berg

2730: To Frederick B. Adams

52 *Tavistock Square, W.C.*1

Typewritten
24th April 1933

Dear Mr Adams,

Many thanks for your letter. Of course you have not 'insulted' me;[1] and I will be perfectly frank with you. As I am as vague as you are about MSS I asked a friend of mine, Lady Colefax, to find out from an expert in MSS what sort of sum the Flush MS would be worth. To my great surprise, he answered, One thousand pounds. This seems to me I admit an absurdly high price. But as the discrepancy is so great between the two I feel myself that it would be better not to attempt to bridge it, but to let the matter rest. But of course if you have any suggestions to make, please dont hesitate to make them.

Anyhow it is a great pleasure to me that you take such an interest in Flush—I only hope you won't be disappointed by the life when it comes out—some time in autumn. May I, though from such a distance, offer my best wishes for your and your wife's happiness?

Yours sincerely
Virginia Woolf

Frederick B. Adams Jr.

2731: To V. Sackville-West   52 *T.[avistock] S.[quare, W.C.*1]

Tuesday [25 April 1933]

Well, Victoria West, here's your horrid little post card.

What I say is come and dine then next Friday? Can you? Only I should

1. By the small sum he offered Virginia for the manuscript of *Flush*. See Letter 2715.

like to see you alone also—Could you come early? Would another time suit better?

I rang you up, all for the sound of your lovely dim voice, like a bird piping through a hawthorn hedge; but heard only buzz buzz buzz. Ring me up, dearest Porpoise West, and say when.

Lord how nice to see the shops pink again!

V.

Berg

2732: To Roger Fry   [52 *Tavistock Square, W.C.*1]

[*First page missing*]
[end April 1933]

. . . . . . predicament, not that I had any lovers, or that if I had they would have suffered from ringworm round the waist.

I met your sister, Margery, the other night—in fact she saved what would have been a most appalling party—dear old Saxon, having grown grey and portly, had taken it into his head to give dinner parties at his Club, not to you and me and Margery, but to the dreariest of dull diplomats, middle aged couples in full evening dress—the lady indeed so bare backed —its the fashion—that had there been a flea on her person, well, one could have caught it. Needless to say, there was not a flea. How women manage to be so exposed, and so clean, and so composed, I cant imagine. Fancy yourself dining out in Pall Mall bare backed. I hope Margery isn't off to the China seas, but she seemed set on it: its the Fry blood: they cant resist natives; I suppose she is going to give them the bible in some form or other.

And you have become a professor,[1] which is of course another form of the same disease. How will you carry out your duties without disgrace?

The latest news in the art world is that Mr Glyn Philpotts has been asked to remove his picture from the R.A. because it represents Satan joining two lovers with his hoof, and might give rise to unpleasant ideas.[2] Nessa and Duncan are, as you may have heard, rising rapidly in the social world; so much so, that having entertained Princess Patricia [Ramsay], they now dine out, even in Lewes high street, with Lord Edward Gleichen.[3] It all

1. In March 1933 Roger Fry was appointed Slade Professor of Fine Art at Cambridge University.
2. Glyn Philpot (1884-1937), the painter and sculptor, had been elected a Royal Academician in 1923.
3. Major-General Lord Edward Gleichen (1863-1937) was the only son of Admiral Prince Victor of Hohenlohe-Langenburg, but served in the British Army. He was an Equerry to King George V.

arose from a portrait of Queen Mary on a plate,[1] but where will it end?
You, as professor, Nessa as Lady Colefax—

But I must bring this horrid flight to a close. Is Helen[2] back? Anyhow,
as she's blackhearted and flint brained, as nothing but bile circulates in her
veins, as far as I'm concerned, I shant hear from her: which does nothing to
cool my regard.

We shall cross the Alps to Siena, and look round at one or two little
places, but only for 3 weeks.

Let me know if there's any chance of meeting you.

Yrs
Virginia

Oh yes I got a lovely long letter from you; and told Leonard what you said
about your book.

Sussex

2733: To Ethel Smyth   52 *Tavistock Sqre.* [*W.C.*1]

Tuesday May 2nd [1933]

I'm sending the letters back today[3]—in the cases, which only need a
tug to open and shut—because, God help me, I'm sunk to the lips in people,
shopping and so on, and cant rescue a single moment before we go. I wonder
if goings worth it—these days are such a panjandrum of misery—people,
people, people.

I dont think the typing so bad—I've seen worse. Still I think she should
buy a new ribbon, and rather thicker paper. Only for a carbon, thin paper
is needed, they say.

If you want to go on. I shd. think Jones as good as anyone; and will
certainly share her bill—gladly.

If you write, which please do, address to the Press, and they'll forward.
Its only 3 weeks after all. Oh to be out of all this! Yes, I feel like a bird who
sees the cage door about to open.

1. Kenneth Clark had commissioned from Duncan and Vanessa a dinner-service
   portraying famous women of history, including Marie Antoinette, Queen
   Alexandra, Ellen Terry and Queen Elizabeth I. (See Shone, *Bloomsbury Portraits*,
   1976, p. 247.)
2. Helen Anrep had been with Fry to Spain, where they stayed with Gerald
   Brenan.
3. The letters to Ethel from Henry Brewster, see p. 74, note 1. For poor typing,
   see p. 176, note 1.

So no more at the moment. We start early on Friday, shall lunch at Monks House, and cross that night, so as to start across France early on Saturday morning

V.

A nice note from Bruno Walter[1]
Here is the cheque .32.

Berg

1. The German-born conductor (1876-1962), who settled in Austria and, after the *Anschluss*, in the United States. He was a friend and admirer of Ethel Smyth, and Virginia had just met him at a London party.

Letters 2734-2739 (May 1933)

On 5 May Virginia and Leonard went on a motoring holiday to Italy, and they were away three weeks. Their route took them through France to the Riviera where they called on the Bussys, and thence to Tuscany, where they spent five days based on Siena. The return journey was through Lerici (where they visited Shelley's house for the second time on this trip), over the Apennines to Parma and Piacenza, and thence back through France by Aix, Avignon and Chartres. They recrossed the Channel from Dieppe on 27 May. Virginia was delighted by Italy, which she enjoyed all the more from having learnt enough of the language to talk to the peasants. They considered, perhaps not very seriously, buying a Tuscan farm.

2734: To Vanessa Bell   *Siena, [Italy]*

Postcard
16th May [1933]

I'm going to try to write you a long letter tonight, but you dont deserve it, dumb deceptive Dolphin. Not a word from you. how foolish you are to prefer Tott. Court Rd. to nightingales, orange flowers, strawberries; I'm just off to buy a farm in the hills [at Fabbria]. This is where we must live.

V.

Berg

2735: To Elizabeth Bowen   *Siena, [Italy]*

May 16th [1933]

Dear Elizabeth,

You see where I am, so I cant come to tea today in Markham Square. But we shall be back in a fortnight, so do ask me again, or come to Tavistock Sqre.

I'm so sleepy I cant write—otherwise I should insult Oxford and Ireland,[1] for I can assure you—not that I've ever been to Ireland, and my relations

---

1. Elizabeth Bowen divided her time between a house at Old Headington, Oxford (where her husband, Alan Cameron, was Secretary for Education to the city), and her childhood home, Bowen's Court in Co. Cork.

with Oxford are formal in the extreme—they cant touch the hem of the dress of this country. I've always been here before in trains—you cant think what a difference it makes driving, or being driven. We stop or go on; and have our lunch under cypresses, with nightingales singing and frogs barking, and climb to the top of hills where no one has ever been before. They are charming people—the peasants, I mean: very melancholy, longing for conversation, offering one wine, or 6 dead fish—I've only 10 words of Italian, but I fire them all perpetually; and so we get led into all kinds of queer places. Today it was a monastery [Monte Oliveto]; where—but no —I will spare you the rest of this letter, because my head is swimming with sleep and wine, but you must pawn your grandfather's gold plate watch or whatever it is, and come next May. Now I must pack, for we are off to

Lucca,
Parma
Piacenza
and so home.

Yrs
Virginia Woolf

I had a letter from Tom Eliot today, apparently very happy in his way, in America, but about to come back, poor man.

Texas

2736: To Dorothy Bussy   *Siena, [Italy]*

May 16 [1933]

My dear Dorothy,

  I'm afraid it looks as if we should not reach Mentone till too late to get to you on Sunday. We are coming back by an unknown road, and cant be sure of our times. So dont expect us—but it was charming to get that hour with you and I still carry my lemon with me.[1]

  Anyhow we shall meet soon, for our annual tea.

  Italy is incredibly lovely—every tree flowering, every bird singing, with the result that I am half tipsy tonight and cant write.

Ever yr
Virginia.

Texas

1. On their journey out, Virginia and Leonard had called on Dorothy and Simon Bussy at their villa near Mentone, in the South of France.

Wednesday May 17th [1933]

Dearest Dolphin

I have tried several times to write to you, but it is almost impossible, owing to every sort of noise, and then I'm so sleepy after a bottle of chianti; and as a matter of fact there is only description of natural objects and works of art to offer you. And you dont write. Post after post comes; none from Dolphin. So far we have had no accidents, but some moments of agony when the fluid wheel has stuck, or the gear gone wrong. And we have been all through France, and as far as Siena; indeed only 50 miles short of Rome. Undoubtedly Tuscany beyond Siena is the most beautiful of all lands anywhere—it is, at the moment, every inch of it laden with flowers: then there are nightingales: but it is the hills,—no, I will not describe for your annoyance. what is to me the loveliest, the most sympathetic, and I may say Virgilian of countries; for its years since we read Virgil together and you very properly told me not to write a word about landscape or art either.

And the peasants are infinitely the nicest of our kind—oh how much preferable to the Sands, the Smyths, the Logans! My Italian lands me in all kinds of wayside conversations, as we generally lunch under olives, beside streams with frogs barking. Why didn't you come? I should have thought the pictures very good at Siena—and then I like the old maids one meets: but the truth is this is only a discovery—we must come and settle at Fabbria [in Tuscany], a little farm we found, for ever and ever. There is no news. We called in at the Bussy's as we passed, and found Janie and Dorothy, perfectly equipped, neat and bright as pins, sipping coffee; I dont care, I must admit for that view, or hill—but then the whole Riviera seems to me Raymonds [Mortimer] country—a pink pyjama country— however they seemed very friendly and want us to sleep the night going back; but I doubt it. Simon [Bussy] appeared, more of an organ monkey than ever, and theyre all about to start for Gordon Square. Why should I be snubbed for asking to be shown the Studio? Sure enough, I was—He said "Not today. Perhaps next time." Considering everything I cant see why I should be snubbed—simpleton as I am. We've seen a great many pictures—San Gimignano today, and yesterday we went to a place where I shall be buried, if bones can walk—that is, Monte Oliveto;[1] oh oh oh— Cypresses, square tanks, oxen, and not big bony hills, little velvety hills— and the monastery: and as hot as August. But I wont deny that we've had some very cold days, and some violent tempests, one at Volterra for example —all because a peasant woman whose vines were perishing, came in and

1. The great monastery of Monte Oliveto Maggiore, near Buonconvento, famous for its frescoes by Signorelli and Sodoma.

offered 2 candles to the Madonna for rain—which promptly came. Now its thundery again, and we've been walking all over Lucca, trying to find an antiquity shop, but the only one there was has gone. Its a most busy town. full of different markets; and the building—but as I said, I wont commit any faux pas on that head.

I suppose London is rocketing like a Catherine Wheel with various splendours—Rumours reach me from Ethel and so on—I hear she came to see you, but you could only talk of her dogs private parts—We now start home, rather slowly, and shall be back on the 27th I think—at Rodmell. The car is miraculous—not a bump comes through—and in France, of course it reaches unparallelled speed;

Shall you be glad to see me? Oh but you never realised I had gone—yet to me it seems years and years and as if I had seen all the countries of the earth spread before me. This is certainly the only way to see Italy.

Are my book cases done?

I'm very excited about them. Do write good Dolphin: the Press will forward. Is it true you've been summoned to tea with the Queen?

Yr
B.

Berg

2738: To Ethel Smyth   *Lerici, [Italy]*

May 18th [1933]

Yes I have meant to write, again and again, but again and again I have fallen fast asleep. Moreover, whats the use of writing? Here am I sitting, by an open window, by a balcony, by the bay in which Shelley was drowned,[1] wasn't he, 113 years ago, on a hot day like this—which indeed I might describe, but how describe the hills, the tall pink yellow white houses, and the in fact, not fiction, purple brown sea, not rolling in waves, as I made my sea [in *The Waves*], but now and again giving a little shiver, like that which runs through a field of corn, or the back of a race horse! No, my good general's daughter, Italy beats me—Tuscany above all, which is incomparably the finest and purest of Italy, where I've been sitting, these 5 or 6 days, on hills like songs, like poems, thought of all in one flash and for ever, you would say by God, but then you're a general's daughter. I'm burnt like a grilled bone, and for the most part a little tipsy; and now we're starting home, over the Apennines tomorrow, to Parma, to Piacenza, so to Avignon,

1. Shelley was drowned on 8 July 1822, together with his friend Edward Williams, when their small schooner capsized in a squall. Their bodies were washed ashore a few weeks later, and were cremated on the beach in the presence of Trelawney, Leigh Hunt and Byron.

which leads to Dieppe, to Monks House, and so once more to the 52nd house in Tavistock Sqre.

Well, what are you doing?—inducing a large penis into a small hole? And I suppose rehearsing masses and comic operas, tippling, browbeating, and leading the forces of womanhood, massed, against ignorance and corruption? I dont like Fascist Italy at all—but hist!—there's the black shirt under the window—so no more.

Addio.
V.

Mrs Shelley and Mary Williams walked up and down the balcony of the house next door [Casa Magni] waiting while Shelleys body rolled round with pearls—it is the best death bed place I've ever seen—

Berg

2739: TO V. SACKVILLE-WEST   *Spotorno, Italy*

May 20th [1933]

This is a strictly business like (only I happen to be tipsy, having drunk more than my half bottle tonight)

1) Would it suit you if we came over to lunch (about 1.30) on Sunday, 28th to fetch Pinka?[1]—not I mean to see you, but to fetch Pinka. Would you send a card to Monks House, which I daresay we shall reach on Friday, to say if yes, if no.

2) Oh God I forgot in London the thing I swore I'd ask you. You know Lyn Irvine?[2] Well she's on the rocks, as its called—as shrunk as a wrung rag—no money—love, I think lost; not a penny to pay for her wretched herring. So I said I'd ask you if she could find any possible opening for articles of any kind in America. She knows all about Eng. lit. But tell me this—only do remember—if I see you. I forgot.

Yes. I am half dazed with travelling, so many cities have I seen, and smelt: now its the waves breaking, and the scent of stocks in the garden—and there is very likely a nightingale, and frogs. But all this you know—and you've heard froggier frogs in the Rockies. Everything I say in future will be thus diminished. Oh Lord I should like to see you without 20 thousand interruptions. We're so brown cheeked red nosed and altogether

1. Pinka (Virginia's cocker-spaniel, and the model for Flush) had been cared for by Vita at Long Barn during their absence.
2. Lyn Lloyd Irvine's book *Ten Letter-Writers* had been published by the Hogarth Press in 1932. She married, in 1934, Maxwell Newman, Lecturer in Mathematics at Cambridge.

dusty shaggy shabby—what a state my clothes are in—even I rather hesitate to wear them—for we lunch in the fields, under olives off ham, and its my duty to wash up, which affects my clothes—so how are we to lunch at Sisst. which is so fashionable? And why did Cynthia M die?[1] And how are you? Writing? Poems?

I'm tipsy

V.

We crossed the Apennines today.

Berg

1. Cynthia, the second daughter of Lord Curzon and Mary Leiter, the American heiress, had married Sir Oswald Mosley in 1920. She died on 16 May 1933, aged 34, of acute appendicitis.

Letters 2740-2767 (June–July 1933)

Virginia at first found it difficult to resume her writing after her return from Italy, but was soon "in full flood" with The Pargiters again. Her London life again became distractingly active, "at its worst" as she described it to Ethel Smyth on 25 June, and Ethel herself was a main culprit, bothering Virginia with her manuscripts and insisting upon being 'seen' at least once a week, but Virginia was now treating her with increasing firmness, though unwilling to break off their friendship. Among others who took up her time were Bernard Shaw, Ottoline Morrell, Vivien Eliot (now distraught by Eliot's decision to leave her) and Vita, whom she visited at Sissinghurst and often met in London.

2740: To Ethel Smyth   [52 *Tavistock Square, W.C.*1]

[31 May 1933]

I forgot Whitsuntide—We're off to Monks tomorrow—But now Nessa rings up and says you put her off on account of cold. Very sorry you've caught one, but imagine it sent by the Gods to remind you in your glory of your flesh. How like your God—that very interfering old Anglo-Indian buffer. But hope to meet in this world soon.

                                           Virginia

What about the MS?[1] I shall have time on my hands at Monks.

Berg

2741: To V. Sackville-West   52, *Tavistock Square, W.C.*1

Thursday [1 June 1933]

Oh dear I was so touched to find your letter here—it was such a nice good hearted letter—that I had meant to give expression to my emotions: but Lord!—what a vain hope. I meant to write a long letter. And this one was to have asked, why is it that I sometimes leave the N.——s [Nicolsons] almost in tears? Not for pity: no: but I do like human life on a large warm adventurous scale—dogs—flowers—boys—building. So that the tears, denied elsewhere,—not altogether rise but gather in the heart. But how I

1. See Letter 2743.

189

raged at your mother!¹ You see, when one's 18, words, news, revelations about ones parents have an immeasurable force; and that she should have taken it on herself to say them—but I am packing and cant finish. It seemed to me so dastardly, so immoral: so fiendishly inhuman.

But we're just off, and this is to say why dont you come to Monks? on your way to or from that old Vipress [Vita's mother]?

Ring up, if you can, as I may have to go to Worthing.

V.

Berg

2742: To Lady Cecil   *Monk's House,*
                                                 Rodmell, [Sussex]

Whitsunday [4 June 1933]

My dear Nelly,

I was trailing along a dusty path in the Loders garden² yesterday when suddenly out of a glade came a woman I thought to be you. So I ran after her—she was walking very fast. And when I got close to her I thought No it isn't her, and if I speak to her she'll look at me with horror and surprise. And so she vanished. Was it you?³ Oh how hot it was! I was trying to find my mother in law, aged 84 who is as spry as a weasel, and had motored over from Worthing by way of a pleasant expedition and we had tea with 500 other old ladies in the stable, where the Loders keep heads of deer and swords. I dont care for that sort of garden—too many glades and rhododendrons and masses of fir trees. Did you like it?—if it was you—if not, did your ghost like it?

We are just back from Italy. We motored across to Siena and back. Almost the loveliest place of all was Lerici, where the Shelleys lived, on the edge of the sea. Now we go back to London and someday I hope we may meet, not like ghosts—

Yr VW

The Marquess of Salisbury (Cecil papers)

1. Virginia and Leonard lunched at Sissinghurst on 28 May, and Ben (Benedict Nicolson, 1914-78) told her that his grandmother, Lady Sackville, had spoken to him "about M. [Vita] getting hold of women and D. [Harold] of men—about Violet Keppel, Virginia Woolf etc." While Ben recounted this story, Virginia "listened . . . with her head bowed. Then she said: 'The old woman ought to be shot.'" For Ben's description of the incident, see *Portrait of a Marriage* (Nigel Nicolson, 1973) pp. 180-3.
2. Leonardslee, Horsham, Sussex, which belonged to Sir Giles Loder Bt.
3. Lady Cecil replied (7 June, *Sussex*): "Oh, Virginia, were you really in that garden? I certainly was—*and* Violet Dickinson, and my old brother D'Arcy . . . I believe that it was *you* who came out of a glade and saw *us* trailing along a dusty path and immediately hid behind an azalea. Tell me the truth for once."

Monks House, [Rodmell, Sussex]

Typewritten

Tuesday 6th June. [1933]

It is far too hot to give any sensible coherent criticism of your paper;[1] so please take what follows as provisional merely—notes merely; but I had better write at once after reading, or my mind will blur.

Yes, I think its well worth saying—well worth printing. I think much of it very convincing, interesting, forcible. I mean by 'much of it' all the impersonal objective part. I mean the facts about education. I think they could not be better, more musically, more persuasively, put. And no one I expect has any notion of them. I am sure they are valuable in the extreme.

I hesitate to go on to criticism; because as you will guess what I criticise is what you say to be necessary—that is the autobiography. I hate it. I dont think it adds any thing to what you have said. I think the personal details immensely diminish the power of the rest. Because one feels——but I wont go on; for I am aware that I may be prejudiced. I hate any writer to talk about himself; anonymity I adore. And this may be an obsession. I blush, I fidget, I turn hot and cold. I want to pull the curtain over this indecency.

My other objection—to have done with them—is to the Unknown Champion[2] and the Statistics. This is largely on aesthetic grounds. I dont think you realise how nauseating press cuttings are—how nobody can read them, served up cold; or if they do, the whole effect of the writing, as a rounded and designed building, is frittered away and teased—Look how Miss [Winifred] Holtby breaks up the design. And those horrid little private letters—I call them 'horrid' because coming in the middle of your long rolling breakers, for which you have such a gift, they affect me with sea sickness. And the dates and the facts—nobody can keep them in mind; it is like the chatter of the parrot house at the Zoo to me. Couldn't you sum the whole thing up, first by saying "See the Burning of Boats;"[3] then a note to the effect that you have private letters which show another side —if you feel that you must give details of your personal lot? I know you have

1. See p. 15, note 2. Virginia was specifically referring to the second chapter in *Female Pipings in Eden* which was entitled *Women's Training Hitherto*, concerning women's lack of opportunities in musical education.
2. At the end of Chapter V of *Pipings* Ethel wrote: "Again and again has the present writer asked of the ambient air when and where a champion will arise who shall say: 'Look here, it's my job to take the part of music's underdog, and see that women composers get a real look-in.'" She cut out most of the Statistics and relegated her press-cuttings to an Appendix.
3. A previous volume of Ethel's autobiography published in 1928. In *Pipings* she could not resist including a chapter about her old friend Henry Brewster, which incorporated several of his letters to her.

good reasons for feeling that you must; I repeat, my dislike of the personal in argument, may be fantastic. And soberly, I think you weaken your case by bringing in VW. I have ventured to put a couple of brackets to show how she could be omitted with advantage,[1] Oh a little mutual admiration society! a nest of friends, people will say.

Now for a few minor points that struck my critical ear; I do not like the title [*Female Pipings in Eden*] It seems to me facetious when you mean to be serious. And its diffuse.

page 3 . . . angelicness but reasonableness—a jingle to me; and a mouthful; why not something like 'it is not owing to inherent goodness of heart, but to reason"[2] This is a very small point.

page 4 . . . differently *to*—should be *from*—to my ear. This happens again somewhere.

page 7—I hate your (?!) No no—Never put two different exclamation marks together while I am within one hundred miles.

General criticism; Too diffuse. [*handwritten:*] (On the other hand, you get a swing and a richness by taking your easy large stride as you do.) [*type-written:*] I think you want to leave out tempting digressions—Bayliss for instance.[3] And I think you are on thin ice when you speak of the Gang— one feels you mean the word in a bad sense; and so father it on to other people when its *you* who call them a gang. It seems to me you must say straight out, this is an abominable set of humbugs, or words to that effect; not "I call them a gang because other people do."[4] It's like ringing the bell and running away, to slip in a very damning indictment and then to gloss it over. Here I may be wrong. Its the heat. But I felt this as I read.

Well then, what it comes to is that I should like it more muscular; drained of water; shorter; terser, less—well, you know what I mean when I talk of the eldritch shriek.

Finally I like immensely the imaginative and tranquil end; the suggestive end; the Pacific and the Hebrides [p. 53 of *Pipings*]. Thats what I call persuasion. In fact I think, even though I'm dripping with heat—oh I had to go round a summer garden with my mother in law, admiring rhodo-dendrons with 500 old Sussex country ladies—with heat, I was saying I think that there are the bones and flesh and sinew of a very important state-ment in this; yet feel that they have not taken on perfect shape; bones flesh

1. Virginia's name is nowhere mentioned in the published book.
2. Changed in the printed text to "not owing to kindliness but to reason".
3. Ethel retained her chapter on Lilian Baylis, who was largely responsible for the success of the Old Vic theatre.
4. Ethel changed 'gang' to 'group', referring to publishers, journalists, patrons of music, etc., who ignored her work.

sinew in one body. Yet I feel reluctant to make this remark, because as I say, my whole bent is away and away and ever so far away from Ethel Smyth, Lilian Bayliss, Virginia Woolf. I hate personal snippets more and more. And the mention of 'I' is so potent—such a drug, such a deep violet stain—that one in a page is enough to colour a chapter. Enough. I will send this off with the MS now as we have to go into Lewes. But please take literally my caution—these are the roughest, most off hand jerks; no doubt, if I read it again I shall see it in much truer perspective. Now I must stop.

Yours
V.

Berg

2744: To Ethel Smyth   52 *T[avistock]* *S[quare, W.C.*1]

Wednesday [7 June 1933]

Yes, I have just heard it (I forget the name) and like it very much.[1] Yes, its quite true—after 4 or 5 times of hearing, an impression begins to come through. I accept this one of your points. And I am therefore made to reflect once more that I was almost certainly patchy, imperfect, too black, too white in my remarks on your article. I'm rather worried to hear, as I thought, on the telephone that you intend altering so much as a word, solely on my outburst. Please consult Lady B. or Miss Steel,[2] or some other person: because I read hastily, and have a horror of inflicting a crude judgment upon what I have not thoroughly grasped.

I purposely said nothing about seeing you tomorrow—if that was your suggestion—I've left your letter at Rodmell and cant be sure—because I think it would be positively suicidal for you to take train or even walk a pavement in this heat—That was why I said nothing. But come, if you can, when it is healthier weather. I'm rather glad to be back—too many moves. Now I hope to settle in and write and write and write.

Let me know about coming when its cooler.

V.

I wont inflict musical, as well as literary, criticism on you. Only that I liked it very much.

Berg

1. A Serenade Concert, including some of Ethel's music, broadcast from the Canterbury Festival of Music and Drama.
2. Lady Balfour; and Ethel Steel, Principal of the Royal School for Officers' Daughters at Bath, where Ethel had been staying.

Thursday [8 June 1933]

Would you dine with me *alone* upon my honour, on Monday next *MONDAY* 12*th*—anytime you like. It is only that I shall be alone. Otherwise, I dont think its worth anyone's while to come to London. Could you angelically ring the telephone?

No, no no—I never boast of American publishers—Scaife?[1] Gods truth I dont—I've not fallen to that degraded state.

A Princess perhaps—not a publisher

Forgive scrawl

Potto is the writer

V.

Berg

2746: To Ethel Smyth   [52 *Tavistock Square, W.C.*1]

Typewritten
Thursday June 8th 1933

No I dont think I put my point effectively; I did not mean that I dislike facts and dates; What I did mean was—oh dear how silly to try and explain —but my conscience is tender about writing—I meant, give all the facts and all the dates; the more the better; but let them be about other people, not E.S. My own longing in reading your article is to escape the individual; and to be told simply, plainly, objectively in 1880 there was not a single woman in an orchestra; there was not a single teacher to teach women harmony; the expense of going to Berlin was 165 pound ten; eight women were educated partly by 1891; in 1902 [Henry] Wood took five violinists women into his orchestra; the number increased, and is now—(here a table) . . . and so on, all the way through. But to be told *My* opera was not played because—*My* mass was only played once, Elgars 17 times—to have to listen to anecdotes, hearsay, verbal anecdotes about how some unknown Austrian said that some unnamed conductor ought to be very proud of ES makes me feel, and will I think make any moderately intelligent moderately sensitive man or woman feel—Oh the womans got a grievance about herself; Shes unable to think of any one else. Now I know that this is deliberate on your part therefore I think you should try to see how very possible it is that your policy is wrong. Leonard to whom I recited passages said exactly the same. I dont believe anyone whose hands have lately been dipped in ink can judge this sort of thng—to give an instance; I was wound to a pitch of fury the other day by a reviewers attacks upon a friend of mine to

1. See p. 169, note 3.

do a thing I have never yet done—to write to the papers a long letter. 'Yes' said L. when I showed it to him; but itll do more harm than good; its all about yourself. When a fortnight later in cold blood I read it, there was 'I' as large, and ugly as could be; thanks to God, I didn't send it. You will say Oh but I must cite my case because there is no other. But my dear Ethel your case is that there are a thousand others. Leave your own case out of it; theirs will be far far stronger. Enough, I only say this because— well, I didnt write 'A room' without considerable feeling even you will admit; I'm not cool on the subject. And I forced myself to keep my own figure fictitious; legendary. If I had said, Look here am I uneducated, because my brothers used all the family funds which is the fact—Well theyd have said; she has an axe to grind; and no one would have taken me seriously, though I agree I should have had many more of the wrong kind of reader; who will read you and go away and rejoice in the personalities, not because they are lively and easy reading; but because they prove once more how vain, how personal, so they will say, rubbing their hands with glee, women always are; I can hear them as I write. One thing more; and silence for ever; Nancy girls to me seems in bad taste.[1] Why? I dont know.

V

Berg

2747: To Lady Cecil   52 *Tavistock Square, W.C.*1

Thursday [8 June 1933]

My dear Nelly,

Yes, I always said you were the best of letter writers—But that's no excuse for running away from old friends down glades. It must have been you—unless a very fine fir tree was Violet [Dickinson], I somehow missed her; and the azalea may of course have been your brother. Anyhow, I'm glad it was you, because, here I am, palpitating from having miscalled, unrecognised, inextricably mixed and introduced wrongly two people I've known these 30 years at a private view today.

If you mean tea next Tuesday I will come with pleasure: at 5: but dont buy a sandwich or butter any bread, because, here at the Press, in order to shorten the anguish of the afternoon we have tea earlier and earlier. I will come all the same with great pleasure, if it is next Tuesday you mean, *in London.*

1. 'Nancy girls' does not appear in the published text. But Ethel ignored Virginia's central message—to omit her autobiographical grievances, with which *Female Pipings* is replete.

Yes, George is always sending me hints how to cook Broad Beans: by Sir G. Duckworth[1] or elegies on his wifes prize pig. What a man!

Yrs V.W

The Marquess of Salisbury (Cecil Papers)

2748: To Daphne Sanger   52 *Tavistock Square, W.C.*1

Private
11th June 1933

Dear Daphne,[2]

I enclose £1.1 for your Carlyle House fund.[3] I feel much more sympathy with Mrs Carlyle than with Mr, anyhow where the house is concerned. I believe if your circular put more stress on her, you would wring more money from our purses. But anyhow I hope you'll get it—and also that some time we may meet.

Yours

James Lees-Milne   Virginia Woolf

2749: To Vanessa Bell   [52 *Tavistock Square, W.C.*1]

Monday [12 June 1933]

Clive has just rung up, and says that the Ott: lunch has been decided on,[4] and that I am to take steps. What steps he didn't seem to know—in fact he was altogether vague.

Could you let me have instructions? I dont know Anreps address, the date, what I'm to do about writing to Ott: in fact nothing. Lord—what a bore poor old Quentin having whooping cough! I intend writing him a long letter. Shall you be there on Saturday? We're coming down on Friday.

Its the Apostle night,[5] and Adrian [Stephen] is dining with me.

B.

Berg

1. Virginia's half-brother.
2. Daphne was the daughter of Charles Sanger, the barrister, to whom Virginia had been devoted. He died in February 1930.
3. She was helping to raise money for the permanent preservation of 24 Cheyne Row, Chelsea, where Jane and Thomas Carlyle lived from 1834 until their deaths in 1866 and 1881 respectively. It was given to the National Trust in 1936 by the Carlyle's House Memorial Trust.
4. Boris Anrep, Clive Bell and Maynard Keynes had proposed that her friends should give a large lunch-party in honour of Ottoline Morrell.
5. The annual dinner in London of the Cambridge Conversazione Society ('The Apostles').

2750: To Lady Ottoline Morrell

52 *Tavistock Square, W.C.*1

Friday [16 June 1933]

Dearest Ottoline,

Yes I confess—in my heart I entirely agree with you.[1] But I hope you realise how it was—I mean the friends were so excited and happy about it, and felt a glow of affection, and therefore I was persuaded to come round to you with the proposal. It was very genuine—dont think it merely pushing and advertising and done from love of publicity. I assure you it was not. I was so touched myself by their feeling—otherwise I would have taken no part in it. However, finally I have to admit that I think you are right, and so will say no more.

Yes, a quiet, cool, dusky tea one of these days without people buzzing about—that's much more to my liking.

Just off to Rodmell for the weekend, so excuse this scrawl. Boris [Anrep] was here when your letter came, so I told him. He was so sure you would agree that he was disappointed—but is writing to you.

Yr V.W.

Texas

2751: To Lydia Keynes

[52 *Tavistock Square, W.C.*1]

Postcard

[16 June 1933]

No, no, no—I cannot face another conversation with B.A. [Boris Anrep]—nor he with me—at the moment. We're sick to death of talking to each other—but united in love of L——a. [Lydia]

V.W.

King's

2752: To V. Sackville-West

[52 *Tavistock Square, W.C.*1]

Monday [19 June 1933]

What luck! Yes we are free dinner on Wednesday. But couldn't you come at 6 all the same, in order to have the rare pleasure of seeing me alone? which I admit I should like.

Could you possibly ring or let me have a card in order that I may be in and alone at 6. Otherwise dinner 7.30

V.

Berg

1. Ottoline refused the proposed luncheon in her honour. She wrote to Virginia (15 June, *Sussex*): "I think that all celebrations are difficult—Christmas, weddings, death—and what would this be? Rather a Death of an Epoch."

52 *Tavistock Square, W.C.*1

Tuesday [20 June 1933]

Dearest Ottoline,

Would Sunday 5.30 suit you? We shall be here, and that would be very nice, but if you're tired or would rather I could come round to you.

Yes I do thank my stars that there's not to be a [Ottoline] lunch at the Savoy with ices, melons, cigars and speeches. What a raving nightmare—still the will was better than the deed.

Old Ethel has just rung me up in a rhapsody about Ly O. [Ottoline] whom she describes all in pink cartwheels and pearls—a siren.

I'm so hot I cant articulate or determine what cartwheels are.

Texas

yrs
V.W.

2754: To Elizabeth Bowen   52 *T.[avistock] S.[quare, W.C.*1]

Wednesday [21 June 1933]

Dear Elizabeth,

I would like to come if I can on Monday, but it wouldn't be till after 5. If I'm prevented (I've made a muddle of my engagements) I'll ring up. Yes, I want very much to come to Ireland. But at present I must try to stick to what I am doing. Siena was debauching enough—another holiday would entirely ruin me. Still—one of these days, without a doubt.

Ottoline refused her luncheon—very rightly, and much to my relief.

Yrs VW

Texas

2755: To V. Sackville-West   [52 *Tavistock Square, W.C.*1]

[23? June 1933]

Potto's love and 10/—to buy him shoes with: and a peasant womans hat.[1] (But *not not not* if theres a pressure or a rush or a difficulty) Lord how happy I was to see you! I forget what I wanted to say—what am I to do about Ethel perhaps? I met Valery Taylor[2] yesterday wheres Vita? she said

1. Vita gave the 10/- to a local cricket club.
2. The actress, a friend of Raymond Mortimer and Vita.

and here's the richest young man in Europe[1] come to dine on peas and bacon in order to pass the Camels eye!

So I must wash.

A thousand blessings.

V. and
P.

Berg

2756: To Molly MacCarthy   52 *Tavistock Sqre*, [*W*.C.1]

June 23rd [1933]

Dearest Molly,

We shall be delighted to dine on Tuesday 11th July at 8.[2] Then it is agreed that you are to read further memoirs—and make them kinder to your old friends—and if Desmond is to talk, and the rest of us are to sit round, happy.

This handwriting, I may point out, is only achieved by having a simple mind and a loving heart. You put it under a microscope and the truth of that will leap to light.

Oh dear how devastating tea parties are! Did you go on to several others? I failed and collapsed in a heap on my doorstep.

Yrs Virginia

Mrs Michael MacCarthy

2757: To Ethel Smyth   52 *T*[*avistock*] *S*.[*quare, W*.C.1]

Sunday [25 June 1933]

I'm sorry to have been so bad about writing—at least I think I've never answered your last letter—but London life has been at its worst. And I suppose you're annoyed with me—I'm sure with every reason. I gather you think I was cold the other day when you came: but then you came at 4.30 when I had said 5.30—praying for one hour between Ottoline Anrep Bernard Shaw etc:[3] in which to write a letter I was ordered to write to the

1. Victor Rothschild (later 3rd Lord Rothschild), who married Barbara Hutchinson in December 1933.
2. For a meeting of the Memoir Club.
3. On 15 June Virginia wrote in the morning, lunched with the Bernard Shaws, went to tea with Ottoline and Boris Anrep, and in the evening Ethel arrived at Tavistock Square. It was a day quite typical of Virginia's life at this period.

New S. etc etc:[1] however thats over. I was dazed with talk. Second: I gather you think me inconsistent. I preach anonymity to you and then have my portrait in mosaics in the Nat. Gall. Yes: but my stipulation was that I was to be Clio: not V.W. Its not my fault if Anrep from motives of his own gives all the names to the papers.[2]

But no more. This is all very petty and trivial. And I daresay you've forgotten by this time if I was cold or warm. And I've forgotten whether you mention yourself or not in your article. Nothing at the moment seems to me to matter one straw. But then I spent 8 hours yesterday at a school treat in a drizzle;[3] listening to children piping, poor little creatures, by the hour: with a mistress hid under a hedge to prompt them. And tomorrow, and tomorrow and tomorrow—I forget Shakespeare: I forget everything

Yr
V.

Berg

2758: TO ALICE RITCHIE   52 *T*[avistock] *S*[quare, *W.C.*1]

25th June [1933]

Dear Alice,

I was so sorry you couldn't come, but we shall be here I suppose, till the end of July; so perhaps we shall see you. Let me know. I'm rather glad to hear that your book is worrying the life out of you.[4] I expect this means that it reads like print and is as deep as the sea. In that case it probably does seem like toothache to you. I write and write with extreme volubility but little success; never mind, if I enjoy myself that is all (being old, disillusioned) that I ask.

We were passing your door yesterday—if your door is at Maldon. We dined at the Kings Head, after spending perhaps the most tiring day of our

---

1. In the *New Statesman* of 24 June Virginia published a letter which supported the demand that the gardens of London squares should be opened to pedestrians during the summer.
2. Anrep's mosaic on the floor of the entrance-hall of the National Gallery incorporated portraits of Virginia as Clio, Clive Bell as Bacchus, Lydia Keynes as the Muse of Song and Dance, Greta Garbo as the Muse of Tragedy, and several others.
3. Angelica Bell's school, Langford Grove, near Maldon, Essex.
4. After her first two novels, *The Pacemakers* (1928) and *Occupied Territories* (1930), both published by the Hogarth Press, Alice Ritchie never published another book, except one for children.

lives—listening to a school reciting plays and playing pianos from 12 to
7.30. I rather like that country, in a damp mist.

Yours
Virginia Woolf

I left this lying in my writing case; and send it to show how punctually I
answer letters.

Mrs Ian Parsons

2759: To Shena, Lady Simon   52 *Tavistock Sqre, W.C.1*

8th July 1933

Dear Lady Simon,

   I would have written to thank you for sending the letters before, but
London has been rather a rush. I read them with great interest and irritation.
They are of course the germ of Margaret B's article.[1] I cant say I like them.
They seem to me peevish and niggling and ungenerous—Nobody can deny
that the man at college has a better time than the woman, but she should
have the wits to see why that is, instead of grumbling like a charwoman
(this remark is for you only!) at authorities.

   It was delightful seeing you, and I hope next time you are in London
you will let us know. There are a thousand things to discuss, about the
future and education; but I am always, if not silenced, rather impeded by my
ignorance of facts. Things are so different for a writer, with anyhow a small
capital to go on.

   I return the letters.

Yours sincerely
Virginia Woolf

Sussex

2760: To Dorothy Brett   52 *Tavistock Square, W.C.1*

Typewritten
8th July [1933]

My dear Brettt, [*sic*]

   (forgive the typewriter which has already converted your name into
another—but my hand is grown cursed and crabbed) I am a wretch to have
delayed writing—but if you live so far away a month or more can't make

1. This article has not been traced, but it was by Margaret Bondfield (1873-1953)
   who had a brilliant career as a Trade Union leader and in women's causes. As
   Minister of Labour in Ramsay MacDonald's second administration she was the
   first woman member of a British Cabinet.

any difference. I was delighted to get your letter and to breathe for a moment the very brilliant queer air in which you live [New Mexico]. No, there's no reason why you should come back to London—here we are, sweating, grimy, full of conferences, ices, parties, and people all lounging back and saying that they can't think how Nancy Cunard can like niggers[1]—etc etc; you can imagine it. But if I'm sincere, then of course I love London and couldnt live with your splendours, not for ever. One of these days I shall pounce or sweep through them and knock at your door as Vita did. She's back, entirely delighted with America, your part that is; not the other. I'm glad you liked her and she you.

I dont know how to fill this page without filling thirty. Theres so much going on and yet it would be useless to begin; Desmond, Ottoline— yesterday Julian had a son[2]—Nessa, Duncan—well, what you must do is to come back some day and put up with us. Dont say *Bloomsbury* in a tone of scorn; for that I will not stand. No, not from Sydney Waterlow even, whose pomp of circumstance surpasses belief.[3]

I looked into your book and shut it;[4] I can't get hold of Lawrence; I like and I dislike; and always feel its a puzzle that I must sit down to one of these days, honestly; to read him through. But at present when there's so much coloured dust about his horizon I leave him there. We saw his grave at Vence[5]—what a fate for a man who loved beauty—a kind of plum pudding it seemed to me, raised by the local mason. I never see Freda, or Murry, or Sullivan;[6] I never knew any of them to count; never spoke to Lawrence or Freda. But anyhow it was very nice of you to give me the book; and I think you get through, as painters do so often, the hide of words with your sincerity. [*handwritten*] Thats why I open and shut and see bright visions; whether I like them or not.

So I've rattled off a page. I'm afraid incoherent and dull; but I'm in a hurry. Do if you will write again. Yesterday I heard from Kot [S. S. Koteliansky].

Yours
Virginia

University of Cincinnati

1. Nancy Cunard took as her lover a black man called Henry Crowder, and in 1931 published *Black Man and White Ladyship*, an attack on her mother Emerald Cunard.
2. Ottoline's daughter, Julian, married Victor Goodman in 1928. She later divorced him, and in 1942 married her earlier love, Igor Vinogradoff.
3. Sydney Waterlow (1878-1944) had been a friend of many Bloomsbury people in their youth, and had once proposed to Virginia even before he was divorced from his first wife. Early in 1933 he was British Minister in Sofia, and later in the year became Minister in Athens.
4. *Lawrence and Brett: A Friendship*, 1933.
5. Near Nice. D. H. Lawrence died there in March 1930.
6. J. N. W. Sullivan, the writer on scientific subjects.

Monday 10th July 1933

Dear Kot,

Do you think I might read the story first? I dont remember it. But I dont want you to send it if you are in a hurry, because though I would like to write a preface to a translation of yours, I feel very doubtful if I can.[1] In the first place, I dont think I have anything interesting to say,—it is a long time since I have read Dostoievsky: and in the second I am writing a book and find it very difficult to stop and turn to other work. But if you would send the story I would read it and let you know as soon as I could.

Yours sincerely
Virginia Woolf

British Library

2762: To Ethel Smyth   52 *Tavistock Sqre.* [*W.C.*1]

Tuesday July 11th [1933]

Yes I have been a brute about writing, but then as you never take offence, so you say, I dont care. And I cant take a pen up in completely stiff fingers. What I write now to say is that, unexpectedly, *Wednesday tomorrow* is free; 4.30. Would you like to come then? All other days this week hopeless; next week there might be another: but its useless asking you when there's Dr. and Mrs Feisl, or Dorothy Bussy: so I cant promise many free days; quite free days. I'm told you rang up about the Letters—just as I was reading them; but I sent them, agreeing that it would be best if I could to have them in one block at Rodmell in August. Already some clearer idea of HB[2] emerges—doubtless not the real one—one I make up. But its certainly coming clearer in the typing.

I'm glad the sun is shaded—I feel very spry and well in the cool, and hope I shant lapse into gloom. But if I do I shall make no bones of it and put you off—if that is you can come, which is not at all likely Dont bother There'll be another day. And all I have to say in my head will keep Lord, I must go and wash and dine with the entirely deaf and therefore rather querulous Molly MacCarthy. Have you finished Pankhurst?[3] I was talking

1. In 1922 Virginia and Koteliansky had collaborated on a translation of Dosto-evsky's *Stavrogin's Confession*, but she did not write the preface which Koteliansky now requested. See Letter 2782.
2. Henry Brewster. See p. 74, note 1.
3. Emmeline Pankhurst (1858-1928), the suffragette leader. Ethel had written about her for *Female Pipings in Eden*, 1933.

to Rebecca West about her. She's been writing on her too, for some omnibus book:[1] said she was a portent. But R's husband [Harry Andrews] is such dead, though excellent, mutton that I couldn't ask as much as I wanted and Rebecca turned formal society, polite

V.

You might angelically, ring up

Berg

2763: To Elizabeth Bowen [52 *Tavistock Square, W.C.*1]

Monday [17 July 1933]

Dear Elizabeth,

I was so sorry I couldnt come today, but a friend whose child has just had an operation wanted to see me,[2] and that meant going in the opposite direction from Chelsea.

But perhaps you'll be up next week, and perhaps that would be possible? We are here till the 26th I think.

Any more news of Vivienne [Eliot]?

Yrs VW

Texas

2764: To V. Sackville-West 52 *Tavistock Square, W.C.*1

Thursday [20 July 1933]

That was the finest breakfast I've had this many a year. They must have grown in a water meadow and been breathed on by cows. (Mushrooms for breakfast, this refers to)

Oh dear how nice it was seeing you the other night! I'm sorry your mother got so largely into the papers, but never mind.[3] And glad Nigel's better. Please give him my love I wonder if there's any Hogarth Book he'd like? Please say if so.

And come to lunch please. Ring up to say if you'd like to. But I don't want to be a Bore.

V

1. *The Post-Victorians*, 1933.
2. Vita's younger son, Nigel, had an emergency operation for appendicitis on 13 July.
3. See p. 216, note 2.

Now must wash and dine with the Hutchinsons and settle what on Earth or Heaven to do with Vivienne.[1] Mary says, put her in a convent. And I told Virginia Isham[2] to write to you.

Berg

2765: To Elizabeth Bowen   52 *T.*[avistock] *S.*[quare, *W.C.*1]
Thursday [20 July 1933]

Dear Elizabeth,

I was so sorry about your cold, which is gone now, I hope.

About Monday or Tuesday—the flat will be shut up so dont telephone: my maid is going to Southsea, and we to Rodmell. Tuesday is no good; I have an engaged couple to see.[3] Monday I may not be back till late. Might I leave it that I'll ring up on Monday morning if I can come—otherwise dont expect me, or put anything off. I'm so sorry, but perhaps there'll be another chance before you go and we go.

Yes, Vivienne [Eliot] seems to have gone crazy poor woman. Tom however is back and safe, but I dare not write down the story as I dont know if its public yet. But I daresay you can guess.[4] Vivienne is in bed and removed from the telephone I hope now.

Yrs
Virginia Woolf

Texas

2766: To Vanessa Bell   52 *T.*[avistock] *S.*[quare, *W.C.*1]
Wednesday [26 July? 1933]

Raymond says he's written a long letter to Clive so there's nothing for me to add.

It seems much better than we thought from R's letter, but I gather that F. [Francis Birrell] saw some ordinary doctor who gave a most alarming account. However, you'll have heard.

1. T. S. Eliot, who had just returned from six months in the United States, had finally decided to separate from his sick wife.
2. The young actress, and Virginia's distant cousin. She hoped to bring a group of Players to Sissinghurst, but the project was later abandoned.
3. Barbara Hutchinson and Victor Rothschild.
4. See letter of 26 July to Quentin Bell.

Here I am sitting among dust sheets, and there of course is the telephone ringing.

I'm longing for Love which I dont get: so write and say if you can come over.

B.

Berg

2767: To Quentin Bell   52 *T[avistock]* *S[quare, W.C.1]*

Typewritten
Wednesday [26 July 1933]

Dearest Quentin,

I'm very sorry to hear that youre in bed.[1] Please recover instantly, as I want you to come and meet Miss Elizabeth Read, a virgin, living with a large dog, rhapsodical, slim—about eighteen; now lodged in an Inn—but for the past six months at Quentins, in the village.[2] I enclose a letter from our dear Cousin James.[3] Never did I see a more dumpish, foolish, chattering ugly man; his trousers stained; his pockets done up with string, bolt eyed, shock headed, with a lolling swollen tongue like a mad dogs. He is a confounded bore and I gave him your address.

Yesterday I went to see the Burne Joneses[4]; no I dont like them; save as remnants of Nessas and my youth—floating lilies; things that have gone down the stream of time; which image is more just than you would think; for every picture has one white face looking down, and another looking up out of water. The suavity, the sinuosity, the way the private parts are merely clouded—it's all a romantic dream, which makes me think of tea at Hyde Park Gate. Oh I'm dripping with heat. Last night we dined with Julia Tomlin, and met Peter Quennell; Dorothy Bussy and Wogan[5] (who asked a great deal after you,) who may spell his other name with two l's or one—I dont know. As youre notoriously indiscreet and Charleston, Nessa

1. He had whooping-cough and mild pleurisy.
2. Elizabeth Read was temporarily lodging at 'Quentins', a house in Rodmell, and admired Virginia's writings. She was a social worker in Stepney.
3. (Sir) James Stephen, then aged 25, who succeeded his father Harry as 4th Baronet in 1945, in which year he was certified insane. He was not discharged from hospital until 1972.
4. An exhibition at the Tate Gallery in commemoration of the centenary of his birth.
5. Wogan Philipps, the painter, husband of Rosamond Lehmann, and later 2nd Lord Milford. Peter Quennell, the poet, essayist, biographer and critic was then aged 28.

says, a warren of literary gents,[1] I will not give you my candid opinion of anybody, but I prefer Wogan to Quennel; on the other hand, Q. has more knives in his brain. And I met a Mlle Chaunèse, and before I knew what was up, she had whipped out a note book and was taking my opinion of Joyce, Lawrence, life, death and the chances of an immortal soul. Then I lost my temper; and told her if she printed a word—shes an interviewer—I'd shoot her dead. This created an incident.

Talking of death and bullets, have you heard that Mrs Eliot is on the war path, said to have a carving knife with which first to skin Tom; then Ottoline; finally me? For she says Ott and I are Tom's mistresses; now as I never had a favour from that man its rather hard to give my life on the pavement.

I'm sending you a book of short stories; one—by [James] Joyce— seems to me very good. The others Ive not read. But please tell me what you think, as I must thank for it. We dined with Jack and Mary [Hutchinson]; Mary is to me ravishing; in chalk white with a yellow turban, like an Arab horse, or a pierrot. And we met two Frogs—Masson[2] and another [Simon Bussy], and went to the Zoo. And now I'm dining with Vita. But I wish I were sitting by my own fish pond with my own nephew writing indecent and vulgar lives of the living. Shall we revive our stories?[3]

I hope to see you soon.

Virginia

Quentin Bell

1. Raymond Mortimer was staying at Charleston.
2. André Masson (b. 1896) the French surrealist painter.
3. When Quentin was younger, he and Virginia collaborated on literary satires of their family and friends, Quentin being the illustrator.

Letters 2768-2800 (August–September 1933)

From late July until early October the Woolfs were at Monk's House, where Virginia intermittently continued The Pargiters (*not yet rechristened* The Years). *It was a glorious and happy summer, but her work was interrupted by a brief illness and many visitors. "I like it when people actually come", she wrote in her diary, but "I love it when they go." Ethel Smyth was away in northern Scotland for several weeks, but twice came to Rodmell, in spite of Virginia's increasing frankness that she did not wish to be disturbed. Among other visitors were Vita, T. S. Eliot (without his wife) and Morgan Forster. Virginia agreed reluctantly to return to London for a single night to review* Twelfth Night, *in which Lydia Keynes was appearing. The serious illness of Francis Birrell troubled her deeply, though she did not know him well. She attended the Labour Party Conference at Hastings in early October, more for Leonard's gratification than her own.* Flush *was published on 5 October, and she was as much dismayed as pleased by its success, for she regarded it as the slightest of all her books.*

2768: To LADY OTTOLINE MORRELL *Monks House, Rodmell, [Sussex]*

Sunday [30 July 1933?]

Dearest Ottoline,

I was so disappointed not to come but we were off that day—I hope they gave you my message. I should have liked to see you again and meant to persuade you to lend me your memoirs—Perhaps I shall have better luck in the autumn—I hope so. Otherwise I am thankful to be out of the hubble bubble—London, which you love.

yr
Virginia

Texas

2769: To ETHEL SMYTH *Monks House, Rodmell, [Sussex]*

July 31st 1933

I seize this moment, having put out a cake and honey and the kettle on the stove, to write: but the Keynes's will be here in a moment and wont go, God bless them and all my friends, till dinner. And then I shall be so talk weary. So now—here's the tip of my little finger or the end of my tail offered to your jaw. You see you're a great lioness and I'm only a dun coloured mouldy mouse. You know how cameleon I am in my changes—leopard one day, all violet spots; mouse today. I've been seeing Nessa (whose boy is ill, but better now: whooping cough: pleurisy and so on—owing to coughing with such violence he seems to have torn his side—he's Quentin; the dreamy charming slow one—but thats too long a sentence) I'm so sorry—yes, really—about your sister[1]—cold as I am, even you sometimes say, I think you're fond of your sister dont you? I hate people being unhappy: because I want all my life now to be hot, burning with happiness. But I've no time to go into that—Anyhow I hope she doesnt have pain. I hope too that your Mrs Pankhurst is done, and done triumphantly. Am I to read it—here they are—

Tuesday

Yes here they were the Keynes's and they stayed till after 8 and the dinner was burnt, but they were very very charming. Maynard prancing all over the world and saying outrageous things, and he and L. quarrelled—Even I was drawn in—about the state of Europe in 50 years: imagine quarelling about Free Trade and Fascism—still we did, and were very fond of each other too—Lydia is now going on the stage, as Rosalind or Ophelia: though she speaks English like a parrokeet:[2]

Well, this is so distracted and disjointed for I'm off now to buy our weeks supplies in Lewes—that I'm ashamed to send it.

What are you doing about Scotland? The Hebrides? How often I dream of the Hebrides! How I long to be walking on some solitary distant shore, with a gull or two, sandhills and a rising moon or setting sun—I dont much mind which: there is a little ship in the bay, one white cottage in the distance, and there am I walking alone by myself—but only in my dreams. Here I walk on the hot downs; but then I see some villa and my gorge rises. And Lord Ethel, there's all my relations in law at Worthing, oh how they turn me sick—coming over in their boots and furs, and talking talking—readymade reach me down chatter—hearts of gold, eyes brimming with sympathy—you'd like them: so do I: in the abstract. But this is my recurring summer malady—Worthing.

Now heres L. So write to me

V.

Berg

1. See p. 176, note 2.
2. Lydia Keynes (Lopokova) acted the role of Olivia in *Twelfth Night* at the Old Vic in September of this year.

Monks House, [Rodmell, Sussex]

Thursday [3 August 1933]

I'm delighted to hear that the old termagant your mother has turned against you again—Much better dig holes in the flower beds than sit poked in her pigstye.

1.) I've answered Carswell.[1]

2.) Leonard says, will you send the poems here.[2] Are they finished? What a triumph! And are they dedicated to B.M?[3] (You see how spiteful I am).

3.) We would like to come over if we can on the 19th—the only thing is that we've got to go up to London and down to Essex one day. D'you want to know?

I'm rather repentant about fastening Virginia Isham and her playery on you. I dont know her, much: only as a child oppressed by a family: and she has grown into a thick but competent young woman, determined to break loose. Anyhow, its a great feather in her cap, if you let her act in flood lights at Sht [Sissinghurst]. And again you show the goodness of your heart.

Yes I do enjoy being here. L. and Percy are talking under the window about fruit and gramophones and racing and clipping hedges. On and on they go—like old gaffers in gaiters. But all the Wolfery is at Worthing; and Ethel coming over, and the Easdales. And Nan's [Hudson] dogs dead and will we therefore go to Auppegard to console her. And I would like to see Vita.

V.

Berg

2771 To Ethel Smyth   *[Monk's House, Rodmell, Sussex]*

Saturday [5 August 1933]

This is not a letter only a deliquescent scrawl. At Worthing [Leonard's Mother] yesterday—oh the heat.

Yes I like it very much indeed.[4] First part first rate. One sentence—about the dawn in the hotel—I should like to crib for myself.[5] The second

1. Catherine Carswell, author of *The Savage Pilgrimage: A Narrative of D. H. Lawrence*, 1932.
2. Vita's *Collected Poems*, Vol. I, published by the Hogarth Press in November. No Vol. II was ever published.
3. 'Bonne Mama', Lady Sackville, to whom Vita did dedicate the volume in spite of a recent row between them.
4. Ethel's short biography of Emmeline Pankhurst, in *Female Pipings in Eden*.
5. "For a second we were standing on the spot in a madly spinning world where nothing stirs, where there is eternal stillness." *Pipings*, p. 194.

part not so exciting; but curious: watered a little by E. P.'s still style. But thats interesting too. A fascinating work. I'll suggest criticisms later. Let me know the exact time of your coming—I'm harassed by possible visitors. Yes, P is very good—

Berg

2772: To Ethel Smyth   *Monks House, [Rodmell, Sussex]*

Monday Bank holiday (7 August 1933]

The letters [Henry Brewster's] came safe this morning, and I shall indulge myself tomorrow in reading them; in beginning anyhow. The heat —oh the heat!—The meadow is like a yellow blanket, burnt up; all the sweet peas dead. Of course, the Pankhurst paper is by far the most convincing suffrage argument there can be—it proved to my entire satisfaction the truth of my attack upon Pipings. Here one is persuaded unconsciously, profoundly from the roots, instead of having one's face smacked by an aggressive charwoman (excuse the metaphor: impute it to the heat) What a remarkable story to be sure—E. P. The four children at the end. Its the end I doubt slightly—the E. P. speaking in person—But I'll read again— when I've time.

It strikes me, to change the subject, that you dont make any allowance, when you twit me for moods and unsociability, for the incessant nibble nibble of my time in London. July was like being a biscuit in the middle of rats. And here its rather a bite—yesterday people; today people; well well: this is only to excuse my acerbity in London. We go to London on Friday next: so dont choose that day and then upbraid me. But come: you'll find me very very nice, and full of admiration—all the more that E.P. proves the justice of my criticism of Pipings—how I hate that little penny whistle title! And what about Maurice [Baring] coming with you?

Yes or no? He wrote to me.

V.

Berg

2773: To V. Sackville-West   *Monks House, Rodmell, [Sussex]*

Wednesday [9 August 1933]

(1) Bumpus (Wilson)[1] wants to exhibit an MS of mine and suggests Orlando.

1. John G. Wilson (1876-1963), Chairman and Managing Director of Edward Bumpus, the bookshop in Oxford Street, London, and author of *The Business of Bookselling*, 1930.

I dont particularly myself wish to be shown up in a glass case along of Priestly and Hugh [Walpole]; so if you like to refuse to lend, please do. But I had to tell him to ask your permission. No, I dont want to be in a glass case at all.

2) What time on 19th is Virginia's play?[1] We would like to come very much, and want to engage seats; and which play is it? So I hear you're off to the Hebrides with Ethel—part of the journey to be in an aeroplane.[2] Well, tastes differ; but I'm not altogether sure that I agree in wishing to fly and fly and fly with Ethel. Dear me, whats the use of joking? She's coming here on Sunday—Oh and we've had the Easdales[3] for 3 hours solid, no 4; as they missed the train; and then all yesterday a positive dangerous woman lunatic from Chicago.[4] Never again do I answer the telephone in person. Please send a line on a card: *also where are your poems?*

And how is Nigel?   V

Berg

2774: To Ethel Smyth   [*Monk's House, Rodmell, Sussex*]

Wednesday [9 August 1933]

L. says he has settled everything with MB. Will you come on Sunday afternoon? L. will call for you at Rottingdean at ¼ to 4.[5]

This will be understood unless you write to the contrary

V.W.

Berg

2775: To Ethel Smyth   [*Monk's House*], *Rodmell, [Sussex]*

Monday [14 August 1933]

Oh dear what a bore! Had it been Wed[y] perhaps I could have seen you. However, can't be helped. I went out on Sat[y]: found people here; had to

1. See p. 205, note 2.
2. Vita did not go with Ethel to Scotland.
3. Joan Easdale, the Hogarth girl poet, and her mother.
4. Elinor Nef, wife of John Ulric Nef, a member of the faculty of the University of Chicago and later Professor of Economic History there. He was the author of many books bridging several disciplines. In his autobiography *Search for Memory*, 1973, Nef wrote about his wife and Virginia: "There was a strange communion between the suffering of the two women. . . . Both suffered illnesses very different in manifestation, but similarly irradicable, and similarly emotional in origin" (p. 147).
5. Ethel was staying with Maurice Baring at Rottingdean.

talk, got another bad head; so whats the use of risking it again? Five minutes I would like; but find the idea bothers L. and it wouldn't be much good. I had been wishing to see the uncastrated cat: am indeed, very fond of that animal. Please tell L. what MSS you can leave. I've not attempted the 2nd version of Pipings: nor read through Mrs P: [Pankhurst] again, so cant give an opinion. Tell L. when you must have them back or the opinion. Also HB [Brewster]—not read—Please write from Shetlands—how I envy you —a land unseen by me. And send one picture postcard of the shore where my Lighthouse was.[1]

Yes. I feel a distinct and odd sensation at the thought of you—can it be affection? Can it be love?

Berg

V.

2776: TO ETHEL SMYTH

[*Monk's House, Rodmell, Sussex*]

Tuesday [15 August 1933]

My own feeling for what it is worth would be in favour of cutting the Pankhurst down.

I believe you could give the essence, fortified, in 30,000. But this means as I know a deadly grind. And I'm sure its all right as it is—only I think there is still vapour adhering—things that could be sat upon and pressed tight.

I venture this however only because you may want another view: its not a trusty one; I only read once, and that for pleasure. If you like to send it back, I wd. read quickly again: But I doubt if this will reach you in time

Better today—sitting up.

Berg

V.

2777: TO QUENTIN BELL

Monks House, [*Rodmell, Sussex*]

Typewritten
Tuesday [15 August 1933]

Dearest Quentin,

Here are the books; but I must explain; the one I admired, perhaps wrongly—but I leave that to you—is Ordinary Families;[2] the other, Night

1. Although the setting of *To the Lighthouse* was vaguely in the Hebrides, Virginia took as her model Godrevy lighthouse in St Ives bay, Cornwall.
2. A novel by E. Arnot-Robertson, 1933.

in May no Frost[1] she calls it, [. . . . . *21 words omitted* . . . . .] She is a friend of Logan's, a Chelsea pensioner, and I daresay worthless; but the erudite say she is full of suppressed ardour, virtue, and it's her own story. So let me have it back. I am dashing off for a day's ride, before the car is decarbonised. We are going to Rye, to eat at the Mermaid [Inn], and drink a cup of tea to the very small ghost of Julian [Bell]; because last time I was at Rye [in 1907]—ask Nessa—Julian was the size of the swallow in the drawing room; featherless; mute; think of it, And Henry James lent us his room; and said Saxon [Sydney-Turner] was a little packet of filth. This is a fragment from my memoirs. I hope you are better. Please get well, because I want you to come here and meet Miss Read.[2]

Virginia

Quentin Bell

2778: To V. Sackville-West   *Monks House, [Rodmell, Sussex]*

Wednesday [16 August 1933]

Poor Virginia has been in bed; and thought how nice it would be to see Vita!: and is now up and says How nice it would be to see Vita! And L says (this is a terrific complement) "I should like to see Vita." What about coming one day next week for the night? Could it be?

And who's Lady Roehampton in the Edwardians?[3] Please tell me. I read The E's all in a gulp with pleasure in bed; very well done I think: also Ordinary Families (thanks to Harold) very good: I thought. Yes, an interesting mind.

But can you come?

If so, Ill write a long long letter. This is only Potto's scrawl

V.

Ethel came and I staved her off.

Sorry Virginias [Isham] play is off.

Berg

1. *Frost in May*, a novel by Antonia White, 1933.
2. See p. 206, note 2.
3. Vita's novel, 1930. She replied on 18 August that the character of Lady Roehampton was based on the Countess of Westmorland (d. 1910), "a lovely sumptuous creature, who came to Knole when I was eight, and who first set my feet along the wrong path" (*Berg*).

2779: To JOHN U. NEF *Monks House, Rodmell,*
[Lewes, Sussex]

16th Aug. 33

Dear Mr Nef

I must apologise for my delay in thanking you for the delightful present that you have sent me,[1] but I have been laid up in bed ever since it came. Even so, I have been dipping into it, and find it full of interest, and of facts of course entirely unknown to me. As a writer of fiction I find books of facts the most delightful relief, and I am enjoying your coal much more than all the MSS about the human heart which I should be reading. Many thanks for sending it to me.

Please remember us both to your wife and thank her for her letter. We both much liked seeing you here.

Yours sincerely
Virginia Woolf

My husband wants me to say how much he thanks you for sending him the book which he will read with great interest.

The University of Chicago Library

2780: To HELEN McAFEE 52 *Tavistock Square, W.C.*1

Typewritten
17th August 1933

Dear Miss McAfee,

I enclose an article on Oliver Goldsmith in case you should like to use it in the Yale Review.[2] It will appear over here in the Times Literary Supplement but I could arrange publication to suit you if you would let me know. I should be very grateful for an early reply. Very stupidly, I have forgotten your dates for copy.

I hope things are going better in America now—we hear, naturally, many different views. At any rate I see that the Yale Review flourishes, which is a good sign, and means I hope that you are well also.

Yours sincerely
Virginia Woolf
(Mrs Woolf)

Yale University

1. Nef's two-volume book *The Rise of the British Coal Industry*, 1932.
2. It was not published in the *Yale Review* but appeared in the *T.L.S.* on 1 March 1934, and was reprinted in *The Captain's Death Bed*, 1950.

2781: To V. Sackville-West

Monk's House, Rodmell,
near Lewes, Sussex

Sunday [20 August 1933]

Yes dearest Creature, that will be very nice: I mean Tuesday 29th. for the night—in a sense.

I was interrupted by the irruption of the Kingsley Martins—not to me an appetising couple.[1] No: I dont want to see another soul: with one exception.

Now can I slip round and take a walk leaving them to Leonard; having provided the bleak Mrs M. [Martin] with a cushion? Can I?

V.

I see Ly Sacklle is again in the dock[2]

Berg

2782: To S. S. Koteliansky

Monks House, Rodmell,
Lewes, Sussex

Typewritten
Aug 21st 1933

My dear Kot,

I am sending back the Dostoevsky with this letter.[3] I think it is an extremely interesting document. But I do not think that I can write an introduction, because in order to say anything of interest about these notes one would have to go deeply into the question of novel writing and into the whole question of Dostoevsky's psychology as a writer. I do not feel that I know enough about him. He is such an extraordinary case as a writer that I should feel it silly to hazard guesses about him; I should want to think a great deal about it. And I feel I should say nothing interesting in the end, because the problems it raises are very difficult ones.

Indeed I do not see why an introduction is needed. Anyone who reads this will be already a Dostoevsky enthusiast; and would, as I myself should,

1. Kingsley Martin was not married, but his lifelong companion was Dorothy Woodman.
2. Vita's mother was so frequently sued for libel, wrongful dismissal, unpaid bills, etc., that she named her house at Brighton the Writs Hotel. The present case was an action brought against her by Thomas Seller whom she had employed to protect her property. She dismissed him for incompetence, ("You have no bloodhound or pistol"), and refused to pay his wages of £3. 10. 0. She lost the case.
3. See Letter 2761.

resent intervention. I would like it published as it stands, with Brodskys[1] introduction but nothing more. I dont much believe in attracting attention by using a well known name—that is only a draw to snobs; and irritates other people.

This is my feeling at any rate. So I am sending it back. I hope I have not kept it too long. I wanted to read it through carefully in peace. And I wish I could be more helpful.

Yours sincerely
Virginia Woolf

British Library

2783: To Ethel Smyth

Monk's House, [Rodmell, Sussex]

22nd August [1933]

No, my dear Ethel, Your psychology is much at fault. If I hadn't a heart of gold under the skin of a shark I should never write to you again, after your comments upon my poor little note.[2] Thats the trouble with the daughters of generals—either things are black, or they're white; either theyre sobs or they're 'shouts—' whereas, I always glide from semi-tone to semitone; and you never hear the difference between one and another. Thats why you dont understand a word I write, either in MS. or print; for its long been plain to me that you dont. Oh no: Dickens is your favourite author; after him Mr. Priestly. Ah hah! (There is an element of very profound truth in this) But I've forgotten now the lecture I meant to write upon your letters. One incident I do however remember. When you came that afternoon, I jumped out of bed and stood outside the drawing room door. I was about to go in. Then I thought, not of you, but of Leonard. Unravel this riddle, as you float above the [Hebridean] islands.

Yes I am much better; I am up. I am about; I have refused to see my mother in law, my sister in law, my brother in law, the Keynes's, and the Gages![3] I have had three entire days alone—three pure and rounded pearls. But then, last Sunday, just as I was writing my hymn to solitude out here in my garden room, with the rooks circling and the cows munching, there's a face at the window: the editor of the New Statesman [Kingsley Martin]

1. Iosif Brodsky, the most talented Russian poet of his generation, who in 1972 came to live in the United States.
2. Ethel had been hurt by Virginia's refusal to see her when she came to Rodmell from Rottingdean on 13 August. She complained that Leonard would not understand that she wished to see Virginia for only two minutes. "Does one want to talk to a landscape? to a fine sunset? No—only to bathe in it for half a second" (Ethel to Virginia, 15 August, *Berg*).
3. 6th Viscount Gage. See p. 137, note 2.

and his wife come to spend the afternoon. So the pearl dissolved; and tasted like a tabloid of quinnine as I swallowed it. What criminals, to waste a pearl; they dont know what they do. However, I write all the morning, which is perhaps all that one should dare to ask.

I wish I knew the geography of the British Isles. I dont at once visualise Hebrides, Skye, and the rest. I only see a black blot in mid air which is you, astride an aeroplane; firmly grasping a rail, keenly envisaging the seascape; and completely master of your feet and faculties. I daresay you drop down upon a British fortress and drink rum with the officers. Do they think you a jolly good fellow? Are you always moving on? Do you ever think?—read?—or are you dazed, as I am in the car, when we drive, and drive and drive, and my mind is a long peaceful smudge? I'm reading a vast number of books—when I'm not getting tea for the Editor of the New Statesman. Turgenev: Shakespeare's life, and huge masses of MSS. Do you know the difference between the Quarto's and the folios? I never did, till last night. Think of having spent a scholars life, correcting misprints! And the garden is—oh but why, when you came, didnt you look at the garden? My plan was to tap on the window: then you'd have come in—for 5 minutes. Why I said that 5 minutes was no good, was based on your own remark—that seeing me with other people there was more torment than pleasure. Lord, what a wild psychologist you are—how random, how violent: but then thats part of being an uncastrated cat, and a generals daughter—which I like: so I dont complain; only marvel admire, and shout with laughter over your letter. Please write another.

V.

Berg

2784: To Hugh Walpole   *Monks House, Rodmell,*
                               Lewes, Sussex

Aug, 23rd [1933]

My dear Hugh,

I was thinking too—Why the devil hasnt Hugh written to me all this time, or come to see me for the matter of that? I'm sorry the reason was such an unhappy one. One's friends ought never to get ill—never to have operations: But they do.[1] I have a theory however—after a bad year, one has a good one. Last year all my friends seemed to die.

Now that is very exciting and good of you—to be sending me Vanessa.[2] I want to read it very much. For one thing it will be about my own age, not my Grandfather's. And then, being in a gloom the other night, I took

1. Hugh Walpole was not himself ill, but Ethel Cheevers, the wife of his devoted servant and companion, Harold, collapsed with pleurisy after an operation.
2. See p. 177, note 2.

down your Apple Trees [1932] and enjoyed it so much, more the second reading even than the first, that I invented a theory to the effect that you being a born romantic, and I not being one, what I like is when you turn your rich lanthorn upon facts, because then they become rimmed and haloed with light but still remains facts in the centre. So I want you to go on writing your memories. It struck me today on my walk, that I like Scott's diaries better than all but three or four of his novels for this reason. And Vanessa —to end the argument—will have more fact in it than the others; what fun, if I'm there in the flesh!—or my name's there.

Its such an age since we met that I cant tell you any news—the voyage to Siena over the Alps is an old story now: so's Flush. No, I dont think it anywhere near a masterpiece. And my opinion of the Book Society has sunk 10 degrees now that theyve taken it. By the way, I couldn't face signing 300 copies as Mr Bott[1] kindly suggested. Ought I to? But I wont and cant.

Well, this sheet of paper seems to hint that I must go and play bowls with Leonard. But there is room to beg that you will soon write again, if you're not too bothered. What a generous man you are to be sure!

Yrs aff VW

When you write, be sure you put plain and large, Virginia Woolf on the envelope, or they open it in the Press d——n them.

Texas

2785: To V. Sackville-West   [*Monk's House, Rodmell, Sussex*]

Wednesday [30 August 1933]

Just to say that I've been talking to Raymond, and I'm glad to say things aren't nearly as bad as it seemed. Francis [Birrell] has been to an expert, who says the growth is small, and he thinks on the outside of the brain. He is going to have the operation next week, but they think he ought to recover completely, though it is of course serious. He's up and about at present only with two paralysed fingers. This I write in haste, thinking you'd like to hear.

Oh it was very nice seeing you, and what a noodle not to stay! as soon as you went, your paramour Mary [Hutchinson] rang up and wanted to come. But no: I'm here. London loathsome

V.

Berg

1. Alan Bott, publisher and author, and Chairman of the Book Society. *Flush* was their selected book for October. It was also the choice of the American Book Society.

[*Monks House, Rodmell, Sussex*]

Typewritten
[30 August 1933]

Dearest Quentin,

Perhaps you could kindly advise me whether I ought to send Miss Lorna Wilkinson, whom you will see is an artist, some cast off clothes?[1] Or do you think her father is a fraud—a have yer, as Lottie [Hope] calls it; as I rather suspect?

Oh what a day was yesterday! The Hon. and Rev. Campbell-Douglas-Douglas-Campbell-Douglas[2] at Ten AM: who said nudity amused him; indecency delighted him; but brutality shocks him; so he walked out of the Movies where his hostess an old lady of Ringmer [Sussex] had taken him with an 18 year old virgin. At Two, Willie Robson.[3] Why Willie I asked; after the German Emperor? No; a mistake of my mothers that has haunted and almost ruined my life. "But will you call me Willie?" On condition I am Virginia for ever, I said being rather flown with the heat. Whereupon the barking of a thousand dogs announced the advent of Vita; and at the same moment Mr Neil Lyons,[4] to beg a spray of bay, because an Italian Lady at Brighton had told him how to pickle herrings in a jar with Bay. But that plant is laurel, I said; and therefore almost instantly fatal. Wait, and I'll fetch Mrs Nicolson who is putting away her car, and is an expert on bays. So I fetched Vita; who said the laurel was a Portugese Juniper; and then flushed red, and whispered to me that Neil Lyons is the lover of the daughter of her sister in laws old flame, Sir Edward Morgan,[5] also the very spit and image of Harolds brother [2nd Lord Carnock], save that Harolds brother weighs twenty stone and is three foot ten; whereas Neil Lyons weighs sixteen stone and is four foot eight. Then Mr Lyons said, Could we oblige him with a spray of hazel, because he suspects himself of power as a water diviner. Not water I should have thought; but let it pass. He is claret coloured and barrel bodied. So it went from lunacy to lunacy, till the moon rose and the dogs bayed.

1. Herbert Wilkinson, a stranger but an avowed admirer of Virginia, had asked whether she could spare some old clothes for his poor but worthy daughter of 16.
2. The Rev. Leopold Douglas Campbell-Douglas (1881-1940), Vicar of Stockcross, Berkshire. He had been a friend of Leonard since Cambridge and was to become 6th Lord Blythswood in 1937.
3. William Robson, Lecturer (later Professor) of Public Administration at the London School of Economics. In 1930 he and Leonard founded the *Political Quarterly*, of which they were co-editors from 1931 until 1959.
4. The novelist and dramatist, 1880-1940.
5. His name was not Edward but Herbert, a man distinguished in industrial and charitable undertakings. He had loved Harold's sister Gwen St Aubyn, later Lady St Levan.

Oh my dear Quentin, that I were a seal lying on a slab of ice in the Hebrides, save that if I were Ethel Smyth would bawl me Brahms in such tones, so she says, that the male seal gives over copulating and dives into the deep. So Orpheus you remember charmed the trees. And just as I was writing this, the telephone rings and theres Mary Hutchinson wants to come tomorrow with Jeremy and Barbara [her children]—Heaven be praised, we shall be in London. Such is life. Kiss your mother and tell her that in spite of everything I adore her. There is a world of meaning in that which she alone will understand.

V.

[handwritten]

Return Wilkinson at your leisure.

Quentin Bell

2787: To Francis Birrell   *Monks House, Rodmell,*
                             [Sussex]

Sunday Sept 3rd [1933]

My dear Francis,

I was just about to write and ask if you would come and stay here, and now I hear that you are to have an operation. What a damned bore for you! We are both miserable to think of it, and wish we could have it for you, or at anyrate, come and see you. A word whispered to Raymond or anyone would always fetch a couple of old wolves to your bedside—but I hope you wont be there long. Please not—there are a million things we want to talk about. And last time [on 5 July] it was such a hubbub—d'you remember: Sashie, Georgia,[1] Brennans and all the rest of them in Helen's [Anrep] bedroom: and Mrs [Peter] Quennell, for whom I have the feeling of a rabbit towards a snake, bending all in black but not I think very agreeably—over the washstand. Why do I always envisage Roger's parties in Helen's bedroom? What they call the pathetic fallacy?[2] Ruskin is that? God knows.

I've been reading a stuck up humbug called Faber on Newman with fury.[3] How my gorge rises at the new generation of virtuous young men, (but I suspect Faber of being bald) who have learnt all their tricks from Lytton, and then accuse him of not loving mankind! Lytton had more love in his little finger than that castrated cat in the whole of his mangy stringy partless gutless tailless body.

1. Sacheverell Sitwell and his wife Georgia.
2. John Ruskin's *Modern Painters*, Vol. III.
3. *Oxford Apostles: A Character Study of the Oxford Movement*, by Geoffrey Faber, 1933. Faber (1889-1961) was President of Faber & Faber, the publishers, and Bursar of All Souls College, Oxford.

That reminds me, rather circumlocuitously, that Tom Eliot's coming here, having first taken every precaution, short of growing a beard, to prevent Vivien following him. I suppose you heard how that man of genius shook off his wife? It was a most interesting process, to one who loves the smell of the rubbish heap as I do, to watch. She sat in her flat under a crowned effigy—that is Toms photo by Elliot Fry, and a wreath of daisies —saying that he was drowned: whereas he was editing the Criterion round the corner. But I dont wonder that he daren't face her—nor could I. The question is, will he drop Xtianity with his wife, as one might empty the fishbones after the herring. (I'm cooking dinner, so forgive the image). I'll write and tell you.

We are going over to Tilton, to be converted by Maynard to what I suspect of being a form of Fascism. My brain soon flags: and I leave it to Leonard, while Lydia sits mumbling the part of Olivia in 12th night which she is to act at the old Vic.

Well, this is only a drivel, from your attached and ancient friend. Leonard sends his love from the top of an apple tree; and we both want to hear that you're all right and will come and see us. I cant tell you how everyone goes on asking for news of you.

Yrs affly
VW

And this needs no answer.

Raymond Mortimer

2788: To Ethel Smyth   *Monk's House, Rodmell,*
near Lewes, Sussex

Wednesday [6 September 1933]

Oh but we're here, thank God, for another month—till Oct, anyhow. Not that there are many empty days, even here: but that as you point out, is the fault of my passion for the aristocracy. My hand shakes so with pulling a dog, not mine, away from sheep I cant write. And I've lost your envelope. But I much admire your Shetland Isles psychology and long to go there, to acquire a touch of it. Oh if I could only control my fingers!

Possibly we go to Bath and Bristol next week, travelling books [later cancelled]. But I'll let you know; if you will write.

What a descriptive writer was lost when you took up the piano. I sat, for 10 minutes, looking at the Orkneys: or was it the Hebrides? Did you fly? Did you buy a picture post card? You see, the dog was very big and young, and when he saw a sheep he ran; and I had to tug. Thats why all I have to say about Shakespeare is so very elliptical. Still, I'm sure you agree.

How's Woking? Hows Kathleen?[1] For Gods sake tell me about the maiden-head removal—what a lark![2]

Shall we go and be done together? Side by side in Bond Street?

V.

Rebecca [West] has written on Pankhurst [in *The Post-Victorians*]; not so much flesh on the bones as yours; and Vera Brittain has written a book which kept me out of bed till I'd read it.[3] Why?

Berg

2789: To ETHEL SMYTH
Monks House [Rodmell, Sussex]

Typewritten
Sunday. [10 September 1933]

Yes a very interesting letter—a good imaginative reasonable interesting mind, Elizabeths [Williamson].

More than can be said for me at the moment—Tom Eliot for twenty four hours solid talk yesterday; Rosamund Lehmann and husband now coming to lunch; Oliver Strachey tea. Lady Colefax I have refused. Lydia makes me write about 12th Night. Must go to London to Old Vic.[4] Must write journalism. Must see friends. Have therefore decided from today on to give up all other writing in order to see that theres beef for lunch and cake for tea. I have just burnt my MS. Sure you'll approve. Am going to spend all my money on clothes, face powder—Mary Hutch. and Jack also came yesterday—She says she'll introduce me to Elizabeth Arden beauty parlour. Fingers to be red. Toes to be silver. Face to be lifted; nose to be filled with wax. I am doing this at your bidding. Oh but my lodge[5] is full of smoke from my burning novel so can not see to write more.

V—who gave up literature at the command of her friends.

Berg

1. Kathleen was the fifth daughter of the 2nd Earl of Balfour, and they were neighbours of Ethel at Woking.
2. Ethel wrote to Virginia on 26 August that she had met a young woman who "tells me lots of girls have themselves operated on nowadays so as not to endure tortures on marriage nights. . . . Why not try it now? (Its never to late to rend)" (*Berg*).
3. *Testament of Youth*, about her experiences in the First War as a Red Cross nurse.
4. Virginia reviewed the play in the *New Statesman*, 30 September.
5. Her garden-hut at Monk's House, where she did most of her writing during the summer.

2790: TO VANESSA BELL   *Monk's House, Rodmell,*
                                          near Lewes, Sussex

Tuesday [12 September 1933]

Angelica and Eve[1] seemed to think they would like to spend a night here. But A. seemed to think that Friday and Saturday were impossible, and Eve goes on Sunday. So that seems to leave Thursday only.

I'm afraid I've left this rather late (but we've been out all day travelling books) but could you bring them to tea on Thursday, and we would bring them back early on Friday afternoon?

Of course it might be simpler if A. could come later alone; only she wanted, I think to come with Eve. About A's birthday present—I dont know what she wants;[2] but I think I'll give her some small present on Saturday; and then perhaps you and she would choose a dress, or whatever she wants in London before she goes back.

Lord! what streams of people we all have—worse than London: so that I never see you for quiet and reasonable talk.

I think you'll have time to send a card about Thursday.

                                                            Yr
                                                            B

Berg

2791: TO VANESSA BELL   [*Monk's House, Rodmell,*
                                          Sussex]

Postcard
[13 September 1933]

P.S.

Or if A. and E. [Angelica and Eve] cant spend the night would they come to a birthday dinner at Shelleys[3] either Thursday or Friday.

Excuse haste

Berg

1. Eve Younger, the orphaned daughter of a Bloomsbury doctor. Angelica had been at school with her.
2. Angelica Bell's birthday was not until 25 December, when she would be 15, but Vanessa gave her an annual 'honorary' birthday party on 16 September, which was also Clive's birthday, to compensate for being born on Christmas Day.
3. Shelleys Hotel, Lewes.

[Monk's House, Rodmell, Sussex]

Typewritten
Thursday [14 September 1933]

Excuse the typing but my hand is perished with cold. Saturday wouldnt do for me either; nieces birthday party. Sunday I can be here; if youd let me know time; but I gather its awkward for you; so what about later? We shall stay on till 3rd or 4th Oct. Next week end is impossible; but after next week end I dont intend to have any more visitors. No; it wasnt your comments on the Waves; it was the insistence of my friends that I should be always at their beck and call that made me resign literature. Two come tonight; and then again on Tuesday; Wednesday we go up to Lydias play; then my horror is that I must write an article on it; all because my friends love me; and again must see Keynes etc. But as I say after next week I shall be freer; so choose which. And let me know. Excuse illiteracy; whistling wind and dead leaves whirling.

V.

Berg

2793: To V. Sackville-West   *Monk's House, Rodmell, near Lewes, Sussex*

15th Sept [1933]

Dearest Creature,

I am a wretch never to have written—not that you care But there has been such a rain of visitors on my head that I couldn't escape. Next week is hopeless—Lord, I have to see Ethel, the Lucas's—Peter [F. L. Lucas], whom Harold so rightly chastises, and a new unknown wife: then go to London to see 12th night, because Lydia is acting; then Morgan Forster: but after the 23rd Heaven be praised, there'll be no one that I know of.

Could we come then? I'm longing to see the Ellen Terry house. Will you thank, rather late in the day, Miss Craig or St John, for offering lunch? I'm going to join their society, I mean nothing more than subscribe to The Barn, as soon as I can summon resolution to write a letter or a cheque.[1]

Yes its very lovely here. Angelica and Eve are shooting bows and arrows on the lawn. Two Comma butterflies have been copulating on the cabbages —but there!—you never collected butterflies, so a comma more or less

1. Christopher St John (the biographer of Ethel Smyth), and Edith Craig, Ellen Terry's daughter, lived at Smallhythe, eight miles from Sissinghurst, in the cottage which belonged to Ellen Terry from 1899 to 1928. Adjoining it was an old barn ('The Barn') which they converted into a private theatre with a subscribing membership.

means nothing to you. All the romance of life is to me centred, not in Vanessa by Hugh Walpole, but in a Red underwing sipping sugar on a beech tree.

My word, what a nice woman you are! Thats the very words I said, on reading your letter to Leonard.[1] Moreover, they confirmed my own saying. He was rather in a stew, and thought we were making demands on your honour, integrity, friendship, magnanimity and so on. I said, Oh but Vita is like that. Then your letter comes to confirm it. It was a noble act though, tossing 1000 guineas into the duckpond, or cesspool, for to tell the truth, I dont like [Rupert] Hart Davies in the flesh, nor [Jonathan] Cape [publishers] in the spirit.

Yes, I'd like to see you again, We stay on till Oct. 6th or so; therefore we may meet. Suggest any day: and I will too.

V.

Berg

2794: TO VANESSA BELL   *Monk's House, Rodmell,*
                                          near Lewes, Sussex

[mid-September 1933]

I've just had this from Raymond which I send in case you've not heard [about Birrell]

Well dinner on Wednesday unless it strikes you that there is something unutterably repulsive about us before that.

B.

Berg

2795: TO QUENTIN BELL   *Monks House, [Rodmell,*
                                          Sussex]

Typewritten
Tuesday [19 September 1933]

Dearest Quentin,

The man has answered—Lorna [Wilkinson] is dressed up in my old clothes[2] and all is well in the worst of all possible worlds. The reason why Ethel Smyth is so repulsive, tell Nessa, is her table manners. She oozes; she chortles; and she half blew her rather red nose on her table napkin. Then she poured the cream—oh the blackberries were divine—into her beer; and I had rather dine with a dog. But you can tell people they are murderers; you can not tell them that they eat like hogs. That is wisdom.

1. Vita to Virginia, 1 September: "Tell Leonard a rival publisher is trying to bribe me away [from the Hogarth Press] with £1,000—but I won't be bribed" (*Berg*).
2. See p. 220, note 1.

She was however full—after dinner—of vigorous charm; she walked four miles; she sang Brahms; the sheep looked up and were not fed. And we packed her off before midnight.

Now the [F. L.] Lucases are coming; and then we go to London; and then—well, have you read the mornings paper on Lydia? The D.T. is scathing.[1] My god; what shall I say? I think the only possible line to take is how very exciting it is to see Shakespr mauled; of course one might make play with the idea that the Elizabethans were just as unintelligible; and throw in a hint about opposites being the same thing as equalities—if you take my meaning. Either the worst, or the best—that sort of remark. Well. Pity me. Yesterday we went and bought yew trees. I heard from Frankie [Birrell] this morning who says he has £4000 of radium in his head; but is as lively as ever. Thats all the news, except that I cant remember Mrs L's name; and am making a shot at Priscilla.[2]

V.

Quentin Bell

2796: To Frances Partridge   *Monks House, Rodmell,*
                                     Lewes, Sussex

Sunday [24 September 1933]

Dear Frances,

We have put off our journey to the west for the time—out of sheer laziness. Otherwise we fully meant to descend upon you [at Ham Spray]. We should very much like to come later in the autumn, if you will have us. No, I had not heard of Oliver's [Strachey] new love, let alone seen her. But he was here the other day, and I thought I felt a change in him. Now several people have told me about her, and I gather that she's no beauty in any way. Isn't it rather hard lines on Ray?[3]—however, I'm always in the dark about peoples loves, so I let Oliver be.

Now I must go off to meet Ethel Smyth—think of me talking at the top of my voice and listening at the top of my ears for the next 6 hours—thats why I snatch my last coherent moment to write this.

Our love to Ralph [Partridge], and hoping to see you.

Yrs Virginia

Frances Partridge

1. The review of *Twelfth Night* was by W. A. Darlington. He wrote: "Lydia Lopokova makes her bow . . . as the most humourless female in literature. . . . What possessed anybody to give the part of Olivia to her?"
2. F. L. Lucas (1894-1967) was the University Reader in English at Cambridge, and the author of many novels, plays and works of criticism. His second wife was called Prudence (*née* Wilkinson).
3. His second wife, Rachel (*née* Costelloe).

2797: To Helen McAfee

Monk's House, Rodmell,
Lewes, Sussex

Typewritten
27th Sept. 1933

Dear Miss McAfee,

Many thanks for your courtesy in cabling to me. Of course I quite understand that Goldsmith is not a subject likely to be of particular interest in America. Your suggestion of an essay upon the modern essayist is interesting, but my time is rather taken up at present. I have promised to do an essay on Turgenev's novels for the Times;[1] and shall try to do that this autumn. But again, I expect that Turgenev is a little remote from your public. In England—or rather in the Literary supplement—we have a habit of reviving old writers from time to time with no particular reason; hence Goldsmith and Turgenev. But if I should think of anything more topical later I will certainly let you know. With many thanks and remembrances from us both,

Yours sincerely
Virginia Woolf

P.S. Unless I hear from you that you would like to see the Turgenev, I will take it for granted that it would not interest you.

Yale University

2798: To Vanessa Bell

Monk's House, Rodmell,
near Lewes, Sussex

[29 September 1933]

Yes, we shall be delighted to dine tomorrow Saturday. But we stay on another week so we may hope to meet later. I'm amazed at the cheapness of the book case [for Monk's House?]. I thought it would be more. I've added a pittance for your share in design. If you object, I'll never ask you to do a job again.

Here's the first, premature review of Flush.[2]

B.

Berg

2799: To V. Sackville-West

Monks House, [Rodmell,
Sussex]

Saturday [30 September 1933]

Would it be possible for you to have us to lunch next Thursday, which

1. *The Novels of Turgenev*, *T.L.S.*, 14 December, was also published in the December issue of the *Yale Review*.
2. *Flush* was published on 5 October.

is, I think, Oct 5th—say about one? Then we could go and see Ellen Terry[1] or not, as turns out convenient: but I'd rather see you than any remains: That's a nice compliment. If you know what a riot of human kind we've had here—Eleven last Sunday; not all to stay thank God, but to talk, and to tea and so on.[2] However they were all, I admit, charming; however I dont want anymore talking; however, thats impossible, because we go back to London But I've just faced Sibyl [Colefax] and told her not to come. All this proves—all those howevers—how fond I must be of you. We've made another pond too. At first the water slanted up one way and down another. And now where can I buy pots, Italian, and a statue? Thats my contribution to the garden.

I've a mint of things to say but I cant remember a single one. How did Passion go at Croydon?[3] Did you enjoy it? Can I see it? Is it coming to London?

And we dined with Mary [Hutchinson], and her Jeremy wants to meet your Ben, so I said I would hand on the message.

Mary makes love to me—yes: other people dont. I daresay at this very minute you're couched with some herring griller in the straw God damn you. A stack here caught fire last week. And the beagles came over today, and my mushroom field was destroyed by them. D'you know, I've had mushrooms every morning. Good; and blackberries, also good. And then we have to go back to Tavistock and Miss West [H. Press] and poetry— Yes I shall read your book, through:[4] and I'll send you Flush, but its only a silly little joke: this is not modesty, nor vanity but sense. Ethel was here the other day: 6 hours: 6 hours really hard work. Let me know about Thursday

V.

Berg

2800: TO LADY OTTOLINE MORRELL   *Monks House, Rodmell,*
                                                        [Sussex]

Typewritten
[7 October 1933]

Dearest Ottoline,

How angelic of you to write—and devilish of me not to answer! Oh how I hated writing that tough little article![5] Poor dear Lydia asked me to

1. See p. 225, note 1.
2. They were mostly members of the Memoir Club, which had met at Tilton the previous evening.
3. *All Passion Spent*, Vita's novel, was dramatised by Beatrice Kelston under the title *Indian Summer*, and first performed at Croydon, with Jean Cadell as Lady Slane, on 23 September.
4. Vita's *Collected Poems*.
5. On *Twelfth Night* at the Old Vic.

do it—she attached great value to her acting—she wants to be an actress—and the whole thing was a dismal farce, and she is out of the Cherry Orchard in consequence. But never will I write about a friend again. They may wear the stones out on their knees before I go through that agony.

I am writing in a hurry and therefore type to spare your eyes. We stayed on here to go to the Labour party [conference] at Hastings, where I sat rather half witted and heard things that I did not understand. But I always enjoy it. And there were ships going by outside, while the tub thumping went on inside; and the old Webbs sitting like idols on the platform and Phil Baker and Irene[1] —do you remember her?

I've just had a letter from Brett. Yes. I think you are right.[2] Something odious oozes through—a kind of thick, impure scent. She says Kot [Koteliansky] is furious with her, for her book;[3] also that she is coming over, and means to see me. But I feel, no, that woman is impure. Now is this your suggestion; or does her letter with its egotism and uneasiness convey some profound truth to me? I do not know.

We are in the middle of packing to come back. I rather dread London. I feel less and less able to control my life and I go on saying yet it is the only life I shall ever have. Why waste it? However, it wont be a waste if you'll come one evening or let me come in the gloaming. I like the October evenings in London. It has been almost beyond belief beautiful here—I walk and walk by the river on the downs in a dream, like a bee, or a red admiral, quivering on brambles, on haystacks; and shut out the cement works and the villas. Even they melted in the yellow light have their glory. But no more. I must pack.

yr Virginia

[handwritten]

You have made a complete conquest of old Ethel. All her love is transferred to you.

Texas

---

1. Philip and Irene Noel-Baker. He had lost his seat (Coventry) in 1931, but was re-elected to Parliament as the Member for Derby in 1936. She, as Irene Noel, was the daughter of an Englishman who owned an estate in Euboea, Greece, where Virginia visited her in 1906.
2. Ottoline had written to Virginia (10 July, *Sussex*): "That cunning, spiteful, evil-smelling little poisonous insect Brett . . . She is a leech, and her apparent devotion is only to suck one."
3. Dorothy Brett's *Lawrence and Brett: A Friendship*, 1933.

Letters 2801-2841 (October–December 1933)

October was a bad month for Virginia. The Hogarth Press was continuing to impose such a burden on her and Leonard that once again they seriously thought of giving it up. Then Leonard had 'flu, and people interrupted, and Quentin was flown by his mother to Switzerland with suspected tuberculosis. Virginia had little time to write, and though she had shown great patience with the drafts of Ethel Smyth's new book, she occasionally burst out (e.g. on 25 October) with annoyance at Ethel's pig-headedness and love of publicity: "We are hopelessly and incorrigibly different". In contrast, Virginia's affection for Vita never wavered, as she explained (in a rare analysis of her feelings for Vita) to Ottoline Morrell on 31 December. Virginia went twice to Oxford, met Walter Sickert amd Michael Arlen, and renewed her friendship with Rebecca West and Stephen Spender. The Woolfs went to Monk's House for Christmas and remained there three weeks.

2801: To David Garnett   52 *Tavistock Sq.*, [*W.C.*1]

Typewritten
Sunday [8 October 1933]

My dear Bunny,
    You were more than generous and wholly delightful about Flush and Virginia last week;[1] and I had meant to write and thank you before, but not being altogether a dog, as you justly observe, had no time to go to the London Library and prove that I'm not so inaccurate as you think. No. I am rather proud of my facts. About license, for instance;[2] surely I made plain that I was referring to nature, not the post office? license natural to his age—well, I ask you, what has that license got to do with the Encyclopaedia? or the Post Office, or six and eightpence? Natures license, sometimes called lust. About the working mans cottage; I agree it looks a farm in the picture; but Mr Orion Horne calls it a working mans cottage; and he saw it; and was not a picturesque artist.[3] Painters at that date always

1. Garnett's review of *Flush* in the *New Statesman* of 6 October.
2. Garnett wrote: "Puppies are unlicensed until six months old."
3. The illustration captioned 'Flush's Birthplace' in *Flush* is a 19th-century engraving, unsigned. Richard Hengist Horne (1803-84), author of *Orion*, collaborated with Miss Barrett on *New Spirit of the Age*, 1844.

231

enlarge houses out of consideration for their owners. Such is my view as a biographer (and oh lord how does any one pretend to be a biographer?) As for asphalt, I admit I have my doubts;[1] but I suspect that the Prince Regent liked asphalt—asphalt seems to me implied by the [Brighton] Pavilion. But how could you let slip the horrid anachronism which stares at you, bright red, on page I dont know what? There were no pillar boxes in the year 1846. They were invented by Anthony Trollope about 1852. Dont expose me. If you do, my sales will prick like a bubble. Old gentlemen will die in fury. I could go on, but will stop, having I hope partly vindicated my claim to truth speaking. Yes, the last paragraph as originally written was simply Queen Victoria dying all over again—Flush remembered his entire past in Lyttons best manner; but I cut it out, when he was not there to see the joke. But what a good critic you are—lots of things you said I think of in the watches of the night; they stick like burs; whereas the others, save Desmond's,[2] run off my coat like water.

Yours affectionate old English springer spaniel Virginia

(Im in such a hurry I cant write sense; but are you in Endsleigh Gardens; will you come and see us; where is Miss Edwards;[3] and how is Francis? [Birrell]

David Garnett

2802: To V. Sackville-West   52 *T.[avistock] S.[quare, W.C.1]*

Tuesday [10 October 1933]

Yes of course it is understood: you come 4.30. Thursday. Yr sister in law [Gwen St Aubyn] after tea; you both bite supper and stay on a little (Julian's coming and wants to see you)

Perhaps we might go to Woolworths or have some other startling adventure. St. [Sissinghurst] cured my head—a miracle.

1. "Is she within her rights in speaking of asphalt paths in Regent's Park in the summer of 1842?"
2. Desmond MacCarthy's review of *Flush* in the *Sunday Times* of 8 October.
3. Dorothy Edwards, the author of *Rhapsody* (1927), a much-praised book of short stories. For a short time in 1933 she lived with David Garnett and his wife in Endsleigh Gardens, and looked after their small son William. Then she returned to her native Wales, had a nervous breakdown, and killed herself.

But I've been listening to Hugh [Walpole] for 3 hours so am not mistress of my wits—he's a dear rosy old bumble bee, and as mild as a shorn Lamb about Vanessa[1]

So 4.30 Thursday.

Berg

V.

2803: To Ethel Smyth   [52 Tavistock Square, W.C.1]

Thursday [12 October 1933]

No I cant manage Monday. There's been a muddle, and I find I have to write and finish an article on Turgenev[2] by Thursday, so that I must try to work between tea and dinner—and dont suppose even so I shall finish it. I'm sorry about your sister—[3] I had not seen it. Also I'm rather worried about Quentin—the dr. seems to think now that it is tuberculosis, and he will have to go to Switzerland. So I'm in no good mood for conversation (I dont mean that Q's really bad: only its a worry for Nessa) No of course I dont mind your not being able to cope with Flush.

So no more at the moment. I'm trying vainly to steer my way through people to considered criticism of art—hopeless! Here's Desmond MacCarthy.

V.

Berg

2804: To Lady Ottoline Morrell   52 Tavistock Sqre, [W.C.1]

Thursday [12 October 1933?]

Dearest Ottoline,

Yes we are just back. It would be very nice to come and see you. If Thursday next week would suit, I would come in after tea, about 5.30— and dont bother to write.

Shall you be here all the winter? That will lend a bustle to London— but I am determined to say nothing nice about you.

your Virginia

Texas

1. Not surprisingly. *Vanessa* had received "nearly sixty reviews, and not one spiteful one", and Metro-Goldwyn-Mayer had bought the film-rights for $12,500. (*Hugh Walpole* by Rupert Hart-Davis, 1952, p. 341).
2. See p. 228, note 1.
3. Alice Davidson (see p. 176, note 2) died on 1 October.

Monks House, Rodmell,
Lewes, Sussex

Oct 13th [1933]

Dear Gladys,[1]

Thank you so much for your letter. I am delighted that my little book on Flush amused you. Yes, they are much alike, Mrs Browning and her dog.

I need hardly say that I remember you and Hilary very well indeed; didnt we all go fishing at St Ives once?—As one grows older, these memories become more vivid.

Thank you again for writing.

Yours sincerely
Virginia Woolf

George Spater

52 *Tavistock Sq.* [*W.C.*1]

Typewritten
Saturday [14 October 1933]

Dearest Quentin,

I saw Julian and hear that though dilapidated and tied up with string, and skidding and skadding you reached home safe. No sooner had you gone, than Hugh Walpole burst in; much elated and also discomposed. He had been to the next door house by mistake; a lady with purple hair and carmine lips answered him. No I am not Mrs Woolf she said—indeed it was obvious what her trade was—not mine; and when Hugh said he must go; Oh no she said, just come in all the same. This was very upsetting Hugh said; his tastes being what they are. He looks down nightly upon the heads of prostitutes in Piccadilly; and never knows more of them than that. With rare tact I said nothing about Vanessa—the book. Then, let me see, Desmond came. Partly because Molly is ill and he wanted to escape; partly to discuss an article he is writing upon Bloomsbury.[2] He is going to tell the true story of that long since dead phantom, with names and facts. No, he would not eat he said—we were lunching; and then he pulled the pie to him and devoured it all.

Then we went to Hendon to fetch the car; there was Vita when we came

1. The daughter of William Holman Hunt, the painter. She and her brother Hilary had spent holidays with the Stephen children in Cornwall.
2. In 1933 Desmond MacCarthy wrote, but left unfinished, an article on Bloomsbury, and the fragment was published posthumously in *Memories* (1953) pp. 172-5. It is reprinted in *The Bloomsbury Group*, ed. S. P. Rosenbaum (1975), pp. 26-9.

back; and soon her sister in law [Gwen St Aubyn] came, whose head has been fractured in a motor car accident, but so neatly that the skull keeps together; and she never knew it; but must now do nothing but feed chickens for months till it grows together. So we gave her a lesson in printing, which is good for setting the skull, so they say. I suppose if she were to jump it might rise like the top of an egg. Then Lyn [Lloyd Irvine] came in the evening; and Julian and Lintott[1] and a mysterious woman speaking with a foreign accent, who makes ties. Who is she? I could not catch.

Lyn after one week on Everyman has sent in her resignation; her conscience—she is the daughter of a Scotch minister—will not stand the lies of Yeats Brown.[2] So now she is on the streets again. She thinks of putting an advertisement in the agony column; spinster of 32 etc. Last night we went to the Cherry Orchard—oh and Lydia came in to see us; and says she is now happier; but they were both in the depths of gloom; and they liked my article on her.[3] So thats all right. We dont think on the whole the Cherry Orchard can be acted by the English. Even the dog is English. I think it ought to be rewritten in sea gulls language like [J.M.] Synge. But they acted very well, but I doubt if it is as great a play as I thought it when I was young. Our Miss Walton [Hogarth Press] waited an hour and a half to see it, and was delighted. Now Kingsley Martin has just rung up to ask L. to go and talk about Hitler. He thinks there is going to be a world revolution. L. thinks he is optimistic and emotional. I dont like his table manners. Have you got Jimmy Sheehans novel?[4] He has sent it to me, but I expect Duncan has it.

Love to your mother. We shall be down on Friday.

Virginia

Quentin Bell

2807: To Ethel Smyth   52 T[avistock] S.[quare, W.C.1]

Tuesday [17 October 1933]

Sorry I didn't write before, but I couldn't make any arrangements. Last week was beyond belief—L. got the flu, people swarmed, I had to finish my article [Turgenev] by Thursday. We went to Rodmell a good

1. (Sir) Henry Lintott (b. 1908), then a civil servant, later High Commissioner in Canada. The 'mysterious woman' was Phyllis Hamerton, whom he married as his first wife.
2. Francis Yeats Brown (1886-1944), the soldier and author whose best-known book was *Bengal Lancer* (1930). He was an editorial consultant for the *Everyman* series of reprints of world classics.
3. See p. 223, note 4.
4. James Vincent Sheean's *The Tide*, 1933.

deal battered on Saturday and have only just got back. I think of giving up London altogether, only, as theyve now started an engine [a pump] which roars all over the marsh at Rodmell, thats no good. I seldom get from 5 to 7 (my time for making up novels) without chatter, chatter, chatter.

So I shall give up novel writing. As for letter writing—no—I *cant* write to you. I know its absurd, but every time I think "This will be shown to someone—" Yes, thats what you said—I re read your letter. What you call "Killingly funny letters" you always show; all my letters are thus parched at birth. I daresay yours is the right method—full of free publicity— but I'm the very opposite—Lord how opposite! You see, I couldnt show a letter of yours to any one, niece or nephew. Well—cant be helped. And I come back to 25 letters, all to be answered. Will I write about William Morris, will I sit, will I see, will I stay—By God, I wont. And I've now lost Time and Tide so I dont know where to send my subscription to. However, L. is recovered, so thats all right; but Nessa is taking Q to Switzerland by air, so thats rather dismal.

So good night.

V.

Berg

2808: To Lady Colefax   52 *Tavistock Sq.* [*W.C.*1]

Sunday [22? October 1933]

Dearest Sibyl,

You are an angel of a woman to write me such an enchanting letter (and the joy of it is that one of your letters can be read 12 times before grasping the full beauty). I'm so glad that you liked Flush. I think it shows great discrimination in you because it was all a matter of hints and shades, and practically no one has seen what I was after, and I was elated to Heaven to think that you among the faithful firmly stood—or whatever Milton said.[1] I cannot collect my wits, because I have to make a dinner do for 4 when it was ordered for 2. And its Sunday and the shops are shut. Why do people ring up at the last moment? But do come yourself, and let us be alone, and ask me to dinner later in the month of Nov. if you will. 29th is a day of entire misery—a dinner of 21 Wolves to celebrate an 85th birthday.

Forgive scrawl, and accept humble homage. What a good critic you are.

V.

Michael Colefax

"... faithful found
Among the faithless, faithful only he"
Paradise Lost, Book I, lines 893-4

236

[25 October 1933]

I could be in tomorrow for a few moments about 6.—if you want to come, as you say. But I feel—I may be wrong, that a meeting at this moment will simply mean raking up Vita, Elizabeth [Williamson], my faults (secretiveness) yours, (bullying)—so we shall go on—and this what you call cutting out an item—this to me at the moment excruciating personal cross examination. And at the moment I am extremely worried, not about your letter, or mine, or anything of that sort.[1] Only a muddle. It'll blow over, in a day or two: meanwhile I admit I'm on edge, and can only read in your letter (just come) the desire to heap abuse on me or rather find fault with my character—quite justly, I'm sure. Only I should put it that we are hopelessly and incorrigibly different, not right or wrong. So choose for yourself. But I admit I'm on edge and loathe these bickerings—these personalities

Berg

2810: To the Editor of the New Statesman

[October 1933]

Sir,

Everybody will sympathise with Mr St John Ervine in his courageous protest last week at the Institute of Journalists against the methods of publicity employed by a certain section of the press. The instances he gave were harrowing enough; Lady Ellerman's account of what she suffered at the hands of photographers when her husband died is still fresh in our minds; and most of us can supplement such stories with cases of a less extreme kind which have come under our own observation. Engaged couples of the upper classes complain that the telephone never ceases to ring until they have agreed to be photographed; the click of the camera is heard behind the altar rails during the marriage service; and at the other end of the social scale a village woman is besieged in her cottage by reporters and photographers because the rumour has reached Fleet Street that the wife of a gardener has received a legacy. The tale is endless.

But are we not ourselves to blame? Open the dailies and the weeklies. Among the pictures of Atlantic flyers and murderers you will find portraits

1. It was not a sudden single disaster, but an accumulation of worries about the Hogarth Press, Quentin's illness, lack of time to write, the pump at Rodmell and Leonard's influenza.   .

of well-known people, and by no means all of them are public people, but private people, musicians, writers, painters, artists of all kinds. Their homes are photographed, their families, their gardens, their studios, their bedrooms and their writing tables. Interviews appear; their opinions on every sort of subject are broadcast. How, then, can we blame the press if it takes advantage of this disposition on the part of well-known people, and infers that on the whole publicity is desired?

Yet this is by no means always the case. If you ask these "celebrities" why they have consented to make their faces or their houses or their views public property they will reply, for the most part, that they have done so unwillingly, but that unless they consent they will be branded as prigs, curmudgeons or cranks. Often, they will add, the request is made by friends whom it is difficult to refuse, or by struggling journalists in urgent need of the few guineas that the interview or the portrait will procure them. In short, a mild form of blackmail is applied, and out of weariness or good nature they succumb. Few are so simple or so modest as to suppose that any compliment is implied, and nobody nowadays believes that a publicity which is so widespread and indiscriminate has any pecuniary or prestige value for the victim.

Surely now the time has come when it is not enough to protest and to sympathise and to succumb. What is needed is a Society, with funds, with an office and some high-sounding title—Society for the Protection of Privacy or the like—to which those who honestly abominate such practices could belong. It is unnecessary to point out how sublime and authoritative sentiments that sound merely priggish when they are spoken by private people appear when issued with the sanction of an institute. A badge might be worn. A pledge might be administered. Members of the literary profession, for example, might take an oath not to allow any photograph, drawing or caricature of themselves to appear in the papers with [sic] their consent; not to give interviews; not to give autographs; not to attend public dinners; not to speak in public; not to see unknown admirers provided with letters of introduction from friends—and so, and so on. The form of the oath could be varied according to the profession. Any surplus funds could be applied to the abolition of steel traps or to the protection of wild animals. Your readers doubtless will be able to amplify and improve these suggestions. But until some society of the sort is founded and supported we have no right to complain if the press assumes that publicity is sweet, and snaps us while we are being born, married and lowered into the grave. As a pledge of good faith, may I add that I am willing to take the above oath myself, and to contribute not less than five guineas annually to any society that will rid us of these pests?

Virginia Woolf

New Statesman, 28 *October* 1933

Sunday [29 October 1933]

First fruits of the N.S. letter.[1]

Friday morning:

Telephone: "Kingsley Martin here. Would you and Virginia dine on Thursday or Friday next to meet Low?[2]

L: Sorry. We're engaged.

K.M.   Oh. Then would you dine Wednesday or Thursday the following week, to meet Low?

L: I must ask Virginia—She's out.

(Virginia; By God I wont dine any day of the year with Kingsley Martin.)

K.M.   Will you ring up when Virginia comes in and tell me what day you *will* dine then?

So we ring off, for the moment. And I've had the supreme joy of telling two persistent friends that owing to my letter I cant sign their books, or send them my phiz [physiognomy]. And orders are issued to the Press. And the bombardment goes on. and I'm having my last list set up and it'll be slipped into envelopes, and I rather think I'm in bad odour with Maynard Keynes, and not altogether popular with my fellow authors.

Tonight I slip on a magnificent dress of purple velvet and old lace and dine with 22 Jews and Jewesses to celebrate my mother in laws 84th birthday. And we shall play Bridge. And it'll be as hot as the monkey house. And tomorrow I shall have a headache and shan't be able to write. And then I shall sit and think of Ethel and wish she would commute herself into the wind of God and blow through my life, chastening but reviving. Psychologically speaking, as a Russian friend of mine says, I believe unconsciousness, and complete anonymity to be the only conditions—dear me what a sentence—but then I'm so hurried—in which I can write. Not to be aware of oneself. And all these people insist that one must be aware of oneself. Thats why I wont see my friends. A woman has written an essay in German on me—would you read it?

V

Berg

---

1. See preceding letter.
2. David Low (1891-1963) the best-known cartoonist of his day. His work appeared mainly in the *Evening Standard*, but he also frequently contributed to the *New Statesman*, for which he was doing a series of contemporary portraits, and wished to draw Virginia.

52 *Tavistock Square, W.C.*1

Tuesday [31 October 1933]

Dearest Ottoline,

I suppose tomorrow, Wednesday is no good for you?
As things have turned out, I think I shall be alone, after tea. We have to go down to Sussex on Thursday partly to see Francis Birrell at Brighton partly to drive Vanessa and Quentin to Croydon, whence they fly to Switzerland. He's been ill all the summer, with some persistent form of pleurisy, and the dr says he must have 3 months in Switzerland.

But I shall be back on Monday, and I daresay the Wednesday or Thursday of that week—8th or 9th—would be free. Perhaps the blessed Milly [maid] would ring up. And do settle some time, so that the stage mayn't be quite empty. I would like to hear about your letter, and Lytton, and the Garsington chapter and everything.

I do nothing but read Borrow,[1] when I'm not dining with 22 Jews to celebrate my mother in laws 84th birthday.

yrs VW

Texas

2813: To V. Sackville-West   52 *T.[avistock] S.[quare, W.C.*1]

Wednesday 1st Nov. [1933]

"I saw Vita lunching at the Café Royal today" said Jack Hutchinson last night

Oh such a pang of rage shot through me! All through dinner, and the supper, which ended with champagne and iced cake at 12.30, I was going back and foraging in my mind for the seed in my pillow: (you know what I mean: the pea under the mattress) and that was it. And I couldn't say "who was with her?"[2] And it burnt a hole in my mind, that you should have been lunching at the Cafe Royal and not come to see me.

How pleased you'll be! You did it on purpose I daresay. But who were you with? You knew I should get wind of it—yes and it was a woman you were lunching with, and there was I, sitting alone and and and . . . . . I break off my writing, which is all dish water, to make this heated exclamation:

1. George Borrow (1803-81), the traveller and authority on gipsy-life. Author of *Romany Rye*, 1857.
2. Vita replied that she had been lunching with her sister-in-law, Gwen St Aubyn. "I can't tell you how gratified I was by your annoyance" (*Berg*).

In fact we've been having the devil of [a] time, what with one thing and another. Quentin's going to Switzerland. Nessa's flying with him to Geneva. We're motoring them to Croydon at 6 on Friday morning: then go to Brighton to see Francis [Birrell], who can only haul himself round a table, hanging on to Desmond and a male nurse. Then back on Monday.

And when shall I see you? Dearest Creature, do write and tell me who you were lunching with at the Cafe Royal—and I sitting alone over the fire!

I've had your book [Collected Poems] in my hands—and very stately it is, like a slab of ivory engraved with steel; but I didn't read it, because you are giving it me.

Oh the Cafe Royal! When Jack said that—not to me, but to the company, you could have seen my hand tremble; and then we all went on talking. and the Rothschild's[1] came in, and a fat man called [Harold?] Shearman, and the candles were lit, and I chose mine, a green one, and it was the first to die, which means they say that out of the 8 or 9 people there, I shall be the first to wear a winding sheet. But you'll be lunching at the Cafe Royal!

Y
V.

Couldnt we lunch together or dine? When? Where? *Not* Thursday 9th.

Berg

2814: To Ethel Smyth   52 *T.*[avistock] *S.*[quare, *W.C.*1]

1st Nov. [1933]

Well, as the door-bell doesn't ring at the moment, I've finished H.B.[2]— some parts indeed I read twice, owing to beginning and being interrupted. Yes. Yes. Yes. That means they're extremely good, judging them as I should a book taken from the Times Book Club. Very witty, easy, well written, full of sparks and faces and shrewdness. I see what I miss—intimacy —is the result of his now coming to life, after being a toad in an oak all those years. I get a little tired of the lunches and dinners and Pasolinis and Contessa this and that. But as I say, I see the reason; and if you send me more—how far do they go?—no doubt that dining out and dissipation will vanish. Thats why, I expect, I dont quite come to grips with him. Rather as if he were always in evening dress—white waistcoat and so on. I cant feel the grain he's made of—cant get the full impression on to the slab of my mind, as I do when I've immersed myself in letters—generally. But of course this may

1. Victor (later 3rd Lord) Rothschild, who married Barbara Hutchinson in December of this year. This was their engagement party (see next letter).
2. Henry Brewster's letters to Ethel.

be the result of some pane of glass between us. Too different? I want more—now what is it?—just saying things as they come into one's head. I cant catch him off his guard. But thats, it may be, because he writes so well. And that, of course, adds to the sparkle and the fun, and the gliding in and out and the quips and cranks which are all very pleasing to me. Yes, I'd like to read the whole series through, and yours in between. Now I get the grain of you printed on the whole of my person.

Ottoline has not come, so I am alone—But stupid and sleepy because last night we sat up till one at the Hutchinsons to celebrate Barbara's engagement to Victor Rothschild, the Jew, the richest young man in England. And they burnt 23 candles round a cake, and we each chose one, and mine—a green one—died first, so they say I shall be the first to leave the room and go out in to what it pleases you to call Heaven. How I'd like to see what you see when I say Heaven!

About the privacy campaign—that stupid, but entirely well meaning, but muddled but incredibly bat eyed, mole snouted, dark, grouting and grovelling in the mine of Fleet Street, man, Kingsley Martin, seemed, from a remark of his to L., to think I was annoyed at *not* being caricatured; assured L. that [David] Low did wish it, and there was still space; so that I finally wrote him a private letter which may open his eyes: but theyre so small, so sealed to everything but his own messy little trade in leading articles, that I doubt it—Anyhow, I said, The reason I wont dine with you is because you have that little guttersnipe Low with a pencil at your table—if table it can be called, I added; for the K M's live in a high airy brainy room at Hampstead, where there's nuts on a check table cloth and autotypes from Albert Durer on a mud coloured wall.

That reminds me—here's L. come in so I must hurry—I'm sending you a paper, written by an exiled Jewess, on me, to read at your leisure; for she offered to pay a translator. And I said, knowing it to be all rot, Ethel will read it. So you will wont you, and tell me if I'm to say she is the only person, short of you, who has yet discovered the meaning of The Waves.

I think Miss Dodge[1] must be all awry with rheumatics, to interfere so unnecessarily, cut out 50 lines, and delay it again 2 days. What a mania for discretion she must be possessed of! I seriously wish to read that book [*Female Pipings . . .*].

Tell me next time you write who to send my cheque to. I've lost the notice giving the names of peeresses. I mean the Smyth fantasia festival.[2]

Nessa flies to Geneva with Quentin on Friday and we shall take her to Croydon about 6 in the morning: then visit Francis Birrell at Brighton—

1. Mary Dodge, Ethel's American friend and patron.
2. A series of concerts, dinners etc, in honour of Ethel Smyth, which took place in January 1934.

a poor good fellow, son of Augustine, who's had a lump cut out of his brain, is paralysed, but likes to see friends for an hour. Lord how we all age and fall! Last night, Desmond MacCarthy said, drinking his champagne, 'Yes Virginia, we are hasting to the grave." So I went and bought a new hair brush this afternoon—to stay away with. You see, L. didnt come, I've had 30 minutes to myself.

V.

What do I owe you for Jones [typing]?

Berg

2815: To V. Sackville-West   [52 *Tavistock Square, W.C.1*]

[8 November 1933]

Yes, very nice indeed—dinner on the 13th. Would you prefer dinner *here* with L. or alone out?

Let me know. Appalling rush. Oh and two such unbelievable days—Nessa flying to Geneva and back and lost in fog over Paris. 2 hours late. Oh my God—how I hate caring for people!

V.

Berg

2816: To Ethel Smyth   [52 *Tavistock Square, W.C.1*]

Wednesday [8 November 1933]

No, tomorrow will be a bad day for me, and ends with 7.30 dinner out. This evening $2\frac{1}{2}$ hours of Ottoline, very lovely, black and white—Yes, I accept your quotation about her. and shall be interested to hear of future developments. But oh how sleepy $2\frac{1}{2}$ hours continuous talk leaves me So I divided this page in two. Oh I've been in such a twitter—Nessa flying to Geneva and back and circling Paris in an aeroplane in a fog. Here was I sitting forced to make sensible remarks to [Shena] Lady Simon about education of women—waiting for a telephone. None came. Then the wrong one. Very well I said there's been a crash—went on making sensible remarks about Newnham [College] and its future. Now this was all very silly I admit. Well I'm ashamed to send this. I'm sorry about the books delay. And I'm sure you'd better send more of H B to the typist, I want to see how *he* develops; but still maintain Ethel should come in between. So good night

V.

Berg

2817: To Benedict Nicolson   52 *Tavistock Square, W.C.*1

Friday [Thursday] 9th Nov 1933

Dear Ben,

I heard from your mother that you very kindly asked me to tea with you when I stay with the Fishers.[1] Could I come this Saturday, 11th, that is day after tomorrow? Leonard and I are driving through Oxford to stay at Ipsden[2] and could be with you for about 4. But very likely this wont suit. I thought I'd ask, as I should so much like to see you, and rather doubt being able to manage it when I stay with the Fishers [on 30 November].

Could you send me a line? I wonder how you like Oxford, if you've met Jeremy Hutchinson, and lots of other things.

Yours ever
Virginia Woolf

Vanessa Nicolson

2818: To Quentin Bell   52 *Tavistock Sq. W.C.*1

Typewritten
Friday 10th Nov [1933]

Dearest Quentin,

Well it has been a very agitating week, waiting for aeroplanes to settle. Nessa seems to have flown round Paris in the fog—and then she mounted into the sun, and then she suddenly saw the Channel beneath her, and Heaven on top and earth below—oh how I envy her, but never never I hope will she fly again. But she says our ancestral mountains [the Alps] rather appeal to her—she begins to feel what father felt—noble, solitary, severe. I must come and see them. Do tell me what you think of them. I daresay they change in the dawn and sunset; and one gets to think them more beautiful than any earth scape.

But to return to human life—last night we had a memoir club meeting at the Gourmet. Naturally, Roger didn't come, having a cold; and Molly forgot to bring her manuscript; so we simply had dinner. Morgan stood it— and for some reason the wine went to our heads, and in the middle of dinner the babble was like all the cormorants, cockatoos and tigers in a tunnel roaring. Your father you see must get his roar above Leonard's; Morgan pipes; I jerk and jibber; and at last had to kiss Duncan in an access of emotion.

1. Ben was an undergraduate at Balliol College. Herbert Fisher was Warden of New College.
2. Near Wallingford, Oxfordshire, where the Woolfs stayed a night with Rosamond (Lehmann) and Wogan Philipps.

Then we went back to Clives: but poor dear Molly cant hear a word, and so Duncan and I talked one to each of her ears, and I couldnt say what the general din was about.

Then Julian came to tea, and made such a wonderful picture of a Miss Raine who was once the wife of Sykes Davis but is now penniless, living with a communist, and he said, six foot two, and noble as Boadicea, so that we must give her a job at the Press. And then she comes, and she's the size of a robin and has the mind of a lovely snowball.[1] How can she run the press? But this is *strictly confidential*, please; Dear old Julian is half seas over what with writing 1000 words daily on Good;[2] and running his museum, for which they need sixty screens of atrocities.[3] They sit there at bare tables typing. Suddenly some one says Isn't it awful—the New Statesman won't take our advertisement? And Julian fires off a furious letter to Kingsley Martin; whereupon the lady—Mrs [Maurice] Dobb—remarks, Oh but what I meant was, the New Statesman wont *give* us an advertisement. From this you may judge the measure of their sanity, Its like giving a party to all London and no cake coming and the butter having gone rancid.

Also Ottoline came to tea, like a weeping willow strung with pearls. She now wears globular moons at her ears—false. But on the other hand she is now all truth, humanity and loving kindness. Nessa and Roger say she bamboozles me. Oh how I wish you were here to take my side. Angelica has just rung up to say I'm to meet her at the dentist at four; Of course I have to go—so will all mankind all her life. I'm sending you the papers. We went to Brighton and had tea with old Mr Birrell,[4] who said, Now theres a chap called Clive; and theres Vanessa and Virginia but who are you? So one has to say I am the wife of Leonard Woolf, and the daughter of Leslie Stephen. Then he remembers exactly what father said in the year 1880. Francis has half his head shaved and looks like a Chinese Idol; Any letter from you will be welcome. But dont bother. Are there any books you want? If so you have only to speak.

Yrs Virginia

Quentin Bell

1. Kathleen Raine, the poet, (b. 1908). Hugh Sykes-Davies, was a fellow-Apostle of Julian at Cambridge. The 'communist' was Charles Madge, whom she later married. She gives an account of this interview in her autobiography *The Land Unknown*, 1975, p. 56.
2. Julian was still hoping to gain a Fellowship at King's, and was writing a new dissertation, this time philosophical, to which he gave the working title *The Good and All That*.
3. A 'No More War' exhibition at Cambridge. (See *Journey to a Frontier* by Peter Stansky and William Abrahams, 1966, p. 107.)
4. Augustine Birrell, Francis's father, the Liberal statesman and essayist. He died only ten days later, on 20 November, aged 83.

Typewritten
13th Nov. 1933

Dear Miss McAfee,

I enclose the proof of my article on Turgenev. You will see that I have made one or two corrections. I hope this may reach you in time for them to be made. I have made them on the proof, but for the sake of clearness, I typed the chief alterations on a separate sheet.

Many thanks for your letter. I am so glad you liked the article. I was greatly impressed by Turgenev, reading him again after many years, and hope that I may lead some of the younger generation to look at him again.

I have left the French to you, as you suggest. The names are given as Mrs Garnett writes them.[1]

Yours sincerely
Virginia Woolf

Yale University

Nov 15th [1933]

Dear David,

Thank you very much for sending me your Scott.[2] I waited to write until I had time to read it. And last night I sat down and read it at a gulp with great enjoyment. I think you make all the points I should have tried to make, and in proportion (which is so difficult) and with great economy. All I could have added would have been something about the dialogue and its relationship—I think the last in fiction of which that can be said—to the drama. But I should never have had the patience to go through the Elizabethans and trace what I mean. I wonder whether you will convert any of the intelligent. Let us flatter ourselves that it needs real intelligence to see the point of Scott against the tide—much more than to see the point of [Gerard Manley] Hopkins with it. I shall read one of my favourites— I only read 4 or 5—at Christmas, thanks to you, and when you next come to tea—but let it be before that—I'll try to find something more intelligent to say about your essay. But I liked it very much, and then lay back in my chair and read it, at ease, instead of bristling all over, as I do when reading in irritation, and jotting down notes with a pencil. There are two misprints:

1. Mrs Constance Garnett, David Garnett's mother, and best known for her translations from Russian literature.
2. David Cecil's essay on Sir Walter Scott in *The Raven Miscellany*, 1933.

sentitive and romatic (a nice new word) which pleases me greatly, because people say I can't spot them. (Flush swarms with them). And if I find 2, I think there must be 20. I can't remember where you live so send this to W.n. [Wellington] Square.[1]

Our love to Rachel.

Yours ever
Virginia Woolf

David Cecil

2821: To Quentin Bell   *Monks House, [Rodmell, Sussex]*

Typewritten
Saturday 18th Nov. [1933]

Dearest Quentin,

Here we are spending a wet dull weeping week end in the country. Weve been walking in the marsh and are all over mud, and we saw two swans, and Pinka flopped in and set them flying. I was very glad of your letter— what a gift for pen and ink you have to be sure. Only now youve sold a picture straight off, you wont give up the brush I fear. I'm told your picture is a lovely one, and I want to go and see it; but Nessa comes round after lunch and paints me. Then it grows dark. We pull the curtains. I've not yet seen the Sickerts.[2]

All my life since I wrote has been a welter of people. Last Sunday we stayed with Rosamond and Wogan [Philipps] in the weeping woods. They've a very nice great big red house with stone passages—unfortunately, to my taste, decorated by Banting[3] in the modern style. And then they throw a few steel chairs about and aluminium tables—in that case I prefer the old mahogany. The truth is Wogan is only a scampering terrier brained painter, and should not decorate; but a very nice gossip and I like Rosamund a good deal better than John. Not so much ego in her composition. She's heavy with child. Oh how we gossiped—Wogan told us such stories of the Partridges, and how poor Fanny [Frances] rang him twice in one day to drive 30 miles to Hamspray. 'Ralph's killing himself. Come at once'. So off he went, and then old Ralph emerged like a great baboon from some bushes. But its over now—Ralph appears stark naked with a cup of tea in his hand by your bed at eight in the morning. I think Lytton's ghost

1. Desmond MacCarthy's house in Chelsea.
2. A retrospective exhibition of Walter Sickert at Thomas Agnew & Son.
3. John Banting, a member of the London Group of artists, was best known for his surrealism, but he was also a decorator, influenced by the cubism of Gris and Braque. For his association with Bloomsbury see *Bloomsbury Portraits* by Richard Shone, 1976, pp. 222-3.

would give a little shiver. It's Lytton played by bumpkins—Lytton acted in the kitchen. So we gossiped, And a man called Harrod of Oxford[1] came and said Oxford is going Communist and Buchmanist[2]—to me all as unreal as gingerbread lions or bonfires—Oxford, I mean. They will talk through their noses and look so spry. Oh dear I've got to stay with the Fishers the week after. I'll tell you all about your cousins.

Then all last week was spent running Jacqueline Stiven to earth. Did you see a passage in last weeks New Statesman called A dinner party [A Dinner]? Well, it was taken from a Room of One's Own [p. 27], and sent in by a school girl ["aged 14"] who swore she wrote it. And Bunny believed her. Then everybody wired and wrote to say it was a hoax. And we thought it must be Logan, because of the name Stiven; and they were having Bunny on for his absurd enthusiasms.[3] So then we all began telephoning—and it was found that Bunny has a niece who knew J. Stiven at Miss Cox's [School] and I had to ring up her mother, and her mother was almost in a fit—said she'd disgraced the family name. And the girl said she had written it herself. And Kingsley Martin was furious. And Bunny as slow as a steam roller with a man carrying a red flag in front. And Leonard suspicious. But thats all over now.

I wonder if you've met Mrs Bottome, Nessa's friend, who is a friend of Vita's—a lady who, being married to a Forbes, sticks to Bottome heroically as her pen name.[4] Dear me—I should never have had the courage to be Virginia Bottome. Or have you preferred, as I should, to lie by yourself sublimely?[5] I used to think it rather sublime, being shut up but then I was not as firm in the wits as you are. I had Ottoline to tea, and now she's sent me more memoirs. Oh and she sent her love. Her memoirs are full of appalling revelations—of course she lies, but not entirely. And how she was torn by Bertie, Lytton, Henry Lamb, Lawrence. Since Helen of Troy I dont think any woman can have launched so many ships. I wish I could lend them to you, to reveal old Bloomsbury at its height; but I dare not.[6] Human nature is an odd mixture—isn't it—Now take Roger. But I leave you to follow up the reflection as I must go and make tea. Its a great pleasure to hear from you, since you write such good letters, but dont if it bores you. I'll send some papers.

1. Roy Harrod, the economist and biographer of Maynard Keynes. He was then aged 33, and since 1929 had been University Lecturer in Economics at Oxford.
2. 'Buchmanism' was the semi-religious movement, known as the Oxford Group or 'moral Rearmament', founded by Frank Buchman (1878-1961), an American by birth.
3. David ('Bunny') Garnett was Literary Editor of the New Statesman at the time.
4. Phyllis Bottome (1882-1963), the novelist, who in 1917 married A. E. Forbes-Dennis. Vita had met her in Berlin.
5. In his Swiss sanatorium.
6. For Ottoline Morrell's Memoirs see p. 15, note 1.

I'm afraid this is very random gossip, but I send it faut de mieux as Clive would say. Julian is coming up tomorrow about a job at the BBC; and we're having him washed and shaved.

Yrs Virginia

Quentin Bell

2822: To Ethel Smyth

Monks House. [Rodmell, Sussex]

Sunday morning [19 November 1933]

Yes, I like it much better so, with the letter 'I' comparatively muted.[1] I'm very glad I made myself a nuisance, because I'm sure its much more persuasive and far carrying this way than the other. I should still like it condensed, pressed, hammered hard; but thats doubtless incompatible with propaganda, people must have things written in chalk and large and repeated over and over again. And I'm sure I'm speaking only as a puritan, the narrow browed and red nosed descendant of the regicide, Venn,[2] when I say I should still prefer the information in the appendix omitted. But I'm glad that Mr Holland[3] doesnt show his brazen face in the text. And I think its very good tempered, and urbane, and, if a little diffuse, still genial, undeniable, and full of truth, and facts. What facts!

How good the others [chapters in *Female Pipings . . .*] are! Thats no doubt why I hum and haw over the first—they seem much more to-gether; profound, and harmonious. But then they dont preach; they expound. There you gallop over turf as springy as a race horse—I'm thinking of Pankhurst and HB, which I've just re-read; and kept thinking how fresh, how full, how wise they are. There you seem to dip your pen into a deeper, richer pot: no vinegar, no sand. I wish, vainly, you'd write more biographies, like the south wind blowing through the grass. I assure you, you have a thousand natural gifts that way which we hacks have long lost. Do consider this should the time ever come when, having lunched with Lady Astor, and had tea off gold plate with Princess Louise[4] (how I adore that side of

1. See Letter 2743.
2. Virginia's grandfather James Stephen (1789-1859), married Jane Catherine Venn. Her ancestor John Venn (1586-1650) was Governor of Windsor Castle in the Civil War and one of the signatories to Charles I's death-warrant.
3. An article by A. K. Holland praising Ethel's music was published in the *Liverpool Post* on 28 November 1932, and Ethel quoted from it at length in an Appendix to *Female Pipings in Eden.*
4. The fourth daughter of Queen Victoria who had married the 9th Duke of Argyll. She was now a widow, aged 85, and lived at Kensington Palace. She died in 1939.

you) you pull off your smart clothes and sit down at Coign at the hideous table into which you once knocked nails.

I am writing in a divided mind—that is I should be packing, writing to Ottoline and Quentin, and at the same time making up my mind about an MS. And it pours

V.

I'll send the book back, but let me have my copy.

Berg

2823: To Ethel Smyth   [52 *Tavistock Square, W.C.*1]

Tuesday [21 November 1933]

I'll send the book [*Female Pipings in Eden*] back today, if I can get the time to pack it. But I'm in a rush, and so shall be for the rest of the week, which is therefore hopeless. I'm amused and delighted to find (in Pipings—odious name) that you attribute Orlando to V. Sackville West.[1] Thats what I'm aiming at—and dont let that enthusiastic and amiable ass Holtby go and write another letter criticising the critics! Surely the horror she produced in T. and T. about the Prison was enough for ever.[2] (This refers to an enclosure, just showing up under a mountain of letters, from which I infer, perhaps unjustly, that the amiable goose—nobody but a goose could have such eyes and nose—has other plans of the kind in her head about the festival. However, perhaps she's meaning something else.) I was enchanted by your courtly grace to HRH. I shall copy it when I'm asked to St James's by Pss Patricia[3]—not that I am asked, but long to know how much cream you drank out of the golden cup. and whether you said as you so often do, Now show me the Klav[4] pulling up your new skirt to adjust the stays, which as you maintain give your figure that monumental majesty which we all admire—Colefax is coming to tea, and I must write to Ottoline, who's—but no, I cant go into that now

V.

I put Surrey because they mistake a solitary Woking for Worthing

Berg

1. Astonishingly, Ethel allowed this sentence to stand in the printed text, (p. 10): "A metamorphosis such as we read of in V. Sackville-West's *Orlando* took place."
2. *Time and Tide.* See Volume IV of this edition, pp. 327-9.
3. Lady Patricia Ramsay. See p. 166, note 3.
4. The manuscript is unclear. It might read 'Klar'.

22nd Nov. [1933]

Oh faithless—why has everybody got a book and not I? Didnt I give you Flush and Orlando? Arent I a critic too—arent I a woman? Dont you care what I say? Am I nothing to you, physically morally or intellectually? Ethel's got one; so has, I daresay, Sibyl, Ottoline, Dotty, Lord Berners and Logan Pearsall Smith. Look here, Vita, you may be putting off humanity and rising, like the day star, a dog—but do let your last act, in the guise of humanity, be to pack a book, called *V. Sackville West Collected Poems* and sign it for me. Then let the hair grow between your toes and catch the running hare and the sleeping partridge as much as ever you like. Anyhow, I wont read a single thing you wrote, or think of you, except as a mangy ill bred cur, with no tail—a dog of all dogs the most worthless, one that bites a widow in a lane. So there.

Sibyl came yesterday and said Lord B.[1] is marrying V. Trefusis, whom you once knew, because they both like poached eggs.

I feel inclined that way myself, in revenge on you. No, I couldn't marry one or t'other. Sibyl is like a signboard that has hung in the rain and sun since the King (George 3rd) was on the throne; and cant even curse poor woman. Her mind flickers like an arc lamp. Oh such a lot of odds and ends she said, but no odd had an end or end an odd—when shall I see you? Oh but that isnt an end is it—what was once a grove of flowering trees, and nymphs walking among them through the daffodils. And I'm dining with Mary [Hutchinson], ostensibly to meet Michael Arlen,[2] but who knows what goes on behind the curtains? Eh?

V.

Do you know a woman called Phyllis Bottome?

And another called Jean Cadell?[3]

Berg

2825: To V. Sackville-West   [52 *Tavistock Square, W.C.1*]
Sunday [26 November 1933]

Yes dearest Creature—that will be very nice, tea on Dec 15th: but let it be as early as possible: its the devil of a long way off.

1. Lord (Gerald) Berners, the gifted amateur painter and musician, had no intention of marrying Violet Trefusis, with whom Vita had eloped to France in 1920.
2. See p. 253, note 1.
3. See p. 229, note 3.

And the book came. And I've read one or two of the new ones. And I liked them yes—I liked the one to Enid Bagnold;[1] and I think I see how you may develop differently. You're an odd mixture as a poet. I like you for being 'out-moded' and not caring a damn: thats why you're free to change; free and lusty. I make up poems. something in the manner of Don Juan, that you might write. But I've only (yes I think I see some very interesting things in your poems) looked between the pages here and there. If you will come Early on the 15th I will tell you more. Did you like Selincourt today?[2] L. says they are 'doing well'—your poems.

I liked Jean Cadell—sandy as a cat, and very nervous. She was making a speech, and I sat by her at lunch.

I gather that thats his Lordships [Lord Berners] joke—the engagement I mean, and rather agree with L. who says that ostlers and barmaids would have better manners.

Old Ethel complains no one notices her book [*Female Pipings . . .*]—its not for lack of trumpeting. And I'm flirting with Ottoline—and who is taking Dial[3] for love of you?

Oh dear me, I wish I could read behind some of the poems!

V.

We will come over from Monks and print.[4] Thats a good idea.

Berg

2826: To Quentin Bell   52 *Tavistock Sq.* [*W.C.*1]

Typewritten
Sunday 26th Nov [1933]

Dearest Quentin,

I read your letter with great pleasure in Time and Tide;[5] it seemed to me put with masterly brevity; most true. But I am no politician—how do you come by that queer instinct? I had such a party the other night at Mary's

1. On pp. 247-8 of Vita's *Collected Poems*. It contained the line, "And I, God's truth, a damned out-moded poet".
2. Basil de Selincourt's laudatory review of Vita's poems in the *Observer*, 26 November.
3. The American cultural magazine.
4. On the original Hogarth printing-press, which Virginia had given to Vita.
5. Attacking the argument that Germany was entitled to claim Austria as part of the German Reich.

—she bet me I wouldn't go, to meet Michael Arlen,[1] who wrote The Green Hat. So I did go; and there he was, and a mort of other notables; including Elizabeth Princess Bibesco,[2] all in flamingo feathers which parted to give view to her own brown down, (how coarse this is; but true). M.A. is a rubber faced little sweaty Armenian monkey, full of protestations, as if I'd just whipped him on the behind for writing the Green Hat. He never stopped apologising, said he only did it to make money, and made fifty thousand pounds; and so married a Greek wife, who was there, silent as an image and stupid, they said, as a mummy; but rather in the style of the Venus of Milo all the same. "She's very silent", he said to me, "but a perfect lady". He is *not* a perfect gentleman. But then he has made fifty thousand pounds, and is now going to write a book for highbrows. Barbara and Victor [Rothschild] were also there;—well, I wont be indiscreet, but between you and me, that's a marriage bound for the rocks.[3] Victor would make me shoot him in ten minutes. He's a Jew; that I rather like but—no, I wont be indiscreet. He had come in the other morning carrying a cardboard box big enough to hold a top hat; and said to B. "Here's a little present". She, thinking it was a muff or a pair of shoes, never cut the string till he'd gone; when out there fell box upon box of pure red rubies—crowns made of rubies, bracelets, rings, breastplates, festoons—all ruby; all red as the morning star and bright as dawn. Jack said the whole room was lit up. They are worth £300,000 pounds. So they can't insure them and they have to be taken to the Bank in a steel lined case and kept there. An old Rothschild bought them 100 years ago for his wife; but she kept them under her bed; I am making Barbara dine here in them next week; and am having the police staff in the Square enlarged. But no—not for all the rubies in the mines of Africa—no, Quentin; no. But I'm discreet.

Then I'm involved with your friend Sickert. I went to his show, and was so much impressed that Nessa made me write to him; and he said "Do me the favour to write about my pictures and say you like them". "I have always been a literary painter, thank goodness, like all the decent painters. Do be the first to say so" he says. I rather think of trying. Nessa is going to take me to tea with him.[4] Do you think one could treat his paintings like novels? I went to Agnews yesterday and Mr Colin [Agnew] had them

1. Michael Arlen (1895-1956), the novelist, was born in Bulgaria of Armenian parents, but was educated in England and became a British subject in 1922. His first book was published when he was 18, and he achieved sudden fame in 1924 with *The Green Hat*, described by one critic as 'a combination of sexual farce and melodrama'. In 1928 he married a Greek Countess, Atalanta Mercati.
2. Elizabeth Bibesco (*née* Asquith), the novelist, married the Romanian diplomatist Prince Antoine Bibesco in 1919.
3. They were married in December 1933, and divorced in 1946.
4. This invitation led to Virginia's *Walter Sickert: A Conversation*, published as a paper-back volume of 28 pages in October 1934.

all brought down, and lined a room; and he asked me to write a book on them. What do you think of Sickert's painting? I gather Roger is rather down on it; so is Clive. It seems to me all that painting ought to be. Am I wrong? if so, why? Are the Alps looking fine? Are there eagles?

So goodbye,

Quentin Bell   Virginia

2827: To Ethel Smyth   *Monks House [Rodmell,*
                                                                Sussex]

Sunday [3 December 1933]

Well, Ethel, Rebecca [West] exclaims with rapture at the thought of meeting the famous woman she calls rather oddly to my ears, Dr. Smyth, on Thursday next at 4.30. So please be punctual and come in your most genial and Bacchic mood, for R. rather raises my hackles, being so insecure herself, and I always, as you know, feel the wind before it blows. A tribute to my own sympathetic nature with which I'm sure you'll agree.

Oh my God, what a lot I've talked the last few days! [at Oxford]—150 boys with some literary tendency (concealed) shook my hand at New College each led like a victim to the altar, by my old bald white priestly cousin Herbert Fisher. We stood in a long gallery, and so it went on till midnight, and I ran out of small talk, and could only think of bargain sales in Selfridges basement to talk about. Why, I ask you as the daughter of a general, why is human society organised on lines which inflict acute agony on the giver and receiver? Why must I stand 3 hours saying Are you first or third year? Are you a cousin of Tom Robertson or his son? Have you read Edith Sitwell—when my lips are parched with thirst and there's an East wind blowing down the corridor? Mrs Fisher is an old hen-wife, by which I mean that she's so nobly (because they're underpaid and must entertain) cheeseparing that they dont allow eggs for breakfast, and I'm so constituted that I loathe salt fish. But there was a certain monastic dignity about the cloisters in moonlight (not that I like colleges) and the young are cool faced and pinked lipped, if only I could have lain on cushions and shied roses at them—instead of standing in a draught handing penny buns. No I dont like institutes where dressing bells ring for dining, and pray-ing bells ring for prayers, and all hours have their duties, which one pretends to observe, but with a lie in ones heart—so that even my kind old cousin, who once loved cricket, I think, is now as hollow as a corn husk. But as you would say

—Well—

Pipings seems to be having a very fine press, which means sales, I hope. So do be punctual on Thursday at 4.30.

V

Berg

254

Monks House, [*Rodmell,*
                                      Sussex]
Typewritten
Sunday 3rd Dec [1933]

Dearest Quentin,

I was much amused to hear of Mr Malcolm Sargent[1] and his sheets—he wrote to the papers saying that he is in the best of health and tempers and proposes to emerge strong as a lion to control the orchestra. Now I thought him a very bad conductor. And you lead me to infer his temper's vile.

I like getting these rounded views of contemporary life. I've seen a good deal of life, so called, since I wrote, I spent a night with the Fishers at the Wardens Lodgings—rather an impressive 14th century house, part tithe barn, but then came the eighteenth century and cut up the barn into bedrooms with panels; and modern youth flourishes, discreetly, decorously, all over the house. I should think there were one hundred promising undergraduates in after dinner; and I shook hands with all; and tried to think what to say, but oh dear what a farce! One might as well go to a school treat and hand out penny buns. There was the great Isaiah Berlin,[2] a Portugese Jew by the look of him, Oxford's leading light; a communist, I think, a fire eater—but at Herbert's everyone minces and mouths and you wouldn't guess to talk to them that they had a spark or a spunk. Herbert is all that is refined and stately; he looks much like Adrian [Stephen]; but office has smoothed out all corrugosities. He told me story after story about the Cabinet of 1916. To him that was what a Christmas tree is to a child, and the poor old moth still haunts those extinct, but once radiant, candles. He adores Lloyd George; he sniffs at Bloomsbury. "No I cannot see much to be said for Mr Eliot; no music". He thinks Winston Churchill a very good painter. He deplores the present state of everything. But he does his bit like a Bishop. And he was very kind to me, and we cracked a little about Madge and Will and George and Uncle Halford—[3] the dead, or practically dead. And there was one lovely girl, I think called Lynd, daughter of Robert,[4] who boards with the Fishers; having been, I gather—but may be wrong—turned out of Somerville for being caught fully dressed talking about the gold standard with a young man. Why are officials so noble but so chilly?

1. Malcolm Sargent (1895-1967) was conductor of the Royal Choral Society from 1928, and became conductor of the B.B.C. Symphony Orchestra in 1950.
2. Isaiah Berlin, the philosopher, aged 24 in 1933, was Oxford Lecturer in Philosophy and a Fellow of All Souls.
3. His uncle, Halford Vaughan, his cousin (and Virginia's) William Wyamar Vaughan, Will's wife Madge, and George Duckworth, Virginia's half-brother.
4. Robert Lynd (1879-1949), the journalist who wrote a notable series of essays for the *New Statesman* under the pseudonym 'Y.Y.'

As for Lettice [Mrs Fisher], she is an old henwife, cheese paring, wispy, all brawn and muscle; no flesh; no humour; but again as kind as they make them—which, if you leave out imagination, humour, music, humanity—doesn't go the whole length. And the beds were hard.

Then we had old Tom Eliot to tea, and sat over the fire and gossiped. He was primed with Clive's brandy, for he had been lunching till tea time on old brandy with Clive, Rebecca West and Lady Colefax. So he was bemused and mellow; and only wanted the W.C. For as he said, he had been drinking since one thirty. What a phantasma one's friends lives are! Tom is writing a pageant [*The Rock*] to be acted at Sadlers Wells in the spring on *London*; in order to collect one quarter of a million to build forty six churches in the suburbs. "Why" asked Leonard. And Tom merely chuckled. I rather think his God is dwindling. But he likes clerical society, and was going to call on the Vicar of Clerkenwell. Dear me, I wish you would come back soon, and then we could go into all these matters together.

Roger and Helen also dined with us. Looked at in a half light Helen reminds me of a red rose just falling on a June night. Dont you think she has a kind of foull (should read 'full') blown beauty? And one or two rain drops might be added. But she was very kind and not too thorny that night. Roger never stops lecturing. So very tactfully we said What is the use of criticism? And he said I think—but its all in his Cambridge lecture[1]—criticism is useless, save as it—but here I lost count, being very sleepy that night. Have you seen his lecture? "Well", he said to me, "you wouldn't find any literature in my paintings—this referred to my essay on Sickert. "What should I find?" I asked. Happily he was stumping down the stairs. So you see old Bloomsbury still crackles under the pot. We have a memoir meeting next week; and I have Ethel Smyth and Rebecca West to tea to discuss the life of Mrs Pankhurst. In strict confidence, Ethel used to love Emmeline—they shared a bed.

Its a howling gale here.

Virginia

Quentin Bell

2829: To Logan Pearsall Smith   52 *Tavistock Sqre. W.C.* [1]

5th Dec. 1933

Dear Logan,

Many thanks for your letter. I have been away, or I would have written sooner.

I am much honoured that the Pronounciating [*sic*] Committee of the

1. His inaugural lecture as Slade Professor at Cambridge. Its subject was 'Art-History as an Academic Study'.

BBC should have considered inviting me to join them and of course I should be delighted—if the duties are as light as you say. But I think I ought to draw your attention to the fact that my education was extremely defective; I have no special knowledge of words or their pronunciation, and frequently find myself at fault in pronouncing biblical or classical names. Whether therefore I should be of the least use on the Committee I am doubtful. But I leave myself in your hands and thank you at any rate for the suggestion.[1]

Yours sincerely
Virginia Woolf

Frederick B. Adams Jr.

2830: TO STEPHEN SPENDER   52 *Tavistock Square, W.C.*1

10th Dec [1933]

Dear Stephen,

Could you dine with us on Tuesday 19th at 8?—without changing of course. I hope you may be able to.

Yours sincerely
Virginia Woolf

Texas

2831: TO DAVID GARNETT   52 *Tavistock Square, W.C.*1

Sunday [10 December 1933]

Dear Bunny,

Well if you persist in being generous, I cant refuse to take the books [*unidentified*], which make a very magnificent row. Whats more, I read them. And if anyone could induce me to write about Shakespeare, it would be you: perhaps I will one day; but apart from wanting to write something quite different at the moment (entirely different from Shakespeare) I have a kind of feeling that unless one is possessed of the truth, or is a garrulous old busybody, from America, one ought to hold one's tongue. So I will: I mean I wont. Send it to Logan is what I mean, and take my blessing. I'm incapable of writing sense at the moment because one of our friends, an intolerable windbag, but golden hearted, is just ringing the bell. But I think you are very generous to your old friends.

Cant I send you a book in exchange?

Here he is   yr affate
V

Berg

1. From Letter 2861, it seems that Virginia agreed to serve on the B.B.C.'s committee on the pronunciation of unusual names and words, but later wished to withdraw. In fact, the Committee did not meet till much later, without Virginia.

Tuesday [12 December 1933]

Here's the cutting.[1] Yes, I see its very gratifying and I've no doubt you are always right about everything.

In fact I thought you perfectly adorable last night and wanted to fling my arms round you, or prostrate myself at your tufted-crow feet; but refrained. Rebecca's [West] an odd mix up, isn't she; like some prehistoric aboreal animal to look at, but an electric mind. No, I had to go to my poor old mother in law; aged 85, going to Epsom and back, back to Epsom and back, with a daughter, to a specialist, husband (daughters) furious; we arrive at 5; choc. cake; "oh my dear V. how you've cheered me after my dreadful day with George—"[2] So there I was, eating choc. cake some of which I conveyed secretly into my pocket, and not listening in But then, as you always say family comes before art, like God and King George—

V

Berg

Typewritten
Tuesday 12th Dec [1933]

Dearest Quentin,

If you were here today—a very foggy cold day—I should say to you, My dear Quentin, if you will take me, I will come. What to? you may ask. To which I reply, number three Belgrave Square. Who the devil lives there? you would say. And in one word I should reply; a cocktail party given by the Hutchinsons to anticipate their daughter's marriage to the richest Jew in Europe [Victor Rothschild]. Oysters and champagne cup. But as youre not here, and its foggy, and its gloomy, and I've no clothes, and cant be bothered to rush out and buy gloves, hat, and shoes, all for a Jew, I sit in my underground vault, with the fog thick on the skylight, writing—oh dear how happy I am not to go! We had the young couple the other night; and they brought a brown bag; and out of this they lifted rubies—rubies set in diamonds. And we all crowned ourselves with the Rothschild rubies; worth £300,000. Well? Nessa and Duncan came in, and said they made just as good in Regent Street. But the diamonds were nice; like spiders webs —immortal spiders webs; spiders webs made in the valleys of the moon. But Nessa will tell you she didn't like the flavour of the Jew. Like raw pork, she said. Surely rather an unkind saying? Barbara I like; I think she's flying

1. Presumably a review of Ethel's *Pipings* . . .
2. George Walker, husband of Leonard's sister Clara. She died in January 1934.

her little flag gamely; but she'll founder they say; in six months, she'll be looking out of the window, and seeing a trim, spare Englishman, and sighing, Oh if I were back in my native fields. Thats Nessa again.

Yesterday I had Ethel Smyth—who adores you, and says you're the image of what she's sought in man all her life, and would marry you, given a dog's chance—and Rebecca West to tea. It was a screaming howling party. Old Ethel meanders so. And she's so deaf. And she's so violent. But she is, to give her her due, very shrewd. And she has battered about the world like a buccaneer, and so when Leonard claps his hand on her mouth, she sits silent, for a second. Rebecca is the oddest woman; like an arboreal animal grasping a tree, and showing all her teeth, as if another animal were about to seize her young. This may be the result of having a son out of wedlock. However, she is tenacious and masterful and very good company, having also battered about in the stinking underworld of hack writers—people like Priestley, [Robert] Lynd, [J.C.] Squire, and others so covered with mud one cant name them even.

They discussed Mrs Pankhurst, and how she smelt when hunger striking; apparently, if you dont drink you smell horribly after three days.

Leonard is at this moment closeted with Lyn [Lloyd] Irvine who wants to start a new paper (keep this to yourself) written entirely by herself; and printed on a cyclo style [*Monologue*]. This is a last effort on her part to speak the truth and make a living. Its to come out fortnightly, and give her views on politics, art, letters, life. Would you do a drawing—but she cant pay, and I daresay the first number will only beget three more; and then it will die. Life and Letters is dying.[1] They all die.

We went to Orpheus [Gluck]—the loveliest opera ever written—at Sadlers Wells; and there was a congeries of old fogies—Ottoline hawking and mousing; Stephen Spender, being hawked and moused; Helen [Anrep], the Russian children; Oliver [Strachey] and a hard featured lady who inspires him with rapture; also a young woman called Lynd, whom I think you might like.

Good bye now, as I am not being very amusing, but then all the time I am feeling, ought I to go to Belgrave Square?

Whats happening to Malcolm Sargent and his sheets? And the Alps your grandfather climbed?

Virginia

[*handwritten*]
I suppose you read Roger's inaugural [Cambridge] lecture. I wonder what you thought of it.

Quentin Bell

1. *Life and Letters* was founded in 1928, and Desmond MacCarthy was its editor until 1933. It survived until 1950.

2834: To V. Sackville-West   [52 *Tavistock Square, W.C.*1]

Wednesday [13 December 1933]

Just to say that you are coming on Friday not later than 4.30—aren't you? and you do still remember me, with affection, in spite of never writing. But then if your hands have turned to paws.

I've a mint of things to talk to you about. What fun to see you at the bottom of the stairs, like a fishmongers shop again. Wasn't it about this time of year we saw the porpoise [in December 1925]? You wore a pink shirt and pearls. Lord how I remember it!

V.

Please sign this for me—I want to send her a guinea [*unidentified*].

Berg

2835: To Ethel Smyth   52 *Tavistock Square, W.C.*1

Tuesday 19th Dec [1933]

Here, after a long interval, is the name and address of the Times Supt. reviewer—G. C. Williams: 16 Aubrey Walk W.8.[1]

So I hope you'll write him a nice kind letter. And oh Lord how I wish M. Baring wouldn't write nice kind letters about you to the N. S.[2] Why drag in these faded testimonials, as if you were a 10th rate and meretorious hack in need of advertisement? How furious I should be if my friends wrote like that about me!—but well intentioned no doubt.

No, we did not go to Rodmell this week end, but must go on Thursday, and see this howling horror through. Again I ask, why is humanity bent on self-torture? I ascribe it chiefly to your religion. Have you read Eliot? I ask, because in the watches of the night I was thinking of the differences between generations: I was thinking how you admire Robert Peckham (by M.B.) [Maurice Baring, 1930] and I hate it, no, not hate; but merely feel that a spider has walked across a garden pond; and then how you hate Eliot; so what happens in the brain of man. What standard is there, and why these diversities. But I must wash

V.

Berg

1. A reviewer of Ethel's book in the *T.L.S.*, where articles were always anonymous.
2. A reply by Maurice Baring to a disagreeable review by Cecil Gray of Ethel's *Female Pipings in Eden*. Baring wrote: "Those who maintain. . . . that Dame Ethel Smyth's music has been inexorably withheld from the public are right" (*New Statesman*, 16 December).

19th Dec. [1933]

Dearest Ottoline,

Now we are off, and I haven't seen you, but what was the use of asking you on top of Ethel Smyth, Rebecca West, Vita Nicolson and so on?—which reminds me that Vita wants to see you, and also reminds me that Rebecca was fascinating—ungainly, awkward, powerful, arborial, like some sloth or mandrill; but oh what a joy to grapple with her hairy arms! I mean she was very upstanding and outspoken, and we discussed religion, sex, literature and other problems, violently, in a roar, to catch Ethel's ear, for 3 hours. This is to corroborate my view, and in oppostion to yours—but who knows? The human soul is deaf, and next time she may bite my fingers to the bone. Did you know Stella Benson? I'm sorry for her death—I think one of these days she might have written something I liked—And I wanted to see her, apart from the dull little man who never left her alone a moment.[1]

Now as I say we are going, why I cant think, to Rodmell, where life will be a flight from the cold to the fire; but perhaps we shall see the downs sometimes. And I cant go on with this scribble, because, owing entirely to you, Stephen Spender is dining here, and I must wash. Mark my words—the whole evening will be spent in talking of Stephen Spender, and when the stars are in the sky, I shall stumble to bed wondering by what alchemy you refine these rough youths to gold. So no more.

yrs V

Texas

Typewritten
21st Dec 1933

Dearest Quentin,

This is a black foggy Christmas week; and the human race is distracted and unlovable. That is, I spent yesterday in Oxford Street buying things like gloves and stockings. A drought is imminent; Rodmell has long ceased to wash; and it is said that Communion is no longer possible, owing to the congealed state of the holy blood. We go down today and I shall think of you when the owl comes out of the ivy bush and the bells toll. It was thus that we ushered out the old clergyman's soul, if you remember.[2] Stephen

1. Stella Benson (1892-1933), the novelist, died on 6 December in Indo-China. Her husband was J. C. O'G. Anderson, of the Chinese customs service.
2. The Rev. Hawkesford, Rector of Rodmell, who died in 1928.

Spender and Miss [Sighle] Lynd—I cant name her, for being Irish her parents have christened her some faery Celtic name—dined here last night. She is dusky, twilit, silent, secretive. He on the other hand talks incessantly and will pan out in years to come a prodigious bore. But he's a nice poetic youth; big nosed, bright eyed, like a giant thrush. The worst of being a poet is one must be a genius; and so he cant talk long without bringing in the abilities and disabilities of great poets; Yeats has praised him; I see being young is hellish. One wants to cut a figure. He is writing about Henry James and has tea alone with Ottoline and is married to a Sergeant in the Guards.[1] They have set up a new quarter in Maida Vale; I propose to call them the Lilies of the Valley. Theres William Plomer, with his policeman; then Stephen, then [Wystan] Auden and Joe Ackerly,[2] all lodged in Maida Vale, and wearing different coloured Lilies.

Their great sorrow at the moment is Siegfried Sassoon's defection;[3] he's gone and married a woman, and says—Rosamond showed me his letter—that he has never till now known what love meant. It is the saving of life he says; and this greatly worries the Lilies of the Valley, among whom is Morgan of course, who loves a crippled bootmaker; why this passion for the porter, the policeman and the bootmaker?[4] Well, we must go into the matter when you come back. Angelica is once more in town; and the place is therefore humming. I suppose in two years there will be a series of bullets flying and knives gashing—for Gods sake dont let her marry a policeman.

Clive gave a party for me to meet Sickert the other night and was at his best; he primed us with wine and turkey; cigars and brandy; in consequence we all kissed each other, and I am committed to write and write and write about Sickert's books—he says they are not pictures. I think Christmas must be better in the Alps than in England. Here is a small present from your poor old doddering Aunt.

Virginia

Quentin Bell

1. Spender, who was then 24, was sharing his flat in Maida Vale with Jimmy Younger, who came from Cardiff, ran away from home aged 18 and joined the Army for three years, but when Spender first met him, he was unemployed.
2. The author (*Hindoo Holiday*), playwright (*Prisoners of War*) and later literary editor of *The Listener*.
3. Sassoon, at the age of 47, married Hester, daughter of Stephen Gatty, K.C.
4. Virginia's descriptions of E. M. Forster's friends are vague. There were John Hampson Simpson (author of *Saturday Night at the Greyhound*), who had worked in hotel kitchens, and Harry Daley and Bob Buckingham, both policemen. The 'bootmaker' is unidentified by P. N. Furbank in his frank account of this period. (*E. M. Forster* II, p. 185).

Typewritten
Dec. 21st 1933

Dear Miss McAfee,

Many thanks for the cheque for the Turgenev article. It is very good of you to trouble about the corrections; owing to Christmas posts the Yale Review has not yet reached me, but as we are just going away, I write now. It is always full of good things, and a great contrast to the usual magazine, either on our side or on yours.

With best wishes for the New Year

Yours very sincerely
Virginia Woolf

Yale University

2839: To Hugh Walpole   *Monks House, Rodmell,*
[Sussex]

27th Dec [1933]

My dear Hugh,

Why didn't you come to tea anyhow?—I wish you had; and even if you hadn't found me there's the lady next door, who's taken to playing Bach so that I think she must be rising in her profession.[1] Even in my comparatively respectable room, you'd have found a mixed company, perhaps to your liking; only I'm not sure whether you, who like everybody, dont for that very reason hate old Ethel Smyth; and loathe Rebecca West—thats my last odd collection. It went very well, though: they bawled about religion and Mrs Pankhurst. Rebecca has a vigorous mind—and I think you do like her. And one day you'd have found me caparisoned in £300,000 worth of rubies, belonging to the Rothschilds. This is by way of asserting myself, rather tamely, against the unparallelled (no—l's wrong as usual) splendours of your progress. Oh but, though I wasn't at Bridgewater House myself, Vanessa was, mine, not yours, and she's become a roaring Tory, instead of a red radical, all because of Mary's heaving bosom blue with sequins, white with diamonds.[2] The majesty of the sight, the way she stooped her neck here and then there, overcame my sister and Duncan, who stood in the gallery, completely. But you shook hands. No, we cant keep pace with you. And I was at Oxford, but not to speak on the English novel. My lips refuse to open in public—and you say yours positively enjoy

1. See p. 234.
2. A reception for Queen Mary at Bridgewater House, which belonged to Lord and Lady Ellesmere.

it! And now you're off to Nassau and Jamaica as easily as I trip up the village to post. Yes please bring me a sponge. There's no water in Rodmell, and I must spend a week in London washing. Mrs Marsh, the horse breeder, has to lodge in Lewes, all for the sake of a hot bath. The Rectorl never washes, so the drought leaves him as it found him. He has married Miss Young-husband—did I tell you?—with his wife still green in the grave. Hence many wont call on her—not that they liked the first wife, but its a question of right feeling.

I've had a sad disappointment—Leons second novel[2]—you remember the Livingstone man—might be a stillborn bantling dropped out of Mrs Humphry Ward. We cant publish it. But this is secret. What a bore! Are you spouting ink like a whale? I am: too profusely. But they cant say of Hugh and Virginia that they're Mrs Ward's miscarriages: we are our own begetters anyhow. Vita and the boys came to recover from the mad bad old woman at Roedean [Lady Sackville]; and Lydia and Maynard: Lydia wants to act but cant: and I'm going to see Bergner,[3] and I wish you'd write to me from the lovely South; and go on with your autobiography, for you're living at the rate of 10,000 words a day: and I must stop this drivel,

with love from us both,
V.

I forgot the one thing I meant to say—we're driving North in the spring—may we call at Brackenburn?[4]

Texas

2840: To Katherine Arnold-Forster

27th Dec [1933]

Monks House, Rodmell,
Lewes, Sussex

Dear Ka,[5]

The gingerbread came in the very nick of time to save my reputation when we had 8 people to tea on Christmas Day. And there's still some left,

1. The Rev. John Webber Ebbs, Rector of Rodmell.
2. The Hogarth Press had published Derrick Leon's *Livingstones* in 1933. His second novel was *Wilderness* (Heinemann, 1935).
3. Elisabeth Bergner was appearing in *Escape me Never!* by Margaret Kennedy, at the Apollo Theatre.
4. Hugh Walpole's house in the Lake District.
5. Katherine Arnold-Forster (*née* Cox) lived at Zennor, near St Ives, Cornwall, with her husband Will, the painter, and their 13-year-old son Mark. Virginia had known her well in their youth, when Ka was loved by Rupert Brooke, and she and Leonard had several times visited them in Cornwall.

in spite of Maynard. I hate it, generally, but this I like, and Leonard adores. Of course Cornwall explains it. I must get the address in Penzance—what an angel you were to send it. Also a large jar of cream arrived: but not, we thought, Cornish. No address on it, so I shall thank you for that too.

I've been walking over the downs, and cant help thinking that of their kind you cant beat them, specially in winter.

In the spring we are going to Ireland and the Hebrides because it seems wrong to see Greece and not the British Isles. But I dont see why Cornwall shouldn't be the next place to Ireland if you're there still. (I mean in Cornwall: too dazed to write)

Give my love to Mark: only he'll be so large now he wont remember the Wolves and the raven. L. is chopping wood, and we shall have more gingerbread with our dinner.

Yrs Virginia

I hope you and Will are going to find a job for Julian—make him speak and drive his car through hostile crowds.[1]

Mark Arnold-Forster

2841: To Lady Ottoline Morrell   *Monks House, Rodmell,*
                                        [Sussex]

31st Dec. [1933]

Dearest Ottoline,

You are a wonderful woman—for many reasons; but specially for sending a present—a lovely original wild and yet useful present—which arrived on Christmas day. I love being 'remembered' as they say; and I hung it on a chair, when the Keynes's lunched here, and boasted, how you had given it me. What a snob I am aren't I! But I cant help it. It was a very nice Christmas, as it happened; I had my shawl, and the turkey was large enough and we had cream, and lots of coloured fruits, and sat and gorged—Maynard Lydia Leonard and I. No, Nessa and Clive were doing penance at the old Bells;[2] and so the moment has not yet come for that remark of mine, about you, over the log fire. But I intend to make it on Sunday, and I shall whisper to myself what you say I may whisper [*unexplained*]. Dear me, how I like people to be fond of me—how deeply emotional or perhaps sentimental I am. Perhaps in another age, one would never have thought of the word

1. Julian Bell was taking an increasingly active part in left-wing politics, particularly at Cambridge.
2. At Seend, Wiltshire, with Clive's mother. His father had died in 1927.

sentimental, and then life would have been simpler. But do lets go on whispering under our breath, so that Bertie and Tom cant hear us.[1]

This morning I had a remarkable letter, for the first time, from Vivienne Haigh Eliot. Happily she doesn't ask me to do anything. She merely says that Tom refuses to come back to her, and that it is a great tragedy—so I suppose I can agree and say no more. She has made Leonard her executor, but writes sensibly—rather severely, and with some dignity poor woman, believing, she says, that I respect marriage.

And Vita came with her sons, one Eton, one Oxford, which explains why she has to spin those sleepwalking servant girl novels. I told her you would like to see her. I remain always very fond of her—this I say because on the surface, she's rather red and black and gaudy, I know: and very slow; and very, compared to us, primitive: but she is incapable of insincerity or pose, and digs and digs, and waters, and walks her dogs, and reads her poets, and falls in love with every pretty woman, just like a man, and is to my mind genuinely aristocratic; but I cant swear that she wont bore you: certainly she'll fall in love with you. But do let her come down from her rose-red tower where she sits with thousands of pigeons cooing over her head.

I'm so cold in the fingers that I cant write, or I would tell you all about Rebecca, Stephen and the rest. R's great point is her tenacious and muscular mind, and all her difficulty comes from the wheals and scars left by the hoofmarks of Wells.[2] Thats why I prefer her to the niminy piminies—the Stephens [Spenders] and the Williams [Plomers], whose minds are refrigerators, and souls blank paper—But Stephen was charming that night, and curbed his egotistic mania.

I'm sending you a little book, Montesqueou (cant spell it) though you will have it, but its small and can be stood in a corner—(or let me give you another)—I was reading it the day Julian was born [in 1908], and have a sentimental feeling for a special page. And that was before I met you.

So goodnight—and tomorrow is 1934, so be well, and happy and come and see me.

yrs Virginia

Texas

1. Bertrand Russell and T. S. Eliot.
2. H. G. Wells, with whom Rebecca West had had a love-affair, and whose son she bore.

Letters 2842-2882 (January–April 1934)

The year opened with an 'Ethel Smyth festival', concerts, luncheons, dinners and tea-parties, some of which Virginia dutifully attended. She had influenza in late January, and it developed into headaches which kept her in bed for about ten days. When she recovered, she finished her article on Walter Sickert's paintings (which delighted him), and resumed The Pargiters, which she temporarily rechristened Here and Now before it became The Years. Her work was distracted by two minor domestic events. 52 Tavistock Square was redecorated from top to bottom by order of the landlord; and Virginia finally steeled herself to give notice to her cook, Nelly Boxall, after eighteen years of intermittent trouble. On 25 April the Woolfs left Monk's House by car for Ireland, where they were to visit Elizabeth Bowen.

2842: TO ETHEL SMYTH   Monks House. [Rodmell, Sussex]

Thursday [4 January 1934]

Many congratulations on terrific ovation last night.[1] I expect you're too overwhelmed, with that and other things to have time to read and write letters—And we've just had news that one of L's sisters is dying.[2] So no more.

V.

Coming to the lunch on the 18th.

Berg

2843: TO V. SACKVILLE-WEST   Monk's House, [Rodmell, Sussex]

4th January 1934

Yes, I listen (but not to the Prison) Please then take a ticket for me for 18th.[3] 7/6. I'll pay: and the food will be horrid—slabs, watery. But I don't come back till the 14th.

1. Sir Thomas Beecham had conducted at the Queen's Hall an entire concert devoted to Ethel's work, including her oratorio *The Prison*.
2. Clara Walker. She died that night, aged 48.
3. A luncheon at Grosvenor House given in honour of Ethel Smyth.

Then of course you go away.[1] Suggest a night for dinner off your own bat. No engagements so far. And L's sister, one I didn't know, but with two small children, is dying today. And my mother-in-law has quarrelled with the husband: son-in-law. What a life in many ways: but are you fond of me?

Who do you think I met galloping on the downs in the gloaming? Your Enid [Bagnold]. And she's coming to tea tomorrow. Shall I fall in love with her?

V.

Come early and lets talk over the fire.

Berg

2844: To Vanessa Bell   *Monks House, [Rodmell, Sussex]*

Friday [5 January 1934]

We have just heard that Leonards sister died yesterday. He has to go to the funeral on Sunday in London, so could you come on Monday instead. I think I shall go up, though not to the funeral. I shall expect you on Monday unless I hear.

V.

Berg

2845: To Quentin Bell   *Monk's House, [Rodmell, Sussex]*

10th Jan. 1934

Dearest Quentin,

It is so cold that I cant go to my outhouse; and as my typewriter is there, I must write in my hand—which you can't read. But there isnt much to say—we are all rusticating very domestically—Charleston, Tilton, Rodmell. It is true that one of Leonard's sisters died last week, and we went up for the funeral. Jewesses are buried without much hope of immortality: at Balls Pond, it is a very severe service, Leonard said. I did not go, as women are happily not allowed. Her husband killed her by neglect, and there are great feelings about it—hatred, bitterness, and a mean sordid desire on his part to cadge money to educate the children—It was all very interesting, as the Jews dress up in black, wear top hats, and look exactly like Hebrew prophets. My brothers in law sat round, cursing, and entirely righteous and hopeless.

1. To Italy and Morocco for a month's holiday.

For the rest, Lady Jones [Enid Bagnold] came to tea. She is an old flame of Desmond's; about 40, with 6 children, and they live at Rottingdean in Burne Jones's house, filled with decayed angels and partless boys. I'm going to see her tomorrow. Julian came over, not partless by any means. He seems to be be firing squibs in all directions, and is coming to town, like Dick Whittington, to find his fortune. Perhaps he will shed Lettice [Ramsay] and acquire a rosy milkman: I hope not: the lower orders should love each other.

Ethel Smyth, who has a passion for you, has been deafening us every evening on the wireless with her caterwauling. At last, she burst into one flame, and had a gigantic party to eat sausages at midnight. And on Tuesday [Thursday] I have to go to a lunch party in her honour. And then I hope the Smyth festival is over. Has it reached Switzerland? Or are the mountains pure?

Are you writing your history of Monaco? Do send it to the Hogarth Press. We badly want a good book. I could illustrate it. Angelica and Eve walked over the downs from Charleston; how the young do grow to be sure! Ann and Judith weigh 10.8 each.[1]

So goodbye
Virginia

Quentin Bell

2846: To Ethel Smyth   *Monks House [Rodmell, Sussex]*

Thursday [11 January 1934]

Yes, I know I ought to have written, but I've been living in such a different world. Leonard's sister you see—no you've forgotten all that, very naturally, in your general helter skelter—died, poor woman; literally was killed by her husband; and I went up to see my mother in law; and really it would have drawn tears from a stone—poor old woman, aged 84, she'd sat up 2 nights with the dying and the husband [George Walker], a cheap American ruffian, with whom she'd quarrelled violently: there they sat side by side and the daughter died between them; and my mother in law, said "She asked so little of life"—an extraordinarily good epitaph: "And why am I left alive?"—and then there was the funeral and all the Jews came to Tavistock Sqre and sat round like prophets in their black clothes and top hats denouncing unrighteousness. But I cant tell the whole story: and you living in a blaze of glory. How odd that two such different versions of life should go on at the same time.

But if it was an 'agony' to you, this celebration, as you say, and I can

1. The daughters of Adrian and Karin Stephen, aged 17 and 15.

well believe, why the devil didn't you wring their necks and say I wont have it? Or do you like some parts and not others?

No no no, we shall never see eye to eye about Keats and Shelley and Vita and Christina [Rossetti] and whats common and whats fine—but it doesnt matter a straw that I can see, since no doubt the God in whom you trust likes diversity among his creatures and is no doubt roaring with laughter both at you and at me. We come back on Sunday I think—In haste and illegibility

V.

Berg

2847: To Donald Brace

Monk's House, Rodmell,
Lewes, Sussex

Typwritten
13th Jan 1934

Dear Mr Brace,

It is very good indeed of you to have troubled to make enquiries about selling the MS of A Room of Ones Own. I am sure you are right, and that it would be better to try to sell it here. Now and again booksellers ask me for manuscripts.

I am very glad that Flush seems to be doing well with you. I had no notion it would be so popular; and as usual, owe you thanks for the trouble you take with my books.

We are just returning to London after a long Christmas here. With best wishes from us both,

yours sincerely
Virginia Woolf

P.S. Your second letter has come. I am refusing Mr Potters invitation [*unidentified*], kind as it is, and flattering But I do not feel that I can lecture, whatever the invitation.

Harcourt Brace Jovanovich

2848: To Lyn Irvine

52 *Tavistock Square, W.C.*1

Wednesday [17 January 1934]

Dear Lyn,

I don't quite know what to say about your suggestion. I am willing, if you wish it to review David Cecil's book [*Early Victorian Novelists*] for you, and of course I don't want to be paid. But I can't help feeling that the people who subscribe to the Monologue[1] want you to write yourself, or the young who have something they want to say. If they find me writing, they'll suspect that I'm there for advertisement purposes, not because I have anything I want to say about Victorian novels (which I havent) And I think they'll feel a little defrauded. At least thats what I should feel if I bought the Monologue on the strength of the prospectus and found say Rebecca West or E. M. Forster, writing reviews.

But let me know what you think. If you want it I am ready, as I say. We're just back from Rodmell

Yours

Virginia Woolf

Sussex

2849: To Ethel Smyth   52 *Tavistock Square, W.C.*1

Sunday [21 January 1934]

I'm sorry I couldn't write yesterday, but we were at Cambridge all day. These are my engagements:

Monday 22nd	Rose Macaulay and friend to tea
Tuesday 23rd	Kept for Vanessa and Angelica.
Wed. 24th	I'm dining out and want to rest my lips (I'm rather afflicted with a little temperature) beforehand.
Thursday 25th	No good for you: an American I think here. (No thats Tuesday next)
Friday 26th	We go to Rodmell.

I know you dont care for mixed interviews, but Lord knows how I'm to sweep a clear space—I'm rather of your opinion that private conversations are the only fruitful, but how is one to give up every day to a separate person? Even the organising energy of the generals daughter couldn't run life on that magnificent scale. But choose what you like and I'll do my best. about Bruno Walter I'm longing to go to his rehearsal and so is L.[2]

No, I've never read anything by C. St John unless she edited Ellen Terry's letters to GBS. which I thought admirable: on the other hand I didnt like the Ellen Terry life edited perhaps by her—but I may be thinking of Edith Craig; and so am at sea.[3] What to suggest for a crossgrained

---

1. Her mimeographed magazine.
2. Bruno Walter was conducting a series of Beethoven concerts at the Queen's Hall.
3. Miss Christopher St John lived with Ellen Terry's daughter, Edith Craig, at Smallhythe, near Sissinghurst, and was in love with Vita. She had edited Ellen Terry's correspondence with Bernard Shaw (1931), and became Ethel's biographer (1959). The *Memoir* of Ellen Terry (1933) was jointly edited by St John and Craig.

Catholic I cant think.[1] Surely the Lovats and Barings and that ilk provide for all their own feather? Yes, she [Christopher] haunts Vita. Oh it was lovely in the country yesterday—and today the Square is like a cage in hell, the railings just visible in yellow fog.

V.

Berg

2850: To Quentin Bell   52 *Tavistock Sq, [W.C.1]*

Typewritten
24th Jan [1934]

Dearest Quentin,

I have now got back to my typewriter, so I can write to you again with some hope that you may be able to read me. Only it is now a ghastly yellow fog so that I can hardly see. Miss Belsher took two hours to get to the press this morning; and Pinka was lost in the vast abyss of the square, Now everybody is coming back to town—Nessa, Julian, Clive, Duncan; old Roger is lecturing; but I did not go; nor have I yet seen the Academy pictures. But Nessa will tell you all that. Here we have had an odd scatter of human beings—Rose Macaulay like a mummified cat; a friend of hers who brought a dog; Vita; and a vast lunch party given to Ethel Smyth. I had to sit next her; there were about 300 people and blazing lights. Sir Thomas Beecham made a speech and brought the house down by saying that he had visited Ethel Smyth in her confinement; "I do not mean what you think" he said; but the roars of laughter continued. (She was in prison as a suffragist.) That was the style. And Ethel got up and said that Sir Thomas conducted—she did not say misconducted—again a roar of laughter. I drank a good deal and got mildly tipsy as was necessary in order to laugh. When I am seventy five, dearest Quentin, please restrain your kind feelings and do not give me a lunch party at the Grosvenor hotel.

Last night I dined with Mary Hutchinson and heard a good deal of vague gossip about Barbara and Victor. They live at the Palace in New-market,[2] a vast Rothschild house with ever so many servants and nothing for Barbara to do. Clive has seen them already quarelling at the Savoy. But then Clive, like a true friend, rather wants them to quarrel. Julian says Victor is very tetchy at the Society [The Apostles]. Julian wears a new blue jumper and looks much thinner. As for Angelica I took her

---

1. Ethel may have asked (letter missing) whether Christopher St John might suit as a biographer for Maurice Baring, a Catholic. Eventually (1938) Ethel wrote it herself, in Baring's lifetime.
2. A large Victorian house belonging to Anthony de Rothschild where Barbara and Victor lived temporarily.

shopping yesterday and we bought a green dress, only as I had forgotten my purse it was rather difficult; but then I remembered my grandfathers [James Stephen] nose and gave myself such airs they let me go off with three pound ten worth. Then we had tea with Nessa; there was Roger, Leonard, Pinka and Duncan. Helen [Anrep] has the flu; and that oaf her son has the congenital idiotcy. I wish Roger could scrape his back of all Russian barnacles. I am writing about sodomy at the moment [*The Pargiters*] and wish I could discuss the matter with you; how far can one say openly what is the relation of a woman and a sod? In French, yes; but in Mr Galsworthys English, no.

How I should like to see you. Do you feel better? Do you go out at all? But dont trouble to write; I will babble on. I hope you get the newspapers. Leonard is caballing with the Labour party as usual. They think Mosley is getting supporters.[1] If so, I shall emigrate. I have to dine with Colefax tonight to meet Noel Coward whose works I despise but they say hes very good to his old mother. And Sybil wont take no, even in the fog. So good bye.

Virginia

Quentin Bell

2851: TO LADY OTTOLINE MORRELL   52 *Tavistock Sqre*, [*W.C.*1]

[end January 1934]

Dearest Ottoline,

Yes I am back—came up and went to that appalling cheap tawdry lunch that Ethel enjoyed so. Really she is like a child with a sugar mouse. Why, as you say, she should enjoy licking pink sweets I cant say. But I'm glad she discharged her energies on you. But next week I shant be able to escape some hours of her: and then there's Ethel Sands and Tom and so on: so it must be the week after if one day would suit you. Monday or Tuesday 5th or 6th? 5.30?

I am in a hurry and illegible

yrs Virginia

Texas

2852: TO LADY CECIL   52 *Tavistock Square*, *W.C.*1

Monday [5 February? 1934]

Dear Nelly,

How very nice to hear from you! I often think of you too. I wish we could come to lunch, but here I am in bed—first a little influenza; which

1. Sir Oswald Mosley's British Union of Fascists.

then gives me a headache, so that I am stupid as—who shall we say? Reginald Smith's[1] horse. If we can, we shall go down to Rodmell on Saturday for a few days change. But we shall then come back here, and why shouldnt you come to tea here soon? That would be a treat, and I deserve it, you've never been here these 10 years, I think. Do let us break this long silence, which the sweetness of our natures, as you say, imposes on us. Never do I get a scrap from you but what I say that woman is the best letter writer I know. And then she won't write. I would have sent you the Brownings dog [*Flush*], but was rather ashamed of my joke.

Excuse this scrawl, and thank you for asking us, which we should have liked—what grammar!—to accept had it been possible.

Yr aff V.W.

The Marquess of Salisbury, Cecil Papers

2853: To ETHEL SANDS   42 *Tavistock Square, W.C.*1

Tuesday [6 February 1934]

Dearest Ethel,

Its very nice of you to ask me to lunch, and I would if I could, but I cant wake up till the lights are lit. I dont suppose you want a fuddled dormouse at your exquisite table. But do come here if you will. On Tuesday next week we have Tom Eliot and an American lady to tea—no, I see you say Wednesday or Thursday. Wednesday I shall be in and alone at 4.30. Thursday I'm trying to summon up courage to go to Sibyls. So come Wednesday if you will (but I shan't have anyone to meet you, I think unless you insist).

Yrs
Virginia

Wendy Baron

2854: To ETHEL SMYTH   52 *T.[avistock] S.[quare, W.C.*1]

Thursday [8 February 1934]

I'm sorry to have been so remiss, but I am still in bed, and have seen nobody, except Vanessa, nor done more than scrawl a note or two. I'm better, but the little temperature I suppose was some influenza germ, which always works its way into my head and doesn't easily move. If I'm all right we shall go to Rodmell for 2 or 3 days this weekend. and I hope come back cured.

1. Editor of the *Cornhill*, to which Virginia and Nelly Cecil had contributed in their youth.

So I've no news whatever, and not much faculty of speech. Why accuse me of bringing this on by love of Society? Since we came back I went (1) Ethel Smyth lunch: (2) dine with Colefax. (3) tête à tête dinner with Mary Hutchinson—thats all. Or do you mean that I'm to cease human intercourse altogether? Or am I only to see Queen Mary?—like a celebrated composer whose Mass is shortly to be played before that unhappy woman?[1] I dont go eating sausages and drinking beer with Ly Cunard and M. Baring— Or am I only to see Ethel Smyth on those rare occasions when she's not gallivanting round London to lunch parties given in her honour! What a humbug and a hypocrite you are! But I've written 130,000 words of my book in 10 months, so say, think, write, do what you like—uncastrated, Christian cat

V.

No word from Bruno W[alter].

Berg

2855: TO LADY OTTOLINE MORRELL

52 *Tavistock Square, W.C.*1

Thursday [8 February 1934]

Dearest Ottoline,

I should have had to put you off anyhow, alas. I caught a slight influenza (the result of Ethel's lunch I think) and this led as usual to the old headache. So I've been in bed these 10 days, and am still too stupid to talk. But we shall go off for a few days to Rodmell on Saturday, and then, I shall be all right and hope you will be back and come and see me, and we can go into every corner and cranny of the universe.

How I wish people would write books I like to read! For instance, Ottoline's memoirs. If I had them, in 6 volumes, by me, I should spend the day in a haze of rapture. As it is I dip into old letters: how tremendously potent they are—any handful of scraps—Charlie Sanger coming to dinner, Goldie all comma's upside down—a line from Lytton—dinner to meet [Roger] Senhouse, a charming boy, at the Ivy—and then I try Lord Berners; and so on. (I mean his Memoirs[2]) but cant face the great at the moment.

yrs V.

Texas

1. Ethel's *Mass in D*, which was performed on 3 March at the Albert Hall.
2. *First Childhood*, 1934.

52 Tavistock Square, W.C.1

Monday [12 February 1934]

Dearest Ottoline,

How angelic of you to send those flowers! They are still burning bright beside me. For I am still in bed, and this blessed disease, even when one is normal, seems to leave a paving stone on top of one's head. All ideas are crushed flat as worms. I hope we shall get away at the end of the week: and I shall come back more amusing, and shall then inflict myself on you. Meanwhile I lie like a torpid alligator and look at your flowers.

yr affate V.W.

Texas

2857: To QUENTIN BELL   *52 Tavistock Sq, W.C.1*

Typewritten
15th Feb [1934]

Dearest Quentin,

I have been very remiss not to write before—I think I am in debt to you for a lovely letter with the picture of a horrid old man in snow boots. Can that be my elegant and handsome nephew? And who is in love with him? All the nurses? And Malcolm Sargent? I daresay. But there must be veils between Aunt and nephew; you see how chastely I observe them. The fact is I have been mewed up in my room for a fortnight, owing to a debauch of society. I got a chill; a violent headache; the blinds were drawn and there I lay. Only Nessa visited me in my confinement. However now I'm about again—in token of which yesterday I had a visit from old Ethel Sands, my first touch with society; and why does one ever need human life? as you once said so truly. Poor old thing, she has rather lost her elegance; has grown a little pouched and dim. But then she lunches out every day of her life and was so fed with food at the Eshers that she could not break a piece of bread and butter with me. When I asked her why she did it, she said that once a year she makes a new friend. But this year she has drawn blank. Now if you must go to three hundred lunch parties and then draw blank, I hardly think it worth while.

I dined with Colefax and met Noel Coward; and he called me Darling, and gave me his glass to drink out of. These are dramatic manners. I find them rather congenial. Anyhow theres no beating about the bush, as Nessa would say, rather coarsely. Then he played his new opera on Sybils grand piano and sang like a tipsy crow—quite without self consciousness. It is about Brighton in the time of the Regency—you can imagine.[1] I am to go and see him in his retreat. He makes about twenty thousand a year, but has several decayed uncles and aunts to keep; and they will dine with him, he says, coming out of Surbiton, and harking back to his poverty stricken days. So he has to combine them with the half naked nymphs who sing his parts, which is difficult.

There is a terrible amount of politics about at the moment. You are nearer Vienna than I am—but everybody says here this is the beginning of the end.[2] We are to have Mosley within five years. I suppose you and Julian will be in for it. What Angelica will live to see boggles me. But after all there are many advantages today over yesterday—one can write to a nephew in a manner that my Aunt Mary [Fisher] could not. Julian is caballing as usual. He darts in, like a very nimble elephant, and seizes books on Manchuria and then departs to his room in Taviton Street. Roger is gone. Clive in Paris. I missed the memoir club owing to my disease; but it sounded rather good.

I have just refused to sit for my portrait for the Nat. Portrait Gallery; dont you agree I am right? They send a wretched boy to draw one in one sitting; then they keep the drawing in a cellar, and when I've been dead ten years they have it out and say Does anyone want to know what Mrs Woolf looked like? No, say all the others. Then its torn up. So why should I defile a whole day by sitting?

What did you think of Lyns organ [*Monologue*]? The second number is out and I will send it you. I don't think she'll be able to keep it up fortnightly. I thought the beginning was amusing. But she has not enough laid down in her cellar I suspect. Only she has worked herself up into such a rage about the world that she cant keep still.

Our house is now in great disorder; they say we must put in an iron pillar to shore up the ceiling because of the weight of our books. Do come back soon, and I will give you the Dictionary of Nat. Biography; which will lighten our burden.

What are you painting? Violet snows? Eddy Sackville has broken his leg in three places skiing; Raymond [Mortimer] his wrist, skiing. And John Lehmann is back in England and is sending us a book of poems. But I dont suppose we shall meet. Rosamond [Lehmann] has a daughter. And the [Cyril] Connollys gave a cocktail party to meet their lemurs to which I did not go.

That is all my news

Virginia

Quentin Bell

1. *Conversation Piece*, a romantic comedy written, composed and directed by Noel Coward. He also acted in it.
2. The Austrian Nazis had staged a *coup d'état* in early February, and during the next two weeks massacred the Socialists and destroyed workers' dwellings.

18th Feb. [1934]

Yes it certainly sounds very nice, your castle.[1] But you will have left it by now. You will be at Marrakesh, with the Princess Royal and Lord Harewood[2]—this piece of news stares me in the face in Sundays paper. Also the King of Belgium has been found killed.[3] Thats all the news in London today.

I've been laid up on the sofa in my dressing gown almost ever since you left—what a bore! I hope I didnt infect you that day in the car: the usual little chill; then the usual damned headache. But I think it has cleared off now, and I actually wrote a few lines this morning. So I've seen nobody, not even Ethel, which is really rather nice—almost as good as a rose-red castle at Portofino. And I've dipped into ten thousand books. That reminds me—I told L., who shouted for joy, to find out about the dark island, and he says he's written to you.[4] We both shouted for joy. Our list was looking very lean and dry—now nature's plenty has descended on it. What a blessing! Pinka is snoring by the fire: there is a thick fog; I ought to be reading an unreadable clever manuscript, which one cant reject or accept; and L. is with his aged mother. Tomorrow life begins again—Ottoline and Ethel, and I think a beautiful lady called Sibyl Cholmondeley[5] Shall I like her?

By the way, do you remember our reckoning of last summers weeks in the car? Well, there was only one month; because you went to Italy, just as we came back. This came into my head the other night. And as soon as you come back, then, I shall go away. Dear me, what a dull letter! But I've got nothing to say, short of writing the history of 3 weeks in the drawing room, and so end, with Pinka's best love, and Potto's too. My love to Harold: I wish I ever saw him—I saw his photograph yesterday.

V

Berg

---

1. Vita, with Harold and Gwen St Aubyn, had taken a short lease of the Castello at Portofino, northern Italy, featured by Elizabeth Russell in *The Enchanted April* (1923). They then went to Morocco for three weeks.
2. Lord Harewood (then Viscount Lascelles) had been in love with Vita before her marriage, and married Princess Mary, the only daughter of King George V, in 1922.
3. King Albert of the Belgians was killed on 17 February rock-climbing near Namur.
4. Vita's new novel *The dark island*, published by the Hogarth Press in October 1934.
5. Daughter of Sir Albert Sassoon, and wife of the 5th Marquess of Cholmondeley.

Monday [26 February 1934]

No "I'll tell this" to copy your style at its sweetest, when I get a letter from you, beating your breast, and going into all the usual attitudes, "how have I wasted my affection—what a serpent Virginia is—what a genius, what an Undine[1]—" then I harden harder, and colden cooler, for I think Ethel Smyths the most attitudinising unreal woman I've ever known—living in a mid Victorian dentists waiting room of emotional falsity—likes beating up quarrels for the sake of dramatising herself, enjoys publicity and titles from universities and Kings, surrounded by flatterers, a swallower of falsehoods, why should I stand this manhandling, this brawling this bullying, this malusage? When I've friends that respect me and love me and treat me honestly generously and according to the fair light of day? Why pray why cowtow to the bragging of a Brigadier Generals daughter? Why?

                                                                    V.

Berg

2nd March [1934]

Dearest Dadie,

There is nothing I would not do for love of you. But—

(1) I have just emerged from three weeks complete inertia (headache; sofa: silence)
(2) I had at once to dash off 4 horrid little articles demanded by friends and importunate editors.
(3) Only this morning did I begin to tackle a vast mountainous, and wholly worthless novel:

Therefore I feel I've not a word to throw at a dog; and cannot for the life of me think of Cleopatra.

If inspiration should visit me—but its useless; I know she wont.

So forgive me once more. Did you see the old Wolves footprints in your room the other day [at Cambridge]?

Hoping to see you, and a thousand thanks for asking.

                                                        Yr ever devoted

                                                                    V.

George Rylands

---

1. *Undine*, a romance by Baron de la Motte Fouqué, published in 1811, about a water nymph brought up by a fisherman.

Sunday [4 March 1934]

Dear Logan,

I am, I admit, relieved to hear that the BBC Comtee. has been put off.[1] In fact I had it in mind to write to you and say that, if no steps had been taken, I would like to withdraw. I more and more doubt that I should do my duty and attend. Therefore, if the scheme is revived, would you—accepting my best thanks for the suggestion—suppress me and invite some one else to take my place? I have never sat on a Comtee. in my life, and feel it is too late to begin.

I am sorry, we cannot come to your party, as we go down to Sussex on Friday.

Yours sincerely
Virginia Woolf

Frederick B. Adams Jr.

5th March [1934]

Yes, I am ever so much better. It was only the usual little temperature, which makes the headache hang about. But I am back in my room again, writing. And it wasn't half as bad as it sometimes is.

Oh Lord though we are in a chaos! Your damned cousin, the Duke [of Bedford]—if he is your cousin disown him—has insisted that we must entirely decorate the house; and every book has to be moved, every piece of type; and here we are, for the next 3 weeks, camped among rolled up carpets and tables on end. Damn all dukes! £270 to spend; and then they pull the house down.

However the fog is over, the King of the B's [Belgians] buried—heaven be praised Ethel's mass has been played—but it was a joke to see her sitting in her triangular hat by the Queen's side in the Royal Box, among all the court.[2] Afterwards she gave a tea party at Lyon's—a more sordid 6d. affair you cant imagine; marble slabbed tables, thick bread and butter, and the populace munching their cream buns. There was Emerald Cunard, Diana, Ly Lovat[3] all eating thick bread and butter. but a little out of their harmony: and Ethel bellowing, as red as the sun, entirely triumphant. and self satisfied.

1. See Letter 2829.
2. On 3 March at the Albert Hall.
3. Lady Cunard, the American-born hostess and intimate friend of George Moore; Lady Diana Cooper; and Laura, Lady Lovat, whose husband, the 16th Lord Lovat, had died the previous year.

That mule faced harridan of yours—this'll make you angry, but there's no accounting for tastes, Christopher St John was there.

And I'm flirting with a rather charming [Lady Cholmondeley?]—oh dear me, this wont make you jealous, sipping roses at Fez. No, we may go to Ireland and the Hebrides, not to Provence, just this minute. I'm afraid it wont be hot yet in Provence. I cant write sense or passion or reason or rhyme—L: will go taking down books and dumping them on the floor. What myriads we've got! And never dusted.

Please write some time to

Potto and V.

Berg

2863: TO QUENTIN BELL   52 *Tavistock Sq,* [*W.C.*1]

Typewritten
March 8th 1934

Dearest Quentin,

I am as usual delighted and shocked by your letter. How you carry on in the High Alps, to be sure—I thought the pure snows had their tempering effect on human passions—but what you tell me of the clergy on the Alp brings a flush even to the cheek of Mont Blanc. And I am not a mountain. No, but I'm hardly distinguishable from an old sack of onions at the moment. That damnable Duke of Bedford is making us entirely redecorate the whole house—from top to bottom; bricks, walls, windows, cellars, cupboards— all have to be painted; rehung; with the result that here I am marooned in a space the size of a rather large tabby cat, books to right of me, pictures to left of me, and not a drop to drink. It is hell—and hell lasting as long as Mr Ridge the builder chooses. We dine on scraps on our knees. Leonard has ardent politicians, five of them at this moment, encamped on the bottoms of cupboards while clouds of dust rise; and our food tastes of plaster; and our noses stink of oil paint. Oh for a whiff of your air, contaminated as it is by the clergy!

Yesterday was a great occasion—Nessa's private view;[1] she will tell you her part in it; mine is that I was caught by several quite unknown admirers, of hers and yours, who said Oh how lovely, oh that bridge—oh that flower, until I had no tongue to praise with left. Old Jack Hutch; bought one for the Contemp; Art;[2] but it turned out already to belong to Duncan. So he cut up crusty, and Jack crusty flushes like a boiling beetroot;

1. At the Lefevre Gallery, King Street. The catalogue had a Foreword by Virginia.
2. The Contemporary Arts Society.

281

it is terrifying. George Booth[1] said he had bought a picture by you, and he liked it very much; and asked after you with all the passion of his old love for Nessa—It occurs to me, are you George Booth's son? I hope so, for then there's capital in the family. He owns a line of ships.

Also there was Lydias Dolls house,[2] which was a triumphant success, much to our surprise. Dear Old Maynard was—this is exactly true—streaming tears; and I kissed him in the stalls between the acts; really, she was a marvel, not only a light leaf in the wind, but edged, profound, and her English was exactly what Ibsen meant—it gave the right aroma. So shes in the 7th Heaven and runs about kissing and crying. Whether it means business I dont know.

Then I was sitting brushing the dust off the bread and butter when Nelly said a very old man called Secker was at the door. I thought she meant a carpenter; but it was old Walter Sickert, come to thank me for my article on him.[3] Up he stumped, in a green peaked cap; and said I had written the only criticism worth having in all his life. That means, it praises him to the skies. He is rather sunk, like a cracked canvas; but he sang a few bawdy songs over his cake, and smoked a cigar. He is bitter though against all Rogers and Clives I imagine; says they dont know a picture from a triangle; here he kissed my hand and said, "Whereas you—youre an angel." Thats what comes of laying it on with skill and thickness, my dear Quentin. However he's 74 and not long for this side of the grave I daresay, so his vanity and weariness must be excused.

Then we had a crazy party in a Lyons tea shop, where half the aristocracy in England sat on hard chairs, drank tea like vinegar and ate rancid butter. This was old Ethel Smyths celebration after the passion of her Mass. "I hate religion" I roared into her deaf ears; and there was lovely Lady Lovat, a Catholic, repining on the next chair. Ethel was in tearing spirits, fresh from the side of the Queen. What a sight they made in the Royal Box together! You are still her paragon. "What a boy!" she keeps on saying. "Were I only sixty years younger—"

Julian is rather bothered about his fellowship which will be out next week.[4] He thinks he may get a job at the BBC. He is writing poetry too, and editing Pope and asking about jobs in China. I've just got a card for

1. Director of the Alfred Booth & Co. Shipping Line, and a Director of the Bank of England, 1915-47. His father, Charles Booth had been a friend of Leslie Stephen, and had employed George Duckworth as a part-time secretary.
2. Lydia Lopokova (Keynes) appeared in Ibsen's *A Doll's House* on 4 March at the Art's Theatre, London.
3. *Walter Sickert: A Conversation.* First published in the *Yale Review*, September 1934.
4. Julian failed in his second attempt to become a Fellow of King's, and was living mainly in London, writing some of the poems which appeared in *Work for the Winter*, 1936, but without paid employment until he went to China in 1935.

Julian Trevelyans show—but I dislike his looks so much I shant go.[1] He should be on the Mappin Terrace at the Zoo. And hes not an honest dog-ape like Bob—theres something shifty about him. What do you think? Its true I've never spoken to him. I suppose you'll be back in a jiffy—are you flying? I shall have a lot to say to you. Yes, Saint Simon was Lyttons great gun—he made me buy him when you were in the cradle. Its sublime, I thought but theres no room to go into all that now, and I must go up and see what colour theyre painting the dining room, and if the five politicians have gone.

If you have time, write and tell me the rest of the story of Miss A and the curate. It made me laugh—but what were the legs in plus fours doing? Your art is too discreet.

Virginia

Quentin Bell

2864: To Lady Ottoline Morrell   *Monks House, Rodmell,*
[Sussex]

Wednesday [14 March 1934]

Dearest Ottoline,

I was about to thank you for your more than heavenly letter when I was struck down by a violent feverish cold—partly because Ethel would come here, all ablowing, all aflowing; and so I didn't write but dreamt of you in bed instead, and your rose-red curtains and your pearls and black velvet. Oh what a bore these little upsets are—not in themselves—I dont mind sneezing and choking—but how I hate not writing! How I hate being again thrown back on my haunches! then all my thoughts whirl round and round: I read Pascal: no: I try Bernard Shaw: no: finally I think of Ottoline, and her red gold curtains conducting a divine symphony in which even the sea lions and cormorants are dulcet as sirens (the reference is to Charles Morgan and E.S.)[2] and wake recovered.

Did I leave a shabby old unbrella in your hall? Well, perhaps you'll bring it one day soon. We shall go back tomorrow to camp out among the painters, puttyers, brick-layers and so on.

Excuse this red nosed sheet.   yrs V

I couldn't come up on Monday, or I would have come to you.

Texas

1. Julian Trevelyan (b. 1910), the painter, was the son of Virginia's old friend R. C. ('Bob') Trevelyan. This first one-man show was at the Lefevre Gallery.
2. Charles Morgan, the novelist, and Ethel Smyth were not acquainted, and Virginia may be making a satirical contrast between the explosiveness of Ethel's music and Morgan's mellifluous prose.

2865: To Lady Ottoline Morrell

[52 *Tavistock Square, W.C.*1]

Postcard
[16 March 1934]

I'll try to come on Monday if I'm not too horribly dirty. I'd like to. But what nonsense—I've met Lady O. [Oxford] scores of times—and we always have the same conversation you'll see. Just back to the full horrors of kitchen being painted.

V.

Texas

2866: To Elizabeth Bowen   52 *Tavistock Square, W.C.*1

26th March [1934]

Dear Elizabeth,

I was hoping to see you, but there seems no chance before Easter. We've been in a horrid state, having the house entirely decorated with us in it. No room to sit and so on.

I wanted to ask you about our Irish tour. Here is our scheme—typed. Would you be so angelic as to make any suggestions—this is only a rough scheme. And could we spend a night with you? Probably not. And are there any books to read?

We go down to Monks House, Rodmell, Lewes, on Wednesday for 10 days, then back here, then Ireland on the 28th—how heavenly! Any ideas that come to you, would be gratefully received.

I hope your book[1] is racing ahead. I'll ring up, but I suppose you'll be out.

yours V. W.

Texas

2867: To Ethel Smyth   *Monks House.* [*Rodmell, Sussex*]

Thursday 29th March [1934]

I have been very remiss—all my letters begin with this, though I dont really feel it, denying as I do all ties, all responsibilities.

Do you know—no you dont—I have gone through almost the most disagreeable six weeks of my life, and I'm so happy, so free today. Well this was what happened; only it sounds a little absurd after this preamble.

1. *The House in Paris*, 1935.

Nelly [Boxall], the cook, the cook we've had 18 years, has been worrying me the past 12 months or so, and gradually I was coming convinced we must part—d'you remember she had her kidneys out, and the dr. appealed to me to take her back, which I did against my judgment? Well, she's been lapsing again into her old tempers and glooms, and I could not decide what to do. In the intervals she was angelic and an admirable cook—and then 6 weeks ago today, when I was ill, there was a row over an electric oven, which we wanted to try; and she wouldn't. And suddenly I felt this is the end; if I let her stay she will grow on us and wither and decay. But I could not face a month with her under notice, so I laid down a scheme to which I kept for 6 weeks, until I almost died of it—that is I kept serenely but severely at a distance; and again and again she tried to break me down; she cajoled and apologised, and half suspected what was up, but not quite. And we had the whole house decorated—floors up, books down, every room a muddle, and agony, and she was determined not to let a word escape her; and so we went on till this Tuesday when I sent for her to the drawing room and told her plainly that I could stand the strain no longer and she must go. And all Tuesday and yesterday we lived in a storm of abuse and apology, and hysterics and appeals and maniacal threats, she entirely refusing to go, and refusing my notice and the cheque—a handsome one— stuffing it back in my pocket, following me about the house, till I was driven in the cold wind to spend yesterday morning parading Oxford Street, as my study is once more in the builders hands.

Well, we had arranged to drive off here at 2.30: and then came the final battle, the final appeal and abuse and tears, and she refused to shake hands with L. and so we left her, grasping a wet cloth at the sink and glaring at us, and off we went, and she still says she will not go. "No, no, no, I will not leave you" I heard her vociferate, to which I said, Ah but you must, and so we slammed the door.

Why does this scene, this long drawn out struggle with a poor drudge demoralise one more than any love or anger scene with ones own kind? I felt such a weight on me all those weeks thinking of how I must dismiss her that sometimes I could hardly sit in my chair. Honestly, I have hardly sat down seriously to a book. Once the moment came, my horror vanished and I didnt mind the abuse and the tears; indeed I saw so deep into her poor muddled terrified but completely self seeking mind that I felt a thousand times reassured. And now its over, and that aching tooth removed for ever! I suppose this reads very absurd, but you dont know how she's clung all these years, or how difficult it was, considering her virtues and her complete determination to stay for ever, to make the effort. So this may excuse some of my stony-hearted silence. In the midst of our house horror—and that was intolerably sordid—every cup tasted of dust—I had to spend every afternoon for ten days dusting books and putting them back, with these awful ingratiating advances from Nelly every hour or so—"Do let me make you a cup of tea—you look so tired" and so on—in the midst of this, Elizabeth [Williamson] came. I took her round to a room I borrowed at the Stracheys. I thought her a most stalwart and upstanding woman (please dont copy this and send it to her) full of character and interest. I shall try to see her again,—oh dear how nice the summer will be without Nelly! I shall only get a daily; I shall be free; I shall dine at the Zoo; I shall make no attachments ever again: oh how cool and quiet I feel this morning; we chuckle and chatter like a pair of pigeons.

I saw Vita who had seen you, and you saw the adored sister in law I hear [Gwen St Aubyn]. I broached the subject of C. St. J [St John]: but V. would have none of it. I expect in her absorption with G. she was blind,—blinder than usual. No, I did not admire St J's article on the Mass: I thought it very skimming and surface interesting only, not criticism, only enthusiasm. But what is the worth of my opinion? On this, nothing. We plan—oh I feel so free, I repeat—a visit to Ireland at the end of the month; and one to Scotland in June, but only short tours. This is a scrabbled dull letter, but the emotions of the last 2 days have made scrambled eggs of my wits; I sit in my lodge and look, like a child of 3, at a bird; at a flower; at a butterfly. There was a butterfly, in spite of the raging wind.

V.

Oh I've said nothing about your ears and your liver—excuse this outburst of egotism: next time I'll be less absorbed.

Berg

2868: TO LADY OTTOLINE MORRELL   *Monks House, Rodmell,*
                                                                    [Sussex]
[4 April 1934]

Dearest Ottoline,

I think Ethel's account [*A three-legged Tour in Greece*, 1927] was exaggerated, as is usually the case with that old sea dog—she likes to pick up the waves and the mountains. Also, she did it on the cheap and did not hire Ghiolmann's car, as we did.[1] If you do it on our system, which worked out fairly cheaply, but then we were 4, and the exchange was in our favour, there are no tramps and no climbs and no starvation. He makes out a tour, gives you an estimate, supplies a driver who talks French, and nothing could be easier. The only necessity is to buy one's own lunch, on occasion, which is easy, and to provide blue spectacles and plenty of veils and cold

1. In Greece, in April 1932.

cream, for the glare can be terrific and the wind—our car was open—
tearing. But on the other hand the air is more exhilarating than any I have
tasted; one feels young, buoyant, vigorous: and sleeps directly one's head
touches the pillow.

We could not manage the long tour, which goes down to Olympia.
But we went to Delphi, as you must; and to Aegina—but thats only a
days expedition, and lovely beyond words, from Athens. And we went to
the Byzantine churches, and Mistra,—coming back from Delphi, and Sunium
—but we had only 3 weeks in Greece; otherwise I should have insisted upon
an island or two. The food in the Inns was always decent; not a bug in the
beds; and the Athenian restaurant, Abemas, (I think) excellent. One can
always get yagourt (how does one spell it?)—that sour milk which is so
delicious, and wild strawberries. I dont think you need prepare for any
worse hardship than you'd find in Italy, and the beauty, the colour of the
sea and the earth, is unspeakable: marble as we know it is mere clay compared
with the marble on a hill there. O how I envy you! We shall be dreaming
and romancing in the mists of Ireland, and spend a night with Elizabeth
Bowen.

yr V.

Texas

2869: To Elizabeth Bowen   *Monk's House, Rodmell,*
                                    Lewes, [Sussex]

5th April [1934]

Dear Elizabeth,

Many thanks for your letter. It was very helpful, and we have altered
some of our plans accordingly.

We are coming back to London on Tuesday next: I suppose there is no
chance that you could come in on the 18th after dinner? Tom Eliot and Maynard Keynes are dining with us—thats why I cant ask you to dinner: but
they would like to see you—and so should we. If that doesnt suit, would
you come to tea on Thursday 19th? Then we could put further questions
to you. We shall be in London till we start, so suggest another day—
I cant remember when you come to London. In fact I can hardly write
sense, owing to the fact that it is the first hot day and I have been walking
on the downs, and found a whole bank of violets—will there be violets in
Ireland? I am very much excited to think of going there at last, and seeing
your house.

Yours
Virginia Woolf

Yes, I've often heard of Stephen Gwynn,[1] somehow through the O'Briens,[2] and I rather think he wrote to me, I'll get his book.

Texas

2870: TO JULIAN BELL

Monks House, Rodmell,
[Sussex]

Postcard
5 April 1934

For Heavens sake tell me where does "Die like a rose in aromatic pain" come from? Pope? And what is the right quotation?[3] And where are your poems.

VW

Quentin Bell

2871: TO ETHEL SMYTH

Monks House. [Rodmell,
Sussex]

Thursday [5 April 1934]

I was lying in bed this morning and saying to myself, "the remarkable thing about Ethel is her stupendous self-satisfaction" when in came your letter to confirm this profound psychological observation. How delighted I was!

"But as regards moral integrity ... I am not sure whether you and I have the same sensitiveness of conscience. Its not a question of whether scrupulosity in such matters is a weakness or a virtue. Its a question of fibre. Thats all. Moral fibre."

"Magnificent!' I cried aloud.

And then this beaming with sensitiveness and righteousness old tom cat goes on about having "pulled off 2 against the grain jobs that nobody else (save the entirely admirable E S) would take on"—surely no one, even in Woking, crowded as it is with city men, can have such an enraptured,

1. Stephen Gwynn (1864-1950), the Irish nationalist, and author of several works of literary biography and poetry. Virginia may have read his *The Charm of Ireland*, of which he published an enlarged edition in 1934. His sister Mary was Elizabeth Bowen's step-mother.
2. Dermod O'Brien (1865-1945), who was active in Irish affairs and a well-known amateur painter. Virginia had vaguely known him since childhood.
3. "Die of a rose in aromatic pain", Pope, *An Essay on Man*, Epistle i, line 200.

childlike admiration for themselves, I cried. And off you went again about not quoting my letters when you discovered that I was "not built on the same lines" as you—but whoever was built in such an orbicular rotundity like the sun in a fog of red hot complacency as Ethel? I asked myself. No, I shall never be able to ask her to come and see me again, I sighed reading on, the sentence that followed about your "rather morbid scrupulousness, as some people would judge it." And when I read that final, if oblique, pat by Ethel on Ethel's own back, I could not help thinking of a man called Pecksniff [in *Martin Chuzzlewit*],—he used to have just that way with him. Seriously, Ethel Pecksniff, with your fine moral fibre, and your perhaps morbid scrupulousness, what are you hinting at? What infamous crime has Vita committed, that she cant speak to me of, coarse of fibre as I am? I understand, I need hardly say, that people like Vita and myself must offend you, with your fine fibre, and all the rest of it, a dozen times a day—its been too good of you to put up with us—still I wish you would say plainly, and simply, if youre not too sensitive, what charge you level at her so cryptically, stopping to pat your own back in between whiles? I'm going to see her, I hope, and I should like to know. What has she done?

Berg

2872: To Ethel Smyth   [*Monk's House, Rodmell, Sussex*]

Sunday [8 April 1934]

This is the letter that roused my anger. I thought, and I think you'll agree that it was natural that I should think, from your language, that C. St John had revealed something extremely discreditable to Vita. And I said, if that is so, Ethel ought either to tell me outright what it was, or to say nothing about it. These dark hints you were so stunned that you couldn't write—yet did hint—put my back up. And now, as far as I can make out from your second letter, C's horrid revelations amount to no more than what Vita told me herself. Hence my irritation when your second letter plumed yourself, as I thought, on your scrupulosity.

We only come up late on Tuesday, And then I shall be faced with domestic horrors. The Nelly [Boxall] affair I'm afraid is not solved yet. But I've no time or room for more. But do read your own words carefully and consider if I was so absurd to be annoyed.

                                                                                    V.

Berg

Tuesday [April? 1934]

Dear Logan

I gave your letter to Leonard, and I think he has answered you. I'm glad you are collecting your essays [*Trivia*], though sorry that they are going to Constable. If by any chance you want to reprint How Little Logan Found Jesus, I shall be proud to publish it—indeed I will print it with my own hands, if only to carry on the work of conversion and find a shorter way to Heaven myself.[1]

Yours very sincerely
Virginia Woolf

Frederick B. Adams Jr.

2874: To Vanessa Bell   *Monks [House, Rodmell, Sussex]*

Thursday [12 April 1934]

Many thanks, good Dolphin, for your information. I have written to Mabel, also to Ha, to find out about her cooking.[2] We rather incline now to have a sleeper in, as the room is there, and it is probably cheaper. But I will see Mabel, as it would certainly be an advantage to have some one used to our habits. Nelly continues to bombard me, through her sister, and I foresee that she'll insist on another interview. Our final day was an incredible misery. Nothing would make me go through it again. I wonder if you've heard of it from Lottie [Hope].

We go up on Tuesday next. Is there any chance of seeing you apart from the general mob? Maynard has rung up and I gather that there's been a muddle about the reading [Memoir Club]. I suppose you couldn't bring Angelica to tea on Monday? We go to Ireland for a fortnight at the end of the month, so I shan't see you for an age. Not that you mind.

However you were very considerate about the Harknesses—[3] that I will say. Lord, what a mercy it is to feel I've not poor old Nelly brooding over me!—Except that she will of course insist on more rows.

Yr
B.

1. This religious tract *How Little Logan was Brought to Jesus* was reprinted in a limited edition of 65 copies by Robert Gathorne-Hardy and Kyrle Long at the Mill House Press in 1934.
2. Virginia was hoping to engage Mabel, Margery Fry's ("Ha" 's) cook, to replace Nelly Boxall.
3. Former Charleston servants.

What about my picture? Shall I write and tell them to deliver it? The post has just sent this.

Berg

2875: To V. Sackville-West   52 *T.[avistock] S.[quare, W.C.1]*

Friday 13th [April 1934]

Yes, I must really write to you, because I want to know what is happening. But that said, I've nothing to say. Thats because you're in love with another, damn you! Aren't I a nice nature, though, like a flight of green birds alighting now and then? I had meant, God knows, to apologise for being so d—d dull, so obtuse, drowsy and dreary that night at Kings Bench.[1] I said to myself, no wonder Vita no longer loves you, because you bore her and if there's one thing love wont stand, its boredom. The truth was Ottoline and Nelly between them—oh what a scene I had—never will I let a servant stay 18 years again—had ground me to a kind of gray dust. That reminds me—your amethyst is on the mantelpiece beneath the stone that came from Persepolis—the 3 curls of the Emperor's head, I always think it is

Shall you be in London this week? Shall you come and see me? I only ask: even a dog can do that.

My God what a rampant rough rowdy dowdy bore old Ethel is! All about you and C St J. I lost my temper, (in writing) whereupon she went to Lady Balfour, who says Ethel is an angel; Lord B. is called in to confirm this;—she cant let a thing be; she's the most ingrained egotist ever I knew. But dont embroil me with her further.

The week after next we go to Ireland, driving all across by land, and then leaping the Channel, and staying with Eli Bowen, and so up to the wildest islands, where the seals bark and the old women croon over corpses of drowned men, dont they. And there I may be windswept in to the sea. But what would Vita care. "No", she'd say, we had Petulaneum Ridentis in that bed last year: we'll try the Scrofulotum Penneum there this." So she'd bury me under, wouldnt she, Vita? And yet how clever, how charming I am!

V.

Berg

1. Virginia had dined with Vita at Harold's flat, 4 Kings Bench Walk, Inner Temple.

2876: To Shena, Lady Simon   52 *Tavistock Square*, [*W.C.*1]

13th April [1934]

My dear Shena,

I wish we could manage Wednesday or Thursday, but I'm afraid both those days are already rather impossibly full. We are just starting for a tour in Ireland, and I have, for some reason, left a mass of things to do.

But would you let us know when you're in London again? We shall be back about May 7th. Wont you and your husband come and dine with us one night? Perhaps you will bear this in mind, and suggest a day. Then, besides education, of which I know nothing, we might discuss the Fishers. Was your remark about daughters and the doting prompted by your tour of Greece? I am very anxious to hear.

Yrs
Virginia Woolf

Sussex

2877: To Ethel Smyth   52 *T.[avistock] S.[quare, W.C.*1]

Monday [16 April 1934]

Yes, I expect Lady B. [Balfour] is perfectly right and that introspection is a bad habit. And the longer I live the less likely it seems that one person can possibly understand another. So let us leave it at that.

No, Wednesday is useless, as I am seeing Tom Eliot, whose poetry you think silly nonsense, and I think real poetry—another instance of the difference above alluded to.

I think the Nelly affair is dispatched, and I am trying another experiment; but my mind which has been chiefly occupied today and yesterday in talking to servants refuses to function. I'm delighted that you saw old Sue Lush:[1] the Gushington we called her when we were children—and I've hardly seen her since, Thank God the workmen have just laid the carpets. and I'm going to Sadlers Wells [*Macbeth*], and must dress, so please pray dear as you would say, God be with you

V.

Berg

1. Susan Lushington, one of the two daughters (the other became Kitty Maxse, the original of Mrs Dalloway) of Vernon Lushington, K.C.

Thursday [19 April 1934]

No, I cannot manage it—I've got into a rush and into a whirl, and nothings done, and so dont come. But do come when we're back—early in May. But I've no sort or hint of 'scunner'—(what an odd word) against E.S. What d'you take me for? I recognise differences—always have—but I dont let them separate; in fact, so contrary are human souls, they serve to ally. I dont require a repetition of V.W—not at all: what I want is a contradiction; and so, though I'm too hurried to elaborate, if you will take the trouble to, you'll find a meaning in this I hope to your liking. No I've put off everyone tomorrow and Saturday—Lady Colefax among them. Every sort of dreary dull business has accumulated. This is always the prelude even to crossing the Irish Channel. I'll write from the Coast. Lord how I long to be out on a rock in mid sea! I had a violent argument about religion etc. with Tom Eliot. He's of your persuasion. So please write, contrary though we are

V.

Berg

20th April [1934]

Dear Bob,

I have read your stories,[1] and with great enjoyment. Perhaps I liked the unchristened one on Love best. I think they are full of interesting and subtle things and beautifully smooth and finished. My only doubt—which rises I know from my novelists prejudice—is about the dialogue form. I am always rather bothered by it. If you bring in people, then I want to know quantities of things about them, and here, of course, as you use them, they are kept severely to the rails. Thence, perhaps, what I used to feel with Goldies' [Goldsworthy Lowes Dickinson] dialogues—something too restricted, too formed. Yet I feel, as I say, the interest, the subtlety of the thought, and the melody of the whole expression. So I am puzzled to see what form there is, save Dialogue, to carry the idea—no doubt, as a novelist, I am bothered by these restrictions more than I should be.

I'm always wanting you (but this is another theme) to break through into a less formed, more natural medium. I wish you could dismiss the dead, who inevitably silence so much and deal with Monday and Tuesday[2]—

1. No stories or dialogues by Trevelyan were published during the 1930s.
2. This advice was paraphrased by Trevelyan in his poem *Aftermath*. See p. 317, note 2.

I mean the thing that is actually in your eyes at the moment. A dialogue between the different parts of yourself perhaps, now, at the moment.

But I liked reading these Dialogues—no St Francis is not that—I'm writing rather hurriedly—very much. I think there is a great deal in them. And if one went into the question of form, it would take a volume to express what I mean. But this is a tribute to the stories, for they make me think of so many things. Suppose you had told me the colour of Miranda's eyes and hair—what would that have suggested? And so on. Excuse this scrawl—we are just off to tour in Ireland.

Yours V.W.

Sussex

2880: To Donald Brace   52 *Tavistock Square, W.C.*1

Typewritten
20th April 1934

Dear Mr Brace,

Many thanks for your letter. I am afraid that there is no chance of my having anything ready for you to include in your autumn list. I have still a great deal of work to do on my new book, and do not expect to have it ready for another year. But I will of course let you know in good time, and will send a description as soon as possible. At the moment, I have not even chosen a name.

I am glad Flush still sells—we have done very well with it here, much better than I thought likely. And I am very pleased with what you have done for it in America.

We are just off for a fortnights holiday motoring in Ireland.

With best wishes from us both

yours sincerely,
Virginia Woolf

Harcourt Brace Jovanovich

2881: To Helen McAfee   52 *Tavistock Square, W.C.*1.

Typewritten
22nd April 1934

Dear Miss McAfee,

I enclose an article on the pictures of Walter Sickert, RA.[1] It will be published over here either this summer or autumn; if you would like to

---

1. *A Conversation about Art* (Sickert), published in the *Yale Review*, September 1934.

have it for the Yale Review I could arrange dates to suit. But of course it may not be of interest to your readers. I dont know how far Sickerts pictures are known in America.

Would you think me mercenary if I asked what fee the Yale Review now pays for articles?

We are just off for a motor tour in Ireland but letters will be sent on.

With kind regards
yours sincerely
Virginia Woolf

If it is too long, the part about poetry could be cut.

Yale University

2882: To Vanessa Bell   *Monk's House, Rodmell,*
                               near Lewes, Sussex
Wednesday [25 April 1934]

I asked Marsh[1] to deliver the cup, which I hope will reach you.

Please write, addressed to 52. They will forward, What did the Dr. say about Quentin? We're just off, and so far it is fine, but why seek the Irish channel?

I enclose a letter[2] which may amuse you—servants psychology. I shant answer. So farewell good Dolph: and dont forget your poor dear Singe. I'll write from Ireland.

B.

Leonard is having asparagus, if any, sent you.

Berg

1. The Lewes butcher.
2. From Nelly Boxall.

Letters 2883-2889 (April–May 1934)

Virginia and Leonard, with Pinka their dog, went to southern Ireland for a fortnight's holiday. It was Virginia's only visit to Ireland. They drove from Rodmell to Pembrokeshire, and embarked at Fishguard on a stormy sea-crossing to Cork. They spent a single night at Elizabeth Bowen's house at Kildorrery, finding Cyril Connolly and his wife there as unwelcome fellow-guests. They continued to south-west Ireland, then turned north to Galway, saw the Aran Islands, and returned through Dublin (for two nights), Holyhead, Worcester, Stratford-on-Avon, and so home to London. They loved Ireland, thought momentarily of buying a house there, but decided that the Irish talked too much for peace. At Waterville, Co. Kerry, they read of the death of George Duckworth, Virginia's half-brother.

2883: To ETHEL SMYTH   *Fishguard Bay Hotel, Goodwick, Pembrokeshire.*

Friday 27th April 1934

The sea is mounting, and a gale is blowing, so perhaps, with luck, I shall never set eyes on England again, but rise, about 2 this morning, and fulfil your hopes—I mean, see God.

We've driven all across Wales today in storms and sudden blasts of sunlight when all the sheep and the gorse blazed white and yellow. The finest thing in England is Salisbury plain, or was, till your cursed army peppered it with huts and bugle calls. How the druids must hate the Colonels! But I'm too dazed to write that chapter of English history. We are sitting in the hotel lounge, with a couple of sporting gentry, who read out from the Times about cricket. I try to read Proust, Then the—the wife—exclaims "But isnt it very odd to try a steeplechaser flat racing?" which he caps with some marvellous 'put'—is that the way you spell it. Lord how I wish I could be them! Their faces have a perfect integrity, a perfect suitability, that seems to me to prove that the world is what they say, and all our alarms are mere flurry. How calm, how right, how deeply rooted they are! Surely they know—oh everything. But they will talk, so I can't write. The lady has just said aloud and cheerfully that she has strained her inside and must see a doctor. Now, I couldn't say that aloud in the lounge. Well, at midnight we cross, and then stay with E^th Bowen at Kildorrery and then go to Galway and then to Arran, and then to Dublin.

She is going to have a whiskey and soda. They have rung the bell. Now I couldn't do that in the lounge of a hotel. No, I quite agree with you, I have missed the bull's eye, and hit only half the rim, the white. "Can I have a small whiskey and soda please?" Yes, thats the way to say it. Well Ethel, this very interesting letter must cease. I cant read Proust though. What do you think of Proust? I'm reading Sodome et Gomorrhe—heres the small whiskey and soda—now how well they drink it! She is knitting. "One and six for that tiny spot!" So it goes on. I dont think society is quite so omnipresent as P. [Proust] makes out. But you have lived with duchesses, so tell me.

V.

Berg

2884: To Quentin Bell   *Fishguard Bay Hotel,*
Goodwick, Pembrokeshire

Friday April 27th [1934]

Dearest Quentin,

You will I know be sorry to hear that this is the last time I shall write to you; all points to death by drowning in the Irish channel. It is pouring and howling. I can see the boat rocking even in the harbour. We are waiting for dinner. Pinka—did I tell you we brought Pinka, with a towel, soap and comb—is with the ship's cook on board. There are several hairy Irish watching me—the Welsh talk a kind of moaning—but the time for moaning will be from midnight to 8. It is now hard on seven.

Well, to say my last words—we had a good deal of rain and storm crossing England, and saw Stonehenge in a wild mist; then we passed within a stone's throw of Seend,[1] and I kissed my hand to the Bells, and their inkpot made out of hunters' hooves.[2] All the same, 6 miles off is the finest country in England. Wales is full of sheep, and salmon rivers. Oh dear, how I envy you, sleeping on dry land. What shall I say to the conger eels? when they nose me at dawn—and its not as if I were Tom Eliot and believed in God. You cant read my writing so its no use taking another page on which to sum up my faith.

Farewell. V.

The A.A. man has just been in, and says it will be very rough.

Kiss Nessa for me for the last time and Angelica and Clinka [dog].

Quentin Bell

1. Cleeve House, Seend, Wiltshire, where Clive Bell's mother lived.
2. For the hoof ink-pot see Letter 335 (Vol. I).

2885: To Lady Ottoline Morrell   *Bowen's Court, Kildorrery,*
Co. Cork

Sunday [29 April 1934]

Dearest Ottoline,

This is where I am, for the moment, so alas I shant be within range of Gower Street before you go. It is a lovely melancholy land and Elizabeth's house is exactly what I imagined,[1] but I cant describe, because of the pen, and breakfast, after wh. we start for the Arran Islands. Love and please tell me about Greece.

V.

Texas

2886: To Elizabeth Bowen   *Eccles Hotel, Glengarriff*
Co. Cork

1st May [1934]

Dear Elizabeth,

Here we are, because it was too beautiful to move. In fact, your island is too seductive, and we have already been asking about houses, whether one can get them easily,—and one can: so expect us as your neighbours in future. But this is largely your doing, as you made us so happy that night and we enjoyed the wishing well, the ducks, the spinning wheel, the plaster, the beds—no I cant make a full catalogue: moreover, what is complicating this letter is that Bostocks[2] has come into being at Eccles Hotel. Everybody talks to everybody and we have struck a fascinating dying lady and a most upright German judge. Excuse this hand—the pens at Bostocks wont write, because talk is so much better.

Yrs V.W.

Remember the Lives of the Bowens.[3]
We are cutting out Galway, because we cant move on, and it strikes me I have never thanked you. Love from us both.

VW.

Texas

1. Bowen's Court was a stone house in which only Bowens had lived since its completion in 1775. Elizabeth inherited it from her father in 1930. She sold it in 1959, and the new owner pulled it down.
2. At Bowen's Court they had talked about "starting a society called Bostocks" (Virginia's diary).
3. Elizabeth did write a history of her family, *Bowen's Court*, 1942.

Thursday May 4th [3rd 1934]

We only got the Times yesterday and read about George.[1] Well, there's nothing much to be said at this distance, in the wilds of Kerry. Poor old creature—I wonder what happened and why he was at Freshwater. But I must wait till I see you, unless you've had the charity to write. Did you go to the funeral? I've just with great labour composed a letter to Margaret [his widow]. Now suppose this had happened 30 years ago, it would have seemed very odd to take it so calmly. As a matter of fact I feel more affection for him now than I did 10 years ago. In fact I think he had a sort of half insane quality—I cant quite make out what—about family and food and so on. But your memoir[2] so flooded me with horror that I cant be pure minded on the subject. I hope to goodness somebody went to the service—I wish I had been able to.

But here we are a great deal further and wilder than if in Italy or Greece. We only see Irish papers, now and then; there are no towns, only an occasional small fishing village and as we changed our plans, all our letters have gone wrong. It was mere chance we found a copy of the Times lying about.

We have had a most garrulous time. We never stop talking. The Irish are the most gifted of people in that line. After dinner the innkeeper comes in and sits down and talks till bedtime, perfect English, much more amusing than any London society, and if its not the innkeeper, as it was last night, then the other guests, if there are any. They all make bosom friends at once, and we're already committed practically, to buy a house at Glengariff. Its a mixture of Italy Greece and Cornwall: I suppose too romantic in parts; but extremely subtle, greys, browns, yellows, an occasional donkey, absolutely deserted, not a house ever to be seen, no gentry, everybody lamenting, because nobody comes any more, and the gentry have all fled. I daresay it would be too depressing to live in, but after Sussex I find it heavenly, and so far we have only had one bad day. We spent a night with the Bowens, where, to our horror we found the Connollys[3]—a less appetising pair I have never seen out of the Zoo, and the apes are considerably preferable to Cyril. She has the face of a golliwog and they brought the reek of Chelsea with them. However Elizabeth was very nice, and her husband [Alan Cameron], though stout and garrulous, was better than rumour reported. It is an 18th Century house, but the remarkable thing about Ireland is that (here Mrs Fitzgerald the landlady broke in for another outburst of conversation: she has given me a receipt for a perfect Onion soup) There is no architecture

1. Sir George Duckworth, Virginia's half-brother, died on 27 April, aged 66, at Freshwater in the Isle of Wight, where he was staying with friends.
2. This memoir has not been traced among Vanessa's published and unpublished papers.
3. Cyril Connolly and his first wife, the American-born Frances Jean Bakewell.

of any kind: all the villages are hideous; built entirely of slate in the year 1850: so Elizabeths home was merely a great stone box, but full of Italian mantelpieces and decayed 18th Century furniture, and carpets all in holes— however they insisted upon keeping up a ramshackle kind of state, dressing for dinner and so on.—Lord! this is all very dull, but garrulity has seized upon me too. Now I must copy out the onion soup, and then we pack and go on to a place called Adare, and so to Dublin and we shall be back on Wednesday.

How is my dear Dolphin? I feel that I have been away a hundred years and dipped in the depths of the sea and anything may have happened.

Leonard says Laura[1] is the one we could have spared.

So goodbye and let me know when we can meet.

B.

Berg

2888: TO VANESSA BELL   *Dunraven Arms Hotel,*
                                          Adare, [Ireland]

Friday 6th [4th] May [1934]

Your letter has just reached me. Well well, I pray to God you may have written an account of the [Duckworth] funeral which I shall find at Dublin:

But this letter, written in a hurry as we're just off, is on business.

Dont you think that it would be much more sensible to let me give you £100 to buy a new car? It seems to me silly to have the old one mended, if it won't be really good. I trust to you to be honest on the matter. What I suggest is that you and Duncan should let me give this as a joint birthday present.[2] I am much better off than I expected, owing to Flush. and it would be a great pleasure to think of you attending family funerals in style.

I'm in a rush, as we are just starting in pouring rain for Galway.

But I trust to your common sense and hope you will order the car at once.

B.

Berg

1. Laura Stephen (1870-1945), Leslie Stephen's daughter by his first wife Harriet (*née* Thackeray). She was mentally disturbed as a child, and for most of her life was confined to an institution, where she died. For the fullest account of her see Jean Love's *Virginia Woolf: Sources of Madness and Art*, 1978, pp. 159-69.
2. Vanessa was 55 on 30 May. Duncan's birthday was on 21 January, when he was 49.

300

May 8th [1934]

Dearest Ka,

Your letter followed me to the wilds of Galway, It is a lovely country, but very melancholy, except that people never stop talking. Now we're in Dublin and still talking—this time to the Aran Islanders who are here making a film.[1] But I cant write with this pen.

Yes, I remember the speech to the man, and my father did say those words, my mother pinned a medal to the man's coat. Can the old doctor have been Dr Nicholls, can he be still alive? He was very handsome once[2].

We are now off to see some pictures, and more talk. It is a wonderful island, only why be so very selfconscious? But I cant go into that, and must stop. Love to Mark. Is he about to go to Cambridge? How terribly time flies.

Why dont you write your life? and let the Hogarth Press publish it?

Yr V.W.

Mark Arnold-Forster

1. *Man of Aran*, a celebrated documentary film produced by Michael Balcon and directed by Robert J. Flaherty, about the islands of Aran off the west coast of Ireland.
2. Dr Nicholls had practised at St Ives, Cornwall, but this anecdote cannot now be explained.

Letters 2890-2914 (May–July 1934)

Virginia caught influenza on her way back from Ireland, and as so often happened, she seemed to recover only to be infected again, and spent several days in bed both in London and at Rodmell. During the unusually hot early-summer months she continued writing her novel, and took French lessons twice a week from Jane Bussy (her progress can be judged from Letter 2911). She was deeply stirred by a monstrous event at the end of June, the 'black weekend' when Hitler murdered some of his closest associates.

2890: TO V. SACKVILLE-WEST   52 T.[avistock] S.[quare, W.C.1]

Thursday [10 May 1934]

Yes we're just back—arrived from Stratford on Avon last night. Oh we've seen such a lot of queer places; and Elizabeth [Bowen] and I clasped hands over the wishing well in her garden—where the poor come and hang rosaries and broken cups—and wished—well, what d'you think we wished? (I must say plainly and frankly, my one wish is to make you jealous.)

So do come on Monday, 4.30, and we'll do whatever the season dictates. But please conceal the fact from Ethel, because I want her to think I'm still in Galway. I wish you'd settle her goose; I get strangulated heart cries about you,—dot, dot, dot, indicating revelations of unspeakable horror. Yes, you ought to go to Stratford, the home of all your tribe.[1] I was tremendously impressed. Poor old George [Duckworth]—no, I'm not seriously sorry, only selfishly, that my past is now further away and the grave I suppose nearer. Also Margaret whom I respect dimly, must be very lonesome —they made such a billing and cooing pair; last time I saw them together the tears came to my eyes.

V.

Berg

2891: TO ETHEL SMYTH   52 T.[avistock] S.[quare, W.C.1]

Wednesday [16 May 1934]

This d——d influenza (though temp. not over 101) has landed me in bed and sofa and complete despair about human life. Oh Lor! To think how

1. The Sackvilles had the living (appointed the Vicar) of Stratford-on-Avon.

I had planned to write and write! And to go to Fidelio! Well it cant be helped. We're off to Rodmell tomorrow for Whitsun. But how does one ever regain those moral heights when it seems right to look down on one's fellows, and take pen in hand and lay down the law? I'm so humble you wouldn't know me.

V

Berg

2892: To Elizabeth Bowen   52 *Tavistock Square, W.C.*1

Wednesday [16 May 1934]

Dear Elizabeth,

I rang you up today on the chance that you were in London and would come and see me—I'm recovering from influenza which struck me the day we got back—but I heard nothing but a buzz, and so suppose you weren't there. I wanted to tell you of our adventures, and how we met a charming Mr and Mrs Rowlands [at Waterville] who said they were old family friends of yours, but knew you only by reputation, as what they called 'extremely clever'. And then we went to Galway and saw the Aran Islands and picked the gentians and were almost blown off the cliff—altogether it was a wonderful time, and we never stopped talking, but it became also very melancholy. However you must come and let us tell you.

Tomorrow we hope to get off to Rodmell for Whitsun. I'm almost recovered, but oh dear, what a bore to start influenza again when I want to write a million words at once and finish with it.

Many thanks for sending the book—the Times book I mean—you didnt send yours.

Yrs VW

I was enraged to see that they gave the £40 to Gibbons;[1] still now you and Rosamund can join in blaming her. Who is she? What is this book? And so you cant buy your carpet.

Excuse this illegible scrawl which I have now made all one blot, the result of writing lying down with what is called a fountain pen.

Texas

1. Stella Gibbons had just been awarded the £40 Femina Vie Heureuse Prize for her novel *Cold Comfort Farm*.

Monk's House, Rodmell,
Lewes, Sussex

May 20th [1934]

Dear Elizabeth,

Yes, do come on Friday 25th, 4.30. The Rowlands—he was a terrific Greek god, but only bodily, not his face or mind—were friends of your Uncle Mervyn; he'd been at Trinity with him he said. Now I come to think of it, I remember Stella Gibbons writing a poem we liked,[1] and so asked her to send us some to print; I cant help thinking you and Rosamond had a better claim[2] That reminds me, I feel guilty about Last September;[3] or perhaps stupid. I thought you were lending me the copy the young man stole. I never meant you to give me one. But I shall be very glad to have it. You must let me give you—I dont know what.

The dr said that influenza takes 40 hours to develop; so I caught mine at Worcester or Holyhead not Ireland. Its gone, and I'm all right, but it leaves one like a watch that doesn't tick. Never have I felt stupider, but I daresay thats good for the soul. And it does't much matter as one can sit under the laburnums and watch a white horse munching in the marsh. Please thank your husband—we thought it was very nice of him to have us.

Yrs V.W.

Texas

Monk's House, Rodmell
near Lewes, Sussex

Monday [21 May 1934]

Yes, I liked your letter very much; but how can you ever write with a fountain pen? This is fountain pen, now writing. Disgusting, slippery, false, yet convenient. Its such a hell of a day—Bank holiday. A mist like a white mare's tail, only uglier, over the marshes, and when I tried to walk there, I found 3 men in yatchting [*sic*] caps with towels under their arms: grocers they looked like, poor wretches pretending to enjoy the white hail, Lord how it stung! So I came back lit the fire; and read Proust, which is of course so magnificent that I cant write myself within its arc; that's true; for years I've put off finishing it; but now, thinking I may, and indeed so they say must die one of these years, I've returned, and let my own scribble do what it likes. Lord what a hopeless bad book mine will be!

1. In the *Criterion*, edited by T. S. Eliot.
2. To the Femina Prize.
3. *The Last September*, Elizabeth Bowen's novel, 1929. Danielstown, the house in the story, is Bowen's Court.

[*The Years*] I tried to start it going; but its verbose, foolish, all about hollow reeds. At lunch I told L: who said anyhow one could burn it. And then I lit the fire and read Mrs Wharton; Memoirs[1] and she knew Mrs Hunter [Ethel's sister], and probably you. Please tell me sometime what you thought of her. Theres the shell of a distinguished mind; I like the way she places colour in her sentences, but I vaguely surmise that there's something you hated and loathed in her. Is there?

But surely a mildly displaced spine is nothing serious? My old half brother, just dead and buried—you must ask Nessa to tell the story of the funeral—lived 66 years with one, and ate and drank till, poor boy, his heart ceased suddenly in a friends house; but I'm sorry if it means Elizabeth [Williamson] whom I much like and respect and hope to see, is ill.

Talk of my obstinacy and folly in not liking my letters to be quoted! I wrote one, casually, to an unknown but accredited American the other day, hinting at a mild literary scandal. She replies that she gave it to a friend of hers who is publishing it in The Atlantic Monthly![2] So thats why I write *Private* or should, in future.

Well Ethel what are you tossing and turning on the point of your horns?

V.

Berg

2895: To Logan Pearsall Smith   52 *Tavistock Square, W.C.*1

23rd May [1934]

Dear Logan,

It is very good of you and your [B.B.C.] Committee to think of asking me again.[3] I wish I could join, because I should so much enjoy meeting the people whom you are asking. But I feel, as I said before, that I should be of no use, and should only take a place that somebody else would fill much better. So I must refuse; but please accept my thanks for thinking of it. I've been away for Whitsun, or I would have written before.

Yours sincerely
Virginia Woolf

Frederick B. Adams Jr.

1. Edith Wharton (1862-1937). Her Memoirs were called *A Backward Glance*, 1934.
2. No such letter was published in the *Atlantic Monthly*.
3. See Letter 2861.

Thursday [24 May 1934]

Dear Janie,[1]

We've just come back from Ireland, and then I had the flu, or I would have asked before this about your father. Now I hear he is getting better, and I'm very glad. What I'm writing to ask is, do you think you could conceivably undertake the task of coming and talking French with me? I mean this as a serious business proposal, of course, and if you consider it, you must tell me what would be the right charge.

The thing is I suddenly discovered, what I have long suspected, that I cant speak a word of French. I read it, but then thats nothing. Also it may be hopeless—our education, ages ago as it was, never ran to grammar.

Let me know if this seems to you possible, And if you cant, can you suggest someone? Lessons at irregular intervals, of an hour you know— that was my idea. And anyhow we hope to see you.

Yours Virginia

I have just caught my finger in the door so cant write.

Please give my love to your mother.

Texas

2897: To Ethel Smyth   52 *T[avistock] S[quare, W.C.*1]

Sunday [27 May 1934]

Well the devil has got me again. We came up on Tuesday—and on Friday the old 101 business started—the dr says a germ still in my throat. Almost normal today but to stay in bed—oh dear—that book! And I had just begun again, and am now reduced to Aldous Huxley.[2] Please write. I think your letters the best I get—so there.

V.

I do sympathise about rheumatism

Berg

1. The daughter of Dorothy (*née* Strachey) and Simon Bussy, the French painter. He lived until 1954.
2. *Beyond the Mexique Bay*, 1934.

2898: To Grace Higgens   52 *Tavistock Square, W.C.*1

29th May 1934

Dear Grace,[1]

Mrs Bell had just told me that you are actually married. So we want to send our best wishes and congratulations. Will you buy yourself a present with the enclosed, which comes with our love, and we hope to see you at Rodmell.

Yrs
Virginia Woolf

Mrs G. Higgens

2899: To Ethel Smyth   52 *T.[avistock] S.[quare, W.C.*1]

Thursday [31 May 1934]

I feel real compunction, Ethel dear, that through me you should sit down dead beat to write. Please dont. It was only the fever that extorted that cry for letters. Write when you're full of words and leisure. I have the sympathy of the old hack for anyone who lifts a pen when their brain is as a dryed yellow sandy sponge, and all that falls is dry yellow sand. I know it—the sensation. Not that your scrawl this morning was of that nature at all.

The fever has gone, and I am left serene, and even begin to feel the stream running and lifting the reeds again. Excuse these metaphors—they come in flocks when I am recumbent—I cant shoo them off: thousands and thousands make themselves in my brain—I suppose the result of not using my brain. The dr. came, 6 hours late of course; had submitted the swab of my throat to a specialist, he finds it swarming with a bacillus called viridans, or green; advises inoculations; "But have you ever known influenza or any other disease cured that way?" I asked; to which she, being Lytton Stracheys niece and an honest woman,[2] said No. One case of eczema was all in her experience. "But I havent got eczema" I said. So we agreed to leave the throat uninoculated—which inoculation is a damnably expensive business—for 3 weeks, and see. The truth is doctors know absolutely nothing, but as theyre paid to advise, have to oblige. I feel much better anyhow. Its very hot today isnt it? Do you sit among the pinks and write your article? And do the pinks, those very sweet white ones, make you think how you brought them up here one summer? and said

1. Grace Higgens (*née* Germany) was employed by Vanessa Bell as her maid from 1920, and after Vanessa's death, by Clive Bell and Duncan Grant, until her retirement in 1970.
2. Dr Elinor Rendel, daughter of Lytton's elder sister, also Elinor.

this was the bloom stage of our friendship which would soon be over? I like your honest mind. That reminds me—see how flighty I am—there's a perfect trumpet if you're getting one: a deaf woman [Molly MacCarthy], to whom to talk to used to be hell—a lovely sentence that—is now as susceptible to my voice without its raising itself, as the fern is to the spring breeze. Go and see T. Eliots The Rock at Sadlers Wells and tell me what you think. I would write more, but my fingers seem rather slippery. How can anyone read this page?

V.

I'm going out today: the dr: advises all possible fresh air

Berg

2900: To Vanessa Bell

Monks House, [Rodmell, Sussex]

Wednesday [6 June 1934]

God! What an utter curse! It seems to me that Mrs Curtis[1] might have kept Angelica, and let her have it there, since there must be arrangements at school. However, I suppose there was some reason against it. Also Quentin might be lodged at Tilton?—but I suppose this also was considered. I believe I've had it—didn't that odious doctor at Welwyn swear I had?[2] But you haven't. As I say, one can only curse God and the school system. Do let me know anything that happens; I expect nothing will, but I'm optimistic.

I'm alone here today, as L. has gone up to a meeting in London, and I wish Dolphin were sitting with me. I've not yet been to any of the operas, but we have tickets for Friday and with luck I may persuade L. to go tomorrow.

My only news is domestic—Annie[3] is getting married to a man called Penfold, which is a damned bore; but she says she must take her chance of settling, though she doesnt seem to know much about him, except that he painted her cottage and breeds rabbits. So we shall probably have an empty cottage and want a cook—I had vague thoughts of Grace [Higgens]: but I suppose it would be too difficult.

Quentin came to tea yesterday. He looks amazingly well and large, and we had a good gossip, like old crones. Certainly he is a most charming

1. Elizabeth Curtis, Headmistress of Langford Grove School, Essex. Angelica had scarlet fever.
2. In 1904, when Violet Dickinson cared for Virginia during her mental breakdown.
3. Annie Thomsett, who had worked at Monk's House periodically since the Woolfs bought a cottage for her at Rodmell in 1929.

brat, and I daresay will do us all credit. He hopes to wangle a ticket for the opera out of Clive; I suppose you've put off your troops of Stracheys. I'm keeping clear of all hospitality but no doubt if I go tomorrow I shall land myself with some undesirables. Anyhow I shall look out for you on Friday.

We shall come back on Sunday.

B

Berg

2901: TO ELIZABETH BOWEN   *Monks House, Rodmell,*
                                          [Sussex]

June 8th 1934

Dear Elizabeth,

My conscience afflicts me for two reasons:—

1) After you had gone that day, I felt livery, took my temperature, found it was over 101, and went to bed for a week with influenza. Did I give it you? I do hope not. But the dr. says it was highly infectious.

2) I never thanked the giver of the Emily Dickinson that I thrust on you. Was her name and address on the letter inside, or the publishers' name? I must write, I suppose; and all traces seem to have vanished. So if you could send a card with this on it, would you.

We came down here to recover, and now I'm all right, and we go back on Sunday I think.

Your VW

I didn't read Last September,[1] because I was in such a state of crass stupidity, but I shall when I get back.

Texas

2902: TO ELIZABETH BOWEN   52 *Tavistock Square, W.C.*1

Monday [11 June 1934]

Dear Elizabeth,

Many thanks for sending the letter. As she's been so tactful, not giving addresses, and writing her name illegibly I think it may lapse.

Of course I am pleased and honoured that Lady Cynthia [Asquith] should want to quote from Mrs Dalloway. If its only a few lines, there is no difficulty: if its a passage, or a page, then the Hogarth Press says will Heinemann write and ask them: as they ask whatever it is—10/6 perhaps—that

1. See p. 304, note 3.

Heinemann in the same circumstances asks them. This is the way publishers behave, and I'm in their hands.

Another thing: did I forget to tell you that we have a friend, Lyn Irvine, who produces what she calls The Monologue? A little typewritten paper. She asked me to ask you if you would consent to send her something. I said I would; now she writes again to ask: so I ask: will you: in case she is too shy to ask. She doesnt pay I think. But she is clever, uncompromising and all that. I'm so grilled that I cannot give you more details.

Yes, how nice it must be, to lie under a tree, having knocked down Lettice Fisher.[1]

Yr. VW

Texas

2903: To Ethel Smyth   [52 *Tavistock Square, W.C.*1]

Sunday [17 June 1934]

No, I cant manage tomorrow. Somebody here. And I suspect you'll be wise for once and sit among your white pinks in the garden. I lie like an alligator basking. Only alligators bethink them of the lotus and the loves of other alligators in this weather; while I think, on the contrary, of slabs of green ice, and green eyed bears, and white birds, and wish I were able to waddle off my ledge into the sea. But I managed to add one staggering nonsensical page to the 700 odd this morning, so I am quite happy; in my grilling.

Why is Mrs Cameron [Elizabeth Bowen?] so touchy? I cant myself feel that even if the aspersions you make were of my dearest I should resent them. An odd trait in human nature: throw it down the WC. if you can spare the water—and think no more of it.

V.

Do you want it back?

Berg

2904: To Ethel Smyth   [52 *Tavistock Square, W.C.*1]

Tuesday [19 June 1934]

Well that was, what they call, a sweet thought of yours; to come in from the roasting grill and find all white, all cool, all as fresh as a laundry. Your Simkins[2]—but this may be the result of sympathy and association—always smell sweeter to me than Oxford Street Barrow Simkins

1. Wife of the Warden of New College, Oxford.
2. *Mrs Sinkins*, a dianthus.

No, tomorrow I have to be out, and praise the Lord, the sun is down, and theres a puddle in the mews at the back. And on Friday I must go, heaven help me, to Worthing. My mother in law, having for the past 5 years, carried on an elderly flirtation with an old man called Legge, who stood her Burgundy and took her on the pier, is now once more desolated, because the old man is naturally dying; which she cant do.

Yes, I liked the tiger story; I thought Stenson was fishy myself—picking up strangers and jumping after hats[1]

V.

Heres the horrors—papers I mean.

Berg

2905: To Ethel Smyth   [52 *Tavistock Square, W.C.*1]

Thursday [28 June 1934]

I am amused, but also rather contrite. I forgot that you cant see the situation at the other end of the telephone. There I was at 4.30 still talking to a charming friend [Desmond MacCarthy] who had asked himself to lunch. Lord love me, will he stay to dinner, I was asking?—and we had people dining—shall I get no respite from talk till one a.m.?—when the telephone rang, and I seized the occasion providentially offered to say, severely, with an eye on him, "No I cant see you. I'm going out." He took the hint and went—you rushed to Staggs and bought lipstick. Such is the power of the human voice. Well my opinion of my own histrionic powers has gone up—so thats all to the good. But let me pay for the lipstick—indeed I think I owe you an umbrella; such a heavenly relief it was to get 2 hours solitude before the diners arrived—much like being given an umbrella in a storm. What about H.Bs [Brewster] letters, that reminds me? Dont I owe you some part of Mrs Jones [typist]? When shall I be alone, and see you—? God knows

V

Berg

2906: To V. Sackville-West   52 *T.[avistock] S.[quare, W.C.*1]

2nd July [1934]

Yes I saw Ben [Nicolson] across the room the other night, and wished and wished I could get at him; but the crowd was too great. What a shindy

1. Stanley Stenson, an employee of Whipsnade Zoo, was mauled to death when he entered the tiger's den to retrieve a stranger's hat, who wagered him that he would not dare to do it.

a party is! I think that one will last me till next July. I'm quite all right—only Elly [Rendel] made me send a swab of my throat to a doctor, who says it is full of germs, and wants to inoculate me, which I wont do: so have kept rather quiet, and so far have had no more flu (as he said I should) I lay it on rather to Ethel, as you divine. Poor old struggler! Now she writes to say she has to pay £2,000 to the Treasury, and is therefore ruined: something about income tax apparently, but I rather suspect exaggerated, like the rest.

I expect L. has already written you a business letter, so that all that is left me is to say that far from thinking you a grasping Jew we always point to you as the one, or the most, perfectly disinterested and incorruptible and mild and modest and magnanimous of all our crew. All I feel sometimes in the grey watches of the night is that *we* are fleecing you; and you have to pull the feathers from your breast to feed the young on our account. The young, Ben, I mean—oh I'm so hot—cant write—looked to me adorable the other night—worth sitting on a felt chair between Sibyl and Jack Hutch. to see, and so I daresay L. ought to pay you one thousand down all to keep him at Balliol.

Here is Osbert [Sitwell] ringing up to ask me to lunch. No I wont. Vita never rings me up; but then she's sitting among the pigeons at the top of the pink tower watching the moon rise between the hop poles—(now, isn't that worth all that Dotty [Dorothy Wellesley] ever wrote and Squire ever praised; so spontaneous, universal, and full of deep feeling). But I wish I ever saw her—Vita I mean; only when she's not on the Tower with the moon in her eyes, she's elsewhere with oh dear me—you see how that sentence must end . . . I had hoped to see Harold—only Raymond came.

V.

Berg

2907: To Ethel Smyth   52 T.[avistock] S.[quare, W.C.1]

Monday [2 July 1934]

I'm seriously much down cast by thinking you have to meet this appalling muddle [her tax demand]. How can it have happened? Still, I cant help guessing they wont exact anything like that amount—not from a Dame, doctor, KCB. and so on, surely. But what a hell of a bore to have to think of it even—and I'm enough of a flibbertigibbet to have panics in the middle of the night about money.—Do you?—When, goodness knows, I've now no need.

Yes, I admit the folly of never seeing you. Not that I had any notion you were going to turn into a brown cocoon so soon (a rhyme—how lucky —like seeing 3 magpies to rhyme unwittingly). And my summer is merely a passive one—here I sit, trying to write, and what drops into my bucket drops. It was Desmond the other day when you rang up. And I seem to be giving offence to my friends by my behaviour. Colefax writes that she is furious. Cant believe that its not a personal insult that I wont roast myself and fry myself talking to her and Noel Coward. Lord—what dusty souls these women get! On the whole—here comes a whopping whale of a compliment, so make ready—I prefer Ethel with all her faults. Yes, really; I think you are worth 4 of Cunard, 6 of Colefax, and 10 of Lady Diana [Cooper]. No, I forget, you have a rapture for her blue eyes and pink bones—to me a little frosty and like the Union Jack on a wedding cake. There used to be one in the hall at Buzzard's [tea-shop]

For the first time almost in my life I am honestly, without exaggeration, appalled by the Germans.[1] Cant get over it. How can you or anyone explain last week end! Their faces! Hitler! Think of that hung before us as the ideal of human life! Sometimes I feel that we are all pent up in the stalls at a bull fight—I go out into the Strand and read the placards, Buses passing. Nobody caring. Well as you would say, Basta. Let me know what happens about the money.

V.

Did I tell you, we have to appear before magistrates on Thursday at Reigate. L. accused of dangerous driving—no, inconsiderate driving[2]

Berg

2908: To Helen McAfee   52 *Tavistock Square, W.C.*1

Typewritten
July 3rd 1934

Dear Miss McAfee,

I must apologise for not having answered your letter before. But it came when I was having rather a troublesome time with influenza, and I put away the MS of the Sickert article to consider in better circumstances.

I have now looked at it; and I think that it will be possible to meet your wishes—I think I can put in a paragraph about Max Beerbohm's Caricatures without interfering too much with the run of the argument. Happily, the dialogue form gives one room for such diversions.

1. In the early morning of 30 June, Ernst Roehm, chief of the S.A., the Nazi private-army, was murdered by Hitler's order, and during the weekend several hundred other prominent Nazis, accused of plotting a coup d'état and other crimes, were ruthlessly executed.
2. Involving a cyclist. Leonard was fined £3.

I am arranging with the magazine here that it shall not come out before October. I will try to send it you in the revised form sometime at the beginning of August. I hope this will suit your dates, but if you want to have it by a fixed date will you let me know?

I quite realise of course that Mr Sickert's pictures are not as familiar with you as with us; he is getting very old and is in very bad circumstances, and this rather led me to write about him, although I have no qualification as an art critic; save admiration for his work.

Yours sincerely
Virginia Woolf

Yale University

2909: TO ETHEL SMYTH   52 *Tavistock Square, W.C.1.*

[5 July 1934]

Well you are without exception the most crossgrained, green eyed, cantankerous, grudging, exacting cat or cassowary I've ever met! Theres Desmond to lunch—Why not Desmond to lunch? I've met Desmond once in 6 months—on 8th April to be precise in a crowd of 10 people: and I've known him 30 years: and by Gods truth, I wont have my meetings or partings altered or dictated by a hair or handsaw by a woman who has spent all her days lunching and dining with Ponsonbys Barings Lovats and Coopers—a little set, if you like, though coroneted. O damn your insolence.

In hurry and heat.

Berg

2910: TO STEPHEN SPENDER   52 *Tavistock Square*, [*W.C.1*]

July 10th [1934]

Dear Stephen,

It was very nice of you to write to me. I love getting letters, but I hate answering them, at least when I've let them, as generally happens, lie about and become mouldy and reproachful. So I'm writing on the nail.

I'm so happy that you read the Lighthouse with pleasure,[1] when there are so many other books you might be reading. Some people say it is the best I wrote—others say the Waves: I never know: do you—I mean about

---

1. Spender had written (4 July, *Sussex*): "It is the only novel, apart from *War and Peace*, which I have read four or five times. I think it is the most delightful book I can imagine."

your own books? It used to worry and puzzle me—this diversity of opinion: no I'm becoming resigned to the fact that one cant get any settled opinion, and its rather a relief, for then one can go ahead on one's own; and merely stop and enjoy the praise if one gets it.

Who was your tutors wife, I wonder?[1] I wish there were some means of circulating the people who are as beautiful and charming as that—As it is, they remain on one shelf, and we on another. I never thought Oxford bred mothers and children—only very distinguished elderly men: but I'm still under the influence as you see, of my party at the Fishers.

I'm very glad to hear that you are writing a long poem [*Vienna*]. Yes, of course I agree that poetry makes statements; and perhaps the most important; but aren't there some shades of being that it cant state? And aren't these just as valuable, or whatever the term is, as any other? I am writing with prejudice, I admit, for I spent last week describing the state of reading poetry together,[2] and I dont think you could say that in poetry.

So with an infinite number of feelings: or such is my feeling. Then I go on to say that prose, as written, is only half fledged; and has a future, and should grow—but thats my private prejudice, and no doubt rises, not from conviction, but because I am in some way stunted. Its all very complex and immensely interesting. I should like to write four lines at a time, describing the same feeling, as a musician does; because it always seems to me that things are going on at so many different levels simultaneously. I shall like anytime to read your poem; I want to read nothing but poetry.

The rock [T. S. Eliot] disappointed me. I couldn't go and see it, having caught the influenza in Ireland; and in reading, without seeing, perhaps one got the horror of that cheap farce and Cockney dialogue and dogmatism too full in the face. Roger Fry, though, went and came out in a rage. But I thought even the choruses tainted; and rather like an old ship swaying in the same track as the Waste Land—a repetition, I mean. But I cant be sure that I wasn't unfairly influenced by my anti-religious bias. He seems to me to be petrifying into a priest—poor old Tom.

What about politics? Even I am shocked by the last week in Germany into taking part: but that only means reading the newspapers. Do write again, should you have time.

Greetings from Leonard
Yrs VW

Texas

1. Winifred Carritt (*née* Etty), wife of E. F. Carritt (1876-1964), University lecturer in Philosophy at Oxford. Spender and his friends tended to identity her with Mrs Ramsay in *To the Lighthouse*.
2. Virginia was revising some of her critical essays for a possible third volume of *The Common Reader*.

[11 July 1934]

Voila, chère Janie, le brouillon que vous avez commandé. Après l'avoir lu, je pense que peutetre il sera mieux de ne pas l'envoyer. Cette image de l'elepant et la sylphe n'est pas tout à fait réussie: c'est un peu—peut on dire 'rosse'?

J'avais l'intention de vous aborder au Square hier soir, mais le sommeil m'a vaincu, et j'ai eu le plaisir en dormant de vous revoir, et de vous entendre dire que vous m'aimez, et que je sais très bien la diffèrence entre les imparfaits et les parfaits—ce qui m'a tellement ravie que je me suis eveillée et hélas—c'était un reve.

A Vendredi, quatre heures.

Texas

July 15th [1934]

My dear Shena,

I didn't at all mean the other night to churn up the foundations of your life! On the contrary what I was feeling, as usual, was envy of other people's experiences—of your and your husband's Manchester education, and so on,[1]—and the desire to combine them with mine. It was modesty that made you think your life was criticised. I become more and more impatient with all these barriers and limitations—so if you will bring Manchester to London, we will send the artists to Manchester, and may I be one of them. It would be a great advantage to know how a university works, or a mill. One gets so dyed in one's own brand of being.

But it is too hot to put this plainly, and I'm only apologising for what must have been a high handed speech. (I've forgotten what I said)

It was very nice of you to come to dinner anyhow—and that reminds me, that the dinner itself is on my conscience still. After 18 years I at last got rid of an affectionate tyrant [Nelly Boxall], and your dinner was the first cooks [Mabel] new attempt—But if you will come again, perhaps she will have improved.

Yrs
Virginia Woolf

Sussex

1. See p. 171, note 2.

18th July [1934]

Dear Bob,

I've been a long time writing about your poem, which delighted me; but the summer in London is distracting. I am very glad I let you off, partly at least, writing the Epistola ad V. W;[1] I don't think it is only because you say so kind a word about me that I find it so sympathetic; of course use the quotation—which gives my meaning fairly.[2] Though of course had I been writing more explicit I should have tried to convey my respect and admiration for the dead, as well as my slight distrust of their dominion over us.

It seems to me that here you have invented or brought into being a method which allows you to be at once personal and poetic. I think the presence of a human being at the end of your poem is an admirable device—because like all good letter writers you feel a little of the other's influence, which breaks up the formality, to me very happily. In particular I like the country part—and the angler watching his "bright line".[3] As for the argument, I daresay my plea for adventurous prose is not disinterested: had I been able to write poetry no doubt I should have been content to leave the other alone. Anyhow, in reading this I see quite plainly what poetry can do and prose can't. So the envy is not all on your side.

A thunderstorm has just broken over Tavistock Square and I am writing in a lurid yellow light, not very connectedly I'm afraid.

Yours,
V.W.

Trinity College, Cambridge

1. In May 1932 the Hogarth Press published Trevelyan's *Rimeless Numbers*, which contained a number of poetic letters addressed to his friends, with titles like, 'Epistola ad D.M.' [Desmond MacCarthy]; 'ad A.W.' [Arthur Waley]; 'ad L.P.S.' [Logan Pearsall Smith] etc. He also addressed one to Virginia and sent her a copy, but did not publish it until after her death, when it appeared in his *Aftermath* (Hogarth Press, 1941).
2. " 'Dismiss the dead, who must silence so much.
   'Forget them, and deal with Monday and Tuesday.'
   Your wise and timely advice to me."
   To Virginia Woolf. (*Aftermath*). See Letter 2879.
3. "The peering angler stalks with cautious stride
   "Waving his bright line." *Ibid.*

[24 July 1934]

My dear Janie,

I must explain that after I had asked you to teach me old Bob Trevelyan came to tea and said he has a friend called Bonamy, a Frenchman, who rides on a horse and teaches French. His charge, Bob said, is always 7/6 an hour, and therefore yours is blacklegging which cant be allowed. So I send a cheque for the proper sum, and even then, considering how you over-ran your hour, and did exercises out of school, I'm probably skimping you.

Talking of the more imponderable element in our lessons (dear me, I've got to wash and dress so I cant furbish up this sentence properly) talking I mean of the pleasures of friendship and human propinquity, so impressed was I by your charm—no, thats not the word either: well, lay charm like a lustre over silver or gold, which is character—do you see that quality in your glass?—in short I was so delighted, interested, and impressed by my teacher that I wrote to her mother [Dorothy Bussy] (thank the Lord I neednt put this ramification into French—I think it savours of St Simon, plus Proust, with just a pinch of Mrs [Edith] Wharton)—I say so, and ask her to tea to express it in so many words, whereupon the clock struck 12: it was a rainy night; Leonard who posts the letters said it was too late to go; so I tore the letter to fragments. When I telephoned in the same connection next day she was midway between one house and the other, so I never saw her to tell her in so many words my opinion of her daughter's charm.

Yes in short, I did very much enjoy the human element my dear Janie, and if you ask Nessa, she will tell you how I sat on the edge of a chair and said Look here, Janie is far and away the best of the younger generation—"So I've always said" she replied, sticking a pin in her mouth; and the conversation then took a turn so flamingly in your praise that had you long ears, with long fur, like a donkeys, nothing could have put out the fire. So there. How would you put that proverb into the French of M. [André] Maurois? By the way he never answered, and thus I fear my likening him to a lark in the sky didnt go down.

                                                                    V.W.

Texas

318

Letters 2915-2937 (August–September 1934)

The saddest event of the summer was the death of Roger Fry on 9 September, by which Virginia was scarcely less affected than by Lytton Strachey's death in 1932, particularly for Vanessa's sake. A few weeks later she completed the first draft of her novel, which we can now begin to call The Years *although she had not yet settled on any title for it. A further 18 months of revision were to follow before it was published. A 'torrent of people' descended on Monk's House, including William Plomer, Saxon Sydney-Turner, Vita (whose latest novel Virginia privately deplored) and Ethel Smyth, who continued to show amazing resilience under Virginia's scathing comments on her religion, friends and literary tastes. An important domestic event was the arrival at Monk's House of Louie Everest, who remained in the service of the Woolfs (and then of Leonard alone) for nearly forty years. A new bedroom was added to the house; and Leonard acquired a marmoset.*

2915: To Ethel Smyth   *Monks House, [Rodmell, Sussex]*

Sunday [29 July 1934]

You would get longer livelier and more frequent letters from me, if it weren't for the Christian religion. How that bell tolling at the end of the garden, dum dum, dum dum, annoys me! Why is Christianity so insistent and so sad? Thats you see, why I dont write page after page: because I lay it down to you, this bell ringing religion; and say to myself, 'She cant have her cake and eat it too.' We got here on Thursday, all Friday was spent at Worthing;[1] today, like a butterfly whose wings have been crinkled up to a frazzle, (American) I begin to shake them out, and plane through the air. I've not read so many hours for how many months. Sometimes I think heaven must be one continuous unexhausted reading. Its a disembodied trance-like intense rapture that used to sieze me as a girl, and comes back now and again down here, with a violence that lays me low. Did I say I was flying? How then can I be low? Because, my dear Ethel, the state of reading consists in the complete elimination of the *ego*; and its the ego that erects itself like another part of the body I dont dare to name.

Yes I will, I suppose, I must I know, get Maurices "Dulwich Lady;"[2]

1. With Leonard's mother.
2. *The Lonely Lady of Dulwich*, Maurice Baring's penultimate novel, 1934.

319

but oh dear me, I dont want to. I never can submit myself to his silvery bald fingers (as a writer I mean) with any gusto. He's too white waistcoated, urbane, and in the old Etonian style for my rough palate. I cant get a thrill or a jar or any kind of acceleration out of him, any more than I can out of my dear infrequently met but always welcome Desmond MacCarthy—No, they're both what the fashion writers call 'immaculate' But I'll try once more in deference to you. But then, since the heart has got into your brain, about Maurice, I dont think you a safe guide in those groves, those scented garden paths, down which he for ever leads some noble crinoline. I am scurrying and hurrying to write this letter, and cover this virgin page, before L: who is reading a vast history of all histories—the sort of book Mr Casaubon tried to write in Middlemarch—finally shuts the page, and says Bed, whereupon Pinka jumps down from her chair, and we go in procession through the garden to my room: where I lie, and look through the apple leaves, at the clouds that hide the stars.

I hear from Nessa by the way that for some sudden inscrutable reason, Bayliss is doing Fête Galante.[1] Gallant old bus horse (this refers to Bayliss, not Smyth) She's a fine figure of a woman—Yes, but I forget where this was leading me. Let me see, I wrote 2 hours this morning, walked by the river and saw a porpoise; then up on the downs by a solitary farm with a fierce chained dog, and so home. and read Timon of Athens. Flaubert; and a modern novel.

Now here is Leonard and I must hastily close; isnt this a gallant effort— only 6 inches left to fill, and the whole letter, brimfull of cogent political argument, love, divinity, literary criticism with some domestic comment thrown in, has wasted precisely 10 minutes of my valuable day. Can you write as quick as this?

Oh how I loathe religion. I was reading the life of an 18th Century Parson Venn.[2] "Mercifully" he says "she swallowed a pin; which led her to thoughts of death; and instead of burning her wings at Assemblies, routs, card parties, she became a shining light." Mercifully she swallowed a pin! How can you belong to such a canting creed?

V.

Berg

---

1. Lilian Baylis (1874-1937) was the manager of the Old Vic, which began as a music-hall and developed during the First War into London's major theatre for Shakespearean productions.
2. Henry Venn (1725-97), the evangelical divine, author of *The Compleat Duty of Man*, 1793. Virginia had been reading *The Life* by his son, John Venn, which was re-issued with selected letters by H. Venn, 1837. Henry Venn was Virginia's great-great-grandfather.

[Monk's House,] Rodmell,
                                        [Sussex]

Wednesday [8 August 1934]

No no, my dear Ethel, you cant possibly get across, I mean get away, with that book of Maurices, No comparison with Mérimée—Oh my God that such a suggestion should have lodged in your otherwise generally clear keen, sagacious head. What a flurry love sets up—what a dust—what, in short, to speak plainly, a vacuum. Carmen![1] Oh dear! Dulwich! Oh my God! Why Carmen, which I read 2 weeks ago by chance, is like an oak tree; this is a piece of chewed string. Every word in Carmen has the thickness of a giants thigh: this is thin as a blade of green that a butterfly makes wobble. *There* the shade is ink black; here thin as weak tea. *There* the sun is blue; here a watered wisp. Its a conjuring trick of a hack. "Behold—my hat! Look well—now there's a rabbit. Now—still keep your eyes on me— behold its gone" Thats all it is—a book without roots; veracity, shade or sun. A parasol of a book—an empty white waistcoat. And that you of all people, with your incorruptible British sense, that you should turn to water and praise this brash*—well, I cant finish this sentence to my liking (having only 5 minutes this time) so must throw it at your unrepentant, uncastrated head, and there leave it of course, its all very pretty and all that.[2]

Then as to Xtianity and egotism. How you religious caterpillars (quotation from [John] Webster) make my gorge rise! 'We' that is Ethel and Elizabeth, having saved our souls, and purged our grossness, faintly and vaguely perceived in you, Virginia, signs of grace—or are they only spots on the sun;? So you say, gazing at me through your sanctimonious spyglasses. Making a corner in virtue; serving it up in pill boxes. Why, I've less egotism in my whole body, Ethel, than some one who likes her music to be played, in her little swollen fingers. Swollen with egotism, thats what you are—gout d'you call it? Ask your doctor next time to purge you of egotism. Lord! How I detest these savers up of merit, these gorged caterpillars; my Jew has more religion in one toe nail—more human love, in one hair.[3]

No time for more. Alas and alas

V
V.

* Brash = babies diarrhoea. Ask Lady B. [Balfour] if it doesnt.

Berg

1. *Carmen*, the novel by Prosper Mérimée, 1847, which was the basis of Bizet's opera.
2. Ethel was unconvinced. In her biography of Maurice Baring (1938) she said that if he had written nothing else, *The Lonely Lady of Dulwich* would alone justify the claim "that Baring is one of the finest novelists England has ever produced".
3. Ethel had written that she and Elizabeth Williamson had often wondered whether Virginia's religious sense would have perished had she not married Leonard (2 August 1934, *Berg*).

2917: To Mrs Easdale   *Monks House, Rodmell,*
                                      Near Lewes, Sussex

8th Aug. [1934]

Dear Mrs Easdale,

You must be accustomed by this time to not being thanked or answered.

But this is a particularly blatant case of ingratitude seeing that I am now sitting under a miraculous glow of your flowers. They have a particular fascination for me—rather like shells, only brighter and odder. How do you get them? I never see them anywhere. Your last years bunch was still in the room—but now they have made room for these. It is very good of you, though far too generous.

We liked so much seeing Joan [Easdale] the other day in London, only I felt guilty that she missed her train.

With best thanks and remembrances from us both.

                                            Yrs sincerely
                                            Virginia Woolf

University of London

2918: To Ethel Smyth   *Monks House, [Rodmell,*
                                      Sussex]

15 Aug. 34

1. FLURRY
2. QUOTATION
3. GROSSNESS.[1]

I hope thats plain—thats what comes of writing 5 minute letters. And this must be perhaps a 2½ minute letter, as I must go and fetch the gammon from the public house.

Religion.

Of course I agree in rating courage and un-egotism among the prime human virtues.

But what warrant have you for assuming that they are more commonly found among those who believe in God than in those who dont? None, I should say. At least thats not my experience. Thats what makes me speak of your 'sanctimonious spy-glasses'. assuming that you have the virtue, by reason of your God.

Vita.

Now there you rather stamp on my corns. What right have you to accuse her, as I think you do, of lack of integrity, weakness and so on? Of course

1. Three words in Letter 2916 which Ethel was unable to read.

you may have personal reasons for feeling less kindly disposed towards her. But I feel that you ought not to say the other thing as positively as you do without giving proof. If I say my maids a thief, I add "she stole 2/6 to my certain knowledge." As a matter of fact, Vita was here last week, and as far as I can judge, she's not capable of stealing (metaphor, you'll observe) one ½d. She quoted, from memory, a letter from C.[1] which made me see the other point of view—what a d——d ass, and a braying hysterical ass at that, C. is. But I dont, on the strength of that letter, inform C's friends that C. is lacking in virtue honour truth. No, no no, I think you're entirely wrong about Vita. As for Dulwich [Maurice Baring], read the dénouement— I mean the chapter about the journalist publishing her life—and ask yourself if anything of such palpable meretricious falsity could be used in that place save in a tenth rate book. Duncan is with me.

V.

Berg

2919: TO SHENA, LADY SIMON   *Monks House, Rodmell,*
                                              Near Lewes, Sussex

15th Aug [1934]

My dear Shena,

We are down here, and shant be back in London till the beginning of October. So would it be possible for us to come later? No, weekends are rather difficult, so that if a night in the middle of the week were possible, it would suit us better. I say 'us', but if Leonard couldn't come, and he is always rather rushed in the autumn, might I perhaps come alone? It is very nice of you to ask us. I wonder if we are still educatable?

Yours Virginia Woolf

Of course I want to see a works.

Sussex

2920: TO DOROTHY BUSSY   *Monks House, Rodmell,*
                                              Lewes, [Sussex]

Aug 22nd [1934]

My dear Dorothy,

I have been looking everywhere for your letter but cannot find it. And as you were somewhere in the country, this will never reach you, unless some

---

1. Christopher St John, whose love Vita did not reciprocate. Ethel had written: "She is less and less like the Vita I was so fond of . . . her integrity seems to have passed" (12 August 1934, *Berg*).

good genius forwards it. It is only to say that we too were very much disappointed—it mustn't happen again—there was your tea waiting and you never came. The truth is the summer is a damnable time in London. The autumn is much better. What about a crumpet in October? Your adorable daughter [Jane] said you might be still in England.

Yes, I think she is a ravishing creature, to me much the most alive and interesting of the younger generation, so French and so English—so cultivated and so fierce. But I am not going to write a character of a daughter to a mother.

Anyhow I enjoyed my lessons greatly, and shall have some more I hope.

Yrs
VW

Texas

2921: To Ethel Smyth   *Monks House, [Rodmell, Sussex]*

Friday [24 August 1934]

No we were up in London all day yesterday—had only just got back when you telephoned.

Can you come tomorrow, which is Saturday, at 5?

I'm afraid we shan't be alone—there's a young man, [William] Plomer, who writes novels and has reviewed Dulwich, and a girl [Lyn Irvine] who wants to write novels. But they'll play bowls, and we can sit in the garden and talk, while pretending to watch. This is the best day, so do come then if you can.

No, I can't understand, seriously, your feeling about Dulwich. If you'd likened it to something say by Edmund Gosse or Andrew Lang, I would have been delighted to praise it—for of course it has its merits—on those terms. But to drag in Stendhal and Carmen! Dear me, how we differ.

But that is no news. And I'll forgive you for having made me order Victoria the Widow,[1] because of one or 2 stories, though there again—dear me, how can you roll out your big guns over that entirely false and feeble and twittering performance.

Tomorrow we will fight

V.

Young Plomer and Lyn Irvine will be excited to see you and hear you, even in the distance.

Berg

1. *Victoria the Widow and her Son*, by Hector Bolitho, 1934.

Monk's House, Rodmell,
Lewes, Sussex

Typewritten
Private
24th Aug. 1934

Dear Mr Oliver,[1]
Many thanks for your letter about my book Orlando. I am much interested in your interpretation, but I know you will understand me if I say
that I am unable to add any comments of my own. This is partly because
I have not read the book since I wrote it, and much is therefore forgotten.
But also I think that the author can scarcely state his meaning except in the
words which he has used in his book. Interpretation must be left to the reader.
This applies also to my relation to literature—I have expressed this as well
as I can in my books of criticism. I fear therefore that I can be of little
help to you.

Yours sincerely
Virginia Woolf

Edward A. Hungerford

2923: To Ethel Smyth *[Monk's House, Rodmell,*
Sussex]

Monday [27 August 1934]

I would have loved to come over to Wootton Manor,[2] my passion for
seeing other peoples houses is inextinguishable—but was too shy to suggest
it; for these reasons (I have just analysed them)

1) You would have told her to admire my books. She wouldn't. That wd.
   have made me shy,

2) You would have said I was good looking, She would have suppressed
   a start at my plainness—Shy again.

Yes, these enthusiastic women—like Ethel—make it almost impossible
for very vain, very shy women, like Virginia ever to meet their, Ethel's,
friends.

1. Robert Oliver (b. 1909), was at this time Dean of Clark Junior College at
   Vancouver, Washington. He was later Speech Professor at Bucknell, Syracuse,
   and at Pennsylvania State University. He is the author of many books on
   communications, history and political science.
2. Near Polegate, Sussex. Ethel was staying there with her friend Alice Hudson.

You were very nice, and very remarkable, to the young[1] the other day;
but Lord! dont count them among my 'clan'; rather among my clientele—
both being almost bankrupt, struggling like flies in saucers; rather desperate;
but *not* among the petit clan. If you go on using that phrase, I shall fire off
a revolver at your head about Barings Balfours and Ponsonbys. As a student
of human nature, isnt it odd what a rise you can always get, out of anyone,
by telling them they live in a 'petit clan'—If I were dead, still my heart
would beat, would beat and blossom in red, at the tread, of that over my
feet.

Maynard. He certainly threw off that remark about Ethel being a national
monument, and she's only got to tell the tax collector so; but I suspect it
was one of his imaginative flights—He has an exaggerated optimism, where
he admires, which is one of his endearing qualities. But of course I'll ask his
advice, if you would like it He knew, of course, all about feluccas [?] (no,
thats not the word)

We drove to Brighton to buy worms today—worms for the marmozet;[2]
left in the greenhouse, they had died. Oh those downs! How you hurt me!
Are they Wilmington downs? Well, there was a horrid little villa, without
a garden, we could have had there; and I've always regretted it, but common-
sense tells me, it is better to be here. Only how fierce and perennial the love
of country is! I remember walking by the Long Man[3]—if thats what you
mean

V.

P.S. Wednesday

But, joking apart, I am quite sure that if the worst should happen,
or the Treasury demands payment [for Ethel's taxes], a letter to the papers,
signed Maurice Baring, or Lord Balfour or both—with Beecham thrown
in—would solve the question in 2 weeks. And also I'm sure that this is the
fitting way to solve it. In fact thats obvious to the meanest capacity. So
please I beg of you devote yourself to memoir writing for posterity and dont
trump up dust and ashes for Peter Davies [publisher]. This I consider your
most sacred duty. Ask Lady Balfour if she doesn't agree.

Berg

1. William Plomer and Lyn Lloyd Irvine, who were staying the weekend at
   Monk's House.
2. Leonard had acquired a pet marmoset, Mitz, on 25 July. See *Downhill all the
   Way*, pp. 186-9.
3. A figure, 226 feet high, of a man holding a club in each hand, cut into the turf
   of Windover Hill, overlooking the village of Wilmington, eight miles east of
   Rodmell.

2924: To Vanessa Bell   [*Monk's House, Rodmell,*
                                          Sussex]

Friday [31 August 1934]

Here's this—

Wolves are on me so I cant write—and I suppose its hopeless ever to
think of seeing you here.

Berg

2925: To Vanessa Bell   *Monks House,* [*Rodmell,*
                                          Sussex]
Wednesday [5 September 1934]

We had a vague hope that we might get over to you on Monday (though
I expect you are happier alone, for a change) but of course Karin Ann and
Judith arrived, the yatcht [*sic*] having broken down at Newhaven.¹ It was
like having a swarm of locusts in the house. Everything disappeared.
We've been living in a torrent of people—in fact I'm thinking next year
of hiring a villa in—God knows where. There are too many Ethels, Lyons',²
[Kingsley] Martins, mothers in law, Keynes', and so on—but this doesnt
apply to the rare blue Dolphin—in Sussex. And here is Mrs Jones' Hugh³
[. . . 3 *words omitted* . . .] asking to come. And tomorrow we go to London:
so is there any chance that you and Duncan could come to tea either Saturday
or Sunday? You might let me have a card. I think we shall be alone.

I'm very glad you are starting Angelica on an allowance, as it is much
more amusing. And I dont see why I shouldnt do what I like with my own
money. By the way, I thought the cover very lovely,⁴ so we're raising the
the price on the strength of it. Ann and Judith had walked from Colchester
to Cowes, lost their purse, and borrowed from lorry drivers on the way.
But this seemed not to matter—We had to visit them in the Atalanta, which
almost made me sick. Even in harbour. Their food is kept in a tin and smells,
and the wc. is next it, and Adrian had hurt his leg in a gale, and they all
wear black trousers. I hope Duncan is now all right⁵—but how we any of us
survive the country doctor God knows. I'm afraid you've had an awful time.

                                                                    Yr
Berg   B

1. Karin Stephen and her two daughters. The 'yatcht' was the sailing-boat *Atalanta*,
   which Adrian Stephen had hired to amuse his children.
2. Neil Lyons (1880-1940), the journalist and novelist, born in South Africa.
3. Philip Hugh-Jones (b. 1917), son of Alice Jones, who had been assistant to
   Leonard when he was Literary Editor of the *Nation*.
4. Vanessa designed the cover for Virginia's pamphlet *Walter Sickert: A Conversation*, and the price was increased from one shilling to one and sixpence.
5. Duncan Grant had had an operation for haemorrhoids.

Thursday [6 September 1934]

That was an angelic thought of yours'—mushrooms for breakfast. I had them with bacon, and thought, how very good and kind Vita is even if she didnt pick them, she must have said, Find string paper, and forked out 9d stamps—all things that only very nice people, about to turn into sheep dogs, do.

By the way, after you had gone that night, I found a nice dinner put away in a corner of the frigidaire.

But theres not much point in saying that now. We're up for the day— London tastes of stale face powder and petrol. But I verified a fact for my book. I am so proud of having one fact that is quite true that I think I shall print it in italics.

That reminds me, owing to the rapacity of our travellers, I've only today got them to give me an advance copy of the dark island (why lower case?)[1] So I shall take it back tonight

I thought the woman who acts the Edwardians looked so divinely and completely to my taste that I almost made an excuse to come to Birmingham.[2]

Are you going to Birmingham?

Are you coming to Rodmell—theres a new bedroom for you.

Oh I have seen so many and so many and so many dull nice good people —chiefly relations. My brother's new yatcht, 15 tons, was blown into Newhaven—his 2 daughters who man it had walked from Colchester to Cowes, lost their purse, borrowed money from men in lorries. How I like the youngest of all the generations! But I must break off in the full flood of inspiration—the marmoset who travels with us, has wetted.

                                                                    V.

And I want to see Harold; and I'm so glad you hated Dulwich ([Maurice] Barings Bastard) and I've been washing up lunch—how servants preserve either sanity or sobriety if thats nine 10ths of their lives—greasy ham— God knows.

                                                                    Potto.

Did I tell you my notion of heaven? All mushrooms,—did I tell you I'd had Ethel down? did I tell you I'm sick of all people called St John? And did I tell you, my God Vita, as you love me, or loved me, write to me.

                                                                    Potto.

Berg

1. *The dark island,* Vita's new novel which the Hogarth Press published in October.
2. Edward Knoblock had re-dramatised Vita's novel *The Edwardians,* and it was first performed at the Birmingham Repertory Theatre on 17 September. The part of Sylvia, the lovely Countess of Roehampton, was played by the young actress Elspeth Duxbury.

2927: TO GEORGE RYLANDS

Monks House, Rodmell,
Near Lewes, Sussex

Sunday [9 September 1934]

Dearest Dadie,

The difficulty about the weekend is that we have Ann and Judith, Adrian's children, here. So could you possibly come for Thursday night (13th)? That would be very nice. Or, if you can't, Leonard says he would fetch you over for dinner Sunday or Saturday and return you, if that's possible, to Tilton. Only the children will be here.

But we want very much to see you.

Your
V.W.

George Rylands

2928: TO JULIAN BELL

Monk's House, [Rodmell,
Sussex]

Sunday [9 September 1934]

My dear Julian,

I enclose the MS. [his poems] Do you mean to publish them separately? I rather doubt that. But then I'm not a student of the time. I think they would do very well in an appendix to your Pope: with an introduction. I'm afraid we dont go to London next Thursday, or at all that week.

Here's Nessa and Clive and the children for tea, while you are being murdered in Hyde Park.[1]

I've heard nothing about Roger yet.[2] Dadie [Rylands] is coming here I hope. I have been on the Stephen's yatcht which broke down in a gale. Ann and Judith come next week—and I hope we shall meet on the birthday.[3] What an amusing and indiscreet letter I would write if you could read! things not to be whispered on the typewriter.[4]

V

Quentin Bell

1. An anti-Fascist demonstration which led to sporadic violence; 18 people were arrested.
2. Roger Fry died of heart-failure on this very day, 9 September, at the Royal Free Hospital, London. He had been taken there a few days earlier after a severe fall which fractured his thigh.
3. A party for Angelica at Charleston on 16 September.
4. This letter is, nonetheless, handwritten.

Monks House, [Rodmell, Sussex]

11th Sept. 1934

That was very nice of you—to send me the Simpkins [dianthus], and it still smelt sweet.

But we've had an awful blow—Roger Fry's death—You'll have seen—It is terrible for Nessa.[1] We took her up to London yesterday and shall probably go up on Thursday again for the service—music only I think. He was to me the most heavenly of men—so I know you'll understand my dumb mood.—so rich so infinitely gifted—and oh how we've talked and talked—for 20 years now.

V.

Berg

2930: To Vanessa Bell   *Monks House, Rodmell, Lewes, [Sussex]*

Wednesday [12 September 1934]

Could you possibly get the paint box for me to give Angelica?
If you've no time, dont bother. I'll give her a tip instead.
I've just heard from Pamela[2] that she wants to see us before the funeral. So I'm asking her to come at 2 tomorrow. She's writing to you. We shant get up till lunch time, or about 12.30 I shall be at the flat till we go to Golders Green.

B.

Berg

2931: To Margaret Llewelyn Davies   *Monk's House, Rodmell, Near Lewes, Sussex*

Sunday [16 Sept 1934]

Dearest Margaret,
It was very nice of you to write—we knew you would understand. It has been a wonderful friendship, and I know we ought to be thankful to have had it. But it is very hard when one's friends die.
We are staying down here till the end of the month. But we shall hope to see you as soon as we get back. Have you been staying in London? It has been a lovely summer—the garden so full of fruit we cant eat it all.

1. They had been in love for several years from 1911, and remained intimate friends until his death.
2. Pamela Diamand, Roger Fry's daughter.

Leonard is now picking apples: and we have our two giant nieces, Adrian's children, staying with us. They walked all the way from Colchester to Southampton last week, sleeping under hedges and borrowing money from lorry drivers when they lost their own. Here they are! one [Ann aged 18] is 6 ft: and means to be a doctor—the other [Judith aged 16] 5 ft 10 and means to be a Civil Servant.

It will be very nice to see you and Lilian [Harris] again.

Love from us both.

Sussex Yr Virginia

2932: To VANESSA BELL   *Monks House, [Rodmell, Sussex]*

Wednesday [19 September 1934]

I forgot to ask you—what do I owe you for Angelica's paint box? Will you let me know.

I was sorry we were out when Julian came yesterday. Do come if ever you would—but I daresay you'd rather be alone for a bit. Today we have a man called Graham[1] about his book, which is an awful bore: tomorrow we have to go to Worthing for the last time thank God. Then I hope we shall be alone

Only as you know this doesn't apply to you. What did Geoffrey Keynes[2] say about Duncan?

So I hope to see you some time   B.

Isnt it extraordinary—Mrs Woolf's niece[3] fell and broke her leg last week— she seemed to get all right—but then suddenly died. Do *take care of yourself*

Berg

2933: To LADY OTTOLINE MORRELL   *Monk's House, Rodmell, Lewes, Sussex*

Friday Sept 21st [1934]

Dearest Ottoline,

Yes, we are all very sad, as I know you will understand. Roger was so much part of our lives—I dont know anybody who gave more and life

1. John L. Graham, whose *Good Merchant* was published by the Hogarth Press in this month.
2. Geoffrey Keynes (b. 1887), Maynard's brother, was distinguished both as a surgeon (in St Bartholomew's Hospital) and as a bibliographer.
3. Charlotte Mannheimer, daughter of Marie Woolf's sister Flora.

seems very dull and thin without him. How I wish you had gone on knowing him—but of course that's useless.[1] He died suddenly, as I expect you have heard. His heart went wrong, and I cant help thinking the doctors completely mismanaged it. But there is this comfort that they found afterwards he was in such a worn out state that he could not have lived long, and might have died at any moment.

We went up for the service, which was very beautiful and nothing but music, and then came back here. I think we shall stay, if we can, another fortnight. It is very lovely up in the downs, where I walk for miles, and never meet anyone but a shepherd.

Yes, I read and write, and we have had a good many people one way and another—the old Buccaneer [Ethel Smyth] among them, much to the surprise and amusement of William Plomer, who happened to be here. He thought her handwriting the worst he had ever seen! I'm sorry about your throat—the only blessing is that you can shut the door on Ethel. But dont shut it on me. I feel stupid and depressed and dull. I hate my friends dying. Roger was so full of his lectures and his plans, and now its all over. But its far worse for Vanessa than anyone. So goodbye for the moment, and excuse this winter fly scrawl. I spent yesterday at Worthing with my old mother in law, aged 86, and as gay as a Robin. Oh these old Jewesses! And do get well.

V

Texas

2934: To V. Sackville-West   *Monks House, [Rodmell, Sussex]*

Sunday [23 September 1934]

It was very nice of you, dearest Creature, to understand how much I should mind about Roger. Its been a horrid time—Nessa was here and rang up and was told he was dead. It was an awful shock. They had thought he was getting better.

I wish you had known him. He was so extraordinarily alive—I still find myself thinking I shall tell him something. And we all lived so much together. Dear me, why must one's friends die? But its far worse for Nessa than for anybody. That I find very difficult to think of in the future. We always saw him with her it was such a complete intimacy—hers and his. We are staying here till the 5th, I hope. Might we come and lunch next Friday, which I think is the 28th? We are travelling our books at T. Wells; and could call in. But will you let me know if it suits?

1. Ottoline and Roger Fry had quarrelled in 1911, when Fry accused her of spreading the rumour that he was in love with her. Their friendship never fully recovered.

No, to be honest as you require, I dont like the Island as well as the others. I cant get Shirin and Venn to come alive.[1] You give me the impression of writing too much in the personal zone, as if you couldnt get far enough off to convey the outside aspect; so that I dont follow her feelings, or gather why she did this or that. But this may be my fault though. I offer it with diffidence, because I suspect that my knowledge of the real people has queered the pitch for me; and no doubt I'm subcutaneously jealous. I liked the still life very much—not Mrs Jolly [a landlady] much—but the island, and the sea; the poetry; but then I always say you are a poet: witness my favourite Sissinghurst,[2] (which Desmond was enthusiastic about the other day by the way). The truth is, I dont grasp the people. And that, I suppose, one must do, in a novel.

It'll be very nice if we may come on Friday. I am very dull and rather dismal.

Yr

V.

I'm delighted that Lady S. has been so well inspired, for a change; and now expect with some confidence that Long Barn will be made over to me, as a token of gratitude and love, by B M.[3]

Berg

2935: To Ethel Smyth

*Monk's House, Rodmell,
near Lewes, Sussex.*

Monday. 24th Sept [1934]

Yes. I know I ought to have written before; but also you dont want me to write when I'm in a silent mood; and I've been in a silent mood.

All the same, I ought to have written, if only to explain that you mistook, no doubt through my own obscurity, the suggestion about the Income Tax.[4] What I meant was, should you have to pay it, a letter say from Maurice Baring, to the papers, saying "Ethel Smyth has to pay—: well we want to pay it for her—" would bring whatevers' needed in 10 days. That was what I meant to say. And I'm sure its true. So dont let a little affair of a few

---

1. Characters in Vita's novel *The dark island.* Shirin was modelled on Gwen St Aubyn, to whom the book was dedicated.
2. Vita's poem *Sissinghurst,* 1931.
3. Lady Sackville ('B.M.') had made up her quarrel with Vita, and in compensation for cancelling her daughter's marriage settlement, bought Long Barn for £8,000, and bequeathed it back to Vita in her Will. She died in 1936.
4. See p. 326.

hundreds stand between you and the immortal page: dont kow tow to mortality.

Here's your letter come, and I'm glad to see that 'you've been delving in immortality—Lady Ponsonby to wit.[1] Theres a violent wind, and all my letters have been dispersed; so I cant refer to the document. I think we shall stay here, save for a day in London, till the 1st week in October, or the 2nd week. And I'm going over to see Vita one day; and my niece is dining here off grouse, and my nephew too; and last week we had 2 more nieces, and such an odd lot of ragamuffins. And I have been thinking about the deaths of my friends. I have been thinking at a great rate—that is with profuse visibility. Do you find that is one of the effects of a shock—that pictures come up and up and up, without bidding or much control? I could almost see Roger yesterday in the room at Charleston. Nessa sits surrounded by her children doing needlework—dear, dear! So I break off. And Maynard is building a theatre, he's so rich, and so enterprising.[2] And I have a vast load of MSS. to read: and go on driving at that interminable book, which has the vitality of a snake—I cant end it.

V.

Berg

2936: To George Rylands   *Monks House, Rodmell,*
                                           Near Lewes, Sussex
Sept 27th [1934]

Dearest Dadie,

I don't know that I had anything very definite in mind about dialogue—only a few random generalisations. My feeling, as a novelist, is that when you make a character speak directly you're in a different state of mind from that in which you describe him indirectly: more 'possessed', less self conscious, more random, and rather excited by the sense of his character and your audience. I think the great Victorians, Scott (no—he wasn't a Vn.) but Dickens, Trollope, to some extent Hardy all had this sense of an audience and created their characters mainly through dialogue. Then I think the novelist became aware of something that can't be said by the character himself; and also lost the sense of an audience. (I've a vague feeling that the play persisted in the novelist's mind, long after it was dead—but this may

1. The widow of Sir Henry Ponsonby (1825-95), for many years Private Secretary to Queen Victoria. She became a Lady-in-waiting after her husband's death and was said to be the only person of whom the Queen was frightened. Ethel's stormy friendship with her lasted nearly 30 years until Lady Ponsonby's death in 1916. Ethel described her at length in *As Time Went On*, 1936.
2. The Cambridge Arts Theatre, opened in February 1936, for which Maynard Keynes initiated the plan and contributed the greater part of the capital.

be fantastic: only as you say novelists are fantastic.) Middlemarch I should say is the transition novel: Mr Brooke done directly by dialogue: Dorothea indirectly. Hence its great interest—the first modern novel. Henry James of course receded further and further from the spoken word, and finally I think only used dialogue when he wanted a very high light.

This is all rather incoherent, and also, as is the case with all theories, too definite. At the same time I do feel in the great Victorian characters, Gamp, Micawber, Becky Sharp, Edie Ochiltree,[1] an abandonment, richness, surprise, as well as a redundancy, tediousness and superficiality which makes them different from the post Middlemarch characters. Perhaps we must now put our toes to the ground again and get back to the spoken word, only from a different angle; to gain richness, and surprise.

I wish you'd look one day and see if there is any sense in this. Also, I wish you'd read the hated Antiquary and see whether you can't discover the last relics of Shakespeare's soliloquies in some of the old peasants speeches.

However, I must stop. It was enchanting to see you again—do let it become a habit—like gambling. And in God's name, why do you call your simple humble straight-forward if mentally muddled old friend Virginia "strange"? R.S.V.P.

Leonard is feeding Mitzy on a grasshopper he caught on an apple tree at this moment or he would send love.

George Rylands

2937: To Pamela Diamand   *Monks House, Rodmell,*
                                 [Sussex]
[end September 1934]

Dear Pamela,

It was very good of you to write to me. No, I dont think I ever realised that I could mean much to Roger—perhaps that was because he meant so much to himself. He was always the giver—no one excited and stirred me as he did.

So I am very grateful to you, because I have felt since his death how little one gave him—how much I wished I had told him what he meant to me. So thank you again. I am very happy to think he even likened me to your mother. Last time he dined with us, in July, he told me his marriage would have been perfect, but for her illness.[2] I always felt this, though I never knew her.

---

1. A character in Scott's *The Antiquary*.
2. Roger Fry's wife, and Pamela's mother, was Helen Coombe, whom he married in 1896. She was a few years older than himself. Her mental health gradually broke down, and in 1910 she became permanently insane. She died in 1937.

We go back to London next week. Do come and see us, if it is ever in your way. And remember me to your husband.

Yours affely
Virginia Woolf

Sussex (typescript copy)

Letters 2938-2970 (October–December 1934)

Virginia put aside The Years *until mid-November. Her* Walter Sickert: A Conversation *was published on* 25 *October, and she was approached by Helen Anrep and Margery Fry to write Roger Fry's biography, a proposal which she greeted with some misgivings. She made a new friend, Victoria O'Campo, the Argentinian intellectual, but an old one, Francis Birrell, was dying.*

2938: To Vanessa Bell   52 *Tavistock Square, W.C.1.*

Postcard
Monday [8 October 1934]

I've had a notice sent me to to say that Fanny Prothero's furniture is to be sold at 24 Bedford Sqre: and it includes some Aunt Julia photographs.[1] Its on view tomorrow till 4: the sale is Wednesday at 12. I think I shall go and look. For some extraordinary reason the Royal Historical Society thinks I might like to buy them. Perhaps I might.

V.

Berg

2939: To Ethel Smyth   52 *Tavistock Square, W.C.1.*

Friday [12 October 1934]

As this will show, we are back again—since Sunday, indeed. And you're at Torquay, rousing sparks in the orchestra,[2] so I read; fanning them to flames and infusing even the old man with the drum, (d'you remember him) with amorosity. I hope you condoled with the Major, the right one, about his wife's death [*inexplicable*]. I've been to Bromley and walked home across the Park. I'm too sleepy to tell you why I went to Bromley.

1. Frances Prothero (*née* Butcher), the widow of Sir George Prothero (1848-1922), the Cambridge historian and editor of the *Quarterly Review*. The Protheros had been friends of Leslie Stephen, and Virginia's mother was a niece of Julia Cameron, the photographer.
2. Ethel was conducting the Torquay (Devon) Municipal Orchestra in a performance of her own work.

337

But I like the London suburbs in autumn and their immense poetry. And I like Hyde Park fading into night, only the flowers burning in a few pale facades. I love overhearing scraps of talk by the Serpentine in the dusk; and thinking of my own youth, and wondering how far we live in other peoples and then buying half a pound of tea, and so on and so on. (You see how sleepy I am.).

I think Gwen [St Aubyn] is almost an—whats the word? [*8 words omitted*] I think the sutures of the skull haven't joined up; and Vitas hot wind puffs too incessantly We lunched with them: she never sits at ease; Gwen: like a scissors. Have you read the book 'their' book[1]. If so, let me have your opinion. I shant give you mine. I'm pestered with visitors: Colefax persistently pecking like a parrot with corns on her toes. No, no, no, I say: it only makes the pecking frantic. Oh dear, is this worth putting in the train to Woking? And you wont be there. You're carousing with the Major; Lord how I should like to peep round the palms and look. You're having a gin and bitters with the widower at this moment—and I not there, but here, but here.

V.

Berg

2940: To Ethel Smyth   52 *Tavistock Sqre*, [*W.C.*1]

Monday [22 October 1934]

This is the only paper I have with holes in it—and I got it at Heffers [bookshop], Cambridge. But its rather small for an author who flows as you do.

I'm so sleepy I cant even fill this little square, and have only $5\frac{1}{2}$ minutes.

1. Yes, if Maurice [Baring] asks me I'll go if I can but I cant possibly write myself.
2. I asked Joyce,[2] but the one impossible night: I'll try again:
3. Colefax says why cant I 'refresh' her: seeing how hard she works—thats her line:
4. What were 4 and 5 and 6? I forget.

Vita has rather bad reviews in London: The grateful provinces adore the aristocracy. I've no strong feeling either way about Gwen: no, I dont think I have any jealousy; only rather a melancholy that V. should invest [her] with superlatives. But I always say, thats the wont of love:

1. *The dark island.*
2. Joyce Wethered, the women's golf-champion, a neighbour of Ethel at Woking, whom Virginia had met there in 1930 and much liked.

and you cant blame the diseased. I've 20 dozen letters to answer. and it is sheer indolence that makes me scribble here.

I'm glad you are launched on the sea of words—and that reminds me the quotation I liked comes at the end of the intron to the 2nd vol of I.

"For I hold that the permanent quality . . . ." down to,
afraid of growing old.[1]

V.

Berg

2941: TO ROSAMOND LEHMANN   *52 Tavistock Square, W.C.*1

Tuesday [23 October 1934]

My dear Rosamond,

Oh dear me, alas, no, we've got hung up with people here both Saturday and Sunday. What a curse! But will you let us drop in some other day, and give us lunch or tea? We would like to come very much: and Mizzy [marmoset] thanks you, and so does Pinka. Remember to tell me when your play[2] is coming on, so that I may sit in the front row of the stalls

The whole room reeks of Ottoline. Leonard has just got up from his chair, saying "I will not sit in this stinking cat house"—but she was all that a lovely leopard should be—and has left me so dazed I cant write sense.

Yr aff
VW

King's

2942 TO ETHEL SANDS   *52 Tavistock Square, W.C.*1

24th Oct. [1934]

Dearest Ethel,

I am so distressed to hear from Vanessa of your accident.[3] What a terrible bore to be laid flat in an hotel!—and it was time too you made your appearance in London, and cheered us all up.

I'm afraid the books I'm sending aren't a very bright lot, but they may do to throw at Nan's [Hudson] head in a moment of exasperation. Crime at Christmas is by a very rich young man who used to work with Philip Ritchie, until he took to the Stock Exchange, and discovered a gift

1. From *Impressions That Remained,* one of Ethel's autobiographies, two vols., 1919.
2. *No More Music.*
3. Ethel Sands had broken her leg in France.

for detective stories.[1] Perhaps you know him. Then there's Vita—about whom, which I mean, I wont express an opinion, but long to hear yours; and Illyria Lady, by an unknown woman who seems to live at Geneva, and appears very smart and witty in her photograph—in fact I thought she was amusing in her book.[2] As for old Virginia on Sickert,[3] which I add, only from affection, not because I'm vain of it, that was written at command of the old tyrant himself, who says no one appreciates him, and has the bailiffs in the basement. No doubt, now I've done his will, he'll commit me to the flames,—that's what artists are—ungrateful, exacting, morbid, impossible. But I like his pictures. Well this is only by way of a call: dont of course bother to answer: but if Nan would send a line on a card to say how you are, then she would prove her heart of gold—which I've always said it was.

London is rather dismal at the moment, and in the devil's own uproar. Rosamund Lehmann is dining here, and her play has been accepted, and Stephen Spender is also coming, and his Epic[4] is appearing, and Ottoline is giving a tea party, and I have no white gloves, and Sibyl is rampant, and Ethel Smyth has arthritis, and Clive almost had a bullet through Benita's[5] head, as they stood in her bedroom in Madrid, and it would be very nice to see Ethel and Nan quietly.

V.W.

Wendy Baron

2943: To Ethel Smyth   52 *Tavistock Square, W.C.1.*

Postcard
[25 October 1934]

Well you horror—not to know your own works: for some obscure reason you print a preface to the 2nd vol. *cheap edition*. of Imps. put a note—this preface is also included in Streaks of Life[6]—and the quote occurs on page VIII of the 2nd vol of Imps: *Cheap* Edition: and is dated 1923. Not a methodical way of composing books, I declare. I dont suppose it occurs in the old edition: but why the 2nd vol, of red edn God knows.

Berg

1. C. H. B. Kitchin's *Crime at Christmas*. The Hogarth Press published the first five of his detective stories, of which the most successful was *Death of My Aunt*, 1929.
2. *Illyria Lady* by Constance Butler.
3. *Walter Sickert: A Conversation* was published next day, 25 October.
4. *Vienna*, 1934, published by Faber & Faber. It was a protest against the suppression of the Austrian Socialists.
5. Benita Jaeger, later Mrs John Armstrong, Clive Bell's companion in the 1930s.
6. Ethel's previous volume of autobiography, 1921.

2944: To Stephen Spender   52 *Tavistock Square, London W.C.*1
Monday [29 October 1934]

Dear Stephen,

I'm very glad indeed to have your book [*Vienna*], which I found last night on getting back from Rodmell. So I havent read it yet; and I shall read it at least 10 times before I know anything about it. I get slower and slower, reading poetry. But I'll write to you and say what I think—or still better, perhaps you'll come and we will talk about it. Thank you very much.

I liked talking to Yeats, but Lord!—what a grind those [Ottoline] parties are! And after an hour's hard work, the occult appeared—an illuminated coat hanger, a child's hand, and a message about an unborn baby in Greek[1]—at which I gasped, like a dying alligator, and Ottoline supplied a Mr Pudney[2] a poet.

No I dont think I could review poetry: for one thing I'm so slow at reading it: and then one always hurts one's friends' feelings: and finally, d'you really think there's any use in writing about contemporaries? Isnt it inevitable that one should Grigsonise?[3] (I mean get into a groove, and write out the malice of one's miserable heart). And how can one know the truth?

But I'm pleased you think me capable—my own criticism always seems to me hand to mouth, done for centenaries and so on: and I've never sat down and thought, as I should, and mean to one of these days.

Yes, it was a great pleasure—seeing you and Rosamond and William [Plomer]. I dont exactly fathom the silent and inscrutable Prof. Read.[4]

Yrs V.W.

Texas

2945: To V. Sackville-West   [52 *Tavistock Square, W.C.*1]
Tuesday [30 October 1934]

Yes, I'll lunch with you on Thursday 8th at Cafe Royal with pleasure. What time? Where meet? How nice: what fun: and then where go?

1. On 9 November Vita wrote to Harold: "Virginia gave me an imitation of Yeats telling her why he was occult. He had been confirmed in this theory because he saw a coat-hanger emerge from his cupboard and travel across the foot of his bed; next night it emerged again, clothed in one of his jackets; the third night, a hand emerged from one of the cuffs; the fourth night—'Ah! Mrs Woolf, that would be a long story; enough to say I finally recovered my potency.'" (Harold Nicolson's Diary, Vol. I, p. 188).
2. John Pudney (1909-78), the poet, novelist, dramatist, journalist and script-writer.
3. Geoffrey Grigson (b. 1905), poet and critic.
4. Herbert Read (1893-1968), poet and critic of literature and art.

As for "forgotten'—Lor lovaduk—the Vet said, when I showed him Potto's mangy tail "Has this animal suffered in his affections, ma'am?" Whereupon such a wail went up: and the name Nick, Mrs Nick resounded: and all the dogs barked and cats wailed. Forgotten, indeed!

I rather hope to come to your lecture this Thursday;[1] but shall in all likelihood be prevented—such a helter skelter, London. Still if you see a mangy woman, and a tailless, in a corner, as you declaim to the shade of Lord Northcliffe on The Loves of The Elizabethans—wave a kiss.

V.

I've been seeing Yeats; and Yeats said, "Mrs Woolf, I've been writing about The Waves!"[2] Hah. Yes. Hah.

I forgot: here's a little feeble joke to add to your collection.

Sickert: he's an old bankrupt and implored me to say a word about him: but words, words, words, What are words?

Berg

2946: To Ethel Smyth   52 *Tavistock Square, W.C.*1.

Thursday [1 November 1934]

In answer to your question about the publisher,[3] L. says he thinks you should ask £200 in advance of Royalty: 15 p.c. on first 2,000 copies sold: 20 pc. on the others:

I hope that is what you wanted to know; but a voice on the telephone is a leaf in the breeze. I sat up so late last night talking to Aldous Huxley a most witty and cosmopolitan minded man that I'm in a state which cant be called either one or other—And Vita is lecturing at 5.30: but I cannot go. for one thing I cant listen; and then—and then—oh all those people. But she is giving me lunch one of these days—herself complained that we never met, or saw each other alone, which touched me, so I'm going to suffer a lunch out—loathe it though I do.

Aldous fired me to read Italian Latin Greek to travel, to see—its true he's blind of one eye, which accounts I think for his erudition—If I had only one eye I should cease to flaunt and flare (I've been walking up Kings-

1. At University College, London, on the Elizabethan Lyricists. Virginia did not attend it.
2. In the Introduction to his play *Fighting The Waves*, 1934, Yeats wrote that Virginia's novel suggested "a philosophy like that of the *Sankara* school of ancient India . . . a deluge of experience breaking over us and within us."
3. Of Ethel's new book *Beecham and Pharaoh*, published in May 1935 by Chapman & Hall.

way merely to gaze my fill) and should (so I say) learn my letters. And you've done it all—thats what I like about you, looked and lusted, and tasted, and learnt, and lolled in a quarry—surely that quarry in the Aldershot region ought to have its tablet "Here Ethel Smyth, dismounted from her bicycle, and lost her virginity." I'll see to it. A chaste circle of blue china. Think of the tourists coming to peer. Do you give me leave? How are you getting on with the memoirs? I'll read or not read just as you like. Did I tell you I met Yeats, at Ottolines? And he said (this is my vanity) "I'm writing about The Waves; which . . ." Now I took that for a compliment, on the lips of our greatest living poet.

V.

Berg

2947: To Donald Brace   52 *Tavistock Square, W.C.*1

Typewritten
2nd Nov. 1934

Dear Mr Brace,

Many thanks for your letter. I think that Miss West [Hogarth Press] only sent you the proofs of my essay on Walter Sickert as a formality. I myself had no thought that you would wish to publish it as a pamphlet. I am sure it would not have any success in America. As a matter of fact, we only published it here separately because old Mr Sickert, who has fallen on bad times financially, was very anxious, in the first place that something should be written about his work, and then that it should be published as soon as possible. Otherwise I should have waited to include it in a collection of essays. With us too the pamphlet is a very difficult matter. But I dont suppose that I shall have enough essays for a book for some time to come. Please dismiss the idea of publishing it in America.[1]

With regard to the novel [*The Years*], I am in rather a perplexity. I have finished it—that is to say I have written what appears to be about 200,000 words; but my feeling is that it will have to be considerably shortened and re-written. I have put it away, so as to come fresh to it; and shall not begin work for another month. And I am quite in the dark as to the amount of revision that will be needed; or the time I shall take. I dont expect to have it ready before next autumn. But I will give you full warning. And it is always on the cards that I shall tear it up; but naturally I hope not.

I am sorry we shall not see you this autumn; but hope we shall have that pleasure in the spring.

With our kind regards,
yours sincerely,
Harcourt Brace Jovanovich   Virginia Woolf

1. The Sickert essay was not published separately in the United States.

343

2948: To R. A. Scott-James   *The Hogarth Press,*
52 Tavistock Square, London W.C.1

Typewritten
5th Nov. 1934

Dear Mr Scott-James,

Many thanks for asking me to review poetry for the London Mercury.[1] It is very good of you but I am afraid that I must refuse. I have come to feel a greater and greater reluctance to write reviews, and seldom do it now. Also in this case as I know both Stephen Spender and Mr Blunden,[2] I should find it very difficult.

But what you say about the scarcity of real criticism of poetry and the absence of any standard of judgment has interested me very much. It applies equally to fiction I think. It seems to me that it might be interesting to discuss the question of contemporary criticism generally, and to try to discover why reviewing is so bad, and how it could be improved. But it would be very difficult. However, I would like to see if I can make anything of it; and should I succeed I will send you the result in case it would interest you.[3]

Yours sincerely

Texas   Virginia Woolf

2949: To Ethel Smyth   *52 T.[avistock] S.[quare, W.C.1]*

Tuesday [6 November 1934]

I dont quite follow your question; if you mean that Longman want to do your new vol. why not ask them what you were going to ask the other publisher? That is £200 advance: 15 p.c. on first 2000; 20 p.c. afterwards? That seems reasonable—But as I say I dont quite follow: you say "Longman rather suggests that I should bring it out as one vol . . ." Does this mean that Longman has suggested taking the book, which Chapman and Hall (I think) had asked you to name a price for? Anyhow, Leonard agrees, that, the above, seems to cover the case: but why has Longman chipped in? I gathered he had let the matter slide: hence C. and Hall.[4]

I long to hear your impressions of Pss. Mary.[5] I'm told she is mutton-faced, mutton-minded, and sheep-natured: that she slightly repels; and has

1. Stephen Spender had suggested this to Scott-James, who was the Editor.
2. Edmund Blunden had just published his poem *Choice or Chance*.
3. Virginia never followed up this suggestion, but she did write *Reviewing* (Hogarth Press, 1939).
4. See p. 342, note 3.
5. Only daughter of King George V, who had married the Earl of Harewood. She had attended one of Ethel's concerts.

only one remark 'Good luck'.—to those who win races. So what did she say to you? And how did she endure the musical harmonies? It is said (I've been seeing a courtier[1]) that H.M. the Queen [Mary] is so constituted that Beethoven causes her acute indigestion. And what about the leg, and the book? And what about life in general? I've worn the napp off my mind trying to concentrate on your question: so no more; and there is no more paper to write on

V.

You'll be amused to hear that Colefax has forced me to see her here: and begs me to remember how she suffers and be kind—Lord! Lord! But poor woman, she sounds and no doubt is distracted

Berg

2950: To Ethel Smyth   52 *Tavistock Square, W.C.1*

Sunday [11 November 1934]

    Tuesday 5 seems the only day of those named.
    Its true Colefax threatens to come at 6 (wh. means 6.30 or 7) but I expect she'll cut me. So come 5 if you can with MSS. and we'll discuss everything then. By the way, its no use addressing to Rodmell, as they only send letters back when we're not there for good.

V.

In a tearing rush: have to cook dinner and go out. Lots of mushrooms. I picked'em this morning in the marshes.

Berg

2951: To Hope Mirrlees   52 *Tavistock Square, London W.C.1*

[13 November 1934]

Dear Hope,[2]
    Will you come and look in on us any time about 9.30 next Monday, 19th? We have Tom Eliot and a young man called Kitchin who writes

---

1. She may mean Kenneth Clark, with whom she had dined on 31 October. He was appointed Surveyor of the King's Pictures in this year.
2. Hope Mirrlees (1887-1978), whose poem *Paris* was one of the first publications of the Hogarth Press, 1920.

detective stories.[1] And bring Marie, I mean the dachshund, to introduce a human note.

And dont dress. And . . . here I am interrupted by that old Brigadier, Ethel Smyth.

Yours
Virginia W.

Mrs T. S. Eliot

2952: To Ethel Smyth   52 *T.[avistock] S.[quare. W.C.1]*

Typewritten
Sunday, [18 November 1934]

(Excuse typing; my hand is illegible today)

Well, Ive read them;[2] and have'nt very many criticisms to make. Of course, obviously, you have a little difficulty at first in getting off the ground. You swoop about a little too vaguely and variously perhaps; but—no, I dont think that could be helped, as you have the awkward join to make. And I think once under way you spin along admirably. I think theres no doubt youve got the whole thing going, and in full train, and the people alive and kicking and your own voice sounding out in its well known emphatic way. What I think you should do is to avoid chops and changes; to give each subject as long and straight a run as you can—skilfully pretending that life allows one a good long look, say at Mrs Benson[3] before bouncing off to Royalty or whatever it may be. Avoid discursiveness, I should say; but otherwise keep on as you're going. I think youve swept in a hundred little sparks of brightness already. Points of style that strike me are; I dont care for your so persistent use of 'one' for 'I'. Its too wobbly for my taste. See page 7. Then page 50; I dont myself like the Beard joke, which reminds me of family tea; not so good in the public world.[4] Then I'm more seriously doubtful about the wisdom of such long extracts from letters. They tend to be facetious. Yet in parts they are most effective like a haul of live water, with crabs and sand in it, out of the real sea. I think H.B.s letters come off very well, though. I believe these scraps of him will

1. See p. 340, note 1.
2. Ethel's draft-chapters for her new volume of autobiography, *As Time Went On*, 1936.
3. The wife of Edward Benson (1862-1925), Archbishop of Canterbury, whose three sons A. C., E. F. and R. H., all achieved literary distinction. Ethel had known the whole family in her youth.
4. A foolish anecdote about Henry Brewster's beard. Ethel did not take Virginia's advice to delete it.

whet the public appetite for more. But do be careful about letters; for one thing they break up the narrative so abruptly that to use them without good reason is a danger.

Then what about libel? Have you considered for example the Bensons? Page 29a. that joke about 'a bachelor and no saint' might (I dont know the old buffer) make him crusty. But this is only remembering Christabel [Aberconway].[1]

Well, I doubt that Ive much of point to say. I read swimmingly and dashingly after the first. And I think it is a gallant start; and now youre in full cry. So go ahead. Aim I should say at continuity, avoid tempting bye paths—I say this, and then half wish to unsay it. Because the longer I live the less I think one person can amend the ways of another; and the more I believe that the soul of writing only issues when the person is open and at full pressure; and at full pressure she must let fall some small inconveniences and oddities. Thats in fact why I never show my own MSS to any one; and only let L. read them when theyre hard and fast finished.

I'm sending the MSS tomorrow. but will post this now, so as to stop your imperious maw.

V.

[handwritten]:

Elizabeth [Williamson] most fascinating. like an old 18th Century miniature, the other night—and an astronomer as well.

Berg

2953: To Susan Buchan   52 *Tavistock Square, London W.C.*1

19th Nov 34

My dear Susie,

It is very nice of you to send me your MS:[2] and it sounds extremely interesting. I'm afraid it may be a little time before we can read it, because at the moment we have a great many manuscripts, and the only way is to read them in turn.

Yes, of course, if ever I find myself in your region I shall certainly try

1. Ethel cut this 'libel'.
2. Susan Buchan (*née* Grosvenor), the novelist and biographer, married John Buchan (later Lord Tweedsmuir), and had known Virginia since her youth. The manuscript was of her *Funeral March of a Marionette, Charlotte of Albany*, which the Hogarth Press published in 1935.

and see you—not only your view and your garden.[1] I too hear of you from Elizabeth Cameron, and wish we ever met.

Your affate
Virginia Woolf

I also heard a wonderful account of Holyrood [Edinburgh] from Enid Jones!

Lady Tweedsmuir

2954: To V. Sackville-West   *52 T[avistock] S.[quare, W.C.1]*

Tuesday [20 November 1934]

No, no no—on no account. Nothing would induce me myself to do it, or Leonard either.[2] It was merely that the people at the Show wanted it, so I was deputed to ask—which I did reluctantly: and I said, if I know Vita, she'll say damn your eyes—and very properly.

It seems to me an iniquity; the idea of standing to be milked by any red handed oaf—no. So let's forget and forgive. You see, though, how if they put it, and say so and so's doing it, then we feel—but no more. And dont for a moment think of coming and doing anything here; that would be simply a silly waste of time. (except kiss me)

Yr in haste
V.

And the idea of signing copies sent to you is quite absurd, L says.

Berg

2955: To Victoria O'Campo   *52 Tavistock Square, W.C.1*

Tuesday [27 November 1934]

Dear Madame Okampo,[3]

You are too generous. And I must compare you to a butterfly if you send me these gorgeous purple butterflies [orchids]. I opened the box and

---

1. The Buchans lived at Elsfield Manor, a few miles from Oxford, where Elizabeth (Bowen) and Alan Cameron were frequent guests. Elizabeth dedicated *To the North* to her.
2. An authors' signing session in a Book Exhibition, which both Virginia and Vita refused to attend.
3. Victoria O'Campo was the most distinguished intellectual in Argentina and editor of *Sur*, its leading cultural journal. Virginia had met her on the previous day at an exhibition of photographs by Man Ray. She was a woman of great wealth and energy, and a dedicated internationalist. She had just returned from Rome, where she had an interview with Mussolini.

thought "this is what a garden in South America looks like!" I am sitting in their shade at the moment, and must thank you a thousand times. On the contrary, it is I who should have apologised for asking questions. It is a bad habit, sprung of terror and delight. But if you will come and see us here I will not ask questions; I will make one sensible remark after another. Would Tuesday Dec 4th at 4.30 suit you? And would you mind finding us alone, at the top of a grimy solicitors office?

It would be a great pleasure if you would come.

With thanks again, and more apologies,

Yrs sincerely

Victoria O'Campo   Virginia Woolf.

2956: To Victoria O'Campo   52 *Tavistock Square, W.C.*1

Thursday [29 November 1934]

Dear Madame Okampo,

Would you come to tea on Saturday or Sunday at 4.30 instead of Tuesday? Either day would suit us, if you would be so kind as to say which. And then that would not interfere with Paris.

It was very good of you to treat my questions so generously. But I am scribbling: I have to go out, so I will leave it—I mean my thanks and interest —unexpressed and ask you to believe in them.

I will read the book again: many thanks.

Yours sincerely

Victoria O'Campo   Virginia Woolf

2957: To Victoria O'Campo   52 *Tavistock Square, W.C.*1

Wednesday [5 December 1934]

Dear Victoria,

Yes, you wrote a very nice, I wont say flattering, but impetuous letter. I agree about hunger: and agree that we are mostly satiated, or so famished that we have no appetite. How interested I am in your language [Spanish], which has a gaping mouth but no words—a very different thing from English. But I'm so befuddled, talking to different people this afternoon, that I am not saying anything to the point: but what I must explain is that we go away on Friday for the week end: shall be back on Monday. Therefore the only chance is, could you dine with us on *Tuesday*, 11th at 8? Then we have a nice quiet boy dining [William Plomer], who was for years on a farm in South Africa; we could sit and talk: I mean, there would be no impediments as

349

we would brush aside formalities. And you should not dress, but come without a hat. There would be Leonard, myself, the boy and you.

Otherwise, my only free time is tea on Monday: but teas are sometimes interrupted. Therefore if you can dine on Tuesday please do: and would you let me know, and forgive this scrappy scrawl written under the glow of the red roses. Ah, but I've no room to describe them, or brain either.

Yr Virginia Woolf.

Victoria O'Campo

2958: To Hugh Walpole   52 *Tavistock Square, W.C.*1
5th Dec [1934]

My dear Hugh,

Well, that was a pleasure—to hear from you. I felt as if you had sunk beneath the rim of the world. (Isn't there a poem, in which sails sink down— no suns—thats what I'm thinking of) Its true I sometimes read that you're acting David Copperfield at Hollywood[1]—but then that seems to me over the rim of the world. Hurry up and come to tea, and tell me all about it.

I have often thought that you were sent into the world (partly at least) to see things on my behalf. An extra pair of eyes. I'm sure that is one at least of your functions. What I'm seeing for you, at this moment, is the Baroness Okampo, the Sibyl Colefax of Argentina, and a M. Gillet, a [French] journalist. And our marmozet is curled round Leonard's neck. She (the Bss) is a generous woman who sheds orchids as easily as buttercups. And we are about to dine off a pheasant.

London is still all garlanded,[2] but the Duke and Dss are—well, what d'you think theyre' doing? You see I've so many things to say that like a bottle of fine old port turned upside down I can say none of them, and this affectionate whisper wont carry, I cant believe, to Hollywood. I've seen a good many of your friends—Plomer, Ottoline, Sibyl et cet:—and they all hope—well, as I say—come to tea. And dont sink behind the setting sun for so long again: the poem says the sun rises from his wet bed: so must you.[3]

Love from us both

Texas   Yr Virginia

1. Hugh Walpole had gone to Hollywood in June to write the script for a film version of *David Copperfield*. He himself took the part of the Vicar of Blunderstone.
2. For the wedding of the King's son, the Duke of Kent, to Princess Marina of Greece, on 29 November at Westminster Abbey.
3. "So when the sun in bed . . .
   Pillows his chin upon an orient wave"
   Milton, On the morning of Christ's Nativity, line 229.

Friday [7 December 1934]

Dear Victoria,

No this is too much—as the old Queen used to say: I mean your flowers. Please dont do it again: please accept my (what she would have called) heartfelt thanks; but hereafter let me go ungiven. I am a graceless woman, who prefers, after one gift (and you have given me orchids and roses) to go ungiven. Thats what comes of having Scotch clergy in my blood—a detestable race. I am, as usual, writing in a whirlwind. The Charwoman's baby has measles. I have to cook the dinner—at our cottage. So come on Tuesday to dinner at 8: because, even if the young man,[1] who will be excited to meet you, because he lived in your country, alone with his flocks—if he's there and falls in love with you, still we can talk separately. And I like the late evening best, and here I'm never alone for certain at tea. So at 8 on Tuesday: without dress.

Excuse this scrawl.

I'm taking your MS to the country.

Yrs V.W.

Victoria O'Campo

Sunday [9 December 1934]

I return, with apologies the article. I used to know L.H. years ago. a mild spectacled youth.[2] Its a little mild and spectacled, but well meaning—his article. Why is all writing about music and most about painting such geese's cackle? Not that its as bad as fiction reviewing. What else! Oh the name of the book [Ethel's]. We are both in favour of "As time went on—" The other seems to us clumsy. It has the advantage of recalling the other book of course.

Couldnt you compromise—then:—

Title page

As time went on
a sequel to
Impressions that Remained.

having only As time went on, on the back.

1. Michael MacCarthy, son of Desmond and Molly.
2. Possibly Lancelot Hogben (1895-1975), the writer on scientific subjects, whom Virginia had met in January 1918. He occasionally wrote on music, but this particular article has not been traced.

I've been rather up to my nose and over my eyes this last week—foreign visitors sent by friends—why do friends do this dastardly act, for which there is no remedy, short of hurting feelings?—and on top of that, Roger Fry's family have asked me to write a life of him:[1] What am I to say? There are masses of private papers, letters, etc: I've refused to write a whole big life; but promised to read through the papers and see if I can do something lesser and slighter. But oh dear what a time it'll all take—what difficulties there'll be! So be patient with the poor donkey Virginia. Madame Okampo the South American visitor was a great friend of Anna de Noailles[2]

Berg

2961: TO VICTORIA O'CAMPO   [*Monk's House, Rodmell,
                                        Sussex*]

Sunday [9 December 1934]

Dear Victoria,

How very badly I must have expressed myself—if you think, through my hurried and illegible handwriting that I dislike your roses. Dear me! I adore them. Its only the lavishness and splendour of your gifts that sometimes makes the great great grandfather in me put on spectacles and take snuff. Nor did I mean (another blow to my pride as a writer) that it was Tuesdays dinner I had to cook. No. Yesterdays. In the country. We were at our cottage. But someone came,—I had no time to read; only cook.

So Tuesday at 8.

Yrs Virginia Woolf

By the way, after all, I am alone tomorrow, Monday, at 6—should you come in: but I expect as indeed must be the case, you are torn into a thousand flying tatters—going away.

Victoria O'Campo

1. The suggestion came first from Helen Anrep, and was supported by Margery Fry, although she had had the notion of writing the biography herself.
2. Anna de Noailles (who was born Roumanian and married Count Mattieu de Noailles) was a poet, and leader of French cultural society. Ethel first met her in Paris in the early 1900s, but later they quarrelled over Princesse de Polignac, with whom Ethel was in love.

[52 *Tavistock Square, W.C.*1]

Sunday [16 December 1934]

Dearest Ottoline,

I would love to come on Thursday if I can. But we go on Friday, and I have the usual hubble bubble to settle before that.

Shant I see you again? Before you start for India?[1] What a romantic sentence—How I shall rig up pictures of you.

But I hope to see you in the flesh if I can escape—oh such a press of bores—3 just this minute gone—on Thursday.

V.

Texas

2963: To Ethel Smyth   [52 *Tavistock Square, W.C.*1]

Typewritten
Monday 17th Dec [1934]

Excuse typing, but Ive been writing all the morning and my hand is shaky.

To begin with, I'm a little doubtful whether I ought to give any opinion, so glibly, on these fragments;[2] because one gets the whole book out of proportion; and I'm not at all sure that I'm saying anything to the point. But on reading again, I still feel here's a high light; theres a dark spot; but what makes the fabric in between? I think it may be that youre writing for your 'petit clan' and therefore they fill in whats not so clear to us outsiders. I mean, you lay so much emphasis upon Lady P's. 'violence'.[3] You give several instances of it. Then you say 'the very greatest of great ladies'— I cant make the connection. Ive got her fixed in my mind as one of those sublime tyrants who stick at nothing; how can I combine this with great lady-hood? I read on; but find no anecdotes or analysis to confirm this statement. So with her intelligence. She read French literature you say; but again, all the emphasis is laid upon her short way with impostors. I cant fit in a keen critical intelligent reflective mind. Then her astonishing kindness; here, if you consult your MS, you will see that you yourself give it up. One cant touch on this side of her you say or words to that effect. And then quote what I have the impertinence to think a very feeble shop soiled specimen of

1. In January Ottoline and Philip Morrell went on an extended tour of India, mainly to collect information for his projected book about Ottoline's ancestor, William Bentinck, the Governor General who abolished suttee.
2. Of Ethel's forthcoming book, *As Time Went On*. It was dedicated to Virginia.
3. Lady Ponsonby. See p. 334, note 1.

dear Maggies unarticulate admiration of her mothers good heart.[1] (How watery she is compared with your vigour). Thats the gist of what I feel. Its a most vigorous and spirited portrait; but only of an outline. You'll say you cant give more in the space. That may be true. But I do feel that you have rubbed in one side to the exclusion of what must have been another side, or indeed several sides, if Lady P. was, as Ive always heard, the very remarkable woman she was. Here I must qualify though. For I dont share your natural admiration for sheer violence. A little of that pulling up of stakes[2] and scene making goes a long way with me. So many of the well bred and well fed have it. Yet I do admire it; and admire and welcome your picture of this indomitable heathen woman. What about quoting a few letters from her? They often shed a whole cuttle fish bag of suggestion, even when theyre not in themselves remarkable. You see I want shades and half lights. But dont mistake me; I think its very brilliant as far as it goes. And I repeat—my own view is so partial, I dont much trust it.

As for the little joke about Sickert, I'm really ashamed now to explain it. Also its faded. I cant remember my own motives. But as you sat talking that night, about your lunch, Maurice Diana, etc.—I was thinking of my own relations with Roger. And then you said something that made me feel you had no notion what a man he was—how he lived—youd never read a word of him. And to me, he is among the finest of critics; and I kept saying to myself, Why does Ethel prefer the Barings and the Coopers of this world? Why is she so anti-Bohemian? And I then said; because shes herself; and thats whats delightful and unique about her. Still, the little voice of the little clan kept chirping; and at last I maliciously thought, Well I'll test her. Ill give her my Sickert. Ill watch her face. She'll dislike the very thought of that old buffoon—yet he's to me the greatest English painter living. But that wont count for anything with Ethel—compared with her Empresses and her Lady Ps. Besides, Ethel once said sharply, I detest being given presents. So I'll rub it in; and say Heres a Christmas present for you. And then having lit the train I shall watch for the explosion.

But it was all very minute and wire drawn; merely what one thinks when someone else is talking—[*handwritten*]: in fun; by way of playing a tune on the bass.

I like trying to play tunes while people are talking—with a view to the whole symphony

Yr V.

I'm sending back the MS separately tomorrow.

Berg

1. The anecdote was omitted from the published book. 'Maggie' was Lady Ponsonby's daughter.
2. With her own hands she demolished a fence erected by a neighbour who disputed the boundary between their properties.

2964: To Lady Ottoline Morrell

52 *Tavistock Square, W.C.*1

Tuesday [18 December 1934]

Dearest Ottoline,

Angelica, Nessa's daughter, is coming to tea with me on Thursday. You and Yeats are her two twin passions. Could I possibly bring her round, after tea? Or would this in any way, (as it so easily may) be a bore for you? She would be content to sit in a corner and look on. If this is all right, dont answer, and we'll creep in at 5.30, but dont hesitate please if theres too many already. She is at the age of great passions for poetry and people and acts Yeats at school, and once saw you, to her eternal marvel.

yrs VW.

Texas

2965: To V. Sackville-West   52 *T.[avistock] S.[quare, W.C.*1]

[19 December 1934]

Nessa wants me to say that she has her Orlando plates done:[1] would you like to go to her Studio, 8 Fitzroy Street and look at them? If so, would you let her know.

They have to be sent off soon. And perhaps, if you do, you'll come and see me. But I daresay you're in your Pink Tower. I wish I were, The 2 Ethel's on me.[2] One of them has scalded her toes; the other has water on the knee. But no more.

Potto

I am in love with Victoria Okampo

Berg

2966: To Victoria O'Campo

Monk's House, Rodmell,
Lewes, [Sussex]

Dec 22nd 34

Dear Victoria,

I told you how very bad I was at writing letters, and now you will believe me, as it is a fortnight since you wrote. But London has been such a confused chaos: a friend very ill [Francis Birrell], and so on and so on.

1. These may have been plates decorated by Vanessa with characters and scenes from *Orlando*, but if so, they do not survive.
2. Ethel Smyth and Ethel Sands.

Yesterday we came down here, and the first thing I did was to read your [Aldous] Huxley—the other. I'm so glad you write criticisms not fiction. And I'm sure it is good criticism—clear and sharp, cut with a knife, not pitchforked with a rusty old hedge machine. (I see one going across the meadow)

I like Aldous's mind immensely: not his imagination. I mean, when he says "I Aldous . . ." I'm with him: what I dont like is "I Rampion—" or whatever the mans' name may be.[1] But you've said all this and much more to my liking. I hope you will go on to Dante, and then to Victoria Okampo. Very few women yet have written truthful autobiographies. It is my favourite form of reading (I mean when I'm incapable of Shakespeare, and one often is) What are you doing in Paris? I have no notion: I did run up a ramshackle South America for you, when I saw you, but what does one do from 10 to 4 in Paris? Whom does one see? And where does one walk? And—but I cant ask all the questions I want answered. Here we are grey and damp and very English: little boys sing carols on the lawn: carts are stumping about the flooded meadows full of turnips: it is a small grey curving landscape—mine: out of the window. I still have a dream of your America. I hope you will write a whole book of criticism and send me, if you will find the time, now and then a letter.

Yes, our evening, our Turkey evening, was much damaged. London's fault.

V.W

Your letter from Madrid has this moment come. And yesterday I sent your MSS to 15 Av de la Bourdonnais. I hope they will send them on. I will write again.

Victoria O'Campo

2967: To Vanessa Bell

Monks House, [Rodmell, Sussex]

Sunday [23 December 1934]

Here is a tribute to Angelica from Ottoline.[2] If you read it carefully you will see that she wants A. to write to her: which I think she must do. After all, it would fill up the time after Christmas lunch; and Ott: leaves for

1. Mark Rampion is a main character in Huxley's *Point Counter Point*, 1928. It was commonly supposed that Rampion was modelled on D. H. Lawrence.
2. Ottoline had written to Virginia (after the Yeats meeting on 20 December): "Angelica is a fresh, lovely and sympathetic creature. I wish she could stay as she is for ever" (*Berg*).

Judea,[1] like the Cameron, at 2.30 the day after or so. I'm sending a fulsome reply on my own.

Here we are—very fine at the moment, but the shade of Christmas has fallen. Why do Marion and Wells Coates send me a Christmas Card? Why does Katherine Furse? Why does Miss Porter? Well, I hope you're all enjoying yourselves. Love to Cory.[2] I'm just getting in to the new garden room. Where's the bill for the carpet? O where?

Berg

2968: To Lady Ottoline Morrell   *Monks House, [Rodmell, Sussex]*

Sunday 23rd [December 1934]

Dearest Ottoline,

What an angel you are! I couldn't help sending on your letter to Nessa—it will please her so. Isn't Angelica a lovely sylph, at the moment? And full of extreme sensibility; also rather mocking and mischievous; but its the boundless enthusiasm of that age that moves one. You should have heard her talking about Lady Ottoline—so wonderful to look at—and Mr Yeats. "Oh how I shall boast about it at school." "But what did he say Angelica?" "Oh I dont know—it was just wonderful—seeing them all." And of course it almost brought the tears to her Aunt's eyes—(hard old sinner though I am) to see you dragging about chairs for those miserable cripples, and putting this straight and that: and to think how often you've done that for all of us, all these years: and there I was, bringing Angelica to share in your bounty. I'd long meant to write to that black faced man, whom I called Scott James, but his name was Ellis Roberts, about Stella Benson.[3] It was on my mind I'd never sent him a few letters from her; and there I settled it all, and heard about her. So I was very grateful, once more: but there wasn't a moment to talk our owls' talk. Of course old Yeats is a magnificent old poet, and I like watching his smoky then fiery eyes.

Peter [F.L.] Lucas—did you know him?—an academic poet; pure Cambridge; clean as a breadknife and as sharp;—he happened to come to tea, and jumped with jealousy when I said I was going to see you—whom

1. Not Judea, but Greece. Cameron was her doctor from Tunbridge Wells.
2. Vanessa was spending Christmas at Cleeve House, Seend, Wiltshire, the home of Clive's widowed mother. Clive's brother, Colonel Cory Bell, was a fellow-guest.
3. Scott-James was Editor of the *London Mercury*. Ellis Roberts had been literary editor of the *New Statesman* before David Garnett. In 1939 he published his *Portrait of Stella Benson*.

he'd only seen once—and Yeats, whom he'd never seen. So I said I'd ring up and ask if he could come. This thrilled him to his immaculate marrow—he lives in the very heart of Kings—and it will put a little live blood in him. So you see you've stirred up a great deal of gratitude and devotion—and here's a book come by this post, unexpectedly: but I mustn't start another page; dear me, what a born giver you are: and thats the quality I humbly adore.

yrs VW

Texas

2969: To Victoria O'Campo

Monk's House, Rodmell,
Lewes, Sussex

28th Dec 34

Dear Victoria,

I have been too stupid for words: I addressed the MSS to Paris; and then wrote to the Recidencea de Senoritas at Madrid, not to the address I found at the end of your letter. Please forgive my incapacity, and I trust the MSS: have been safely sent on. But it was very careless of me, and its what comes of being practical.

This is not a letter, only an apology, written in a howling gale and a blowing rainstorm, so that I cant go out to my garden house, where I should be able to think what I'm writing. I'm talking while I write. I'm talking to Leonard who is mending an electric lamp, and the marmoset crosses from him to me, always with the same look, as if the world were a question. But this is no news to send to Madrid; unless indeed the marmoset were suddenly to come out with the answer.

The Lawrence has come—a magnificent looking book, though I cant read a word of it, and I shall be proud to see A Room look like that.[1] I I think the Room is the best to begin on: then perhaps, if you want another, Orlando or The Lighthouse. I heard from your Agent this morning; and oddly enough by the same post got a copy of Mrs Dalloway in a Spanish translation. (Catalan I think) so dont do that. I've never read any of them since I wrote them, and they look to me like faces seen in my childhood—those remote books, about which I felt so passionately, as I wrote them. I have been sitting and reading, walking and dreaming, pouring out tea for the Keynes's; and writing a book (again with passion) But this does not mean that I have forgotten you: or your orchids and roses: only what are you doing in Madrid? Does it rain there? I only know it in fine weather.

Salutations. V.W.

Victoria O'Campo

1. Spanish editions published by Victoria O'Campo in Buenos Aires.

Monk's House, Rodmell,
near Lewes, Sussex

29th Dec. 34

Potto said he was drawing you a picture—3 robin red breasts against the moon—but its still unfinished. (Did you know that he has taken up art, to cure his heart? Neglect broke it. I told you didnt I, what the Vet. said) Are you coming this way to see the old termagant? I allude to your mother. If so, wont you dine or sleep or lunch or something? We have a very fine Peach fed Virginia [ham] in cut; another over the fire. I had such a lovely divine lonely walk this afternoon, to a ruined farm up behind Tarring Neville[1] How I long to live there—a mile from any road, down behind. Coming back I saw 3 great black cormorants on the river. And I've got a new garden room, in which I'm going to sleep o'summer nights.

It was very nice and kind of your husband to dine with us. I like him very much. We told Everybody on Xmas day (thats the Keynes's) about Lindbergh.[2] So one lives on one's friends.

A HAPPY NEW Year. (Potto wrote that.)

—V.

I have had to stop Victoria Okampo from sending me orchids. I opened the letter to say this, in the hope of annoying you.

Berg

1. A village three miles from Rodmell, in the Downs on the east bank of the Ouse.
2. Harold Nicolson had been staying with Charles and Anne Lindbergh at Englewood, New Jersey, where he was writing the life of Dwight Morrow, Anne's father.

Letters 2971-3014 (January–April 1935)

Virginia's diary for this period is much fuller than her correspondence, and her letters give us no further information about the progress she was slowly making with The Years. *There were the usual social distractions, including the re-writing and rehearsal of her only play,* Freshwater, *which had but a single amateur performance, on 18 January. Unexpectedly, she found herself involved in political activity, as a supporter of an anti-Fascist exhibition, and André Malraux was one of those she met in connection with this theme. Another friend, Francis Birrell, died. While she maintained with Ethel Smyth the same volume of correspondence, often mutually reproachful, she acknowledged in her diary that her friendship with Vita was beginning to lose its intimacy.*

2971: To Elizabeth Bowen *Monk's House, Rodmell, Lewes, Sussex*

6th Jan [1935] *See Erratum, p. x.*

Dear Elizabeth,

I'm so glad you're back, but I'm afraid I shant be in London till after the 14th. Let me know if you're coming up again.

I'm much tempted by the idea of your fortnight in America. I expect that thats the solution, only is it very expensive? No, the dollar is now shrunk isn't it—I must find out, and make a push next year.[1]

I had a hard night's work at the Fishers [in Oxford], due to their excessive kindness. I dont think I said more than three words to anyone, but then I said them to about 150 undergraduates. I never realised which of them Mr Berlin[2] was, but had to piece him together from descriptions afterwards. Rosamond Phillips [Lehmann] was talking of him. Wont you bring him to dinner one night?

I'm glad you're starting a book;[3] that is when you have answered your letters. By the way, Rose, old Rose, Rose Macaulay rang up and asked, among other things, for news of you, which I invented on the spur of the moment, so dont be surprised if she takes a rosy view of your career.

1. Virginia never visited the United States.
2. (Sir) Isaiah Berlin was then 25. He was a Fellow of All Souls and Lecturer in Philosophy at New College, Oxford, and already had the reputation of one of the most brilliant scholars and talkers of his generation.
3. *The House in Paris.*

I'm listening [on radio] with one ear to a profound, but to me caco-
phonous work by Ethel Smyth—so excuse the scrawl.

Yrs
V.W.

Texas

2972: To H. A. L. Fisher

Monk's House, Rodmell,
Near Lewes, Sussex

6th Jan. 35

My dear Herbert,

It is extremely good of the English association[1] to ask me to speak.
I wish I could. But I have come to the conclusion that lecturing is not my
line, and have given up making the attempt—even in the most flattering
circumstances, like these. So I am afraid that I must refuse. But will you
thank Mr Nowell Smith[2] on my behalf? It is very good of them.

Now I am going to be shameless and make a request of you. If you
have finished your great book,[3] wont you consider writing something of
an autobiographical kind for the Hogarth Press? I know you dont want
to write about politics, but how fascinating it would be if you would write
down something of earlier days—the family—and so on? At least I throw
it out as a suggestion; in case you ever have a spare moment.

Your affectionate
Virginia Woolf

Bodleian Library, Oxford

2973: To Ethel Smyth

Monks House, [Rodmell,
Sussex]

Tuesday 9th [8] Jan. 1935

It is so cold I cant stretch out far enough from the fire to get a blameless
sheet. I think this one has been sat on by the marmozet. I admit I've been
silent—oh but what a compliment to you that is! Every day I polish off
a crop of nettles; never do I get any letter (except from Woking) of pure
affection. All the rest implore, command, badger, worry. Here's Lady
Rhondda, heres a man who wants a puff, a woman who wants a preface;
and that d——d ass Elizabeth Bibesco—So we go round and round the

1. Founded in 1906 to promote the advanced study and teaching of English
literature.
2. Nowell Charles Smith (1871-1961), formerly Headmaster of Sherborne School,
and Chairman of the English Association, 1941-43.
3. His *History of Europe*, 3 vols, 1935. He never offered any book to the Hogarth
Press, but his *Unfinished Autobiography* was published posthumously in 1940.

prickly pear: only Ethel remains unredeemed, a very flagstaff of British oak. Its an age since I unloaded my breast. In the first place did I tell you about the death of that dear bright little—no rather heroic—Francis Birrell?[1] He had cancer of the brain, and I had to go and sit with him 2 or 3 times after he knew he was dying; might linger paralysed, or die mad. And did he show it? No, in spite of being an atheist, there he lay cracking his little jokes, with his face paralysed. But what, my dear Ethel, do you think it all means? What would you have said to a friend—25 years I've known him—dying at 45, full of love of life,—just beginning to live? And we both knew he was dying: and what was there to say about it? Nothing. I feel like a dead blue sea after all these deaths—cant feel any more.

So to the Sitwells. One night before coming here I met Osbert, who said Hows Ethel Smyth? Do ask her when you see her,—did my father propose to her? Because thats the family story. So I ask you. Did he? And was that why he married the woman who went to prison,[2] (hereby breeding O. and Edith and Sashy [Sacheverell]—nor I think to the ultimate glory of the British tongue, fond as I am of parts of them.)

At the same time how happy we are here! Cooking dinner; and walking —oh what miles I've walked, right into remote valleys; with a thorn tree, and a shell. I always think the ice has only melted off the downs a year or two ago—the primeval ice—green ice, smooth ice

Its true, we had a childrens' party and I judged the clothes. All the mothers gazed, and I felt like—who's the man in the bible—?[3] Which by the way, I have bought and am reading. And Renan.[4] And the New Testament; so dont call me heathen in future. I'm pained, rather, to use my grandmother's language, about Vita and Gwen. I had a moments talk with Harold, and he hinted, and I hinted: the upshot of it being he thinks V. has grown very slack. So I said, 'she sits in her red tower and—dreams'. Upon which he cocked his eyebrow and said 'Thats precisely it. She refuses to see anyone but'—Now this has taken me 7 mins. ¾ to write. And all the MSS. remain unread. And the log is blazing. And I shall sleep sound. And write in my new garden hut which looks over the marsh:—did I tell you? So raise your voice and thank me for this now 10 minute letter; and hook the ink to you and reply.

Yr V.

Berg

1. He died on 2 January.
2. Sir George Reresby Sitwell 4th Bt. (1860-1943), married Ida, daughter of the Earl of Londesborough. She fell heavily into debt by gambling, borrowed from a money-lender, and when Sir George refused to pay her debts, was sentenced to three months imprisonment in March 1915.
3. Probably Solomon—I Kings 3, vv. 16-28.
4. Ernest Renan (1823-92), the French historian, Hebrew scholar, philologist and ritic.

Monk's House, Rodmell,
Near Lewes, Sussex

Typewritten
8th Jan 1935

Dear Mrs Easdale,

I am delighted to hear that you have written your autobiography. I hope I had some share in suggesting it. And it is very good news that Constable is going to publish it.[1]

My own feeling is that it is far better not to have any preface by another hand. When some years ago Bernard Shaw was ready to write a preface to a book of my husbands, we refused;[2] because if a book is worth publishing, it is much better that it should stand on its own feet. I am always put off myself by being 'introduced' to a writer. And again, a well known name means that the introduction gets all the attention and not the book. I'm sure your book doesnt want anyone to praise it. It is good news too that they are anxious to do work by your son. I always like the way they get up their books.

We are down here, almost rained out, and with damp everywhere; but all the same the downs are at their best, without trees or leaves, and we hate the thought of London.

Remember us to Joan [her daughter]; I have it on my mind that she asked me about a room in Bloomsbury. I haven't heard of one; but the whole place seems thick with house agents boards. I will write if I hear of anything going.

I hope the book will be out this spring.

University of London

Yours very sincerely
Virginia Woolf

52 Tavistock Square, W.C.1

Typewritten
15th Jan. 1935

Dear Miss Brewster,

Some time ago I received a copy of Modern Fiction.[3] I do not know

1. *Middle Age 1885-1932*, by Gladys Ellen Killen (Mrs Easdale) published by Constable, 1935.
2. *International Government*, 1916. But Shaw did contribute an Introduction to the American and French edition. See Leonard's *Beginning Again*, pp. 122-3.
3. Dorothy Brewster was Professor of English at Columbia University from 1915 to 1950. She wrote *Modern Fiction* in 1934 in collaboration with Angus Burrell. It included some thirty pages about Virginia. Later she wrote *Virginia Woolf's London*, 1959, and *Virginia Woolf*, 1962.

whether I owe it to your courtesy; but may I take this opportunity of thanking you for the very sympathetic article which I find you have written on my own work? Many thanks.

Believe me, yours sincerely
Virginia Woolf

Columbia University

2976: To Hugh Walpole   *52 Tavistock Square, W.C.*1

Sunday [20 January 1935]

My dear Hugh,

I was talking to William Plomer the other night, and about you, and all sorts of things were said you would have blushed for shame to hear: but one thing was distressing: he said you had been very ill. How are you? This is what I am writing to ask. I would really like to know, if you can tell me without bother. I hope anyhow you are now up and about. And if you're not off to Hollywood, may we meet.

I wrote to you, to that fabulous address just before Christmas. Then I hear you flew across America on a stretcher.[1] Then I hear you had Mrs Galsworthy to tea: there are intriguing points in your narrative, but much lies hid between.

I cant write—I'm so cold. This is the party at which I talked to William [Plomer], to which I would have asked you: it was a childrens' party.[2] And I daresay you'd have been the making of it.

We are just back from a cursed cold but lovely week end; hence my chapped hands, frayed wits, but enduring affection.

Yrs V.W.

Texas

2977: To Victoria O'Campo   *52 Tavistock Square, W.C.*1

22nd Jan 35

My dear Victoria,

I have just telegraphed in answer to your telegram. I am horrified to think that my extreme distaste for letter writing has made you for a moment suspect me of coldness,—I assure you I am not addicted to the vice of taking offence. And why should I take offence with you? But please bear in mind I have no secretary; I deal with the dull letters first, and put away the

---

1. Walpole had had an acute attack of arthritis in Palm Springs, California, and was flown to a hospital in New York. From there he sailed home early in December 1934.
2. The *Freshwater* party on 18 January, given to celebrate Angelica Bell's recent birthday. See next Letter.

interesting ones until I have time. And for a fortnight now I have been unable to write a word, because I had to teach actors and then rehearse and then act a play I wrote.[1] Its true it was only for friends—but oh the time it all took! This is the first day I've been free of an evening. So please forgive. And do remember in future that I am capable of infinite silence, but incapable, I hope and believe, of taking offence—if you did, I should at once wire to you and put the case under your nose in so many words. But enough of this. I am so sorry to have seemed for a moment inconsiderate when in fact you were so generous in writing the letter to me. I mean the pages you sent me. I dont usually like appearing as a private person in print, but on this occasion I can find no fault, and like what you say very much and thank you for it. When will the book be out?[2]

I have been living a chattering agitated life since we got back from Sussex. I have done no writing to speak of. I have stood for hours in a studio, repeating my own words [*Freshwater*]. It was to amuse my sisters children. Now I am settling in again. And you are about to voyage to the land of great butterflies and vast fields [Argentina]: which I still make up from your flying words. What a strange broken life we live—what phantoms! But do not let me drift into the bog. Tell me what you are doing: whom you see: what the country looks like, also the town: also your room, your house, down to the food and the cats and dogs and what time you spend on this and that. And please never never think me cold, because I do not write. But I get so tired of writing.

Yr V.W.

I have not got your address in Buenos Aires. Please tell me where I am to write to.

Victoria O'Campo

2978: To Ethel Smyth   52 T[avistock] S[quare, W.C.1]

Wednesday [23 January 1935]

Well, how harr you? Castrated, no entire, wild cat? Gnawing the stump of your pen still? How well I remember the taste of pen holders—But

1. *Freshwater*, a comedy about Mrs Cameron and her circle, which Virginia had first written in 1923. She now wrote a second version, and it was performed on 18 January in Vanessa's studio at 8 Fitzroy Street before an audience of about eighty friends. Julia Cameron's role was taken by Vanessa, her husband's by Leonard, and Ellen Terry's by Angelica Bell. Other parts were allotted to Duncan Grant, Adrian Stephen and Julian Bell. Virginia was the prompter. See *Freshwater*, edited with a preface by Lucio P. Ruotolo, 1976.
2. *Testimonio*. Buenos Aires, 1935.

this is a mere parenthesis. I forget where we left off. And I have 3½ mins: before settling down to read the Bible. Why did you never tell me what a magnificent book it is! And the Testament? and the Psalms! Every half hour I get a wire from Paris asking me if I've quarrelled with a beaming South American [O'Campo] because I dont write. Poor woman—she hasn't much idea of my gift for silence yet. And has rooked me of 2/6 on wires.

I agree with you entirely about death from Cancer: I forget how you said it: something about having a chance to die standing up. That is a very true remark, and sometimes you say a thing that I had it in mind to say. But why ain't I to come when you, if you, die? Why? Aren't I capable of comfort? No—a mere reed, floating along a sugary stream, in your view. And so you dont want to see me. Also; why do you always compound 'intelligence' with destructive criticism? Roger [Fry], who was the most intelligent of my friends was profusely, ridiculously, perpetually creative: couldnt see 2 matches without making them into a boat. That was the secret of his charm and genius. Its some grit thats got into your eye from meeting Peter Lucas here—a prig and a pedant if ever there was one: but a sweet prig: and anyhow he's the only one. And you're always protesting and self-conscious and with your hackles pricked about critics. But enough as Lady Ponsonby used to say. What a convenience it is to make your friends speak for me! Oh I've been in such a howling duststorm—to sit alone and read the Bible is like drawing into a sunny submarine hollow between deep waves.

Adieu

Berg   VW

2979: To Rupert Hart-Davis   52 *Tavistock Square, W.C.*1

Typewritten
24th Jan 1935

Dear Mr Hart-Davis,

Many thanks for sending me the notes on the novel.[1] I cannot remember anything about them; and as it seems to me that they are very disjointed and not of much interest, I do not wish them to be republished in book form. I am sorry to appear disobliging, but I cannot think that they would add to the value of your book.

Yours sincerely
Rupert Hart-Davis   Virginia Woolf

1. In 1935 Rupert Hart-Davis edited for Cape a small book called *Then & Now*, which consisted in past contributions to Cape's house-journal *Now & Then* (1924-35). He had asked Virginia for permission to include one of her articles, but she refused.

2980: To SUSAN BUCHAN

52 *Tavistock Square, W.C.*1

30th Jan 35

Dear Susie,

I'm afraid I have kept your funeral March even longer than I threatened.[1] But there was a great rush of MSS. Now we have both read it, and think it extremely interesting. We should like very much to be able to publish it, but it seems to us that it is rather too slight as it stands. Do you think anything could be done to make more of a book of it? Could you print some of the letters in full? And what about portraits? If you think it would be possible to do something of this sort, and would let us know, Leonard would write you a business letter—which this does not pretend to be! But I found the story fascinating.

Yours ever

Lady Tweedsmuir   Virginia Woolf

2981: To VANESSA BELL

[52 *Tavistock Square, W.C.*1]

Wednesday [6 February 1935]

Yes of course—we are delighted; and it seems a very small sum. Let us know if there's any difficulty, as we could easily send more.

Theyve never sent me a bill by the way for [Duncans] carpet.

I suppose you wouldnt like to dine alone with me tomorrow night— —L. is at the Cranium [dining-club].

B.

We bought 3 pictures yesterday!

Berg

2982: To R. C. TREVELYAN

52 *Tavistock Square, W.C.*1

7th Feb 1935

My dear Bob,

I dont know what your politics are, or whether you have any sympathy with the enclosed.[2] As you see I, as well as Donald Tovey,[3] and other of

1. *Funeral March of a Marionette* by Susan Buchan (Lady Tweedsmuir) was published by the Hogarth Press in October 1935. It was about Charlotte of Albany (1753-89), the illegitimate daughter of Charles Edward Stuart (the Young Pretender) and Clementina Walkinshaw.
2. A Communist-inspired anti-Fascist exhibition. See Quentin Bell II, p. 187.
3. Sir Donald Tovey (1875-1940), the pianist, composer and conductor, who was Reid Professor of Music at Edinburgh University.

your friends, am on the Committee (for the first and I hope last time in my life). So they asked me to ask you; which I do: the money is wanted to hire the Show and pay for the Hall here. But if you dont want to be bothered, I shall understand, and hope you wont bear me a grudge for asking.

Yours ever

Sussex   Virginia Woolf

2983: To Clive Bell   52 *Tavistock Square, W.C.*1

Thursday [7 February 1935]

Dearest Clive,

Here I am pestering you: but you will see the reason and please bear me no grudge.[1] And could you ask Cory [Clive's brother] if you should see him. This is the way my life is spent—torturing my friends in the cause of freedom which is truth, truth which is moonshine—where does the moon shine for ever? In India.[2]

I am imbecile after 2 hours of Ralph Wright.[3] How many wives has he?

Yrs V.W.

Quentin Bell

2984: To Ethel Smyth   *Monks House, Rodmell*
                                                             [Sussex]

9th Feb: [1935]

When a person's thick to the lips in finishing a book, (like you) its no use pretending that they have bodies and souls so far as the rest of the world is concerned. They turn the sickle side of the moon to [the] world: the globe to the other. This profound psychological truth I've so often proved, and now respect in you, so dont write. One of these days our moons shall shine broad in each others' faces—when I come to Woking.

I forget where we left off. Oh you praised Colefax; and now I have to see her. But the trouble is that a woman whose soul has been eaten away by the world, has no surface one can cut into. So I cant settle my wretched little quarrel: it drags on. She muling and puling. If it had been the uncast-rated cat, one spring, one claw,—all's over.

Joyce[4] dined the other night—what a nice woman—the soul of pan,

1. See previous letter.
2. "For the moon ever shines, on youth, on truth, in India." *Freshwater* (Ruotolo, p. 7).
3. The literary critic, and a frequent contributor to the *New Statesman*. He had been lunching with the Woolfs, and they discussed the anti-Fascist Exhibition.
4. Joyce Wethered, the women's golf-champion.

in a woman's body: sheepdog Pan, not God. She has a queer Cockney accent. Why? Next week I have to see the sister [Margery] Fry about the Roger book—oh dear, she's accumulated so many papers; and what am I to do? I cant get rid of my own burden before August: what a labour writing is: re-writing; making one sentence do the work of a page: thats what I call hard work.

This is all very disjected; but you'll only have scraps of the day, and threads of a mind. And I have to write to all my friends, that is the political and the rich, to ask for money to fight Fascism. And its withering cold; even I couldn't walk. And the logs green; and I must put the chicken in the oven—

So I kiss the top of your head and farewell

V.

What a comfort to think that nothing I could say or do would make you think better or worse of me.

Berg

2985: To Ethel Smyth   [52 *Tavistock Square, W.C.*1]

Friday [15 February 1935]

Look here, it suddenly struck me in the night, please dont breathe a word, even to Elizabeth [Williamson], about the Frys or the biography. You wont, I know. Only I saw her (the sister) and the position is delicate and difficult, and things get repeated and distorted, as you know, and she might easily round on me. In fact, she was far more tolerant and sympathetic and well informed than I'd given her credit for.

I sent my cheque to Ly. Ravensdale.[1] And here, to my surprise, is a letter from Vita asking to see me.

All right. I had meant to come on Sunday, of course, chiefly with a view to tapping that bottle of champagne before its empty: but now you shall drink it to the health of the book How do you manage to write as you do? I can only wish I had a vine press (what you press grapes with) so that I could squeeze my innumerable watery pages into one liqueur glass Oh the grind!

V.

I'm sorry old Vernon[2] is dead. I had hoped rather to see her. But she was far sunk in age, I suppose.

Berg

1. Irene Ravensdale, eldest daughter of Lord Curzon, who devoted her life to women's emancipation, social causes, music and travel.
2. Violet Paget, the novelist, who wrote under the name Vernon Lee. She died on 13 February at the age of 78.

Friday [15 February 1935]

Yes, any day, anytime. You have only to suggest which and when. I'm longing for an adventure, dearest Creature. But would like to stipulate for at least 48½ minutes alone with you. Not to say or do anything in particular. Mere affection—to the memory of the porpoise in the pink window.

I've been so buried under with dust and rubbish. But now here's the spring.

Look at this—did I ever encourage Mr Nicolson to leave his publisher and go to mine?[1] I cant remember it, but am very glad to accept the credit.

My mind is filled with dreams of romantic meetings. D'you remember once sitting at Kew in a purple storm?

On the contrary, we thought *you* had been very nice and generous to us. How unlike most of our authors! I'm sorry Mr whatshisname is doing Joan too.[2] But never mind. I think I could tell you all about her Voices by the way. And have you heard the bells at Chillon (is it?)[3]—a rusty clock that still strikes, and she heard?

So let me know, and love me better and better, and put another rung on the ladder and let me climb up. Did I tell you about my new love?

Yr.

V.

Berg

[19? February 1935]

Yes, I'll come if I can, on the 3rd. but I cant be dead sure; and oh Lord how I hate afternoon concerts![4] But as I say, if I can, from love of you, I'll come. Only we may be away Let me know times and meetings, drink the champagne—no I daresay its drunk already. So here's my blessing on the new baby.[5] And when will it be seen in its long white draperies, taking the air in Hyde Park?

V.

Berg

1. The Hogarth Press published only one book by Harold Nicolson, *The Development of English Biography*, 1928.
2. Vita was beginning to write *Saint Joan of Arc*. Before she completed it, Milton Waldman published his *Joan of Arc*, 1935, to Vita's great distress. She had asked Leonard whether he would consent to her temporarily abandoning the Hogarth Press to publish *Saint Joan* with Cobden Sanderson, and he agreed.
3. Chinon, which Virginia herself had visited in April 1931.
4. Sir Thomas Beecham was conducting the Prelude to Ethel's *The Wreckers* at the Queen's Hall.
5. Ethel's new book, *Beecham and Pharaoh*, 1935.

52 *Tavistock Square, W.C.*1

Typewritten

19th Feb 1935

Dearest Clive,

Mr Bluit of the Fascist Exhibition has been to see me about a letter that you have written to the Committee. He seems to think that you are annoyed (in part at least) by a phrase that you quote as coming from me—"Virginia Woolf, who invited me, in a covering letter, to "strike a blow for freedom." The phrase certainly seems to me a silly one, but I dont think I used it.[1] I didnt keep a copy, naturally; but as far as I can remember what I said was "a blow for freedom which is truth, for truth which is moonshine, and where does the moon shine for ever? "which was a quotation from Freshwater and meant to be humorous. Mr Bluit seems to think that you are going to publish your letter. If so, will you leave out the quotation from me, because as you use it, nobody could see that it was meant for a joke. And it wasnt meant for publication anyhow.

Excuse this typing, but my hand is illegible,

Yrs V.W.

Quentin Bell

---

52 *Tavistock Square, W.C.*1

Typewritten
20th Feb 1935

Dear Mr Harcourt,

Many thanks for your letter. We only mentioned my book [*The Years*] in our spring list by way of advertisement. I dont think there is any chance that it will be ready before the autumn—if then. And of course I will give you due warning. I hope that it will be published, like my other books, simultaneously here and with you.

I am so glad that Harold Nicolson is bringing you his new book [*Dwight Morrow*]. I am sure it will be of the greatest interest. He has an enthusiastic public here, and from what he has told me about this book, I expect it will be of particular interest in America.

I am sorry that we shall not see Mr Brace this spring—but Florida sounds a better holiday resort than England at the moment.

With our kind regards
Yours sincerely,
Virginia Woolf

Many thanks for sending me the reviews of Flush.

Harcourt Brace Jovanovich

1. See Letter 2983.

2990: To Ethel Smyth   [52 *Tavistock Square, W.C.1*]

Monday [25 February 1935]

I should say: the only *possible* sentence is "if I did not shrink from even the semblance". The other, with *'incurring'* seems to us both—ahem—damned nonsense. So there—flat[1].

I'm sorry you have castrated the hermaphrodite;[2] but you cant be too sure, the public being what it is. No I cant manage Thursday But I *think* Sunday is free—so I'll go if I can to the concert. Let me know what time. I should pocket my afternoon prejudice. Only its not at the moment altogether free from—I forget. what—but some horror; Sunday Pm I mean.

So let me know the time, and the ticket—

and forgive incoherent haste—so much to do so little done

VW.

Berg

2991: To Victoria O'Campo   52 *Tavistock Square, W.C.1*

Feb 26th [1935]

My dear Victoria,

Your magnificent book has come.[3] How tempting it is—I cant read a word of it, and yet every other word is almost one I know. I must wait for the French edition—or shall I begin to learn Spanish? By this time you are among the butterflies, and I am still in London in the room which you describe except for an occasional weekend here and there in the country. All very tame and about the size of a molehill outwardly. But then London is full of people I know, and their souls are generally pouring out lava—flame: I mean they talk a great deal, and not always gossip. You are now—doing what? An elderly Colonel has been talking to me about the difficulty of starting a village Club. I imagine you hear the wind bending a million acres of pampas grass. I dont know what is happening about A Room of One's own [Spanish edition]. I will ask. How disconnected this all is! But then I cant yet rig up a picture of you. I think of you playing tennis on board ship with a dark gentleman something like the King of Spain. Let me know the truth, one of these days: and send me a very exact picture of your house; and accept my salutation and thanks for the tantalising Book.

Yrs VW.

Victoria O'Campo

1. Ethel's letter which referred to these alternatives is lost.
2. A key incident in *Beecham and Pharaoh* is Ethel's meeting with a hermaphrodite, the cast-off 'wife' of a Sheik, in the Nubian desert.
3. See p. 365, note 2.

Typewritten
27th Feb 1935

Dearest Quentin,

Here is our Christmas present and it would have been sent long long ago, when the snow was on the ground and the holly on the bough, but for your own illiteracy. I can't remember to write to you when I'm in touch with a typewriter; and you cant read me when I'm in touch with a pen. I am longing for news of you. Please write a full and indiscreet account of your amorous adventures—la vie amoureuse de Quentin; or I shall be forced to invent one, with coloured pictures. Nessa says you are hobnobbing with the wise the great and the fair. How I envy you.

There are plenty of mouse coloured virtues here, but nothing shining. However we see a good many odds and ends. Last week we had an amazing interview with Hugh Walpole; who has shrunk to an old pantaloon, because when he was acting Micawber[1] at Hollywood his right hand was struck with arthritis. He was only rescued from the grave and from agony unspeakable by a bottle of quack medicine called Cleano administered by his chauffeur. Such and so great is it to be a romantic novelist with a taste for ones own sex in the lower orders.

I am having tea with Nessa today; Clive will come in; we shall discuss the Anti Fascist Exhibition; and Clive's last letter—a very violent one, which poor Ralph Wright took much to heart. But as you see I cant go into this as you're so distant. It reads like nonsense instead of rather profound political wisdom. L. has today finished a book called Quack Quack.[2]

Ethel Smyth, your lover, has been rooked 1600 pounds by the Income Tax authorities—all for telling the truth. She is more harum scarum, rag tag hobbledehoy than ever; but always collects her fifteen wits to ask after you. That reminds me—what about the History of Monaco?[3] You know what I mean—the great and exciting narrative. Please write it and let me see it. And dont do the donkey work for any one else. Because if one collects facts, they are ones own; and cant be used by a second hand. This I tell you because I myself have a passion for truth.

Have you seen any of the Cambridge gamblers? They will come with the swallow—old palsied Shepp[4] and dear Dadie [Rylands], whom Duncan wdnt ask to our [*Freshwater*] party. I wish you had been there to see Nessa and Angelica and Duncan and the marmoset wetting on Leonards arm.

1. Actually, the Vicar of Blunderstone in the film of *David Copperfield*.
2. An attack on Nazi Germany and Fascist Italy, and the philosophy of Spengler and Bergson. It was published by the Hogarth Press in May 1935.
3. Quentin wrote, but never published, this book.
4. J. T. Sheppard, the Cambridge classical scholar, who was a keen gambler at Monte Carlo.

A great deal of pain was given to many of our friends by that party; so all went well, as you can imagine. Julian is to be seen stealing through the square at night with a woman. I wave my hand and pass on. Either they change or my eyes fail me. He seems to be writing three books at once; and comes round now and then to tear his hair—so that he's bald. Cory [Bell] came to see me yesterday. We had a fascinating talk about Peggy and Michael and the army in India;[1] I dont think he's altogether a happy man. He walks two hours on the downs alone with the dogs every morning. We think of coming to Italy in May. Where shall you be? And how is Janie [Bussy]?— that divine woman, whose French has landed me in an amour with a Brazilian beauty [O'Campo]. Oh and M. Gillet.[2] He came—for hours. We talked of Janie, in the language of Madame du Deffand talking to Saint Simon. But theres no room, or could run on, and must now wash, and face facts! the rain and the mud and the glow in the sky is Quentin. So please write a full life of him.

Yr V.

And my love to Dorothy[3] of course.

Quentin Bell

2993: To R. C. Trevelyan   52 *Tavistock Square,* [*W.C.*1]

Feb 27th 1953

My dear Bob,

Many thanks for writing so fully. Of course, I quite understand and in many ways agree with your views. The difficulty is that one hears such different accounts from different people, and at the time I was asked to join,[4] some months ago, Mr Blackett,[5] and Mr [Ralph] Wright and others seemed very convincing. But I'm not a politician, and have too little first hand grasp of these things to join in any movement really.

From what I hear, I think it doubtful that they [will] get enough money to hold the Exhibition. Many people hold off because they think it absurd not to expose the other tyrannies at the same time. What a horror it all is!

But this is only to thank you for your letter. And I hope you will let

1. Cory's children, Margaret and Michael Bell. Michael became a regular soldier.
2. Editor of *Revue des Deux Mondes.*
3. Dorothy Bussy (*née* Strachey), with whom Quentin was staying at Rocquebrune in the south of France.
4. The anti-Fascist Exhibition committee.
5. P. M. S. Blackett (later Lord Blackett, O.M.), then Professor of Physics at Birkbeck College, London.

us know if you are in London and come and see us—not to discuss politics, but happier subjects. I was hearing of you at Florence from my enormous niece, Ann [Stephen].

Yours ever
Virginia Woolf

Sussex

2994: To Hugh Walpole   *Monks House, Rodmell,*

Near Lewes, Sussex

2nd April [March? 1935]

My dear Hugh,

No, you're quite wrong. I mean, that wasn't what I said to Leonard. What I said was, By God! Here's dear old Hugh! not who the devil *is* Hugh? That's what comes of being a romantic novelist—you will invent things that dont fit with fact. You're altogether at sea in the world of reality. There my footing is firm; and what I said was, "Now there's a man I'd like to see. But how? when?" Because I said, I want to hear all about Hugh at Hollywood. Has he shot a man? Has he raped a woman? But here I checked myself, remembering that I'm not a romantic novelist.

We come back on Sunday, tomorrow. I'll drop you a line in case you're free before the 9th. I dont know, being vague in the head, to what horrors we're committed. We've been having the devil of a time with the Press. But that'll keep. A young man, called Christopher Isherwood, admires you and is grateful to you and wants to meet you. So I'll try and bring you together.

This is only a hasty scrawl—hand much worse than yours—to put you right about what I did say or didn't say.

Yours
VW

Texas

2995: To V. Sackville-West   52 *Tavistock Sqre.,* [*W.C.*1]

Thursday [7 March 1935]

Telegram just come. Tea, say at 5, will do just as well, if it's honestly not a bore having us.

It suddenly came over us, in Holborn, that we would like to see you, once more.[1]

---

1. Harold and Vita were going on holiday to Greece. Virginia and Leonard went to Sissinghurst on 10 March.

But if this is at all awkward, (tea on Sunday,) would you ring up Lewes
385 where we go tomorrow night. late.

And do you love me?[1]

No.

Berg

2996: To Hugh Walpole   52 *Tavistock Square, W.C.*1

From Leonard Woolf, handwritten by Virginia

7.3.35

Dear Hugh,

I am going to ask you something which as a publisher I have never
asked before of anyone, and only on the understanding that you wont
do it if you feel the slightest degree averse. I am told that you think very
well of Isherwood's novel.[2] If you do, would you possibly let us have a
line or two which we could quote over your name? It would be extraordinarily good of you if you would.

I hope you admire my new secretaries* writing: she is very expensive.

Yours

Leonard Woolf

[*in Leonard's handwriting*]

*She does not know grammar

Texas

2997: To Vanessa Bell   [52 *Tavistock Square, W.C.*1]

March 11th [1935]

I entirely forgot that it was so late in the month. I thought it was still
February in fact.

Lord—we drove 40 miles last night back from Sissinghurst in a driving
snowstorm and bitter gale, and I thought we should perish. And you would
then have shed one tear (perhaps) But it [was] a lovely sight.

Berg

1. It was on this occasion, writes Quentin Bell (II, p. 183), that "Virginia realised
   that their passionate friendship was over".
2. *Mr Norris Changes Trains* by Christopher Isherwood, published in March
   1935 by the Hogarth Press.

Tuesday [12 March 1935]

Yes, of course I will read Ly Ponsonby[1] if you will send her me. Now: attend.

1) I want to have a drawing of you.
2) There is a Miss Preece,[2] much admired by Roger and Vanessa.
3) She is poor.
4) She longs to draw you.
5) She is shy.
6) She lives at Cookham.
7) Will you sit?

If she did a passable drawing, I want to try and get it published in Time and Tide. Could you go to Cookham? I think one sitting would be enough. She's afraid of failing in a strange studio. But I said; through Vanessa, that to drag to C^m. seemed extortionate. Let me have a line.

She—Preece—is in a twitter.

Why has Shelley no heart? I dont mind being in his boat.

We went to Siss^t [Sissinghurst] in a snowstorm on Sunday. Saw Gwen and Vita—Yes—yes.

No time for more.

                                                      VW.

Berg

2999: To Vanessa Bell   [52 *Tavistock Square, W.C.*1]

Thursday [14 March 1935]

Here is my due for the unequalled entertainment; give Duncan the extra in part payment of cabs etc.[3]

Would you like me to come in to tea, or after, tomorrow? We shall be away this Sunday—thats why I presume. But let me know

                                                      B.

Berg

1. Ethel's article on Lady Ponsonby (see p. 334, note 1) in *As Time Went On*, 1936.
2. Patricia Preece, despite considerable talent, achieved no great success as an artist. At this period she was intimate with Stanley Spencer, the painter, who also lived at Cookham, Berkshire, and in 1937 she married him as his second wife.
3. The Woolfs had been to a Busch concert on 13 March.

March 14th [1935]

Yes, Ethel dear, I think its improved out of all knowledge.—[1] how, I dont quite know, or whether I'm reading in a more cordial mood and was too stingy before: Anyhow you seem to me to have deepened and shaded it so that its a mass, not an outline, and the qualities melt together instead of being separate, disconnected, and thus unintelligible prominences as I thought them before. And it has, (the supreme excellence in this kind of writing), suggestiveness; so that the sentence runs on, I mean breeds meaning, after it is finished. I should now rest content that you've raised, not a monument, but a ghost; not a ghost but a presence. In fact I congratulate you, and whats more to the point, feel I know her so well I wish I'd known her better. My only cavils are 3 little trifles: (marked in the margin) 119, why 'they'?: 122. should be 'from'; not to; and, 135: neglect: is this the right tense, after the past 'endangered'? It sounds to me wrong; but I'm no grammarian. Dear me, if I could write about Roger like that! Isnt it odd, this is sincere, but your swing and ease sometimes affect me like Joyce [Wethered] playing a ball. I can feel the bat (thinking of cricket) melt into the ball, both become one. And I'm an old trained writer, and cant do it.

No news from Miss Preece. Of course you shan't plod to Cookham, if thats what she insists: we will convey you. I once tried to arrange a series with T and T: of her things, and Roger muddled it; and she is on my conscience rather—a very gifted (they say) extremely odd woman, who is being quite soberly, done to death by a business father, who wont allow her a penny, or a day off. So she's now at her wits ends. But that doesn't excuse her for not writing: I'll let you know when I hear. And by God, remembering the Tomlin horror,[2] I cant conceive a worse than this; but she needs at most 2 sittings.

I dont follow your flight about the heartlessness of Shakespeare. Do you lump him with the frog footed Shelley and Virginia Woolf—the web footed; your grammar leaves me doubtful. However, Shelley is good enough company for me, much though I prefer Sh[re].

I heard [Donald] Toveys quartet last night, and liked it. Right or wrong?

Let me know about the ray of sunshine, or whatever you call it; I mean the possible hope about the Tax. In haste

V.

Berg

---

1. *Lady Ponsonby.*
2. The bust of Virginia by Stephen Tomlin, 1931. She meant that the tedium of sitting to him, not the bust itself, was horrible.

3001: TO ETHEL SMYTH   [52 *Tavistock Square, W.C.*1]

Tuesday [19 March 1935]

No, Wednesday is hopeless. I'm condemned to go to a meeting: did I tell you about my Anti Fascist fiasco? And Elizabeth Bibesco's rudeness? I forget—And Wickham Steed?[1] Anyhow, tomorrow a French novelist Malraux[2] is going to unite us all at Hampstead. And there I must talk my broken French in honour of liberty.

V.

Berg

3002: TO ETHEL SMYTH   52 *T.[avistock] S.[quare, W.C.*1]

Monday [25 March 1935]

Yes, we were at Monks House—oh the sun and the bees = the flowers and the trees!—I've read the letters and destroyed. Of course I dont altogether see eye to eye with you, as I said. I mean, love seems to me to queer all pitches. But given your relations with Vita—and the St John complication[3] —I daresay you're right to shoot this sad and severe dart. Whether it'll do any good to the person herself [Gwen St Aubyn], I doubt; whether any writing or speaking can; but I daresay it will clear the air between you, which is in itself a good, of course. I shall be much interested to hear if she answers, and what. You wont—but this I needn't stress, because I know you wouldnt—say or write anything to bring me in: because I wouldnt like Vita to hear a word about my feelings except through me. And I'm not by any means clear what I do feel—Its all such a silly mess—I rather think the [Violet] Trefusis affair was the same sort of smudge too. dear me— I didnt take to Trefusis either, and loves the devil, as I said

Nessa tells me that Preece cant face Smyth: in that case she's a silly ass, and there's no more to be done about it, for which I thank the Lord, and I daresay you do too.

Written in haste as usual.

V.

Berg

1. Wickham Steed (1871-1956), editor of *The Times* 1919-22, and lecturer on Central European history at King's College, London, 1925-38.
2. André Malraux, the French novelist and essayist. In 1936 he took part in the Spanish civil war on the Republican side.
3. Christopher St John (Ethel's future biographer) had fallen in love with Vita. For Ethel's relations with Vita see Letter 3004.

Wednesday [27 March 1935]

Yes, thats all very interesting. I suppose I couldn't see V's and G's letters?[1] Psychologically, they would interest me; but no doubt it wouldn't be fair. I hope the Treasury is turning like the worm it is.[2] And here I am, scribbling—such d——d dull letters—involved in such boring politics—that my brain turns, worms, and burns. What did you think of Stanford? C.V.?[3] I'm reading his life.

Berg

3004: To V. Sackville-West   52 *T[avistock] S.[quare, W.C.1]*
Friday [29 March 1953]

Lord what a nuisance about old Ethel!

I'm afraid I cant throw much light on it because I dont understand it myself.

She came here about a week ago and talked in much the same way that she has written to you. As far as I could make out, she had come to the conclusion that her relations with you were on a false footing, and she didn't like taking presents from you without explaining. But why she had suddenly come to this conclusion I couldn't make out. I did my best to persuade her not to write, but of course she wouldn't listen. I think she has got into a thorough turmoil over her income tax etc. and anything may start her off. I've had the most violent letters from her simply because of some silly joke of mine, and Elizabeth W. [Williamson] and Maurice Baring both told me she's always doing it to them too. The only comfort is I dont think people believe any of it. Certainly, I've heard no echoes; if any should reach me, I will let fly at her. Or would you like me to write to her? I dont expect to see her until after Easter. But to do her justice, I dont think she would ever abuse one to enemies or acquaintances, only to old friends, whom one hopes can be trusted to discount it. But its always worrying I know. Tell me what you'd like me to do.

We go abroad in May—did you ever drive from Naples to Rome? Can you give us any information? Love from Mitzi [Marmoset].

V.

Berg

1. Vita and Gwen St Aubyn.
2. About Ethel's debt to the Inland Revenue.
3. Charles Villiers Stanford (1852-1924), the Irish composer. His biography (1935) was by Harry Plunket Greene.

3005: To VANESSA BELL   [52 *Tavistock Square, W.C.*1]

Monday [1 April 1935]

Vita writes that she is sending her motor car to Rome, leaving England on April 19th

"Sooner than let it go empty I would offer anybody a seat in it for a very small proportion of the expense.... It is a comfortable car, wh. wd. take 2 or 3 passengers and all necessary luggage." She thinks you might like it. So I scrawl this out, marmozet ridden and bitten as I am.

B.

Let me know at once if its any use, as she's going to Greece. Perhaps some of your cronies

Berg

3006: To PHILIPPA STRACHEY   [52 *Tavistock Square, W.C.*1]

Tuesday [2 April 1935]

Dearest Pippa,

I dont expect the following is any use to you, but I said I would ask in case you thought of going South.

Vita Nicolson's car is leaving England on April 19th. She would offer anybody a seat in it for a very small proportion of the expense. It would take 2 or 3 passengers and luggage—and is a comfortable Humber Saloon. It is going to Rome, driven by her Chauffeur, and would pass through Roquebrune, I suppose, as it goes via the French riviera. She's leaving for Greece on Thursday, so if you should have any thought of it, let me know as soon as you can. But I don't suppose its likely.

Yr Virginia

Sussex [typewritten copy]

3007: To QUENTIN BELL   52 *Tavistock Sq. [W.C.*1]

Typewritten
3rd April [1935]

Dearest Quentin,

I was very glad to get your letter, and as you are such a stingy beast, only writing when written to, I must take up my typewriter. By the way, I have just bought a picture of yours—a collage, as you call it. I think it is very lovely; it reminds me of an old pavement that peacocks walk on among ladies in old silk. From this description you will of course recognise the one I mean; pink and blue; a little battered, as if the mosaic had been rubbed. But the feet were beautiful; and they went to passionate meetings, hundreds of years ago over those tiles. I am hanging it on the W.C. door. Your private view was as usual my abomination;[1] all the dandies and the epicures tasting and twitting; Clive; in blue; Benita [Jaeger] in black; Duncan in pale grey with patched boots; all the fawn coloured and the ecstatic. I hope they did more than ecstasise. Cash is whats wanted at the moment. So I had to go again in my humble serge and I think in short you have a great gift with the scissors and chalks; but you will only jeer at my criticism. I dont think I like writing on a typewriter. It breaks up sentences, and imposes a technique of its own. Is it the same thing with brushes—does the hog scrape and the camel swish? What a business art is to be sure; why in Gods name do we all bow under it like spavined mules?

As for news I have seen a mint of curiosities; your old friend Jeremy Hutch[inson]. last night; rather a taking youth, who's coming to stay. He has built himself a bungalow at Chichester to be away from the pride and glory of Albert Road. Barbara [Rothschild, *née* Hutchinson] was presented at Court last week, wearing all the rubies. So many and so heavy they had to fix a panel to her side of white satin on which to wear them. But she said it was a great fraud. The King and Queen are rooms away; you no longer touch them; and the telephone broke down, and there wasnt a car to be had; and they handed thick ham sandwiches and slices of plum cake to all the Duchesses. She says she is a democrat for life.

I had a meeting with M. Malraux; and trotted out fragments of Janie's [Bussy] French; he is as voluble as a fountain in June; but cant understand or speak English. All the second rate literary gents were there; and he wanted them to form a centre of culture and stem the tide of tyrrany. Whereupon a little horror called Louis Golding[2] spoke about his own spotted soul for twenty minutes; Amabel[3] translated sections of it into sound middle class French; and I gave one gulp—I hate anchovy sandwiches —I had to hide it in my bag—and fled. So this is my last dabble in politics. Lord Ivor [Churchill] tells me the other Fascist Exhibition has been proved a Communist plot; and I'm to have my five pounds back. But I forgot if I told you.

Ann has got a scholarship. Isnt she an odd upstanding unmitigated Stephen? We took her to Bengal Lancers,[4] about a handful of Englishmen ruling eighty million natives; and she was simply bored. She said such things

1. At the Redfern Gallery.
2. The novelist, essayist, traveller and lecturer. His best-known book was *Magnolia Street*, 1932.
3. Amabel Williams-Ellis (*née* Strachey), wife of the architect, Clough Williams-Ellis.
4. The film of the novel by Francis Yeats-Brown, 1930.

dont seem to her even funny. You imagine the old Colonel gashing his arm on a wild boars tusks and saying A mere scratch—for the honour of the Regiment. Now I shed a tear; thats what comes of being one generation nearer to Uncle Fitzy [Sir James Fitzjames Stephen].

Nessa is flourishing about, talking of driving in Vita's car to Rome. That is all my doing. But though the idea seems good, I doubt if it can be worked as Vita is off to Greece, and she means to pick you up by the way and they will have to haggle on the telephone about terms. We think of flying to Rome by way of Holland. I think to wander on a flat field among tulips would be very soothing after these incessant politics. Leonard says we shall shortly be poisoned by the Germans; not only you and Julian, which I dont so much mind, as your young; but even myself! Yes, as I walk down Oxford Street I shall see a yellow fume, and sink down some gutter; and the tide of Teutons will roll on and on—engulphing what was once Bloomsbury but will be, I suppose, a Platz with a statue of The Leader. Bloomsbury is having a very bad press at the moment;[1] so please take up your hammer and chisel and sculpt a great flaming Goddess to put them all to shame. Excuse this random letter; which I write waiting for the bell to ring.

We go to Angelica's last [school] concert tomorrow. Thank the lord its the last. But then Judith [Bagenal] wants us to go to her play. Julian is walking with a woman—which? Does it matter? Now dont repeat this or I shall have my neck wrung, when all I mean is kindness sweetness and truth. I hope to meet you in Rome in May. We will sit in the Forum we will sport in the Boboli—unless as I rather think thats in Florence.

Love to everybody; and please write.

Virginia

Quentin Bell

3008: To Ethel Smyth   52 T[avistock] S.[quare, W.C.]

Thursday [11 April 1935]

No, dont keep Monday or Tuesday for me. I've been rather knocked up all this week with the usual headache, and it would be ruining my peach (thats you) to mumble it, half torpid, as I am. But we only go to Rodmell for Easter; and are back directly the holiday abates, So come, if you will then: when I shall be fresh and brisk and we can go into all the doors and corridors and banqueting halls your letters open. Yes—how we differ! I suspect your incurable optimism has always landed you in believing more than can be established. And why you want affirmation in books is that at heart you dont believe as much as you say—is that possible? and . . . .

1. From Wyndham Lewis, Prince Mirsky and Frank Swinnerton.

thats why you're unfair on Vita: first Bengal Lights, then London fog. I liked E's [Elizabeth Williamson] testimony to the Waves; but I dont believe (this is the truth) I mind much if you care or dont care for it, or any of them. Its not at all that I doubt your good taste. But always at the back of my mind I'm sure you would never like my books if you hadnt met me. Our minds are too entirely and integrally different: which is why we get on; and though I dont want you particularly to like my books: I do like Eth to like them.

What a bore relations—Ponsonby's—are! Why show it? Oh I'm so sleepy! So dumb—so glad to sit quiet—Did I tell you all my politics have gone phut for ever! What a satire on the practical! I earned a headache simply because their heads dont ache.

V.

We dont go abroad till May 1st

Berg

3009: TO ANGUS DAVIDSON   52 *Tavistock Square, W.C.*1

April 11th [1935]

Dear Angus,

Here is the poem. I'm afraid there's not much hope of inducing Tommy [Stephen Tomlin] to produce enough to print, so that it had better be in your safe keeping. Should any more ever be written, then perhaps we could have this again.

Your state must be one of complete happiness. I wont threaten to come and disturb it, though I always feel that I am the original owner of Cornwall, and everyone else is a newcomer—But you will excuse this peculiarity. We are going to Italy, through Holland, through Germany in a car in a short time; so perhaps we shall never meet again; but I hope so.

Leonard sends his love. He is sitting with a marmozet on his neck.

Yrs Virginia

Angus Davidson

3010: TO VIOLET DICKINSON   52 *Tavistock Sqre., [W.C.*1]

[18 April 1935]

Look what came this morning! Tear it up, and even if you're not the Miss Dickinson who was so kind to the lady at St Johns [College, Oxford] when she was a new girl (and I've just written to say on the contrary you're entirely different) dont altogether forget your old attached Sp:[1] (to whom you *were* very kind when she was an insufferable hobbledehoy.)

We're just off motoring to Rome to meet Nessa who's there educating her daughter to go on the Stage (she's a lovely creature) and as we go through Germany, and as Leonards nose is so long and hooked, we rather suspect that we shall be flayed alive; but if not, I hope some day we may meet again.

How are you?

V.

Leonard wishes to be remembered to you.

Berg

3011: To Susan Buchan   52 *Tavistock Square, W.C.*1

25th April [1935]

My dear Susie,

I'm sorry to be so long in writing, but I've been waiting for other people to settle their plans and they wont—everybody seems to have dashed off abroad. They are having an opera festival at Glynde[bourne], which is 3 miles from Rodmell, all June, and as we've asked various people to stay I think it would be safer if I asked if I might come in July instead of June. Would the 2nd, which is Tuesday, or the 4th, Thursday suit you? Please dont bother to ask 'interesting people' as you suggest—it would be so nice to see you and your family quietly. Elizabeth Bowen often talks of them. Let me know some time about dates.

We are driving through Germany to Rome, so perhaps we shall be in trouble with the Nazis. But I hope not.

Your affate
Virginia Woolf

Lady Tweedsmuir

3012: To Ethel Smyth   [52 *Tavistock Square, W.C.*1]

Friday [26 April 1935]

I did, though you wont believe it, want to see you today, and had written to say so; but found L. was so agitated that I obediently tore up my letter. The fact is I rather spoilt our Easter and feel guilty—(I mean not being able to knock about but lying on a chair) and cant face spoiling

1. 'Sp.' stood for 'Sparroy', the affectionate nickname which Virginia used for herself in writing to Violet during their long intimacy before Virginia's marriage.

Holland, Germany, Italy too. But as usual, he exaggerates. Yes. I will give you our address, for even though I always read your letters carefully, never do I so gloat and glimmer as when, waiting behind the bars in Poste Restantes, there they are, under letter W. But 52 T.S. Hogarth Press, is always best: they have the latest chops and changes. Oh so many dreary little miseries to dispatch—German Embassy today to get a letter out of Prince Bismarck,[1] since our Jewishness is said to be a danger—(not seriously) We have one week in Rome. back June 1st. thus missing George and Mary —[2] Piccadilly with its silver hatchets looks rather nice—Now I must put off Colefax and Miss [Lyn] Irvine. But I must see my mother in law, who is rapidly going blind. The dr. says the only chance she has is to remain 'perfectly cheerful'—What are doctors made of?

Hugh Walpole wrote to me today from Greece; so did Vita.[3] But Vita never says a word that couldnt be heard by all Oxford Circus.—at least to me. I will write again. This is only an apology for L's outburst. But you will understand my difficulty—I mean my guilt—I mean how I cant risk his unhappy wrinkles. Cant spell or write.

V.

When does Beecham [and Pharaoh] come out? Can I have a copy before I go?

Berg

3013: To Vanessa Bell   52 *T.[avistock] S.[quare, W.C.*1]
Sunday 28th April 1935

I was very glad to get your letter, and hope you are now safe in Rome. How clever of me to plan that tour! I wonder if you've seen Vita and Gwen and Hugh and Harold—but I daresay with your usual badger skill you've escaped. We set off on Wednesday, and I am beginning to make lists of underclothes and things—but God knows, I hate buying suspenders. I wish Angelica would do it all for me. Also it is perishing cold here, black as a raven, and wet as a sealion. Are you hot? Are the hydrangeas blooming, and the nursemaids sunning themselves in—whatever the gardens are called [Borghese]. London is all a fuzz wtih silver poles and paper crowns and festoons; but as I say, black as the pit, and not a ray of sun. Julian and Alix [Strachey] dined here last night, James having a cold. We couldn't have much gossip, as we got into a political argument which lasted all

1. Prince Otto von Bismarck, who had served on the Russian front in the First War. He had been Counsellor in the London Embassy since 1928.
2. The Silver Jubilee celebrations of King George V and Queen Mary.
3. Vita and Harold, with Hugh Walpole, Gwen St Aubyn and Lady Ravensdale, were passengers on an Hellenic Travellers cruise in S.S. *Letitia*.

night. But Julian said [Lord] Gage had been over, and asked, not Julian, but Playfair[1] to tea: where he met the Keynes's. We had the Wigrams[2] over, as we had shamelessly asked them about Jews in Germany. And now we're for ever committed to know them. She has an idiot child, and he, though a nice honest Englishman is all paralysed. Hence her extreme discontent. And she is not a sympathetic beauty—rather like an old daisy, And then to my horror, Kingsley Martin arrived and wasted the one fine day, talking incessantly about that damned dull paper [*New Statesman*] and his own health—He is suffering from egomania, and the egg is bad—which is a joke. But I am writing rather in a hurry, so you must excuse your poor Singe. I have managed to put off till June, Ethel, Sibyl, Lyn, Hugh, and so there isn't much news. I asked Duncan to dinner, but it is said he is still away, and I'm afraid I shant see him. Your cat is very well. I enclose these cuttings to show what is up in the art world.

I gather that Julian is having a prickly time with Ha [Margery Fry] over Mallarmé:[3] I've not heard a word from her. I am longing not so much to see you, as to sit in the sun and see a bird on a bough. Still, if you will kiss me I will simulate emotion. Will you give us your address, and write to (paper enclosed). Please write often.

Prince Bismarck of the foreign office sent for Leonard and gave him a letter recommending the Germans to treat us with respect. They say we might be glad of it should we find an anti Jewish riot on, but there's not much risk of that. Tell Quentin he is a devil never to have written to me. We arrive in Rome on 16th, afternoon. I'll write cards on the way. So God bless you and kiss my niece and nephew.

B.

[*paper enclosed*]

If you write on 4th

address to	Poste Restante Amsterdam
... on 11th	Poste Restante Verona
... on 12th	P. R. Bologna

Berg

1. Edward Playfair, Julian's greatest friend at Cambridge. He had a distinguished career in the Civil Service, and later became Chairman of the National Gallery Trustees.
2. Ralph Wigram (1890-1936), a brilliant younger member of the Foreign Office, who had just visited Hitler in Berlin with Sir John Simon. He and his wife Ava lived at Southease, the next village to Rodmell.
3. Roger Fry's translations of Stéphan Mallarmé's poems, which were published posthumously in 1936, with a commentary by Charles Mauron.

3014: To Margaret Llewelyn Davies

52 *Tavistock Square, [W.C.*1]

Typewritten
Sunday 28th April [1935]

Dearest Margaret,

We were so glad to get a word from you. We hadnt tried to see you as we heard from your charming nephew Richard who dined with us the other night that you were knocked up.[1] Now we hope you and Lillian [Harris] are settled in and enjoying this abominable spring. You cant think how hideous London is at the moment, all blue and black with wreaths and festoons of yellow paper shivering in the rain. We are just off, on Wednesday, on a grand expedition through Holland, Germany and Italy to Rome; driving our car. Whether we shall ever get to Rome, Heaven knows. We have got a letter from Prince Bismarck in our pockets, as people say we might be unpopular as we are Jews. But I dont think there's much danger, and it will be the greatest fun—at Rome Nessa is having her daughter taught to speak Italian; We shall be a week there, and then drive back through France. Then may we come and see you and have a good gossip in the old style. You remember how we used to talk at Cliffords Inn.[2] I hope you have a garden and a tree to sit under.

Leonard has just finished his book, called Quack Quack which will be out in June. I expect it will get him into hot water with all classes, as it is a very spirited attack upon human nature as it is at present. I think you'll enjoy it. Then he is going to return to the Deluge.[3] But at the moment I cant think of books and writing or politics either, as we are in the midst of getting ready, and it will be such a mercy to be quit of politics and books for a month. We liked your nephew Richard so much. He is lodging with the Stephens round the corner and I hope we may see more of him. I suppose you have a great many neighbours—Trevelyans and so on. I dont think one is ever alone in the country, what with motor cars. But this isnt what I meant to say—for I hope you will let us come some time; but not till you and Lilian are rested.

Love from us both
Yr V

Sussex

---

1. Richard Llewelyn-Davies, son of Margaret's brother Crompton. He was then aged 22, and had been an undergraduate at Trinity College, Cambridge. His later career was in architecture and town-planning, and he was created a Life Peer in 1964.
2. In 1913, where Virginia and Leonard first lived after their marriage.
3. *After the Deluge*, of which Leonard had published the first volume in 1931.

Letters 3015-3025 (May 1935)

On 1 May the Woolfs left England by car for their annual holiday, taking with them Mitz, Leonard's marmoset. They crossed from Harwich to Holland, (which Virginia compared to Shakespeare's England), and drove through a large part of Germany to Austria. In every German town they were confronted by anti-Semitic placards, and near Bonn found themselves marginally involved in a Nazi demonstration. From Innsbruck they crossed the Brenner Pass into Italy, and slowly made their way by Florence and Perugia to Rome, where they spent a week with Vanessa, Quentin and Angelica Bell. The return journey took them along the Italian and French Rivieras and through central France to Chartres and Dieppe. They arrived back at Monk's House on 31 May to find their dog Pinka had just died.

3015: To Vanessa Bell   *Hotel des Pays-Bas, Utrecht, Holland*

May 7th [1935]

Here we are in the middle of Holland. So far it has been perfect—blazing sun, until today no accidents, except killing one hen, but it was the hen's fault. It is extremely difficult driving however, as the streets are very narrow, and there are millions of cyclists—like flocks of swallows, and innumerable racing cars. Even Cousin Thea[1] would cycle if she were a dutchwoman. We have been to Amsterdam, Dordrecht, Zutphen and Haarlem. Its all next door—I mean towns are only across 6 fields. The great point about it is the beauty of the architecture; and the awnings, which are all colours, and the canals, and the tulips, and flowering trees, weeping their reflections into the water—can such a thing be said? I'm so cold, and my face burns like a flayed herring. I can hardly write sense. We are so burnt it is hardly nice to dine with an English clergyman. The only Englishman we have seen by the way. I've also seen some of the best Rembrandts in the world; and Vermeers, but you wont want descriptions. But I dont see how to avoid them, as we are cut off from civilisation completely. I've just got 3 letters—one from Ka [Arnold-Forster], to ask me to visit her in a nursing home, one from Violet Dickinson, to ask me to tea, one from David Cecil who wants to have tea with us—Thank God, none of these things can be done at Utrecht. What a blessing the Channel is, in intercepting ones friends once in a way.

1. Dorothea Stephen, aged 64.

389

By the way, as I was leaving, Saxon [Sydney-Turner] rang up to ask our opinion of Judith [Bagenal], as Barbara [her mother] wanted to know. Happily Leonard answered, and made a gallant effort. But how can you say that the lot of the friends of parents is either easy or honest? This paper makes calligraphy impossible. Its like writing on a biscuit. Tomorrow we start for Germany: but I dont think we shall be interned, owing to Mitzi [the marmoset]. We are received everywhere like film stars, generally there is a crowd of 20 round the car when we stop. All the children come running; old ladies are sent for: they always end by offering to show us the way or do anything for us—such is their love of Apes[1] (please consider this). I'll write from Verona. I expect we shall go to Hasslers, but I'll let you know. Please write to me as often as you can.

Its very expensive here, and I think we have spent more in one week than in 3 elsewhere. and there is not much human beauty, but every virtue—cleanliness, honesty and so on: bad coffee; delicious biscuits: the cows wear brown holland coats; and its amazingly lovely—the streets and the water and the marshes and the barges and the . . . . . . but I will stop this sentence, for the plain fact I cant form my letters only I must say you ought to paint the tulip fields and the hyacinth fields all laid out flat with about 20 miles of water in and out, 18 sheep, 6 windmills, sun setting, moon rising. So goodbye. I agree about Vitas transformation. Harold says its the Change of life—I say its love—

B

Berg

3016: To Ethel Smyth   *Roermond, Holland*

8th May [1935]

I doubt that any remarks of mine about B and P[2] have any value, as I've been half asleep in the evenings—and read it in between great gulps of somnolence—So this is only an impression: that is, I dont care as much for the Beecham as for some of your characters, the reason being, I think, that you hold your hand from those incisions that cut deep, because the fish is alive that youre skinning. Thus I feel you skirmish round and toss balls in the air, and dont settle down and pull up your sleeves—but thats the inevitable drawback with a living subject. And its very lively and spirited—what I miss is the innards. But I've only read it once, and in gulps as I say. The Pharaohs seemed to me to strike more boldly and, directly and I enjoyed the desert and the little snatches of travellers figures seen against

1. She was also referring to the nickname 'Apes', by which she was known to her family in childhood and later.
2. Ethel's book, *Beecham and Pharaoh*, which had just been published.

the hotel lounge greatly. There you seem to swing out free and come down hard. The B. as I say had for me rather the air of skating and flaunting where, with my passion for fact, I wanted "then Sir T: [Thomas Beecham] unlaced his boots and went to bed with her."

I found the same slipperiness overcame me when I wrote about Sickert—But I'll read again and no doubt revise.

Oh we're having such a time—sliding from one town to another—figure to yourself Shakespeare's England still lived in, with Canals and whole banks of red tulips, yellow laburnum, showering down: but very crowded, too many people, too little country, now and again a long low shore with a windmill. Here we are on the verge of Germany—we cross the frontier tomorrow

V.

Berg

3017: To Katherine Arnold-Forster   *Roermond, Holland*
8th May [1935]

My dear Ka,

Your letter has just reached me—this is the last town in Holland, and tomorrow we cross into Germany and drive down to Rome, so I'm afraid there's not much chance of seeing you. We shan't be back till the 1st of June. I hope it doesn't mean that you're having an operation or something: but the address sounds suspicious. Let me know if you're in London in June. What a woman you are for these nursing homes—but I hope its not much. Bruins ought to keep to the hills and the rocks:[1] not Weymouth St. W.1.

About Gwen [Raverat] and The Land—it doesn't rest with us—we only had the right to include it with the other poems. Heinemann publishes it; but the simplest thing would be for Gwen to write straight to Vita—Sissinghurst Castle, Kent. I rather think there was an illustrated edition, but I'm not sure.[2]

I'm writing in a room full of old Dutch officers, listening to the loud speaker, so cant spell or think. But we are enjoying ourselves immensely—oh what a mercy to be out of reach of London: and Holland is full of cows, and canals and houses that were built 500 years ago and are precisely the same with old ladies combing their cats in the window. Did I tell you we

1. 'Bruin' was Virginia's name for Katherine Arnold-Forster. Her home was in western Cornwall, near Zennor.
2. The first (limited) edition of Vita's long pastoral poem *The Land* was illustrated with woodcuts by George Plank. The poem was included in Vita's *Collected Poems*, Hogarth Press, 1933. Gwen Raverat now wished to reissue it with her own illustrations, but the proposal did not mature.

travel with a marmozet of Leonard's! Crowds collect to gaze at it at every
stopping place—we hope even Hitler will soften to us.

How odd to see your hand! Only the day before I had been thinking
of you with intensity and affection (cant spell) and meant to take up my pen.

Please get well. Love from L

Yr VW

Mark Arnold-Forster

3018: To Stephen Spender   *Innsbruck, [Austria]*

12th May [1935]

Dear Stephen,

Your book arrived just as we were making ready to start on our travels.[1]
(We've been cruising about in Holland and Germany and are about to
cross into Italy and come to rest in Rome) so we didn't read it, but we
will when we get back. It was very nice of you to send it, and especially
as I cant remember saying anything about Henry James. There's lots to
say though; and I expect you've said many things I've never thought of.
He loomed up in my young days almost to the obstruction of his works.

I'm writing in a hotel lounge, half asleep after 10 hours motoring.
There is also a great deal to say about Germany. But again sleep forbids.
We almost met Hitler face to face.[2]

I'll try to remember what I thought about Vienna:[3] but d'you think
criticism is any use? If so, why? I mean of the living, by the living?

We shall be back in June. Leonard sends his love. He drives with the
marmozet on his neck. And all the children cried Hail! as we passed.

Yrs V.W

Texas

3019: To Vanessa Bell   *Verona, [Italy]*

13th May [1935]

We have just arrived, and found your letter. Would you be so angelic
as to take 2 single rooms for us at The Albergo d'Inghilterra [Rome] from
the 16th for one week. That seems best on the whole—If one of the rooms

1. *The Destructive Element*, 1935, which discussed the forces threatening our
   civilisation, as analysed by Henry James, Joyce and Eliot.
2. When they were near Bonn, they found themselves driving through crowds
   awaiting the arrival of a Nazi leader, possibly Hitler, more probably Goering,
   and their car was diverted across the Rhine. See Leonard's *Downhill all the Way*,
   pp. 189-91, where he describes how the crowds "shrieked with delight" at the
   sight of Mitz.
3. Spender's poem *Vienna*, 1934.

could have a bath, we are prepared to pay 20 lira a day extra If you cant get them, would you get them somewhere else, and leave a note at the Inghilterra, saying where. We will come round to you some time late in the afternoon. I'll keep my news till then. In fact I'm so sleepy with driving over the Brenner and so drunk with a bottle of wine I cant write.

I hope you've got your passports. Please make out a list of all to be done and seen in a week. Its been grilling hot coming across Germany, till the last day, when it rained, and its raining here at Verona.

It will be a great treat to see you, but dont bother about us, as we shall have plenty to see.

No—I cant speak any more Italian but I can still read.

B.

P.S.

I forgot to say that old Ethel did force her way in before we left in high feather because she has got let off £600 [income tax], owing to the pressure put on the Treasury by her rich friends. This however is not enough—In the night it struck her that she might as well ask to be quit of another £200 on the plea that she is going to produce the Ballet. Which is the ewe lamb of her eye with you.[1] She was therefore stumping off to the Treasury where I gather they're so cowed and coerced they drop £50 every time they see her to be rid of her.

I didnt see Duncan, as he was staying with Bunny [Garnett], but I heard him on the telephone and he sounded composed and serene and all in his right mind. And I didnt see the Jubilee, as we were in Dordrecht, but hope to see some movies—unless the King was killed, or the Queen dropped in a fit at the altar—as may have happened. Now I must stop, but please excuse this random and rapid rate. (the Dilkes[2] couldnt have said that) at which I write. in the cold.

B.

Berg

3020: To Vanessa Bell   *Modena, [Italy]*
Postcard
[14 May 1935]

We will call in before dinner on Thursday and hope you will all dine with us.

V.

Berg

1. Vanessa had designed the stage-settings for Ethel's ballet *Fête Galante*.
2. Ethel (*née* Clifford) and Sir Fisher Wentworth Dilke Bt., friends of Virginia's youth.

3021: To Clive Bell   *Siena, [Italy]*

Postcard
May 15th [1935]

It was on the spot now marked by a cross that Clive Bell quarrelled with his sister in law in Sept. 1908.[1] I dropped memory's tear there today under the orange blossom

V.W.

Quentin Bell

3022: To Clive Bell   *Perugia, [Italy]*

Postcard
16th May [1935]

Do you remember Perugia, Mugliston, and the lady who fell out of the train?[2]

Here we are.

V.W

Quentin Bell

3023: To Ethel Smyth   *Rome*

19th May [1935]

But its impossible to write letters, travelling. I cant collect any force—all is splintered—or theyre playing pianos or bells are ringing and L. is making out roads on a map. This is the only town I love—as you love [King] George and Mary. Patriotism? My word, it seems a lodging house virtue here. Think Ethel, of the [Borghese] Garden, all a blowing, of the sun on the domes—of the Forum, and then you go grubbing in your back garden for geranium roots. However, I admit I like hearing about our Kings and Queens driving down Piccadilly—here one would blow off the end of the pipe like a bubble. Its so irresponsible—sitting in cafes, watching lovely, but Lord how soulless, women, with white cheeks and a dab of rouge: and then a vast old beggar, praying; thats when my niece takes me to the Church. But you will be tired of these unlinked melodies. Last night at the Café Angelica was reading a library book.[3] Couldnt stop.

1. The picture on the reverse side showed the ramparts of Siena. Virginia's 'quarrel' with Clive during their Italian tour in 1908 is discussed by Quentin Bell, I, p. 139, with reference to this postcard.
2. This incident, presumably during the 1908 tour, cannot now be explained.
3. Ethel's first autobiography, *Impressions that Remained*.

And I said, thats a bad habit, reading, at meals. And then she showed me the picture of the 6 Miss Smyths with their donkey, and we read the page together, where you say you're afraid of being with child. "This is so exciting I cant stop" she said—thats the way you corrupt youth—

Of course, I was bitterly disappointed that you took Maurices £900.[1] Isnt that odd? I wanted to think of you romantically insurgent, refusing; its then that one likes to make what is called a vicarious sacrifice: but I see that common sense says no. I only record my disappointment as a psychological phenomenon. Nessa has got B amd P [*Beecham and Pharaoh*]: and will give, in a day or two, a far sounder judgment than mine: I reserve mine for London—Reading is a kind of rhapsody here—I snatch a page to match it with the mood—I cant collect all my little knives and probes. I'm reading Stendhal and a profuse woman called Mitchison.[2] We are going to drive off into the country buying pottery and then home I suppose. But heavens! The relief of being quit of seeing people! Nessa lives a completely detached but entirely satisfactory hand to mouth life, with son and daughter, old woman to wash up, dipping into an occasional Salon, lunching off cold ham—which I must now go and eat. Oh and I had a little Birthday honour offered me![3]

V.

Berg

3024: TO VICTORIA O'CAMPO   *Moulins, France*

May 28th [1935]

Dear Victoria,

I got your letter in Pisa, (we are driving home from Rome where we've been staying with my sister) and hastily write, in this hotel bedroom by a vile light, to say we cant think why you havent heard from the Hogarth Press about A Room [*of One's Own*]. Leonard says they wrote long ago to Madrid. But he'll look into it when we go back next week. I need'nt say that I shall be delighted if you find you can do it. The Press will write again.

We've been in Holland, Germany and Italy, and seen ever so many different civilisations; in fact my brain is so crowded I want to subside into a coma, like a spinning top and cease spinning.

Alas, though, I've used all my holiday this year, and shant get as far as South America. Another time? Yes, I hope so. I'm still imagining vast

1. Maurice Baring's contribution to her income-tax debt.
2. Naomi Mitchison's *We have been Warned*, 1935.
3. The C.H. (Companion of Honour), an order limited then to the King and 50 members. Virginia refused it.

yellow butterflies and your room and the flowers. And I've forgotten the address! But rather than wait to get it in London I will send this illegibile scrawl to the English Minister [in Buenos Aires] and trust to him to forward.

And dont forget me either.

Yrs V.W.

Victoria O'Campo

3025: To Ethel Smyth   [52 *Tavistock Square, W.C.*1]

[2 June 1935]

I'm sorry I've been so incommunicative, but I can only write letters when my mind is full of bubble and foam; when I'm not aware of the niceties of the English language. You dont know the bother it is, using for one purpose what I'm perpetually using for another. Could you sit down and improvise a dance at the piano after tea to please your friends? And now, home here, I shall drink no more wine—now we're landed, and are strewn with bills, letters, manuscripts, dark men from the East who must see Leonard—etc etc. I cant count the number of flies settled on this dead horse.

And talking of death, the first thing that happened as we drew up at Monks House was meeting poor old Pinka's dead body. She had a fit and died the day before we came. and here was Percy [Bartholomew] burying her in her basket and we were both very unhappy—This you'll call senti-mental—perhaps—but then a dog somehow represents—no I cant think of the word—the private side of life—the play side.

Did I tell you in my drunken bout that I was offered a red ribbon, and to be one of the 18 or so ladies and gentlemen calling themselves Com-panions of Honour, and to walk into the room behind you, the Dames? I said No thanks; I dont believe in Honours, though Ethel Smyth, I said, does. Was I right?— Would you like to see me wearing a red ribbon and walking behind you? Oh what d——d nonsense it all is!

I see your point about MB and the £900:[1] but cant you see mine about wishing to have a friend who was a perfect stark rock of incorruptible severity? Cant you see how I shuddered when that dream was dashed? Have you no romance in you. Yes, I think 800 copies very good; so does L: it means 2 or 3000 in the long run.[2] Oh we saw the loveliest places in the world, driving home by the coast—between Rome and Civita Vecchia: pines, sands, sea and low hills, all whispering together in perfect solitude.

So farewell

V

1. See p. 395, note 1.
2. Sales of *Beecham and Pharaoh.*

I wrote this last night, Sunday, but forgot to post—Here's your card. No I cant manage—I wish I could—tea today; and our gramophone wireless I mean, has been smashed in spring cleaning. So what a bore—neither ES. in spirit nor in flesh. But soon I hope.

Berg

Letters 3026-3066 (June–September 1935)

June and July were very sociable London months, and August and September were as usual spent at Rodmell. Virginia was finishing the first draft of The Years *(she decided on this title in September), and while she was pleased with it, she found the penultimate stage hard going. At the same time she was beginning to read Roger Fry's letters, having more or less committed herself to writing his life, and she spoke in Bristol on 12 July at an exhibition of his pictures. Honours were offered to her (the C.H., the Presidency of P.E.N.), but she refused them all. Vanessa was in Rome and at Cassis for most of this period, but returned home to see her son Julian who was about to take up a three-year Professorship at a Chinese University. On 4 October, the day before the Woolfs returned to London, a new political crisis opened with Mussolini's invasion of Abyssinia.*

3026: To V. Sackville-West   52 *Tavistock Sqre*, [*W.C.*1]

Wednesday [5 June 1935]

Yes, we're just back, but going down to Monks for Whitsun. And I got your letter, with pleasure, but didn't think I could hit you off, flying about as you were. And we've been through Germany, Holland Austria, Italy—And we came back to find Pinka dead. Isnt it a miserable thing— Leonard is so unhappy. But the marmoset went to Italy and is well.

By the way, Gwen Raverat wants to illustrate The Land.[1] I told her to write to you.

V.

Back here on Tuesday.

Berg

3027: To Ethel Smyth   52 *T*[*avistock*] *S.*[*quare. W.C.*1]

Thursday [6 June 1935]

Another large blue sheet, as you like them; but God knows why I thus embark, except that I'm waiting for L: who has a man called Pannikar with

1. See p. 391, note 2.

398

him—an Indian, a Knight, a very important man.[1] Our house is a mere meeting place for the winds of heaven: last night they blew the most detestable Polish Count,[2] who said—but no: that man, whining and cringing, made me so physically sick (he's the one who was in prison for writing about Venus and Penis, and L. paid £20 and so on) well, I'm so sick with the vanity of the human race, and their pertinacity, that when Rebecca West asks me to lunch—how can I write novels, with these secretaries needing instant replies?—I say violently No. (I'm waiting to go out with L.)

What I meant to say was

1) Dont bring the roses—no the pinks though the faraway smell on the stairs that far away summer brings tears to my eyes, and d'you remember how you'd packed them in ferns?—because we go after dinner through the summer rain to Rodmell tonight for Whitsun: back next Tuesday late at night after The Magic Flute:

2) The man who was talking to L. when you rang up yesterday was Ralph Brewster;[3] and he stayed on and on, showing his photographs, I was so hungry. Then I said at lunch, very cross, perhaps he's HB's grandson? L. said Not likely. But he was. He has a factotum, on Mount Athos. I gather from your letter its another case of Venus and Penis—the Factotum.

3) A very good review of B. and P. in Man Guardian. I wish Nessa had finished the Book. You must lend me a copy. I want to read at leisure. Her leisure, with books, is so prodigious: it reminds me always of the gestation and copulation of elephants. "No, I cant say I've read more than one sentence . . . but when I read, I read" And thats true. It'll take her six months. So lend me another.

4) How can I cure my violent moods? I wish you'd tell me. Oh such despairs, and wooden hearted long droughts when the heart of an oak in which a toad sits imprisoned has more sap and green than my heart: and then d'you know walking last evening, in a rage, through Regents Park alone, I became so flooded with ecstasy: part no doubt caused by the blue and red mounds of flowers burning a wet radiance through the green grey haze: and I assure you I made up pages of stories I shall never write. And then that d———d Count. But the truth is I am in the cavernous recesses (excuse this language) because Roger is dead (I never minded any death of a friend half so much: its like coming into a room and expecting all the violins and trumpets and hearing a mouse squeak) And Nessa is staying

1. Kavalam Madhava Panikkar (1895-1963), editor of the *Hindustan Times*. Leonard was still secretary of the Labour Party's advisory committee on Imperial Affairs which consistently advocated self-government for India.
2. Count Potocki de Montalk. See p. 20, note 2.
3. Author of *The 6,000 Beards of Athos*, with a preface by Ethel Smyth, published by the Hogarth Press in October.

abroad till October: and Vita, I foretell, is dead and buried for 3 years to come. So forgive moods—incurable moods—here is L: and Pannikar has gone.

Yr V.

Berg

3028: To Elizabeth Bowen

Monk's House, Rodmell,
Lewes, [Sussex]

Friday [7? June 1935]

Dear Elizabeth,

I wish I had known you were going to Dieppe. You might have looked in on us. But wont you come down for a night before you go to Ireland? Its very nice here, sitting in the garden, and we're alone, and have no servants, in the house, so I cant promise much comfort, but there's a bed in a shed and so on. Do come. I'm afraid we shant manage another holiday in Ireland this year.

By the way, your publisher sent me what they call a proof copy of your book[1] the other day, but I put it away to wait till I was free, and now if you're going to send me a real copy, I shall wait for that. But I begin to think I know nothing about fiction—I'm so muddled by reading a mass of manuscripts. But I shall, all the same, read yours.

Yrs
V.W.

I'm so glad you've got the house in Regents Park.[2] I often walk by the lake, and think how nice it must be to live by it.

Texas

3029: To V. Sackville-West

Monks House, [Rodmell,
Sussex]

Sunday [9 June 1935]

Thats very nice of you, about giving L. a dog. But at the moment I think he feels too melancholy. I will let you know later—he must have another. Pinka's death was a mystery. We left her in perfect health with Percy, and she was in the highest spirits for the first fortnight. Suddenly she had three fits; they got the vet. who said he didn't know what it was: but she grew weaker and weaker, wouldn't eat, and died the night before

1. *The House in Paris*, 1935.
2. 2 Clarence Terrace, where she lived for the next seventeen years.

we came. The woman dog breeder here says she never saw a case like it in an old dog (Pinka was only 8) and so we're quite in the dark. The vet. at one moment called it meningitis.

No, I wish we could come, but we go back at midnight on Tuesday, after The Magic Flute at Glynde[bourne], and I dont suppose you want to be knocked up off the Pink Tower at dawn. Dear me, what a lovely day it is!

V.

Berg

3030: TO ETHEL SMYTH   [52 *Tavistock Square, W.C.1*]

Typewritten
[19 June 1935]

Excuse typing—I'm in such a rush. Here they are, and think theyre very good and seem sincere not forced out drop by drop like most reviews.[1] When shall I have time to read B and P. God knows. Or to write, or to read? The white pinks are exquisite cool as ices, and fresh as the songs of robins —or should it be wrens? Ive not read or answered the german lady [*unidentified*]; and must do both before I throw it over to your waste paper. Its only worth that. so I guess. I will write to the most kind and charming Lady B. [Balfour]

V.

Vita lunches on Monday

Berg

3031: TO VANESSA BELL   *Monks House, [Rodmell, Sussex]*

21st June [1935]

Well at last I got a letter from you—which I started to answer—the very same day, but I was interrupted. No, of course I wont show the letters to anybody—they're safely stowed away in the Studio;[2] and I'll consider what you say about Helen's [Anrep] possibly seeing them some time. Mrs Jebb[3] hasn't yet sent any more; but I dont suppose I shall begin to read

1. Reviews of *Beecham and Pharaoh.*
2. Letters to Vanessa from Roger Fry.
3. Cynthia, wife of Gladwyn Jebb, who was then serving in the British Embassy in Rome. She sent the letters through the diplomatic bag.

them till August, as I must try to finish this long weary dreary book, which wont be done till the middle of August I daresay. I know once I start on Roger I shall get so absorbed I shant be able to write fiction. I've just let myself in for rather an awful, and I daresay unnecessary undertaking—to go down to Bristol and open a show of Rogers pictures next month [12 July]. Ha [Margery Fry] rang me up, and as she was very considerate and said I mustn't do it, but of course it would make the Exhibition known etc; I felt I must. It only means speaking for 15 minutes, and we shall go on to Weymouth for a treat. I gather it has been got up entirely by the Frys— have you heard about it? Helen dined with me the other night, but said nothing about it. Then Ha rather alarmed me by saying that she has been collecting a great number of documents, and, as I thought, rather took it for granted that I was going to produce a large book—at least, she seems to be putting it all in my hands, instead of getting the Maurons, Wedds etc[1] to write. However, I may be mistaken—I'm going to see her. You'll probably have heard from Julian that the Mallarmé[2] has broken down for the moment, as the Cambridge Press wont do it without a large subsidy. But Julian's off to Dublin, and I've not seen him again.

London is swarming, as you can imagine. I dont think you deserve gossip, as you maintain this regal seclusion—but my heart is too good to be silent; and thank God, here we are, mercifully alone (though we should be having Pippa, let alone James [Strachey] and Margery [Fry] to stay) There was the Apostles dinner on Tuesday—made memorable by the astonishing apparition of Norton,[3] in the highest spirits, quite recovered, nobody knows how or why. But he seemed to have forgotten 20 years of insanity, went back to James's and stayed cracking jokes till 3. am.

Old Sir Fred,[4] however was the hero of the night, as he has been 70 years an Apostle. He will be 90 in a few days, and George Trevelyan made a most eloquent eulogy on him, after which he was led away. But he seemed practically intact. There was a very short speech about Roger, and the dinner was not very exciting, Leonard said, as very few people came. Maynard had the flu, and instead therefore of dining with us at Lady Rhondda's, we had to take Lydia alone, and she seemed, I thought, greatly in the dumps about life and death and everything, and said she felt very sad. I expect this will please you. I think time drags on her, and she cant learn The Master

1. Charles Mauron (1899-1966), the French writer and translator, and Nathaniel Wedd (1864-1940), Fellow of King's College, Cambridge, both intimate friends of Roger Fry. It had been suggested that they and others should contribute to a book about him, but Margery Fry turned down the idea in favour of a book by Virginia alone.
2. See p. 387, note 3.
3. H. T. J. Norton (1886-1937), the Cambridge mathematician. He suffered from what the doctors then termed 'hypomania'.
4. Sir Frederick Pollock (1845-1937), the distinguished jurist.

Builder for ever.[1] I was amused by the party,—Lady Rhondda in white trousers, Miss [Theodora] Bosanquet in black, and some oddities, among them a Mr Hay, an art teacher, and a Miss Stanhope, an aristocrat, who found life in drawingrooms so intolerable that she took to journalism, and is now a stout capable, bobtailed advertising manager. But I didnt listen much; Leonard says if I had I should have been bored. Then—oh dear me —there's Ralph Brewster who's been living in Mount Athos and says the monks the hens the dogs are all sodomites. he's H.B's grandson and has written a book; but sodomy is rather dull in the lump: we've asked him to cut it down; then there's Viola Tree,[2] who arrived carrying two family bibles wrapped in blue plush which contain all Alans notes on life: a mixture of quotations, invitations, scraps from the Daily Mirror, fragments from Sappho and Homer, letters about buying dogs—complete chaos, but she says, showing beyond a doubt what a beautiful nature and brilliant mind he had "though a bit narrow till I married him" She expects us to edit this rubbish heap. Then old Tom [Eliot] came to dinner, and was so easy and charming, in his rather obscure way, that I (Good Lord—can I take another sheet—when you never read what I write?—and the marmoset is just about to wet on my shoulder—we're buying another dog—probably go to Chichester tomorrow to see one) well: I almost kissed him; and he made me go into a long hyena shriek by describing how John Hayward,[3] the paralysed man, gave a party to [Herbert] Read, your man, Ludo,[4] and the two stout German girls. Thinking to Egager them (I'm having lessons from Janie, but have refused to go to the Paris Conference today)[5] he went to Gamages and bought some sugar which let out small fish on being dropped into coffee; some fireworks, and some chocolates which he thought were filled with sawdust, but were in fact filled with soap. The German girls love chocolates and ate greedily. Suddenly they began to foam at the mouth with soap, and set on Tom and almost tore his collar off. After that the evening

1. Lydia appeared as Hilda Wangel in Ibsen's *The Master Builder* at the Criterion Theatre in March 1936.
2. Viola Tree (1884-1938) was the eldest daughter of Sir Beerbohm Tree, the actor-manager. She was trained as an actress, and the Hogarth Press had published her reminiscences *Castles in the Air* in 1926. She married Alan Parsons, the dramatic critic.
3. John Davy Hayward (1905-65), the bibliographer and anthologist.
4. Margaret Ludwig, Herbert Read's second wife.
5. The anti-Fascist conference of intellectuals organised by André Malraux. Among the British delegates were Forster, Aldous Huxley and John Strachey. See Furbank, *E. M. Forster* II, pp. 192-6. Forster had written to Virginia (6 June 1935, *Sussex*): "I don't suppose the Conference is of any use—things have gone too far. But I have no doubt as to the importance of people like ourselves *inside* the conference. We do represent the last utterances of the civilised."

was such a failure that he forgot about the fireworks till they were going, when he exploded them on the doorstep. He is having a great success with his religious play at Canterbury[1]—success is very good for people. I wish I were successful. But I gather, from dining with Clive, that you re all the rage now, and people say you're the best painter of your time, which seems to me a silly and rather exacerbating remark—if one wants to be a success oneself—Still I think its time to produce a book on you all the same, and wish you would seriously consider it.

This is the first fine day we've had since we came back—literally this is true. Rain and wind, thunder and lightning; all fuss and waterproofs in the streets. And you are so hot you cant peel an onion. No, you misunderstand me about maternity. (Annie Thompsett [Rodmell helper] had a son last night) I adore all mothers and babies, but detest the child being covered with maternal spit (the foam one sees on hedges) after the age of 10. Thats what queers the pitch, and makes Aunts detest their nephews. But up till 10—there I am with you. By the way, Janie can talk of nothing but Quentin: says theyre all in love with him; he's so wise, so learned, so modest, reads books at a stretch and understands them; has tact, charm, sympathy—in fact she says, all Roquebrune[2] says Where's Quentin? We must consult Quentin, whether its a question of love, or politics, or art, or cookery; alas, I had to agree: I admire Quentin greatly myself. Now I cant take another page. Next week we're dining with the [David] Cecils and with Rebecca West: Leonard then dines with Raymond [Mortimer] and I go for my penance to the Buchans: but not a word will I tell you, not a word—unless you write to me. I'm not going to hope to see you before October. I dont say 'wish'— I say 'hope'. Life has taught me these lessons.

B

Berg

3032: To Victoria O'Campo

Monk's House, Rodmell, Lewes, [Sussex]

21st June 1935

My dear Victoria,

What a chapter of accidents! But of course I want you to do A Room of One's Own. I wrote from France the other day to say so, but sent it to the British Minister at Uraguay [Argentina], not having your address. Now the manager of the Press went and did the same thing: so that probably you never got the letters, and before that they wrote to Madrid. By this time I hope you will have heard from them, and that the matter is settled.

1. *Murder in the Cathedral.*
2. The Bussys (Simon, Dorothy and Jane) lived at Roquebrune in the south of France, where Quentin had been staying.

What reason could I possibly have for not wishing you to do it? No: I shall be honoured and delighted. I want to write a sequel to it, denouncing Fascism: but must finish my novel first, and then I've been asked to write something about Roger Fry, the critic. So my time is full. But I want to write an article or two—Heaven knows about what. May I send you one—should I? But only if you promise to refuse it. You tempt us greatly with your South America. We try to plan a journey to America next spring—but that depends on so many things: the office, time, books—and so on. Tell me about the butterflies and your riven asunder soul—these 'nostalgics' —that is what I mean by a "riven asunder". At last it is fine here, but how it has rained and snowed! And London is very full—buzzing with people, and I wish you were driving about in your slim white car. Then we go back again: I only get time to write at weekends.

Yr Virginia.

Victoria O'Campo

3033: To Lady Tweedsmuir   *Monk's House, Rodmell,*
                                  Lewes, [Sussex]
Typewritten
June 21st [1935]

My dear Susie,

That sounds very exciting—I mean about the necromancer;[1] and I much look forward though with fear.

I'm afraid I must be back on the 3rd though. I'll come some time on the afternoon of the 2nd. I'll look out a train and let you know.

You must be having a rush—please put me off if it becomes intolerable. And excuse my incompetent typing—not a patch on yours.

Yr affate
V.W.

Lady Tweedsmuir

3034: To Vanessa Bell   52 *Tavistock Sqre.* [*W.C.*1]
Sunday 23rd June [1935]

I've just got back from Rodmell and found the packet of Rogers letters. But Mrs Jebb sent them through the post and they were so badly done up

1. The 'necromancer' was Charles Wade of Snowshill Manor, Gloucestershire, who filled his beautiful house with a curious assortment of objects including a stuffed crocodile and glass retorts which he used for experiments in alchemy. Virginia, with Lady Tweedsmuir and Elizabeth Bowen, visited him there on 3 July. See Susan Tweedsmuir, *A Winter Bouquet*, 1954, pp. 81-2.

that the parcel was practically open—I'm afraid some packets may have dropped out. Have you a list so that you can check them? These are the ones that have come:—in order of date.

1	packet	1922		1—1931
1	,,	1924		1—1932
1	,,	1925		1—1933
1	,,	1926		1—1934
1	,,	1927		
1	,,	1928		
1	,,	1929		
1	,,	1930		

The only thing that makes me doubtful is the gap between 1922 and 1924.

Let me know as soon as you can, and I'll go to the Post office if there's any missing.

Anyhow she was a perfect idiot not to tie it up properly.

Roasting hot for a wonder.

Do write

B.

Berg

3035: To Geoffrey Tillotson   52 *Tavistock Square, W.C.*1

June 24th 1935

Dear Mr Tillotson,[1]

Many thanks for sending me a copy of your book.[2] I suppose the printing is not strictly professional, but I like it all the better for that, and think it harmonises very well with the poem.

With best wishes for the success of your press.

Yours sincerely
Virginia Woolf

Kathleen Tillotson

1. Geoffrey Tillotson (1905-69) was at this time Reader in English Literature, University College, London. His many books on 18th- and 19th-century literature included *Mid-Victorian Studies*, 1965, written in collaboration with his wife Kathleen.
2. A recently discovered 17th-century poem *The Larke* by Arthur Duke, which Tillotson had printed on a hand-press at University College.

3036: To Theodora Bosanquet   52 *Tavistock Sq.* [*W.C.*1]

June 25th [1935]

Dear Miss Bosanquet,

I've been looking to see if I could find one of the older copies of Jacobs Room [1922], which I like better than the little edition [1929], to send you. But the only one I have is in such a state of moth and dust that I think I had better send the other. I would have gone on to say how very nice it is of you to want to have it, but that I am just in the middle of Miss Martineau.[1] She has started for America, and I'm so anxious to see what becomes of her —you have so aroused my curiosity about that queer old bird—that I cant tear myself away and must at once go back. But this is your own fault, and you'll agree that to have overcome one author's vanity is a great triumph for another author.

Yours very sincerely
Virginia Woolf

Houghton Library, Harvard University

3037: To Stephen Spender   52 *Tavistock Square, W.C.*1

Typewritten
25th June 1935

My dear Stephen,

I've read your book[2]—in fact I've read it twice—and I wish we could discuss it. I think it most interesting especially the first part on Henry James. I think you've got hold of something very hard and genuine, which nobody else, as far as I know, has seen. I suspect you are quite right about his development, and it puts him in a new light.

I think of course that you see him too much from the 1935 angle—that is you have to re-arrange him rather forcibly at times to make him fit in with your scheme. But what a mercy not to have the usual floating film— the film that floats on the top of the mind. Ought you not, perhaps, to argue your case a little more drastically? Now and then I slipped about rather not knowing what your definitions might mean. But that is not very material.

The last part of the book, about the living writers and Lawrence, seems to me more doubtful. I think it reads a little scrappy. But I am not a good judge, as you deal with contemporaries who seem to me much less important than they seem to you. But that again is the effect of the 1935 angle; if youre writing from a point of view in time then things have value for you which

1. *Retrospect of Western Travel*, by Harriet Martineau, 1838.
2. *The Destructive Element.* See p. 392, note 1.

is their value to you *now*—not to me, who am *then*. (I'm writing in a hurry, and anyhow cant write out criticism except in a hurry; its so complex that I should want reams and months and have only this hot afternoon)

It seems to me that artists can only help one if they dont try to. Again, living writers are to me like people singing in the next room—too loud, too near; and for some reason I am so exacerbated by their being flat or sharp; as if I were singing my own song, and they put me out. Hence my unfairness to Lawrence; but how can you put him with the very great? How can you call him a great psychologist? To me hes like an express train running through a tunnel—one shriek, sparks, smoke and gone. As for sitting down to think him out—as for reading him again (and I've read very little)—no. Of course I feel the 'genius'; the power of vision. But how distorted and of the surface. (Excuse this). Then of course I cant feel that William [Plomer] and [Laurens] Van der Post and [Ezra] Pound and Tom [Eliot] are of the calibre you make them out. Never mind. I think it is very penetrating and acute and new and honest. Also very generous, and imaginative. I hope you'll go on and do some more.

This will lead me back to Vienna [Spender's poem], about which I expect I feel something confused; as that youve not got the elements yet rightly mixed; that your desire to teach and help is always bringing you up to the top when you should be down in the depths. That hints at the reason why I feel it jerked broken incomplete. The transitions from poetry to prose are not natural yet. But I'm sure its vigorous and on the lines of something big, which is more than most of them are. Here again my hatred of preaching pops out and barks. I dont think you can get your words to come till youre almost unconscious; and unconsciousness only comes when youve been beaten and broken and gone through every sort of grinding mill. But then for your generation the call to action in words is so much more strident than it was for mine. But I'll have another look; and see if I cant get something more coherent. But is there any good in criticising poetry unless one can criticise the words—and only a poet, practising, can do that. I've not read Auden's play;[1] but I am reading Toms.[2] I dont like Christianity though i.e. Church of England.

Love from us both and write if you will. It is very hot and very crowded in London and we see more people than is good for the soul. No room to tell you about Germany.

Yours V.W.

And why say 'Bloomsbury' when you mean Clive Bell or Roger Fry. Out of sheer malice you'll lead me to talk of 'Maida Vale', meaning school-masters.

Texas

1. *The Dog Beneath the Skin*, written in collaboration with Christopher Isherwood.
2. *Murder in the Cathedral*.

3038: To V. Sackville-West   [52 *Tavistock Square, W.C.*1]

Postcard
[27 June 1935]

How are you? What is happening? I hope its not you who are ill?[1]—
and that its over? and that I shall see you some time:
Heres Mitz.[2]

Lorraine Helms

3039: To Ethel Smyth   52 *Tavistock Sqre.* [*W.C.*1]

July 2nd [1935]

I'm so sorry to have been so incommunicative, but I dont suppose it
matters a straw, at our mature and sublimely tolerant age. I've been let in
for ever so many unnecessary external distracting affairs. Why have I
promised to go and stay with the Buchan's tonight?[3] A wave of old senti-
mentality: I used to know her as a girl: then I go to Bristol to open a show
of Rogers pictures: this was another wave. I dont think rightly speaking,
I should have done—and theyre still to do—either.
1) Have you heard from Vita? Thats more to the point. About Gwens
"terribly serious operation?" Vita put me off, and wrote this explanation.
What will happen if Gwen dies? Have you any news?
2) Did you send a young man in blue to leave pinks at the door last week,
with a mysterious card in a feigned hand, saying "these broken petals from
an ex-Stormy Petrel"—enclosing a piece of sponge and a yard measure
and a bill from a Gloucester coal merchant? I used to call somebody "Stormy
Petrel"—was it you? I dont think so.[4]
We've bought a dog[5] who is at once passionately in love with Leonard.
Its a curious case of hopeless erotic mania—precisely like a human passion.
Then, I've been toiling and toiling; because the Frys cluster round, and I
swear I wont glance at biography till I'm quit of fiction. Dear me—I must
go and see if I've a clean nightgown and pack.
Please answer, if on a card, about the blue young man and the pinks.
I doubt that your [Ralph] Brewster is a very clear judge of character.
He seems to me to jangle, like a bell wire after the bell's rung—something

1. Gwen St Aubyn was told that she must have a major operation.
2. The reverse of the card was a photograph of Leonard's marmoset.
3. At Elsfield Manor, near Burford, Oxfordshire.
4. The 'Stormy petrel' was a maid called Lily whom the Woolfs temporarily
   employed at Asheham in 1914.
5. Sally, a cocker spaniel.

very unstable—And, my nephew says, a well known homosexual, but liked, and thought honest by his contemporaries. As for Mr Peploe[1]—well, our Miss West [Hogarth Press] says there cant be two opinions as to what *he* is!

V.

Berg

3040: To Vanessa Bell   52 *Tavistock Sq.* [*W.C.*1]

July 3rd [1935]

I am slightly puzzled by your letter, as you say that the 1922 packet got separated: but that is among the Jebb lot: it is 1923 that is missing. Then you put at the end "did the letters I gave you include 1 packet for 1923? and perhaps one for 1922?" But it is the 1923 that is missing: all the others are there. So I take it you have got the 1923. I had to tell the Jebbs, as the Post office wanted details—that was before your letter came. Jebb rang me up in a great state, and said that what had happened was that the Customs had opened the parcel to see that there was nothing dutiable—the size would make them suspicious. They are always doing this to the foreign office bag much to their fury. But why the F.O. shouldn't have done up the parcel before sending it on. God knows. Obviously it had been opened on purpose: the string was quite loose, and one end opened—It was a miracle that nothing was lost—I've told the Jebbs that I think you didn't include the missing packet: let me know.

I'm just back from staying with the Buchans or Tweedsmuirs as they are now called. At first I thought it was going to be a complete frost—Susie awaited me in a typical shabby but large country house drawing room, alone, with a dog. She has grown very ample, and carries a faint flavour of Lushingtons. But by degrees we got warmer; and there was a dinner party, —the Camerons,[2] Isaiah Berlin, an Oxford undergraduate, a son, a daughter, and the daughter of Mamie—if you remember Mamie.[3] Happily John[4] was in London being given a dinner, or seeing the King, and it wasn't so bad. They're rather out at elbows, and have holes in the carpet and only one family W.C. I twitted Susie about her grandeur, and had the usual undergraduate Oxford talk, and argued with Isaiah, who is a very clever, much

1. William Peploe, who married Clotilde Brewster, a grand-daughter of Ethel's friend Henry Brewster and a sister of Ralph. Peploe was a partner in the Lefevre Gallery, and although he looked homosexual, he was probably not.
2. Elizabeth Bowen and her husband Alan Cameron.
3. Mary Caroline (d. 1941), daughter of James Stuart Wortley and second wife of the 2nd Earl of Lovelace. She was Susan Buchan's aunt.
4. John Buchan, who had been created Lord Tweedsmuir in May 1935.

too clever, like Maynard in his youth, don: a violent Jew. So the shades fell. and I had forgotten my loofah, and felt endlessly old; talking about the Lyulph Stanleys [of Alderley] and the [Marquess of] Sligos with Susie, and then about films and modern poetry with the boy,[1] who is a simple, and rather shaggy,—And all today we spent driving about the Cotswolds, which were about as beautiful, or is it my eyes are going?—as the Campagna? Really the country was astonishing, and all the villages made of yellow stone, and not a new house anywhere. We went 40 miles to see a necromancer[2]—that is a retired East Indian planter who lives in a mediaeval farm [Snowshill] which he has filled with old clothes, bicycles, mummies, alligators, Italian altars—not, I thought, very interesting, and I think rather a fraud, as he pretended to have no watch, and so I lost my train, and only got back at 8.30. to find Leonard dining with Raymond and no letter from you. But the drive was very lovely. You see I'm trying to tempt you back —England is now and then the most poetic of all countries. Why. I wonder? It almost brought tears to my eyes, sitting beside Susie who went cooing on about our youth; and asked a great deal after you, and wants you to do a jacket for her book—one on some historical character that we're publishing.[3] So will you? I'm so sleepy I can hardly write. I'm getting very queer and crusty without you. Do come back in August; however I see your point about family life. I had such a dose of Woolves at Rodmell the other day— all family gossip: it feels like wet ducks padding about one's head. That reminds me—Judith Bagenal suddenly appeared the other evening, and said Mrs Curtis[4] and another girl were in the basement, come to fetch Angelica's present—So we had to have them up to unpack it. And I thought she would never go: she quacks; I dont think I could stand her for long; she trails so, and enthuses so: and nothing would make her go. She was laden with bits of stuff for their play, to which she invited us. And she raved about A: and said she must be a great actress: but so she goes on about everything. However, in default of A:, Judith had a certain hard crude charm I thought —youth is certainly a great appetiser:

Julian came in 2 nights ago, and was also very charming and full of sense and character. I got the impression he hadn't much enjoyed Dublin: Moya[5] I gather, is a little too Irish, and does the Ottoline of Dublin too much for him. But he had been driving about with Janie, and I wish to God she didn't look so like an old French postmistress with a bristly chin. Otherwise I wish she would marry him. Not that he thinks of it I imagine.

1. William Buchan, then aged 19, at New College, Oxford.
2. See p. 405, note 1.
3. *Funeral March of a Marionette*, about Charlotte of Albany.
4. Elizabeth Curtis, headmistress of Angelica's school, Langford Grove, Essex.
5. Moya Llewelyn Davies, who entertained extensively at her house just outside Dublin.

Clive is dining here to meet Odette Keun,[1] next week; and I've fallen in love with a charming Marchesa Origo,[2] Sybil Scotts daughter—who has an Italian farm near Siena. I think you'd like her. and she's asked us to stay. But then Leo Myers[3] is in love with her, and he looks like a duke of a sort, so well got up, so what chance have I? We dined with the Cecils who are a piping pair of love birds, but no young, and met her and him there. And Mary's [Hutchinson] back from Vienna, where Barbaras been having an operation, and Vita is in a great taking because Gwen has to have a very serious operation—thats all my news.

Yes, do buy me any brooch, necklace, pin, or ring; I lost 2 brooches coming back; up to £5 I will go—any trifles. And please love me—I'm such a darling—and getting very wild without you

B

We have just got a new dog—black and white—and it is passionately in love with L.

Berg

3041: TO LADY TWEEDSMUIR   52 *Tavistock Square, W.C.*1

Thursday [4 July 1935]

My dear Susie,

Here I am on a hot dusty windy day, plodding along Holborn (this refers to an hour ago) to Gamages to buy worms for a marmozet, while I try to describe to Leonard what it was like yesterday looking over the Cotswolds. I can hardly get my bearings, after that miraculous expedition, and you have the satisfaction of knowing that you ruined a page of fiction this morning. But anyhow for me, it was well worth it. I enjoyed myself immensely, and send you my inarticulate thanks.

I hope you will come one of these days before you are an entire Royalty[4] to discuss advertising with the Hogarth Press. Leonard thinks your idea very interesting—I mean about the reminders.

    Thank you again.   Yrs aff
                                       Virginia Woolf

1. Odette Keun took the place of Rebecca West in H. G. Wells's life in the late 1920s, but in 1934 she attacked him in three *Time and Tide* articles.
2. Marchesa Iris Origo, daughter of Lady Sybil Scott by her first marriage to the American, Bayard Cutting. She wrote several excellent books, and lived in Val d'Orcia, south of Siena.
3. Leopold Hamilton Myers (1881-1944). A novelist, a founder of the Society of Psychical Research, and a founder-patron of the London Artists' Association.
4. As wife of the Governor General of Canada.

I am sending a little pamphlet to your son,[1] because he pleased me so much by saying that he liked it. I wish I had seen more of your son and your daughter. I wanted to discuss the young with her.

We're just off to see what Stephen Tennant[2] has done to Monk's House. Bath salts—scents everywhere I expect, if not Stephen himself.

Lady Tweedsmuir

3042: TO ETHEL SMYTH   52 T[avistock] S.[quare, W.C.1]
Sunday [7 July 1935]

Well, thats a relief about Vita and Gwen[3]—I was picturing all kinds of horrors—I hope needlessly.

I cant manage tomorrow (if that is you were able to come) but dont, in this heat—no hurry, I imagine—a post wd. bring the MS.) Tomorrow I must keep all my wits for an appalling infliction—Odette Keun—who *must* see L: *must* dine here. And after Oxford my weekend was spent with my head on a pillow. But after Bristol (which is, God help me) on Friday I hope for some free spacious days like those of Q. Elizabeth was it?[4] Freedom slowly broadening down. As Woking depends on the car, the car on L: L. on freedom from blacks and coffee colour and Odettes—his book [*Quack, Quack*] is bringing in the usual crop—how can I say to Lady B [Balfour] as I should like—yes we'll come at once? I always think of her as the most reasonable persuasive and sweethearted of women—but this is not for her ears, only a sheet for you: like a bed of pinks in this swelter. You see I cant form my letters: but if you can, do.

V.

I am greatly relieved to hear that you sent the pinks—(but why disguise your hand) Years ago a girl in some sort of fix haunted us, and I called her The Stormy Petrel.[5] Now I thought she's turned up again, and will be on me, after this douceur. And I cant remember who it was or why I so christened her. Imagine therefore my relief—call yourself in future uncastrated cat.

Berg

1. Virginia sent William Buchan *A Letter to a Young Poet*.
2. They had lent Monk's House for the weekend to Stephen Tennant, the son of Lord Glenconner. He was a painter, aged 29.
3. Gwen St Aubyn's major operation was now said to be unnecessary, but she had a minor one.
4. "The spacious times of great Elizabeth." Tennyson, *A Dream of Fair Women*.
5. See p. 409, note 4.

3043: To T. S. Eliot   [*Monk's House,*
                                                       Rodmell, Sussex]
Sunday [7 July 1935]

My dear Tom,

It is extraordinarily nice of you to give me your book,[1] and I wish I could thank you as you should be thanked. I am sure, soberly speaking, that it is a very remarkable work, and will put all my critical faculties to the stretch. I have only had time, though, in this world of interruption to read it once, and so, though I am sure, as I say, I will keep any further remarks, should I venture to make them, until you come and stay with us. And that reminds me—where have I been staying? With the great novelist (of the school of Scott) who is now Governor of Canada [Buchan]. Forgive this boast, but in sober truth, I am not nearly so proud of that as I am of my copy of your play, and beg you to believe me with all my faults thick upon my head still your admiring and attached old friend.

                                                       Virginia W.
                                                       (as you call her)

No: we enjoyed having you immensely the other night. This refers to your circular.

Mrs T. S. Eliot

3044: To V. Sackville-West   52 *T.*[*avistock*] *S.*[*quare, W.C.*1]

[10? July 1935]

I'm so glad that the operation [Gwen's] isn't to be as bad as you thought. And it would be very nice and refreshing to see you. But it must be before the 25th: as thats the day we go to Rodmell. So let it be the 24th if you *can.* Would you send a line sometime?

Oh dear, I've got to go to Bristol and make a speech about Roger Frys pictures! Why must one do these things? Excuse the holes in the sheet. We've got a black and white dog—a perfect lady. But I'm so hot; and I would like to see you; and I'm so badgered by Ethel—so no more.

A man[2] came and asked me to be President of the PEN: and I said, Try Mrs Nicolson: at which they jumped. Forgive my malice.

Berg

1. *Murder in the Cathedral.*
2. Ellis Roberts, formerly literary editor of the *Nation.* The previous President of P.E.N. (the international authors' society) was H. G. Wells.

3045: TO LADY OTTOLINE MORRELL   [*Stratford-on-Avon*]

Postcard
Saturday [13 July 1935]

You see this is where I am. I had to come to Bristol to open a show of
Roger's pictures. Back on Monday and will hope to see you next week, and
write. Oh the heat of Somerset today!

Texas

3046: TO LADY OTTOLINE MORRELL
                                        *52 Tavistock Square, W.C.*1
Sunday [14 July 1935]

Dearest Ottoline
    This week seems to be a perfect hurly burly; but still I wonder if you
would come in without of course dressing, on Friday night, anytime about
9.30? Edith Sitwell is dining here, and anyhow it would be very nice to see
you, in the comparative cool—the day's too hot to broach all we want to
talk about. But I'll tell you all I know—not much—about Dotty [Wellesley],
and describe my downfall in the matter of Charles Morgan: but there'll
still be India.
    I can't describe the horror of Bristol on Friday—200 stout burgesses,
crammed and dripping, and having to talk about art after losing my way in
the most hideous of all towns—but its too hot. But we cooled down at
Lechlade, and saw Kelmscot[t][1] today—why dont we all live in a silver grey
manor house, and sit on the Thames banks, and watch the moon rise, as I
did last night—it was incredibly lovely—like a rose petal in the sky.

                                                            yrs VW
Texas

3047: TO VANESSA BELL   *52 Tavistock Sqre. [W.C.*1]

17th July [1935]

    I was just sitting down to write to you last night when Julian came in to

1. The 16th-century house near Oxford, which was William Morris's summer
   home from 1871 till his death in 1896.

415

say that he has got the Chinese professorship.[1] You will have heard from him already. He seemed very excited, though also rather alarmed at the prospect. I wish it weren't for so long—though he says he can come back after a year. Still I suppose its a great chance, and means that he will easily get something in England afterwards. Leonard thinks it an extraordinarily interesting job as it will mean being in the thick of Chinese politics, and Julian also felt this—what it means Chinese politics, I dont know, nor I suppose do you We had a long talk, and he was very charming and said that he felt it was time he made a complete break. In the middle, Mrs Pirrie[2] rang up, but he said she wasn't as much upset as he expected. Of course he's got a mass of things to do and was going to see the Board again, in order to find out more details. Well, its all very upsetting: I shall see him on Friday, and try to find out more. He was still vague about the house and the pay. We urged him to find out all about the climate and conditions—he's going to see Tawney[3] who has been there; and also Margery [Fry]

This is the most exciting news naturally. Otherwise I was going to tell you about the horrors of going to Bristol to open Roger's show. Really the Frys—in the first place, it was broiling hot; then we lost our way and only got there just in time. Then there was a large audience, all of the most stodgy and respectable; then they kept an electric fan going so that I could hardly make myself heard—then I felt in my bones that neither Margery nor Pamela [Diamand] much liked what I said. In short it was all rather an absurd waste of time and energy, I felt—though I thought Roger's pictures, as far as I could see them in the crowd, a good deal better than I expected. Margery never wrote and thanked me—and in fact I feel that the Frys view of Roger is completely different from ours, and I'm in rather a puzzle to know what to do about seeing Margery before I go. I'm sure she'll disapprove of anything I write. Yet I feel she means to hold me to it. Julian agrees—thinks her almost crazed on the subject, and advises me to keep clear of her: but how am I to? Anyhow, I feel sure she didn't like my innocent and highly eulogistic speech for some reason.

I've now been through both parcels of your letters, and I find that you had put a 1923 packet among the letters you gave me. Also there are 2 1922 packets. As the 1923 was the missing one, I suppose now nothing was lost —no thanks to the Foreign Office though: (I've just heard from the Post Office that they have searched in vain)

1. Julian Bell had applied more than a year before to the Cambridge Appointments Board for a teaching job in a foreign University, preferably in the Far East. He was now offered, and accepted, the Professorship of English in Wuhan University, 400 miles up the Yangtze River from Nanking, China. His letter to Vanessa is published in *Journey to the Frontier* (Stansky and Abrahams, 1966), pp. 250-1.
2. Antoinette Pirie (*née* Patey), wife of N. W. Pirie, the Cambridge biochemist.
3. R. H. Tawney (1880-1962), the distinguished economic historian.

I hear Quentin is back [from Rome]—he was dining with Kapp[1] last night, Julian said. Both he and Julian, I hope, are coming on Friday to help us with Edith Sitwell and Ottoline; such is my penance; but I hope the last before we go to Rodmell next Thursday. Lord what a mercy to be there, out of this racket and uproar! Clive is giving a farewell dinner on Sunday; we gave him an appalling one to meet Wells's old mistress, Odette Keun, one of the most raddle faced bitter tongued women I've ever met. And I must say Clive was good natured in the extreme. Gerald Brenan and his wife came in—a dried up pair, I thought, and Gerald apologising for his book [*Jack Robinson* 1933], for which apologies are useless. That same night Frances Marshall [Partridge], dining with the Bussys, was taken with child and removed on a stretcher: a boy [Lytton Burgo], all well, as I daresay you've heard.

This is a very dull letter, but its been so hot, and I've talked such a lot the past 2 days, my wits are roasting: twice I dreamt I was kissing Angelica passionately, across a hedge, from which I can only deduce that incest and sapphism embrace in one breast. But neither the one nor the other come within a thousand miles of me when seeing Susie Buchan or Ethel Smyth—both of whom came here yesterday. Adrian is said by Julian to be openly and outrageously in love with Mrs [Henry] Lintott so that people laugh at her car in front of his sitting room window, in which, the room I mean, there's no light, owing to the bedroom being at the back. How I wish I could see you, even across a hedge! But I must wait till September. I wish old Julian werent going: he's such an angel; but still, its done him a lot of good, I see; Simpson[2] was rejected—How are your Queen Mary paintings?[3] I met Kauffer[4] at the Hutches. [Hutchinsons] and he said that they were such asses, the architects, asking him to do Britannia with a shield, that he thought he should refuse. But I hope you're all right. Now please write. We go to Monks House on the 25th.

B.

I have been asked to be President of the P E. N Club in succession to Wells: this is about the greatest insult that could be offered a writer, or a human being.

Berg

1. Edmond Kapp (1890-1978), the portrait-painter and lithographer. His first wife wrote under the name of Yvonne Cloud (see p. 7, note 3.)
2. The latest novel by John Hampson Simpson, whose *Saturday Night at the Greyhound* was published by the Hogarth Press in 1931.
3. Vanessa and Duncan had been commissioned to paint panels for the new Cunard liner *Queen Mary*.
4. Edward McKnight Kauffer (1890-1954), the American painter whose best-known works were posters for the London Underground.

*52 Tavistock Square, W.C.*1

Wednesday [17 July 1935]

Dearest Ottoline,

I'm so sorry you've been ill, and had to retire to Clifton.[1] I wonder if you saw the dancing nuns—thats my impression: Nuns dancing in a convent: one looks down from a terrace: rather like birds doing some ceremony.

I would have given you the Roger[2] if I'd thought you would like it. But I think speaking in public always makes one tell lies and puts a throttle round ones throat. I didn't get anything out naturally; and it was so hot, and such a plum pudding crowd. I hated the whole thing.

We shan't go away just yet, so I hope we may owl again. But please dont hang too many of us round your neck. Kot [Koteliansky] came here the other day, just the same, the same schemes and curses. Murry came in for a sound shower. I've not read Shakespeare, and I cant.[3] Why let that smell pervade him even for a moment? But I read Murry on Murry[4] because carrion has its fascination, like eating high game. I'm so sleepy I'm writing nonsense. Old Ethel has been making the telephone rattle—How are we to provide for her now her book's done? You see how I pile things on to you —If you dont take care, you shall have Mrs Grosvenor and my half brother [Gerald Duckworth] and old [Sir] Harry Stephen and Elizabeth Robins.[5] E.R. however is a bird of a very different feather, something like a humming bird stuffed.

We go to Rachel and David [Cecil] for the weekend, where I hope to meet Desmond. So no more.

V.

nodding over the fire

Texas

1. From 1935 onwards Ottoline's health declined slowly, and she visited a series of clinics. This one was at Clifton, Bristol.
2. Her speech about Roger Fry's paintings at the Bristol Art Gallery was published as a pamphlet in September 1935 in a limited edition, not for sale. See Kirkpatrick, A 21.
3. John Middleton Murry's *Shakespeare*, 1935.
4. His autobiography, *Between Two Worlds*, 1935.
5. The American-born novelist and actress (d. 1952) who had been a friend of Virginia's mother. She lived in Brighton with Octavia Wilberforce, who became Virginia's doctor at the end of her life.

Typewritten
18th July 1935

Dear Miss McAfee,

Thank you so much for your charming letter and for the suggestions it contains.

I had at the back of my mind an article that I hoped to write for your autumn number [*Yale Review*], but I never got time, and that, I am afraid, is the reason why I must not accept the tempting invitation to write an open letter—even a short one. I have promised to finish a book by August, and it is now past the middle of July, and the book is still on my hands. I am therefore refusing to let myself break off into any other activity until I have done with it. In fact, I have written no articles since November—but I hope to be freer in the autumn, and then perhaps you will let me send you something.

We have not yet escaped, as you see; but hope to get into the country next week. Meanwhile, it is refreshing to think that somebody else is enjoying Jane Austen in peace. Here, as far as I can make out, nobody reads anything but the newspaper.

With our best regards,
yours sincerely
Virginia Woolf

Yale University

3050: To Ethel Smyth   52 *Tavistock Square,* [*W.C.*1]

Sunday [21 July 1935]

Dossier.

(1) Yes. I think I recognise the pink rimmed handkerchief as one I bought to assuage hay fever in Marlborough, going to Bristol. But keep it. The memory is detestable.

(2) Ottoline says you are entirely adorable, and seduced Hope Mirrlees from the holy Ghost.[1] What a press you're having![2]

(3) Read the enclosed—fulsome praise I hope—at your leisure, and tell me if I must answer.

V

Berg

1. See p. 345, note 2.
2. For her book *Beecham and Pharaoh*.

52 *Tavistock Square, W.C.1*

21st July 1935

Dear Logan,

Thank you very much for sending me the little tract[1] which I shall, of course, put on my shelves in the hope, as you suggest, that I may profit by it.

With regard to the essay [*unidentified*], charming as it is I am afraid that it would be no use for us to attempt to publish it. The public appetite for separate essays seems to be exhausted, so far as we are concerned, and we have had to bring our essay series to an end. And even if we tried the experiment of beginning another series with your essay, the fact that you are so soon going to include it in your book of essays[2] would, we fear, be a fatal drawback. Our autumn list is already made up, and we could not bring it out therefore till next year, by which time, I gather, your book would be almost ready.

Therefore I am reluctantly returning it, but we are very grateful to you for giving us the opportunity.

Yours sincerely
Virginia Woolf

Frederick B. Adams Jr.

3052: To Elizabeth Bowen   [52 *Tavistock Square, W.C.1*]

Postcard
Monday [22 July 1935]

Many thanks for taking so much trouble. I've told my brother in law [Clive] what you say. We go away on Thursday but could you come in on Wednesday, any time after 9.30? Do if you can. Rosamund's brother John [Lehmann] is coming and Lytton's sister Dorothy [Bussy]. Many congratulations—what fun to take a house.

V.W.

Texas

3053: To V. Sackville-West   *Monks House, [Rodmell, Sussex]*

Saturday [27 July 1935]

I wrote you a long and loving letter, and left it on my table in London unstamped, so it wont go. It was only to say we couldn't come in on our

1. *How Little Logan Was Brought to Jesus.* See p. 131, note 1.
2. *Re-perusals and re-collections*, 1936.

way yesterday—but perhaps you'll ask us over, which would be simpler, when we're here: or come in yourself. Do you still visit your mother? We visit L's mother, at Worthing, and its a dismal grinding visit, as the poor old creature is rapidly growing blind, yet is so strong she may reach 100;— But this scribble is only to say I hope you won't have a devilish time in London,[1] and wish I were there to go on a jaunt, to Kew.

I saw Ottoline the other night and heard about the visit to Yeats, which should set Dotty up there 15 years, and I hope will plume her feathers for her, and make her sing like a nightingale.[2] Not that it alters my own opinion one jot.

I've got such a mass of writing and reading to do down here and can only sit on the terrace and look at a swarm of bees, and read Captain Marryat.[3] I've seen too many humans, and would like a long dose of donkeys. So come and see us; or let us come to you, and, as I say, please get through all these horrors and come out at the end still caring for the poor Potto without a tail. Oh Ethel!

The royal garden party etc—but no room or time for more.

V.

Berg

3054: To Vanessa Bell

Monks House, Rodmell,
[Sussex]

Monday [29 July 1935]

Well, this is very nice, that Dolphin should be in town again,[4] though I'm afraid not so nice for the poor brute itself. I was beginning to write to you when the whole [Joan] Easdale family broke in, and we had to spend the afternoon with them. Stephen Tennant who's lodging at Piddinghoe, has already been round this morning—what can be done about people?— (I dont mean the Bells). However, what I was going to say was: if you want your tea set, it is in the Bathroom at 52; still packed in the box they sent it in, and I hope unhurt—If you want it, and Mabel's not there, they have a Key in the Press. The other china is here. Also: have you got a copy of

1. For Gwen St Aubyn's minor operation on 29 July.
2. Dorothy Wellesley had formed an intimate friendship with W. B. Yeats, who greatly admired her poetry and whose *Letters on Poetry*, 1940, were addressed to her.
3. Frederick Marryat (1792-1848), author of *Peter Simple, Mr Midshipman Easy*, etc. Virginia published an article about him in the *T.L.S.* of 26 September 1935 under the title *The Captain's Death Bed*, later reprinted in the volume of that name, 1950.
4. Vanessa had just returned from Cassis.

Rogers Transformations?[1] a small one? I cant find mine, so could you lend me one? If not, I can easily get it from the Library. I'm afraid Ha is going to be rather difficult—but I'll keep that till we meet.

Let me know when and where.

B.

Berg

3055: To John Lehmann   *Monk's House, Rodmell,*
                                         [Sussex]

1st August [1935]

Dear John,

It is difficult for me to say if you're right or wrong.[2] Its very interesting anyhow. But I've not read The Waves since I wrote it, and I'm now doing something so different that I can't get back into the mood. Of course, my attempt was to get that kind of effect, by those means—metaphors, rhythm, repetitions, as you say. But in actually writing one's mind, as you know, gets into a trance, and the different images seem to come unconsciously. It is very interesting to me, though, to see how deliberate it looks to a critic. Of course most of the work is done before one writes and the concentration of writing makes one forget what the general effect is. But I'm very pleased it strikes you like that—as a whole.

But if you print it, as I hope you will, leave out Shakespeare, because I don't think anyone in their senses can have mentioned him in that connection. (I almost put a capital H, and that is rather my feeling).

The village is playing stoolball, and I must go and sit on the grass and watch.

Yours
V.W.

Texas

3056: To Ethel Smyth   *Monks House, [Rodmell,*
                                         Sussex]

Saturday [10 August 1935]

Well my dear Ethel, how delightful this silence is—how fertile, how satisfying: I'd just made up my mind never to break it by a single word when I looked up and caught the shine of the coachman's hat in your portrait

1. Roger Fry's collection of essays and lectures published in 1926.
2. Lehmann had written an article on the pattern and imagery of *The Waves*. He sent it to Virginia in typescript, but there is no record of its publication.

[photograph], which so titillated my wish to know what the devil the uncastrated cat is doing at the moment—there seems to be only one obvious employment for such an animal—that I take up my pen, as they say. Since coming here I have poured out tea for 15 self-invited guests: I have been to London; I have read a dozen MSS. of tepid trash and then you call me lazy! Then you say I forget old friends!—ranking yourself apparently with the fairy who bent over my cradle and whispered music in my ear. Well, aint it odd, how, a mere four year old like you—for it is now precisely four years since you caught me a cuff over the head for telling you—I forget what, but I remember falling flat on the drawing room floor—aint it odd how free and easy we are together: and what pains over your heart is like a breeze over corn in mine. Now any critic, anyone trained in the art of letters at Cambridge, like your friend Peter Lucas, could tell from that last sentence, with its recurring rhythm, and visual emblem—why dont they make me Prof. of English—I'd teach em—would know from that sentence that I've just come in from a long hot walk over the downs and sat by myself in a cornfield. If ever you come this way, I'll take you to Muggery Poke. There we'll seal our love on a floor where the nettles push among the cow droppings. It was deserted 50 years ago, and I go there every Saturday to muse upon my youth—

Did I tell you—no—I never boast—I'm one of the most modest people, come to think of it, there's ever been—that Wells having retired from the PEN Club they asked me to suceed him? Upon which I flicked my hand, as a greek woman flicks a bug off her childs head. Conceive the damned insolence! Ten dinners a year, and I to sit at the head of this puling company of back scratchers and administer balm. I thought of you. Why? In what connection? Ah-hah, thats my secret.

Vita wrote today and asked me to go to S^t. [Sissinghurst], where Gwen is lying in bed with 2 nurses I gather; and it was a very nice affectionate letter. Have you heard?

Now L. calls me to bowls

So no more

Berg

V.

3057: To Jane Bussy

Monk's House, Rodmell,
[Sussex]

Saturday [10 August 1935]

But, my dear Janie, this is too silly. Even I can count, there are six black marks in my diary, every one of which stood for Janie. And I think its damned cheek on your part to rate our interviews [French lessons] at a mere 5/bob. However, have it your own way: I only stick to my point—since it affects accuracy—that there were 6 lessons, not 4.

I have been trying all this week to continue a diary in French: but life flies so fast, and French verbs—dear me, I shall never forget saying beut instead of boit in front of Clive of all people—life, that is my mother in law, the Keynses, Stephen Tennant etc, flies so fast, and I've got to finish a book of 150,000 words all in a jiffy, that I cant get on with the diary. Never mind, I will tell it you when we meet.

It is roasting hot here, and incredibly beautiful at the moment—orange fields, yellow grasses, and a green running river with a schooner on it. I stopped to admire the view, and what d'you think happened? A fox got up at my feet! But then you dont care about animals.

I wish I had a library of French books within reach. I should like to lie in a deck chair and absorb French with my feet. They say now one can see with ones back. But its too hot to read a vast work called My Life and my Love, by the widow of a headmaster which has just been sent us.

Love to any Stracheys who may be doing crossword puzzles at the moment.

V.W.

Texas

3058: To Vanessa Bell

Monks House, [Rodmell, Sussex]

Postcard
[21 August 1935]

Margery [Fry] only arrives rather late on Friday afternoon and goes early on Saturday, so I dont [*sic*] there will be much chance of coming over. But I'll tell her of the invitation.

(Written in the car.)

3059: To Vanessa Bell

[Monk's House, Rodmell, Sussex]

Sunday [25 August 1935]

Julian suggested a meeting before he goes.[1]

Would you and he dine here on Tuesday—or if you'd prefer it—should we dine with you?

We have to go to Sissinghurst but should be back by 8. But dont do either if a bother. We shall be out to lunch and tea on Tuesday.

Would you send a line.

Berg

1. Julian Bell left Newhaven for China on 29 August.

3060: To Ethel Smyth   *Monks House, [Rodmell,*
                                         Sussex]

Tuesday [3 September 1935]

I have lost your letter in the general chaos of MSS. and dont know what
day you said you were coming. So let me know possible dates. I remember
all the soul of the letter, about the dog and Vita; its only the facts.

I went to Siss^t: and Vita was so seductive in her sailors trousers, and we
had 15 minutes alone—the first this year—and I'm sorry you dismiss her.
G. [Gwen] was there, like a drowning cat; wet, white, and Harold—Red,
robust.

                                                          V.

I've been up in London all day, and so cant write

Berg

3061: To Margaret Llewelyn Davies
                                         Monk's House, Rodmell,
                                         Lewes, [Sussex]

Typewritten
6th Sept [1935]

Dearest Margaret,

We were just about to write to you to suggest a visit—would next
Friday, 13th, suit you? We would turn up about four [at Dorking]. If that
is all right for you, dont bother to write. I'm so sorry you havent been well
—dont hesitate to put us off, if it should seem a burden, as I know visitors
can seem. Our telephone number is Lewes 385.

You may be amused by the enclosed letter and article which I've just
had sent me by Mrs Leavis.[1] I dont know her, but am told that she and her
husband represent all that is highest and dryest at Cambridge. So I rather
feel from reading her article; but I suppose she means well, and I'm glad
that she should feel sympathetic in her high and dry way to our book. I
wish we could produce another. Could we? It didnt do so badly. I dont
want Scrutiny or the letter again.

So it will be very nice to see you, and we shall turn up in our car on
the Friday, unless stopped. Love from us both.

                                                          Yours
Sussex   V.W.

1. A review in *Scrutiny* (a quarterly) of *Life As We Have Known It*, edited by
   Margaret Llewelyn Davies with an Introduction by Virginia, 1931. For the
   Leavises, see p. 22, note 2.

Monk's House, Rodmell,
Near Lewes, Sussex

13th Sept [1935]

Dear Mrs Easdale,

It is extremely good of you to have sent me your book,¹ and I write at once, as I am afraid it will be a week or two before I can sit down in peace to read it. But of course I have looked to see the quotation from the diary that you told me about. It gives a most glowing account of eating crumpets at Monk's House, and is more than kind.² But I admit that it makes me a little shy. I cant feel that Mr and Mrs Woolf are quite so exciting when they come to tea as you make out, but I dont want to shake your generous illusion. (And I have just had a dip in, and couldn't stop though I tried, reading the account of 'my first corpse', and the large linen sheet upon which your grandfather blew his nose. Compared with the book I ought to have been reading, all about Jowett and Oxford, how delightful yours is!)

I'm afraid it looks as if we shouldn't get a day off to come to Kent this autumn. We are both trying to get a good deal of work done before we go back, and have to deal with a good many interruptions here. But if we can, I will write and suggest it. I am much excited by the thought of more flowers—they last year in year out here.

Thank you again for the book. I shall keep it till I have done my duty by manuscripts; meanwhile I shall watch for reviews, and feel sure of its success.

Yrs sincerely
Virginia Woolf

University of London

Monk's House, [Rodmell,
Sussex]

Wednesday 18th [September 1935]

I have a terrible but I hope fugitive confession to make: I read your chapter;³ put it away, and now can't find it. L. is out at the moment, and may have it in his keeping. But please get it retyped at my expense. I am furious, with myself, for this slovenliness. My only excuse is that we have the floor littered with MSS: and I'm going through all the Fry papers, and am rather dazed. And no doubt it will turn up. But please God you have a

1. *Middle Age 1885-1932.*
2. Mrs Easdale and her daughter Joan had tea at Monk's House on 27 September 1931. There were crumpets with honey, which Virginia had bought specially for them.
3. Of Ethel's next autobiographical volume *As Time Went On*, 1936.

copy, which your man can do again—at my expense. Hence I cant answer your question about the paragraph at the moment. My impression of the whole was that it was an excellent fragment, by itself; and very vivid. Only I think I had read it before? I seem to remember the incident of your hearing the Mass and not knowing what it was. But perhaps you showed me this with the Ponsonby Chapter? Anyhow, it reads very fresh and free; yes, no doubt about it. (Oh dear, oh dear—that I should add to the losses and worries.—but its the first time) About Miss Gordon.[1] I have had a thick dossier from her. But I cant possibly read the MS yet: I have to read our Press books in rotation, and shant get through to hers for a time. The season of books is on me. I'll let you know my opinion when I have one.

Meanwhile, as I say, I am facing my 3 large boxes of Fry, in the vain hope that I may make some way in them before London begins. And there's a whole room full more, I believe. But its fascinating work; save that handwriting strains the eyes, and I have to read every note with a view to some light or hint. So excuse me for scrawling: you'll have to make even more than the usual allowances for me till I'm through this thick hedge

V.

Berg

3064: To Lady Tweedsmuir   *Monk's House, Rodmell,*
                                 Near Lewes, Sussex

20th Sept [1935]

My dear Susie,

We are bringing out your book[2] about 8th Oct. Yes, of course we will send an advance copy to Miss Garvin. Would you like us to send it to you, so that you could put a note in it? Or if you sent us a note, we could put it in. Or we could send it without. One line on a card to the Hogarth Press, and they will do whatever you wish. But please use your secretary. I'm sure you must be worn to bits. I cant say its been altogether balmy down here the last few days—all our fruit and most of our hedges are blown down; but I've just picked a hat full of mushrooms in the marsh so I cant complain.

Yes I hope we shall see you before you go.

Yrs ever
V.W.

Lady Tweedsmuir

1. Mary Gordon, *Chase of the Wild Goose. The story of Lady Eleanor Butler and Miss Sarah Ponsonby, known as the Ladies of Llangollen*, Hogarth Press, May 1936.
2. *Funeral March of a Marionette.*

3065: To Donald Brace   *Monk's House, Rodmell,*
                                         Lewes, Sussex
Typewritten
29th Sept. 1935

Dear Mr Brace,

With regard to my novel—it is taking me longer than I expected; but I hope that it may be ready by Christmas. I have decided to call it "The Years", but I should much prefer not to give any description of it until I have read it through, as you are so good as to say that this is not essential. I have still a good deal to do in the way of revision; and it is still much too long. And in these circumstances I find it difficult to give an intelligible account of it.

We had a very interesting and varied trip, through Holland, Germany, Italy and France in the spring. But that now seems a long time ago, and we are preparing to go back to London next week for the winter.

I hope you are well, and that affairs in America are prospering.

                                         Yours sincerely,
                                         Virginia Woolf

Harcourt Brace Jovanovich

3066: To Lady Ottoline Morrell   *Monks House, Rodmell,*
                                  [Sussex]
Oct 4th [1935]

Dearest Ottoline,

I am a wretch never to have written—I liked getting your letter so much. But we have been trapesing off to Brighton to listen to the vociferations of the Labour party, and then dashing up to London—in short, thinking you didn't hold by your pound of flesh I never wrote. Now we are just about to come back. It is a flooded and stormy world here, with the marsh overflowing and gigantic storms coming over the hills; but all very lovely as usual. I wish public affairs wouldn't jerk their ugly heads up. When even I cant sleep at night for thinking of politics, things must be in a fine mess. All our friends and neighbours talk politics, politics.[1]

Tom Eliot was here the other weekend, very mellow, charming and humane. I no longer feel a crashing vulgarian, an upstart illiterate in his presence—after 20 years thats something. I'm beginning to read a huge collection of Roger's letters that Margery has deposited with me. On and on and on I go, but whether anything can be done with them I'm not sure,

1. On this very day Mussolini launched his attack on Abyssinia. The League of Nations, following Anthony Eden's lead at Geneva, voted for economic sanctions against Italy.

and it will take me six months, only to read the letters at this rate. I skimmed Elizabeth's book[1] in a rush: I must read it again. I thought it a little tight and hard, but very good—much the best of hers I've read.

Now Leonard has turned on the wireless to listen to the news, and so I am flicked out of the world I like into the other. I wish one were allowed to live only in one world, but thats asking too much. But I hope you'll let me come owling round in the dusk one of these evenings. I heard a brilliant account of your losing a dog on a Common from Ethel. (We are now hearing about the war, so I cant write sense). Aren't I right though to make her take to her pen, not her harp?

yrs VW.

Texas

1. *The House in Paris*, by Elizabeth Bowen. For Virginia's reaction to it, see *Elizabeth Bowen: Portrait of a Writer* by Victoria Glendinning (1977), p. 94.

Letters 3067–3091 (October–December 1935)

Virginia was still working on The Years, *which she described to her new friend Victoria O'Campo on 29 October as "a corpulent and most obstinate novel: I think I've finished it, and then it springs back in my face, like a bramble, all prickles". She was also ruminating on a book about women's professions (which she eventually wrote as* Three Guineas), *and was intermittently reading Roger Fry's letters for her biography of him. It was an autumn of great political activity, beginning with the Abyssinian crisis, followed by the General Election on 14 November, and then by the resignation of the Foreign Secretary, Sir Samuel Hoare, over his pact with Pierre Laval. Julian Bell left England to take up a three-year appointment in a Chinese University, and for a time he became Virginia's main correspondent. At the end of December she suffered from severe headaches, not least because of the demands of the Hogarth Press, which once again the Woolfs thought of abandoning or selling.*

3067: To Lyn Newman   52 *Tavistock Square*, [*W.C.*1]
Oct 6th [1935]

Dear Lyn,

We have just got back to London after rather a distracted summer. At least it ended with the Labour party at Brighton and began with Germany and Italy. Did we tell you how the marmoset saved us from Hitler?[1]

We're so glad that you are going to have a baby, and hope to see you both this autumn. Where is Comberton?[2] I've no notion. Grantchester I know and Madingley, but thats all. Leonard is in a great rush with politics as you can imagine, and we are both at the moment regretting Monk's House, which we left almost flooded, but very lovely in its ruined way. The storm turned half of every tree deep brown.

Well, we shall hope for news of you, and shall turn up when we're travelling our books if we may. Now by the way, I have a niece at Newnham: a very charming niece, Ann Stephen.

Leonard sends his love and congratulations

Yrs

Sussex   Virginia Woolf

1. See p. 392, note 2.
2. Lyn Newman (*née* Lloyd Irvine) lived with her husband Max at Cross Farm, Comberton, near Cambridge.

3068: To Ethel Smyth

52 *T.[avistock] Sqre. [W.C.1]*
Tuesday [8 October 1935]

I have a thousand apologies to make—but no MS.![1] We had a comb out through every jungle before leaving Monks House, and found nothing. What is most likely is that I stuffed it between the leaves of a huge MS. novel I was reading and rejecting, and that it was sent back to some infuriated author who kept it in revenge. At the same time I lost a letter I had to answer —containing not mere praise but 3 pocket handkerchiefs. You must tell me faithfully what the bill for retyping is. I'm getting so casual and submerged in things—all these Fry papers—I lose something daily. The theory is that I'm so careful of the Fry letters, all my care is spent.—thats what I say. I heard from Vera Brittain, a heart broken letter poor woman. And I'm told (not by her) that what killed poor Winifred was first an African germ, which they thought was cured; then Vera B's father jumped into the Thames and drowned himself; Vera and W. spent several days searching for the body; found it; Vera broke down thereupon; Winifred was sent to look after the children; suddenly the germ revived; she was too exhausted to struggle, and so died; but this comes only second hand.[2]

I hope to keep freer next week than this: Athos is out;[3] R.B. has written fairly mildly in answer to a sound drubbing by L: all the bookshops praise the set up; and first sales not bad—I mean advance sales. but we must wait. I had to send the Ladies of Ll: back to the hermaphrodite.[4] I cant repeat my reasons on this slip; but perhaps, she'll tell you. I thought it quite well done in its way.

V

Remember the Bill

Berg

3069: To Julian Bell

52 *Tavistock Square, [W.C.1]*
Typewritten
14th Oct 1935

Dearest Julian,

Nessa says it is possible to write to you, which for some reason I had

1. See beginning of Letter 3063.
2. In her book about Winifred Holtby, *Testament of Friendship*, 1940, Vera Brittain records that her father died "suddenly and tragically" in July while she was in France, and Holtby came over to break the news. There was no searching for his body. Holtby herself died, aged 37, in a London nursing-home on 29 September. Her most famous novel *South Riding* was published post-humously in 1936.
3. Ralph Brewster's *The 6,000 Beards of Athos*.
4. See p. 427, note 1.

thought doubtful. Now the great thing is to make a beginning, and then to trust that you will answer. So I lead off—only I'm told one must be careful. Well, we had a great family meeting the other night and Nessa read your journey letter aloud and it was we all said a very good letter; only rather melancholy. You were on board ship, and it had been very hot in the Red Sea. Then she had a cable to say youd arrived. Now I suppose you are teaching the Chinks about Mrs Gaskell—which seems an odd thing to do. Oh dear how I wish television were now installed and I could switch on and see you, instead of tap tapping, which curtails my ideas and castrates my style. But then, I take it, you cant read the only hand that gives me any currency.

As for news—well, after you left we had old Tom [Eliot] to stay the week end; he was urbanity itself, and we had a good deal of old crones talk about people like Middleton Murry, Wyndham Lewis and so on. He's determined to write plays about modern life in verse, and rather crusty when reviewers say he's an old fogy. In fact I think he feels that hes only just beginning to write what he wants. Whether hes on the turn, religiously speaking, I'm not sure. He had an early cup of tea on Sunday and went to Communion. It was a wet morning too, and when I came down to get breakfast there he was dew sprinkled, saying that he had met three old women in the churchyard and one of them said, as he passed, "Yes, there she was lying in bed with a still born child by her side". A nice way of beginning Sunday. We dined with the Keynses, and Maynard commissioned him to write a play for the new theatre.[1]

Then we went to the Brighton conference, which was better than any play. To hear first old Lansbury[2] a true Christian, but with an eye, I thought to the gallery—I mean the [Brighton] Dome, not Heaven; and then [Ernest] Bevin like a snake whos swallowed a toad, denouncing him, crushing him 'Some people like to go hawking their consciences about" he said—while poor Lansbury squirmed behind him; this was as good as any play—not that Ive seen one. But I wont write politics; They are now all in a stir about the election, said to come off in November.[3]

I am beginning to work at Rogers letters, and have by the way had a scrawl from Ha to say that the Mallarmé[4] is all off, owing to the monstrous behaviour of the Mallarmé people in Paris. I gather theyve refused to have any further dealings; but on what grounds I dont know. Doubtless she'll

1. The Cambridge Arts Theatre, which Keynes inspired and helped to finance. It opened in February 1936. Eliot did not write a play for it.
2. George Lansbury (1859-1940), the Labour leader and pacifist, opposed the imposition of sanctions on Italy, and finding himself supported by only a small minority at the Brighton conference, resigned his leadership of the Parliamentary Labour Party.
3. Polling Day in the General Election was 14 November.
4. See p. 387, note 3.

tell you. Rogers letters are fascinating; an awful mix; the family ones very stiff; the travel ones rather dull; but always some flash of interest; and some to Basil Williams[1] extremely amusing. But I cant think how to deal with it —or whether to deal with it. I wish you were here to discuss the whole thing. Did you write anything [about Fry]? I hope so. One might write a whole long book; I rather suspect its a case either of a long book or a short essay. But I must go on reading. Your C.O. book has come for L. to review.[2] I thought Adrian very good—the only one Ive looked at.

Last night we dined with Clive; present, Nessa, Duncan and Sally [dog]. We discussed criticism; and at what point the critical faculty dies. I think mine is just able to deal with poetry this year; but will be dead next year. So hurry up and write some.

We are all well in health, and spry in spirit; but rather miss you, and I wish Q. wasnt going up to the potteries,[3] however I rather suspect we shall make a push and come to China.

I must now go and see an importunate and unfortunate Gerwoman[4] who thinks I can help her with facts about Women under Democracy—little she knows—what you do about your poor old Virginia.

Quentin Bell

3070: To Ethel Smyth   52 *Tavistock Sqre.* [*W.C.*1]

Monday [21 October 1935]

I've now got completely muddled;—you will not be surprised to hear, and can only say will you let me know when you appear at the Old Bailey in order that I may be there.[5] I must if I possibly can. So send me a line that I mayn't be closeted here with some inescapable grub. I sat next Elizabeth [Williamson] at a concert the other night, and she told me that you were off somewhere in the country with Mrs Wodehouse.[6] (Please convey her

1. Professor of History at Edinburgh University, 1925-37.
2. *We Did Not Fight*, 1935, a collection of eighteen autobiographical essays by British conscientious objectors in the First War, edited with an Introduction by Julian Bell. Among the contributors were Adrian Stephen, David Garnett, Norman Angell and Siegfried Sassoon.
3. To learn the craft of pot-making at Stoke-on-Trent.
4. Ruth Gruber, who wrote, in English, *Virginia Woolf: A Study*, (*Kölner Anglist. Arbeiten*, Vol. 24, 1935).
5. On 14 November Ethel successfully sued the British General Press for the return of some articles she had offered them for publication.
6. Violet Gordon-Woodhouse, the harpsichordist, with whom Ethel often stayed in her beautiful house Nether Lyppiat, Gloucestershire.

my respectful homage. Ought we to buy the Scarlatti records?) Elizabeth looked—but I'm no judge of 'looks',—very well, and we had a little back chat over our seats. It was Bach, and the flute didn't carry round the corner —is that a legitimate criticism? I'm too shy of you to venture many such you'll admit.

I've had a poetess reading her works aloud [Easdale]; I've had a French socialist declaiming against Fascism [Walter]; I've had a German Jewess [Gruber]—no, I cant go into all the vociferations and gesticulations that are our lot in Tavistock Sqre.—but you'll admit that it is difficult to wedge in even an hours reading of old letters (Rogers) and a morning at my own script, and taking Sally round the square;—she wont make water except in Leonards presence, which has introduced an additional complication: Such is love! Venus toute entiere—etc.[1]

But for Gods sake. let me come to the Old Bailey

V.

"Gerald Balfour[2]—surely the handsomest man I've ever seen" I've just read this in an old letter of Rogers.

Berg

3071: TO ETHEL SMYTH   52 *T.[avistock] S.[quare, W.C.1]*

Thursday [24 October 1935]

I'm very sorry you're not well enough to come, and very sorry too about the death of that nice man.[3] But Lady Simon stayed here talking about politics till 6.45. and I daresay you'd have been bored. (She's a rather nice woman though, something to do with Newnham, something to do with Manchester, and a great admirer of a Room of Ones Own—hence her visit —hence her demand that I must write a sequel)[4]

Well, I must leave the future to you. This is a stupid page, but I cant strike any romantic line of thought. At the moment L. is telephoning to a lady who insists that she must see Miss Virginia Woolf—do you mean Mrs says Leonard; upon which she cries off into the night. Now what did she want to see me for, and then get my name wrong? I am about to attempt to

1. *Vénus toute entière à sa proie attachée.* Racine, *Phèdre.*
2. Fellow of Trinity College, Cambridge, and brother of A. J. Balfour, the former Prime Minster. Ethel's friend, Betty Balfour, married Gerald's nephew.
3. Frederick Ponsonby, Lord Sysonby, the son of Ethel's friend Lady Ponsonby, died on 20 October, aged 68.
4. For Shena, Lady Simon, see p. 171, note 2. The 'sequel' was *Three Guineas.*

read the Life of Bishop Gore;[1] I am about to decide whether I can possibly refuse my old mother in laws birthday party, and go to tea instead. Can I? She is blind as a bat, and croons with dismal persistency over all the anniversaries of all the deaths, which conglomerate this month. What about the Van Dams, and your ballet?[2] What about the Hermaphrodite? [Mary Gordon] She's writing a sequel to Orlando. What about Gwen and V [Vita]? I've never a word from V. which rather hurts me, save that I know what is to be has to be. And whats the good of complaining? I am rather ravaged and harassed by Fry relations and friends: and can only hug my freedom, and refuse to commit myself to any work till my book is on the Atlantic waves. I read The Temple last night: George Herbert.[3] Why cant I believe too? only I think my own beliefs so much more exciting. Yet Gore, they say, was a good man. But I cant get into the romantic vein tonight.

V.

Athos [Brewster] has had quite good reviews. L. says it is selling "quite fairly well."

A cheap edition of the 2nd Common Reader has just come out. Shall I give you a copy to give your friend?

Berg

3072: To Julian Bell   52 *Tavistock Square*, [*W.C.*1]

Typewritten
Oct 25th 1935

Dearest Julian,

Nessa says you get a letter if its sent on a Friday. (I wrote you one the other day, but lost it; if I find it I'll put it—[*later*] I put it in) Your letters are read aloud and seem to us very good indeed, only they take so long to come that when we read them you are already in another part of the world. I heard of you yesterday though from old Mrs Woolf, who says you visited Bella[4] and she thought you a most charming young man. I gather that you

1. Charles Gore (1853-1932), Bishop of Oxford. His Life was written by G. L. Prestige.
2. Vivian Van Damm (d. 1960) was General Manager of the Windmill Theatre in London. He did not produce Ethel's ballet *Fête Galante*.
3. *The Temple, or Sacred Poems and Private Ejaculations*, 1652.
4. Bella was Leonard's eldest sister (1877-1960). Her second husband was (Sir) Thomas Southorn, who was Colonial Secretary, Hong Kong, 1926-36.

were tactful in the extreme; at least, my mother in law was delighted that according to you I am very fond of her. That was a master stroke—I am, in a way; but how did you know it?

Then Leonard heard from Tyrrell,[1] whom you had also charmed. And now you are in your official residence on the banks of the Yangste. Its useless to ask what youre doing at this moment much though I want to know. Here at this moment it is a bright cool October evening; Miss West [Hogarth Press] has twice run in to say the Sunday Times wants to know can we get someone to introduce Mr Day Lewis when he speaks at their Book show; and I have had to ring up Morgan [Forster]; and have just got him to promise to be chairman. Leonard is having tea with him in Brunswick Square to meet Mr Kidd[2] because Janie [Bussy] brought M. Walter[3] round here, imploring us intellectuals to stand by the French anti-fascists. And now Charles Mauron wants us to go to a conference in Paris. And then there will be the general Election. But I gather that politics are best avoided; and in any case my views are likely to be inaccurate and perhaps partial—all politics be damned.

I am beginning to read Rogers letters, and wish to goodness you were here to consult. It seems to me either one must write a long book; or a short essay. There are masses of documents; and still more to come when Margery returns next week. The bother is he writes a dull letter for the most part, and then theres a flash of great fun. And his love letters are prolific; he must have had a love every new year; and most of them are foreigners. So I am plodding away, when the light fails, and I can no longer write my long dull novel, And now the Stracheys want me to write about Lytton. By the way your C.O. book[4] was reviewed at length in the New Statesman today and also in the Times. It seems to be taken very seriously and much praised. I looked at Adrians thing and thought it very good. Humanly speaking we are all as busy as bees—Nessa painting, Duncan painting, Clive dining out, Leonard as usual balancing twenty balls on top of his toes. As for youth and beauty, I have seen Rose Macaulay and Elizabeth Bowen; and Morgan and Joe Ackerley.[5] But they are all past their prime. I wish— but whats the use of wishing?—that you and Angelica and Quentin and Ann [Stephen] were all round the corner. Tomorrow perhaps we shall go to Cambridge for the day and call on Ann. Today as I was walking along

1. William Tyrrell (1866-1947), who had retired in 1934 as Ambassador in Paris. He had met Julian in London.
2. Ronald Kidd (1889-1942), founder of the National Council for Civil Liberties. Forster was President of its Executive Committee.
3. Francois Walter, editor of the French journal *Vigilance*, which was also the name given to an anti-Fascist group of intellectuals.
4. See p. 433, note 2.
5. J. R. Ackerley, author, future literary editor of *The Listener*, and an intimate friend of E. M. Forster.

the Strand I saw up "Public entrance" and so went into the Law Courts, and heard the Judges in the Appeal court try a case about land at Enfield—not very exciting, but fun to hear. I'm glad on the whole youre not a lawyer. Jack Hutchinson fell down in a fit the other day, said to be through over eating; but thats malicious. Anyhow hes all right again. I am reading old plays; do you find that your mind works oddly, about poetry? I can read it for an hour with rapture but without understanding a word. And the first of my senses to wake is the colour sense. Did you manage to write anything about Roger? Do when you can—not that I shall begin to write before the spring at earliest. I heard from Margery that the Mallarmé has fallen through owing to the malice of the family. No doubt shes told you. I think they objected to her terms. Peter Lucas writes to the Times; Lyn [Newman] has a son. Peter has the dons way of being clever about politics—about Shaw and Abyssinia.[1] Are there any books youd like? I see Empsom has written another on some critical theory;[2] but I shant read it. We are all very well. Nessa seems quite gay; and the other night at a concert she had painted her cheeks; but for sentimental reasons I dont like it. Would you? Certainly she looked very lovely. Clive is giving a lunch party to me and Christabel [Aberconway] and Desmond next week; and is shooting I think at Seend this Sunday. I will write these scraps often. But you mustnt expect much sense or polish or wit or fancy if I type, because the typewriter always pecks my poor brain to pieces. But you see how much we wish you were here my dearest Julian.

Quentin Bell

3073: To Philippa Strachey   52 *Tavistock Square, W.C.1*
25th Oct 1935

With Mrs Woolf's compliments, in order that Miss Strachey may buy something at the Bazaar,[3] as she wont accept her stamps.

    (And many thanks. The pamphlets just what I want to read)

Sussex (typed copy)

---

1. In *The Times* of 24 October Lucas wrote: "Mr Bernard Shaw in his letter of October 22nd is in raptures about the Italian invasion of Abyssinia, on the grounds that the Italians will make such good roads."
2. William Empson, *Some Versions of Pastoral*, 1935
3. In aid of the London-National Society for Women's Service, of which Philippa Strachey was Secretary.

Typewritten
25th Oct 1935

Dear Mr Ould,[1]

I am in receipt of your letter of the 25th inst.

I have had no communication from Mr Ellis Roberts[2] and I do not know therefore why he has informed you, as you say, that I have "agreed to join the P.E.N."

For reasons with which I need not trouble you I am unable to join the Club, and it is therefore impossible for me to sign the resolution which you have so kindly forwarded to me.

I need not say how much I appreciate the kindness of the Committee in making the suggestion.

Yours sincerely
Virginia Woolf
(Mrs Woolf)

Texas

3075: To Victoria O'Campo   [52 *Tavistock Square, W.C.*1]

Tuesday Oct 29th 1935

Dear Victoria,

A week ago—no, I'm afraid it is more than a week ago—two mysterious foreign ladies arrived in the hall just as I was saying goodbye for 5 years to an old friend who has been jumped up to the ridiculous and exalted station of Governor of Canada (his wife I mean) [Tweedsmuirs]: and they pressed into my hand a large parcel, murmured some musical but unintelligible remarks about "giving it into your own hands" and vanished. It took me at least ten minutes to realise that this was your present of South American butterflies. What could have been more fantastically inappropriate! It was a chilly October evening, and the road was up, and there was a row of little red lights to mark the ditch: and then these butterflies! And people were dining with us, and I had no time for anything but to take off my dress, and come down to the sitting room, and stand the butterflies on a chair: and at intervals all through the evening (we had E. M. Forster and a B.B.C. official [Ackerley] dining with us) I looked over their heads at the butterflies and thought of the difference between two worlds. I must say it was an extraordinarily imaginative thought on your part. I cant, in spite of my

1. Dramatist, poet and critic, and General Secretary of the International P.E.N. Club.
2. See p. 414, note 2.

puritan ancestor, disapprove and regret it. So what I have done is to hang the butterflies over his portrait on the stairs, in the mystic hope that somehow they may persuade each other of the error of their ways. The butterflies, so far, are having much the best of it.

But will you thank the veiled and mysterious ladies, and explain how it was that I was so flabbergasted and inexpressive, and did not show them any hospitality, as I should like to have done? As I say, they vanished, and there was no card, or anything, to which I could send my thanks.

I wrote you a long letter in August, about the PEN and Buenos Aires: to say they had invited me, and offered to pay my expenses. But I cant talk about literature; thats not my line; so I cant accept their generosity, which, without any proof to go on, I connect with you. All the same, one of these days I shall come. Only you can't think how fast we are tied to England, even to 52 Tavistock Sqre, by the Hogarth Press: by politics (now its the General Election) by the necessity I am under of finishing a corpulent and most obstinate novel: I think I've finished it, and then it springs back in my face, like a bramble, all prickles, and I have to begin again, cutting and pruning. As I say I wrote all this in a letter in August, but was interrupted; saw it lying about; got sick of it and so threw it away. But you wont want letters, written in this scrawl, which is partly due to a pen with a split nose.

Perhaps someday you will write.[1] How remote and sunk in time and space you seem, over there, in the vast—what d'you call them—those immense blue grey lands with the wild cattle and the pampas grass and the butterflies? Every time I go out of my door I make up another picture of South America: and no doubt you'd be surprised if you could see yourself in your house as I arrange it. It is always grilling hot, and there is a moth alighted in a silver flower. And this too in broad daylight. I must hurry to lunch. So goodbye.

Yrs gratefully
Virginia Woolf

Victoria O'Campo

3076: To Lady Ottoline Morrell
52 *Tavistock Square, W.C.*1
3rd Nov [1935]

Dearest Ottoline,
I wish I could come, but I'm afraid I cant on Tuesday. I have promised to be in to see a dull little man, and I dont suppose he'll go in time. But

1. Victoria O'Campo replied: "I am a very voracious person. And I believe hunger is all. I am not ashamed of being hungry. Dont you think life is *the hunger* to love?" (*Sussex*)

may I come another day, evening rather, when you're alone, if you're not too busy? We are just back from Rodmell, where we had Labour Party meetings in the schoolroom—not a chance of getting in of course.

Give the great poet [Yeats] my humble duty, and thank you for asking me.

yrs Virginia

Texas

3077: To Mrs Easdale   52 *Tavistock Square*, [*W.C.1*]

7th Nov. [1935]

Dear Mrs Easdale,

It is most good of you to send the flowers again—it makes me feel guilty, putting you to all this trouble every autumn. At the same time I am very glad when they do come, because they always look as if they were in the south in the sun. At the moment it is drenching wet and a fog: so they have their work cut out for them. Thank you very much—and I should include the box they came in as part of the present, since it is so distinguished looking: I'm very glad of the Honesty[1] too, but this we can get at Rodmell, so dont dream of sending any. We are going down there next week end, or before, but only to take voters to the Poll.

Please accept my annual and very sincere thanks. I hope your book is doing well—but I suppose its too soon to know.

Yrs very sincerely
Virginia Woolf

University of London

3078: To Ethel Smyth   52 *T-[avistock] S.[quare, W.C.1]*

[9 November 1935]

But why am I in your bad books? What have I done thats wrong? Or do you scold me on principle like the nurse in Punch. Go and tell Charles he mustn't.[2] Here I've been merely dealing with the usual pack of cards— people, people:—one by the way rammed on me by Ethel Sands—was a

1. The dried seed-pods of *Lunaria annua*.
2. "Go directly—see what she's doing, and tell her she mustn't." *Punch*, vol. lxiii, p. 202, 1872.

niece of Hindenburg,[1] and said you used to come to her mothers who helped you with an opera: this woman is marmoreal and monolithic, and precisely like a statue in a street: well, here I sit dealing with these for ever falling cards: reading Fry papers; toiling away at fiction, going to Labour party meetings at Rodmell—and my word, the little Quakers in the village schoolroom lit by one oil lamp, (and they mostly smelt,) brought the blood to my head—a natural easy hoarse orator—making metaphors—and whats been my crime towards you? Merely existing? Merely breathing the November air? Oh what a tyrannous heart you have to grudge me a gulp of fog! You'd have laughed to see me leading our 5 clerks at a gallop across the Sqre. and mounting a bed, so as to cheer the ducal couple—just in time—past they came—and she tossed me a kiss.[2] So there. More than you do

V.

Berg

3079: To V. Sackville-West 52 T[avistock] S.[quare, W.C.1]

Sunday [10 November 1935]

Yes, the 28th lunch would suit perfectly, and be a great treat.

I wish we could lunch alone; but lunching out is rather a noisy bore, so lets lunch here, with L. and Mitzi, and then perhaps you needn't hurry off at once?

I heard you were in France, so didn't write: then that you were canvassing in Leicester.[3] Perhaps that was only an excuse to get out of the horror of the Sunday Times show:[4] which has been wasting my time, but then so has the Election. On Thursday I have to walk Brighton pier for 4 hours while Leonard takes voters to the Poll. I think I shall call on Lady Sackville and ask for a cup of tea. Then I should drop dead foaming at the mouth, poisoned. All the placards would say, Lady Novelist poisoned by Peeress; and the sale of my books would bound up—but I must not continue this harrowing story as its dinner time. I must take the pot from the oven.

1. Baroness Nostitz. A Nazi sympathiser, who was in London hoping to persuade young English critics to lecture in Germany on poetry. See Quentin Bell, II, p. 191.
2. The wedding of the Duke and Duchess of Gloucester on 6 November. She was Lady Alice Montagu-Douglas-Scott.
3. Vita had been visiting Joan of Arc sites in France for her book. She refused to visit Leicester, where Harold Nicolson was standing as National Labour candidate in the General Election. See *Harold Nicolson's Diaries and Letters*, I, pp. 220-1.
4. The Book Exhibition at Dorland Hall, which was opened by Princess Louise.

What about Joan of Arc? Thats a book I shall like; a long, true, passionate yet absolutely matter of fact book. about 500 pages. with pictures

> So the 28th at one.
> Only you'll be late
> And wear yr pearls
> > for Bosman Potto's[1] sake

V.

Berg

3080: TO ETHEL SMYTH 52 *T.[avistock] S.[quare, W.C.1]*

Wednesday [13 November 1935]

Oh my God! What a fraud! Here's the one thing I wanted—to go to Kings Bench[2] tomorrow and this intolerable election has put a spoke in my otherwise so rapid rolling wheel. I must go with L. to Brighton—he says, (and this I feel you'll understand) "I should be dull without you." Now isn't that a compliment? And there I shall be, knocking in and out of the Pavilion, up and down the Pier instead of seeing the magnificent sight of Ethel confronting British Justice.

Ottoline has just gone. I feel like an old Pander handing bouquets from lover to lover: *She* says youre a trump: a great card; a magnificent English-woman; one of Shakespeares—I forget what—whores I daresay. And how you kept 'em all in a roar the other day; and put some red blood into that lily livered man.[3] I went to his play last night, and came away as if I'd been rolling in the ash bin; and somehow filled my mouth with the bones of a decaying cat thrown there by a workhouse drab. But I'm dazed with talk, and were it not for my sense of being unfairly treated by the Laws—all other days I could have gone—should spare you this scrawl.

Well: back on Monday. Let me know all about it; and for Heaven's sake keep yourself alive and brisk in a world which needs sanity and sub-stance and not the puling of green sick American eunuchs: though I love him in my own spasmodic fashion.

Ottoline says your her ideal of a great and noble nature—(these are very nearly her exact words: I'm too sleepy either to lie or to write)

V.

Berg

1. Virginia's full nickname for herself in writing to Vita. A potto is an African lemur.
2. See p. 433, note 5.
3. T. S. Eliot. Virginia had been to a performance of his play *Murder in the Cathedral*.

Saturday [16 November 1935]

I was very glad of the telegram,—glad you've scotched that viper, though I dont suppose it'll do you any good—the majesty of the Law.[1] Do you get your articles back? or had he sold them and forgotten where? Anyhow, I cursed my lot; not merely that I missed the sight (one day last week I walked in and sat through a dull case for the sake of the sight) but it was almost what they call a wash out my coming to Patcham,[2] and blessing the insurance agent who was running the Labour candidate with my smile. L had to drive voters for 3 hours in a downpour, so I toiled back to Rodmell; had to stand in the rain waiting for buses, took two and a half hours coming back, and so spent yesterday with a headache. But its exciting, too getting these odd glimpses of people I never meet nor you neither: and very good for my conceit and ignorance to have to pass the time of day with Mr Fean the postman, and Hancock the Quaker. Poor wretch! After slaving for a month, 7 meetings daily and so on, he's 10,000 votes behind Loder.[3] Harold's in—how astonishing![4] What a tribute to a good heart and the upper class manner! I admire his gameness. Out of the diplomacy into the frying pan: and so to make an omelette. Vita wrote me a dear loving kind letter asking to come to lunch and saying she had 5 years of talk to have with me about her book [*Saint Joan of Arc*]. I know—since youre so steadfast—you never said a word to her of any complaint of mine. I'm frying sausages for dinner as I write; and have just turned them delicately with the holder of this pen, having left the spoon in the kitchen. Then we dine off chicken and oatcake: L. makes a brew of coffee; and so to bed or rather to read a whole wall of Manuscripts. Yes, I was sorry not to see you too in that becoming light

V.

No, my criticism of the Murder [*in the Cathedral*] was a violent flare, not to be taken as serious criticism. Though violent flares are always good evidence. The truth is it acts far less well than reads: cant manage the human body: only a soliloquy

Berg

1. See p. 433, note 5.
2. A suburb of Brighton.
3. In the Lewes constituency Captain J. de V. Loder (Conservative) defeated his Labour opponent, F. R. Hancock, by a majority of 14,085.
4. Harold Nicolson was elected National Labour M.P. for West Leicester with a majority of 87 votes. The National Government (under Stanley Baldwin) won the Election with 425 seats. The Opposition held only 180, of which 154 were Labour.

52 *Tavistock Square,* [*W.C.1*]
(*but we're really at Monks
House for the moment.*)

Typewritten
Sunday Nov. 18th [17th, 1935]

Darling dearest Pix;

Here we are, in a down pour; frogs weather; but I was so delighted to get your deceitful letter that I try to dry my webbed claws, having become to all purposes a toad, and write. Again once again you took me in. "Beale Cunningham as I live!" I howled, seeing your envelope on my plate.[1] How do you know precisely how to take me in with her writing?—And then it turns into you. And then the very next day comes her book; which is all about keeping goldfish in Paris; and falling in love with Jews; and it begins well; but swells into such a mish-mash of words, about love and Jews and how to train vines over pergolas and wear silk pyjamas—In fact I think she must be mad; and I ought to write and tell her so. If you should meet a dumpy but washy woman, who loved a Jew in the Palais Royal, drop a pebble down her back and tell her to empty her ink pot into the Seine and never write another word, with my love.

We came down here on Thursday for the Election. Leonard had to drive voters to the Poll—not parrot—would that it had been—for three hours in a downpour. And after all our Mr Hancock was ten thousand votes behind Mr Loder. However I will not send politics to the Asses house, for thats what he lives on. I imagine you coming down to breakfast, lifting the cover off your plate and finding nothing but AntiFascist hay, chopped very fine; with a few old herring bones. However this is not strictly according to fact;[2] for from what you say I think you have a good eye for a witch.

Oh I liked your visit to the black sea [*inexplicable*].

I was oh so happy to read a little common sense in your letter about sunsets and witches. The woman who thought you such a good actress was Elizabeth Bowen; whos a very good writer in her way; and moves about the world and sees all sorts of actors and actresses; and she said she could see you had the real gift. We went to see Tom Eliot's play [*Murder in the Cathedral*] the other night. I think what is wanted is for some actress to make plays in which people are like ourselves only heightened; what is so bad is the complete break between the acting, the words and the scenery. Thus you lose all feeling of harmony. Why dont you make a play all in one? Thus it is much better to read plays than to see them. I am almost

1. Beall Cunningham, novelist. Angelica Garnett cannot now (1979) remember the significance of this joke, but Virginia may have been teasing her for her bad handwriting.
2. Angelica was in Paris, learning French. She was lodging with Francois and Zoum Walter.

dazed with writing my book; and think it would be better acted. I shall make
the end into a play for you to act. Some of it is good; most of it is bad.
It is too long. And I have to write about Roger. At least Nessa wants me to;
and Margery Fry has given me masses of letters; and all his diaries; how he
dined out or went to Paris. Do you think it is possible to write a life of anyone? I doubt it; because people are all over the place. Here are you, for
instance, walking in the Tuileries; and buying necklaces; and seeing the
sunset; and writing to me; now which is you? Eh? I will give Mummy all
your messages; only some of them are scratched out on the envelope. I like
dinner better than tea; but when one has to see people one doesnt know,
tea is over quicker.

Ive been seeing E.M.Delafield, who writes the Provincial Lady; she is
called Dashwood really; Elizabeth Dashwood;[1] and lives in an old house
like a character in Jane Austen; whom she adores. But she has to scribble
and scribble to pay for it and her children.

I'm dining with your admirer Raymond [Mortimer] tomorrow; to meet
Aldous Huxley; oh you dont like Raymond;—Tom is bringing an American
[Emily Hale] to tea; and I had a long visit from Ottoline. I was late; and
found her curled in my chair like a viper reading a book. We had a vipers
talk; fascinating; about her life when she was a Duke's sister and wore a
great hat and sat on the box seat of his four in hand and went to Ascot.
That was thirty years ago. She took the Duke of Portland, her brother, to
tea with [J. T.] Sheppard at Kings; and Maynard was there and Lydia. The
Duke said, 'Who was that Don, who married the dancing girl?' He'd never
heard of Maynard. So Ottoline said, "Hes Maynard Keynes. Very well
known." And the Duke said, "Maynard? Any relation of the Miss Maynard
who married Lord Warwick?" So you see Bloomsbury is still very very
obscure.

Sally has just run in to send her love to you; but the truth is shes so
passionately in love with Leonard that she cant stay in my garden room,
and has just galloped off in the pouring wet because she thinks Leonard is
taking flowers out of the greenhouse. And heres Leonard; and he sends his
love. We want to come to Fontainebleau after Christmas. What are your
plans?

Ginny

[*handwritten*]

I think I shall call my book "The Years". Do you think it a good name?
Mummy is going to do a jacket full of Donkeys Ears.

Angelica Garnett

1. She was born Elizabeth de la Pasture, married Major Arthur Dashwood, and
   wrote under the name E. M. Delafield. Her best-known book *The Diary of a
   Provincial Lady*, 1931, had first appeared as weekly articles in *Time and Tide*.

3083: To Stephen Spender   52 *Tavistock Square, W.C.*1

Tuesday [19 November 1935]

Dear Stephen,

I'm sorry I've been so long answering; but the Election muddled everything.

Could you dine here on Monday 25th at 8? I hope so: then we can discuss the interesting case of the Murder in the Cl. I rather suspect it is human nature that floors him: when its in the flesh.

I'll try to get Rosamond [Lehmann].   Yrs V.W.

Texas

3084: To Ethel Smyth   52 *T[avistock] S.[quare, W.C.*1]

Tuesday [26 November 1935]

Haven't I been good in respecting the furies of literary composition? Silence has dropped its mantle between us; and thats the greatest homage I can pay you. As a matter of fact though I did write, and was interrupted, and so sickened of the faded sheet, and thereupon invented this theory to justify myself, and became so enamoured of my image of the mantle of silence that I inhibited my own pen. What a thing it is to be a writer—to be so suggestible by one's own words that all ones instincts lie flat at their command, like sheep under a cloud: a fact which I think I've observed on the marshes at Rodmell. But no one respects my furies of composition: I swear to finish this incredibly tough old serpent [*The Years*]—a serpent without any of the charm of the Nile, only with all the toughness of what is evil and perennial—by Christmas; and to make this out of the question all my friends give letters of introduction to all their friends; I cant get rid of them —Cards, deeply black edged, are handed in. Will I see so and so? No, I say: whereupon the door is thrust open, and there are M. and M^m Gillet,[1] .... on top of Tom Eliot, who was just saying how much he admired you, and why had I never asked you to meet him, and his dull impeccable Bostonian lady.[2]

1. Editor of *Revue des Deux Mondes.*
2. Emily Hale, formerly from Boston, who taught at Claremont College, California. Her letter to Ruth George describing the visit is preserved at Scripps College, Claremont. She was astonished by Mitz: "Mr Woolf carries on his shoulder a tiny marmoset . . . all day long, peering out at one, first from one side, then the other; this tiny furry ball has a long tail which hangs down from his master's neck like a short queue, slightly confusing at first." Of Virginia she wrote: "She addressed several questions directly to me, suddenly but very carefully, so to speak, as if it really mattered what you answered her. . . . The impression of cool half-mocking detachment began to lessen, it became a reserve, a shyness, a husbanding of fine abilities."

So my book decays upon me like the body of the albatross. Next week by the way I have to break all my rules and lunch with Clive to meet the lady he calls gloriously Mme de Polignac, and I call Winnie Singer.[1] Shall I like?—shall I, shant I? God knows why I should be introduced to anyone —Then Vita came; and you'll be amused to hear that though my love of her character, so modest so magnanimous, remains unimpaired, I cant really forgive her for growing so large: with such tomato cheeks and thick black moustache—Surely that wasn't necessary: and the devil is that it shuts up her eyes that were the beaming beauty I first loved her for, and altogether reduces her (to look at) to the semblance of any fox hunting turnip stalking country lady. You'd never think she could turn a phrase; only whip a dog; but she remains, as I say, to me always modesty and gentleness no longer incarnate, but as it were hovering above her, in a nimbus. She seemed gloomy about Gwen; but our communications on that head are formal.

So goodbye. But wont you praise me for respecting the cloak of silence?

V.

Now I am going to Romeo and Juliet. Do you think he could love Juliet so soon after Rosalind? Doesnt Shakespeare spoil his psychology on account of the play?

Berg

3085: To Julian Bell   52 *Tavistock Square, [W.C.1]*

Typewritten
1st Dec 1935

Dearest Julian,

Your letter about Roger[2] came the other day, and I was very glad to get it, though you say that some of the pages flew in to the China seas. I wish you could rethink them—I thought it full of interesting and what is more, suggestive things. I wished there were more childhood stories; because Ive not got any that give that side of him. Also I'm very glad to have what you say of his work; perhaps some time you could go on with it. Any odds and ends about him come in useful. And you give the feeling of him extremely well I think. I am now reading the letters to Helen [Anrep], and get more and more involved in his mind and character, for though he

1. See p. 148, note 3.
2. Julian had drafted a letter about Roger Fry, hoping that the Hogarth Press might publish it. But the Woolfs thought there was too little in it about Fry, and too much about Julian, and declined it. See *Journey to a Frontier*, pp. 277-83.

is a bad letter writer mostly, to her he was extremely free and easy and self analytic. What to do with it all, I dont even try to think yet—theres so much to read. But I shall stodge on, and trust for some flash of illumination. Old Mrs Bridges, widow of Robert,[1] sent for me to talk about Roger; but she hadnt much to say, and was chiefly anxious I think to plaster over the quarrel about Rogers portrait of the old man. She said however that once when R. was grown up, Robert stayed with him at Failand; and wanted to play bowls on a Sunday. Roger hummed and hawed, and at last went off to ask Sir Edward's[2] permission; which was only given grudgingly. So you see how our ancestors lived. Gerard Hopkins she said used to come, very seldom though, because he had to celebrate mass daily.

Oh Lord—how I hate these parsons! We went to Toms play, the Murder, last week; and I had almost to carry Leonard out, shrieking. What was odd was how much better it reads than acts; the tightness, chillness, deadness and general worship of the decay and skeleton made one near sickness. The truth is when he has live bodies on the stage his words thin out, and no rhetoric will save them. Then we met Stephen Spender, who also was green at the gills with dislike, and came on to dinner one night; and told us how he has quarrelled with your friend John [Lehmann]. He wrote a story and put John in; then he sent the proofs to John, who was furious; whereupon Stephen stopped the story from appearing and rewrote it; but Johns vanity —for such I suppose it to be—was outraged; and they are on tiger-cat terms; in fact, broken off entirely. Stephen is off to Portugal with Isherwood and a friend; two friends I think; of the lower orders and the male sex.

Who else have I seen likely to amuse you? Janet Vaughan;[3] just had another baby; a girl; very nice; rather beautiful; will write us a book, we hope, on medicine; a little touchy about her husband; but has a good job at Wormwood Scrubs. Sally Graves; niece of Robert, Oxford; 22; a York-shire tyke, clumsy; touseled headed, nice, will also write us a book.[4] But sometimes I long for the Hogarth Press to end—then my task of reading novels would be over. And I wish L. would get on with his [After the] Deluge.

3rd Dec. I see Id better make this a diary letter; as I never get time to write for more than a minute or two. I try to read Roger in the lapses of finishing my book; but it won't finish; its like some snake thats been half run over but always pops its head up. Ive just come on this in one of

1. The poet-laureate, who had died in 1930. Mrs Bridges was Fry's cousin.
2. Sir Edward Fry, the judge, was Roger's father.
3. Daughter of Virginia's friend Madge Vaughan. In 1930 she married David Gourlay, co-founder of the Wayfarers Travel Agency. She was Assistant in Clinical Pathology, British Post-Graduate Medical School, 1934-39.
4. In 1937 she married Richard Chilver, and later became Principal of Bedford College, London, and of Lady Margaret Hall, Oxford. She never published a book.

Rogers letters from Charleston 1926:—youd all been to dine with the Keyneses, and Lydia would talk, "I felt hardly able to play up and relapsed into talk with Julian and Quentin who accompanied us. Julian's very beautiful, and very charming and extremely intelligent. Hes got much of Clive but is a more serious character with bigger ambitions and altogether more to him. I've been teaching him chess and hes got on with astonishing rapidity so that I have to reduce my handicap every day." I like compliments myself; and so hand this on. There are others equally good; but be discreet; for he says very sharp things about Clive. In fact his irritation with Clive seems to become almost an obsession—about his bagging Rogers ideas; his lack of understanding of art; his reverting to the Bell type and so on. I must ask Nessa.

Friday 6th Dec. Heres your letter this morning! a great pleasure. Do please go on writing—any scrap; then we shant turn into stiff old boots. If you dont mind these scraps, I'll send them as they accumulate. And we wont try to make sentences that will seem to the Chinese models of what we ought to write, English prose.

We had such a meeting at Adrian's last night to form a group to encourage the French; Nessa will tell you what for. I was dumb with helpless wonder at the competence of the political; and his loquacity. There was dear old Peter [Lucas] and Aldous and Auden; besides a mass of vociferous nonentities, chiefly journalists and scrubby men with rough hair—you know the sort. Anyhow L. is doomed to another Committee; much may it profit the world. Peter's in a fuss because no one reviews his two latest efforts; and then the N.S., that is [G. W.] Stonier, comes out with what I thought the most immoral review I almost ever read; unfair; untrue; written with a squint and a bitter poison; to which Peter, like an ass, thought good to reply, and only to say 'What a great poet am I'. Better leave others to say it. He's parching and tanning; red as a herring; and one that has no roe.[1] (See Romeo and Juliet)—to which we went two nights ago; and how it curled up Tom's Cathedral, and dropped it down the W.C.! Do you appreciate Shakespeare? I think you used not to. To me he becomes so miraculous, I felt, sitting there—not that Romeos one of the best—like the crowd who watch a rope go up into the air with a heavy basket on top. A thing one cant account for. Still acting it they spoil the poetry.

I'm glad, to return to your letter, that you are platonically in love.[2] Thats one of the best ways—and if you ever have a moment, fire off to me some crude, rude, brief remarks on the book of mine you are going to read to the pupils.[3] I get no criticism; and feel now and then it would help me.

1. See *Romeo and Juliet* II, iv, line 40, where Mercutio describes Romeo as "Without his roe, like a dried herring".
2. With the wife of one of his professorial colleagues at Wuhan.
3. Julian had written to her, "I think they [his Chinese pupils] must do you, Tom and Yeats."

One only gets mere slobber or mere abuse. Neither are of the least help. L. has written a blurb for your poems;[1] which I'll enclose.

Last night I met Margery Fry; she took a part in the debate; and made L. furious, by her reasonable but meddlesome ways. Then she cornered me and said she has a vast mass of Roger's papers; which I must come to tea to carry off. All his letters to the first Helen[2] I gather; and masses more of all his old papers; reviews &c. Lord! I wish you were here; I should make you do some of the reading; or we might consult. As it is I go on making extracts which is laborious, but may help you or another should there ever be a wish for a full life. His letters to Helen (Anrep) are far the most like him Ive yet struck.

I hope you wont follow Dadies [Rylands] example; I see in the paper hes been made [Cambridge] University lecturer in English for three years. But why teach English? As you say, all one can do is to herd books into groups, and then these submissive young, who are far too frightened and callow to have a bone in their backs, swallow it down; and tie it up; and thus we get English literature into ABC; one, two, three; and lose all sense of what its about. Thats why Auden, Spender and Day Lewis are bound together in a holy trinity—nobody reads with open eyes. All are mere catalogue makers; and thats what comes of teaching in a Chinese university. I make no doubt though that they scoop up pailsfull of what is worth having from seeing you walk about the fields with your glasses in your hands, and no nonsense about being a learned man. In fact, as the ambassador of reason and love, I can quite see you wearing a halo, bright winged, with eyes—dear me, I had thought of such a nice phrase for you, as the Chinese, of both sexes see you —and now its lunch time; and I must rush up.

P.M. We have just been to the Chinese show;[3] about which I dont expect you want information; and there met Jack Hutch; and Monty Shearman;[4] Jack grown pale and thin, speaking comparatively; and very cordial; but plagued by Mrs [Vivien] Eliot who has taken to the stage. She wears a black shirt, believes in Mussolini, and accosts Tom just as hes about to lecture on the Future of Poetry before a devout and cultured audience. Such are the chief events in the world of letters. Nobodies written a book you could touch with a barge pole, as far as I know. We are all well—Duncan and Nessa and Helen [Anrep] dined here last night; Helen I like better and better. Nessa begins to grumble about Christmas at Seend; Cory [Bell] has sent me a brace of pheasants. Adrian found a burglar in his bath, and put him in

1. *Work for the Winter*, Hogarth Press, March 1936.
2. Helen Coombe, Roger Fry's wife, whom he married in 1896. She gradually became insane.
3. The exhibition of Chinese Art at the Royal Academy.
4. Sir Montague Shearman, the judge, died in 1930. Virginia may have meant Harold Shearman, see p. 241.

a taxi and sent him to the hospital. I enclose my speech on Roger;[1] but its purely formal and not at all satisfactory; one always lies when one speaks in public; still in case you might like it, I send it. So good bye for the moment dearest Julian but let us continue this spasmodic chirp, as it is a way of converse. Love from L.

V.

Quentin Bell

3086: To Clive Bell   52 *Tavistock Square, W.C.*1

Wednesday [4 December 1935]

Dearest Clive,

I didn't know that I was still capable of blushing. However, when I read your letter that old accomplishment of mine, said to be connected with vanity, said to be one of my ancient foibles, came alive: and I had a happy morning. How absurd! but once in a way how delightful!

So you see you could ask me a much greater favour than to come to lunch to meet the Princess [de Polignac]—who must I think be Ethel's old flame—and I shall come with pleasure on the 12th Dec. at 1.30. Havent I always said that Clive—but no: I wont write out my affectionate praises lest you should think, what isnt true, that I'm sitting with my paws dangling and my nose twitching asking for more. And oh I'm so dusty in the throat and dumpy in the head after 3 mortal hours of Tom Eliot × rich American snob lady [Emily Hale], × Stephen Spender × M. et Madame Gillet over for the Chinese show and a rapid rifling of the flowers of old Bloomsbury; so forgive this scrap, and read into it some ancient kisses.

Yrs Virginia

Quentin Bell

3087: To Ethel Smith   [52 *Tavistock Square, W.C.*1]

Thursday [5 December 1935]

But what can have happened? L. posted that letter [No. 3084] with his own hands about 6 I shd. say 2 nights ago—just before you rang up. I'm slightly anxious, remembering that it was rash and hasty and said some wild things—thinking I may have sent it to the wrong person. So let me have a card; if you would. No doubt only the beginning of the Christmas curse: crowded posts.

V.

Berg

1. See p. 418, note 2.

Typewritten
17th Dec 1935

Dearest Julian,

I must begin another snatch of diary letter, or I shall never get started again. I hope youre making an effort in spite of Platonism and the Chinese version of it to do the same. By the way give your lover, if she's my lover, my love. Thats a Chinese box of a sentence for you! And by rights I should be lunching with Margery to meet the head of the Chinese in London—whats his name I dont know; over here to do the Show.[1] But I've compromised; and am going to tea now, to go over Rogers papers, with her.

This week end Quentin was up; and we had a crack on Sunday at Nessas. I was glad to find that we could still argue with some heat the question of palmistry. Aldous Huxley asked me to have my hand told by his friend—Maria's rather—Lotte Wolff;[2] so I did; with the result that some things she got hopelessly wrong; others she guessed amazingly right. And for two hours poured forth a flood of connected and intense discourse. Leonard said it was all humbug; disgusting humbug; Clive said That's not the scientific spirit; you must try things. Nessa was on L's side. I kept my distance, having the idea that after all some kind of communion is possible between beings, that cant be accounted for; or what about my dive into them in fiction? But why marks on the hand? Why should deaths and other events indent the palm of the hand? Anyhow, old Quentin, who has a sagacious clear sure footed mind like a handy little Scotch pony—but he's grown very fat—put us through our paces admirably. I was glad to argue again; how I miss Roger on Sundays for then there was always a substance, not mere froth in the talk. Yes I wish Roger were here more and more. So hurry up and come back.

Thursday 19*th.*
I went to Margery and ferreted among her dusty papers. She hadnt done much to get them ready—in particular I dont think shes found the Roger-Goldie letters; only a mass of quite illegible Goldie.[3] She told me she thinks she settled with Chatto and Windus to bring out the Mallarmé—on very bad terms; what, I dont know. Shes not a model of simple sense, which is I

1. The Chinese Exhibition at the Royal Academy, Burlington House.
2. Dr Charlotte Wolff, the palmist, author of *The Human Hand*, 1942, and *A Psychology of Gesture*, 1945. Virginia had spent two hours with her. Dr Wolff, sponsored by the Huxleys, moved from Paris to London, and read not only the hands of leading British intellectuals, but of the monkeys at the Zoo. See Sybille Bedford, *Aldous Huxley*, 1973, I, p. 314.
3. Goldsworthy Lowes Dickinson (1862-1932), the Cambridge historian and philosophical writer.

believe always so with the truly administrative mind. Because they make others do the facts; but no doubt she could marshall an army over an Alpine pass as soon as say Jack Jones.

Last night I dined with Ethel Sands to meet an incredible collection of petrified culture-bugs—Eric Maclagans, Leigh Ashtons, and Bruce Richmonds.[1] Its dressing up and being ladies and gentlemen that finally slows down the blood; so that all the knowledge, all the cleverness in the world— and Eric Maclagan told me many facts, as we pecked our fish, about Shakespeare which I dont know and only half believe—none of this survives dressing up and being respectable. Take my warning to heart. Leigh Ashton told me he wanted to have your job; must go to China; but as he's swollen to the size of a muffin in water I doubt that he ever leaves his Museum.

Leonard fetched me on a cold foggy night all agog, having just heard of Hoares resignation.[2] What is to come next? But what is to come will have come by the time you get this, You can imagine the hubbub here among those who go into details. Tomorrow we go to Rodmell for Christmas, in which silence I hope to finish my book and perhaps write you a less jumped and jerked letter. The truth is, I never sit down in London but what someone doesnt ring up or come in. Morgan has had to have the same operation—for prostate—that Goldie had. But hes having it in the best way—that is in two gos.[3] We're going to ask this afternoon; it was done— the first part—this morning. He put it off for four years thinking that it impairs the mind—but there seems no truth in this, and I think it might freshen him up; and make him write something. But hes oddly despondent always.

Friday. Ackerley has just rung up to say that Morgan is going on very well; and there ought to be no danger. And as we're hurrying off, on a fine frosty morning and all my packings still to do, I'd better stop. I had tea with Nessa yesterday and the bell rang and rang; Popkins,[4] Clive, Benita [Jaeger]; all for Duncan though, who complicated matters by hanging OUT on a placard; though he was in. Nessa and I stole a few moments from the hubbub and agreed we wanted no dressed society; which entirely destroys our work next day. Shes still got her huge canvas there with its face to the wall.[5] And Seend [Wiltshire] looms; and everythings much as it always is, come

1. Maclagan, Director of the Victoria and Albert Museum; Ashton, his successor in 1945; and Richmond, Editor of the *T.L.S.*
2. Sir Samuel Hoare, the Foreign Secretary, resigned as a result of his nefarious deal over Abyssinia with Pierre Laval, the French Foreign Minister, known as the Hoare-Laval Pact.
3. The second and main operation was in February 1936.
4. Percy Popkin, the accountant, much patronised by Bloomsbury for their Income Tax affairs.
5. Possibly one of the panels for the *Queen Mary*.

Christmas. We're sending you a book wh Leonard says is very good and fully documented on Robespierre [by R. Renier]. It wont come till the new year though; or later; And to think of you on the banks of the yellow river enjoying life—So good bye dearest Julian; I'll try to write more coherently next time. Love from us both.

Virginia

You may be amused to hear that I've just had a request from Virginia Isham, on behalf of a repertory Company to bring my troupe down to a barn at Chesham Bois and act Freshwater or will I let them—professional actors—do it themselves? I had to say Mr Craig[1] is in China, and it cant be done without him.

Quentin Bell

3089: To Virginia Isham   52 *Tavistock Square, W.C.*1

Dec 17th [1935]

Dear Virginia,

I am greatly flattered that you should wish to do Freshwater; and so is the Caste (no, I didn't act; only prompted, which was very necessary) But the caste is partly in China, and partly in Paris—that is Julian and Angelica; and even if they were here, I'm afraid its so purely a family joke, that though you and Mary [Fisher] might see the point, I dont think anyone else would. Also, its a mere Christmas scrap, and not actable in a serious sense. But if I ever do write a play, and I always want to, I shall certainly submit it to you. What fun it would be!

Are you ever in London, and would you suggest a time for coming here? Vanessa wants me to say how much she would like to see you. Angelica aged just 17, wants to go on the stage, and any advice you could give would be much appreciated.

I hope Mary's humourous Virgin was a success.[2]

Yrs V.W.

Northamptonshire Record Office

1. In the January 1935 production of *Freshwater*, Julian had taken the part of Lieut. John Craig, R.N.
2. Mary Fisher (daughter of Herbert Fisher, and later Mary Bennett, Principal of St Hilda's College, Oxford) played the Madonna in a production of a Miracle Play at Chesham Bois. This was the first production of Ida Teather's new Theatre Club, which shortly afterwards collapsed for lack of funds.

Monks House, [Rodmell,
                                         Sussex]
Christmas day [1935]

I am greatly touched by the calendar because I cant think how you remember these things, seeing you have now 105 presents to give—and then a calendar on top. Isnt it odd how much more one sees in a photograph than in real life? I never noticed the pillars before.[1] I'm deep in Roger Fry and trying to master his aesthetics. What he says is if you cut off your practical senses, the aesthetic then work: so now I'm not warding off [Vita's] Alsatians, I can see the door.

But this letter is in fact to ask if you and Harold wont come to lunch one day next week? Leonard wants to talk politics; and I, in my humbler sphere, would like to see you both. Could you? Both, or separate; or with the boys. Only let me know so that I may put a fowl in the pot. And also I must know whats the secret about Byron that Harold wont tell? Some one has sent me a book with a very good article of Harolds in it; and there he lets slip this amazing fact.[2]

Its a gale here, and I've been walking in the marshes and put up two great cormorant. Now at Sissinghurst you only have small blue fancy birds [budgerigars]—because its a castle: thats my little dig. I daresay you might net a Sturgeon in the lake, but then you'd have to give it to the King. Oh how heavenly it is to hear nothing but the wind! In London, there'd be dear old Ethels scrannel shriek.

Telephone number is 385 Lewes.

                                                    Yr.
Berg   V.

Monks House, [Rodmell,
                                         Sussex]
Dec 31st 1935

Thats where we are—thats why I spoke of getting a fowl: for in London they are common birds. We rang up Harold, and explained. But I dont suppose you'll want to come over here in these floods; so we must wait till you're up. I hope you're not anxious about Gwen [St Aubyn's illness]? Didn't you say they would know more in January?

1. The calendar was gummed to a photograph of the tower at Sissinghurst.
2. In *What Is A Book* (edited by Dale Warren, 1935) Harold Nicolson hinted at certain hitherto unknown facts concerning Byron's decision to leave England in the last years of his life. To disclose them, he said, would have thrown a bad light on Byron's character, and he decided to suppress them in his own book *Byron: The Last Journey*, 1924.

Soon the bells will be ringing and a new year beginning; which is, as you see, a kind of lyric. That reminds me—Brighton Corporation—to whom I applied about Cooking classes—are teaching [Vita's] The Land this term. So why dont you produce another poem at once?

I want a long poem to read now.

V.

T.O

I've been in bed with a cursed headache for 2 days, so forgot to send this—not that its worth sending, except as an expression of faithful devotion on the part of poor dear Bosman. We go up on Sunday I think and hope to see Harold in London.

Jan. 2nd 1936
Happy New Year

Berg

Index

The numbers are page-numbers, except in the 'Letters to' section at the end of individual entries, when the letter-numbers are given in italics.

Abbreviations: V. stands for Virginia Woolf; L. for Leonard Woolf: Vita for V. Sackville-West; ES. for Ethel Smyth.

Crabbe, George, 14
Craig, Edith, 47 & *n*, 225 & *n*, 271
Cranium Club, 163, 367
Crete, 50, 51, 52, 62
Cromer, Norfolk, 35*n*, 38
Crowder, Henry, 202*n*
Croydon, 229 & *n*, 240
Cunard, Lady Emerald, 158 & *n*, 202*n*, 280
Cunard, Nancy, 158 & *n*, 202 & *n*
Cunningham, Beale, 444
Curtis, Elizabeth, 308 & *n*, 411

Daley, Henry, 262*n*
Dalloway, Mrs: Septimus, 36; MS of, 41*n*; quoted from, 309; Spanish edition, 358
Daphnis, Greece, 52
Darlington, W. A., 227*n*
Davidson, Alice, 176*n*, 209, 233*n*
Davidson, Angus, 384
    Letter to: No. *3009*
Davies, Emily, 125 & *n*
Davies, Peter, 30 & *n*, 39*n*, 326
Davison, Ivy, 170 & *n*
Day Lewis, Cecil, 82, 436, 450
Delafield, E. M., 445 & *n*
Delattre, Floris (book about V.), 37 & *n*, 38, 79, 114
Delius, Frederick, 178 & *n*
Delphi, Greece, 54-7, 61
Desborough, Lady, 118
Dial, The (N.Y.), 252
Diamand, Pamela (Fry), 50 & *n*, 63 & *n*, 330, 416
    Letters to: Nos. *2584, 2937*
Dickens, Charles, 2, 217, 289, 334-5
Dickinson, Emily, 309
Dickinson, Goldsworthy Lowes: dies, 85 & *n*, 87, 128; dialogues, 293; Fry letters, 452
Dickinson, Violet: in Greece, 56 & *n*; in Sussex, 190*n*, 195; helped V. in her madness, 308*n*, 385
    Letter to: No. *3010*
Dilke, Sir Fisher Wentworth and Ethel, 393 & *n*
Dobb, Mrs Maurice, 245
Dodge, Mary, 77 & *n*, 242
Dodsley, Robert, 14 & *n*
Donne, John, 16 & *n*, 86
Dordrecht, Holland, 389, 393
Dostoevsky, Feodor, 203 & *n*, 216-17
Dreadnought hoax (1910), 109
Dryden, John, 13 & *n*
Dublin, 301, 411 & *n*
Duckworth, Sir George: V.'s early memories of, 13 & *n*; writes on beans and pigs, 196; secretary to Booth,

282*n*; dies, 299 & *n*, 302; funeral, 300, 305
Duckworth, Gerald, 418
Duckworth, Lady Margaret, 299, 302
Duke, Arthur, 406*n*
Duxbury, Elspeth, 328 & *n*

Easdale, Mrs G. E., 95, 212, 322, 363, 421, 426.
    Letters to: Nos. *2917, 2974, 3062, 3077*
Easdale, Joan, 95 & *n*, 212, 322, 363, 421, 426*n*, 434
Ebbs, Rev. J. W., 264 & *n*
Eden, Anthony, 428*n*
Edward VII, King, 121
Edwards, Dorothy, 232 & *n*
Elgar, Edward, 47 & *n*
Eliot, George, 120, 335
Eliot, T. S. ('Tom'): his first wife, 71; his poetry 'violent', 83; his marriage breaking up, 99, 107; 'trim as a bank clerk', 100; *Sweeney Agonistes*, 139 & *n*; in America, 150 & *n*, 151, 184; literary influence, 151; separates from wife, 205*n*, 207, 222, 266; H. A. L. Fisher on, 255; *The Rock*, 256, 308, 315; V. to ES. on his work, 260, 292; argues with V. on religion, 293; 'petrifying into a priest', 315; dines with V., 345; at Hayward party, 403; *Murder in the Cathedral*, 404, 408, 414, 442, 443, 444, 446, 448; 'not top calibre', 408; 'mellow, charming', 428, 432; religion at Monk's House, 432; 'lily-livered', 442; Emily Hale, 446 & *n*; Mrs Eliot reappears, 450
    Letters to: Nos. *2696, 3043*
Eliot, Mrs T. S. (Vivien): forces herself on V., 71; marriage collapsing, 99, 107; appearance and whims, 100, 107; separates from Eliot, 205 & *n*, 207, 222, 266; takes to acting, 450
Ellerman, Lady, 237
Ellesmere, Lady, 263*n*
Elsfield Manor (Buchans), 348*n*, 409*n*, 410-11
Empson, William, 437 & *n*
Ervine, St John, 237
Eugénie, Empress, 101 & *n*, 105 & *n*
Everest, Louie, 319

Fabbria, Tuscany, 183, 185
Faber, Geoffrey, 221 & *n*
Falmer, Sussex, 169
Farrell, Sophia, 133 & *n*
Fascists, British, 273 & *n*; Italian, 187; Austrian, 277 & *n*
Feisl, Dr and Mrs, 203

Isherwood, 376 & *n*; ending essay series, 420; V. longs to finish with, 448. *See also under employees,* Belsher, Cashin, Perkins, Scott-Johnson, West; *and* Woolf, Virginia, *under* Hogarth Press, her work for

Hogben, Lancelot, 351 & *n*

Holland: V. and L. visit, 389-92

Holland, A. K., 249 & *n*

Holman Hunt, William, 234*n*

Holtby, Winifred: book on V., 97 & *n*, 102, 108, 114 & *n*, 125, 191; on ES.'s music, 250 & *n*; dies, 431 & *n*

Homosexuals, 262 & *n*, 273

Hoover, President, 156 & *n*

Hope, Lottie (maid), 46, 126, 161 & *n*, 220, 290

Hopkins, Gerard Manley, 44, 246, 448

Horne (Vita's butler), 148

Horne, R. H., 231 & *n*

Hosias Loukas, Greece, 54, 57

Houghton Mifflin, 169 & *n*; *see* Scaife, Roger L.

Hudson, Alice, 325*n*

Hudson, Nan, 17 & *n*, 45, 148, 210, 339

Hugh-Jones, Philip, 327 & *n*

Hungerford, Wiltshire, 3, 5; *see* Ham Spray

Hunt, Hilary, 234 & *n*

Hunter, Mary, 64, 151 & *n*, 152

Hurst, Sir Arthur, 5

Hutchinson, Barbara (Rothschild): engaged to Rothschild, 205 & *n*; engagement parties, 242, 258-9; Rothschild jewels, 253, 258; Newmarket house, 272 & *n*; presented at Court, 382; operation, 412

Hutchinson, Jeremy, 221, 229, 244, 382

Hutchinson, Mary: Lytton Strachey, 18 & *n*; Aldous Huxley, 55; parties, 115, 133; her dresses, 157-8; appearance, 207; at Monk's House, 221, 223; V. dines with, 229; Barbara's engagement parties, 242, 258-9; party for Michael Arlen, 253; tête-à-tête with V., 275

Hutchinson, R. W., 49 & *n*

Hutchinson, St John ('Jack'), 18*n*, 28, 151, 223, 240, 242, 281, 437, 450

Huxley, Aldous and Maria: 55 & *n*; D. H. Lawrence letters, 117 & *n*; *Brave New World*, 139 & *n*; *Beyond the Mexique Bay*, 306 & *n*; 'witty and cosmopolitan', 342; *Point Counter Point*, 356 & *n*; anti-Fascist conference, 403*n*, 449; palmistry, 452 & *n*

Ibsen, Henrik, 282 & *n*, 403*n*

Ilbert, Margaret ('Mora'), 57*n*, 61

India, 399 & *n*

Innsbruck, Austria, 392

Ipsden, Oxford, 244, 247-8

Ireland: V. and L. prepare to visit, 291; 1934 visit: summary, 296; Fishguard-Cork, 297; Bowen's Court, Kildorrery, 298-9; Glengariff, 298-9; Co. Kerry, 299; Adare, 300; Galway, 301; Dublin, 301, 411 & *n*; Aran Islands, 301, 303; Waterville, 303

Irvine, Lyn Lloyd (Newman): no money, 187 & *n*; marriage, 187*n*; resigns from Everyman, 235; edits *Monologue*, 259, 270-1, 277, 310; visits Monk's House, 324, 326; lives near Cambridge, 430 & *n*
Letters to: Nos. *2848, 3067*

Isham, Sir Gyles, 145 & *n*, 149

Isham, Virginia: wants to broadcast *The Waves*, 145 & *n*, 149; wants to act at Sissinghurst, 205 & *n*, 210, 212, 214; wants to act *Freshwater*, 454 & *n*
Letters to: Nos. *2690, 2695, 3089*

Isherwood, Christopher, 375, 376 & *n*, 408*n*, 448

Italian language: V. learns, 157, 173, 175; speaks in Italy, 185, 393

Italy: V. in Venice, 49-50, 51, 63; Brindisi, 50; Italian holiday (May 1933), 183-8; Fascism, 187; V. in Verona and Rome, etc., 392-6; invasion of Abyssinia, 428 & *n*, 429

Ivers, Dorothy (Easton), 88 & *n*

Ivinghoe Beacon, Chilterns, 166

Jaeger, Benita (Armstrong), 7 & *n*, 340, 382, 453

Jamaica, 176

James, Charlie (milliner), 157-8

James, Henry: Hugh Walpole on, 92*n*, 142; T. Bosanquet, 135*n*; V. met in Rye, 214; use of dialogue, 335; 'loomed up' in V.'s youth, 392; Spender on, 407

Janin, René, 37 & *n*

Jebb, Cynthia, 401 & *n*, 405, 410

Joan of Arc, 370 & *n*

Johnson, Dr Samuel, 15

Jones, Alice, 164 & *n*, 176*n*, 181, 243, 311, 327 & *n*

Jones, Lady: *see* Bagnold, Enid

Joyce, James, 207

Kapp, Edmond, 417 & *n*

Kapp, Yvonne (Cloud), 7 & *n*, 417*n*

Kelmscott (William Morris), 415 & *n*

Kent, Duke of (Prince George), 17 & *n*, 350 & *n*

Keppel, Mrs George (Alice), 31 & *n*, 118, 121 & *n*

Keun, Odette, 412 & *n*, 413, 417

Keynes, Geoffrey, 331 & *n*

Keynes, Lydia (Lopokova): retiring from ballet, 94, 97; portrait in mosaic, 200*n*; acts in *Twelfth Night*, 209 & *n*, 222, 223*n*, 227 & *n*, 229-30, 235; cant act, 264; triumph in *Doll's House*, 282 & *n*; 'very sad', 402; acts in *The Master Builder*, 403 & *n*
    Letter to: No. *2751*

Keynes, Maynard: on *Three Guineas*, xv; Barbara Bagenal, 27; Ethel Smyth, 97; at King's, 97*n*; on ES.'s ballet, 113; at Monk's House, 139, 209; V. at Tilton, 222; weeps at Lydia's Ibsen performance, 282; on ES.'s tax problem, 326; Cambridge Arts Theatre, 334 & *n*, 432; unknown to Duke of Portland, 445; *mentioned*, 39, 45, 137, 148, 196*n*, 239, 265, 290, 359, 411, 449

Kidd, Ronald, 436 & *n*

Kilbracken, Lord (Arthur Godley), 88 & *n*

Kildorrery, Co. Cork, 298-300

King's College, Cambridge, 31, 33*n*, 97*n*, 245*n*, 282*n*

King's Lynn, Norfolk, 34

Kitchin, C. H. B., 339-40*n*, 346

Knoblock, Edward, 328*n*

Knole, Kent, 41*n*

Koteliansky, S. S. ('Kot'): on Lytton Strachey, 42 & *n*; V. revised his translations from Russian, 91 & *n*, 203 & *n*; Dostoevsky, 203 & *n*, 216-17; Dorothy Brett, 230; 'schemes and curses', 418
    Letters to: Nos. *2566, 2761, 2782*

Labour Party: conferences, 39, 108, 124, 230, 428, 432; committees at Rodmell, 86, 440-1; imperial affairs, 399*n*; General Election (1935), 432 & *n*, 440-4

Lamb, Henry, 130 & *n*, 248

Lansbury, George, 432 & *n*

Lascelles, Sir Alan, 53 & *n*

Laski, Harold and Frida, 153 & *n*, 154

Laurence, Samuel, 68 & *n*

Laval, Pierre, 453*n*

Law, Alice, 80 & *n*

Lawrence, D. H.: his letters, 117 & *n*; not first-rate genius, 121-2, 408; Carswell on, 130 & *n*, 139, 157; at Taos, 157 & *n*; Murry on, 159; his reputation muddied, 167; Brett's book on, 202 & *n*, 230; his grave at Vence, 202 & *n*

Lawrence, Frieda (Mrs D. H.), 157, 159, 167, 202

Leavis, F. R., 22 & *n*

Leavis, Q. D. ('Queenie'), xviii, 22 & *n*, 425 & *n*

Lee, Vernon (Violet Paget), 137 & *n*, 146 & *n*; dies, 369 & *n*

Lehmann, John: works at Hogarth Press, 14 & *n*, 62; *Letter to a Young Poet*, 22 & *n*; V.'s reply to his letter about, 82-3; difficulties with L., 64 & *n*, 69; remains 'adviser', 72*n*; resigns from Press, 85; on *The Waves*, 422 & *n*; Stephen Spender, 448; *mentioned*, 17, 103, 227, 420.
    Letters to: Nos. *2583, 2615, 3055*

Lehmann, Rosamond: at Bloomsbury party, 72; at Monk's House, 223; V. stays with, 244 & *n*, 247-8; daughter born, 277; *No More Music*, 339; Isaiah Berlin, 360; *mentioned*, 37, 148, 304
    Letters to: Nos. *2601, 2941*

Leicester, 108, 124, 441 & *n*, 443*n*

Leon, Derrick, 19 & *n*, 21, 142 & *n*, 175*n*, 177, 264 & *n*

Leonardslee, Sussex, 190*n*

Lerici, Italy, 186 & *n*, 187, 190

Lessore, Thérèse, 138 & *n*

Letter to a Young Poet, A: 22 & *n*; published, 75*n*; V. replies to Lehmann about, 82-3; U.S. edition, 33 & *n*, 44; copy for William Buchan, 413 & *n*

Lewes, Sussex, 96, 224*n*

Lewis, Wyndham, 82 & *n*, 383*n*

Lily (maid), 409*n*, 413

Lindbergh, Charles and Anne, 359 & *n*

Lindsay, Elizabeth, 156*n*

Lintott, Sir Henry, 235 & *n*, 417

Little Innocents, 134*n*, 135, 140, 143

Llewelyn Davies, Margaret, 20 & *n*, 425 & *n*, 330, 388
    Letters to: Nos. *2530, 2664, 2931, 3014, 3061*

Llewelyn Davies, Moya, 411 & *n*

Llewelyn Davies, Richard, 388 & *n*

Loder, Sir Giles, 190 & *n*

Loder, J. de V. (Lord Wakehurst), 443 & *n*

London: V.'s walks in, 10-11, 72, 338, 399; London squares, 200 & *n*

London National Society of Women's Service, xiv, 43 & *n*, 136*n*, 156 & *n*, 437*n*

Long Barn, Kent (Vita's house), 3 & *n*, 333 & *n*

Lopokova, Lydia; *see* Keynes, Lydia

Louise, Princess, 249 & *n*, 441*n*

Lovat, Lady Laura, 280 & *n*, 282

Love, Jean, 300*n*

Moore, George, 152 & *n*, 154 & *n*
Morgan, Charles, 24 & *n*, 25, 283 & *n*, 415
Morgan, Sir Herbert, 220 & *n*
Morocco, 278
Morrell, Julian (Goodman, Vinogradoff), 202 & *n*
Morrell, Lady Ottoline: praises *The Waves*, 6; her Memoirs, 15 & *n*, 162, 248; Lytton Strachey, 16, 18, 130 & *n*; D. H. Lawrence, 121-2*n*, 167; 'better alone', 151; illness, 159; passion for life, 162; her letters, 167; very deaf, 175; refuses luncheon in her honour, 196 & *n*, 197 & *n*, 198; accused by Vivien Eliot, 207; on Brett, 230*n*; 'very lovely', 243; 'loving kindness', 245; her love-affairs, 248; 'hawking and mousing', 259; V.'s fondness for, 265; V. on Vita, 266; Roger Fry, 332 & *n*; 'lovely leopard', 339; Yeats's party, 341; to India, 353 & *n*; Angelica and Yeats, 356*n*, 357; declining health, 418 & *n*; on ES., 442; her early life, 445
Letters to: *passim* (total of 43 in this volume)
Morrell, Philip, 99, 353*n*
Morris, William, 236, 415*n*
Mortimer, Raymond: *The French Pictures*, 7 & *n*, 8; 'Raymond's country', 185; Francis Birrell's illness, 205, 219, 226; at Charleston, 207*n*; accident to, 277; with V. and Huxley, 445; *mentioned*, 31*n*, 138, 148, 312, 404
Mosley, Lady Cynthia (Curzon), 4 & *n*, 188 & *n*
Mosley, Sir Oswald, 3 & *n*, 273 & *n*, 277
Moulins, France, 395
'Much Muckle', 51 & *n*
Muggery Poke (Rodmell), 423
Muir, Edwin, 24 & *n*
Mulock, Gladys, 234 & *n*
Letter to: No. *2805*
Munthe, Axel, 140
Murry, Middleton, 51 & *n*, 157, 159, 418 & *n*
Mussolini, Benito, 348*n*, 428*n*
Mycenae, Greece, 59 & *n*
Myers, Leopold, 412 & *n*

National Gallery, mosaics, 200 & *n*
National Portrait Gallery: K. Mansfield portrait for, 135 & *n*; V. refuses to sit for own portrait, 277
Nauplia, Greece, 54, 59, 61
Nef, John Ulric and Elinor, 212 & *n*, 215 & *n*
Letter to: No. *2779*

Newbolt, Sir Henry, 92 & *n*
Letter to: No. *2623*
Newhaven, Sussex, 328
Newman, Cardinal John, 221 & *n*
Newman, Mrs Max: *see* Irvine, Lyn Lloyd
New Mexico, 157 & *n*, 202
New Statesman: Kingsley Martin's editorship, 41*n*; V. will not review for, 68, 117-18; V.'s letter on London squares 200 & *n*; V.'s letter on hating publicity, 237-8; David Low, 239 & *n*, 242; V. plagiarised in, 248; 'damned dull', 387. *See also* Martin, Kingsley
Letter to: No. *2810*
Nicolson, Benedict (Ben), 190 & *n*, 229, 244, 266, 311-12
Letter to: No. *2817*
Nicolson, Harold: failure of *Action*, 3 & *n*; dines with V., 41; reviews her *Letter to a Young Poet*, 75 & *n*; reviews Yeats Brown, 88 & *n*; on modern writers, 93; American lecture tour with Vita, 141*n*, 143, 169; *Peacemaking*, 178 & *n*; in Italy and Morocco, 278 & *n*; Charles Lindbergh, 359 & *n*; *Dwight Morrow*, 359*n*, 371; *Biography*, 370 & *n*; in Greece, 386*n*; M.P. for Leicester, 441*n*, 443 & *n*; suppresses facts on Byron, 455 & *n*; *mentioned*, 53, 214, 220, 225, 362, 425
Nicolson, Nigel, 204*n*, 212, 266
Noailles, Anna de, 352 & *n*
Noel-Baker, Philip and Irene, 230 & *n*
Norfolk, 32, 35 & *n*
Norton, H. T. J., 402 & *n*
Nostitz, Baroness, 441 & *n*
Nussey, Ellen, 80

O'Brien, Dermod, 288 & *n*
O'Campo, Victoria: V. first meets, 348 & *n*, 349-51; friend of Anna de Noailles, 352 & *n*; V. 'in love with', 355, 359; autobiography?, 356; publishes Spanish editions of V.'s books, 358, 404-5; writes about V., 365 & *n*, 372 & *n*; V. offers her article, 405; gives V. butterflies, 438-9
Letters to: Nos. *2955-7, 2959, 2961, 2966, 2969, 2977, 2991, 3024, 3032, 3075*
Oliver, Robert T., 325 & *n*
Letter to: No. *2922*
Olivier, Lord (Sydney), 175 & *n*
Olympia, Greece, 58
Origo, Iris, 412 & *n*
Orlando: sale of MS?, 40-1, 43, 156; MS at Knole, 41*n*; give MS to Bodleian?,

Radnor, Lady, 141 & *n*
Raine, Kathleen, 245 & *n*
Ramsay, Lettice, 269
Ramsay, Lady Patricia, 166 & *n*, 167, 170, 173, 174, 250
Ravensdale, Lady, 369 & *n*, 386*n*
Raverat, Gwen, 11 & *n*, 15, 391 & *n*, 398
   Letter to: No. *2516*
Raverat, Jacques, xii, 11*n*
Rayleigh, Lady, 93 & *n*
Read, Elizabeth, 206 & *n*, 214
Read, Herbert, 341 & *n*, 403
Reinhardt, Max, 46*n*, 73*n*
Rembrandt van Rijn, 389
Renan, Ernest, 362 & *n*
Rendel, Dr Elinor, 97 & *n*, 121, 123, 307
Reiner, R., 454
Rhondda, Viscountess, 167 & *n*, 173, 175, 402-3
Richards, Noel (Olivier), 73*n*, 74
Richards, Virginia, 73 & *n*, 74
Richardson, Dorothy, 91 & *n*, 97
Richmond, Bruce, 453 & *n*
Richmond Park, 136, 173
Ridge, Mr (builder), 281
Riley, R. E., 106 & *n*
Ritchie, Alice, 7 & *n*, 87 & *n*, 90, 200 & *n*
   Letters to: Nos. *2618*, *2621*, *2758*
Roberts, Ellis, 357 & *n*, 414*n*, 438
Roberts, Michael, 177 & *n*
Robins, Elizabeth, 418 & *n*
Robinson, J. C. (Rodmell), 138 & *n*
Robson, William, 220 & *n*
Rodmell, Sussex: cement works at Asham, 10, 39-40, 41, 46, 138; V.'s love of the Downs, 105, 140, 141, 169, 230, 358; pump-noises, 236; habits of villagers, 264
Roehm, Ernst, 313*n*
Roermond, Holland, 390-1
Roger Fry: A Biography: V. invited to write, 352 & *n*, 369; letters to Vanessa, 401 & *n*, 405-6, 410, 416; V. alarmed by prospect of book, 402, 416, 422; begins reading letters, 427, 428-9, 433; plans book, 436; letters to Helen Anrep, 447; Mrs Bridges on Fry, 448 & *n*; letters to G. L. Dickinson, 452. See also Fry, Roger
Rome: V. in, 392-5
Room of One's Own, A: origins and method, xiv; not autobiographical, 91 & *n*, 195; V. expert on schools?, 95-6; proposed sale of MS, 136 & *n*, 156, 169, 170, 270; plagiarised by schoolgirl, 248; *Three Guineas*, a sequel to, 405, 434; Spanish edition, 358, 372, 395, 404-5
Rossetti, Christina, 270

Rothenstein, Sir William, 116 & *n*
   Letter to: No. *2655*
Rothermere, Lord, 3 & *n*
Rothschild, Victor (Lord Rothschild): dines with V., 199 & *n*; engaged to Barbara Hutchinson, 205*n*; engagement parties, 242, 258-9; his family jewels, 253, 258, 382; Newmarket house, 272 & *n*
Rowlands, Mr and Mrs, (in Ireland), 303-4
Ruskin, John, 221 & *n*
Russell, Bertrand, 248, 266
Rutherford, Mark (William Hale White), 95 & *n*
Rye, Sussex, 214
Rylands, George ('Dadie'): produces *Hamlet*, 24, 34; V. visits in Cambridge, 31, 33, 279; Dialogues, 35 & *n*, 39, 155, 334; new theatrical productions, 155*n*; invited to Monk's House, 329; lecturer in English, 450; *mentioned*, 20, 170, 373
   Letters to: Nos. *2536*, *2554*, *2561*, *2701*, *2860*, *2927*, *2936*

Sackville, Lady (Vita's mother): 'ought to be shot', 190 & *n*; 'Writs Hotel', 204, 216 & *n*; 'old termigant', 210; 'mad, bad', 264; buys Long Barn, 333 & *n*; V. proposes to call on, 441
Sackville-West, Edward (Eddy): 26 & *n*; *Simpson*, 31 & *n*; temporary row with V., 66-7*n*, 152; row made up, 69-70; his childhood story, 140, 143; letter 'a masterpiece', 129; breaks leg skiing, 277
   Letters to: Nos. *2591*, *2598*
Sackville-West, Victoria (Mrs Harold Nicolson, 'Vita'): V.'s changing attitude towards, xiii; her affair with V. revealed to her son Ben, 190*n*; interest in religion, xiii; MSS of V.'s novels, 41 & *n*, 43, 66; V. visits Sissinghurst, 45, 189, 232, 376, 425, 454 & *n*; depressed, 61 & *n*; V. needs her affection, 72; visits Monk's House, 93, 219, 220, 264; success of *Family History*, 110; reviews *Common Reader*, 111; Hilda Matheson, 111 & *n*; Violet Trefusis, 121 & *n*, 190*n*, 379; 'innocence', 135; lecture-tour of America, 141*n*, 143, 147-9; V. misses her, 144, 148-9, 153; dines at White House, 156 & *n*; meets Brett, 157*n*; in California, 169*n*; returns home, 177; V. and Lady Sackville, 190 & *n*, 216*n*; Nigel's operation, 204 & *n*; origin of her Sapphism, 214*n*; wont desert

469

473

Election, 442-4; visits Ireland with
V., 296-301; *Quack, Quack!*, 373 & *n*,
388, 413; *After the Deluge*, 388 & *n*,
448; acts in *Freshwater*, 365*n*; with V.
to Holland, Germany, Austria and
Italy, 389-97; Monk's House garden,
210; his sister dies, 268; his 'religion',
321; his marmoset, 326 & *n*, 446*n*; on
Indian politics, 399 & *n*; Abyssinian
crisis, 428-30

(No letters to him in this volume)

Woolf, Marie (Leonard's mother): birthday parties, 23, 239; visits Monk's
House, 89; illness, 154 & *n*; 'indomitable', 173; with V. at Leonardslee,
190*n*; her relations 'turn me sick',
209; daughter Clara dying, 258 & *n*;
Clara dies, 267-8, 269; V. visits in
Worthing, 311, 319, 332; going
blind, 386, 421, 435

Woolf, Virginia

Life (main events only; summary of
1932-35, xi)

1932: aged 50, 1; visits Lytton
Strachey on death-bed, 5 & *n*, 6;
his death, 8-9; meets Elizabeth
Bowen, 14 & *n*; writing *Common
Reader* (2nd series), 16, 40; at
Cambridge, 24, 34; refuses Clark
lectures, 26 & *n*, 27, 34-5; stays
with ES., 29; visits Carrington,
31-2; Carrington's suicide, 32 & *n*,
34, 38; holiday in Greece with L.
and Frys, 49-63; depression, 67;
faints, 75; *Letter to a Young Poet*
published, 75 & *n*, 82-3; interrupted by visitors, 74, 76-8; *Flush*,
83; faints again, 89, 94; Eliots at
Monk's House, 100; *Common
Reader* published, 111; dispute
with Pearsall Smith, 118-20;
Leicester conference, 124; progress
with *The Years*, 127

1933: new car, 146, 154; missing
Vita in America, 148-9, 153; learns
Italian, 157ff; in Chilterns, 166;
refuses Manchester degree, 171-2;
motoring holiday in Italy, 183-8;
criticises ES.'s egotism, 191-3,
194-5; portrait in mosaic, 200 & *n*;
summer at Rodmell, 208; repels
visitors owing to illness, 217;
Flush published, 228*n*; attends
Labour conference, 230; protests
against publicity, 237-9; stays with
Rosamond Lehmann, 247-8; meets
Sickert, 253, 262; visits Oxford,
254-6; Christmas, 265; feeling
about Vita, 266

1934: Ethel Smyth Festival, 267-73,
280; influenza, 273-6, 283; writing
The Years (*Pargiters*), 275; angry
letters to ES., 279, 288-9; Tavistock Square redecorated, 280ff;
dismisses Nelly Boxall, 285-6; visit
to Elizabeth Bowen etc in Ireland,
296-301; George Duckworth dies,
299 & *n*; influenza again, 303ff;
The Years going badly, 304-5;
learns French, 306ff; death of
Roger Fry, 329ff; *Sickert*
published, 340; finished first draft
of *The Years*, 343; invited to
write Fry's life, 352ff; meets
Victoria O'Campo, 348ff

1935: *Freshwater* performed, 365;
on anti-Fascist committee, 367-8,
374, 379, 382; end of love for
Vita?, 376 & *n*; with L. to Holland,
Germany, Austria and Italy,
389-97; refuses CH, 395-6; death
of Pinka, 396, 400-1; speaks at Fry
exhibition, 415-16; stays with
Tweedsmuirs, 410-11; declines
Presidency of PEN, 414, 417, 423;
working simultaneously on *The
Years* and *Roger Fry*, 427-8, 434,
445; invasion of Abyssinia, 428-9;
Julian Bell goes to China, 432;
Labour party conference, 432;
General Election, 440-4; headaches
at Christmas, 456

Publications: See separate headings for:
*Common Reader, The; Dalloway,
Mrs; Flush: Freshwater; Letter to a
Young Poet, A; Orlando; Years, The
(The Pargiters); Roger Fry: A
Biography; Room of One's Own, A;
Three Guineas; Waves, The*

Life as we have Known it, 20 & *n*,
425 & *n*; *Mark on the Wall,* 37;
translations from Russian, 91 & *n*,
203 & *n*, 216-17; article on Leslie
Stephen, 100, 102, 132; *To the Light-
house,* 213 & *n*, 314-15; *Oliver
Goldsmith,* 215 & *n*, 228; *Twelfth
Night* review, 223*n*, 227, 229-30;
Turgenev, 228 & *n*, 233, 235, 246;
Walter Sickert: A Conversation, see
Sickert, Walter; Foreword to
Vanessa catalogue, 281*n*; *Jacob's
Room,* 407; speech on Roger Fry,
418 & *n*, 451

Literary development and method: V.'s
education, 91, 195, 257, 306; knowledge of history 'rudimentary', 20;
dont publish till thirty, 83; V. 'never
wrote for money', 91 & *n*; no literary

474